Events Management

Third Edition

Other books in the Events Management series

Marketing and Selling Destinations and Venues: A Convention and Events Perspective by Tony Rogers and Rob Davidson

The Management of Events Operations by Julia Tum, Philippa Norton and J. Nevan Wright

Innovative Marketing Communications: Strategies for the Events Industry by Guy Masterman and Emma H. Wood

Events Design and Experience by Graham Berridge

Human Resource Management for Events: Managing the Event Workforce by Lynn Van der Wagen

Event Studies: Theory, Research and Policy for Planned Events by Donald Getz

Conferences and Conventions: A Global Industry, 2nd edition by Tony Rogers

Risk Management for Meetings and Events by Julia Rutherford Silvers

Events Management

Third Edition

Glenn A J Bowdin
*Head, UK Centre for Events Management,
Leeds Metropolitan University, UK*

Johnny Allen
*Foundation Director, Australian Centre for Event Management,
University of Technology, Sydney, Australia*

William O'Toole
International Events Development Specialist, Sydney, Australia

Robert Harris
*Director, Australian Centre for Event Management,
University of Technology, Sydney, Australia*

Ian McDonnell
*Senior Lecturer, School of Leisure, Sport and Tourism,
University of Technology, Sydney, Australia*

ELSEVIER

AMSTERDAM • BOSTON • HEIDELBERG • LONDON • NEW YORK • OXFORD
PARIS • SAN DIEGO • SAN FRANCISCO • SINGAPORE • SYDNEY • TOKYO

Butterworth-Heinemann is an imprint of Elsevier

Elsevier Butterworth-Heinemann
Linacre House, Jordan Hill, Oxford OX2 8DP, UK
30 Corporate Drive, Suite 400, Burlington, MA 01803, USA

First published in Australia by John Wiley & Sons Australia Ltd
33 Park Road, Milton Q 4064
© Johny Allen, William O'Toole, Robert Harris, Ian McDonnell 2008

First published in Great Britain 2001
Second edition published in Great Britain 2006
Third edition published in Great Britain 2011

British Library Cataloguing in Publication Data
A catalogue record for this book is available from the British Library

Library of Congress Cataloguing in Publication Data
A catalogue record for this book is available from the Library of Congress

ISBN: 978-1-85617-818-1

For information on all Butterworth-Heinemann publications
visit our web site at http://books.elsevier.com

Printed and bound in Great Britain
11 12 13 10 9 8 7 6 5 4 3

Contents

SECTION 1   THE EVENTS CONTEXT

SECTION 2 PLANNING

CHAPTER 12   **Promotion: integrated marketing communication for events**.. **421**

CHAPTER 13   **Sponsorship of events** **441**

List of figures

List of tables

The authors

Glenn A J Bowdin is Head of the UK Centre for Events Management, Leeds Metropolitan University, where he has responsibility for leading a dedicated team of events educators and researchers. He is co-series editor for the *Elsevier Butterworth-Heinemann Events Management Series*. His research interests include the area of service quality management, specifically focusing on the area of quality costing, and issues relating to the planning, management and evaluation of events. He is a member of the editorial boards for *Event Management* (an international journal) and *Journal of Convention & Event Tourism*, Chair of AEME (Association for Events Management Education), a founding director of the International EMBOK (Event Management Body of Knowledge) and a member of Meeting Professionals International (MPI).

Johnny Allen AM was Foundation Director of the Australian Centre for Event Management (ACEM) at the University of Technology, Sydney, and continues teaching and research activities with that organisation. He was event manager for the Darling Harbour Authority from 1989 until 1996, and special event manager for Tourism New South Wales from 1996 to 1999. Johnny has an extensive career in event planning, including public events and festivals in both urban and regional areas. He was made a member of the Order of Australia in 2007 for his services to the events industry and event education.

William O'Toole is an International Events Development Specialist. He assists councils, cities, regions, countries and companies to grow their events portfolio and write their strategies. For five years he advised the Supreme Commission for Tourism in the Kingdom of Saudi Arabia on the development of their tourism event program in the thirteen provinces. Bill trains and assists the United Nations event organisers in places such as the Sudan and Uganda and is facilitating the development of the event industry in Kenya. He is a founding director of the Event Management Body of Knowledge and key advisor to the International Event Management Competency Standard. From Scotland to San Jose to Johannesburg, he has trained events staff in the application of project and risk management to their events. Bill has been involved in events innovation, creation, operations, management and strategy in over 30 countries. He is currently writing a textbook on *Events Feasibility and Development*.

Rob Harris is a Senior Lecturer and the Director of the Australian Centre for Event Management, University of Technology, Sydney. Rob has been involved in event management training, education and curriculum development for more than 10 years and was a foundation director of the Festivals and Events Association of Australia. He has an international reputation as an event management educator, having delivered short executive development programs through to Masters level courses in a variety of locations around the world, including the United Kingdom, Malaysia, China and New Zealand, as well as throughout Australia. Rob is a co-author of the texts *Festival and Special Event Management* and *Regional Event Management Handbook*, as well as a number of event-related journal articles. He is on the editorial board of the international journal *Event Management*, and is the founder of the recently established Event Education and Research Network Australasia.

Ian McDonnell is a Senior Lecturer in the faculty of Business's School of Leisure, Sport and Tourism at the University of Technology, Sydney, where he teaches management and marketing of leisure and tourism services, including the very popular event management subject. In 1996, along with Johnny Allen, he started the first higher education course in event management, the Executive Certificate in Event Management. This book came from the lack of a text that could be used in such courses.

Series editors

Glenn A J Bowdin is Head of the UK Centre for Events Management, Leeds Metropolitan University, where he has responsibility for leading a dedicated team of events educators and researchers. His research interests include the area of service quality management, specifically focusing on the area of quality costing, and issues relating to the planning, management and evaluation of events. He is a member of the editorial boards for *Event Management* (an international journal) and *Journal of Convention & Event Tourism*, Chair of AEME (Association for Events Management Education), a founding director of the International EMBOK (Event Management Body of Knowledge) and a member of Meeting Professionals International (MPI).

Donald Getz is Professor Emeritus at the University of Calgary, Canada, and Adjunct Professor in the Haskayne School of Business there. He is a Distinguished Fellow in the International Academy for the Study of Tourism. Donald maintains strong research links in Australia, New Zealand, Sweden and Norway, including that of Guest Professor at the University of Gothenburg. His ongoing research involves all aspects of event studies, and he consults in the event management and tourism fields. He is author of a number of books including *Event Management and Event Tourism, and Event Studies.*

Conrad Lashley is Professor and Director of Research in the Department of Hospitality, Leisure and Tourism Management at Oxford Brookes University. He is also series editor for the *Elsevier Butterworth Heinemann series on Hospitality Leisure and Tourism* and co-editor of the *Gastronomica Book Series*. His research interests have largely been concerned with service quality management, and specifically employee empowerment in service delivery. He also has research interest and publications relating to hospitality management education. Recent books include *Organisation Behaviour for Leisure Services*, *12 Steps to Study Success, Hospitality Retail Management, and Empowerment: HR Strategies for Service Excellence.* He has co-edited, Hospitality: A Social Lens, and *In Search of Hospitality: Theoretical Perspectives and Debates.* He is the past Chair of the Council for Hospitality Management Education. He is a Chair of the British Institute of Innkeeping's panel judges for the NITA Training awards, and is advisor to England's East Midlands Tourism network.

Series preface

The events industry, including festivals, meetings, conferences, exhibitions, incentives, sports and a range of other events, is rapidly developing and makes a significant contribution to business and leisure related tourism. With increased regulation and the growth of government and corporate involvement in events, the environment has become much more complex. Event managers are now required to identify and service a wide range of stakeholders and to balance their needs and objectives. Though mainly operating at national levels, there has been significant growth of academic provision to meet the needs of events and related industries and the organizations that comprise them. The English speaking nations, together with key Northern European countries, have developed programmes of study leading to the award of diploma, undergraduate and post-graduate awards. These courses focus on providing education and training for future event professionals, and cover areas such as event planning and management, marketing, finance, human resource management and operations. Modules in events management are also included in many tourism, leisure, recreation and hospitality qualifications in universities and colleges.

The rapid growth of such courses has meant that there is a vast gap in the available literature on this topic for lecturers, students and professionals alike. To this end, the *Events Management Series* has been created to meet these needs to create a planned and targeted set of publications in this area.

Aimed at academic and management development in events management and related studies, the *Events Management Series*:

- provides a portfolio of titles which match management development needs through various stages;
- prioritizes publication of texts where there are current gaps in the market, or where current provision is unsatisfactory;
- develops a portfolio of both practical and stimulating texts;
- provides a basis for theoretical and research underpinning for programmes of study;
- is recognized as being of consistent high quality;
- will quickly become the series of first choice for both authors and users.

Preface

Each year, events occur throughout the United Kingdom and around the world. They dominate the media, fill transport systems, hotels and venues, meet business objectives, motivate communities and create positive and negative impacts. For example, the Notting Hill Carnival can trace its origins back to 1964 when, established as a festival, it provided an opportunity for West Indians to celebrate and commemorate their ancestors' freedom from slavery. Over the years, the event grew slowly, from 200 visitors, to some 3000 in the early 1970s. The turning point for the Carnival came in 1975, when the Carnival was promoted by Capital Radio, resulting in 150,000 people from the West Indian community attending. In the last decade, the Carnival has boasted audiences up to 1.5 million people from all communities — attracting attention from Greater London Authority and other stakeholders who fear for the safety of visitors and wish to support its future development.

The UK events industry is wide ranging, incorporating many different sectors from the smallest of exhibitions, conferences and parties, through to large-scale sport and entertainment events. Although definitive data are not available, due to the complex nature and diversity of the industry, figures suggest that the economic impact of business visits and events alone (e.g. conferences, exhibitions, incentive travel) is over £22 billion. This suggests that the industry offers significant income to the UK economy, which has not gone unnoticed by local and national governments, regional development agencies, and other public sector bodies. Increasingly, they are using events as a means of serving a host of policy objectives — from delivering tourists, regenerating communities and celebrating moments in time (such as the extensive range of events during the Millennium) to arousing civic pride, inspiring the arts and stimulating regional economies, illustrated by the increasing number of events strategies across the UK and support for large scale events, including the successful London 2012 Olympic Games and Glasgow 2014 Commonwealth Games bids among many.

The UK has developed an enviable programme of events, including The Championships (known the world over as simply Wimbledon), Notting Hill Carnival, The Open Championships, Glastonbury Festival, Royal Ascot, Edinburgh International Festival, the British Grand Prix, Belfast Festival at Queen's, Eisteddfod and the FA Cup — together with many others that cover the full spectrum of business and community interests. These events and others, which are discussed in later chapters, illustrate in various ways the power of events to raise the profile of their host cities, attract visitors, deliver economic benefits and create jobs. They also show the various origins of events, ranging from community celebrations growing out of protest, to international events supported for political and economic needs. They raise issues of the costs, benefits and impacts on their host communities and serve as models for event management, development and marketing.

Until relatively recently, events have been seen as part of hospitality, tourism, leisure and recreation industries, or as a support service to businesses. However, the environment is changing and the events industry is emerging in its own right. In the past decade or more, events management has shifted from being a field of dedicated and resourceful amateurs to being one of trained and skilled professionals. There are several reasons for this shift.

First, events management has emerged as the umbrella profession for a diverse range of activities that were previously viewed as discrete areas. These activities include festivals, sporting events, conferences, tourism and corporate events. This change has led to the need for a methodology broad enough to service this wide range of event types, but also flexible enough to encompass their individual needs and differences.

Second, the environments in which events operate and the range of stakeholder expectations have become much more complex and demanding. This change has led to the need for a robust methodology that is responsive to change and able to manage and encompass risk.

Third, corporate and government involvement in events has increased dramatically, in terms of both companies mounting events for their own purposes, and companies and governments investing in events through sponsorship and grants. This change has led to the need for management systems that are accountable and able to measure and deliver return on investment.

In response to these challenges, the events industry is seeking to increase professionalism and has relatively quickly developed a body of knowledge of industry best practice, supported by qualifications, training and accreditation. To do so, it has borrowed much from other disciplines and adapted this knowledge to the event context. This textbook attempts to capture and refine this emerging body of knowledge, and to document it in a useful form for students, researchers and practitioners in the field. As authors, we each bring to the textbook the benefits of our own discipline and perspective, reflecting the many facets of events management.

Events Management examines these and other aspects of events from a UK perspective. Specifically, the book aims to:

- Introduce the concepts of event planning and management
- Present the study of events management within an academic environment
- Discuss the key components for staging an event, covering the whole process from creation to evaluation
- Develop an understanding of key areas required for planning and managing events, including planning, project management, logistics, risk management, legal considerations, human resources, budgeting, staging, marketing planning, integrated marketing communications and evaluation
- Examine the events industry within its broader business context, covering impacts and event tourism
- Provide an effective guide for producers of events

Section One deals with the context for events — the reasons human societies create events and the events culture that has evolved are examined, as are the range and types of events and their impacts on their host communities, environment, economy and tourism. The section also examines sustainable development and perspectives on events. Section Two illustrates a methodology for the planning of events by examining the processes involved in conceptualising, developing, project planning, implementing, marketing and sponsoring events. The section also examines the formation, leadership and training of event teams. Finally, Section Three looks at event operations and evaluation in detail and focuses on the systems event managers can use to manage events, discussing staging events, logistics, legal issues, risk management and the process of monitoring and evaluating events and reporting back to stakeholders.

The book is conveniently divided into eighteen chapters, which may be used to structure teaching sessions. Each chapter commences with clear objectives and ends with review questions in order to assess the students understanding. The book is also amply illustrated throughout with case studies, which assist the reader to relate the theory of events management to the real world of events practice, with all its challenges, frustrations and rewards. The book provides the reader with both a tool for greater understanding of events management and a framework for planning and implementing events.

The events industry is emerging, supported by an increasing body of knowledge, education, research and industry professionals; hopefully, the third edition of *Events Management* will contribute to this evolution and to a better understanding of how events enrich our lives, and it is hoped that the reader will in turn contribute to the future of this young and exciting industry.

Acknowledgements

Glenn wishes to thank Johnny, Bill, Rob and Ian for collaborating on this exciting project, and the publishing team at Elsevier for all their support, advice and professional guidance during the production of this text. Special thanks and appreciation to current and past colleagues and students from the UK Centre for Events Management, Leeds Metropolitan University and members of the International EMBOK (Event Management Body of Knowledge) Executive, for their ideas, advice and suggestions, together with members of the Association for Events Management Education (AEME) for their feedback on the earlier editions. Finally, Glenn dedicates this edition to his wife Eileen and their children Peter, Sean, David and Niamh.

The authors and publisher would like to thank the following copyright holders, organisations and individuals, for permission to reproduce copyright material in this book.

p. 37 (Figure 1.3) and p. 38 (Figure 1.4): © International EMBOK Executive 2006, reproduced with permission; p. 56 © Hammersmith & Fulham Council, 2009, reproduced with permission; pp. 77 (Figure 2.2): The City of Edinburgh Council; p. 100 (Figure 3.1), 101 (Figure 3.2), p.102 (Figure 3.3): © 2006 UK Sport; p. 220 (Figure 6.9), 222 (Figure 6.10), 224 (Figure 6.11), 225 (Figure 6.12), p. 226 (Figure 6.13): Ian Alker; p. 140 (Figure 4.5): © Events Tasmania 2006; pp. 161-2 (Figure 5.1): © David Suzuki Foundation (2010) www.davidsuzuki.org); p. 162 (Figure 5.2): © 2007, The London Organising Committee of the Olympic Games Limited; pp. 165-6 (Figure 5.3): Department of Sustainability, Victoria; p. 167 (Figure 5.4): © Government Office for the South West, 2010; pp. 170-1 (Figure 5.5): Greenpeace Olympic Environmental Guidelines, 2003, Greenpeace Australia Pacific; p. 174 (Figure 5.6): Xerox Corporation, *Guide to Waste Reduction and Recycling at Special Events*, 1998, reproduced with permission of Xerox Corporation, New York; p. 174 (Figure 5.7): BSI, 2010; pp. 175-6:): © 2009, The London Organising Committee of the Olympic Games Limited; pp. 191-2: © Bristol City Council Arts Festivals and Events Service (2008), reproduced with permission; p. 194 (Figure 6.3), p. 262 (Figure 8.1), p. 270 (Figure 8.3), p. 282 (Figure 8.6), p. 299 (Figure 9.2), p. 597 (Figure 17.2): William O'Toole, Event Project Management System Pty Ltd, EPMS. net; p. 196 (Figure 6.5): Roskilde Festival; p. 197 (Figure 6.6): Commonwealth Games Foundation, supplied courtesy of the Commonwealth Games Federation, London; p. 199 (Figure 6.7): Jim Sloman, Sloman, J. (2006), Project Management (course notes), Major Event Management Program 9–14 June, Sports Knowledge Australia, Sydney; p. 231. (Figure 7.2), p. 324 (Figure 10.1): Manchester City Council, Manchester Archives & Local Studies, Central Library; p. 297 (Figure 9.1): John Aitken; p. 310 (Figure 9.9): Adapted from Burke, R. (2003). *Project Management: Planning and Control Techniques*. 4th edn. Chichester, John Wiley & Sons. © 2003 Johns Wiley & Sons Limited. Reproduced with permission; pp. 321 (Figure 9.11): Edinburgh International Festival Society, 2010, reproduced with permission; p. 325 (Figure 10.2): adapted from Getz, D. (2005), *Event Management and Event Tourism*, reproduced by permission of Cognizant Communications Corporation, New York; p. 331 (Figure 10.3), p. 338 (Figure 10.6): Harrogate International Festival; p. 333-4 (Figure 10.4): Sport and Recreation Victoria, Melbourne 2006 Commonwealth Games; p. 341 (Figure 10.8): School of Volunteer Management, 2004; p. 343 (Figure 10.9): Bradner, J. (1995) Recruitment, orientation, retention. In: Connors, T. ed., *The Volunteer Management Handbook*, New York, John Wiley and Sons. Copyright © 1995 T Connors. This material is used by permission of John Wiley & Sons. Inc.; p. 345 (Figure 10.10): UK Centre for Events Management, Leeds Metropolitan University 2010; p. 346 (Figure 10.11): Buckler, B. (1998), Practical steps towards a learning organization: applying academic knowledge to improvement and innovation in business performance, *The Learning Organization*, 5(1), pp. 15−23, reproduced by permission of MCB University Press, Bradford; p. 347 (Figure 10.12): R. Stone (2002). *Human Resource Management 3rd edn*, John Wiley & Sons, Brisbane. This material is used by permission of John Wiley & Sons, Australia; p. 351 (Figure 10.13): California Traditional Music Society; p. 353 (Figure 10.14): Peach, E. and Murrell, K. (1995), Reward and recognition systems for volunteers. In: Connors, T. ed., *The Volunteer Management Handbook*, New York, John Wiley & Sons. Copyright © 1995 T Connors. This material is used by permission of John Wiley & Sons. Inc.; p. 353 (Figure 10. 15): from *Organisational Behaviour: a global perspective*, 3rd edition, Wood, Chapman, Fromholz, Morrison, Wallace, Zeffane, Schermerhorn, Hunt, Osborn. This material is used by permission of John Wiley & Sons. Inc; p. 353 (Figure 10.16): Adapted and Reprinted by permission of Harvard Business Review. [Exhibit]. From "One More Time: How Do You Motivate Employees?" by F. Hetzberg, 01/03, p. 90. Copyright © 2003 by the Harvard Business School Publishing Corporation, all rights reserved; p. 378 (Figure 11.5): Adapted with the permission of The Free Press, a Division of Simon & Schuster Adult Publishing Group from COMPETITIVE STRATEGY: Techniques for Analyzing Industries and Competitors by Michael E. Porter. Copyright © 1980, 1998 by The Free Press. All rights reserved; p. 389 (Figure 11.6): Marketing for Leisure and Tourism by Michael Morgan, Pearson Education Limited. Copyright © Prentice Hall Europe 1996; p. 396 (Figure 11.7): Principles of Marketing by Frances Brassington and Stephen Pettitt, Pearson Education Limited. Copyright © Frances Brassington and Stephen Pettitt 1997 © Pearson Education Limited 2000, 2003; p. 402 (Figure 11.8): Reprinted by permission of Harvard Business Review. [Exhibit]. From "Strategies For Diversification" by I. Ansoff, September-October, pp. 113-124. Copyright (c) 1957 by the Harvard Business School Publishing Corporation, all rights reserved; p. 404 (Figure 11.9): SERVICES MARKETING: PEOPLE, TECHNOLOGY by Lovelock and Wirtz Adapted and reprinted by permission of Pearson Education Inc., Upper Saddle River, NJ; p. 436 (Figure 12.6): Peter Kerwood, Dave Quainton, Event Magazine 2009; pp. 437-40: Confex Group; pp. 444 (Figure 13.1): Sponsormap.com; pp. 448 (Figure 13.2): Adapted from Crompton, J. (1994), Benefits and risks associated with sponsorship of major events, *Festival Management and Event Tourism*, 2(2), pp. 65−74, reproduced by permission of Cognizant Communications Corporation, New York; p. 451 (Figure 13.3): Meenaghan, T. (2001). Understanding Sponsorship Effects. *Psychology and Marketing*, 18(2), pp. 95–122. Copyright © 2001 John Wiley & Sons Inc. This material is used by permission of John Wiley & Sons Inc.; p. 457 (Figure 13.4): Kevin Gwinner, Gwinner, K. & Bennet G. (2007) The impact of brand cohesiveness and sport identification on brand fit in a sponsorship context; p. 467 (Figure 13.5): SAGA Group Ltd; 2010; pp. 470-1 (Figure 13.6): Adapted from Crompton, J. (1994). Benefits and risks associated with sponsorship of major events', *Festival Management and Event Tourism,* **2**(2), pp. 65-74. Reproduced by permission of Cognizant Communications Corporation, New York; p. 499 (Figure 14.4): Roger Foley, Fogg Productions; p. 526 Figure 15.2): 490 adapted from 'Three Die in IKEA Stampede' by K. S. Ramkumar & Hassan Adawi, *Arab News*, 2 September 2004; pp. 541 (Figure 15.10): Slice PR, London; p. 545 (Figure 15.12): © Wiltshire Council, 2009); p. 548 (Figure 15.13), p. 615 (Figure 17.6): Crown copyright material is reproduced with the permission of the Controller of HMSO and the Queen's Printer for Scotland; p. 567 (Figure 16.1): Allen, K. and Shaw, P. (2001) *Festivals Mean Business: The Shape of Arts Festivals in the UK*, reproduced by permission of British Arts Festivals Association, London; p. 569 (Figure 16.2): Chris Hannam, Stagesafe Limited; p. 570 (Figure 16.4): O'Toole, W. and Mikolaitis, P. (2002). *Corporate Event Project Management*. New York, John Wiley & Sons. © 2002 O'Toole and Mikolaitis. This material is used by permission of John Wiley & Sons Inc.; p. 576 (Figure 16.6), p. 577 (Figure 16.7), p. 596 (Figure 17.1): Crown copyright material is reproduced with the permission of the Controller of HMSO and the Queen's Printer for Scotland; p. 581 (Figure 16.8): Hiscox, 2010; p. 599 (Figure 17.3): *Sydney Morning Herald*, 1 November 2005 by Nick O'Malley; p. 603 (Figure 17.4): *Sydney Morning Herald*, 27 February 2006, Alexa Moses; p. 609 (Figure 17.5), p. 617 (Figure 17.7): Commonwealth Copyright Administration, *Guidance on the Principles of Safe Design for Work*, Australian Safety and Compensation Council, Canberra, May 2006. Both copyright Commonwealth of Australia, reproduced by permission; p. 618 (Figure 17.8): Ministry of Civil Defence & Emergency Management, New Zealand; p. 647-8 (Figure 18.3) Manchester City Council, 2009; p. 649 (Figure 18.4), pp. 650-1 (Figure 18.5), p. 652 (Figure 18.6): © UK Sport 1999, reproduced with permission; p. 656 (Figure 18.7): Dr Leo Jago (2006), *Encore Festival and Event Evaluation Kit*, draft document prepared for CRC for Sustainable Tourism, Melbourne.

TEXT

p. 12 (Table 1.1): PSI (1992), Arts festivals, *Cultural Trends*, 15, reproduced by permission of Policy Studies Institute, London; pp. 44-7 Steven Wood Schmader; pp. 47-9 2002 Manchester The XVII Commonwealth Games: Post Games Report. London, Commonwealth Games Federation, pp. 18–19. Reproduced with permission; p. 66 (Table 2.2): Hilbers, J. (2005) Research and evaluation of "communities together" festivals and celebrations scheme 2002—04: building community capacity © Australian Centre for Event Management 2005; p. 67: IAP2, International Association for Public Participation; pp. 70-1: WorldEvents™; pp. 72-7 Kenneth Wardrop, The City of Edinburgh Council; p. 74 (Table 2.3, 2.4), 75 (Table 2.5): SQW/TNS; p. 88 (Table 3.2): © 2004, The London Organising Committee of the Olympic Games Limited; pp. 103-5 (Table 3.3): Fredline, L., Deery, M. and Jago L. K. (2005) Testing of a compressed generic instrument to assess host community perceptions of events: a case study of the Australian Open Tennis Tournament; © Australian Centre for Event Management 2005; pp. 111-4: The NEC Group, Birmingham; pp. 114-7: Richard Cashman; pp. 135-7: Lars Blicher-Hansen, Danish Tourist Board, Copenhagen, Denmark; pp. 148-51: © EventScotland 2009, reproduced with permission of EventScotland; pp. 151-4: Claire Holder; pp. 178-181: Glastonbury Festival of Contemporary Performing Arts; pp. 181-4: © BSI, reproduced with permission; pp. 215-8: Randle Stonier; pp. 219-27: Ian Alker; pp. 241-3 Manchester City Council, Manchester Archives & Local Studies, Central Library; pp. 252-5: Jane Ali-Knight, Kath Mainland, General Manager, Amanda Barry, Marketing and PR Manager and all the staff at the Edinburgh International Book Festival for their kind support when putting this case study together; pp. 287-91: Neil Timmins; pp. 291-3: Jack Morton Worldwide; pp. 319-22: Edinburgh International Festival; p. 356 (Table 10.1): Peach, E. and Murrell, K. (1995), Reward and recognition systems for volunteers. In: Connors, T. ed., *The Volunteer Management Handbook*, New York, John Wiley & Sons. Copyright © 1995 T Connors. This material is used by permission of John Wiley & Sons. Inc.; pp. 363-4: Manchester City Council's Games Xchange; p. 394 (Table 11.3): Crown copyright material is reproduced with the permission of the Controller of HMSO and the Queen's Printer for Scotland; p. 395 (Table 11.4): adapted from Getz, D. (2005), *Event Management and Event Tourism*, 2nd edn. reproduced by permission of Cognizant Communications Corporation, New York; p. 397 (Table 11.5): © 2006 CACI Limited, London. All rights reserved; pp. 414-5: Imagination; pp. 416-9: Media 10; p. 463: CAT Publications Ltd, 2010; p. 479: Terri Meadmore: Terri Ferguson, Manager Sponsorship; pp. 481-4: Rachael Church, Editor, Sport and Technology; pp. 484-7: Cheltenham Festivals Ltd; pp. 514-5: Lisa Gudge, Access All Areas; pp. 518-9: David Jamilly, Theme Traders; pp. 519-22: Paul Milligan, AV magazine; pp. 558-60: Bill Egan, Aggreko UK Ltd; pp. 560-4: Belfast Festival at Queen's; pp. 586-8: Logistik Ltd; pp. 589-91: Paul Jonson; pp. 619-623: Tim Roberts; pp. 624-7 Patrick Loy; pp. 658-60: Scottish Enterprise Edinburgh and Lothian, City of Edinburgh Council and EventScotland; pp.660-3: DF Concerts and Tennent's Lager.

Every effort has been made to trace ownership of copyright material. Information that will enable the publisher to rectify any error or omission in subsequent editions will be welcome. In such cases, please contact Elsevier's Science & Technology Rights Department in Oxford.

The Events Context 1

The first part of this book looks at the history and development of events and the emergence of the event industry in the United Kingdom. It examines the impact of events, including their social/cultural, physical/environmental, political and tourism/ economic implications. This section also deals with the nature and importance of event tourism and includes a chapter on sustainable development, an increasingly significant factor influencing overall events planning.

An overview of the events field

1

LEARNING OBJECTIVES

After studying this chapter, you should be able to:

- define special events, mega-events, hallmark events and major events
- demonstrate an awareness of why events have evolved in human society
- describe the role of events in the UK, and the UK tradition of events
- describe the rise and effect of the community arts movement and its influence on the development of festivals and public events
- understand the growth and emergence of the events industry
- distinguish between different types of events
- list and describe the components of the events industry, including associations
- discuss the attributes and knowledge requirements of an events manager
- describe the types of organisation involved in the delivery of events management training.

INTRODUCTION

Today, events are central to our culture as perhaps never before. Increases in leisure time and discretionary spending have led to a proliferation of public events, celebrations and entertainment. Governments now support and promote events as part of their strategies for economic development, nation building and destination marketing. Corporations and businesses embrace events as key elements in their marketing strategies and image promotion. The enthusiasm of community groups and individuals for their own interests and passions gives rise to a marvellous array of events on almost every subject and theme imaginable. Events spill out of our newspapers and television screens, occupy much of our time and enrich our lives. As we study the phenomenon of events, it is worth examining where the events tradition in the United Kingdom has come from, and what forces are likely to shape its future growth and development. As events emerge as an industry in their own right, it is also worth considering what elements characterise such an industry and how the UK events industry might chart its future directions in an increasingly complex and demanding environment.

Events Management. DOI: 10.1016/B978-1-85617-818-1.10001-5

EVENTS AS BENCHMARKS FOR OUR LIVES

Since the dawn of time, human beings have found ways to mark important events in their lives: the changing of the seasons; the phases of the moon; the eternal cycle of birth, death and the miraculous renewal of life each spring. In Britain, the early folk festivals were associated with Plough Monday, May Day, Midsummer Day and Harvest Home — the latter celebrating the final gathering of the grain harvest (Oxford Interactive Encyclopaedia, 1997). From the Chinese new year to the Dionysian rites of ancient Greece and the European carnival tradition of the middle ages, myths and rituals have been created to interpret cosmological happenings. To the present day, scratch the surface of the symbols of Old Father Time on New Year's Eve, Guy Fawkes on 5 November Bonfire Night, Halloween, or Father Christmas on 25 December — and remnants of old myths, archetypes and ancient celebrations will be found underneath.

Both in private and in public, people feel the need to mark the important occasions in their lives and to celebrate milestones. Coming of age, for example, is often marked by rites of passage such as initiation ceremonies, the Jewish bar and bat mitzvahs and the suburban twenty-first birthday party. At the public level, momentous events become the milestones by which people measure their private lives. We may talk about things happening 'before the new millennium', in the same way that an earlier generation talked of marrying 'before the Depression' or being born 'after the War'. Occasional events — the 1966 World Cup, the new millennium, and the Manchester 2002 Commonwealth Games — help to mark eras and define milestones.

Even in the high-tech era of global media, when people have lost touch with the common religious beliefs and social norms of the past, we still need larger social events to mark the local and domestic details of our lives.

THE RICH TRADITION OF EVENTS

The UK and the various countries and cultures within it, have a rich tradition of rituals and ceremonies extending over thousands of years. These traditions, influenced by changes within society, including urbanisation, industrialisation and the increasingly multicultural population, have greatly influenced many events as they are celebrated today. Palmer and Lloyd (1972) highlight that Britain has many customs and traditions that are tied in with the changing seasons and country life. In addition, they note that with developing immigration, particularly after the war, settlers brought their own customs and traditions that have now become part of Britain's heritage. In the cultural collision with the first migrants from the former colonies of India, Pakistan and the Caribbean, new traditions have formed alongside the old. However, many events that people take for granted today have been taking place in one form or another for hundreds of years. These include fairs, festivals, sporting events, exhibitions and other forms of public celebration.

The Lord Mayor's Show provides an example of this — originating from 1215 when King John granted a Charter confirming the right of the citizens of London to choose their own mayor. One of the conditions of the Charter was that the man chosen as mayor must be presented to King John for approval and had to swear an oath of allegiance. This was the basis for the original show — literally, the mayor has to go to Westminster to be shown to the king. The Lord Mayor's Show is now the largest parade of its kind in the world — with 6000 participants, 2000 military personnel, 200 horses, 220 motor vehicles, 56 floats, 20 marching bands, and the state coach, all involved in the procession that is nearly 2.5 miles long, yet travels a route of less than 2 miles (Lord Mayor's Show, 2000).

The term 'festival' has been used for hundreds of years and can be used to cover a multitude of events. The Policy Studies Institute (PSI, 1992, p. 1) notes that:

'A festival was traditionally a time of celebration, relaxation and recuperation which often followed a period of hard physical labour, sowing or harvesting of crops, for example. The essential feature of these festivals was the celebration or reaffirmation of community or culture. The artistic content of such events was variable and many had a religious or ritualistic aspect, but music, dance and drama were important features of the celebration.

The majority of fairs held in the UK can trace their ancestry back to the Charters and privileges granted by the Crown. The original purpose of the fairs was to trade produce — much the same as with exhibitions today. For example, the famous Scarborough Fayre dates back to 1161. The first recorded Charter granted to King's Lynn was granted in 1204, with the Charter for the Valentine's Day fair granted by Henry VIII in 1537. Cambridge Fair dates back to 1211 and provides an excellent example of a fair that started out as a trade fair run under the auspices of the local religious community; it continues today as a pleasure fair. Hull Fair, the largest travelling fair in Europe, dates back to 1278 and Nottingham Goose Fair to 1284 (National Fairground Archive, 2007).

Encyclopedia Britannica (2009) notes that the term 'festival', as commonly understood today, was first used in England in 1655, when the Festival of the Sons of the Clergy was first delivered at St Paul's Cathedral, London. Established as an annual charity sermon, it assumed a musical character in 1698. Other examples of early festivals include the Three Choirs Festival (1713), the Norfolk and Norwich Festival (1789) and the Royal National Eisteddford of Wales, (revived in 1880 although it originates from 1176) (PSI, 1992). Festivals of secular music started in the eighteenth century — the first devoted to Handel took place in Westminster Abbey in 1784 — with many continuing well into the twentieth century (Britannica. com, 2005).

INDUSTRIALISATION, FESTIVALS AND THE SPORTING EVENTS CALENDAR

Exhibitions and trade shows have taken over much of the traditional purpose of the fairs. The Exhibition Liaison Committee (1995, pp. 2–3) noted:

> Since pre-Biblical times producers and merchants have displayed their wares at fairs. However the present UK exhibition industry can trace its origin back to the first industrial exhibitions held in London in 1760 and 1791. These were organised by the Royal Society of Arts and culminated . . . in the Great Exhibition of 1851 which was housed in the impressive 'Crystal Palace' erected in Hyde Park.

Dale (1995) highlights that the Great Exhibition was a triumphant success, with over six million visitors – around 25% of the population. It proved to be an excellent promotional tool for Britain, British industry and related trades, and was the first international trade show (Cartwright, 1995). The exhibition generated profits of over £180 000 (Exhibition Liaison Committee, 1995). The following years saw the development of many exhibition facilities that are in existence today, including Alexandra Palace and the Royal Agricultural Hall (1862), Olympia (1886) and Earls Court (originally opened 1887, current structure from 1936).

Sport provides many of the UK's most significant and enduring events. As well as attracting large crowds and media attention, they help to create a national identity and are important to the country's tourism appeal. As the originator of most team sports, Britain has an international reputation for sport, and stages many international world-class events each year, drawing in large numbers of visitors and providing major benefits for local economies (English Tourism, 1999). Many of the most famous UK sporting events have their origins in the eighteenth and nineteenth centuries, including equestrian events such as Royal Ascot (1711), the Epsom Derby (1780) and the Aintree Grand National (1839, name adopted 1847), water-based events, such as the Oxford and Cambridge Boat Race (1829), Cowes Week (1826), Henley Royal Regatta (established 1839, named Henley Royal Regatta from 1851) and the first Americas Cup race off the Solent, Isle of Wight (1851). Other major events from this period include The Open Championship (Golf) (1860), the FA Cup (1872), The Championship (Wimbledon) (1877) and Test cricket (England vs. Australia, 1882).

During the eighteenth and nineteenth centuries, festivals that were predominantly choral developed in cities across England, including Leeds. However, further trends included local singing competitions in taverns in the eighteenth century, and amateur singing and brass band competitions in the nineteenth century (Britannica. com, 2005).

Wood (1982) observed that due to the dual forces of industrialisation and Christianity in the mid-nineteenth century, many of the traditional festivities that developed alongside folklore were lost. In the emerging climate of industrialisation, the working classes had little time for traditional celebrations, with the new National Police Force disciplining the working classes through the criminalisation of many traditional festivities. The middle of the nineteenth century saw at least forty saint days in the year, although not all were public holidays in all areas. However, the Victorians believed that it was not economical for workers to have so much free time; as a result, they abolished a number of festivals and tidied up the public holidays. Later, they introduced a week's paid holiday to replace lost Bank holidays (Harrowven, 1980). Wood (1982, p. 13) noted:

> *'The assumed irrationality of festivity underlay the bourgeois social order of industrial life and for the working classes this meant that old ways of thinking about the future, steeped in folklore and superstition, were slowly obliterated. The emerging morality of industrialism insisted that personal security could only be gained by thrift, diligence and abstinence from the pleasures of the flesh. There was little place for riotous assembly in this code of ethics until far sighted [sic] commercial entrepreneurs began to discover in the frustrated needs of the working class a whole new sector of the industrial market. Celebration was then resurrected as the Leitmotif of the emerging leisure industry and has remained a key element of mass entertainment ever since.'*

Palmer and Lloyd (1972) acknowledge that weakening community life and the increasing pace of progress led to folk festivities that had lasted hundreds of years being changed — a trend which they note will continue with the rapid change in civilization. However, they highlight that British resolve has prevented the complete extinction of these celebrations, with many of them too deep-rooted in communities to completely disappear. Although many do not take place as spontaneously as previously, the folk rituals continue to survive or be revived, with some of the modern revivals adding new energy to old traditions. They explain:

> *'It is said that if you scratch civilisation you find a savage. If you scratch the owner-occupier of a desirable semi-detached residence you will a find a man who is unconsciously seeking something safe and familiar, something with roots deep in the forgotten past. He may call Morris dancers "quaint" . . . and refuse to appear as St. George in a mummer's play, but he will still eat hot cross buns on Good Friday, hang up mistletoe at Christmas and give a Hallowe'en party . . . Modern man is what history has made him, and one facet of history lies in the popular customs that have their beginnings in cults almost as old as man himself.'*

(Palmer and Lloyd, 1972, pp. 9–10)

Records of amateur festivals taking place across Britain date from as early as 1872. The 1870's witnessed the spontaneous birth of local competition festivals alongside developments of intense competition in industry. The first recorded festival was Workington Festival, which is still running today (BFF, 2005). Perhaps one of the most famous music events in the world, the Last Night of the Proms, originates from this period with the first Proms concert taking place in 1895.

BIRTH OF THE EVENTS INDUSTRY?

Wood (1982) highlighted the birth of what is now becoming known as the events industry. She identified that commercialisation of popular celebrations required wealth for people to participate and therefore involved selecting suitable elements of the traditional festivities and adapting them for 'vicarious consumption'. Consequently, celebrations that were traditionally seen as indecent or immoral were restricted. The Hoppings in Newcastle (now one of Britain's biggest fairs), provides a good example of one approach; it was founded in 1882 as a temperance festival, in conjunction with race week. The idea of using a fair to advise people to act morally and not drink was in contrast to the London Council and the Fair Act of 1871, which asserted that fairs were places of ill repute and dangerous for residents. The purpose of fairs has changed over time, and they are seen today as events that mainly operate for enjoyment, with rides, sideshows and stalls (Toulmin, 1995).

With the increase in work through industrialisation, the practicalities of celebration meant that people were too tired to celebrate as they had done previously. Thus, celebration and commercial celebration provided the opportunity to relax from working life, and from a government perspective, it provided the basis for ensuring that celebration and the traditional pleasure culture did not interfere with work. Wood (1982, p. 15) noted:

> 'In order to remove the guilty feelings attached to the pursuit of 'sinful pleasure' by the legacy of the Protestant Work Ethic, it became necessary to firstly earn the material means of acquiring product of the entertainment industry and secondly, to ornate the rituals of mass celebration with an aura of professionalism and beneficient spectacle strong enough to dispel the appeal of popular home-spun amateur entertainment and pleasure seeking.'

In 1871 Bank holidays were made lawful, with the days dictated by the government and the monarch. Since that time, the monarch has retained the power to proclaim additional holidays, with the approval of Parliament, as illustrated by the extra Bank holidays given for the 1977 Silver Jubilee and the 2002 Golden Jubilee celebrations (Harrowven, 1980).

Speak to any international visitor and it is likely that comments relating to Britain's rich history will emerge. The monarchy and anniversaries of major historic events have played a key role in public celebrations and the traditions, image and culture of Britain for hundreds of years. Royal events encourage patriotic fervour and serve not only to involve the general public in celebrating the monarchy itself, but have also contributed much to the UK's position as one of the leading international tourist destinations, attracting millions of tourists each year. Judd (1997) notes that Queen Victoria's Diamond Jubilee celebrations in June 1897 were staged mainly to display the achievements of Britain and the British Empire. Patriotic sentiment, lavish receptions and balls, street parties with flags and bunting, shows and military and naval displays marked the festivities — similar displays have been witnessed since, for example, at the Coronation of Queen Elizabeth in 1953 and the Queen's Silver Jubilee in 1977.

According to Rogers (2007), the origins of the UK conference industry lie in political and religious congresses, and the trade and professional association conventions in America of the late nineteenth century, though recognition of the industry itself is more recent, dating from the middle to latter half of the twentieth century. Shone (1998) supports this and notes that although the emergence of the conference industry dates from the last thirty years, and to some extent, the past two hundred and fifty years, this would ignore the development that took place for the preceding thousands of years. He goes on to discuss the development of meeting places for trade, supported by the growth in appropriate facilities, from public halls (first century AD), churches (tenth and eleventh centuries), market towns (thirteenth century), and guildhalls (fourteenth century), through inns and coffee houses (seventeenth century), assembly rooms, town halls and universities (eighteenth century), to specialist banqueting and assembly facilities such as the Café Royal and Connaught Rooms in London, and meeting rooms within hotels (nineteenth century).

Some of the leading exhibitions today have their origins in the early part of the twentieth century. The Ideal Home Show is a prime example. The show was launched in 1908. Since that time, it has mirrored changes in Britain's social and lifestyle trends. The show is dedicated to setting and reflecting trends from the 1930s when plastics and stainless steel made their first appearance, through the 1960s with the introduction of American-style kitchens as an international dimension was introduced, to the twenty-first century when the exhibits continue to be at the forefront of innovation and still include the 'House of the Future' — one of the show's most famous features. Who would have thought in 1908 that technological concepts then showcased at the exhibition as futuristic and innovative, could become part of everyday life?

Significance of events established

In 1915, the British government realized the value of exhibitions to the country and held the first British Industries Fair at the Royal Agricultural Hall (now the Business Design Centre), London. This event proved to be a great success and grew rapidly over the following years, to the stage where it ran in Earls Court, Olympia and Castle Bromwich (Birmingham) simultaneously. However, due to the increasing demand from trade associations and exhibitors for more specialized events, the final British Industries Fair took place in 1957 (Cartwright, 1995). The period is also notable for the 1938 Empire Exhibition at Bellahouston in Glasgow, which attracted 12.6 million paying customers (Dale, 1995).

Following the World Wars, the promotion of popular celebration became a thriving sector of the new industrial economy. The Policy Studies Institute (PSI, 1992) notes that since 1945, arts festivals have become a prominent feature in the UK. It adds that over 500 festivals now take place each year, in addition to hundreds of one-day community festivals and carnivals. Some of the most famous festivals, including Cheltenham (1945), the Edinburgh International Festival (1947) and the Bath Festival (1948 — then named Bath Assembly) were developed by arts practitioners following the two World Wars, as a means of encouraging contact between European countries (PSI, 1992). Although some arts festivals have been in existence for hundreds of years, over half of all festivals have been established since 1980, with only six festivals within the PSI research established before the twentieth century and a small number held before the end of the Second World War. Those taking place before 1945 tended generally to be music festivals, — for example, the Glyndebourne Festival (1934) which focuses on opera, — as arts festivals are more contemporary.

The 1951 Festival of Britain was held at South Bank Centre, London, to celebrate the centenary of the Great Exhibition and to provide a symbol for Britain's emergence from the Second World War. It proved to be a great success, yet it underlined the fact that Britain had lost its early lead in staging international exhibitions (Cartwright, 1995). As a result, in 1959 the Pollitzer Committee inquiry identified that the shortage of quality exhibition space was damaging the UK's ability to compete in the global marketplace and recommended that further development was required. Rogers (2008) points out that since the 1960s significant investment has been made in the infrastructure to support conferences, meetings and related events, with the 1990s showing the highest sustained growth in venue development, illustrated, by the developments in Birmingham (International Convention Centre) and Glasgow (Scottish Exhibition and Conference Centre).

Emergence of professional events

The 1950s and 1960s were also notable for other factors that shaped events as they appear today. First, the period saw the rapid increase in communities from the West Indies and South Asia and the establishment of events to celebrate these cultures. For example, the Notting Hill Carnival was established in 1964 by the West Indian community to celebrate their ancestors' freedom from slavery (see the case study in Chapter 2). Second, the period saw the emergence of festival culture that is still around today. McKay (2000) highlights that contrary to popular belief, festival culture was established in the 1950s rather than the 1960s. He states:

> The early roots of British festival culture in the jazz festivals run by Edward (Lord) Montagu at Beaulieu (1956–1961) and in Harold Pendelton's National Jazz Federation events at Richmond then Reading (from 1961 on) indicate the perhaps surprising extent to which the trad and modern jazz scenes of the 1950s and early 1960s blazed the trail for the hippy festivals of the later 1960s and beyond.

This period saw the appearance of a number of popular music festivals, including the Bath Blues Festival (1969), the Pilton Festival (1970) — the forerunner of the Glastonbury Festival), and the Isle of Wight Festival (1968, 1969, 1970). The Isle of

Wight Festival 1970 is believed to be the largest UK festival ever, and over 600,000 people are believed to have attended. This event illustrated the need for professional organisation and control as the organizers ended up making the event free when they lost control of admissions. The promoters, Fiery Creations, are said to have made this their last festival on the island owing to concerns that the size of the festival had made it unmanageable.

The 1970s and 1980s saw a range of multipurpose venues being built, funded predominantly by local authorities including the National Exhibition Centre (NEC) in Birmingham (1976) and the Wembley Exhibition Centre (1977) (Exhibition Liaison Committee, 1995). Since then, the pace of development has continued with the addition of exhibition space alongside or within football stadia, an increasing number of multipurpose indoor arenas (e.g. Sheffield, Manchester, Birmingham, London, Newcastle, Cardiff and Belfast), additional exhibition space at the NEC and Earls Court (Greaves, 1999), plus the launch of Excel in London (2000); yet demand apparently still outstrips supply given the continuing development and re-development taking place.

The growth in community festivals in the 1970s allowed professional artists to measure their skills against ordinary working people, and provided a means of harnessing community spirit by focusing attention away from social deprivation and unrest. Funding for such celebrations came through art associations, with the events developed within the umbrella of social welfare and community development. Thus, community festivals and festivities were used by governments to provide a focus for society, in order to rejuvenate communities and to provide a base for social and economic regeneration (Wood, 1982). Festivals had become part of the cultural landscape and had become connected again to people's needs and lives. Every community it seemed, had something to celebrate and the tools with which to create its own festival.

Closely allied to sporting events is the area of corporate entertainment and hospitality. Crofts (2001) observes that Britain has one of the most sophisticated corporate hospitality markets, due in part to the concentrated summer social season that includes many of the distinguished events highlighted earlier. Peter Selby of Keith Prowse Hospitality noted that corporate hospitality in the UK is believed to originate from the early 1970s when the Open Golf Championship let Gus Payne erect a catering tent at the event. Other events saw this as a means of generating revenue and keeping control of their events by limiting their reliance on sponsors, and quickly followed suit. Further, in the mid to late 1970s, Keith Prowse Hospitality was established. Initially selling incentive packages for staff, clients began asking to use the facilities for entertaining their customers as well; at this point, a new industry was born (Crofts, 2001). Greaves (1996, p. 46) notes: 'with the blip of the recession putting a stop to the spiralling extravagance of the 1980s, a more targeted and cost efficient display of corporate entertainment has had to step into the shoes of the last decade, re-fashion them and then carry on walking down a different path'.

Through the 1980s and 1990s certain seminal events set the pattern for the contemporary events industry as we know it today. The Commonwealth Games in

Brisbane in 1982 ushered in a new era of maturity and prominence for that city and a new breed of sporting events. It also initiated a career in ceremonies and celebrations for the former ABC rock show producer Ric Birch, which led to his taking a key role in the opening and closing ceremonies at the Los Angeles, Barcelona and Sydney Summer Olympics and the Turin Winter Olympics.

The Olympic Games in Los Angeles in 1984 demonstrated that major events could be economically viable and blended the media mastery of Hollywood-style spectacle with a sporting event in a manner that had not been done before and it set a standard for all similar events in future. The production and marketing skills of the television industry brought the Olympics to a wider audience than ever before. Television also demonstrated the power of a major sporting event to bring increased profile and economic benefits to a city and to an entire country. The 1980s saw a rapid increase in the use of spectator sports for corporate hospitality, with international sporting events such as the Open Golf Championship, Wimbledon, Royal Ascot, the British Grand Prix and rugby events at Twickenham still popular today. Roger de Pilkyngton, marketing director of Payne & Gunter noted that the focus changed from entertaining for the sake of it, to a more strategic use of hospitality. The mid to late 1980s saw an expansion of teambuilding and multi-activity events (Greaves, 1996), with market growth continuing into the twenty-first century.

In 1985, Live Aid introduced the era of the telethon, followed by the BBC's Children in Need and Comic Relief's Red Nose days (Anon., 1998). Live Aid was a unique television event — it was a direct plea to the audience of 1.5 billion people in 160 countries to give Ethiopia famine relief. It resulted in £200 million being raised (Younge, 1999).

Table 1.1 illustrates the origin dates of arts festivals. It shows particularly that the 1980s benefited from significant expansion, due to success observed in established festivals, supported by increased funding from the Arts Council and regional arts associations (now boards). New Leisure Markets (1995) note that as a result of festival development and re-development in the 1970s and 1980s, the typical festivals are modern events. Further, the 1980s saw increasing links with local authorities as they recognized the role of the arts in regeneration and tourism.

Table 1.1 Year of origin of UK arts festivals

Year of origin	Percentage of total
Pre- 1940	4
1940s	4
1950s	3
1960s	12
1970s	21
1980s	51
1990/1	5

(Source: PSI, 1992, p. 14)

These festivals gave the cities and towns a sense of identity and distinction and became a focus for community groups and charity fund-raising. It is a tribute to their place in the lives of their communities that many of these festivals still continue a century later.

During 1995, extensive VE Day and VJ Day commemorations, parades and celebrations marked the fiftieth anniversaries of the end of the Second World War in Europe and Japan. A series of events was staged not only to celebrate victory and to thank those that fought for their country, but also to look forward to the future and meet former enemies in a spirit of reconciliation. The finale to the VE celebrations was the biggest celebration of reconciliation in European history. Taking place in Hyde Park, London, it was attended by the Queen and members of the royal family, leaders and representatives of fifty-four countries touched by the war, and a crowd of 150,000 people (Hardman, 1995).

The UK enjoyed success throughout the twentieth century in hosting some of the world's major international sporting events. These became more than the particular sport — many are 'festivals of sport', reflecting the package of events taking place alongside the main event and also the increasing crossover between sport, leisure, festivals and public events. These develop interest in the event, encourage festive spirit and community involvement and enhance the image of the event in the host community. For example, during the twentieth century, the UK hosted the 1908 and 1948 Olympic Games in London, the 1966 World Cup in London, the 1986 Commonwealth Games in Edinburgh, the 1991 Rugby Union World Cup in England, the 1975, 1979 and 1983 Cricket World Cups and the 1991 World Student Games. In the past fifteen years alone, the UK has hosted in quick succession the UEFA European Football Championships (1996), the Rugby Union World Cup (1999), the Cricket World Cup (1999), the Rugby League World Cup (2000), Ryder Cup (2002), the Commonwealth Games (2002) and the World Indoor Athletics Championships (2003). More recently, England spent £10 million bidding for the FIFA Football World Cup in 2006 — a bid subsequently awarded to Germany, and also bid for the 2007 Rugby Union World Cup — an event awarded to France, while a joint Scotland/Ireland bid for the 2008 UEFA European Football Championships was awarded to Austria and Switzerland. Wales (Celtic Manor) will be hosting the Ryder Cup in 2010 while Scotland (Gleneagles) holds this privilege in 2014. Finally, the UK is becoming increasingly successful at winning bids for major events, with England hosting the 2010 Women's Rugby World Cup, London hosting the 2012 Olympic Games, the UK hosting the 2013 Rugby League World Cup, Glasgow hosting the 2014 Commonwealth Games, England hosting the 2015 Rugby World Cup and England currently bidding to host the 2018 FIFA World Cup. The pursuit of major events such as these forms part of government strategy implemented through UK Sport (discussed further in Chapter 3). Since 1997 when the strategy was launched, UK Sport has supported over one hundred and twenty events of European, World or Commonwealth status. They are also pursued by national agencies such as EventBritain, EventScotland, the Northern Ireland Tourist Board (with the Welsh Assembly consulting on a major events strategy with a view to forming EventWales) and regional agencies or local authorities — for example, the North West Development Agency, Yorkshire Forward, Events for London, and the Sheffield City Council Major Events Unit (discussed in Chapter 3).

The spirit of Live Aid was rejuvenated in 1999, with the NetAid fundraising concerts and again in 2005 for the Tsunami Relief Concert at Millennium Stadium in Cardiff and Live 8 (see event profile and case study in Chapter 14). Using modern technology not available at Live Aid in 1985, the NetAid concerts took place simultaneously in London, Geneva and New Jersey, with a combined live audience of 110 000. However, the difference with this event was that 2.4 million people watched the live Internet broadcast of the event in one day, setting a new world record; and worldwide television, radio and Internet coverage has so far generated over 2 billion impressions on the NetAid.org website. NetAid illustrates the potential use of the Internet as a medium for social change, through its use of the Internet to provide a global resource against extreme poverty. NetAid has also been credited with helping to secure $27 billion in US debt relief by U2's Bono (NetAid.org, 1999). Live 8 took place in July 2005. Timed before the G8 Summit of world leaders (Canada, France, Germany, UK, Italy, Japan, Russia and USA) at Gleneagles Hotel in Scotland, Live 8 was developed not to raise money, — which had been the aim of Live Aid, — but to campaign for justice by putting pressure on the G8 leaders to end poverty in Africa by cancelling debt, increasing aid and delivering trade justice. What had originally been planned as five concerts (Berlin, London, Paris, Rome and Philadelphia) expanded to twelve, with events taking place in Barrie, Berlin, Cornwall (Eden Project), Johannesburg, London, Moscow, Paris, Philadelphia, Rome and Tokyo. The main concert took place in Hyde Park where an audience of over 200,000 watched acts including U2, Sir Paul McCartney, Robbie Williams, Cold Play, Madonna, Dido, Pink Floyd, The Who, REM, and a host of other leading artists perform in the ten hour event. Live 8 was watched by an estimated three billion people worldwide with the event broadcast through television, radio, the Internet and mobile phones (Live8, 2005).

Into the new millennium

The trend in local authority funding for arts festivals has continued into the twenty-first century. Allen and Shaw (2001) found that, of the 137 festivals responding to their study, 82% received part of their funding in 1998/9 from local authorities, with 51% gaining grants from arts councils and 42% from the English Regional Arts Boards. In the updated BAFA commissioned study, based on 2006/7 data, Sam and the University of Brighton (2008) reported that of the one hundred and ninety three festivals responding to the study, around £5.2 million of their £21.3 million combined total funding came from local authorities and councils, compared to £5.4 million from Arts Councils, £4 million in grants from Trusts and Foundations and £6.7 million from business. New Leisure Markets (1995) concludes that festivals are attractive to local authorities because they provide visitors/tourists, encourage commercial sponsorship, present cultural experiences for residents by taking arts to a wider audience, give staff a focus and can motivate involvement from the local performing arts community.

Commenting on their study (BAFA, 2000), Tim Joss Chair of BAFA and Director of the Bath Festivals Trust, highlights the modern role of festivals. He comments:

> *It's time for many people — in the arts, in national and local government, and elsewhere — to change their attitude to festivals. The old view that festivals are flashes in the pan contributing nothing to long-term development must go. This valuable research paints a very different picture. It makes an impressive case for arts festivals as flexible, efficient, contemporary enterprises rooted in their local communities. And thanks to their special freedom to collaborate with artists, venues, and artistic and other partners, they are proving themselves valuable catalysts for cultural, social and economic development.*
>
> **(BAFA, 2001)**

Across the UK the new millennium brought an unprecedented level of funding for community projects, including events, and firmly focused the spotlight on the events industry. North West Arts Board (1999) note that community festivals and events such as melas, the Chinese new year and carnivals are extremely important, providing not only the opportunity for communities to celebrate their identity and presence in the UK, but also a stage for creative expression within the context of their cultural heritage. The year-long Millennium Festival, supported with £100 million from the National Lottery-funded Millennium Commission, saw communities take part in around 2000 events across the UK, including major celebrations in twenty-two towns and cities on New Year's Eve 1999, a further thirty-two events closing the year in 2000 and over three hundred and seventy large-scale festivals. Steve Denford, Senior Festival Manager at the Millennium Commission Press Office (2000) noted: 'The Millennium Festival is the largest programme of year-long celebrations ever mounted in the UK with an opportunity for all communities to come together and celebrate the year 2000. Throughout the year, the diverse programme of events is offering something for everyone and something happening everywhere.'

One of the largest combined events was the Beacon Millennium Project, whereby 1400 beacons were lit across the UK on 31 December 1999, providing the focal point for community-level celebrations. Further initiatives included investment of over £1.3 billion in around 200 new buildings, environmental projects, visitor attractions and a total of £200 million provided as 40,000 grants or 'Millennium Awards' for individuals to put their ideas into action for their communities (Millennium Commission, 2000).

The Millennium Festival caused communities across Britain to pause and reflect on identity and the past and to look forward to the future. It also changed forever the nature of our public celebrations as a new benchmark has been created, against which all future events will be measured. The millennium also left a legacy of public spaces dedicated to celebrations and events, and government, both local and central, supportive of their social and economic benefits. For example, the Millennium

Square in Leeds opened on 31 December 2000 as a multipurpose event and leisure space in the heart of the city, – to provide a relaxing environment for the people of Leeds, while incorporating a range of services to reflect the needs of events organizers.

Major events are continuing into the twenty-first century with increasing recognition of the role that events can play beyond merely entertainment, linking in to cultural, arts, regeneration, education, tourism and other strategies. A series of festivals and events were planned as part of the Sea Britain Festival 2005, coordinated by the National Maritime Museum, 'to celebrate the ways in which the sea touches all of our lives.' The centrepiece of the festival was the Trafalgar Weekend in October to mark the 200th anniversary of Nelson's victory (National Maritime Museum, 2005). Liverpool successfully hosted the European Capital of Culture 2008. This prompted a series of events before, during and after 2008 and significant investment in cultural infrastructure, revitalising the city (Liverpool Culture Company 2005a; Garcia, Melville and Cox 2010). The other unsuccessful bidding cities, including Newcastle Gateshead and Bradford have capitalised on their bids to take forward cultural programmes in their cities. For example, Newcastle Gateshead Initiative implemented an ambitious programme of world-class events, festivals and initiatives in 2003 through the culture[10] project (Newcastle Gateshead Initiative, 2010).

The business world was quick to discover the marketing and image-making power of events, and events were established through the 1990s and early in this decade as an important element of the corporate marketing mix. Companies and corporations began to partner and sponsor major events, such as Microsoft and Adecco's involvement in the 2002 Manchester Commonwealth Games. Other corporations created events as vehicles for their own marketing – for example, Sundae on the Common, a festival on Clapham Common in London developed for Ben & Jerry's ice-cream. By early this decade, corporate involvement in events had become the norm, so sponsorship was perceived as an integral part of staging major events. Companies became increasingly aware of the role that events could play in promoting their image and increasing their market share, but they also became more focused on event outcomes and return on investment. It became common for large companies to have an in-house events team, focused not only on the company's involvement in public events but also on the internal role of events in company and product promotions, staff training and morale building. Events became not only a significant part of the corporate vocabulary but also a viable career option with employment opportunities and career paths.

This brief outline of the history of modern events relates primarily to the UK situation, but a similar story has been replicated in most postindustrial societies. The balance between more traditional festivals and contemporary corporate events changes according to the nature of the society in a given geographic area. Nevertheless, there is ample anecdotal evidence to suggest that the growth of events is a worldwide phenomenon. In Asia, the staging of the Summer Olympics in Beijing in 2008, the World Expo in Shanghai and the Commonwealth Games in Delhi in 2010 will see these cities use major events to showcase their emerging prominence to the world. This increasing interest in events in Asia is reflected in the establishment of the International Festivals and Events Association affiliates in Beijing, Singapore and South Africa (International Festivals and Events Association, 2006). In Australia, the state governments events corporations and the staging of the Sydney Olympics, the Rugby World Cup and the Melbourne Commonwealth Games are regarded as international benchmarks for best practice in the field. The UK is widely recognised as a leader in the events field, for example, with successful events such as the Edinburgh International Festival, the 2002 Manchester Commonwealth Games and the opening and closing ceremonies of the 2004 Athens Olympics organized by Jack Morton UK, helping shape the future bidding for events in the UK.

WHAT ARE EVENTS?

Before exploring events in further detail throughout the following chapters, it is important to clarify the terms used. Many authors have discussed the definition of 'events' and the various terms used to describe these; however, there is little agreement on standardized terms or categories. A useful starting point when looking at definitions and terminology is The Chambers Dictionary (1998, p. 560) which defines an event as:

> *anything which happens; result; any incidence or occurrence esp a memorable one; contingency or possibility of occurrence; an item in a programme (of sports, etc); a type of horse-riding competition, often held over three days (three-day event), consisting of three sections, ie dressage, cross-country riding and showjumping; fortune or fate (obs); an organized activity at a particular venue, eg for sales promotion, fundraising.*

It can be concluded from this definition that the term event may be viewed in a variety of ways, with other texts and dictionaries offering similar definitions. The Accepted Practices Exchange (APEX) Industry Glossary of terms (CIC, 2005) defines an event as, 'An organized occasion such as a meeting, convention, exhibition, special event, gala dinner, etc. An event is often composed of several different yet related functions.' Getz (2005, p. 16) notes that a principle applying to all events is they are temporary and that: 'Every such event is unique, stemming from the blend of management, program, setting, and people.'

Special events

The term 'special events' has been coined to describe specific rituals, presentations, performances or celebrations that are consciously planned and created to mark special occasions and/or to achieve particular social, cultural or corporate goals and objectives. Special events can include national days and celebrations, important civic occasions, unique cultural performances, major sporting fixtures, corporate functions, trade promotions and product launches. It seems at times that special events are everywhere; they have become a growth industry. The field of special events is now so vast that it is impossible to provide a definition that includes all varieties and shades of events. As an early pioneer in events literature, Goldblatt (2008, p. 5), highlighted the human aspect of events, defining special events as, 'a unique moment in time, celebrated with ceremony and ritual to satisfy specific needs.' In his groundbreaking work on the typology of events, Getz (2005, p. 16) suggests that special events are best defined by their context. He offers two definitions, one from the point of view of the events organiser, and the other from that of the customer, or guest:

1. A special event is a one-time, or infrequently occurring event outside the normal program or activities of the sponsoring or organising body.
2. To the customer or guest, a special event is an opportunity for an experience outside the normal range of choices or beyond everyday experience.

Getz believes that among the attributes that make events special are festive spirit, uniqueness, quality, authenticity, tradition, hospitality, theme orientation, affordability, convenience and symbolism.

It is clear from the above discussion that whether an event is special or not depends in some degree on the viewpoint of the practitioner or person experiencing the event, or indeed the author, researcher or student in the field. However, it is clear that 'special event' is again being used as a term that includes many other categories.

Jago and Shaw (1998, p. 28) express another view from a tourism context. Based on their research which explored and developed a definitional framework for special events, they suggested six core attributes of special events. These were that a special event should attract tourists or tourism development; be of limited duration; be a one-off or infrequent occurrence, raise the awareness, image, or profile of a region; offer a social experience and be out of the ordinary. In their summary definition of a special event they draw together a number of the above attributes: 'A one-time or infrequently occurring event of limited duration that provides the consumer with a leisure and social opportunity beyond everyday experience. Such events, which attract or have the potential to attract tourists are often held to raise the profile, image or awareness of a region' (Jago and Shaw, 1998, p. 29).

TYPES OF EVENTS

There are many different ways of categorising or grouping events, including by size, form and content. This text examines the full range of events that the events industry produces, using the term 'events' to cover all of the following categories.

Size

Events are often characterised according to their size and scale. Common categories are major events, mega-events, hallmark events and local/community events, although definitions are not exact and distinctions become blurred. Following an extensive review of classifications, typologies and terminology in use within the literature and published research, Jago and Shaw (1998) proposed mega-events and hallmark events as subcategories of major events, while other authors present these categories on a scale according to size and impact. This is illustrated in Figure 1.1.

Local or community events

Most communities produce a host of festivals and events that are targeted mainly at local audiences and staged primarily for their social, fun and entertainment value. These events often produce a range of benefits, engendering pride in the community, strengthening a feeling of belonging and creating a sense of place. They can also help to expose people to new ideas and experiences, encourage participation in sports and arts activities and encourage tolerance and diversity. For these reasons, local governments often support such events as part of their community and cultural development strategies. Janiskee (1996, p. 404) defines local or community events as:

> *family-fun events that are considered 'owned' by a community because they use volunteer services from the host community, employ public venues such as streets, parks and schools and are produced at the direction of local government agencies or non-government organizations (NGOs) such as service clubs, public safety organisations or business associations.*

Janiskee also comments that community festivals can become hallmark events and attract a large number of visitors to a community. He estimates that community

FIGURE 1.1 Categorisation of events

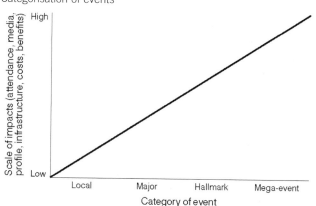

celebrations in the USA have been increasing at an annual rate of 5% since the 1930s, and anecdotal evidence suggests that it is reasonable to assume a similar growth in the UK.

Another growing subsection of community is the charity fund-raising event, which seeks to increase the profile and raise funds for a particular charity. Well-known examples include 'BBC Children in Need' and Comic Relief's 'Red Nose Day'. Although these events often have key financial objectives, they are generally seen as part of the not-for-profit community sector.

Major events

Major events are events that by their scale and media interest, are capable of attracting significant visitor numbers, media coverage and economic benefits. The Isle of Man hosts the TT Races and Silverstone has the British Formula One Grand Prix, both significant annual major events. Cowes Week, hosted on the Isle of Wight each year, provides a focus on maritime pursuits as well as attracting international prestige and media attention. The Open Championship, staged at different golf courses each year, attracts strong destination promotion around the world for the host region. Many top international sporting championships fit into this category and are increasingly being sought after and bid for, by national sporting organisations and governments in the competitive world of international major events. UK Sport (1999a, p. 4) considers that three elements are required for an event to be classed as a major sporting event:

1. It must involve competition between teams and/or individuals representing a number of nations.
2. It must attract significant public interest nationally and internationally, through spectator attendance and media coverage.
3. It must be of international significance to the sport concerned and feature prominently on its international calendar.

Hallmark events

The term 'hallmark events' refers to those events that become so identified with the spirit or ethos of a town, city or region that they become synonymous with the name of the place and gain widespread recognition and awareness. Tourism researcher Ritchie (1984, p. 2) defines them as: 'Major one time or recurring events of limited duration, developed primarily to enhance awareness, appeal and profitability of a tourism destination in the short term or long term. Such events rely for their success on uniqueness, status or timely significance to create interest and attract attention.'

Classic examples of hallmark events are the Carnival in Rio, known throughout the world as an expression of the Latin vitality and exuberance of that city, the Kentucky Derby in the USA, the Chelsea Flower Show in the UK, the Oktoberfest in Munich, Germany and the Edinburgh International Festival in Scotland. These events are identified with the very essence of these places and their citizens and generate huge tourist revenue as well as a strong sense of local pride and international recognition. Getz (2005, pp. 16—17) describes them in terms of their ability to provide a competitive advantage for their host communities:

> *In other words, 'hallmark' describes an event that possesses such significance, in terms of tradition, attractiveness, quality, or publicity, that the event provides the host venue, community, or destination with a competitive advantage. Over time, the event and destination can become inextricably linked, such as Mardi Gras and New Orleans.*

Examples in the UK might include the Notting Hill Carnival, the Grand National at Aintree, the FA Cup Final (mostly associated with Wembley Stadium, except during the recent redevelopment, when it took place at the Millennium Stadium, Cardiff) and The Championships at Wimbledon, all of which have a degree of international recognition. Commenting on the value of The Championships, John Barrett, author and Senior BBC Commentator stated: '"Wimbledon", as The Championships are universally known, has become over the years, an established part of the fabric of British life. It is more than a tradition, more than just the world's most important and historic tennis tournament. It is a symbol of all that is best about sport, royal patronage, and social significance that the British understand so well — a subtle blend that the rest of the world finds irresistible' (Jones, 2000).

Mega-events

Mega-events are those events that are so large that they affect whole economies and reverberate in the global media. These events are generally developed following competitive bidding. They include the Olympic Games, the FIFA World Cup and World Fairs but it is difficult for many other events to fit into this category. Marris in Getz (2005, p. 18) defines mega-events in the following way:

> *Their volume should exceed 1 million visits, their capital cost should be at least $500 million, and their reputation should be that of a 'must see' event.*

Getz (2005, p. 6) goes on to say:

> *Mega-events, by way of their size or significance, are those that yield extraordinarily high levels of tourism, media coverage, prestige, or economic impact for the host community, venue or organization.*

Hall (1997, p. 5), another researcher in the field of events and tourism, offers this definition:

> *Mega-events such as World Fairs and Expositions, the World Soccer Cup Final, or the Olympic Games, are events which are expressly targeted at the international tourism market and may be suitably described as 'mega' by virtue of their size in terms of attendance, target market, level of public financial involvement, political effects, extent of television coverage, construction of facilities, and impact on economic and social fabric of the host community.*

Finally, Jago and Shaw (1998, p. 29) define mega-events simply as, 'A one-time major event that is generally of an international scale.' In relative terms by these definitions the Great Exhibition in London in 1851 was perhaps the UK's first mega-event. Although belonging to an era of less encompassing media, other early examples may include the 1908 and 1948 London Olympics, the 1938 Empire Exhibition in Glasgow, the 1951 Festival of Britain and the 1966 World Cup. Modern events such as the 1991 World Student Games in Sheffield and the Euro '96 football championships would struggle to meet all of Getz's criteria. More recently, the UK Millennium Festival in 2000, if taken as a national event, would probably qualify, as may the Manchester 2002 Commonwealth Games with the associated national Spirit of Friendship Festival, the London 2012 Olympic Games and the Glasgow 2014 Commonwealth Games.

Form or content

Another common means of classifying events is by their form or content. Cultural events, including festivals, are a universal form of events that pre-date the contemporary events industry and exist in most times and most societies. Sports events have grown out of similar roots to become a sizable and growing sector of the event industry. Business events, sometimes called MICE (Meetings, Incentives, Conventions and Exhibitions) events, are an established arm of the events industry, and generate considerable income for their host cities and, increasingly, for regional centres.

Cultural events

Cultural events can also be major events. For example, major musicals such as *Phantom of the Opera, Sound of Music, Joseph* and *Cats* reap considerable tourism revenue for London's West End. Annual events such as Edinburgh festivals are an important expression of human activity that contributes much to our social and cultural life, while the hosting of London 2012 Olympics provides further cultural opportunities through the Cultural Olympiad. A further highly visible example of this was the extensive programme of events for the Liverpool 2008 European Capital of Culture. Cultural events are also increasingly linked with tourism to generate business activity and income for their host communities. Councils and related organisations supporting both private and public sector initiatives, have developed an enviable reputation and tourism bonanzas through staging a wide range of festivals that cater to different market needs. Cheltenham has developed the Cheltenham Jazz Festival, Cheltenham Music Festival, Cheltenham Science Festival and the Cheltenham Literature Festival; Bath and North East Somerset have developed the Bath International Music Festival and Glyndebourne has the developed the world-famous opera festival. Each has an eye to positioning itself in the tourism markets as well as in the arts world. Some local authorities and government/regional agencies are taking these initiatives one stage further, by developing an event-focused arts strategy (e.g. Bath and North East Somerset Council)(Arts

Development Service, 2004), using events to deliver the cultural strategy (e.g. Brighton and Hove, Newham Council) or developing a specific events/festivals strategy (e.g. Edinburgh District Council, EventScotland, North West Development Agency). The value and role of carnivals within cultural events has been recognised with the recently published National Carnival Arts Strategy (Nindi, 2005). Event tourism and event strategy are further discussed in Chapter 4.

Arts festivals share a number of characteristics, including intense artistic output, and a clear, time-specific programme delivered with a clear purpose and direction (Rolfe, 1992). South East Arts (1998, p. 2) have developed seven categories for festivals within their region based on the overall purpose and size, which can usefully be applied to classify festivals in other regions. These are:

1. *High-profile general celebrations of the arts*: these address an ambitious agenda and a multitude of aims — to reach the highest standards, to achieve a high media profile, to reach a broad audience, to generate high levels of income.
2. *Festivals that celebrate a particular location*: from small villages to large towns, these festivals aim to bring people together to celebrate their local area, often featuring a large number of local groups. These festivals subdivide into those run by voluntary groups and those run by local authorities. Festivals run by voluntary groups tend to be smaller.
3. *Art-form festivals*: focused on a specific art form, offering unique opportunities for audiences to see particular kinds of work, they may also address the development of that artform by providing a focus for critical debate, master classes, commissions of new work etc.
4. *Celebration of work by a community of interest*: these festivals highlight work by specific groups of people, for example disabled people, young people or women and often contain a large proportion of participatory workshops.
5. *Calendar*: cultural or religious festivals. Indigenous traditions of large-scale assembly have largely died away in England, but the Asian and Caribbean communities have brought carnivals and melas to enhance the cultural mix of festivals in the UK.
6. *Amateur arts festivals*: a large but low-profile sector that involves thousands of people. Many of these festivals are competitive.
7. *Commercial music festivals*: a hugely popular phenomenon; some local authorities also run outdoor pop music festivals that adopt a similar model.

New Leisure Markets (1995) notes that UK festivals are divided between single-theme and multi-theme events. The main themes for single-theme festivals are folk (35%), classical music (15%), jazz (15%), literature (5%) and film (5%). Page and Carey (2009) note that in 2008 live music, based on ticket sales and ancilliary sales (food, drink and merchandise), was worth in the region of £1.4 million. Further, AFO (2003, 2004) estimated that there are now over 350 folk festivals taking place in the UK, generating over £77 million, while Sam and the University of Brighton (2008) reported that the 193 arts festivals in their study generated around £41.8 million for the UK economy.

Sports events

The testing of sporting prowess through competition is one of the oldest and most enduring of human activities, with a rich tradition going back to the ancient Greek Olympics and beyond. Sports events are an important and growing part of the events industry, encompassing the full spectrum of individual sports and multi-sport events such as the Olympics, Commonwealth Games and Masters. Their ability to attract tourist visitors and to generate media coverage and economic impact has placed them at the forefront of most government events strategies and destination marketing programs. Sports events not only bring benefits to their host governments and sports organisations, but also benefit participants such as players, coaches and officials and bring entertainment and enjoyment to spectators. Examples of sports events can be readily identified in each of the size categories listed earlier.It is interesting to note that UK Sport (1999a) classifies the sporting calendar into four groups within the overall umbrella of major events, including mega, calendar, one-off and showcase events.UK Sport (2004) reclassified these as Type A, Type B, Type C and Type D events. There is some duplication with the points discussed earlier. However, the categories are included in order to illustrate the need to clarify terminology before commencing a study of events or bidding, and provide a useful illustration of potential objectives and means of attracting these events.

- *Type A (Mega events)*: i.e. irregular major international spectator events generating significant economic activity and media interest such as the Olympic Games. Includes the Summer Olympics, the Paralympic Games, the FIFA World Cup.
- *Type B (Calendar events)*: i.e. major spectator events generating significant economic activity, media interest and part of an annual domestic cycle such as the FA Cup Final.
- *Type C (One-off events)*: i.e. irregular one-off major spectator/competitor events generating an uncertain level of economic activity such as Grand Prix Athletics;.
- *Type D (Showcase events)*: i.e. major competitor events generating little economic activity and part of an annual cycle such as the national championships in most sports.

(UK Sport, 2004, p. 11).

Business events

Business events include meetings, conferences, exhibitions, incentive travel, and corporate events. These industries are sometimes grouped as discretionary business tourism, MICE (meetings, incentives, conventions and exhibitions/events), MEEC (meetings, expositions, events and conventions)(Fenich, 2008) or under a variety of other terms. Internationally, in April 2005 the Joint Meetings Industry Council recommended adopting the term The Meetings Industry as a unifying term at the launch of its "Profile and Power" campaign which seeks to distinguish these activities from tourism and other industries (JMIC, 2005). This sector is largely characterised by its business and trade focus, although there is a strong public and tourism aspect to many of its activities. The following section provides an overview of some of the sectors. Market data should be viewed with some caution, as much of it is based on estimates and the methodologies used are not always comparable; however it is useful in providing a general understanding of the market size.

The Business Visits & Events Partnership (BVEP) suggests that conferences, exhibitions, incentive travel, corporate hospitality and business travel combined account for 28 per cent of inbound visitors in the UK. This equates to an estimated tourism income worth £22 billion, not including business travel or business transacted at the events estimated to be worth £100 billion (BVEP, 2007).

According to the Convention Industry Committee (CIC) APEX initiative, the term 'meeting' is generally used to refer to "a gathering for business, educational or social purposes" (Fenich, 2008, p. 9) and therefore internationally the term has been adopted by some in industry to cover many sectors; however in the UK, the term is generally used to refer to smaller gatherings. Conferences can be very diverse, as revealed by the definition of the in the APEX Industry Glossary (CIC, 2005):

1. Participatory meeting designed for discussion, fact-finding, problem solving and consultation.
2. An event used by any organisation to meet and exchange views, convey a message, open a debate or give publicity to some area of opinion on a specific issue. No tradition, continuity or periodicity is required to convene a conference. Although not generally limited in time, conferences are usually of short duration with specific objectives. Conferences are usually on a smaller scale than congresses.

For the UK Events Market Trends Survey and the Business Meetings & Events Industry Survey, a more succinct definition is used: 'an out-of-office meeting of at least four hours' duration involving a minimum of eight people' (Rogers, 2008, p. 22). Conferences can be categorised according to their primary market focus generally as corporate or association. The conference market is worth an estimated £10.3 billion per annum (BVEP, 2007). Many conferences are relatively small scale, for example, the average number of delegates at corporate conferences is around 140 and 123 is the average delegate strength for association events (based on 2006 UK Conference Market Survey) (Rogers, 2008); the average attendance at annual association conferences is 289 (Rogers, 2010), though during the economic downturn these delegate numbers are likely to have reduced. However, there are larger examples that may illustrate the scale of the sector. The Rotary International World Convention brought 24,000 big-spending delegates to Glasgow in 1997, while the 1998 Lions International Convention at Birmingham NEC brought in 25,000 delegates from 180 countries (The NEC Group, 2005). Bournemouth International Centre hosted the biggest political conference so far in the UK − around 20,000 delegates, journalists, exhibitors and technicians attended the Labour Party Conference in September 1999 (Barnes, 1999). A further example from the Scottish Exhibition and Conference Centre (SECC) in Glasgow was seen in September 2004, where they hosted over 14,000 delegates for the 14th Annual Congress of the

European Respiratory Society which led to the injection of £10 million into the local economy (SECC, 2005). Finally, Excel London hosted Gastro 2009, UEGW/WCOG London in November 2009, which for the first time brought together almost 14,600 delegates from four of the leading gastroenterology organisations (Association Planner, 2009).

Exhibitions are a considerable and growing part of business events. Exhibitions can be defined as: '...*a presentation of products or services to an invited audience with the object of inducing a sale or informing the visitor. It is a form of three dimensional advertising where, in many instances, the product can be seen, handled, assessed by demonstration and in some cases even smelt and tasted.*' (Exhibition Liaison Council, 1995).Exhibitions were more recently and succinctly defined as 'an event that enables buyers and sellers to meet together in a market situation' (Exhibition Audience Audits Ltd, 2005). Internationally, the terms exposition, expo, (trade/consumer) show, trade fair are sometimes used interchangeably, though the term 'exhibition' has been adopted in the UK as the overarching term. Research undertaken in 2005 by KPMG on behalf of the Events Industry Alliance (EIA, 2007) suggests that the exhibitions sector was worth around £9.3 billion and attracted 17 million people to the UK. Exhibitions bring suppliers of goods and services together with buyers, usually in a particular industry sector. The British International Motor Show, the Ideal Home Show and the International Boat Show have been three of the largest exhibitions in the UK over the past ten years, each generating tens of thousands of visitors. The Exhibition Liaison Committee (1995, p. 8) identified that there are four main categories of exhibitions in the UK:

- *Agricultural shows*: held in the countryside on open sites (including purpose-built show grounds). They normally occur once a year, with attendance ranging from 5000 to 200,000 at the largest events within a period of one to five days. Examples include the Balmoral Show and The Royal County of Berkshire Show.
- *Consumer shows*: aimed mainly at the general public, although may have a trade element. They include subjects such as gardening, home interiors, motoring and fashion. These are extensively promoted by the media, for example, the Ideal Home Show (established in 1908) or Clothes Show Live.
- *Specialised trade shows and exhibitions*: the product emphasis and target buying audience are generally defined and controlled by the organiser. These are sometimes referred to as business-to-business (B2B) events. For example, International Confex and PLASA (Production Light and Sound) held at Earls Court, EventUK at NEC, the Event Production Show at Olympia, and The Showman's Show at Newbury Showground all focus on various aspects of the developing events industry.
- *Private exhibitions*: include product launches and in-store and concourse displays, which are exclusive to one or a defined group of manufacturers. The audience is normally informed by direct invitation.

A further category is one which combines trade and consumer markets, which Morrow (2007) refers to as the combined or mixed show; for example, the London

International Music Show or the London Boat Show. Finally, a new term to emerge over recent years is the confex — an exhibition and conference combined. These take one of two forms: they are either professional, scientific and medical conferences that offset their overheads from income generated by associated trade shows or exhibitions that enhance visitor numbers by featuring linked conferences in their show (Exhibition Audience Audits Ltd, 2005).

Exhibitions can also be categorised according to the industry sector that they focus on or by size. The Exhibition Industry Research Group (Exhibition Audience Audits Ltd, 2005) agreed to a new categorisation system in 2001, using four categories:

- **Category 1:** Exhibitions held in qualifying venues (a qualifying venue is one offering more than 2000 m^2 of continuous covered space).
- **Category 2:** One day public exhibitions held at qualifying venues.
- **Category 3:** Exhibitions that are primarily held outdoors in qualifying and non-qualifying venues (i.e. major agricultural and horticultural events attracting more than 50,000 visitors, trade or public and trade events that are held primarily at non-qualifying outdoor venues).
- **Category 4:** Exhibitions held at non-qualifying venues (venues that offer less than 2,000 m^2 for indoor exhibitions)

The modern exhibition industry is clearly structured, taking in venue owners, exhibition organisers and contractors from the supply side and exhibitors and visitors generating the demand. Major conference and exhibition centres in the main cities and many regional centres now vie for their share of the thriving business events market.

Another lucrative aspect is incentive travel, defined by the Society of Incentive Travel Executives (2006, cited in Rogers, 2008, p.67) as 'a global management tool that uses an exceptional travel experience to motivate and/or recognise participants for increased levels of performance in support of organisational goals'. The UK's unique locations and international popularity as a tourism destination make it a leading player in the incentive travel market, with the inbound incentive travel market estimated to be worth an estimated £1.2 billion in 2007 (BVEP, 2007).

A final category that may be included within business events is 'corporate events', which includes corporate hospitality, incentive travel, client entertainment, staff entertainment, team building, meetings and conferences (Rogers, 2008). Although definitive data does not exist due to difficulties with definition and the cross-over with other sectors, the client and staff entertainment aspects may be reflected in data collected on corporate hospitality, which indicates that the sector was worth around £1 billion (BVEP, 2007). In addition, a survey by the International Visual Communications Association (IVCA), found that audiovisual communications represented an industry sector set to be worth an estimated £3 billion in 2008 (International Visual Communications Association, 2008) — up from £2.62 billion in 2004, of which £578 million was attributable to business events (Anon., 2005a).

According to the UK Event Marketing Survey the events industry in the UK experienced a downturn in 2006-2008, with an estimated value of £7.2 billion compared to £8 billion in 2005-2007 (Rogers, 2010). It could be argued that this financial downturn in some ways mirrored the downturn in the wider economy brought about by the banking crisis and the longest recession in recent history, which stretched through 2009 with its impact continuing to reverberate around the economy into 2010. The recession had a major impact on the events industry, with a number of established companies going into receivership, organisational down-sizing leading to redundancies and increased consolidation of organisations within the market place. Many sectors from the automotive to the financial sector and from construction to the public sector, were severely affected with funding sources drying up and the role and value of events being questioned.

As a response, industries in the UK and overseas rallied together to demon-strate the value of their products and services. In the UK, National Meetings Week in 2009 took on added emphasis with a high profile Keep Britain Talking campaign (managed by Business Visits and Events at VisitBritain) which focused on the importance of meetings for achieving business objectives and demonstrated the economic benefits that they bring to the UK economy. As they noted, the meetings and events industry is worth £22 billion, contributes £3.8 billion in tax revenue and creates over 1.8 million jobs. The core messages were to 'buy meetings and events', 'buy British' and understand that 'Britain means value.' (Keep Britain Talking, 2009). The campaign was supported by a website (www. keepbritaintalking.co.uk), media campaign, events and ongoing discussions with the government. The campaign mirrored and supported activities in America, where the Keep America Meeting (KAM) project was established to draw the industry together to demonstrate the importance of meetings, events and incentive travel. This was particularly necessary due to the introduction of regulations surrounding the Troubled Asset Relief Program (TARP) — the government funding for struggling industries, —that required CEOs to justify expenditure on meetings, events and incentives and to ensure that they were not 'excessive or luxury items',' which resulted in a large number of cancellations (Keep America Meeting, 2009). The KAM campaign was supported by other initiatives including Meetings Mean Results (www.meetingsmeanresults.com) and Meetings Mean Business (www. meetingsmeanbusiness.com).

A major issue to arise over the past few years is the role of procurement/purchasing departments when putting business out to tender, which has led to heated discussions at industry events and in industry magazines. The tension has arisen due to a potential lack of understanding about the role that event management companies play in developing events and the differences in aims and terminology in use. In a bid to increase understanding of the roles of both parties, initiatives are being developed; for example, the Chartered Institute of Purchasing and Supply (CIPS) working with Eventia, organised the production of guidelines and workshops to educate procurement officers about the best way to work with event management companies (CIPS, 2007).

One positive consequence of the attention that was focused on events was an increasing interest in and application of Return On Investment (ROI) methodologies to the industry, with organisations now having a clearer understanding of their objectives when funding events and events managers now offering more sophisticated evaluation as part of their offering. The Meeting Professionals International (MPI) Foundation has undertaken research and produced a number of articles on ROI, together with industry projects (visit www.mpifoundation.org for further details).

All market data discussed in this section and to some extent elsewhere in this text, has to be considered in this context − that with regard to much of it, it is not clear whether the data was collected before or during the recession. If before, it is likely that the value of the industry overall reduced during the following period. If during, it is possible that it is understating value, as the industry has started on the road to recovery. As there continues to be a lack of agreement on what is covered within particular sectors, any data reported should be considered as an indication of the large scale of the industry being discussed and therefore demonstrating that it has a significant impact on the economy of UK (and the world). However, caution should be applied when adding figures together for each sector to indicate the value of the events industry overall, as there is at least a risk of double counting. What is clear is that there is a clear need for accurate market intelligence to support the development of the events industry.

THE STRUCTURE OF THE EVENTS INDUSTRY

The rapid growth of events in the past decade led to the formation of an identifiable event industry, with its own practitioners, suppliers and professional associations. The emergence of the industry has involved the identification and refinement of a discrete body of knowledge of industry best practice, accompanied by the development of training programs and career paths. The industry's formation has also been accompanied by a period of rapid globalisation of markets and communication, which has affected the nature of, and trends within, the industry. Further, it has been accompanied by an era of increasing government regulation, which has resulted in a complex and demanding operational environment. The following sections describe the key components of the event industry.

Events organisations

Events are often staged or hosted by events organisations, which may be event-specific bodies such as the Harrogate International Festival or the Glastonbury Festival of Contemporary Performing Arts. Other events are run by special teams within larger organisations, such as BBC Good Food Shows organised by BBC Haymarket Exhibitions or ITMA2003, which was organised by a team within the NEC Group. Corporate events are often organised by in-house events teams or by project teams within the companies that are putting on the event.

Events management companies

Events management companies are professional groups or individuals who organise events on a contract basis on behalf of their clients. The BBC, for example, may contract an event management company to stage an event or organise in-house through, for example, BBC Worldwide; or the Microsoft Corporation may contract an event manager to stage the launch of a new product such as Windows 7. The specialist companies often organise a number of events concurrently and develop long-term relationships with their clients and suppliers.

Events industry suppliers

The growth of a large and complex industry has led to the formation of a wide range of specialist suppliers. These suppliers may work in direct events related areas, such as staging, sound production, lighting, audiovisual production, entertainment and catering; or they may work in associated areas such as transport, communications, security, legal services and accounting services. This network of suppliers is an integral part of the industry, and their increasing specialisation and expertise assist the production of professional and high-calibre events.

Venues

Venue management often includes an events management component, whether as part of the marketing of the venue or as part of the servicing of events clients. Many venues such as historical houses, galleries, museums, theatres, universities and libraries create additional revenue by hiring their facilities for functions and corporate events. Merlin Entertainments Group (2009) encompasses a wide range of venues including Madame Tussauds, London, The London Eye, Alton Towers Resort, LEGOLAND®, Windsor and Warwick Castle. Types of venues that commonly include an event management component include hotels, resorts, conference, convention and exhibition centres, sports and fitness centres, sports stadiums, performing arts centres, heritage sites, theme parks, shopping centres and markets.

Industry associations

The emergence of the industry has also led to the formation of professional associations providing networking, communications and liaison within the industry, training and accreditation programs, codes of ethical practice and lobbying on behalf of their members. Because the industry is so diverse the UK has a multitude of industry associations that represent the various sectors within the industry, with some serving more than one sector and others competing for members within the same sector. Some are international associations with affiliated groups in countries such as the UK; others are specific to their region or country. Events managers should identify the association(s) that best suits their individual situation and the needs of a particular organisation; some associations promote individual membership, whilst others promote membership on an organisational basis. Some of the main trade and professional associations covering the events industry are listed below:

- *Associations*: European Society of Association Executives (ESAE)
- *Conference/meetings*: Association for Conferences and Events (ACE), Association of British Professional Conference Organisers (ABPCO), European Cities Marketing (ECM), International Association of Congress Centres (AIPC), Eventia, Institute of Travel & Meetings (ITM), International Association of Professional Conference Organisers (IAPCO), International Congress & Convention Association (ICCA), Meeting Professionals International (MPI), Meetings Industry Association (MIA) and Society of Association Executives (SAE).
- *Exhibitions*: Association of Event Organisers (AEO), Association of Shows and Agricultural Organisations (ASAO), Exhibition Supplier and Services Association (ESSA), National Exhibitors Association (NEA).
- *Incentive travel*: Eventia, UK Chapter of the Society of Incentive Travel Executives (SITE).
- *Festivals*: British Arts Festivals Association (BAFA), Association of Festival Organisers (AFO), British & International Federation of Festivals (BIFF), International Festival and Events Association (IFEA), Europe.
- *Corporate hospitality*: Eventia, Institute of Hospitality (IoH).
- *Music events/event production*: Concert Promoters Association (CPA), Production Services Association (PSA), Professional Light and Sound Association (PLASA), United Kingdom Crowd Management Association (UKCMA).
- *Event (other)*: Event Hire Association (EHA), Institute for Sport, Parks and Leisure (ISPAL), International Special Events Society (ISES), International Visual Communications Association (IVCA), National Outdoor Events Association (NOEA), The Event Services Association (TESA), Society of Event Organisers (SEO).
- *Venues*: Association of Event Venues (AEV), Meetings Industry Association (MIA), National Arenas Association (NAA), UK Stadium Managers Association (UKSMA)
- *Miscellaneous/suppliers*: British Hospitality Association (BHA), Hotel Booking Agents Association (HBAA), Independent Street Arts Network (ISAN), Made-Up Textiles Association (MUTA), Nationwide Caterers Association (NCASS), Society of Ticket Agents and Retailers (STAR).

It should be noted that although categorised for convenience, in reality many of these associations work across sectors and categories. In addition, organisations representing the hospitality, tourism and leisure industries and the professions associated with these, for example, the Tourism Alliance, British Hospitality Association, Institute of Travel & Tourism and The Tourism Society, also have a role in the events industry as the boundaries are not clearly defined.

There has been some discussion over whether there is a need for the consolidation of associations to ensure that the industry can move forward and its needs effectively lobbied to government. Although this has not happened across the board, there are a number of initiatives taking place where associations are effectively working together, forming federations and alliances. The Business Visits & Events Partnership (formerly Business Tourism Partnership) represents leading trade associations (ACE, AEME, AEO, APCO, BACD, BHA, EVA, Eventia, ICCA, MIA, MPI, NOEA, SITE Global) and government related agencies and departments (Department of Culture, Media and Sport, Northern Ireland Tourist Board, MeetEngland, UK Inbound, UK Trade & Investment, VisitBritain, VisitLondon, VisitScotland, VisitWales) involved in conferences, exhibitions, meetings and incentives. Eventia has been formed from the merger of the Incentive Travel and Meetings Association (ITMA), Corporate Events Association (CEA) and British Association of Conference Destinations (BACD). The Events Industry Alliance manages AEO, AEV and ESSA. The Events Industry Forum has been formed as an informal body to enable discussion on topics of interest to the events industry, for example, the rewrite of The Event Safety Guide (HSE, 1999). The European Live Music Forum (ELMF) draws together eight national and European associations with an interest in the live music industry in Europe, including CPA and IFEA, with the aim of developing the market and working effectively with the European Union Commission. European Federation of the Associations of Professional Conference Organisers (EFAPCO), including ABPCO, has been formed to enhance the image of Europe for hosting meetings, to promote the European Professional Conference Organisers (PCOs) and to maintain standards. An extended list of national and international associations is available on the website WorldofEvents.net.

External regulatory bodies

As noted, contemporary events take place in an increasingly regulated and complex environment. A series of local government and statutory bodies are responsible for overseeing the conduct and safe staging of events, and these bodies have an integral relationship with the industry. Councils often oversee the application of laws governing the preparation and sale of food, street closures, waste management and removal. In addition, events organisers have a legal responsibility to provide a safe workplace and to obey all laws and statutes relating to employment, contracts, taxation and so on. The professional event manager needs to be familiar with the regulations governing events and must maintain contact with the public authorities that have a vested interest in the industry.

Publications

In order to support the development of industry and education, an increasing number of books have been written, particularly over the last decade. There has been a significant increase in the number of books focusing on events planning and management over recent years, including Getz (2005), Goldblatt (2008), O'Toole and Mikolaitis (2002), Shone and Parry (2010), Raj, Walters and Rashid (2009), Silvers (2004b), Tassiopoulos (ed.)(2010), Van Der Wagen (2008), and Watt (1998). Getz (2005) and Goldblatt (2008) are generally acknowledged as the pioneers of the subject with the first editions of their books having been published in the mid-nineties. Getz (2007) is also advancing the development of the field beyond events management with his exploration of events studies, a move supported by an increasing range of research based texts, including Aitchison and Pritchard (eds.) (2007), Ali-Knight and Chambers (eds.)(2006), Ali-Knight, Robertson, Fyall and Ladkin (eds.)(2009), Baum, Deery, Hanlon, Lockstone and Smith (eds.)(2009), Fleming and Jordan (eds.)(2006), Horne and Manzentreiter (eds.)(2006), Picard and Robinson (eds.)(2006), Robertson (ed.)(2006), Robertson and Frew (ed.)(2008) and Weber and Chon (eds.)(2002). Building on the growth in interest and the number of courses studying the subject, two dedicated series of events books are available — The Wiley Event Management Series (edited by Dr Joe Goldblatt, published by John Wiley & Sons, Inc, Hoboken, New Jersey) and the Events Management Series (edited by Glenn Bowdin, Professor Donald Getz and Professor Conrad Lashley, published by Elsevier Butterworth-Heinemann, Oxford).Both series, together with a range of events-related texts from other publishers are beginning to address specific gaps in events management literature, including interaction with the range of disciplines for both professional development and for higher education markets. The emerging discipline is served by an increasing range of dedicated journals, including *Event Management* (formerly *Festival Management and Event Tourism*), *International Journal of Event Management Research, International Journal of Event & Festival Management, International Journal of Planned Events, Journal of Convention and Event Tourism* (formerly *Journal of Convention and Exhibition Management) and the Journal of Policy Research in Tourism, Leisure and Events*, alongside an increasing volume of events and festivals research being published in journals for related fields such as tourism, sports and leisure and established disciplines including management and marketing. Finally, this wealth of knowledge is enhanced with a range of periodicals and an increasing number of websites and e-newsletters providing contemporary articles and industry news, including: *Access All Areas, AV, Conference & Incentive Travel, Conference News, Event, Event Organiser, Event & Venue Specialist, Exhibition Bulletin, Exhibition News, Expoabc.com, Lighting & Sound International, Live!, Meetings & Incentive Travel, MeetingsReview.com, Stand Out, The Main Event Magazine and Total Production International*. For extensive links to event-related books, research journals, periodicals, e-newsletters and publications, please visit WorldofEvents.net.

EVENTS MANAGEMENT EDUCATION AND TRAINING

As the size and needs of the events industry have grown, event management training has started to emerge as a discrete discipline. In the early years of the industry the field was characterised by a large number of volunteers. Those events managers who obtained paid positions came from a variety of related disciplines, drawing on the knowledge gained from a particular discipline and skills learnt on the job. Many came from allied areas such as theatre and entertainment or audiovisual production and film, and adapted their skills to events. Others came from working for events suppliers such as stage, lighting and sound production companies, having discovered that they could expand and build on their existing skills to undertake the overall management of events. However, as the use of events by government and industry has grown, events budgets have increased and the logistics of events have become more complex, the need has emerged for skilled events professionals who can meet the industry's specific requirements. Education and training at a number of levels have arisen to meet this need.

Identifying the knowledge and skills required by event managers

Research for the Institute of Management (Coulson and Coe, 1991) identified the qualities that future events managers should possess. These included the ability to communicate, flexibility, adaptability, a broad perspective on organisational goals, a balanced perspective overall and an understanding of the business environment. Further, nine out of ten believed that managers should have an ability to assume greater responsibility, contribute to teamwork, handle uncertainty and surprise, be aware of ethics and values and have a commitment to ongoing learning. Later research by Katz (1974, cited in Mullins, 2005, pp. 211-212) identified the qualities possessed by effective managers, which were grouped under the headings of technical competence (specific knowledge, methods and skills applied to discrete tasks), social and human skills (focusing on interpersonal relationships, motivating staff, effective teamwork and leadership, sensitivity and style of management) and conceptual ability (the ability to envisage the complexity of situations, decision making and contributions related to the objectives and strategy of an organisation.). Mullins (2005) notes that as managers progress within an organisation, more emphasis will be placed on conceptual ability and less on technical competence. In addition to generic management skills, Getz and Wicks (1994, pp. 108–9) specify the following event-specific areas of knowledge as appropriate for inclusion in events management training:

- History and meanings of festivals, celebrations, rituals and other events
- Historical evolution; types of events
- Trends in demand and supply
- Motivations and benefits sought from events
- Roles and impacts of events in society, the economy, the environment and culture
- Who is producing events, and why?
- Program concepts and styles
- Event settings
- Operations unique to events
- Management unique to events
- Marketing unique to events

Limited research has been conducted within the events industry to identify the skills, qualities and attributes of successful event managers, particularly in the UK. The Business Tourism Forum and the Business Tourism Advisory Committee (1999, p. 36) found that the conference and event industries required enhanced negotiation skills, higher client management skills and a detailed knowledge of specific venues. In addition, the industry requires people with an informed understanding of and ability to anticipate client needs and to suggest solutions to problems and improvements to plans. Further research conducted in Canada and Australia provides a useful insight into the attributes and knowledge required specifically by event managers. While developing occupational standards for events managers, the International Occupational Standards for Event Management (also known as IEMS) (CTHRC, 2009), the Canadian Tourism Human Resource Council (CTHRC, 2005, p. 6) identified that an event manager is responsible for:

- determining parameters, policies, and procedures
- planning, designing and producing
- overseeing coordination
- developing and implementing the marketing plan
- preparing financial, business and evaluative reports
- developing a risk management plan
- overseeing financial management.

(CTHRC, 2009) (CTHRC, 2005, p. 6).

CTHRC groups skills under six broad headings of administration, event planning and management, marketing, risk management, human resource management and professionalism. Goldblatt (2008) highlights six qualities of leading event management leaders with integrity being highlighted as paramount, followed by confidence and persistence, collaboration, problem solving, communications skills and vision.

Further research conducted in Australia provides useful insight into the attributes and knowledge required specifically by events managers. Perry, Foley and Rumpf (1996) described the attributes and knowledge required by events managers identified from their survey of 105 managers attending the Australian Events Conference in Canberra in February 1996. Seven attributes were frequently mentioned, of which vision was listed as the most important, followed closely by leadership, adaptability and skills in organisation, communication, marketing and people management. Knowledge areas considered most important were project management, budgeting, time management, media relations, business planning, human resource management and marketing. The graph in Figure 1.2 shows some of the results of the survey. Respondents were asked to indicate how strongly they agreed or disagreed with a statement such as 'An events manager requires skills in project management'.

Later studies by Harris and Griffin (1997), Royal and Jago (1998), Harris and Jago (1999) and Arcodia and Barker (2002) confirmed the importance of these knowledge/skill domains. Allen (2005) focuses on the skills of time management and explores the techniques event managers can use for smooth event implementation.

FIGURE 1.2 Knowledge required by event managers — results of survey

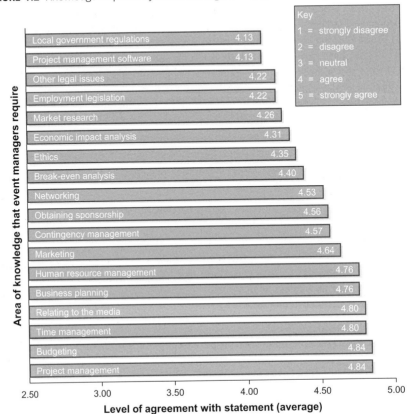

(Source: Perry, Foley and Rumpf, 1996)

RECOGNITION OF EVENTS MANAGEMENT AS A PROFESSION

When considering the events industry, it is easy to be misdirected and conclude it is only about events. Events can be compared to any project-based industry. Civil engineering, for example, is not just about the product; it is a description of the process needed to create that product. Event management, therefore, is about the processes that are used to create and sustain an event. Recognition of this process is the basis for recognising event management as a profession.

A profession is characterised by:

- *a body of knowledge* — this is the library of the profession. It is made up of information from other professions such as logistics, contract management and marketing. Journals and textbooks describe the body of knowledge and continually refine it.

- *a methodology* — this is made up of a series of processes or tasks, which can be described and taught. The risk management process is an example.
- *heuristics* — these are 'rules of thumb', stories and descriptions of experience that can be learned only 'on the job'.

Event management is gradually collating and describing these three areas. In the past, 'rule of thumb' was the main method of organising events. The recognition and description of the processes used to create the event — that is, the methodology — is the 'eureka' moment when events management progressed from being a skill to becoming a profession.

The events management body of knowledge (EMBOK)

The events management body of knowledge (EMBOK) is being defined and developed. O'Toole (2002) and Silvers (2003) began developing categories for EMBOK, as described in Chapter 9, with the work further progressed by the International EMBOK Executive. The purpose of EMBOK is, 'To create a framework of the knowledge and processes used in event management that may be customised to meet the needs of various cultures, governments, education programs, and organisations.' Figure 1.3 illustrates the EMBOK structure. Building on earlier work of O'Toole (2002) and Silvers (2003, 2004), International EMBOK Executive settled on five over arching domains: administration, design, marketing, operations and risk management (Silvers, Bowdin, O'Toole and Nelson, 2006). Figure 1.4 provides a breakdown of each knowledge domain. For further definition of the knowledge domains, core values, phases, classes and processes and to view how the

FIGURE 1.3 International EMBOK structure

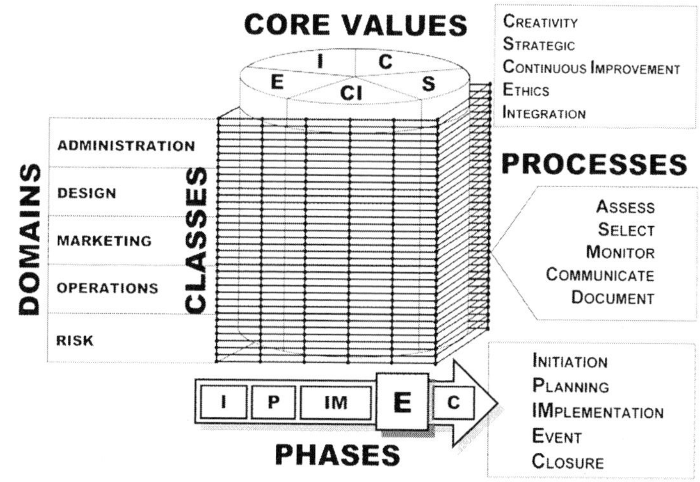

(Source: International EMBOK Executive, 2006)

FIGURE 1.4 Event management body of knowledge domain and classes structure

ADMINISTRATION	DESIGN	MARKETING	OPERATIONS	RISK
Financial	Catering	Marketing Plan	Attendees	Compliance
Human Resources	Content	Materials	Communications	Decisions
Information	Entertainment	Merchandise	Infrastructure	Emergency
Procurement	Environment	Promotion	Logistics	Health & Safety
Stakeholders	Production	Public Relations	Participants	Insurance
Systems	Program	Sales	Site	Legal
Time	Theme	Sponsorship	Technical	Security

(Source: International EMBOK Executive, 2006)

EMBOK is developing, please visit www.embok.org. Despite occasional differing emphases and nuances, the field is beginning to agree on the specific body of knowledge of best practice appropriate to the training of professional events managers.

The content of this book broadly covers the knowledge domains and classes. Part 1, Event Context, provides a general background to the events industry, the range of perspectives on events and event impacts. Part 2, Planning, deals with the knowledge areas of administration and marketing and the phases of events. Part 3, Event operations and Evaluation, deals with the areas of design, operations, risk management and associated issues.

Standards

Combined with the advance of the EMBOK is the development of competency standards for events management. For example, in the United Kingdom, competency standards were developed for the National Vocational Qualifications, while comparable standards have also been developed in Australia, South Africa and Canada. A competency standard for events management gives the industry a benchmark to measure excellence in management. Previously this benchmark was the success of the event; however, stakeholders cannot wait until the event is over to find out whether the event management was competent — by then it is too late.

Linked to the development of standards is the interest in ethical standards for events. Many associations have codes of conduct, codes of ethics or standards which their members agree to abide by. These standards are designed to ensure best and honest practice and are in place throughout the industry. Although there are many professional organisations operating within the events industry, there are still some examples of poor practice; for example, the theft of ideas and poaching of clients/business or the ethics of (hidden) commissions. Allen (2003), Goldblatt (2008) and Sorin (2003) provide a detailed discussion of this important issue.

The search for standards has led to the development of guidelines including outdoor events (BSI, 2004), sustainable events (BSI, 2009b) and stewarding (BSI, 2009c). With a constantly changing business environment, risk management is perceived as the way to handle uncertainty. The requirement for accountability is behind the adoption of International Standards Organisation (ISO) standards implemented in the UK through British Standards. Many government departments and large companies are investigating their events to see whether they comply with ISO certification standards.

Training delivery

As training has become needed, it has been delivered in a range of formats by a variety of institutions. Industry skills development within the UK falls within the remit of a range of Sector Skills Councils (SSCs), which are state-sponsored, employer-led organisations, set up with the aim of reducing skills gaps, improving productivity, boosting skills and improving learning supply (People 1st, 2010). People1st, the Sector Skills Council covering hospitality, tourism, leisure, events and related industries, was established in 2004 to replace the Travel, Tourism Services and Events National Training Organisation (TTENTO) and the Hospitality Training Foundation (HTF), and support the industry in furthering the agenda toward a fully trained workforce. Their remit includes developing occupational standards, producing industry research and labour market data (for example, Bowdin, McPherson and Flinn, 2006 and People 1st, 2010) and encouraging communication between education providers, employers and industry associations. The events industry, depending on the sub-sector, is also served by other SSCs including Creative and Cultural Skills (live music), SkillsActive (sport), Skillset (creative media), and Skills for Security (security) (People 1st, 2010).

Industry associations

The major event industry associations have all been involved in the delivery of training and certification programmes and are beginning to recognise the benefits that these, together with the developments in formal education, can deliver in addressing the shortfall in qualified professionals that some areas of the industry are experiencing. These programmes typically involve a points system whereby accreditation can be gained from a mix of dedicated training programmes, participation in the association, contribution to the industry, attendance at conferences and seminars and often a written paper or examination. Pre-requisites often include membership of the association, industry experience and allegiance to a written code of conduct or ethics. Accreditation programs are usually supported by educational provisions such as seminar training programs, online training courses and self-directed learning resources. For example, ISES offers an examination-based accreditation as a 'Certified Special Events Professional' (CSEP); MPI offers examination-based accreditation as a 'Certified Meetings Manager' (CMM) and supports the Convention Industry Council's 'Certified Meeting Professional' (CMP), together with a range of education opportunities; MIA, Eventia, PSA, AEC/AEO/AEV and other associations provide training courses focusing on topics including health and safety, sales and procurement. Thus, each area of industry is increasingly investing in training and education in order to ensure that there is a sufficient qualified staffing base to support the developing industry.

Universities and colleges

Universities and colleges have become involved in events education, with many offering events management or marketing subjects as part of tourism, hospitality, leisure, recreation or sport management courses. The George Washington University in Washington DC was an early pioneer in offering a concentration in events management within a graduate program; in 1994 it commenced a complete certification program in events management (Getz and Wicks, 1994).

Dedicated, or combined, courses in events management are being delivered at colleges and universities across the UK at foundation degree, diploma, degree and masters level. These courses focus on providing education and training for future events professionals. Generally built on or around a management core, they cover areas such as management, marketing, human resource management, finance and operations together with event specific modules such as event planning, production and risk management. The establishment of events as a subject has been reflected as a specific strand within revised Quality Assurance Agency benchmark statements (QAA, 2008), which provide an indication of what degree level events courses should cover. Universities & Colleges Admissions Service (UCAS, 2010), the organisation responsible for processing applications to higher education in the United Kingdom (UK), currently list 68 colleges and universities offering undergraduate, events related courses in the UK, though this figure is likely to be on the low side when taking into account additional courses already being offered or in development. In addition, over twenty universities are known to be offering postgraduate masters courses in the UK. For example, the UK Centre for Events Management (Leeds Metropolitan University) launched the first events management degree in the UK in 1996. This has now been established in the market and has been joined by a range of specialised one-year (top-up) degrees in conferences and exhibitions management, sport events management, managing cultural and major events and fundraising and sponsorship, and also masters degrees including an MSc International Events Management and MSc Events Management by distance learning. Further research undertaken in development of WorldofEvents.net, an online directory, indicates that these developments are being mirrored internationally with dedicated events-related courses being offering in Ireland, Germany, France, Australia, Canada, USA and elsewhere.

To recognise these developments, AEME (the Association for Events Management Education) was formed in 2004 in order to further develop events education and best practice and to act as the events management subject association particularly within the UK. Featuring many of the UK providers of events education together with trainers, associations and educators from Ireland and elsewhere among its members, AEME hosts an annual Events Management Educators Forum to further the association's aims. For further information about AEME, please visit www.aeme.org.

For links to events-related courses and qualifications offered by training companies, associations and further/higher education internationally, please visit WorldofEvents.net.

CAREER OPPORTUNITIES IN EVENTS

As demonstrated above, events are an expanding industry providing new and challenging job opportunities for people entering the field. Roles, titles, salaries and job descriptions are not yet standardised in the industry and details vary from city to city and between countries. However, the International Special Events Society has been consulting with its members and the industry in order to achieve some degree of general agreement on these issues. Landey (2006) lists the following roles as having some degree of general acceptance among events management companies (see Table 1.2), while People 1st (2010) has reviewed roles as part of their labour market study.

Table 1.2 Roles in the event industry

Role	Qualifications
Event professional	Certified professional
Event producer	5 years experience Major role in at least 10 events
Event manager	Three to 5 years experience Major role in at least 5 events
Event coordinator	Up to 3 years experience
Event support	Entry level into industry

A career in the events industry is not limited to just these roles or to events management companies. There is a vast array of events positions available in different sectors of the industry including corporate and government institutions, public relations companies, the media, arts and sports organisations, not-for-profit groups and charities and non-government and community organisations, to name just a few. Inside these and the companies that supply them there is a variety of roles to suit all interests and backgrounds, including project managers, stage managers, technicians, graphic artists, set designers, costume makers, make-up artists, marketers, publicists, photographers, entertainers, comperes, caterers, pyrotechnicians — again, the list is seemingly endless. It is in the nature of the industry that much of this work is freelance and spasmodic, with many events staff working on a short-term contract basis for a series of employers and events.

A successful career in events depends on applicants identifying their own skills and interests and then matching these carefully with the needs of prospective employers. Areas of expanding activity — such as corporate events, conferences, local government and tourism — may be fruitful areas to examine. Employers often look for a mix of qualifications and experience, so intending job seekers may be advised to consider volunteering and/or taking entry-level positions to take that important first step towards a satisfying and rewarding career. Although to date, limited information has been developed about careers in events, this is beginning to change with the Association of Graduate Career Advisory Services (AGCAS), other associations (for example, ACE, AEO, MIA and MPI) and other organisations producing careers information; much more information is likely to be available in the near future.

Meeting Professionals International (MPI), one of the leading industry associations worldwide with around 24,000 members, has developed the 'MPI Knowledge Plan' for meeting professionals to build a body of knowledge, research and study. The initiative identifies six levels of knowledge covering introduction, basics, intermediate, advanced, strategic and executive levels and links these to a series of courses including global certificates and a executive leadership programme (MPI 2010).

For links to events-related careers information, vacancies, recruitment companies and related resources, please visit WorldofEvents.net.

SUMMARY

Events perform a powerful role in society. They have existed throughout human history in all times and all cultures. British cultures have a rich tradition of rituals and ceremonies. The events tradition in modern Britain began to take off towards the end of the nineteenth century, with industrialisation reducing spontaneous celebration and increasing professionally organised events. The ruling elite often decided the form and content of public celebrations but an alternative tradition of popular celebrations arose from the interests and pursuits of ordinary people. Many nineteenth century leisure pursuits such as race meetings have survived to the present day. Through the twentieth century, changes in society were mirrored by changes in the style of public events. A tradition of city and town festivals evolved in the post- Second World War years and was rejuvenated by the social movements and cultural changes of the 1970s. Notions of high culture were challenged by a more pluralistic and democratic popular culture, which reinvigourated festivals and community events. With the coming of the 1980s, governments and the corporate sector began to recognise the economic and promotional value of events.

The 1990s saw the events industry emerge; various sectors, particularly those focused on business-related events, pushed forward the claim for the industry to be recognised, supported by dialogue with government and backed by an increase in training and support for the industry-related NVQs. The period since then has seen the growth in events-related education in colleges and universities, with dedicated courses and modules being developed to support the emerging industry. Events vary in their size and impact, with terms such as special events, mega-events, hallmark events and major events used to describe and categorise them. Events are also categorised according to their type and sector, such as public, cultural, festival, sporting, tourism and corporate events. The business events sector (including meetings, incentives, conventions and exhibitions) is one of the fastest growing areas of events. With increasing expansion and corporate involvement, events have emerged as a new growth industry capable of generating economic and job creation benefits.

The emerging events industry with its needs, challenges and opportunities will be examined in the following chapters.

QUESTIONS

1. Why are events created and what purpose do they serve in society?

2. Do events mirror changes in society or do they have a role in creating and changing values? Give examples to illustrate your answer.

3. Why have events emerged so strongly in recent years in the UK?

4. What are the key political, cultural and social trends that determine the current climate of events in the UK? How would you expect these to influence the nature of events in the coming years?

5. Identify an event in your city or region that has the capacity to be a hallmark event. Give your reasons for placing it in this category.

6. What characteristics define an industry and using these criteria do you consider that there is an events industry in the UK?

7. Do you agree with the attributes and knowledge areas required by events managers listed in this chapter? Make an inventory of your own attributes and skills based on these listings.

CASE STUDY: THE POWER OF CELEBRATION – THE GLOBALISATION AND IMPACT OF THE FESTIVALS AND EVENTS INDUSTRY

Building legacies

For as long as anyone can remember, people have celebrated. Celebration itself is perhaps the most common denominator that we have, with the unique ability to cross all barriers of race, religion, ethnicity, age, politics, economics, education and geography.

From small, localised celebrations to mega-events with global outreach, festivals and events bring hope and joy that burns bright in the unlikeliest of locations; they range from the Afghan travelling holiday festival now enjoyed by children in Kandahar, Afghanistan – a treat forbidden under the Taliban,to the Olympics, which shares a vision beyond just being a great sporting competition and as a result, has succeeded in bringing the world together for a few brief weeks to celebrate our differences. In fact, events have brought more people together, peacefully, than any other world entity or profession and that may be the greatest legacy that we leave.

The changing migration patterns of events and culture. Building legacies, however, takes time. Sometimes it takes a very long time – as we discover when we consider where those legacies and traditions began and how they have shaped our identities and our world.

The National Geographic Society has undertaken an ongoing program called the Geno-graphic Project. Using DNA, a worldwide team of experts have tracked human ancestry – all the variously shaped and shaded people of Earth – to African hunter-gatherers some 150,000 years ago. Their research reminds us that the world's population shares a common link.

Using further DNA research, these experts have been able to determine the patterns of human migration as we slowly populated the Earth. Humans migrated from the African cradle some 60,000 years ago – moving into Australia 50,000 years ago, Europe and Asia a short 40,000 years ago, and populating the Americas only 15,000 to 20,000 years ago, which is practically yesterday in world history terms!

With that migration came not only new languages but religious beliefs, political systems and cultural identifiers. It is easy to conjecture that when these wanderers decided upon the location of their new homes, especially given the challenges that they must have faced along the way, the first thing they would have done is celebrate. Before governments were formed, before cities were built, before laws were established – humans celebrated. We continue that pattern today cele-brating traditions, victories, life, death, birthdays, anniversaries, love, remembrance, achieve-ments, war, peace, belief systems, change, agricultural products, education, patriotism and so on. The need to celebrate seems inherent in everything we do. Governments celebrate; scientists celebrate; institutions and corporations celebrate; communities and countries celebrate; and, on occasion, the world celebrates.

Over time, these celebrations became the roots of our culture and heritage. Through music, clothing, dance, food and storytelling we created our identities, our comfort zones, our brands and images – the things that told others who we were and what was important to us, what we were proud of, and what our accomplishments were. Internally, these elements bonded us. Externally, they became our cultural markers, much like the genetic markers on our DNA.

As migration patterns continued and continue today, many of these traditions were carried to other places and evolved into their own legacies. New traditions held on to some components of the past, added new ones and quickly distanced themselves with others.

As time passed and people were able to travel more easily many of these traditions were translated or shared with others. The carnivals of Nice, France and Viareggio, Italy found the seeds of their events growing in the Mardi Gras of New Orleans, the Pasadena Tournament of Roses in Los Angeles and the Carnivals of Brazil. Oktoberfest in Munich, Germany, spawned countless worldwide imitators; Chinese New Year is now celebrated in many places outside of

Asia and on 17 March every year, many of our global citizens become Irish if only for a day, as we celebrate St Patrick's Day.

Interestingly, you may be more likely to find an authentic version of cultural traditions and celebrations taking place in those locations where ethnic populations have settled rather than in their original homelands. Immigrants continue celebrating and holding fast to what they remember while those who remained celebrate who they are and who they have become today. In either case, it is our perceived identities that we celebrate.

Today, the world is flat. What took our ancestors 150,000 years, we can do in seconds. With the speed and capabilities available today via travel, technology, the Internet and the media, the speed at which ideas, images and information travel has reconfigured the world as we know it. Investors in one part of the world work with manufacturers in another; educators in the west exchange concepts with counterparts in the east; trade routes for all industries crisscross like global spider webs; and the 'middle of nowhere' no longer exists. Virtually every continent on our planet is becoming a melting pot of international diversity. 'International' is the new status symbol of businesses and events worldwide.

The effect of this globalisation process can be found throughout today's festivals and events industry as professional peers worldwide continuously share and learn from each other every day. Whether it is the large-scale spectacle and pageantry of Chinese events; the iconic holiday parades of North America; the envelope-pushing artistic creativity of European festivals; the colour and energy of Latin America's carnivals; the culturally rich, tourism-driven events of the Middle East; or the 'downunder' cutting-edge ambience created by Australian events– every region, country, province, state and city provides a new window and view to unlimited creativity.

The growth and changing face of our industry. As far back as celebration and events can be traced, however, it is only in relatively recent history that we left behind the days of 'spare time' event marketing and management.

Over time, celebrations began to change from often informal affairs to spectacular productions requiring new sets of skills, experience, creativity, financing, planning and leadership. As a result, celebration evolved into a business as well as a growing and vital global industry with new demands, needs and challenges every day.

Festivals and events have proven to be among the most successful tools available to communities, states, regions and even countries to

- increase tourism
- create powerful and memorable branding and imaging opportunities
- bond people
- encourage positive media coverage
- enhance economic wellbeing
- add to the quality of life for those who live in its immediate environment.

Extrapolating from recent IFEA industry surveys the special events industry today, worldwide, is estimated to include four to five million regularly recurring festivals and events large enough to require municipal support services. Add to this figure those one-time or less-than-annual major events such as the millennium celebrations, the Olympics and world fairs and the incalculable number of smaller, more informal events, such as corporate celebrations, weddings, religious gatherings and school carnivals, and you start to understand the huge outreach of our industry. The special events industry has an estimated combined economic impact in the trillions of dollars and combined attendances that touch virtually every life on the planet several times over.

Over time, as our industry began to take shape and recognise itself as an industry, professional associations like the International Festivals & Events Association (IFEA) naturally emerged out of the process to respond to and support the many changing needs of this dynamic industry.

Continued

CASE STUDY: THE POWER OF CELEBRATION – THE GLOBALISATION AND IMPACT OF THE FESTIVALS AND EVENTS INDUSTRY—*CONT'D*

The IFEA reached the fifty-year milestone in event leadership in 2005. From small beginnings of simply sharing ideas, the IFEA today represents a true global industry and professional network including IFEA Asia, Australia, Europe, Latin America, Middle East and North America. Today's industry professionals understand, as did IFEA's founders fifty years ago, the enormous value and power created through an international network of professional peers, for the purpose of sharing ideas, successes and creative new solutions.

On a parallel track, educational programs have grown and prospered to support both experienced professionals and those new to this quickly developing industry. From professional certification programs such as the CFEE (Certified Festivals & Events Executive) programme offered through the IFEA to formalised college and university programmes, there are now more than three hundred institutions of higher learning offering courses, certificates or degrees in events education worldwide, supported by an ever-growing library of resources and research.

As we move forward, a natural and expanding alliance between these two tracks will grow, forged by the increased needs of the professional industry itself and the research capabilities that the academic world brings to the table.

The flattening of the world will open up many new opportunities in the years ahead. New possibilities for exchanging ideas, entertainment, traditions and experiences worldwide will be reflected in how we think and operate; in the events that we produce; in where we seek funding and support; in how and where we market and promote our events and in the relationships that we establish and enjoy. As we continue our evolution as an industry, so too will the professional credibility and public awareness of our field evolve enabling us to create a strong and positive brand identity for our industry.

A globally united industry. Our first and most important challenge as we look to the future will be our ability to unite our industry globally – something many others have struggled to do throughout history. We must form a global partnership of cooperation and communication in all directions that crosses all barriers, assumptions and beliefs that we may have about the world around us. This partnership must allow us to see each other as a true global network of peers and an unlimited source of creativity and support.

Further, we must commit to our own personal use of and ongoing support of this global network to ensure its success. All of us freely talk about the power of our events and industry to bring people together; now we must show that we are capable of doing that among ourselves.

At the IFEA fiftieth anniversary world convention we featured a global panel session that looked at the next fifty years for our industry. On that panel were professional representatives from Asia, Australia, Europe, Latin America, the Middle East and North America. There were no egos, no discussions about what shape the table should be or who could sit beside whom and no hesitations about sharing viewpoints that would benefit us all. It was a shining example of what we can build, a reminder of the many lives that we can touch as a result and the catalyst for a new IFEA World Forum conference that will be held annually beginning in 2008 in tandem with the Olympic Games in China – further underlining the important role of festivals and events.

The power of celebration. From the earliest migrations out of Africa to today and continuing well into the changing future ahead of us we are part of a dynamic global industry that will ensure that the world does not lose touch with itself. Such is the power of celebration and such can be the power that we create by working together as a common global industry in the years ahead.

For further information about the International Festivals & Events Association, please visit: www.ifea.com.

By Steven Wood Schmader, CFEE, President and CEO, International Festivals & Events Association, World Headquarters

Questions

1. Identify three events in your city or region that celebrate diverse cultures within your area. Investigate how and when these events were started and what they aim to achieve.
2. Identify a traditional event in your region that has been running for many years or decades or perhaps even longer. How and why was the event started? How has it changed over time?
3. Identify a global event in your region that takes place either simultaneously or consecutively in a number of different regions or countries. Identify who owns the event, and discuss how it is transmitted from one location or region to another.

CASE STUDY: MANCHESTER 2002 THE XVII COMMONWEALTH GAMES – KEY LESSONS

Introduction

Every city bidding for a major sporting event, particularly one of the top multi-sport events in the world, spends considerable time, energy and resources assessing the financial, economic and social viability of the event. There is no right or wrong answer. Every city and every Games will deliver a different event unique to its own place, time and cultural setting.

Following the Commonwealth Games, a Post Games Report was produced to pull together an overview of the challenges and questions involved, while a project (Games Xchange) implemented in Manchester manages the archive of documents and records and ensures that the knowledge is transferred to future events and projects. The report covers the questions that M2002 asked, the process the Organising Committee (OC) went through and most importantly, the lessons learned during the planning and implementation of the Manchester 2002 Commonwealth Games. It is only through sharing this information that the Commonwealth Games (and indeed other multi-sporting events) can raise the bar and communicate through sport.

There are many lessons and recommendations contained throughout the Post Games Report; however, there are core fundamentals that are vital to all multi-sport events. These are summarised below.

Maximise Potential. It is more than a sporting event. Whilst the sporting competition sits at the core, it is also the pebble that is thrown into a pond creating ever widening circles of opportunities that encompasses more and more people and includes ever increasing opportunities, activities and programmes that can use sport to develop host cities and communities and harness greater human values.

Partnerships. Partnerships provide not only funding but expertise and experience, that is priceless and should never be underestimated; particularly at every level of Government; from national to local and all key sporting bodies; from the crucial funding and strategic partners; from operational stakeholders such as transport and the Police; national and regional stakeholders to the critically important sponsors, partners and supporters.

Planning. Organisational and operational planning are the life blood of a successful event – from designing and building the venues, through to holding test events, planning risk management, timetabling reliable transport and other essential services.

Continued

CASE STUDY: MANCHESTER 2002 THE XVII COMMONWEALTH GAMES – KEY LESSONS—*CONT'D*

Infrastructure. Infrastructure planning, construction and Games operations of venues, villages and transport not only provide the legacy but form the stage upon which the sporting drama unfolds. It is the physical and visible manifestation of years of planning, the public face of the organisation and the Games experience of both athletes and spectators.

Technology. With each major event, sporting technology moves forward in leaps and bounds. It is important to remember that the technology landscape may well change over the planning and implementation period due to developments in timing and scoring devices, telecommunications, results services and even broadcast formats such as the Internet. By way of example, Manchester 2002 (M2002) was the first multi-sport event to pilot delivery of results to PDAs (Personal Digital Assistants) over GPRS (General Packet Radio Service). This will be standard in forthcoming events. The technology infrastructure and operating platforms for any Games must be flexible, as it is initially created far in advance of many functional needs.

Human Resource. People (whether paid staff, volunteers or contractors) are the wheels that keep the Games moving forward both in the planning stages and during the event itself. The task of creating a workforce that is the equivalent of a FTSE 100 company and then disbanding the majority of staff post-Games is unique only to this type of event and takes great human resource skills and courage to meet both the needs of the Games and the needs of the individuals involved. Different skills are often required for planning and operational phases and individuals need to understand this and appreciate that their roles may evolve over time.

Financial. The financial and commercial requirements of an event of this scale provide the oxygen that keeps the organisation alive. Transparency, accountability and exceptional corporate governance are critical to ensuring that funds are received in a timely manner. It is also important to remember that plans for every Functional Area (FA) will need to be reassessed in the planning, testing and operational phases since having adequate contingency funds is vital to operational success.

Marketing and Communication. No event can achieve its full potential without creative and impactful marketing and communication strategies. Whilst so much is being created in terms of infrastructure, venues and legacies it is sometimes easy to forget that the signature of an outstanding event is full venues and community support and involvement at Games time. The media together with marketing campaigns play a decisive role in influencing the public to attend and in shaping their memories of the event itself. Much of this work needs to be done many months before the Games through community and educational campaigns such as The Queen's Jubilee Baton Relay and the Spirit of Friendship Festival.

SUMMARY

If there was a multi-sport mantra it would have to be plan, plan, plan, test, test, test, communicate, communicate, communicate.

These core fundamentals shaped the planning and implementation of the 2002 Commonwealth Games in Manchester. Many are lessons learned as the programme developed and grew. The Post Games Report illustrates in detail the points made above and gives further details and recommendations that may assist cities hosting future multi-sport events. The report itself has been put together in sections, however, for ease of reference; those who do not wish to go into great depth in every section will find Executive Summaries of the key sections in Volume I.

For further information about the Commonwealth Games, please visit www.thecgf.com. For further detailed information on the legacy of the Manchester 2002 Commonwealth Games and to access the Post Games Report online, please visit http://web.archive.org/web/ 20070621192427/www.gameslegacy.com.

Source: Manchester 2002 (2003) The XVII Commonwealth Games: Post Games Report. London, Commonwealth Games Federation, pp. 18-19.

Questions

1. What type of event is the Commonwealth Games? Explain your answer.
2. Running festivals alongside sporting events is becoming increasingly popular. What can these bring to the event?
3. Using other materials at your disposal, for example, the official legacy website, conduct research into the Manchester 2002 Commonwealth Games. What facts can be ascertained from this material regarding the size, nature and management of the event?
4. How would you expect the experience of organising the Manchester 2002 Commonwealth Games to influence bidding for and management of large-scale events within the UK in the future? Explain your answer.

Perspectives on events

LEARNING OBJECTIVES

After studying this chapter, you should be able to:

- list the range of roles that governments play in events
- describe the nature and function of government event strategies
- discuss the use of events by governments as tools for economic regeneration and development
- discuss the use of events by the corporate sector
- describe the role that events play in integrated marketing strategies
- list and describe methods used by the corporate sector in measuring the return on investment (ROI) of events
- discuss the benefits that can result to communities from the staging of events
- list the range of strategies available to event managers to promote community engagement in events
- discuss the implications for event managers of differing perspectives on events in the event planning process

INTRODUCTION

As we have seen in Chapter 1, events take place across the full spectrum of society leading to differing contexts, goals and objectives. In this chapter we will look at events from the perspectives of the three major sectors — government, the corporate sector and community — and examine how these perspectives vary and their implications for event managers.

Governments play a leading role in events and increasingly employ event strategies in order to guide their involvement, priorities and decision-making. In recent years, many governments have created dedicated celebration spaces for the staging of public events and some have consciously used them in tandem with other policies and strategies as tools for urban regeneration and development.

The corporate sector is a major player in events using them regularly in the course of business administration, staff motivation and training, and as a significant element of the integrated marketing mix in the sale and promotion of goods and services. Companies also sponsor public events in order to demonstrate product attributes, build brand awareness and reach target markets effectively.

Events Management. DOI: 10.1016/B978-1-85617-818-1.10002-7

Events have long played a universal and enduring role in communities whose prime focus is on their direct entertainment, social, cultural and sporting benefits. In planning events, event managers need to devise and incorporate appropriate strategies for community ownership, participation and engagement.

THE GOVERNMENT PERSPECTIVE

All levels of government, national, regional and local, make frequent use of events, both in conducting the affairs of government and as part of their service delivery. They will often combine in the celebration of significant national anniversaries and events, as seen in Britain with Royal Weddings, the Queen's Golden Jubilee and the Millennium celebrations. In addition, almost all government departments make extensive internal use of events in order to train staff, develop networks and communicate with the public.

National government

However, it is the national governments that usually have the prime carriage of major celebrations of national significance. It will then work closely with other levels of government to augment related programmes at state and local levels.

National governments are also increasingly involved with hosting and organising major international political and economic gatherings; for example, the Commonwealth Heads of Government Meeting (CHOGM) and The London Summit 2009 of the world leaders of G20 group of countries. Such events present increasing logistic and security challenges but confer significant prestige on their host governments. National governments also make significant use of cultural events in the promotion of trade through their foreign affairs departments, as was seen recently in the Year of Paris in Beijing and the corresponding Year of Beijing in Paris.

The staging of major sporting and cultural events on home soil is more the province of state and city governments, though interestingly the International Olympic Committee has stated that the Olympic Games will not be awarded in future to cities that do not have the express underwriting and support of their national governments. For example, the successful London 2012 Olympic Games bid included messages of support from the then Prime Minister Tony Blair and the then Mayor of London Ken Livingstone.

Regional Development Agencies

In the UK, at the time of writing Regional Development Agencies currently play a major role in bidding for and staging major events of economic and tourism significance, often setting up events organisations and convention and visitor bureaus for this purpose as discussed in Chapter 1. Most Regional Development Agencies are involved in staging or assisting events as part of their portfolio — for example, major festivals, sporting competitions, events celebrating ethnic diversity or flagship tourism events. They may sponsor or be involved in events that carry messages relevant to their remit. For example, the Yorkshire Forward sponsored the UK's largest medical networking conference, Driving Competitiveness Through Innovation, at York racecourse, to demonstrate their support for healthcare technologies and biomedical medicine industries (Yorkshire Forward, 2009); and One Northeast joined with Business Link to sponsor the Celebrating Learning and Skills Success (Class) Awards in 2010 as a celebration of learning and skills. From One Northeast's perspective they emphasised, "the key message about the importance of retaining and rewarding skills excellence in the region" (One Northeast, 2009).

Local government

Local authorities are also increasingly involved with events, seeing them as an important means of creating quality of life for their constituents and attracting tourism and economic benefits to their regions. Local authorities are now some of the biggest players in the events field, with almost every local government body employing an event manager or team and with most providing funding and support for a wide range of local events.

The role of government in events

Governments commonly perform a wide and complex variety of roles in events, particularly in the arena of public outdoor events and festivals. The extent and scale of these roles will vary according to the size and level of governments and to the degree of their resources and commitment. However, the roles listed below and the issues that arise from them are common to most governments and provide the impetus for them to form events departments and create strategies in order to delineate and implement their role in events.

Venue owner/manager

Governments are often the owners of parks, playing fields, streets, town halls, stadiums, and sports and community centres where events are staged. They are responsible for the development and maintenance of these assets, as well as managing them on a day-to-day basis. They therefore need to employ staff to run them and to set and administer policies and charges for their use.

Consent authority and regulatory body

Governments also set and administer many of the laws and policies that govern the staging of events in matters such as the creation of temporary structures, the sale of food, noise restrictions, street closures and traffic and parking requirements. Local councils often work closely with other government agencies such as road and traffic authorities, health departments and police, in the drafting, implementation and monitoring of rules and regulations governing these areas. For large public events attracting over 500 people in England and Wales, councils will require a premises licence (under the Licensing Act 2003) and for major events this will require close liaison with the responsible licensing authorities, with the applications addressing issues such as environmental impact, traffic management and safety; smaller events will simply require the issue of a licence.

Service provider

The successful staging of major events involves coordinating a wide range of infrastructure and support services including venues, transport and communications; and liaison with public authorities such as police, fire, ambulance and emergency services. Many of these services are provided by government, so many event strategies include a 'one-stop shop' approach to their coordination and management. The staging of major events has increasingly underlined the importance of such coordination. The Edinburgh Event Planning and Operations Group (EPOG) is a best-practice example of such a coordination group. Working alongside a council-established Event Management Team, EPOG consists of government and non-government agencies including council public safety staff, emergency services and other agencies. According to its terms of reference, the EPOG exists to:

- Coordinate the operational planning of all major events
- Ensure that a responsible person is nominated for each event from within or outside the Council, as appropriate
- Liaise with the Emergency Services, Local Health Authority, Council Departments and any other appropriate bodies
- Develop road closure/traffic management plans for all events
- Produce event/area layout plans, as required
- Ensure the production of Event Safety Plans where appropriate.

(City of Edinburgh Council, 2002, p. 4).

Funding body

Governments often establish funding programmes that aim to develop and assist events. This may be at a community level, where assisting events is seen as part of the overall provision of services to the community. In such cases the scale of funding is likely to be modest and guidelines are likely to focus on community/cultural services and outcomes. See for example, the approach taken to providing funding for community events through local councils in Northern Ireland. In other cases, governments may support events because of their perceived economic and tourism benefits and will seek to fund and develop events that match this agenda. Clear funding criteria and guidelines need to be established and procedures need to be put in place for the monitoring of event implementation and the reporting and measurement of event outcomes.

The event organiser

Governments may also themselves be event producers or host organisations. This may involve the organisation and protocol of official visits and ceremonial events or the celebration of national days and important anniversaries such as the Queen's Golden Jubilee, St Patrick's Day or Homecoming Scotland 2009. Governments may also choose to mount a programme of local events and celebrations in order to animate civic spaces, to enhance the quality of life of residents or to attract visitors.

The event/destination marketer

Governments may assume some responsibility for the compilation and promotion of an annual calendar of events, both as a service to residents and as part of the overall tourism promotion of the city or destination. Such events calendars may be supported by a communications strategy, with highlight events being the subject of individual campaigns. The use of events as part of destination marketing strategies will be discussed further in Chapter 4.

Event strategies

Increasingly governments are developing event strategies in order to coordinate their overall involvement in events, to plan the use of resources and to improve and measure the outcomes of programmes and services. Such strategies ideally dovetail with other policies and strategies in the areas of urban planning, community and cultural services, economic development and tourism. They also establish strong links with agencies at other levels of government, and the private sector.

Event strategies seek to delineate government objectives in the events area and to identify the appropriate policies, infrastructure, resources, staffing and programmes needed to achieve them. They often include the development of a portfolio or annual programme of events designed to reflect the particular characteristics and needs of a city or region. Such a portfolio may include a broad range of events, including signature or flagship events that are intended to promote the destination, and other events designed to serve particular cultural, sporting, economic or tourism goals and objectives. Events portfolios may involve both existing events and the sourcing of new events by bidding for suitable events properties or by developing events from the ground up. Event strategies provide a framework for the appraisal of proposed new events in order to determine their fit with strategic objectives.

An event strategy will often include the creation of a 'one-stop shop' for event organisers, in order to bring together and coordinate various government departments and services related to events. This will greatly assist in the efficient planning and delivery of events and create an 'event friendly' culture and working environment that will strengthen the role of events and the outcomes of the strategy.

An example of a clear and focused local government event strategy that incorporates many of the roles discussed above is the London Borough of Hammersmith and Fulham's event strategy (see Figure 2.1). This strategy defines the

FIGURE 2.1 Hammersmith and Fulham events strategy 2009–12

The Hammersmith and Fulham Event Strategy covers all types of events in Borough venues, including those organised by the Council and those that are staged by private individuals or organisations.

Vision
To develop and deliver an events programme that creates a lively and vibrant place to live, work and visit, whilst ensuring the sustainable use of the Borough's venues.

Strategic Priorities
The strategy has three main priorities, each with a number of strategies:
Priority 1: Celebrate Hammersmith & Fulham and engage its residents through diverse events

1.1. Provide enjoyment, learning and value for local residents and visitors through events

1.2. Widen audiences and participation in events

1.3. Celebrate the cultural heritage of Hammersmith & Fulham

Priority 2: Facilitate neighbourhood events and the animation of local open spaces

2.1 Empower local neighbourhood groups to organise their own events

2.2 Increase the number of volunteers at events

Priority 3: Ensure the sustainable use of Hammersmith & Fulham's parks, open spaces and indoor venues for events

3.1 Ensure regular consultation with local stakeholders

3.2 Collect feedback and evaluation to inform future event planning

3.3 Promote the use of Borough venues for events to maximise income potential

3.4 Ensure effective event management planning and health & safety systems for events

3.5 Manage the impact of events on parks, open spaces and indoor venues

(Source: Hammersmith & Fulham Council, 2009)

roles of Hammersmith and Fulham in events and identifies clear goals, strategies and key performance indicators for the efficient implementation of these roles. It supports a range of other strategies and policies including the Mayor of London's "Cultural Metropolis" and London 2012 strategies, the West Wedge (West London 2012 Partnership and its action plan for promoting arts and culture across West London), the Community Strategy, the Parks and Open Spaces Strategy and the Decent Neighbourhoods programme, to lay a clear framework for the strategic development and enhancement of events (Hammersmith and Fulham Council, 2009, pp. 6-7).

Creating celebration spaces and precincts

The relationship between entertainment and commerce has a long history that dates back at least to mediaeval times, when town markets and fairs attracted not only traders and their customers but also a colourful bevy of minstrels, jugglers and acrobats. Indeed, the origins of the street theatre of today can be traced back to the bazaars and marketplaces of the ancient world.

Many cities and towns now consciously set out to create civic areas and public celebration spaces that perform much the same function as the traditional city square or village green. A seminal example in the 1960s was the development of the Inner Harbor of Baltimore in Maryland, USA. Initially a community celebration was held in order to promote cultural diversity in a derelict downtown area that had been the site of riots in the city. This ultimately inspired the regeneration of the Inner Harbor shores, with a festival marketplace, museums and hotels transforming the rundown area into a lively urban precinct. This in turn became the model for similar water-front precincts in other parts of the world, including Darling Harbour in Sydney, Cape Town in South Africa, Yokohama in Japan, Fisherman's Wharf in San Francisco and the Singapore riverfront.

The Millennium celebrations were the catalyst for the Millennium Square in Leeds, transforming the streets and gardens around the Civic Hall into a £12 million, multi-purpose, public square and event space.

Town and city councils and urban planners everywhere have been influenced by national and international developments, with waterside areas in Liverpool, Leeds, Glasgow, Edinburgh and Dundee serving as just a few examples of the creation of public recreation and celebration spaces that have become widespread in the UK and other western nations. Festivals, concerts, markets, public art programmes and street theatre are tools commonly used to animate these spaces and to make them congenial spaces for people to congregate in and enjoy.

Events and urban development

Governments have increasingly come to see events as potential tools for urban regeneration and renewal. They can provide the impetus for development and become catalysts for the commitment of public funds and the investment of private capital needed to secure it. Integrated with other strategies such as town planning, commercial development, arts and cultural development and tourism, they can become powerful drivers in changing the image of destinations and in bringing new life and prosperity to communities. Clark (2008) highlights that if local development benefits and a long term legacy are to be achieved, effective planning is required.

An early example in Australia illustrates the point. The America's Cup was being hosted by Fremantle, Western Australia in 1986–87. An icon of the sport of yachting with one of the world's oldest sporting trophies, the race had been dominated for most of its long history by North American yachting teams. When in a surprise coup a West Australian syndicate led by Perth entrepreneur Alan Bond snatched victory, tradition decreed that the team's home city would host the next event.

The port city of Fremantle, which had suffered a long economic downturn due to the slow decline of the shipping industry, had been the subject of various government regeneration and improvement proposals. The momentum of hosting the America's Cup was used to fast-track these proposals, to attract finance and generate the will to transform the city. Motivated by the promise of a tourism bonanza and the stimulus that 'the eyes of the world will be on Fremantle', an enthusiastic wave of refurbishment and new building transformed the sleepy working class port into a popular tourism destination. While some of the visitor predictions ultimately proved an exaggeration, the city of Fremantle emerged with a greatly improved image and higher self-esteem, though arguably at the expense of its original working class character and values (Hall and Selwood, 1995). The spell of the Americans having been broken, the America's Cup was hosted by Auckland, New Zealand in 1999–2000 and 2002–2003. The somewhat dilapidated Auckland harbourside was transformed into an upmarket restaurant precinct, with positive urban redevelopment and tourism outcomes for the city.

Perhaps nowhere has the use of events as tools for urban regeneration been as striking as in the United Kingdom. From having been the leader of the industrial revolution, by the mid-twentieth century many of the UK's major industrial cities, particularly in the north of England and in Scotland, were in an advanced state of decay. Typically, the inner-city urban areas where industrial plants had congregated were subject to high levels of unemployment, high rates of crime, substandard housing and low self-esteem.

With strong initiative and ingenuity, the UK tackled this problem to become a pioneer in urban regeneration and the use of event-based strategies. A series of five National Garden Festivals during the 1980s and early 1990s in Liverpool, Stoke-on-Trent, Glasgow, Gateshead and Ebbw Vale were used to transform derelict sites into attractive housing estates and parkland (Shone with Parry, 2001). The Glasgow site now houses the Glasgow Science Centre and a digital media village on the banks of the River Clyde. Glasgow went on to use the accolade of European City of Culture in 1990 and the UK City of Architecture and Design in 1999, to transform its image from that of a decaying industrial city into that of a dynamic centre with a strong arts and tourism base.

Probably the most outstanding example of the use of events in urban regeneration in the UK in recent times is that of the Manchester 2002 Commonwealth Games.

Background: Manchester in decay

By the 1990s Manchester, once known as 'the workshop of the world' during the industrial revolution, had been in a period of steady decline for several decades (Hughes, 1993; Manchester 2002, 2003). With the economic recessions of the 1970s and 1980s, it lost 60% of its employment base. Between 1981 and 1991 the resident population fell by 11.5%, leaving a demographically unbalanced population with heavy concentrations of the old, the young, ethnic minorities and the economically disadvantaged. By August 1992, unemployment had risen to 17.5% (compared with a UK average of 9.9%), and more than a third of the population received income from social security. An IRA bomb explosion in 1996 led to the further demoralisation of the city.

Government strategies for urban renewal

In the 1990s a comprehensive and integrated approach was established to regenerate the city (Manchester City Council, 2005). The area was identified as one of 17 national pathfinders under the New Deal for Communities (NDC) Initiative in 1998. The East Manchester Plan, Beacons for a Brighter Future, was the first successful NDC scheme in the country, securing funding of £51.7 million. Its key themes were tackling crime and the fear of crime; improvements to housing and neighbourhood management; the provision of positive open space; an emphasis on education, skills and training to help local people take advantage of employment opportunities; capacity building within the community to increase confidence and promote sustainability and projects aimed at promoting the health and well being of the community. Subsequently, complementary UK government funding of £25 million from the Single Regeneration Budget, enabled the activity and benefits from the NDC to be rolled out across the wider area.

East Manchester was the location of one of three pilot urban regeneration companies in the UK, with New East Manchester Limited set up by the government in 1999 to provide an integrated and coordinated approach to regeneration. Formed as a partnership between the City Council, English Partnerships, the North West Development Agency and the local communities covering the wider East Manchester area, its charter was to prepare and implement a strategic framework for the area, secure additional funding, take the lead on particular development projects, secure inward investment and coordinate the range of initiatives in East Manchester.

The Commonwealth Games serve as a catalyst

An important strategic initiative of the regeneration programme was to utilise the hosting of major events as a tool for urban regeneration and economic development. The City of Manchester bid unsuccessfully for the 1996 and 2000 Olympic Games and was finally awarded the 2002 Commonwealth Games in 1995. The staging of the Games became a catalyst to inspire commitment and fast-track much of the planned regeneration and development. The building of venues was used to rejuvenate East Manchester and to upgrade the transport and accommodation infrastructure of the city. The successful hosting of the Games not only brought visitors and media attention to the city but also attracted further business investment and support. The final Games report (Manchester 2002, 2003) stated that over the following 15 years, New East Manchester was expected to secure more than £600 million in public and private funding, with the New Business Park development expected to create more than 6000 jobs and a new retail centre, a four star hotel and new housing developments expected to create another 3800 jobs for the people of East Manchester.

The legacy continues

Manchester has continued to pursue a major events strategy, with a Five Year Regional Event Strategy drawn up by the North West Development Agency in 2004. Manchester City Football Club, as the new resident in the City of Manchester stadium draws 40,000 people to the streets of East Manchester for each of its home games. Concerts by U2 and Oasis in the summer of 2005 attracted 360,000 music fans. In 2005, Manchester Event Volunteers, an outgrowth of the Games, had a database of over 2000 volunteers taking part in a wide range of events including the Salford Triathlon, the Great Manchester Run and the World Paralympics event.

The final Games report (Commonwealth Games Legacy, 2003) concludes that:

> This event had to be about more than municipal ego. More than an opportunity to bathe in the reflected glory of a world event successfully staged. Manchester was always explicit in its intention. In bidding for the Commonwealth Games its aim was not only to deliver a world-class event but also to create a lasting legacy for Manchester and the region. A unique and innovative approach was taken to the legacy of the Manchester Games. Any city or organisation would expect the successful delivery of such a huge event to deliver benefits to tourism, sporting infrastructure and measurable commercial gains. Manchester went further.
>
> The aim was for the hosting of the Games to provide the catalyst for the whole scale regeneration of a large area of the city.

THE CORPORATE PERSPECTIVE

Events have a unique ability to bring people physically together and to inspire and communicate with them in ways that cannot be easily duplicated by other means or by media. This has been recognised by the corporate sector, which as we saw in Chapter 1 increased its use of events rapidly in the 1990s, establishing a trend that has continued unabated until the global banking crisis and downturn from 2008, with recovery out of recession in late 2009. In a survey of event industry representatives including corporate event planners undertaken by *Meetings & Incentive Travel Magazine* in April 2010 (Anon., 2010), 64% expected to stage more events in the coming year compared to 2009, and 82% are feeling more confident about the future than six months ago. This upward trend reflects the recognition of the power of events by the corporate sector and its increasing use of events as tools both to improve company morale and business procedures and to increase profitability and income.

Corporate use of events

Silvers (2010) describes corporate and business events as 'Any event that supports business objectives, including management functions, corporate communications,

Table 2.1 Corporate use of events

Internal	External
Annual General Meetings (AGMs)	Grand openings
Corporate retreats	Product launches
Board meetings	Sales promotions
Management meetings	Media conferences
Staff training	Publicity events
Team building	Photo opportunities
Staff social events	Exhibitions
Incentive events	Trade missions
Award nights	Trade shows
Sales conferences	Client hospitality
Dealer network seminars	Event sponsorship

training, marketing, incentives, employee relations, and customer relations, scheduled alone or in conjunction with other events.'

The use of events by companies and businesses may be focused internally and aimed at their own business practices and staff, or it may be focused externally and aimed at their customers and clients (see Table 2.1). The common thread is the demonstrated ability of events to deliver results in terms of business objectives and therefore to provide a return on investment.

Internal events

Internally, companies make significant use of events such as management meetings and staff training in the day-to-day conduct of their business. Given the modern corporate environment, major internal company events such as Annual General Meetings (AGMs), corporate retreats and board meetings are often treated as significant occasions deserving of dedicated organisation and meticulous attention to detail. Other internal events such as staff social events, team building, incentives and award nights are seen as valuable tools to inspire and motivate staff and as contributing to the development of a successful corporate culture. Sales conferences and product seminars are used to extend this culture further to company representatives and dealer networks. Many companies contribute considerable resources towards ensuring that such events are perceived as part of their corporate identity and style and they are conducted with high standards of professionalism and presentation skills.

A prime example of the internal use of events is that of satellite broadcaster Sky, who held Skyfest for 20,000 of their employees, friends and families. Their two-day event in London in July 2009, was repeated for their Scottish staff in September 2009 and took on different formats in London and Scotland, with the London event becoming more of a family-friendly festival while the Scottish event was child-free. For example, the London event included an over-18s event featuring entertainment by Will Young, DJ Seb Fontaine and comedian Frankie Boyle, while the following day featured family entertainment, with a funfair, dance lessons with Strictly Come Dancing stars and music from Bjorn Again (O'Donovan, 2009).

External events

Externally, events are highly valued for their ability to communicate corporate and sales messages and to cut through the clutter of advertising and media to reach customers and clients directly and effectively. As detailed in Table 2.1, grand openings, product launches, sales promotions, media conferences, publicity events and photo opportunities are just some of the wide variety of events that are used to gain the attention of potential customers and to create a 'buzz' around new products and services. Companies also use exhibitions, trade missions and trade shows to reach distribution networks and to maintain a company presence in selected markets.

An example of the use of events to promote a corporate image and launch new products is provided by Tesco's "Enjoy the Taste of Scotland: Get to Know your Locals" food and drink event. Produced in collaboration with Denvir, the event included the aims of attracting Scottish suppliers to promote and sell their products, building awareness of Tesco's Scottish supplier base with at least 20,000 attendees and driving sales of local products through stores (Denvir, 2009).

Another growing corporate use of events is the entertaining of clients in order to build and nourish business relationships with them. This can take the form of hosted cocktail parties, dinners or receptions or hospitality at company sponsored public events. Often the sponsorship of events can bring many of these aspects together, enabling companies to reach event attendees and demonstrate product attributes through associating their product with the event, while at the same time hosting clients in a convivial atmosphere.

The sponsorship by Asos.com of the Global Radio 95.8 Capital FM Summertime Ball in London allows the company to bring its brand to life, as Asos aims to promote its online store as 'first for fashion, first for trends, the UK's largest branded fashion offer.' It is aiming to associate itself with a popular event among its target audience and also to demonstrate its product attributes by linking fashion and music (Baker, 2010).

Association conferences

Another corporate-related use of events touched on in Chapter 1 is that of conferences and business meetings. A large and growing number of professional, academic and industry associations use meetings, congresses and conferences to communicate with their members, to explore relevant issues and to disseminate information to their respective audiences. These can be local, national or international in scope, with many international associations maintaining a structure and bidding process similar to that of major sporting bodies. An important aspect of these events is the opportunity provided by participants to keep abreast of developments in their professional fields and to network with colleagues and associates. There has been recent speculation in the industry that increasing environmental impact, travel costs and security issues, coupled with the increasing technological capacity for online meetings and video conferencing, will slow the growth of the industry. However, to date the advantages of direct networking and face-to-face contact seem to override the disadvantages, as the meetings industry continues to thrive and prosper.

Return on investment

The growth in the use of events by the corporate sector has been accompanied by an increasing desire and need to evaluate their outcomes. With the increasing amount spent on events, companies understandably want to know what their events are achieving and their effectiveness and return on investment (ROI) compared with other marketing tools and strategies. This has led to a greater emphasis on the establishment of measures or metrics to benchmark events and to quantify their outcomes.

However, many of the benefits and outcomes of events are difficult to quantify in monetary terms, and different companies use different measures and yardsticks. Myhill (2005) maintains that the ROI for meetings and training events can be calculated by the use of careful data planning and analysis, using the Phillips ROI methodology developed in the 1970s. Phillips, Breining and Phillips (2008) have developed a methodology specifically for meetings and events, with Phillip's ROI methodology also providing the framework for the European Events ROI Institute. The ROI methodology uses five levels of evaluation, leading to the full numerical calculation of return on investment:

- Reaction and planned action — measures attendee satisfaction, usually by the use of generic questionnaires. While important, attendee satisfaction does not in itself guarantee the acquisition of new skills, knowledge or professional contacts.
- Learning — uses tests, skill practices, group evaluations and other assessment tools to ensure that attendees have absorbed the meeting material and know how to use it properly. However, it does not guarantee that what has been learnt will be used on the job.
- Job application — used to determine whether attendees applied what they learnt from the meeting on the job. While it is a good gauge of the meeting's success, it does not guarantee a positive business impact for the organisation.
- Business results — focuses on the results achieved by attendees as they successfully apply what they have learnt from the meeting. Typical measures include output, sales, quality, costs, time and customer satisfaction. However, this still does not provide a measure of the financial value of the meeting or event.
- Return on investment — compares the monetary benefits gained from the meeting with the costs. A numerical ROI percentage can be obtained using the formula:

$$\frac{\text{Meeting benefits} - \text{Meeting costs}}{\text{Meeting costs}} \times 100$$

This formula can be used to compare the ROI of meetings and events with alternative events and strategies. However, Myhill suggests that it is not appropriate to conduct such a study on all meetings and events. She recommends that ROI should be applied to only five to ten percent of events, with the most suitable being those linked to the operational goals and/or strategic objectives of the organisation and which incur significant costs and staff/participant time.

Events aimed at external stakeholders are typically measured by attendance numbers, sales leads obtained or changes in attitude or perception. It is often as much about brand awareness and enhancement as it is about actual sales or measurable outcomes. Jeff Kline (Hurley, 2005), Executive Vice President of Business Affairs at California based TBA Global Events, comments:

> 'ROI is very important, but it is measured differently by each client. The return could be measured by the number of people attending the event, how the event looked and was perceived or how attendees felt as they left the event. We believe that the ROI of events can be somewhat intangible; but the true value resides in that moment when the brand achieves relevance and preference to the audience and that is what we focus on.'

THE COMMUNITY PERSPECTIVE

Most public events are either community events or major events that take place in host communities that have a particular interest and attitude toward the event. Thus the community is a major stakeholder in events and it is incumbent on event managers to consider the community perspective and to include this in the event planning process.

Community events

As discussed in Chapter 1, some form of festivals and events can be identified in every human society and in every age. They are part of how we interact as humans and form part of the social fabric that binds our communities together. This can be seen in many country town and regional festivals, where the main social event of the year is often the town festival. The myriad social interactions that go into creating the festival — the committee meetings, the approaches to local businesses for support, the involvement of local arts and sports groups, the contacting of service groups and volunteers — all help to create social capital and community wellbeing. In many cases, these festivals provide an annual opportunity for local clubs and societies to fundraise and recruit new members and are therefore crucial to their survival. Communities of course are not always heterogeneous, and festivals can provide the stimulation for healthy disagreement and debate about their priorities and identity. In many very real ways, therefore, these festivals help to create and strengthen a sense of community and belonging. For this and related reasons, they are often supported by local governments and other government agencies concerned with maintaining and supporting healthy communities.

The individual perspective

From the perspective of community members, their requirements and expectations of community events are often very simple and direct. They want to participate and be entertained — to have a social and enriching experience beyond their everyday reality. They may want to participate as a family so that they can enjoy the experience together and so that children are provided a special treat at an affordable cost. They may want to showcase their creative talents in the case of arts or cultural festivals or to enjoy friendly competition in the case of sporting events. In some cases they may want the satisfaction and achievement of being involved as organisers or to achieve social contact and recognition by being involved as volunteers. They may have some awareness of the larger role of the event in their community but are likely to be more interested in the social and cultural benefits than the business and economic outcomes of the event.

The Centre for Popular Education (UTS) conducted an evaluation of 20 festivals funded by the Communities Together: Festival and Celebration Scheme of VicHealth in Victoria, Australia, from 2002–2004 in order to determine the outcomes of the programme (Hilbers, 2005). The study found evidence that community based celebrations contribute positively to the mental health and wellbeing of communities. It concluded that there were opportunities for communities to work together to create and manage celebrations that enable people to engage in creative activity, express themselves and socialise, lead to bonding within groups strengthen relationships between communities and foster skills development and dialogue across communities. However, the nature and extent of benefits identified by the study varied according to the histories of the communities and their societal influences, the purpose of the celebrations, the mode of practice adopted, the skills of the organisers and the level of engagement.

The process also identified potential indicators for future evaluations that are summarised in Table 2.2.

Major events and the community

The community perspective changes when we examine major events within the community that attract many visitors. Community members may still look forward to enjoying the event as participants or spectators. However, as the event organisation becomes larger and more professional, much of the event planning is often taken out of the hands of members of the host community. They are now more likely to be concerned with the wider impact of the event, which may include a sense of pride in their community, economic and job creation benefits, and physical implications such as traffic restrictions and crowd congestion. Their relationship with the event is likely to be less direct and the media may become the main source of information on the planning of the event and predictions of visitor numbers, media coverage, economic benefits and job creation. Under such circumstances, it is easy for members of the community to become distanced from the event and to fluctuate in their perceptions and expectations of the event experience and outcomes.

Table 2.2 Potential individual, organisational and community capacity building indicators for community celebrations and festivals

Individual	Organisational	Community
Learning new information	New membership to existing groups	Increased ability to access skills and resources within the community
Self-reflection opportunities	Provision of formal and informal learning opportunities	Trial activities within the festival/celebration context
Access to formal and informal learning opportunities leading to skill development (for example, planning, promoting, managing events; creative and artistic skills, community development, technical, planning and evaluation, administration, interpersonal skills)	Increased ability to access skills and resources within the group	Increased creative capacity of the community
Experience and confidence	New or existing groups demonstrate ability to work together	Creation and management of whole of community activity
Employment	Learning culture	Continuation of community activities
	Advocacy about the value of community celebrations	Interest and action in other community initiatives (for example, community celebrations, provision of physical resources)

(Source: Hilbers, 2005)

For the event organisers, keeping the host community informed and on their side becomes a vital task in the event planning process. Not only is it important to keep the community engaged with the event but if it becomes disaffected, then this attitude is likely to affect the experience and enjoyment of visitors to the event. The negative reaction of some residents to the National Lottery funds spent on the 2007 'Heart of the Dragon' festival in Newcastle Emlyn, Wales, is an example of the negative impact of community disengagement with an event. Event organisers therefore need to develop strategies to involve the host community in the planning of the event, to maintain good community relations, and to monitor the community's perceptions of and attitudes to an event.

An excellent example of establishing good community relations is provided by the St Patrick's Day community events in Belfast, funded under the St Patrick's Day

Grants Scheme from the Good Relations Unit. This fund aims 'to promote good relations between people of different religions, political beliefs and different racial groups', and since it commenced in 2004 it has provided nearly £155,000 to over 364 projects (Good Relations Unit, 2010).

Strategies for community engagement

Community perceptions of an event will depend to a large extent on the levels of community engagement and on the efforts made by event organisers to involve the community in the planning, implementation and evaluation of the event. Appropriate liaison with stakeholders will ensure that the event represents the true values of the community and will often serve to resolve many of the potential community conflicts and disruptions in relation to the event.

Harris and Allen (2006), in a study for artsACT, examined 22 medium- to large-scale public events in Australia and overseas in order to identify the strategies employed by event managers to facilitate community engagement. They posited core values for public engagement and participation based on those of the International Association for Public Participation (IAP2, 2007):

1. The public should be consulted and should have a say in decisions about actions that affect their lives
2. Public participation undertakes that the public's contribution will influence the decision-making process
3. The public participation process communicates the interests and meets the process needs of all participants
4. The public participation process identifies those potentially affected and facilitates their input.
5. The public participation process involves participants in defining how they participate
6. The public participation process provides participants with the information they need to participate in a meaningful way
7. The public participation process provides feedback to participants on how their input affected the decision (IAP2, www.iap2.org)

In practice, the study found that the extent and type of community engagement varied widely in the events that they studied, with some events much more proactive than others in seeking to involve and engage the community. Mechanisms for community engagement in the events examined by the study included:

Participation facilitation
- Free or discounted provision of transport
- Provision of on-site facilities and services for specific groups, such as marquees for elderly people and creches for young families
- Radio broadcasts for community members who are housebound
- Free access to aspects of the programme

- Discount ticket prices for selected groups — such as the unemployed, pensioners and students — and access to free tickets for selected groups
- Provision of specific services and facilities for people with disabilities
- Embracing a variety of geographic locations within a community when delivering the event programme or when engaged in outreach activities

Community input and feedback facilitation

- Public meetings
- Community based 'whole of event' strategic reviews
- Festival workshops designed to seek input with regard to event design and programming
- Open calls for membership of an event organising committee
- Dedicated local radio talk-back sessions with event organisers
- Community advisory committees or consultation groups that serve to provide input to the event or the inclusion of community representatives on the organising committee
- Inclusion of a feedback or contact facility on the event website

Inclusive programming

- Targeting of specific community groups to deliver or assist with one or more aspects of the event programme. Such groups included the unemployed, at-risk youth and special interest groups such as environmental organisations
- Designing programme elements with the needs of specific groups in mind (for example, the participation of schools by incorporating an 'education day')

Incentives

- The provision of free stall space to non-profit organisations and charities to raise funds, attract new members or raise awareness of a particular issue or cause
- Competitions and contests that serve to encourage involvement by particular community groups such as school children, local artists and sporting groups

Outreach

- Profits from the event used to engage in extension activities to specific, often disadvantaged groups in the community
- Shop fronts that provide an ongoing connection between the event and its community
- Involvement of schools by seeking inclusion in school curriculum activities or by creating lesson plans for use by teachers that deal with various aspects of events in general
- Access to event websites for non-profit organisations, so that they may enhance their community presence
- The use of symbolism to reach out to communities on an ongoing basis (for example, a public installation or sculpture to remind local people of the ongoing connection between the town and the event)
- Broadening the local community by expanding the footprint of the event into nearby areas

Community development and capacity building
- Internships, traineeships and work experience programmes that provide opportunities for young people to learn new skills and knowledge that can in turn be used within their communities on a paid or voluntary basis
- Provision of volunteering opportunities, training sessions and volunteer social events that facilitate the creation of new networks within the community and may result in new business and other opportunities for volunteers
- Enhancement of the community's capacity to deal with a specific issue or problem
- Providing financial resources from an event into the development of various non-profit community organisations in order to progress a community's development efforts

Friends of the event/event alumni associations
- The creation of 'friends' or 'alumni' groups to integrate an event further with its community

Local business engagement
- Encouragement of attendee expenditure at local businesses through the creation of special incentives tied in with the event
- Giving preference to local businesses for the supply of services

This study is primarily an exploratory one, and more research needs to be devoted to identifying community engagement mechanisms and their relative effectiveness. Nevertheless, for the event manager it indicates that there is a broad range of initiatives available to engage the involvement and participation of host communities in events. However, considerable care must be taken to ensure that the particular strategies chosen are best suited to the particular community and its needs and are most likely to achieve results. This in turn will reap rewards in terms of a greater sense of community ownership of the event and a more positive perception of its benefits and impact.

SUMMARY

This chapter examined a number of important perspectives that have implications for event managers in the planning and delivery of events. From the government perspective, a number of disparate roles and functions in events are often integrated through the use of event strategies, as illustrated by the North East England Festival and Events Strategy (One NorthEast, 2007). Governments may also create dedicated celebration spaces and use events as tools for urban renewal. Event managers need to be aware of government regulations and requirements and to see governments as key stakeholders and potential partners in events. The corporate sector uses events to achieve both internal and external goals and objectives, and sponsors public events in order to obtain commercial benefits. Event managers need to be aware of corporate objectives and the increasing need of companies to identify the return on investment (ROI) of events. From the community perspective, community members are often focused on the direct, personal impact and the benefits of events for the individual personally and for the community in general. Managers of public events need to carefully choose and implement appropriate mechanisms for communication and engagement with the community.

QUESTIONS

1. Does local government in your area have an event strategy? Analyse the roles that your local government plays in the regulation and coordination of events.

2. Can you identify a dedicated celebration space in your city or region? How is the space managed and what role does it play in the life of the community?

3. Choose a corporate event. Investigate why it was staged and how its outcomes were measured.

4. Analyse the corporate sponsorship of an event and identify the main benefits that were obtained.

5. Choose a community event with which you are familiar and identify the benefits to individuals and to the community from the staging of the event.

6. Identify the community engagement strategies of a large community event in your city or region.

7. Discuss the implications for event managers that arise from the analysis of the government, corporate and community perspectives on events.

CASE STUDY: EUROSTAR FORUM BY WORLDEVENTS™

This case study provides a powerful example of how WorldEvents™ – a global player in corporate events and motivational, incentive and teambuilding programmes – provides effective communications, production, team building and on-site event management. The case study is concerned with the use of an event to motivate management teams and to communicate brand messages, based on the Eurostar Managers Forum, an annual meeting arranged for Eurostar Group.

The Eurostar Group, responsible for determining the communication direction and service direction of the overall Eurostar business, comprises train-operating companies from the UK (Eurostar UK), France (SNCF) and Belgium (SNCB). As a result of geographic and cultural diversity, it is essential that management have a clear understanding of the organisation. In order to facilitate this, Eurostar hold an annual two-day meeting of managers from all divisions of the three companies. For this year, the venue chosen for the event was The New York Convention Centre at Disneyland Paris, with the client managing their own travel via the Eurostar, and their own logistics at the Sequioa Lodge Hotel, Disneyland, Paris.

Diversity of the audience can present a significant challenge. The event was aimed at train operators, not marketers, plus key distributors and contractors, and therefore the event had to be designed to ensure that the communication message was clear. The task of taking into account the requirements of 195 managers from three railway companies based in London, Paris and

Brussels, speaking three different languages, and each having distinctly different cultures – required clear objectives to be formulated to ensure success. These were identified as follows:

- To understand the power of branding and the Eurostar brand
- To give information about performance, future developments and plans
- To encourage a very mixed group to get to know each other better
- To move the meeting format forward from the last meeting

Based on these objectives, WorldEvents™ developed a conference that involved and surprised the audience throughout the two days, based around a clear theme and using a host/facilitator, video inserts, table challenges, breakout workshops and two, very different team building activities.

The theme was developed around a key message – 'Making Our Marque' – to communicate the power of branding, the power of the Eurostar brand and its relevance to an audience of French and English speakers.

The Event Format. For the brand exercises, the audience was challenged to map out and present their current and future perceptions of the Eurostar brand. Real customer views were presented as video inserts – in three languages – to add the customers' perceptions into the discussion. During plenary sessions, simultaneous translation was provided in two languages.

The day ended in the early evening with a final team activity – 'Trading Brands' – which focused on using the power of brands to increase company value.

Day 1. For the first day, the audience was seated at round tables for the workshop and for reporting back

The delegates were divided into teams by badges with different famous brand names

In order to keep the day informal, no lectern was used – instead, all messages were presented in discussion format. A facilitator was used to introduce the theme, key messages, interact with audience and host discussions with all five speakers.

For the brand exercises, the audience was challenged to map out and present their current and future perceptions of the Eurostar brand. Real customer views were presented as video inserts – in three languages – to add the customers' perceptions into the discussion. During plenary sessions, simultaneous translation was provided in two languages.

The day ended in the early evening with a final team activity – 'Trading Brands' – which focused on using the power of brands to increase company value.

Day 2 (1/2 day am). On the second day, workshops were used where the audience, in mixed groups, were challenged to develop action plans to improve customer service and company performance. The findings from this were collated but not formally presented back to the group.

In the late morning, the audience took part in a final team activity – 'T-shirt Masterpiece'. The teams summarised the Eurostar brand and message on T-shirts, then each team in turn presented their message on stage.

Evaluating the results. As a result of the event, the following outcomes were achieved:

- A better understanding of the company's service culture and future strategies and improved working relationships between delegates
- Enthusiastic participation in both team activities

WorldEvents™ designed, produced and managed the theme, title and conference logo, the event format, running order, speaker support on screen, the two team activities, customer interview films, simtran (simultaneous translation), set and staging, technical support and all stage management.

For further details about WorldEvents™, please visit www.world-events.com.

By WorldEvents™

Continued

CASE STUDY: EUROSTAR FORUM BY WORLDEVENTS™—*CONT'D*

Questions

1. Why was this an 'event'? How is it different from and similar to other events that you know of?
2. Who were the event stakeholders?
3. What stakeholders' needs were satisfied by this event?
4. The case illustrates the use of events for motivational purposes. How can events such as this be used to motivate employees and managers? What other needs do they satisfy? On what basis can participants be selected to take part?

CASE STUDY EDINBURGH'S WINTER FESTIVALS

1. Changing market profile. A visit to Edinburgh's Hogmanay is listed in a book called '*One hundred things to do before you die*'.. Scotland can rightly claim to be the home of New Year's Eve celebrations and Edinburgh, Scotland's capital, hosts the biggest and best of parties. With its iconic castle, Edinburgh offers a natural and unique events arena. Scotland has its own name for New Year – 'Hogmanay', derived from a seventeenth century Norman French term meaning 'New Year's gift'.

The strategic objective set out by the City of Edinburgh Council for Edinburgh's Winter Festivals is to stimulate tourism and related business in Edinburgh throughout the winter months from November to January. Edinburgh's Hogmanay celebrations in their current form as a four day festival dates from 1993, while Edinburgh's Christmas festival dates from 1999. Together these two events make up Edinburgh's Winter Festivals (EWF).

In February 2004 the two events were brought under a single management within the City of Edinburgh Council. The primary reasons for this were to achieve economies of scale, maximise synergies between the two events and exploit marketing opportunities. The two event programmes have distinct brand identities aimed at specific target audiences:

- the Christmas festival is aimed at families and retail focused visitors to the city
- Hogmanay is aimed at city break visitors and attracts more international visitors.

Edinburgh's Christmas festival is a month-long series of mostly free public events held in the city's public open spaces and runs from the end of November until Christmas Eve. The festival events are focused on the festive lighting of the city centre (the 'switching on' of the festive lights on 'Light Night' on the last Thursday of November, is a highlight of the festival), a central events arena in Princes Street Gardens including the Winter Wonderland ice rink, the Edinburgh Wheel, the traditional German Christmas market (staged by the City of Frankfurt, Germany) and a series of special events such as the Great Scottish Santa Fun Run, Santa Comes to Town, Norwegian Advent Concert and the Nativity Carol Service. As a central development aspect of the events' programming and promotion, the Edinburgh Winter Festivals management team has encouraged promoters of events, exhibitions and Christmas-related activities, to brand these as Edinburgh's Christmas events and include them in the promotional programme.

Edinburgh's Hogmanay kicks off on 29 December, again made up of mostly free open air public events, and includes the 15,000 strong torchlight procession and the burning of a Viking long boat on Calton Hill. On 30 December George Street plays host to more than 20,000 people for the Night Afore International (international street theatre, world music and street ceilidh – traditional Scottish social dances.). On 31 December (New Year's Eve or Hogmanay) is the street party, with 100,000 party goers listening to a variety of international live music acts on a number of stages in the city centre, as well as various indoor and outdoor ceilidhs; on 1 January are events such as the Loony Dook and the One o'Clock Run.

Prior to the development of the Winter Festivals, December and January was traditionally a quiet period for hotels in Edinburgh. The city was generally shut for business, with most shops and visitor attractions such as museums being closed on 1st and 2nd January. The Winter Festivals programme and the active encouragement of businesses and attractions to open for business have changed that situation.

Evidence of the impact of the EWF is demonstrated in occupancy rates in the city's hotels and guest houses of 76% for November and 64% for December, compared with an average 75% occupancy rate for the year. In 2005, 43% of visitors to the festivals were on a short break or more than a three-night stay (*Scotsman Newspaper*, 2006). The Scottish Retail Consortium also reported a two percent increase in retail spending over the period compared to the previous year. In December 2005 the number of passengers at Edinburgh Airport grew by three percent on the previous year. The draw or appeal of the city because of the Winter Festivals programme has been assisted by the development of 'no frills' airlines primarily connecting Edinburgh to its main markets in the south-east of England, and also more direct international air routes into the city.

In December 2006 the travel website Trip Advisor put Edinburgh in the world top 10 of 10 great places to ring in 2007 with the headline 'Edinburgh's Hogmanay howls' (PR Newswire 2006).

2. Benefits to the city. In 2004–2005 EWF attracted an audience of approximately half a million people and generated £44.4 million for the Scottish economy (SQW/TNS, 2005b). This supported 930 full-time equivalent (fte) jobs. This figure is included in the overall economic impact of Edinburgh's 17 major festivals totalling £184 million and 3900 fte jobs (*Summary of economic impact study* 2005, p. 2). This economic impact study follows studies in 1991 (*The economic impact of Edinburgh's festivals*), 1996 (*Edinburgh festivals economic impact study*) and studies in 2002–2003 and 2003–2004.

The 2004–2005 Edinburgh Festivals study was funded jointly by the City Council, participating festivals, EventScotland and Scottish Enterprise and was undertaken by two Edinburgh based companies, SQW and TNS. The main objectives of the Edinburgh Festivals 2004–2005 study were to:

- identify and quantify the full economic impact of each festival in Edinburgh, Lothian and Scotland, including the number of jobs created and protected
- develop a profile of the audiences for each of the festivals and for all of the festivals as a whole
- obtain consumer perceptions of the festivals from both local residents and visitors

More specifically, the rationale for undertaking this research was to:

- track the evolution of the festivals over time (against previous strategic objectives)
- assist in business planning and the strategic development of the festivals (both programming and product)
- ensure continued market fit
- inform future marketing strategies
- support justification for specific project funding
- provide advocacy for further funding bids

For EWF the study outcomes have been central to the reshaping of the new five year (2007–2012) business plan and current marketing plans. In 2005–2006 further audience research was conducted online rather than face-to-face and this will be repeated annually until the next major, full-scale face-to-face visitor survey and economic impact assessment is undertaken.

Continued

CASE STUDY EDINBURGH'S WINTER FESTIVALS—*CONT'D*

As it formed part of a wider piece of year round festival research, the base research for the 2004–2005 study involved face-to-face visitor surveys with 335 of the audience for Edinburgh's Christmas and 406 of the audience for Edinburgh's Hogmanay out of a total of 4129 interviews for all of the 17 major festivals in the city. The survey questionnaire was made up of 20 questions. In addition, the 2004–05 study contained interviews with 115 performers and delegates, 25 journalists and media representatives, 19 major hotels and 26 guest houses.

This research also showed that 78% of residents questioned believed Edinburgh to be a better place to live in because of the Winter Festivals. For visitors to Edinburgh, 70% stated 'I am more likely to come back to Edinburgh after having been to the Winter Festivals'.

The City Council also perceives a major benefit of EWF and in particular Edinburgh's Hogmanay, to be the positive and high media profile it generates both domestically in the UK and internationally. Edinburgh is featured in news broadcasts along with New York, London and Sydney when there is coverage of New Year's Eve celebrations. In 2005–2006 there were 50 media organisations registered for the Hogmanay Street Party with television coverage being achieved in more than 30 countries. A good example of the international media exposure achieved was that Chinese Television covered the 2005–2006 event, by broadcasting a feature on EWF on New Year's Eve. China is considered a good potential visitor market for Edinburgh and Scotland. Development of stronger media partnerships and profiling of the festival and the city in key target visitor markets is a major aspect of the new EWF five year business plan for 2007–2012.

Table 2.3 shows the home location of visitors to EWF and Table 2.4 shows the primary reason for their visit.

Table 2.3 Home location of visitors to EWF

	Christmas (%)	Hogmanay (%)
Edinburgh	38	33
Lothians (City region)	7	4
Elsewhere in Scotland	13	9
Elsewhere in Britain	25	31
Overseas	16	23

(Source: SQW/TNS, 2005a, Table 2.1, p. 5)

Table 2.4 Reason for visit

	Christmas (%)	Hogmanay (%)
Sole reason for coming	25	46
A very important reason	22	29
A fairly important reason	16	13
Only a small reason	17	8

(Source: SQW/TNS, 2005a, Table 2.5, p. 6)

In 2005, 66% of visitors came specifically for EWF (up from 57% in 2004). Visitor experience versus expectation is shown in Table 2.5.

Table 2.5 Visitor experience versus expectation

	Better than Expected (%)
The atmosphere in Edinburgh with the festive/ Christmas lights switched on	75
Overall experience of the Winter Festivals	75
Overall experience of Edinburgh as a place to visit	67

(Source: composite of Tables 127 (p. 150), 131 (p. 154) and 133 (p. 156), SQW/TNS, 2005b)

In 2005, audiences rated all of the events four out of five (with five standing for 'excellent').

3. What does it cost?. The budget for the Winter Festivals programme in 2004–2005 was just over £2.6 million with £1.9 million of this being spent on the Festivals programme, £0.3 million on marketing and communications and £0.44 million on operations and management. The City of Edinburgh Council has a competitively tendered contract (which under EU rules, has to be advertised across all EU states), with Unique Events to perform the role of producers of both Edinburgh's Christmas and Edinburgh's Hogmanay. Unique Events, an Edinburgh based company, has created, produced and delivered Edinburgh's Hogmanay celebrations for its 13 year history and Edinburgh's Christmas for the last five years.

Just over half (51%) of the funding or income for the festival comes direct from the City of Edinburgh Council, with the balance being generated from earned income (34%) and sponsorship (15%). The continued rationale for the large sums of tax payers' money being invested in the Festival is the total economic benefit accruing directly to the City from the Festival (£36 million), the civic pride generated in the city and the positive profiling of the city to key national and international audiences.

The Festival also attracts funding support from the Scottish Government primarily through 'Scotland the Place', EventScotland and 'in-kind' and marketing support from VisitScotland. The Hogmanay street party has attracted blue chip sponsors such as the Royal Bank of Scotland and is currently sponsored by Scottish and Newcastle Brewers, who are promoting their Foster's brand.

Generation of new sources of income and sponsorship remains a major focus and challenge of the Winter Festivals management team and has been assisted since 2004 by the appointment of a full-time sponsorship and commercial development manager. The new five year (2007–12) business plan focuses on ways of enhancing components such as the Hogmanay Club, which offers premium products and exclusive benefits, as a source of revenue generation.

Just under half of the total budget for the five week festival is taken by the Hogmanay street party. The biggest cost component of this event is related to public safety measures. In the 2005–06 event, for the first time a street party pass administration charge of £2.50 was levied to cover the significant administration costs associated with the distribution of street party passes. The control of numbers entering Princes Street is one of the primary mitigating public safety measures. EWF's exemplary public safety record is one that requires significant investment to maintain. The winter weather of course can create its own public safety issues, which require investment in robust weather proofing of the infrastructure, especially after the weather related cancellation of the Hogmanay street party in 2004.

Continued

CASE STUDY EDINBURGH'S WINTER FESTIVALS—*CONT'D*

4. Management structures. The management structure of the event involves a policy advisory group overseeing an event planning and operations group (EPOG), a sponsorship and commercial development group, a marketing and PR group and an event liaison group (see Figure 2.2).

The event planning and operations group (EPOG) is considered a best practice example for public safety management, much copied by other events and typifying Edinburgh's 'belt and braces' approach to public safety. For large street-based public events, the changed security environment caused by 9/11 enhances the central role of EPOG and public safety considerations in the planning and operation of EWF. Increasingly, the linked issue of insurance and the escalating cost of public safety measures will be a central challenge for the festival in the future.

The management structures are constantly kept under review to ensure that they remain 'fit for purpose' as the festival evolves. This is an especially important consideration in the light of the ongoing debate about whether the future development of the festival is supported or hindered by being operated from within City Council structures (with the associated governmental bureaucratic and accounting procedure constraints), and whether it would be better as an independent entity, set up as a company. Ongoing sustainability of funding and public safety issues remain at the centre of the pros and cons of this debate.

5. Going forward. The festivals' strategy is events led. According to EWFs' *Annual Review 2005–06* (p. 3), 'The role of Edinburgh's Winter Festivals is to be imaginative and inspirational and create seasonal experiences to delight visitors and residents'.

Issues facing the festival include increasing costs and the challenges of identifying effective and efficient sources of income generation – a challenge for the future development of the festival programme. Investment in essential, state-of-the-art infrastructure in the public events arena also remains a challenge. Exploitation of information and communication technology as a distribution route for income generating activities and as a marketing tool is a key action in the festivals' business plan for the next five years.

For EWF as well as Edinburgh's summer and other festivals there is a perennial debate on how to unlock some of the significant economic benefits generated in the local economy from these largely free public events, against a backdrop of tight central government funding and competing demands on the funding from the city. This repeatedly leads stakeholders to consider alternative funding mechanisms, such as transient visitor taxation or a bed/tourism tax. The argument does seem to have been won that the festivals will struggle to be self-financing and that based on wider economic benefits, should continue to receive a continuing level of public subsidy. However, securing 'cash in hand' from central government sources remains a challenge.

Edinburgh is not complacent and is acutely aware of what competitor cities are doing. Retaining market appeal, distinctiveness and competitive advantage in the environment of a dynamic market and evolving a consumer base are top strategic objectives.

The task is to identify market developmental opportunities that appeal to identified key target markets that will attract support from key partners in the city such as national government agencies and commercial partners such as visitor attraction operators and retailers. At the same time, Edinburgh must maintain its special local character, appeal to civic pride and ensure that 'in the bleak mid-winter Edinburgh continues to sparkle'.

6. A last word from the consumer. 'Sixty-five percent of online visitors said they would come again and 65% said they would recommend it' (*Edinburgh's Winter Festivals Annual Review 2005–06*, p. 19).

Kenneth Wardrop, Interim Head of Economic Development, City Development, The City of Edinburgh Council

FIGURE 2.2 Organisational structure of Edinburgh's Winter Festivals

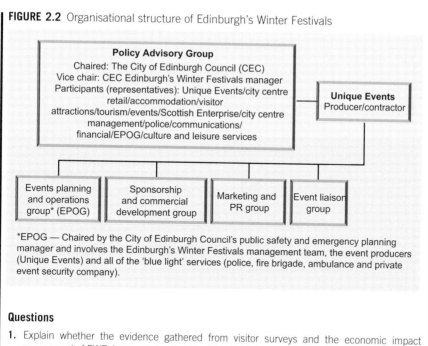

Policy Advisory Group
Chaired: The City of Edinburgh Council (CEC)
Vice chair: CEC Edinburgh's Winter Festivals manager
Participants (representatives): Unique Events/city centre
retail/accommodation/visitor
attractions/tourism/events/Scottish Enterprise/city centre
management/police/communications/
financial/EPOG/culture and leisure services

Unique Events
Producer/contractor

Events planning
and operations
group* (EPOG)

Sponsorship
and commercial
development group

Marketing and
PR group

Event liaison
group

*EPOG — Chaired by the City of Edinburgh Council's public safety and emergency planning manager and involves the Edinburgh's Winter Festivals management team, the event producers (Unique Events) and all of the 'blue light' services (police, fire brigade, ambulance and private event security company).

Questions

1. Explain whether the evidence gathered from visitor surveys and the economic impact assessment of EWF demonstrates that the City of Edinburgh Council's strategic objectives for supporting and investing in this programme of events is being realised.
2. What is the City Council's (and partners') rationale for undertaking an economic impact assessment of Edinburgh's Winter Festivals?
3. What are the financial challenges for Edinburgh's Winter Festivals as they go forward?
4. Public safety is a priority for the city and the event organisers. What measures are being applied to tackle this?

Event impacts and legacies

3

LEARNING OBJECTIVES

After studying this chapter, you should be able to:

- explain the role of the event manager in balancing the impacts of events
- identify the major impacts that events have on their stakeholders and host communities
- describe the social and cultural impacts of events and plan for positive outcomes
- describe the physical and environmental impacts of events
- discuss the political context of events
- discuss the tourism and economic impacts of events
- discuss why governments become involved in events
- describe the use of economic impact studies in measuring event outcomes
- discuss methods for identifying community perceptions of the impacts of events.

INTRODUCTION

Events do not take place in a vacuum — they touch almost every aspect of our lives, whether they are social, cultural, economic, environmental or political aspects. The benefits arising from such positive connections are a large part of the reason for the popularity and support of events. They are increasingly well documented and researched and strategies are being developed to enhance event outcomes and optimise their benefits.

The recent explosion of events, along with the parallel increase in the involvement of governments and businesses, has led to an increasing emphasis on the economic analysis of event benefits.

Understandably, governments considering the investment of substantial taxpayers' funds in events want to know what they are getting for their investment and how it compares with other investment options. This climate has given rise to detailed economic studies of events and to the development and application of increasingly sophisticated techniques of economic analysis and evaluation. However, events can also have unintended consequences that can lead them to have public prominence and media attention for the wrong reasons. The cost of event failure can be disastrous, turning positive benefits into negative publicity, political embarrassment and costly lawsuits. An important core task in organising

Events Management. DOI: 10.1016/B978-1-85617-818-1.10003-9

contemporary events is the identification, monitoring and management of event impacts. In this chapter, we examine some of the main areas affected by events, along with the strategies that event managers can employ to balance event impacts.

BALANCING THE IMPACTS OF EVENTS

Events have a range of impacts — both positive and negative — on their host communities and stakeholders (Table 3.1, page 81). It is the task of the event manager to identify and predict these impacts and then to manage them to achieve the best outcomes for all parties, so that on balance the overall impact of the event is positive. To achieve this, the event manager must develop and maximise all the foreseeable positive impacts and counter all the negative impacts. Often, negative impacts can be addressed through awareness and intervention — good planning is always critical. Ultimately, the success of the event depends on the event manager achieving this positive balance sheet and communicating it to a range of stakeholders.

Great emphasis is often placed on the financial impacts of events, partly because of the need of employers and governments to meet budget goals and justify expenditure and partly because such impacts are the most easily assessed. However, local and national government policies commonly acknowledge the 'triple bottom line' of social, economic and environmental goals/yardsticks in relation to events. Event managers should not lose sight of the full range of an event's impacts and the need to identify, describe, manage and document them. It is also important to realise that different impacts require different means of assessment. Social and cultural benefits, for example, are vital contributors to the calculation of an event's overall impact but describing them may require a narrative rather than a statistical approach. The literature relating to the impacts of events is continually expanding and maturing as more is understood about events, their significance and effects; for example, Langen and Garcia (2009) provide a detailed review of studies measuring the impacts of cultural events as part of the Impacts 08 programme, while Horne and Manzenreiter (eds., 2006) draw together researchers interested in the sociological, economic and political aspects of sports mega-events. In this chapter, we discuss some of the complex factors that need to be taken into account when assessing the impacts of events.

Social and cultural impacts

All events have a direct social and cultural impact on their participants and some-times on their wider host communities, as outlined by Hall (1997) and Getz (2005). This impact may be as simple as a shared entertainment experience, such as a sporting event or concert. Events can also result in intense national and community pride, as evidenced by the outpouring of emotion by many English fans that greeted the England team's performance at the 2005 Ashes Test Series; and the euphoria in

Table 3.1 The impacts of events		
Impacts of Events	**Positive Impacts**	**Negative Impacts**
Social and cultural	• Shared experience • Revitalisation of traditions • Building of community pride • Validation of community groups • Increased community participation • Introducing new and challenging ideas • Expansion of cultural perspectives	• Community alienation • Manipulation of community • Negative community image • Bad behaviour • Substance abuse • Social dislocation • Loss of amenity
Physical and environmental	• Showcasing the environment • Providing models for best practice • Increasing environmental awareness • Infrastructural legacy • Improved transport and communications • Urban transformation and renewal	• Environmental damage • Pollution • Destruction of heritage • Noise disturbance • Traffic congestion
Political	• International prestige • Improved profile • Promotion of investment • Social cohesion • Development of administrative skills	• Risk of event failure • Mis-allocation of funds • Lack of accountability • Propagandising • Loss of community ownership and control • Legitimation of ideology
Tourism and economic	• Destinational promotion and increased tourist visits • Extended length of stay • Higher yield • Increased tax revenue • Business opportunities • Commercial activity • Job creation	• Community resistance to tourism • Loss of authenticity • Damage to reputation • Exploitation • Inflated prices • Opportunity costs • Financial mismanagement • Financial loss
(Source: adapted from Hall, 1989)		

the Iraqi community resulting from their Asian Football Championships victory in 2007. Other impacts include increased pride — which results from some community events and celebrations of national days — and the validation of particular groups in the community. Some events leave a legacy of greater awareness and participation in sporting and cultural activities. For example, the sporting legacies stated for the

2002 and 2014 Commonwealth Games and the London 2012 Olympic Games. Others broaden people's cultural horizons, and expose them to new and challenging people, customs or ideas. For example, the melas held in Bradford, Leeds, Manchester, East London (Newham) and Edinburgh each summer, have introduced the Asian tradition with its strong religious and cultural associations, to wider audiences. The City of Bristol illustrated the benefits to be gained through social inclusion, from hosting the West Indies cricket team during the Cricket World Cup 1999. The council in partnership with Gloucester County Cricket Club and First Group developed a range of events targeted at schoolchildren and the local Afro-Caribbean community, including free access to warm-up sessions, coaching clinics and school visits (Select Committee on Culture, Media and Sport, 1999). In 1997, the ceremonies for the handover of Hong Kong from Britain to China had great symbolic importance for both countries. World media coverage of the ceremonies provoked emotions ranging from pride to sadness, jubilation to apprehension. On a different front, the installation of the Ice Cube outdoor ice-skating rink at Millennium Square in Leeds and similar events in Edinburgh and Somerset House in London, illustrate the trend in finding innovative alternative uses for city centre space.

Events have the power to challenge the imagination and to explore possibilities. The Long Walk to Justice, a series of marches in Edinburgh and around the world to coincide with the G8 Summit at Gleneagles in 2005, served to draw attention to the plight of Africa due to debt and the Make Poverty History campaign, and brought this issue powerfully to the attention of the leaders of the G8 nations and the media. The start of the week of events was marked with the Live 8 concerts taking place in Hyde Park, London and eight other countries: France, Italy, Germany, USA, Japan, Canada Russia and South Africa. The estimated audience for the concerts was three billion people worldwide (Live 8, 2005). Research undertaken to assess the impact of the 2200 funded Millennium Festival events (Jura Consultants and Gardiner & Theobold, 2001, p. 55) found the following social benefits:

- communities were mobilised and involved
- there were high levels of community integration
- organisers and volunteers benefited from significant personal development opportunities
- high numbers of volunteers were involved, giving significant amount of their time
- the creation of educational and recreational opportunities
- participation from a cross-section of the community
- a vast majority reported a strengthening of links in the local community
- an increased sense of local pride.
- entertainment provided in a friendly atmosphere.
- likelihood of the festivals continuing in some form in the future.

Events can also contribute to political debate and help to change history, as demonstrated by the watershed United Nations Conference on Environment and Development ('The Earth Summit') in Rio de Janeiro, Brazil in 1992 and the World Summit on Sustainable Development in Johannesburg, South Africa in 2002.

Further, they can promote healing in the community, as demonstrated by events dedicated to the victims and survivors of the terrorist attack in New York on 11 September 2001, the Bali nightclub bombing in October 2002, the South Asia Tsunamis on 26 December 2004 and the London transport bombings on 7 July 2005.

Events can form the cornerstone of cultural strategies. For example, Newham Council developed a local cultural strategy, entitled 'Reasons To Be Cheerful', at the heart of which is the vision that people will choose to live and work in Newham by 2010. In order to achieve this, events are used in a number of key areas. The strategy includes the following themes, illustrated with selected key points from the action plan:

- *New governance arrangements*: work with the Mayor and the Greater London Authority (GLA) to ensure Newham plays a full part in London's cultural strategy and in bids for major events such as the Olympics.
- *Showcase developments and a strengthened economy*: establish Three Mills as a major centre for creative industries, as a regional performance venue and visitor destination.
- Promote *an environment which supports a good quality of life*: establish mechanisms to attract major events to the area.
- *Local area strategies*: plan celebrations of local cultures to increase community cohesion.

(Newham Leisure Services, 2000).

Events can be developed with the aim of having a major impact on culture, as demonstrated by Liverpool's European Capital of Culture (ECoC) initiative in 2008. Liverpool 08 had the objectives of confirming Liverpool's position as a premier European City, to empower an inclusive and dynamic community and to achieve long-lasting cultural and economic benefits for Liverpool and future generations (Liverpool Culture Company, 2005c). In order to evaluate the impact, Liverpool City Council commissioned the University of Liverpool and Liverpool John Moores University for Impacts 08 – The Liverpool Model as a European Capital of Culture Research Programme. This programme aimed to develop a research model for evaluating culture-led regeneration programmes, with research focusing on social, cultural and economic impacts grouped around five themes: cultural access and participation; economy and tourism; cultural vibrancy and sustainability; image and perceptions and governance and the delivery process (Garcia, Melville and Cox, 2010, p. 5).

Research suggests that local communities often value the 'feel-good' aspects of hallmark events; they are prepared to put up with temporary inconvenience and disruption because of the excitement generated and the long-term expectation of improved facilities and profile. The Virgin London Marathon provides the opportunity each year for professional and amateur athletes to participate in a great international sporting event. For the professionals, this is an opportunity for them to prove their sporting excellence against the world's elite. For others, it provides an opportunity to prove their endurance to family, friends and relatives. However, for the majority of the runners it provides an opportunity to raise funds for their favoured charities. Charities benefit each year from the millions of pounds raised through sponsorship. A survey after the 2009 marathon found that £47.2 million had been raised for good causes, up from £46.7 million in 2008 and £46.5 million in 2007 and totalling over £450 million since 1981, with the organisers, The London Marathon Ltd, having also raised £28 million (London Marathon, 2010a), making it the largest annual fundraiser according to Guinness World Records (London Marathon, 2010).

A study of Leeds residents' and visitors' views of Euro '96 for Leeds City Council, indicated that the success of the tournament nationally and regionally had impressed people who traditionally had little to do with football, leading to civic pride. For a proportion of Leeds residents, the football stadium would be associated with the spectacle of the France vs Spain game rather than the long-held association with hooliganism (Tourism Works, 1996). However, the same level of support was not received from Leeds residents for Leeds Love Parade or the Leeds Festival, with the result that the former did not gain approval for 2001 and moved to an alternative city and then later, moved from Temple Newsam to Bramham Park near Wetherby.

The All England Lawn Tennis Club and The Championships attempt to take a socially aware attitude to the organisation of the championships, using the event to encourage junior interest and participation in tennis. In addition to the proceeds of the tournament being ploughed back into tennis development each year, specific local benefits include:

- Sponsoring hanging baskets and planters for Wimbledon in Bloom and Wimbledon Village Summer Fair
- increased trade for local businesses and employment opportunities
- offering local schools and tennis clubs the use of Raynes Park Sports Ground and covered courts
- financial assistance to Merton Borough's tennis development programme
- financial donations to local charities
- improvement to infrastructure e.g. Wimbledon Mainline Station, contribution to CCTV in Wimbledon Town Centre
- renewal of 15 tennis courts in Wimbledon Park in 1988 and again in 2003 and provision of floodlighting
- Merton Youth Concert Band and Jazz Orchestra get the opportunity to play on both the semi-final days of the championships (All England Lawn Tennis Club, 2009)

A public opinion study by UK Sport (1998) found that 87% of the public believe it important that the UK host major events, with 88% believing that success on the world sporting stage creates a national 'feel-good' factor. In developing a UK strategy for major events, UK Sport highlights the role that events play in sport, and as a result, in society as a whole. They state, 'Events matter . . . because they are the heart and soul of the experience for everyone involved in sport — athletes, coaches, officials, volunteers, media, sponsors and fans. Our attitude to events is ultimately our attitude to sport: the hosting of major events should therefore be a key part of any sports system which aims to be a world leader' (UK Sport, 1999a, p. 4).

However, such events can have negative social impacts. Bath and North East Somerset Council conducted a resident survey to canvas opinion on the local impact of events staged at Royal Victoria Park. The survey found that of the 303 returned questionnaires (27% response rate), a significant number (almost 25%) said they had planned time away from home to coincide with events to avoid noise or disruption. Further, although over 75% of the sample had attended some of the events in the last 12 months, including Bath Festival Opening Night, the Spring Flower Show and the Fringe Festival, respondents considered the Festival Opening Night, the Fringe Festival and the Funfair to be the most intrusive events in terms of both amplified music and general disturbance. As a result of these disruptions, most respondents considered that finishing times for events between 10.00 p.m. and midnight would be most appropriate (Howey, 2000).

The larger and more high profile the event, the more potential there is for things to go wrong, and to create negative impacts. A study into the impact of the Network Q Rally 1999 on Lanidloes and the forest of mid-Wales, found that 48% of respondents had a negative attitude towards spectators, with main reasons being that the spectators were prone to drive recklessly, imitating rally drivers and that they showed lack of respect for the locals (Blakey et al., 2000). In 1997, the bomb scare at the Aintree Grand National, one of Britain's most popular sport events, had an unforeseen impact on the local community, when 60,000 racegoers were evacuated. Due to the security alert, thousands of people were left stranded with 20,000 cars and hundreds of coaches trapped inside the grounds overnight. With all hotels fully booked, Merseyside Emergency Committee was convened and schools, leisure centres, church halls, together with generous local families, provided emergency accommodation (Henderson and Chapman, 1997).

Events, when they go wrong, can go very wrong indeed. Consider the impact of gatecrashers on Glastonbury 2000 – immediately, pressure was placed on facilities, food and other resources; in the long term, the Glastonbury Festival in 2001 was cancelled amid worries of crowd safety and the organiser was prosecuted for breach of the entertainment licence. More seriously, the tragic death of 96 Liverpool fans at Hillsborough in 1989, the bombing incident at the Atlanta Olympics in 1996, the death of eight fans at Roskilde Festival in 2000 and the death of over 100 people at a rock concert in Rhode Island, together with other disasters, shocked the world (for further data on crowd-related disasters, visit Crowd Dynamics at www. crowddynamics.com). Such events have far-reaching negative impacts, resulting not only in bad press but damage or injury to participants, stakeholders and the host community.

Managing crowd behaviour

Major events can have unintended social consequences such as substance abuse, bad crowd behaviour and an increase in criminal activity (Getz, 2005). If not managed properly, these unintended consequences can hijack the agenda and determine the public perception of the event. In recent years, English football clubs have successfully implemented strategies to manage alcohol-related, bad crowd behaviour in order to protect their reputation and football's image and future. However, the image was tarnished by the alcohol-fuelled violence of fans abroad during the World Cup 1998 in France and the European Championships in Holland and Belgium in 2000, which some believe to be the main factor in England losing their bid to host the World Cup in 2006. It should be remembered that football is not the only sport to suffer, with 'yobbish' behaviour spreading into the summer Test cricket programme and Royal Ascot. For example, in the 1998 Test cricket series between England and South Africa, Old Trafford Cricket Ground banned non-members from bringing alcohol into the games and — bizarre as it would seem to some — the wearing of novelty clothing, as a result of 'rowdyism' at the previous match at Edgbaston. Deeley (1998) noted:

'At Edgbaston there were many complaints about the behaviour of groups of bizarrely dressed young men in the cheapest seating on the Rea Bank stand, chanting football fashion, shouting obscene remarks and dancing in the aisles. At Old Trafford people wearing dress deemed offensive and 'full body suits' (pelicans, teddy bears and the like) will be refused admission. The county say hats, wigs and headdress restricting the view of others will not be tolerated.'

Deeley goes on to investigate the possible causes, as similar behaviour was not demonstrated at either Lords or the Fosters Oval grounds. He found that availability of alcohol could have a significant effect if the grounds did not have an effective bar management policy (either leaving bars open or unnecessarily closing them could influence the mood of the crowd). The other issue, the so called 'rowdyism', could be managed through strictly limiting tickets to avoid large groups sitting together (for example, Lords limited tickets to four per person) and banning or ejecting those who turn up in eccentric costumes or cause disturbance to others through chanting or taking part in congas. However, this may take away from the atmosphere at games. Other events such as the Notting Hill Carnival, the summer music festivals (e.g. Glastonbury and Reading) and dance events have in some years been tainted by a perceived drug culture, which some believe is encouraged by tolerant policing.

Crowd behaviour can be modified with careful planning. Sometimes, this is an evolutionary process. The organisation of New Year's Eve in London and Edinburgh have seen a series of modifications and adjustments. In 1999, at the launch of the Millennium Festival year, around 3 million people partied along the banks of the River Thames and around Trafalgar Square to witness the largest firework display ever staged in Britain. An estimated 2 million of these, used the London Underground to access Central London between midday and midnight, with only a temporary closure of Underground stations to alleviate safety fears. Police made 99 arrests (more than half for drunkenness) and three police officers were attacked in two separate incidents; but generally the celebrations passed off without serious incident (Harrison and Hastings, 2000).

However, Londoners were to be disappointed in 2000 when Greater London Authority cancelled celebrations due to a clash between crowd safety management and commercial viability. The main issue raised was a fear that the transport system would be dangerously overcrowded, as seen the previous year, which lead to the Underground and train operators proposing a restricted service and transport unions threatening industrial action unless safety concerns were addressed. A strategy proposed to manage this — restricting transport, cancelling the midnight firework display and moving an earlier display from 7 p.m. to 5 p.m. — proved unpopular with sponsors due to the reduced audience, leading to the largest sponsor, Yahoo, withdrawing their £350,000 offer and, ultimately, led to the cancellation of the event (O'Neill, 2000). Subsequently, a review of major events in London by a Greater London Authority London Assembly Committee identified a number of conditions for successful major events in London, including sufficient lead time of at least 18 months, a dispersed event, sufficient resources, empowered leadership, a committed multi-agency partnership, effective project management and effective decision making(Major Events Investigative Committee, 2001). Edinburgh's Hogmanay Street Party had its capacity reduced from a record 200,000 in 1999 to 100,000 for New Year 2000 and onwards in order to increase safety. As a result of better crowd management and improved strategies, global celebrations of the New Millennium were largely reported as good-spirited and peaceful.

Since the terrorist attack in New York on 11 September 2001, the threat of terrorism has resulted in increased security at major events worldwide. However, due to appropriate precautions, events such as the FIFA World Cup in South Korea and Japan in 2002 and the Rugby World Cup in Australia in 2003, the Commonwealth Games in Melbourne, Australia in 2006 and the FIFA World Cup in Germany in 2006 were conducted safely without major incident. Security for the Olympics was increased from 11,500 (including 4500 police officers) for the Sydney Games in 2000, to 45,000 (including 25,000 from the police force) for the Athens Games in 2004 (Kyriakopoulos and Benns, 2004). Further, security was a key theme of the successful London 2012 Olympic bid with the government taking ultimate responsibility through the Home Office and guaranteeing to make every effort to ensure a safe games. Estimates at the bid stage indicated that it would require 14,800 trained police together with 6,500 private security staff and 10,000 volunteers for stewarding a marshalling (London 2012, 2004). Table 3.2 illustrates security levels in previous major international events in London and England.

Community ownership and control of events

Events can also have wider effects on the social life and structure of communities. Traffic arrangements, for example, may restrict residents' access to their homes or businesses, as experienced for the G8 Summit at Gleneagles in 2005. Other impacts may include loss of amenity owing to noise or crowds, resentment of inequitable distribution of costs and benefits and cost inflation of goods and services that can

Table 3.2 Major international events

	Year	Event	Duration of Event [Days]	Number of Participants	Number of Dignitaries and VIPs	Number of Attending Spectators	Number of Security Personnel
London	Annual	Notting Hill Carnival	2	10,000	n/a	850,000	12,000
	Annual	London Marathon	1	34,000	n/a	26,000	850
	Annual	Wimbledon Tennis	14	950	56	539,000	11,900
	2002	Golden Jubilee Weekend	4	15,500	540	1,000,000	10,180
	2002	The funeral of The Queen Mother	9	5,476	585	400,000	12,887
	2000	Millennium Celebrations (London)	1	2,000	500	1,000,000	4,500
England	Annual	Epsom Derby	2	1,000	3,000	100,000	1,000
	Annual	Royal Henley Regatta	4	16,000	12	60,000	320
	2003	UEFA Champions League Final	1	30	10	67,000	700
	2002	Manchester Commonwealth Games	10	5,717	30	900,000	22,500
	1996	UEFA European Championships	21	500	100	1,236,000	18,500

(*Source: London 2012, 2004b, p. 43*)

upset housing markets and impact low-income groups most, as outlined by Getz (2005). It follows that communities should have a major say in the planning and management of events. For example, the then Mayor of London, Ken Livingstone, initiated an extensive review of the management, organisation and funding of the Notting Hill Carnival, together with longer-term trends and opportunities for the event's development. This included the views of stakeholders, including relevant community organisations and the general public (Mayor's Carnival Review Group, 2004). However, Hall (1989) concludes that the role of communities is often marginalised and that governments often make the crucial decision of whether to host the event without adequate community consultation. Public participation then becomes a form of placation designed to legitimise the decisions of government and developers, rather than a full and open discussion of the advantages and disadvantages of hosting events.

This makes it all the more important for governments to be accountable, through the political process, for the allocation of resources to events. Hall (1997) maintains that political analysis is an important tool in regaining community control over hallmark events and ensuring that the objectives of these events focus on maximising returns to the community.

Allegations of corruption within the International Olympic Committee (IOC), the scandal over ticketing strategies by the Sydney Organising Committee for the Olympic Games (SOCOG) and the outrage over a loan from the English Football Association to the Welsh Football Association — allegedly in return for their support of the England 2006 World Cup bid — are examples of the increasing pressure for transparency and public accountability in the staging of major events. Reviews of these issues have resulted in changes being made to policies, procedures and bidding processes to ensure that issues such as these do not arise again.

Physical and environmental impacts

An event is an excellent way to showcase the unique characteristics of the host environment. Hall (1989) points out that selling the image of a hallmark event includes the marketing of the intrinsic properties of the destination. However, host environments may be extremely delicate, and great care should be taken to protect them. A major event may require an environmental impact assessment to be conducted before council or government permission is granted for it to go ahead. Even if a formal study is not required, the event manager should carefully consider the likely impact of the event on the environment. This impact will be fairly contained if the event is to be held in a suitable purpose-built venue, e.g. a stadium, a sports ground, show ground, conference or exhibition centre. The impact may be much greater if the event is to be held in a public space not ordinarily reserved for events, such as a park, town square or street. For example, Birmingham city centre was brought to a standstill in 1993 when an unforeseen number of residents turned up to witness the relaunch of local radio station, BRMB, leading to a reprimand for organisers from police and the council. Another example is the 13 tonnes of litter left after the Oasis concert in the Haymarket, Roseburn and Murrayfield areas. Not only did Edinburgh Council arrange the cleanup from this event, which they acknowledged was only one-third of the litter created by New Year/Hogmanay celebrations, disturbingly, their cleanup staff came under attack from people throwing bottles and their vehicles had to be escorted off site by police (City of Edinburgh Council, 2000a). Aspects such as crowd movement and control, noise levels, access and parking will be important considerations. Other major issues may include wear and tear on the natural and physical environment, heritage protection issues and disruption of the local community.

Effective communication and consultation with local authorities will often resolve some of these issues. In addition, careful management planning may be required to modify impacts. In Liverpool, organisers of the John Smith's Grand National have worked over several years to progressively reduce the traffic impact of visitors to the event by developing a park-and-ride system of fringe parking and shuttle buses to the event area. A similar park-and-ride system is operated at the Royal Norfolk Show held at Norfolk Show Ground, Norwich. Many festivals and outdoor events have reduced their impact on the environment by banning glass bottles, — which can break and get trodden into the ground — and implementing effective waste management strategies. Event managers are discovering that such measures make good financial as well as environmental sense, for example, by generating savings in the cost of the site clean-up.

When staging large events, the provision of infrastructure is often a costly budget component; but this expenditure may result in an improved environment and facilities for the host community and provide a strong incentive for the community to act as host. Many of London's landmark venues have been the legacy of major events, including Crystal Palace (1851 Great Exhibition), Earls Court/Olympia (1887 to 1890 American, Italian, French and German Exhibitions), Royal Festival Hall and South Bank (1951 Festival of Britain) and more recently the Millennium Dome (1999/2000 Millennium Festival) (Evans, 1996). Similarly, Sheffield profited from an investment of £139 million in the development of state-of-the-art facilities for the 1991 World Student Games, including Ponds Forge International Swimming Pool, the Sheffield Arena and the Don Valley Stadium (Select Committee on Culture, Media and Sport, 1999). Manchester benefitted from investment in facilities for the Commonwealth Games 2002 and London and Glasgow will benefit for many years to come, from significant investments in facilities for the London 2012 Olympic Games and the Glasgow 2014 Commonwealth Games. All these examples illustrate the lasting benefits that can result from the hosting of large-scale events.

Political impacts

Politics and politicians are an important part of the equation that is contemporary events management. Ever since the Roman emperors discovered the power of the circus to deflect criticism and shore up popularity, shrewd politicians have had an eye for events that will keep the populace happy and themselves in power. No less an authority than Count Nicolo Machiavelli, adviser to the Medicis in the sixteenth century, had this to say on the subject:

'A prince must also show himself a lover of merit, give preferment to the able and honour those who excel in every art . . . Besides this, he ought, at convenient seasons of the year, to keep the people occupied with festivals and shows; and as every city is divided into guilds or into classes, he ought to pay attention to all these groups, mingle with them from time to time, and give them an example of his humanity and munificence, always upholding, however, the majesty of his dignity, which must never be allowed to fail in anything whatever.' (Machiavelli, 1962, pp. 112–13)

The Royal Family took this advice to heart, providing some of the most popular events of the last century with the Coronation of Queen Elizabeth II and the fairytale-like wedding of Prince Charles and Lady Diana Spencer. Following the tragic, untimely death of Diana, Princess of Wales, in 1997, more recent royal events have attempted to reflect the modernisation of the monarchy and the mood of the people, with the wedding of Prince Edward and Sophie Rhys-Jones in 1999, the one-hundredth birthday of the Queen Mother in 2000 and the wedding of Prince Charles to Camilla Parker Bowles in 2005. An extensive programme of events was organised for the Queen's Golden Jubilee in 2002 (BBC News, 2002a) — which coincided with the Commonwealth Games in Manchester — with a year of events planned around six themes: celebration, community, service, past and future, giving thanks and Commonwealth, with an extra bank holiday to mark the occasion. The celebrations culminated in a concert in the grounds of Buckingham Palace for 12,000 people who had won a ticket by national ballot, while over one million people congregated on The Mall and in various London parks to watch the concert on giant screens and hundreds of street parties took place across the UK (BBC News, 2002b). Queen Elizabeth The Queen Mother's funeral in April 2002 marked a return to tradition, with over 200,000 people walking past her coffin during a period of lying in state and over one million people lining the streets of London around Westminster Abbey for her funeral. Successive British politicians have continued to use the spotlight of events to build their personal profile and gain political advantage. Commenting on the Great Exhibition of 1851, Asa Briggs noted how criticism of the project disappeared as the crowds flocked to see the event — crowds that were encouraged to attend through the equivalent of a Travelcard (Carling and Seeley, 1998). In 1951, Foreign Secretary Herbert Morrison received significant criticism due to his enthusiasm for the Festival of Britain project, leading an opposition MP to label him 'Lord Festival', a title that stuck (Carling and Seeley, 1998). Former Prime Minister John Major was frequently seen at major cricket matches during his term in office. In 1997 his first year in office, the Prime Minister, Tony Blair, continued with the Conservative government planned Millennium Dome project, attempting to use the Dome as a symbol of 'New Labour, New Britain', and of himself as a visionary and enlightened leader.

When details of the Dome's contents were first published, he summarised the aim of the festival:

> '*In this Experience I want people to pause and reflect on this moment, about the possibilities ahead of us, about the values that guide our society . . . It will be an event to lift our horizons. It will be a catalyst to imagine our futures . . . As we approach the Millennium we can boast that we have a richness of talent in this country that is unparalleled: the finest artists, authors, architects, musicians, designers, animators, software makers, scientists… so why not put it on display?*'
>
> **(Carling and Seeley, 1998, p. 5)**

However, although the year-long exhibition, the Millennium Experience, achieved over six million visitors during its year of operation, this was significantly less than the predicted twelve million. In addition, the project was plagued by financial problems during the year due to the lower than expected visitor numbers, leading to additional funds being provided by the Millennium Commission (The Comptroller and Auditor General, 2000). Although to some extent a success, the Millennium Dome may be remembered more for the lack of legacy planning and the spiralling costs both during and after the Millennium Experience. Although the Dome has been used for a small number of events since 2001, it did not fully re-open until 2007, when it became an entertainment venue including a 23,000 seater arena, a 2,000 capacity music club and an ice rink. Following a £6 million per year sponsorship deal, the venue, now owned by Anschutz Entertainment Group (AEG), is known as 'the O2' (BBC News, 2005).

Arnold, Fischer, Hatch and Paix (1989, pp. 191–2) leave no doubt of the role of events in the political process: 'Governments in power will continue to use hallmark events to punctuate the ends of their periods in office, to arouse nationalism, enthusiasm and finally, votes. They are cheaper than wars or the preparation for them. In this regard, hallmark events do not hide political realities, they are the political reality.'

Governments around the world have realised the ability of events to raise the profile of politicians and the cities and areas that they govern. They have also realised the ability of events to attract visitors and thus create economic benefits and jobs. This potent mixture has led to governments becoming major players in bidding for, hosting and staging of major events. The UK government has undertaken two major inquiries into the staging of major events. In 1995, the National Heritage Committee ran an inquiry into 'Bids to Stage International Sporting Events', which identified how bidding for and staging international events could be improved. They found that, 'unless Britain does coordinate the multitudinous and sometimes apparently conflicting organisations that are involved and is given a clear focus, then our country is unlikely to be successful in any bid for which there is fierce competition' (House of Commons National Heritage Committee Report, 1995, cited in UK Sport, 1999b, p. 5). This led to the GB Sports Council (the forerunner of UK Sport) being given the responsibility for sport event development in the UK (English Sports Council, 1999).

In 1998 a second Select Committee was established to investigate all aspects of staging international sporting events from bidding through to the economic, environmental and regeneration legacies of these events (Select Committee on Culture, Media and Sport, 1999). The committee took comprehensive evidence from associations and groups representing all major sports, government ministers and tourism bodies, together with information from organisations with experience of hosting major events (including fact-finding trips to Australia and Malaysia). The ensuing report detailed 32 principal conclusions and recommendations including:

- the need for further research into economic benefits and impacts, and the incorporation of an independent assessment as a requirement for future funding
- support for the proposed UK Sport Major Event Strategy
- the need to vet the qualifications and ability of suitable candidates for committee posts of international sporting events, to ensure the effective representation of British interests
- the need for central government to partner local authorities to gain national benefits from events, including the Manchester 2002 Commonwealth Games
- the need for a 'Minister for Events' with responsibility for an events strategy incorporating sport and non-sport events.

(Select Committee on Culture, Media and Sport, 1999, s. IX).

The outcomes of the committee have been reviewed to monitor performance, with generally positive feedback gained (see Select Committee on Culture, Media and Sport, 2001).

Established in 1996, UK Sport includes the aim to, 'promote the UK or any part of it as a venue for international sports events and to advise, encourage and assist bodies in staging or seeking to stage such events'. It aims to provide a one-stop shop for event advice and support. In keeping with this, it established a Major Events Steering Group in 1999, which includes members with a range of experience in areas including legal issues, media, marketing, sponsorship, event management, local authority involvement and the international politics of sport (UK Sport, 1999a). Elsewhere, EventBritain, the Northern Ireland Events Company and EventScotland have been established (discussed in Chapter 4). Edinburgh has built up a strong international reputation as a festival city, with an extensive programme of major events including the Edinburgh International Festival, Edinburgh Fringe, and Edinburgh's Hogmanay.

This involvement of governments in events has politicised the events landscape, as pointed out by Hall (1989, p. 236):

Politics is paramount in hallmark events. It is either naïve or duplistic to pretend otherwise. Events alter the time frame in which planning occurs and they become opportunities to do something new and better than before. In this context, events may change or legitimate political priorities in the short term and political ideologies and socio-cultural reality in the longer term. Hallmark events represent the tournaments of old, fulfilling psychological and political needs through the winning of hosting over other locations and the winning of events themselves. Following a hallmark event some places will never be the same again, physically, economically, socially and, perhaps most importantly of all, politically.

It is important to acknowledge that events have values beyond just tangible and economic benefits. Humans are social animals, and celebrations play a key role in the well-being of the social structure — the common wealth. Events have the ability to engender social cohesion, confidence and pride (Wood, 2002). Therein lies the source of their political power and influence and the reason why events will always reflect and interact with their political circumstances and environment.

Tourism and economic impacts

A primary concern of an event entrepreneur or host organisation is whether an event is within budget and, hopefully, results in a surplus or profit. This is a simple matter of whether the income from sponsorship, merchandise and ticket sales exceeds the costs of conducting and marketing the event. However, from the perspectives of the host communities and governments, a wider range of economic impacts is often of equal or greater significance.

Governments are increasingly turning to tourism as a growth industry capable of delivering economic benefits and job creation. Events are also seen as image-makers, creating profile for destinations, positioning them in the market and providing competitive marketing advantage. One of the most important impacts is the tourism revenue generated by an event. In addition to their spending at the event, external visitors are likely to spend money on travel, accommodation, goods and services in the host city or region. This expenditure can have a considerable impact as it circulates through the local economy. Effective tourism promotion can result in visitors to the event extending their length of stay and visiting other regional tourism destinations and attractions. In addition to the tourism generated during the event, events may attract media coverage and exposure that enhance the profile of the host town or city, resulting in improved long-term tourism image and visits. Chapter 4 discusses these and other aspects of the tourism impact of events.

Business opportunities

Events can provide their host communities with a strong platform for showcasing their expertise, hosting potential investors and promoting new business opportunities. The media exposure generated by the success of an event can dramatically illustrate the capacity, innovation and achievements of event participants and/or the host community. Advantage West Midlands secured European Union funding of £1.2 million to launch a major marketing campaign for the British International Motor Show with the objective of raising attendances and generating tourism revenue. In addition, with the automotive industry being a major provider of employment in the region, this was seen as a potential showcase for industry in the region (Advantage West Midlands, 2004). After a 30 year absence, the event moved back to London in 2006 where it was relaunched with a range of new features at Excel London, achieving 415,536 visitors (IMIE Ltd, 2008). This success was repeated again in 2008; however, due to the global recession and the impact it has had on the automotive industry, the event in 2010 was cancelled.

During the Sydney Olympics in 2000, the New South Wales Government spent $3.6 million on a trade and investment drive coinciding with the event (Humphries, 2000). This effort led to more than 60 business-related events, board meetings of international companies, briefings and trade presentations being held in Sydney at the time of the Olympics. Forty-six international chambers of commerce were briefed on business opportunities, and more than 500 world business leaders, Olympic sponsors and New South Wales corporate executives attended four promotional events. State Treasurer Michael Egan was quoted as saying, 'We'll be benefiting from the Games well after we think the benefits have worn off and in ways that will never show up in statistics' (Humphries, 2000).

Similar business development strategies are accompanying preparations for the London 2012 Olympics. However, little research has been done on analysing business development strategies for events and quantifying the amount of business that these strategies generate. More work needs to be done so that event enhancement frameworks are better understood and their outcomes can be assessed.

Commercial activity

Whatever the generation of new business at the macro level, the suppliers of infrastructure, goods and services undoubtedly profit from the staging of major events. The construction industry — witness the construction boom resulting from the Commonwealth Games 2002 in Manchester, London 2012 and the redevelopment of Wembley National Stadium — is often stimulated by the need for new or improved facilities required to stage a major event. But do these benefits trickle down to traders and small business operators? A survey of 1000 tourism-related businesses was conducted in relation to the Rugby World Cup in Wales in 1999 (Anon., 2000). The accommodation sector fared best, with two-thirds of accommodation providers experiencing improvements in business performance, and a 7.5% increase in room rates by operators in Cardiff and the south-east of Wales. Around half of food and drink outlets reported increased performance. This sector also reported having made considerable investment in promotional activities and small-scale product development. However, over half of those who responded from the retail sector, thought that despite improvements in average spend, the event had impacted negatively on their overall performance. As another example, the World Masters Athletics Championships 2000 in Gateshead were expected to lead to an estimated 150,000 additional bednights, adding a minimum of £12 million to the local economy (Select Committee on Culture, Media and Sport, 1999).

Muthaly et al. (2000) used a case study approach to examine the impact of the Atlanta Olympics on seven small businesses in Atlanta. The case study included:

- a wholesale restaurant equipment dealership, which expanded its existing business and current line of equipment, resulting in a 70–80% increase in revenue as a result of the Games
- a one-person home rental business specifically started to provide bed-and-breakfast housing for Olympic visitors, which lost US$23,000 due to lack of any significant Games business
- a frozen lemonade stand franchise that employed up to 50 people at four fixed and three roving locations, which failed due to problems with inventory and staffing, unanticipated and unregulated competition and lower than expected attendance at the Games
- an established beverage distributor, who became an approved Games vendor and reported increased profits through additional sales to usual customers and a firm policy of not extending credit to new customers
- a craft retail location at Stone Mountain Park, a major tourist attraction for Atlanta and the south-east, where some Olympic events were located. The owner lost about US$10,000 on a special line of Olympic theme dolls, sculptures and so on, as a result of added costs and a lack of customers.
- a UK-based currency service and foreign exchange business that established two locations downtown near the Olympic Park and two uptown near the retail and residential heart of the city. The principal felt that it was not a very successful business project, given the changing nature of the market (people using credit or debit cards in place of currency) and lack of communication with Olympic organisers.
- an established sporting goods retail store that reported increased sales of established lines and regular merchandise, but not of Olympic merchandise stocked to sell in front of the store. The owner reported considerable staffing difficulties due to poor transport planning and absenteeism as a result of the Games.

The study team concluded that large businesses such as Delta Airlines, local construction companies, local law firms associated with the Olympics and niche players that watched their risk carefully fared very well. However, for many small operators, dreams of big profits turned into heartache. Visitors did not come in anticipated numbers and those who did come did not spend the amount of money expected. Olympic visitors proved to be sports mad, tight fisted and uninterested in traditional tourist attractions.

From these and other studies, the anticipated benefits of major events to traders and small business operators appear to be sometimes exaggerated, with the results often being sporadic and uneven. Benefits also seem more likely to accrue to those businesses that are properly prepared and that manage and invest wisely in the opportunities provided by events. More research needs to be done in this field to identify appropriate strategies to enhance the benefits of events to small business.

Employment creation

By stimulating activity in the economy, expenditure on events can have a positive effect on employment. Employment multipliers measure how many full time equivalent job opportunities are supported in the community as a result of visitor expenditure. However, as Faulkner (1993) and others point out, it is easy to over-estimate the number of jobs created by major events in the short term. Because the demand for additional services is short lived, employers tend to meet this demand by using their existing staff more rather than employing new staff members. Existing employees may be released from other duties to accommodate the temporary demand or requested to work overtime.

However, major events can generate substantial employment in the construction phase, as well as during the staging of the event. The 2002 British Grand Prix at Silverstone was estimated to support 1150 full time equivalent jobs in the United Kingdom, including 400 full time equivalent jobs within 50 miles of the circuit (MIA, 2003). The 2002 Manchester Commonwealth Games was estimated to have generated 6,100 jobs, of which 2,400 are additional jobs in Manchester (Cambridge Policy Consultants, 2002). The America's Cup in Auckland in 2000 was estimated to have generated 1,470 new jobs in construction, accommodation, marine and related activities (Scott, 2003). The 2000 Oktoberfest in Munich generated employment for an estimated 12,000 people through the 0.7 billion euro that 5.5 million visitors to the event spent over 16 days (Munich Tourist Office, 2000, cited in Richards and Wilson, 2002).

ECONOMIC IMPACTS AND THE ROLE OF GOVERNMENT

The strong growth of the events industry is part of a general economic trend away from an industrial product base to a more service-based economy. Traditionally, communities and governments have staged events for their perceived social, cultural and/or sporting benefits and value. This situation began to change dramatically in the early 1980s when major events in many parts of the world began to be regarded as desirable commodities for their perceived ability to deliver economic benefits through the promotion of tourism, increased visitor expenditure and job creation.

Major events with international reputations have appeared on the sporting calendar in the UK for many years on an annual basis, however, their value has not always been recognised. Changes began to emerge in the mid to late nineties when the National Heritage Committee (1995) and the Select Committee on Culture, Media and Sport (1999, 2001) fully investigated the value of hosting major sporting events which gathered evidence on the value of events. As a result, events began to be recognised, for example, with UK Sport establishing a major events strategy in 1999 (UK Sport, 1999a).

As outlined elsewhere, various local and national governments have pursued vigorous event strategies since the 1980s, building strong portfolios of annual events and aggressively bidding for the right for their city, region or country to host major one-off events. Apart from international and regional rivalry and political kudos, what is it that motivates and justifies this level of government involvement in what otherwise might be seen as largely commercial enterprises? According to Mules (1998), the answer lies in what he terms the 'spillover effects' of events. While many major events might make an operational loss, they produce benefits for related industry sectors such as travel, accommodation, restaurants, hirers and suppliers of equipment and so on. They may also produce long-term benefits such as destination promotion resulting in increased tourism spending. However, a single organisation cannot capture this wide range of benefits. Governments thus sometimes play a role in funding or underwriting events so that these generalised benefits might be obtained. For example, the UK government has underwritten the London 2012 Olympic Games (London 2012, 2004). A further example is the role that regional development agencies (RDAs) are playing in supporting events in their regions which have the potential to promote the region or bring in tourists, for example, when a number of RDAs sponsored the 2004 Tour of Britain Cycle Race and together with other agencies sponsored the event again in 2005 (SIRC, 2005).

ECONOMIC IMPACT STUDIES

In deciding what events should be funded and what levels of funding are appropriate, governments need to obtain a full picture of the event's costs and the anticipated return on investment. To do so, they sometimes undertake economic impact studies, which seek to identify all of the expenditure involved in the staging of events, and to determine their impacts on the wider economy. The impacts of an event derive from three main sources (Faulkner, 1993; Jago and Dwyer, 2006):

1. expenditure by visitors from outside the region
2. capital expenditure on facilities required to conduct the event
3. expenditure incurred by event organisers and sponsors to stage the event.

However, this expenditure has flow-on effects that need to be taken into account in calculating the economic impact of an event. For example, money spent on a meal by an event visitor will flow on to businesses that supply the restaurant with food and beverage items. The money spent on the meal is direct expenditure, while the flow-on effect to suppliers is indirect expenditure. The event may also stimulate additional activity in the economy, resulting in increased wages and consumer spending. Further, sales of goods at exhibitions result in jobs being supported elsewhere, for example, at the International Spring Fair at Birmingham NEC in 1997, it was estimated that over £1.6 billion of orders were taken. This is referred to as induced expenditure.

The aggregated impact on the economy of all of the expenditure is expressed as a multiplier ratio, a concept used widely by economists. Multipliers reflect the impact of the event expenditure as it ripples through the economy, and they vary according to the particular mix of industries in a given geographic location. The use of multipliers is controversial and some studies prefer to concentrate on the direct expenditure of an event as being more reliable, although this does not give a true picture of the complex impact on the economy of the event expenditure.

Conducting economic impact studies that account for all of the myriad factors of the event expenditure and environment is quite complex and usually undertaken by specialist researchers with an economics background. However, a considerable body of literature is available to provide an insight for event managers, into the process of conducting economic impact studies on events (see, for example, Burgan and Mules, 2000; Crompton and McKay, 1994; eventIMPACTS, 2010; Giddings, 1997; Hunn and Mangan, 1999; Jackson, Houghton, Russell and Triandos, 2005; Jago and Dwyer, 2006; Mules, 1999; Mules and McDonald, 1994).

Example of government use of economic impact studies

A good example of government use of event impact studies to compare the economic impacts of events is provided by *Measuring Success 2 — The Economic Impacts of Major Sports Events* (UK Sport, 2006). This research examined the economic impact of 16 major sports events held in the UK since 1997 (see Figure 3.1). The report drew on the findings of individual studies, including 11 events funded under the auspices of the World Class Events Programme, with commercially successful events such as Test Cricket, Women's Open Golf and the Flora London Marathon also included for general interest. In each case, the studies used a common methodology to calculate the total amount of additional expenditure generated within a host city (or area), which could be directly attributed to the staging of the event. Economic multipliers were not used, as the purpose of the research was to compare events and not economies.

The conclusions arising from the study (see Figures 3.2 and 3.3) include the following:

- The most significant economic impact was the 2000 Flora London Marathon, which generated five times the impact of the next most significant event, Test Match Cricket
- Nine of the 16 events generated incomes of more than £1.45 million, which might be termed a major impact
- A major event in spending terms does not necessarily generate a major impact, for example, the IAAF Grand Prix
- World Championships do not necessarily generate a major impact, for example, the 2003 World Indoor Athletics and 1997 World Badminton

Following this research, UK Sport commissioned further research covering six events in 2005 and 2006 (reported in UK Sport, 2007) and a further six in 2008. This study resulted in a major joint project by UK Sport, Visit Britain, EventScotland, the

FIGURE 3.1 Events included in the study to measure the economic impact of major sports events

EVENT	HOST CITY/AREA
World Badminton Championships	Glasgow
European Junior Boxing Championships	Birmingham
First Ashes Test — Cricket	Birmingham
IAAF Grand Prix 1 Athletics	Sheffield
European Junior Swimming Championships	Glasgow
Women's British Open Golf Championship	Sunningdale
European Short Course Swimming Championships	Sheffield
European Show Jumping Championships	Hickstead
World Judo Championships	Birmingham
World Indoor Climbing Championships	Birmingham
Flora London Marathon (FLM)	London
Spar Europa Cup — Athletics	Gateshead
World Amateur Boxing Championships	Belfast
World Half Marathon Championships	Bristol
World Cup Triathlon	Salford
World Indoor Athletics Championships	Birmingham

(Source: Adapted from UK Sport, 2006)

London Development Agency, the North West Development Agency, Yorkshire Forward and Glasgow City Marketing Bureau which developed the eventIMPACTS Toolkit (available from www.eventimpacts.com) to enable those organising major sporting and cultural events to better evaluate economic, environmental, media and social related impacts. The eventIMPACTS Toolkit provides useful guidance and examples of good practice, including case studies on the six events evaluated in 2008, a process to follow and sample survey instruments for gathering data.

COMMUNITY PERCEPTIONS OF EVENT IMPACTS

For annual events, surveys of the host community's perceptions of an event can provide valuable tools for identifying and addressing community concerns in the

FIGURE 3.2 Economic impact of 'major' sports events (1–8)

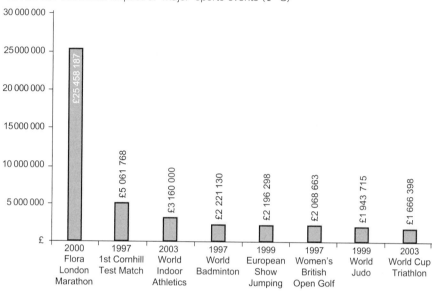

(Source: UK Sport, 2006)

planning of the next event. A number of researchers have sought to establish a generic survey instrument capable of accurately and reliably measuring such perceptions, and to track changes in them over time.

A study funded by Australia's Sustainable Tourism Cooperative Research Centre (Fredline, Deery and Jago, 2005) surveyed attitudes of the Melbourne community to the Australian Open Tennis Tournament in 2003. For the study they developed a survey instrument using 12 items compressed from a 42-item scale that had been previously tested in a range of case studies. This survey was administered four to five weeks after the event via a telephone interview to 300 subjects chosen at random from the Melbourne telephone directory. For each of the 12 items, the respondents were asked whether they agreed or disagreed with the statements, then whether the impact affected their personal quality of life and the community as a whole. If they perceived an impact, they were asked to rate this in terms of its direction (positive or negative) and intensity on a scale ranging from −3 to +3. The summary of responses to these specific impacts is illustrated in Table 3.3.

A study undertaken by Motor Sport Association on the Network Q Rally, one of the largest spectator sports with 134,921 paying spectators, found that it pumped £11.1 million into the local economy, 60% of which was from outside the area. Those benefitting included local accommodation providers, restaurants, retail outlets and transport providers. They noted that the event also generates an additional £17 million from tourism stimulated by the television coverage (Lilley III and DeFranco,

FIGURE 3.3 Economic impact of 'major' sports events (9–16)

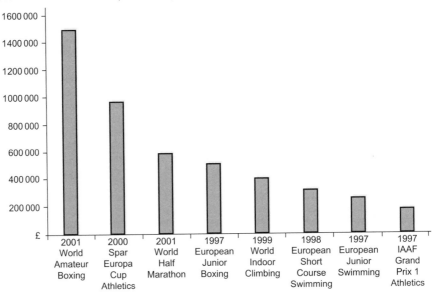

(Source: UK Sport, 2006)

1999a). Impacts could indeed be greater, as later research by Blakey et al. (2000) indicates that in 1999 there were over 1 million live spectators and 11,000 volunteer officials, which would make it the largest sporting event in the UK. The British Grand Prix 1996, seen by many to be one of the showcase UK events, had an economic impact of £28 million, £25 million from outside the local area (Lilley III and DeFranco, 1999b). In the most recent study of the 2002 FIA Foster's British Grand Prix, expenditure had risen to an estimated £34.7 million; and income to the UK was £17.2 million (£5.6 to the region), equating 1 148 jobs, of which 403 were within the region (MIA, 2003). British International Motor Show, held at Birmingham NEC in June 2004 branded as The Sunday Times Motor Show Live, played host to an estimated 461,000 visitors, bringing an additional £61.4 million into the local economy with gross spending amounting to £105.5 million (SMMT, 2004).

Table 3.4 summarises the economic benefits of a number of recent events in the UK. The results are not strictly comparable, as the methodologies for evaluating events vary widely. However, the table does demonstrate the considerable tourism and economic benefits that flow from major events. UK Sport is attempting to address comparability issues through proposing a standard methodology, discussed in Chapter 18.

Events have the potential to provide niche development opportunities for city and regional governments. Research conducted on behalf of the Society of London

Table 3.3 Summary of responses to specific impacts

	Part A			Part B	Part C
	Agree	Disagree	Don't Know	Personal Impact Mean	Community Impact Mean
Entertainment: The Australian Open gave Melbourne residents an opportunity to attend an interesting event, have fun with their family and friends, and interact with new people.	94.0%	3.3%	2.7%	0.92	1.53
Public money: The Australian Open was a waste of public money; that is, too much public money was spent on the event that would be better spent on other public activities.	6.7%	80.3%	13.0%	−0.02	−0.04
Economic benefits: The Australian Open is good for the economy because the money that visitors spend when they come for the event helps to stimulate the economy, stimulates employment opportunities and is good for local business.	95.3%	2.3%	2.3%	0.38	1.52
Disruption to local residents: The Australian Open disrupted the lives of local residents and created inconvenience. While the event was on, problems like traffic congestion, parking difficulties and excessive noise were worse than usual.	20.6%	66.9%	12.5%	0.02	−0.10

Continued

Table 3.3 Summary of responses to specific impacts *(Continued)*

	Part A			Part B	Part C
	Agree	Disagree	Don't Know	Personal Impact Mean	Community Impact Mean
Maintenance of public facilities: The Australian Open promoted development and better maintenance of public facilities such as roads, parks, sporting facilities, and/or public transport.	56.0%	15.1%	28.9%	0.38	0.97
Bad behaviour: The Australian Open was associated with some people behaving inappropriately, perhaps in a rowdy and delinquent way or engaging in excessive drinking, drug use or other criminal behaviour.	11.4%	78.3%	10.4%	−0.03	−0.03
Community pride: The Australian Open made local residents feel more proud of their city and made them feel good about themselves and their community.	80.3%	5.3%	14.3%	0.70	1.45
Environmental impact: The Australian Open had a negative impact on the environment through excessive litter and/or pollution and/or damage to natural areas.	3.3%	89.0%	7.7%	0	−0.01

Regional showcase: The Australian Open showcased Melbourne in a positive light. This helps to promote a better opinion of our region and encourages future tourism and/or business investment.	97.7%	1.0%	1.3%	0.48	1.53
Prices: The Australian Open Tennis 2003 led to increases in the price of some things such as some goods and services and property values and/or rental costs.	29.0%	27.0%	44.0%	−0.02	−0.06
Community injustice: The Australian Open was unfair to ordinary residents, and the costs and benefits were distributed unfairly across the community.	6.7%	68.7%	24.7%	−0.02	0
Loss of use of public facilities: The Australian Open denied local residents access to public facilities, that is, roads, parks, sporting facilities, public transport and/or other facilities were less available to local residents because of closure or overcrowding.	15.1%	66.2%	18.7%	0	−0.10

(Source: Fredline, Deery and Jago, 2005)

Table 3.4 Examples of economic benefits of events

Event	Total Attendance ('000s)	Total Visitors from Outside Local Area ('000s)	Total Expenditure from Outside Local Area (£M)	Total Economic Impact (£M)
European Football Championships (Euro'96), UK, 1996		280	120	195
1st Cornhill Test Match England v Australia, 1997	72,700	66.9 (92%)	4.6	9
World Badminton Championships & Sudirman Cup 1997	21,700	13.5 (62%)	.386	1.9
British Grand Prix 1997	170,000	136(80%)	25	28
Weetabix Women's British Open Golf Championship, Sunningdale 1997	50		.207	2.1
Network Q Rally of Great Britain 1998	135	81 (60%)	6.7	17
Leeds Love Parade, 2000	250	165 (66%)		12.8
British Grand Prix 2002	160,000		5.6	17.2
ITMA, Birmingham, 2003	125,500		85	110
Matthew Street Festival, Liverpool, 2004	335,000			25
Brighton Festival 2004	430,000			20
British International Motor Show, 2004	461,000		61.4	105.5
UEFA Cup Final, Glasgow, 2007	47,000		10	16.3
Glastonbury Festival, 2007	177,500	97.8%		73
Manchester International Festival, 2009	231'445			35.7
Celtic Connections Festival, Glasgow, 2010	100,000		6,4	11.9

(Source: Baker Associates, 2008; BBC, 2010; Bernstein, 2009; Lilley III & DeFranco, 1999a, 1999b; Liverpool Culture Company, 2005c; MIA, 2003; The NEC Group, 2004; SMMT, 2004; Sussex Arts Marketing, 2004; The Tourism Works, 1996; UK Sport, 2000a; Yorkshire Tourist Board, 2000)

Theatre demonstrated that theatre can have a major impact on tourism and the economy, with the 1997 West End theatre season worth £1075 million to the city of London, supporting 41,000 jobs (Travers, 1998). A study on behalf of the London Development Agency (LDA, 2003) into the Notting Hill Carnival, found that it brought an estimated income of £93 million into London in 2002, supporting in the region of 3,000 full time equivalent jobs. This study, together with a review of other aspects of the carnival (Mayor's Carnival Review Group, 2004) has lead to increased attention being paid to the carnival by the Mayor of London and other interested stakeholders.

Birmingham maximised the benefits of successfully staging the G8 Birmingham Summit, the Eurovision Song Contest and the Lions Clubs International Conference in 1998, which had a combined impact of £35.65 million additional spend and highlighted the city's ability to successfully stage international conferences. Following these high-profile events, a national telephone survey of 1000 people by Birmingham Marketing Partnership (BMP), found that 68% believed that Birmingham had improved as a city, 55% thought it was a friendly city and 70% considered Birmingham to be a leading event city. Further research by the City Council and BMP established that the media impact was eight times greater than could be expected for major news stories, equating to approximately £1.8 million of media coverage (Notman, 1999). Birmingham NEC successfully hosted ITMA 2003 (the International Exhibition of Textile Machinery) — the world's largest exhibition. This was the first time the event took place in the UK since its launch in 1951. Taking over 200,000 square metres of stand space, with 1275 exhibitors from forty countries, the event attracted an audience of 125, 500 from 129 countries. Independent research by KPMG estimated that the event resulted in £85 million additional expenditure in the West Midlands, equivalent to 1550 full-time equivalent jobs for the region or £110 million spending in the UK as a whole (The NEC Group, 2004). Birmingham has continued to capitalise on its image as a major event city, through promoting itself as 'Europe's meeting place' and expanding the NEC complex, the UK's largest exhibition space, which according to research in 1999 generated £711 million impact — supporting nearly 22,000 jobs (The NEC Group, 2005).

There is increasing interest in the impacts of festivals, illustrated by the recent completion of two large scale studies. For example, on a national level, a study conducted on behalf of The Association of Festival Organisers (AFO) by Morris, Hargreaves, McIntyre (AFO, 2004) discovered that folk festivals generate spending of over £77 million. In addition, their study found that festivals have a role in developing audiences and in training, launching and supporting artists and administrators. Further, on a regional level, a picture begins to emerge of the potential scale of the impacts of festivals. A recent study of 11 festivals in the East Midlands (Maughan and Bianchini, 2003) found that the festivals spent just under £990,000 in the region with an additional £570,000 estimated due to multiplier effects, while money spent by audiences amounted to some £7 million, with an additional £4.16 million additional income estimated for the region. Developing a programme of festivals or events for a region can also pay dividends, as illustrated by the study commissioned for Cheltenham Borough Council into Cheltenham's Festivals (Brookes and Landry, 2002). This study found that the programme of thirteen festivals generated close to £34 million income for the town, sustaining some 300 jobs. In addition, as they noted, the town receives a wealth of positive media coverage that adds to the town's image and attracts new investment and employment.

COST-BENEFIT ANALYSIS

Money spent on events represents an opportunity cost of resources that may have been devoted to other needs in the community. This has caused governments to look at the cost-benefit analysis of events, and has given rise to a specialised branch of economic study. As discussed earlier, Edinburgh has developed a year round strand of economic activity based on its positioning as the festival capital of Europe. For example, the City of Edinburgh Council (2000c) notes that Edinburgh's Hogmanay is now in the same league as the Edinburgh International Festival in terms of both its image and the impact it has on the city's economy. For an outlay of around £1.4 million the event generates an economic return in the region of £30 million.

An extensive evaluation commissioned in 1990 by the Department of the Environment of the Liverpool International Garden Festival (1984), Stoke National Garden Festival (1986) and Glasgow Garden Festival (1988) found that Liverpool and Stoke cost in the region of £40 million to stage, with an additional local impact of £21 million (1985 prices). Costs of staging the Glasgow festival were higher at around £69 million, due in part to greater sponsorship and franchising. The benefits generated, fit under three broad headings of reclamation (increased speed and higher-quality reclaimation of the site), environmental gains (visual impact during and after the festival, image-building for the cities) and economic impact (1,400–2,500 jobs) (PA Cambridge Economic Consultants, 1990).

MONITORING LONG-TERM IMPACTS

Impacts that are calculated during the actual timeframe of an event tell only part of the story. In order to form a full picture of the impact of an event, it is necessary to look at the long-term effects on the community and its economy. The case of the 1991 World Student Games give some indication of the aftershock of the event. Bramwell (1997) notes that there is a temptation to evaluate mega-events too soon after an event before the full impact can be assessed. He points out that, despite the debt incurred by Sheffield during the event, five years after the games, the city had been designated a City of Sport, had benefited from an extensive programme of national and international events and the development of a further £20 million private leisure scheme next to the arena. The city was left with a legacy of infrastructure and quality tourism development that were either initiated or speeded up by the event. On a wider level, an event-led city strategy grew out of the games (Destination Sheffield, 1995). With a brief to attract or initiate events each year that would profile the city, by 1997 it had already hosted 160 national, 19 European, 10 world championships and 48 other international events (KRONOS, 1997).

SUMMARY

All events produce impacts, both positive and negative, which it is the task of the event manager to assess and balance. Social and cultural impacts may involve a shared experience, and may give rise to local pride, validation and/or the widening of cultural horizons. However, social problems arising from events may result in social dislocation if not properly managed. Events are an excellent opportunity to showcase the physical characteristics of a destination but event environments may be very delicate, and care should be taken to safeguard and protect them. Tourism and economic impacts include the expenditure made by visitors to an event, the promotion of business opportunities, the creation of commercial activity and the generation of employment. Events may involve longer-term issues affecting the built environment and the legacy of improved facilities. Increasingly, environmental considerations are paramount, as shown by the environmental guidelines that have been developed by UK Sport to be considered when bidding for and staging events, to manage their environmental impact and their inclusion in the eventIMPACT Toolkit.

Governments have long recognised the political impacts that often include an increased profile and benefits to the host community. However, the emotive power of events can also be subject to manipulation and abuse. Political impacts have long been recognised by governments and often include increased profile and benefits to the host community. However, it is important that events fulfill the wider community agenda. Governments are attracted to events because of the economic benefits, job creation and tourism that they can provide. Events act as catalysts for attracting tourists and extending their length of stay. They also enhance the profile of a destination and can be designed to attract visitors out of season when tourism facilities are underutilised. In considering appropriate levels of funding for events, governments and organisations use economic impact studies to predict the likely impacts of events and then determine the wider outcomes. Methodologies are also available to identify community perceptions of event impacts, so that strategies can be developed to incorporate community participation and feedback in the planning of events. Large events also serve as catalysts for urban renewal and for the creation of new tourism infrastructure. Events bring economic benefits to their communities but governments need to weigh these benefits against costs when deciding how to allocate resources.

QUESTIONS

1   Describe examples of events whose needs have been perceived to conflict with those of their host communities. As the event manager, how would you have resolved these conflicting needs?

2   Identify an event that you know has been marred by social problems or bad crowd behaviour. As the event manager, what would you have done to manage the situation and improve the outcomes of the event? In your answer, discuss both the planning of the event and possible on-the-spot responses.

3   Describe an event that you believe was not sufficiently responsive to community attitudes and values. What steps could the community have taken to improve the situation?

4   Select a major event that has been held in your region and identify as many environmental impacts as you can. Evaluate whether the overall environmental impact on the host community was positive or negative. Recommend steps that could be taken to improve the balance.

5   Select an event that you have been involved in as a participant or close observer. Identify as many impacts of the event as you can, both positive and negative, and then answer the following questions:

   (a) Did the positive impacts outweigh the negative?

   (b) What measures did the organisers have in place to maximise positive impacts and minimise negative impacts?

   (c) As the event manager, what other steps could you have taken to balance the impacts and improve the outcomes of the event?

6   List and describe what you consider to be the main reasons why governments support events.

7   Obtain three event reports that have been compiled on events in your area. Compare and contrast these reports in terms of (a) the methods used to compile them and (b) how they have been used to communicate and promote the outcomes of the event.

CASE STUDY ITMA 2003, THE NEC, BIRMINGHAM

Introduction

ITMA (International Textile Machinery Exhibition) is one of the largest trade exhibitions – and the largest single sector trade show - in the world. Staged every four years, ITMA is a peripatetic exhibition - travelling around venues in Europe. Until recognising the facilities on offer at The NEC, Birmingham, the only countries assumed capable of staging the event were France, Germany and Italy, who have shared the show for the past 30 years.

ITMA 2003 ran from 22 to 29 October 2003. Over the eight days of the event, 1,275 exhibitors took part from 40 countries, with the show having an overall attendance of 125,500 visits from 129 countries. To give some idea of the magnitude of the exhibition, the show used all 21 exhibition halls at The NEC and required every piece of mains cable, with extra supplies being brought in from London, Manchester and Glasgow, while more than 2,500 articulated trucks were required to deliver all the exhibition stands and display material.

Why The NEC?. Co-ordination between The NEC, the Airport and Rail station ensured a seamless journey for visitors. An event like ITMA needs a massive supporting structure, which is where The NEC comes into its own. There are currently close to 75,000 bed spaces within 1 hour of The NEC (30,000 within 30 minutes), from 5 star to quality budget, guest houses, self catering accommodation, and even some private homes. A specialist web site was created to assist visitors through online booking facilities, while a close partnership with the Birmingham Convention and Visitor Bureau meant that visitors were also able to reserve:

- a wide range of other services including shuttle bus services between The NEC and the main hotels
- air and rail tickets
- airport transfers to The NEC from all major UK airports
- coach and car hire
- sightseeing and social programmes
- events
- receptions
- theatre tickets.

More than 500 restaurants in the city provided a variety of culinary delights, and the new Mailbox and Bullring developments offered visitors a multitude of shopping options.

Uniquely, there were also some world-famous performers appearing at The NEC Arena, with pop superstar Christina Aguilera performing at The NEC Arena on Saturday, October 25 and Mariah Carey appearing three days later.

The Organiser

ITMA 2003 was organised in-house by The NEC organising division Centre Exhibitions, on behalf of show the owners, industry body CEMATEX (Comité Européen des Constructeurs de Machines Textiles/European Committee of Textile Machinery Manufacturers). CEMATEX is made up of eight member associations from the UK, France, Germany, Italy, Switzerland, The Netherlands, Belgium and Spain. Other key markets represented at ITMA include Turkey and China.

The Exhibitors. ITMA 2003 used the whole of The NEC site - 200,000 square metres of space. The tenancy covered 38 days - 22 build days, eight open days and eight breakdown days.

The exhibition was clearly international, including 1,275 exhibitors from 40 countries, with the top 10 exhibiting countries (in order of space taken) being as follows:

1. Italy
2. Germany
3. Switzerland

Continued

CASE STUDY ITMA 2003, THE NEC, BIRMINGHAM—*CONT'D*

4. Spain
5. Belgium
6. Turkey
7. UK
8. France
9. USA
10. Austria

In terms of space taken, 78% of exhibitors came from the CEMATEX, with the greatest increase in exhibitor numbers (compared to ITMA 1999) from the following non-CEMATEX countries: Turkey (from 33 to 61 exhibitors); India (from 41 to 86 exhibitors) and China (from 10 to 28 exhibitors). The largest product sectors were Dyeing and Finishing, taking 33% of the total space, followed by Spinning (24%) and Weaving (17.7%).

The Visitors. Despite the perception of economic and political concerns, visitors to ITMA 2003 travelled from all over the world, with an average of over 15,600 each day of the show. Analysis revealed that 64% of the visitors came from Europe, and over 24% from Asia/SE Asia and the Middle East. The top visiting countries, after the UK, were Turkey, Germany and Italy, with the breakdown of visitors shown below:

1. UK 15%
2. Turkey 7.82%
3. Germany 7.49%
4. Italy 6.55%
5. Pakistan 6.03%
6. India 5.09%
7. France 4.82%
8. Belgium 3.87%
9. Spain 3.45%
10. USA 2.78%
11. China 2.69%

Most visitors came for the Weaving Sector (18%), followed by the Spinning Sector (15%) then Dyeing and Finishing (12%), although a large percentage of the visitors (20%) were involved in more than one sector. For the first time, ITMA 2003 introduced a separate sector for Non-wovens.

Unique Features

Despite The NEC's wealth of experience, the demands of a show the size and scope of ITMA required a wealth of innovative approaches. This was the first ITMA, since the first show 52 years ago, to have an industry forum addressing the strategic issues that face the textile machinery field. It was also the first to fully embrace the opportunities presented by the Internet, and to endow the exhibition with an element of showmanship and 'pizzazz!'

Additionally, a radical approach was implemented for developing relationships with customers, with a decision to make the exhibiting process simpler by supplying as many services as possible through a single source, equipped with multi-lingual staff. Working alongside service suppliers, this dedicated team was able to liaise directly with exhibitors, presenting a 'one-stop-shop' for exhibiting queries. The feedback from exhibitors suggested that they welcomed this approach as a way providing cost-effective and simplified solutions.

Key Moments

The "Forum" (a conference that discussed the key business issues facing the industry) was a first for ITMA. Previous events had only run conferences addressing technical issues; never before had the event seen such high profile and significant presentations. The opening session was particularly interesting as the topic was the impact of China joining the World Trade Organisation in 2005. The consequences will affect the whole business world not just the world of textiles. The event was attended by the Chinese Government Minister for Textiles who engaged in a "full and frank" debate with a high profile industry lobbyist from the USA, addressing such issues as "dumping", tariffs, and unfair trading practices.

The sound effect of John Betjamen's poem The Night Train which accompanied a famous film about the Royal Mail trains or those old films of Lancashire cotton mills all thundering away churning out fabric,was created within the exhibition halls used to display weaving equipment; for 20 minutes in every hour, the dozens of huge looms all began operating at once. It was a powerful visual and auditory experience that really did conjure up the industry at its most dynamic.

Watching the machines turning out a full Axminster carpet, six metres wide, at the rate of 2 metres a minute, was really quite mesmerising; 14,000 threads on the weft and a warp introduced with shuttles (mechanical, water jet or air jet), moved too fast to be seen.

Business and Economic Impact

As the UK's largest ever international exhibition, ITMA generated an estimated £85 million for the West Midlands economy in visitor spending, according to research undertaken by KPMG, which also found that the show supported the equivalent of more than 1,500 full-time jobs. To place these figures in context, this represents the largest impact of any single show ever staged in the UK – activities at The NEC Group each year generate spending of more than £1 billion and ITMA alone added an additional eight percent to the figure during 2003. Total spending within the UK, as a result of ITMA, is estimated at £110 million. The KPMG study also found considerable positive feedback about Birmingham and the West Midlands region as a destination; almost half (45%) of the visitors surveyed, said that they were likely to bring friends or family back to the area in the future.

ITMA helped Birmingham International Airport (BIA) break performance targets. In October 2003, the airport handled 881,709 passengers, an increase of 11.4% on the previous year, and its busiest October on record. During the event, BIA also handled more than 100 special charter flights along with larger aircraft on scheduled routes to deal with the exhibition traffic. Most exhibitors (63%) and nearly half of all visitors (47%) flew directly into Birmingham International Airport as their gateway into the UK. ITMA was also the first major test for the Monorail link, which connects the airport directly with Birmingham International station and The NEC. It transported – without a problem – more than 22,000 people during the show.

As might be imagined, there were a few nerves amongst exhibitors at the thought of ITMA running in the UK for the first time; however, these proved to be completely without foundation. Feedback from exhibitors in every sector has been extremely positive, with reports of a considerable amount of business being done during the show. Indeed, 60% of all visitors were of Director level and above and this clearly was an important factor in the quantity of orders placed during the show.

It is clear from the above case study that ITMA was successful on a number of levels. Major exhibitions, such as ITMA, clearly have a range of impacts which organisers have to manage effectively to maximise the positive effects and ensure that the exhibition meets all exhibitor, visitor and stakeholder requirements. ITMA demonstrated the ability of The NEC to organise and host exhibitions of this scale, while also demonstrating the positive benefits of working with a range of partners from across Birmingham and the West Midlands. After ITMA, The NEC was

Continued

CASE STUDY ITMA 2003, THE NEC, BIRMINGHAM—*CONT'D*

recognised for its work in bringing international visitors to the region for ITMA 2003, with The NEC Group also recognised for its commitment to language and communication at the National Language for Export Awards 2003. Knowledge, skills and experience developed from ITMA will help The NEC move forward as one of the major European exhibition centres and it has illustrated the potential of The NEC, Birmingham, the West Midlands and the UK to host large-scale international exhibitions.

For more information about The NEC Group, please visit www.necgroup.co.uk.

By The NEC Group.

Questions
1. From the case study, identify the main stakeholders in ITMA.
2. In evaluating the impacts, what are the long-term benefits to Birmingham of hosting the ITMA show?
3. What factors contributed to the success of the show?
4. The case illustrates the impact of the external environment on the event itself with rail disruption causing a reduction in target numbers and a change in transportation. What other issues from the external environment could have had an impact on the show? What strategies could event managers implement to minimise the impact of such issues?

CASE STUDY IMPACTS OF THE SYDNEY 2000 OLYMPIC GAMES

The importance of impacts

Impacts are immensely important because they relate to issues of sustainability and accountability. In 2002, International Olympic Committee President Dr Jacques Rogge warned about the danger of luxury developments made in the name of the Olympic Games that become white elephants — costly extravaganzas with no long-term benefit. It has also become clearer that greater attention needs to be paid to the development of post-Olympic evaluation by appropriate authorities to minimise negative impacts and maximise positive ones.

There had been too little evaluation of the Olympic Games and their impacts in the past. Maurice Roche, who has written extensively on mega-events, noted in 1992 that 'pre-event projections are seldom tested against post-event accounting'. The organisation of an international conference at Lausanne in 2002 on 'The Legacy of the Olympic Games 1984–2000' and the publication of its proceedings, made a cogent case for greater focus on Olympic outcomes. Scholars pointed to the need to canvas a wide range of outcomes relating to global promotion; economic benefits; the built and physical environment; public life; politics and culture; sporting infrastructure and participation; education and information and symbols, memory and history. It was also noted at the conference that while a legacy is invariably regarded as something desirable, Olympic impacts could be both positive and negative.

The International Olympic Committee (IOC) had earlier recognised the importance of impacts when it created the Olympic Games Global Impact (OGGI) program in 2001. OGGI operates over an 11-year cycle, from two years before the selection of an Olympic city to two years after the staging of an Olympic Games; and during this period there is a sustained effort to collect and capture the social, environmental and economic impacts of the Games. OGGI assists with the transfer of Olympic knowledge from one Olympic city to another and it enables the IOC to better understand and manage future Olympic Games. There was an OGGI program in place at the time of the Sydney Games.

Sydney's bid promises and its Olympic vision

Impacts are best measured against the bid promises that set out the rationale for hosting the event. Promises are made to the host community to gain their support for a bid that is essential for its success. The main promise to the Sydney community was the creation of a super sports precinct at Sydney Olympic Park that was linked to environmental measures there. The park, it was suggested, would provide facilities both for high profile and community sport and would encourage greater sports participation. A second strand of Sydney's Olympic vision was that the Games would enhance the global positioning of Sydney and benefit the tourism industry in particular.

Sydney Olympic Park was the city's major Olympic infrastructure project. The majority of Olympic venues were located at the park and almost without exception, were new and state of the art. The park was framed by the parklands of Millennium Park and by Bicentennial Park, which included significant wetlands and facilities for passive leisure. It also included the Olympic village that later became the suburb of Newington and the show grounds that are the site of an annual agricultural show. The Olympic vision for the park was multi-dimensional. The super sports precinct was located in western Sydney where sports facilities were most needed. The parklands provided facilities for active recreation (cycling and walking paths) and passive leisure. The park also had the potential to act as an environmental showcase and to host cultural activities.

It was forecast before the Games that Olympic tourism would generate handsome and long-lasting benefits for Sydney and Australia. Backed by Australian Government funding, the Australian Tourist Commission developed ambitious programmes to leverage Olympic tourism, including a visiting journalist program from 1996 to 2000 and the creation of the Sydney Media Centre for non-accredited media. The Tourism Council estimated that as a result of the international exposure from the Games there would be an increase of 1.6 million additional tourists from 1997 to 2004.

Measurement of impacts

An interest in post-Games impacts had been limited and haphazard in the past as most cities had been content to bask in the accolades handed out at the closing ceremony. This had occurred because organising committees closed down soon after the Olympic event and there was no post-Games authority to undertake sustained evaluation.

The measurement of Olympic tourism is equally imprecise because there is no agreed methodology as to how an Olympic factor can be extracted from general tourist figures. Despite the optimistic predictions of international tourist growth in Australia after 2000, there were three years of unprecedented decline in 2001, 2002 and 2003 because of international terrorism, SARS and the increased value of the Australian dollar. The tourist industry has recovered since 2004 but it is unclear whether the ongoing impact of the successful Olympic Games contributed to this. However, an impressive growth in convention tourism before and after the Games was a positive Olympic outcome.

There was much rhetoric at the time of the Sydney Games that the staging of the event would lead to greater sports participation. Scholars have questioned whether the Games produced a bounce in sports participation. They have also noted the absence of data to confirm (or deny) that an increase in sports participation has occurred.

Media reporting of post-Games impacts has been spasmodic and largely consists of the occasional reporting of post-Olympic problems. Sydney Olympic Park was frequently empty in 2001 and 2002 and serviced by inadequate public transport except when a major event was staged there. It soon became apparent that the park was struggling to realise its vision. One commentator dismissed the park as a ghost town and another referred to it as a 'wasteland of white elephants'.

Continued

CASE STUDY IMPACTS OF THE SYDNEY 2000 OLYMPIC GAMES—*CONT'D*

Continuing impacts

It has become clear that impacts – direct and indirect, planned and unplanned – continue to resonate in an Olympic city years after the Games. For instance, the strategic plan developed on behalf of the New South Wales Government for Sydney Olympic Park in 2007 and 2008, envisaged a second commercial and residential building boom comparable to the spurt of 1996 to 1999, when the Olympic venues were erected. The establishment of this permanent residential population and enhanced commercial presence was a response to the underutilisation of the park in 2001 and 2002, immediately after the Olympic Games... The re-creation of the Olympic Park as a multipurpose facility was an attempt to ensure that Sydney's Olympic legacy was sustainable and positive. The commercial and residential development of the park since 2001 represents a creative modification of the original Olympic plan. With a permanent population of 30,000, greater numbers of Sydneysiders will make use of the sports, recreational and cultural assets of the park.

The new plans for the park occurred in part for political reasons. Had Sydney Olympic Park continued to struggle, in 2003 it could have become a potential political liability at the March 2003 state elections because it was the state (and the taxpayers) that had underwritten Sydney Olympic Park. The successful commercial and residential development from 2006 to 2009 removed it as an issue in the March 2007 elections.

Unplanned outcomes. Although Sydney's legacy plans were developed belatedly, there have been some remarkable success stories as government and individuals have responded creatively to new post-Games opportunities that were not apparent in 2000.

The Sydney-Beijing Olympic Secretariat (SBOS), which was established in February 2002, is a prime example of a shrewd and timely response to Beijing's success in winning the bid for the 2008 Olympic Games in July 2001. SBOS was established within the Department of State and Regional Development (DSRD) in the New South Wales Government. Its aim was to assist local Australian business to gain access to the Chinese Olympic market. SBOS has worked well because it enlisted the active support of individuals, such as Sandy Hollway, who had been CEO of the Sydney Organising Committee for the Olympic Games (SOCOG).

SBOS has been a great success story as it has promoted an Australian Olympic export business, based on Australia's admired event management expertise. Individual firms have won important contracts to design and build venues in Beijing and many other Olympic, Commonwealth and Asian Games cities. Many individual Australians have also secured Games oriented employment as consultants and advisers.

SUMMARY

Given Sydney's sizeable investment in the staging of the Olympic Games, it is appropriate that the city should seek positive outcomes. However, like most previous Olympic cities, insufficient plans were in place in 2000 to implement Sydney's post-Olympic vision. There was inadequate evaluation of Olympic tourism and sports impacts.

Fortunately plans were put in place belatedly to harness positive impacts and there are two outstanding examples of significant post-Games benefits. With the commercial and residential development of Sydney Olympic Park, it is no longer the city's white elephant. The development of an Olympic export industry since 2001 is another success story. Both these examples demonstrate that impacts continue to resonate in the Olympic city.

By Richard Cashman, Director, Australian Centre for Olympic Studies.

Questions
1. Why was it important for impacts of the Sydney 2000 Olympic Games to be measured?
2. Who should measure the impacts of such mega-events?
3. When and how can impacts best be measured?
4. What lessons can future Olympic Games take from the Sydney's approach to and experience of organising the games?

Event tourism planning

4

LEARNING OBJECTIVES

After studying this chapter, you should be able to:

- describe event tourism and the destination approach to event tourism planning

- conduct an event tourism situational analysis to create a foundation for goal setting and strategic decision making

- describe the range of goals that a destination might seek to progress through an event tourism strategy

- list and describe organisations that might play a role in a destination's efforts at event tourism development

- describe generic strategy options available to organisations seeking to develop event tourism to a destination

- list and discuss approaches to the implementation and evaluation of event tourism strategies

- discuss the potential event tourism has to generate positive outcomes in small communities.

INTRODUCTION

This chapter will explore the relationship between events and tourism from the viewpoint of destinations (cities, towns, counties, regions or countries) that are seeking to develop and implement strategies to increase visitation. The chapter begins with an overview of event tourism, before moving on to propose and discuss a strategic approach to event tourism planning. This approach involves: conduct of a detailed situational analysis; the creation of event tourism goals; the establishment of an organisational structure through which event tourism goals can be progressed and the development, implementation and evaluation of an event tourism strategy. It is argued in this chapter that the value of this process lies in its capacity to generate a coordinated strategic approach to a destination's overall event tourism efforts. The final part of this chapter seeks to redress the tendency in dealing with event tourism to focus on cities, regions and countries. It does this by briefly examining the significant, positive role that event tourism can play in the context of small communities.

Events Management. DOI: 10.1016/B978-1-85617-818-1.10004-0

DEVELOPING DESTINATION-BASED EVENT TOURISM STRATEGIES

Government support at all levels has been integral to the expansion of event tourism. Not only have governments invested in the creation of specialist bodies charged with event tourism development but many have also funded, or contributed significantly to event-specific infrastructure, such as convention and exhibition centres and stadiums. In the specific case of China, for example, there was only one convention and exhibition centre larger than 50,000 square metres in 1992. By 2003 this number had risen to 16 (Kaye, 2005). The willingness of governments to support event tourism through policy initiatives, financial support and legislation is also increasingly evident. Once the London 2012 Olympics bid was won, for example, the UK Government moved quickly to pass legislation to create organising bodies, ensure Games security, and allow and expedite Olympic-related developments, including the appointment of an Olympics Minister to oversee the projects. Such willingness, however, can sometimes create problems due to the public's lack of participation in decision making, as Waitt (2003) noted in connection with the Sydney Olympics.

The willingness of governments to support event tourism through policy initiatives, financial support and legislation is increasingly evident. For example, following the launch of the North East Tourism Strategy in 2005, the regional development agency One NorthEast lead partners including Sport England, Arts Council England, North East, Culture North East, the Culture10 team within the NewcastleGateshead Initiative and the private sector, to develop a North East England Festival and Events Strategy. The strategy is designed to help the partners improve the economic and social impact of festivals and events and to clarify strategic relationships within the regional and sub-regional economy (One North-East, 2007, p. 1).

Responsibility for progressing event tourism efforts varies from destination to destination. In the context of smaller destinations, such as towns and regions, involvement may be limited to organisations such as tourism promotional bodies, local government and the local chamber of commerce. Larger destinations (cities, regions, countries) are likely to have an expanded range of organisations involved in the event tourism area, including conference and exhibition centres, conference and visitor bureaus, tourism commissions/agencies, festival/public event bodies, major event agencies, government departments involved in areas such as sport and the arts and specialist event organising companies.

THE EVENT TOURISM STRATEGIC PLANNING PROCESS

A strategic approach to a destination's event tourism development efforts offers significant benefits. These benefits lie primarily in the areas of coordination and in the building of an event tourism capacity that represents the best strategic fit with the area's overall tourism efforts and its current and projected business environment.

FIGURE 4.1 Event tourism strategic planning process

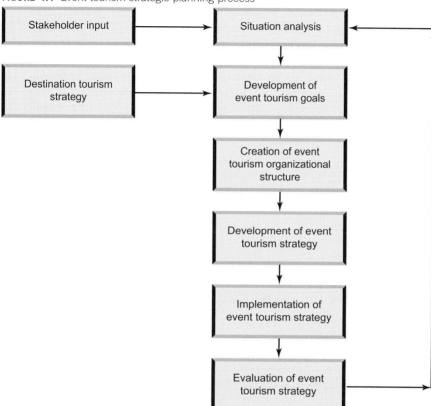

This approach is presented in Figure 4.1 as a series of sequential steps, each of which is discussed in this section.

The timeframe in which event tourism strategic plans operate will vary from destination to destination, but 5–15-year planning horizons are not uncommon. For example, EventScotland's major events strategy spans the period 2003–15 (see the case study on pages 148-51) and Events Tasmania employs a rolling 10-year events plan (Events Tasmania, 2006a). Similarly, Event South West has a ten year strategy for winning or creating major sporting events for the South West of England (Event South West, 2008).

SITUATIONAL ANALYSIS

A detailed situational analysis should underpin the decisions made on the event tourism goals to be set for a destination. This analysis should reflect the various perspectives of key stakeholders in the event area, such as tourism bodies, the destination's community, government agencies associated with areas such as the arts and sport and major event organisers. In preparing the major events strategy for Scotland, for example, the consultancy company charged with this task (Objective Performance Limited) spent 18 months engaged in research, including interviewing more than 80 individuals and organisations involved in major events in Scotland and overseas (Scottish Executive, 2002). In the case of Victoria in Australia, the Victorian Government's event tourism strategy, more than 70 formal submissions were received in response to an initial discussion paper and a further 50 interviews were undertaken with industry and government organisations (Victorian Government 2006, p. 43).

A strengths, weaknesses, opportunities and threats (SWOT) analysis (see Chapter 6) is a useful way of assessing the situation that a destination faces in its efforts to develop event tourism. Figure 4.2 lists a range of factors that might feature in such an analysis, undertaken as a precursor to developing a destination's event tourism strategy.

DEVELOPMENT OF EVENT TOURISM GOALS

The role that event tourism is required to play in a destination's tourism development efforts will vary according to the overall tourism strategy that is being pursued. An understanding of this strategy is important as it provides, for example, the basis for establishing event tourism visitation targets, as well as insights into destination branding and positioning efforts that an event strategy may be required to support. While each destination's event tourism goals differ, common considerations in setting such goals can be identified and these are discussed below.

Leveraging events for economic gain

A key consideration in any event tourism strategy is the potential for events to bring 'new' money into a destination from outside visitors (see Chapter 2). For example, a single large-scale event, such as the Manchester International Festival, has the potential to contribute significantly to a destination's economy. When this event was proposed in 2004, research for the feasibility study suggested that it could initially bring in 160,000 visitors, rising to 270,000 in future years, with an estimated economic impact of £34 million (Davidson, 2004). A major research study of the summer and winter festivals in Edinburgh, Scotland produced the following key findings in this regard:

- *65% of all visitors to Edinburgh, said the Festivals were their sole reason or a very important reason for visiting Edinburgh*
- *70% of people attending Edinburgh Festivals came from outside of the city, with 15% coming from countries outside the UK*

FIGURE 4.2 Possible factors for inclusion in a destination's event tourism SWOT analysis

Strengths/weaknesses
Existing stock of events
- Type
- Quality
- Uniqueness/competitive advantage
- Number
- Duration/timing (for example, whether most events are scheduled at a particular time of the year, such as summer, and whether this clustering is advantageous or disadvantageous from a tourism perspective)
- Current financial situation
- Image/reputation (particularly in visitor markets) of individual events
- Level of current demand from regional, intrastate, interstate and overseas visitor markets
- Level of understanding (developed through market research) of the needs of visitor markets
- Current economic, social and environmental impacts
- Existing links between events and the destination's tourism industry (for example, level of packaging evident and level of partnering with tourism industry marketing bodies)
- Stage of individual events in terms of their 'product' life cycle
- Evidence of long-term strategic planning

Venues/sites/facilities/supporting services
- Number, type, quality and capacity of venues/outdoor event sites
- Capacity of local suppliers (for example, equipment hire, food and beverage services) to support various types of event
- Stock of supporting local tourism services (for example, accommodation suppliers, transport suppliers, tour operators)

Human resources
- Level/type of destination event venue/event management expertise
- Capacity of a community to provide volunteers to support event delivery
- Range/type of event-related training conducted in the area, or accessible to people from the area

Stage of event sector development
- Existence of organisations such as event industry associations, convention and visitors bureaus and major event agencies

Destination location relative to major tourist markets
- Travel time and costs
- Types and frequency of public transport to and from the area

Degree of political support
- Level of available funding for event tourism
- Level of/potential for legislative support
- Level of coordination/cooperation between local, state and national governments (and associated agencies) in the event area

Level of community support
- Prevailing community perspectives on the economic, environmental and social impacts of events
- Level of anticipated local patronage for events (necessary to underpin the economics of many events)
- Level of willingness of the community to absorb short-term negatives, such as crowding and traffic congestion

Continued

FIGURE 4.2 *Continued*

- Willingness of the community to support events via volunteering and the provision of home hosting services, etc.

Opportunities/threats
Potential for partnering with selected organisations to progress one or more event tourism goals
- Possible partnering bodies include:
  - Government departments
  - Cultural organisations
  - Tourism bodies
  - Chambers of commerce
  - Tourism businesses (to package events)
  - Environmental groups (to minimise impacts/maximise environmental outcomes)

Level and type of competition from events in other destinations
- Direct competition from similar events
- Indirect competition from dissimilar events taking place within the same time period as the existing/planned events

Market tastes/preferences for events
- Ability of an area to respond to changing market needs through existing and new events
- Impact on existing/planned events of changes in such areas as family structures, community age profiles, patterns of work/retirement and attitudes to health, etc.

Availability of external funds
- Capacity to attract government grants or loans
- Likelihood of attracting sponsorship

Potential to link events with overall destination branding efforts
- Strength and nature of existing destination brand

Local cultural/environmental attributes that have the potential to be leveraged for event purposes
- Capacity of an area's flora or fauna, Indigenous culture, history, ethnicity, architecture, local agricultural pursuits, etc. to be embraced within an event context

Presence of local chapters/bodies with affiliations to parent organisations that regularly conduct events
- Capacity of local sporting/business/cultural bodies to bid for and host events owned by their respective parent bodies; for example, national/international conventions, annual industry trade fairs and regional/national/international annual sporting competitions

Environmental and social impacts
- Capacity of a destination to absorb event tourism impacts without negative environmental or community outcomes. Potential problem areas associated with events include waste generation, anti-social behaviour, crowding and the inability of local area infrastructure to cope with large, temporary population increases
- Existing community perspectives on the environmental and social impacts of events

General economic conditions
- Employment levels
- Interest rates
- Inflation
- Consumer confidence levels
- Recession

FIGURE 4.2 *Continued*

Other
- Changes in weather patterns due to global warming
- Security and health issues (for example, terrorism, SARS)
- Political climate (for example, the extent to which events involving particular groups or nations will be supported by key stakeholders, such as local authorities or national governments).

- *£76 million was spent by festival visitors through accommodation providers in Scotland, with £49 million of this being in Edinburgh itself.*
- *70% of hotel occupancy in some months could be attributed directly to festival activity*

(Edinburgh Fringe Festival, 2006)

Even in developing countries events can generate significant tourist demand (and therefore export income). In the Caribbean, for example, peaks in visitation in many countries often coincide with an event (Nurse, 2003).

Geographic dispersal of economic benefits flowing from tourism

When the destinations seeking to engage in event tourism are large geographic entities, such as regions or countries, it is not uncommon for them to use events as a means of encouraging travel to areas outside major tourism counties. In this way, the economic benefits from visitation are more widely spread.

Destination branding

A destination's 'brand' can be thought of as the overall impression, association or feeling that its name and associated symbols generate in the minds of consumers. Events are an opportunity to assist in creating, changing or reinforcing such brands. According to a study by Jago et al. (2003) in Australia, such efforts at using events for destination branding purposes depend greatly on local community support and on the cultural and strategic fit between the destination and the event(s) conducted there. This study also found that in the context of individual events, event differentiation, the longevity/tradition associated with an event, cooperative planning by key players and media support were central factors in the successful integration of individual events into a destination's overall branding efforts.

The Edinburgh International Festival, one of the UK's best known events worldwide, is an excellent example of the use of an event for destination branding purposes. This event has been extensively leveraged to create a 'brand' for the city of Edinburgh. The city is now firmly established as the UK's festival city, a position it has sought to strengthen via a variety of means. These means have included the drawing together of a range of festivals into a programme of events, encouraging the development of new festivals, building a festival theatre and developing The Hub as Edinburgh's Festival Centre. Another example of 'identity' creation through events can be observed in Birmingham. This area claims to be 'The world's meeting place' (Marketing Birmingham, 2010) and conducts multiple events to reinforce this position, appealing both to business and leisure markets.

Many other examples of branding through events can be identified. The general category of food and/or wine festivals, for example, perform this function for a number of destinations, reinforcing to the broader market the destination's status in connection with these products. Ludlow Marches Food & Drink Festival and the Abergavenny Food Festival are indicative of such events, showcasing quality food from the region.

Another aspect of the link between events and destination branding is the use of events by tourism marketing bodies as integral parts of broad 'theme' years. Liverpool Culture Company developed a series of themed years in the build up to hosting the European Capital of Culture in 2008, to reflect aspects of the Liverpool culture covering learning, faith, sea, performance, and the city's 800th anniversary, with environment and innovation planned for the two years after 2008. The programme of events and activities attracted 9.7 million additional visits to Liverpool (Garcia, Melville and Cox, 2010). Events are also sometimes used as the basis for theme years, an example being SeaBritain in 2005 coordinated by the National Maritime Museum. The goal of this themed year was to celebrate 'the ways in which the sea touches all of our lives' with the main event being a celebration of the Trafalgar Festival to mark the 200th anniversary of Nelson's victory (National Maritime Museum, 2005).

Destination marketing

Associated with the issue of destination branding is the more general one of destination promotion. Destinations often use the opportunity provided by events to progress their overall tourism promotional efforts; a range of destination marketing organisations have been established throughout the UK over recent years to further this aim, for example, Marketing Leeds, Marketing Manchester, Marketing Birmingham, Glasgow City Marketing Bureau and Experience Nottinghamshire (see Davidson and Rogers, 2006, for a detailed exploration of destination marketing).

The Wales Tourist Board (now called Visit Wales) undertook a major marketing and promotional campaign in relation to the Rugby World Cup in Wales in 1999. Its overall aim was to use the tournament as an opportunity to attract additional visitors, in order to raise the profile of the host nation and to secure lasting tourism benefits. Over 330,000 people were estimated to have visited Wales as a result of the event. In a survey of international rugby fans conducted before and after the Rugby World Cup, fewer than 20% had visited Wales. Of those who had, almost 70% thought it likely that they would return on holiday. Amongst those who had seen coverage of the event on television, 25% thought that they would be much more likely to visit Wales on holiday as a result. Research indicated that around 135,000 trips could have been generated from the UK over the succeeding five years, potentially worth around £15 million (Anon., 2000).

If events are to be effective in positioning their destinations in the market, they must strive for authenticity and the expression of the unique characteristics of their communities. Visitors want to do what the locals do and experience what the locals enjoy. The UK government report 'Tomorrow's Tourism' (DCMS, 1999, p. 7) argues that:

> *Tourism is based largely on our heritage, culture and countryside and, therefore, needs to maintain the quality of the resources upon which it depends. Tourism can provide an incentive and income to protect our built and natural environment and helps to maintain local culture and diversity. Where tourism is popular, it underpins local commercial activity and services and it can help to regenerate urban and rural areas.*

Conversely, destinations that produce events for the tourists rather than events that have meaning for their own communities, run the danger of producing inauthentic, shallow events. Exploitative or badly run events with inadequate management or facilities can damage the reputation of a destination.

For example, Smith and Jenner (1998) point to the dramatic rise in visitation to Atlanta, Georgia (a 78% rise in overseas visitors and a 35% rise in domestic visitors) over the three-year period following the announcement in 1990 that it was the site of the 1996 Atlanta Olympics. They attribute this increase in part to the publicity that Atlanta was able to obtain as a result of hosting the Olympics. Such tourism-related outcomes are common in the context of mega-events, with De Groote (2005) providing a more extensive listing of such benefits in the context of the subsequent summer Olympic Games in Sydney, including:

- acceleration of Australia's tourism marketing efforts by 10 years. This outcome was in large measure due to the generation of an additional A$3.8 billion in publicity for Australia between 1997 and 2000, with a further A$300 million in additional advertising exposure coming from partnerships with major Olympic sponsors such as Visa, McDonald's, Kodak and Coca-Cola.
- increase in international visitation (by 10.9% in 2000 to almost 5 million visitors). This outcome was in part due to post-Games tactical programs conducted by the Australian Tourist Commission (now Tourism Australia), which saw some 90 campaigns launched, involving 200 industry partners worth a total of A$45 million. These programs were intended to convert interest and awareness into actual visitation.
- rising interest in Australia and Sydney as a destination by potential travellers and as a location for the conduct of conferences. This interest was in part due to a campaign by the Australian Tourist Commission which saw some 100 business events conducted off the back of the event.
- high level of intended return visitation, with an estimated 88% of the 110,000 international visitors who came to Australia for the Olympics indicating that they were likely to return to Sydney as tourists.

Weed (2008) has provided an extensive exploration of the nature and potential of Olympic tourism, including guidance on partnerships and other factors are required in order to successfully establish Olympic tourism. He concludes that empirical evidence is still quite limited; however, his findings suggest that there are temporary opportunities pre- and post-games for increasing tourism, not only in the host city, but within the wider host country as well. These findings are reflected in the approach taken by the government. The UK, — national and regional governments and the tourism industry in the UK — are seeking to capitalise on the tourism benefits of hosting the London 2012 Olympics and have been working on this since before the handover in Beijing in 2008. For example, the Department for Culture Media and Sport have launched the 2012 tourism strategy for the UK which seeks to, 'maximise the financial benefits of the 2012 Games for the tourism industry' (DCMS, 2008, p.4). The vision is to engage all UK tourism businesses in a national campaign; improve international perceptions of Britain; deliver a first class welcome; improve the skills of the workforce; drive up the quality of accommodation; maximise opportunities from increasing business visits and events; spread the benefits across the UK and improve sustainability (DCMS, 2008b, p. 4).

Creating off-season demand for tourism industry services

Events have the capacity to be scheduled in periods of low tourism demand, when airline and accommodation providers often have surplus capacity, thereby evening out seasonal tourism flows. Skiing centres, for example, often use events as a means of generating demand during non-winter periods. Getz (2005, p. 142) describes the way that events can overcome seasonality by capitalising 'on whatever natural appeal the off-season presents, such as winter as opposed to summer sports, seasonal food and produce, and scenery or wildlife viewed in different places and under changing conditions'. He also notes that 'in many destinations the residents prefer the off-season for their own celebrations, and these provide more authentic events for visitors' (Getz, 2005, p. 143).

Many UK destinations have developed events to enliven off-season periods. Within 'Achieving Our Potential: A Tourism Strategy for Wales' (WTB, 2000, p. 53) Visit Wales notes the benefit that events can bring to Wales, highlighting that, 'Festivals and events, for example, can play a key role in attracting larger numbers of overseas visitors and in developing new markets within the UK throughout the year'. However, Visit Wales goes on to note that due to a previously uncoordinated approach to developing the events programme, the best known events within Wales are in the main summer months which reinforces seasonality. As a result, the tourism strategy recommends the development of an events/festival strategy to distribute events throughout the year and a more coordinated approach to marketing in order to gain full benefit from business tourism (including meetings, incentives, conferences and exhibitions). This is now being progressed, with proposals for the formation of EventWales as part of a major events strategy. A further example is Edinburgh, which in 2000 launched the new Capital Christmas winter festival to extend the traditional New Year Hogmanay celebrations and attract visitors in the off-season winter months. Donald Anderson, Leader of the Council, noted, 'Edinburgh attracts thousands of visitors all year round and our world renowned festivals play a major part in this. Capital Christmas and Edinburgh's Hogmanay together offer the best winter festival programme in the world and I know of no other city that hosts a full month of family entertainment throughout the festive season' (City of Edinburgh Council, 2000b).

Events can also be used as a means of extending the tourist season by conducting them just before or just after the high-season period. In connection with the use of events for this purpose, acting in this way can serve to move market perceptions of a destination from that of a single season only location to one providing year round leisure opportunities.

Enhancing visitor experiences

Events add to the range of experiences a destination can offer and thus add to its capacity to attract and/or hold visitors for longer periods of time (Getz 2005). Resorts, museums, historic districts, heritage sites, archaeological sites, markets and shopping centers, sports stadiums, convention centers and theme parks all develop programmes of events. Built attractions and facilities everywhere have realised the advantages of 'animation' — the process of programming interpretive features and/or events that make the place come alive with sensory stimulation and appealing atmosphere. In this regard, destinations often seek to add to their stock of existing events. National Media Museum in Bradford, Alton Towers in Staffordshire and Blackpool Pleasure Beach all use extensive event programmes to increase market profile and attract repeat visits. These offerings in turn are communicated to their potential visitor markets by such means as web-based event calendars.

Extenders

Another important aspect to consider is the opportunity to keep visitors or tourists in the region when they have attended an event, — in other words, to extend their stay. Davidson and Cope (2003) note that delegates or visitors to business events are generally being funded by their organisations to attend at their employers' expense. As a result, they may bring along partners or family; attend other business or social events; extend their visit either before or after the event to spend some of their leisure time (and money) in the area or return at a future date — this is particularly true of international delegates. As a result, it is important that organisers, tourism agencies and other stakeholders consider the opportunities that this may bring and ensure that delegates are provided with sufficient information before attending, to influence their decision. VisitBritain and the Business Visits and Events Partnership provide useful guidance on ensuring that the benefits from business tourists are maximised (Davidson, 2002).

Catalyst for the expansion and/or improvement of destination infrastructure and tourism infrastructure

Events can enhance the quality of life and thus add to the sense of place and the residential amenity of neighbourhoods. Events can also provide a significant spur to both public and private investment in a destination. Many writers (for example, Carlsen and Millan, 2002; Carlsen and Taylor, 2003; Clark, 2008; Getz, 2005; Hiller and Moylan, 1999; Jones, 2001; Muñoz, 2006; Mules, 1993; Ritchie, 2000, 2001; Roche, 2000; Selwood and Jones, 1993) have highlighted the role that particularly large-scale events can play in urban renewal and in the subsequent development of a destination's attractiveness and capacity as a tourist destination. For example, Millennium Square, a £12 million project funded by Leeds City Council and the Millennium Commission, is used for events but also provides traffic-free leisure space for residents to enjoy. Leeds' annual multicultural programme of events is the envy of many cities and ranges from Opera in the Park and Party in the Park, through to the Irish and Chinese festivals.

Investment by the private sector in restaurants and tourist accommodation, for example, is often central to this process and may sometimes extend to the building of large-scale infrastructure items. The Sheffield World Student Games in 1991 provided major facilities, including Ponds Forge International Pool, the Sheffield Arena and the Don Valley Stadium that have contributed to Sheffield's reputation as a sporting city. The 2002 Manchester Commonwealth Games led to the regeneration of East Manchester, including development of the City of Manchester Stadium — now home to Manchester City Football Club following the Games — to ensure a legacy and long-term after-use (see, Carlsen and Taylor, 2003, for a discussion of the policies linking the Commonwealth Games to regeneration). Other examples include the Millennium Dome (now known as The O$_2$) and the surrounding area in Greenwich (East London) developed as the focal point for the Millennium Festival celebrations and the Festival Hall and South Bank Centre developed for the Festival of Britain in 1951, both of which gained infrastructural development stemming from the hosting of large-scale events. Hotel and facilities development, better communications and improved road and public transport networks are some of the legacies left by these events.

One of Edinburgh International Festival's founders, Henry Harvey Wood, noted in 1947 the role that the festival could play in regenerating the economy. He stated, 'If the Festival succeeds, Edinburgh will not only have scored an artistic triumph but laid the foundations of a major industry, a new and exciting source of income' (EIF, 2000, p. 2). The festival has succeeded and his prediction has come true. Edinburgh International Festival continues to be of substantial economic importance, as does the programme of events that have developed around it. In 2004 alone Edinburgh's summer festivals generated an estimated £135 million for the economy, sustaining the equivalent of 2900 full time equivalent jobs (SQW Ltd and TNS Travel and Tourism, 2005).

Liverpool's European Capital of Culture 2008 was used to great effect in regenerating Liverpool. In the formal evaluation report of the programme, undertaken within the Impacts 08 research programme, Garcia, Melville and Cox (2010, pp. 12-13) note that the European Capital of Culture operated on three levels: 1) the main branded programme of events, Liverpool '08; 2) linking with the wider city regeneration and re-imaging programme, which saw over £4 billion invested over eight years; and 3) engagement with European Capital of Culture stakeholders from across Europe. The physical investment in infrastructure peaked in 2008 with £1.5 billion worth of project being completed (Garcia, Melville and Cox, 2010, p. 11). They noted that the programme generated £130 million in income, the largest to date of any European Capital of Culture programme; and the visitors generated £753.8 million in economic impact — additional visitor spend. (Garcia, Melville and Cox, 2010, p. 25).

Progression of a destination's social, cultural and/or environmental agenda

A range of agendas may be pursued through the conduct of events — tourism development is one example. These other agenda may serve to condition how event tourism is approached or may be independent of such considerations. It is not uncommon for major event agencies to also concern themselves with a range of non-tourism goals. Government tourism and arts bodies often consciously use events to position their destinations in the market and deliver tourism, culture and art strategies. For example, Hampshire County Council noted that 'festivals can provide high profile opportunities to celebrate communities, to promote artistic excellence and innovation, and to improve the image, identity and competitiveness of particular localities' (Fuller, 1998). The Events Unit (now repositioned within the Belfast Waterfront & Ulster Hall and Events team of Belfast City's Development Department) aims to 'promote and develop a high quality, sustainable, inclusive programme of public access events in a safe enjoyable environment, in order to help raise the profile of Belfast in support of regeneration' (Belfast City Council, 2000a, p. 2). Key objectives of the Events Unit Strategy, mapped into the Development Department Strategy are:

- Develop and promote a high-quality, sustainable, inclusive programme of public access events to raise the profile of Belfast and utilise the common Belfast branding to ensure that Belfast is an attractive and welcoming city.
- Work in partnership with the Tourism Development Unit and the Arts Unit to ensure the development, packaging and promotion of events which will enhance Belfast's reputation.
- Ensure that all promotional tools including literature, advertisements and press releases provide an appropriate range of information for residents and visitors to the city.
- Work in conjunction with the Tourism Unit and the Belfast Visitor and Convention Bureau (BVCB) to ensure that the common branding of the city is adopted appropriately (Belfast City Council, 2000b).

Another example is the key role that events play within the arts strategy of Bath and North East Somerset Council (B&NES) for the period 2008 to 2011 (Cullis and Salt, 2007). The strategy includes festivals and events development as one of its ten strategic priorities, with three clearly identified outcomes that they are looking to achieve by 2011:

- Increased and improved reputation, profile and visibility for festivals and major events
- A proactive and 'festivals friendly' Council
- A 'one-stop', coordinated approach by the Council

To achieve this, B&NES have set the following four objectives for 2008-11:

- Learn about and implement good practice in the promotion, support and monitoring of festivals and events by researching festivals and events promoters and local authorities around the UK and abroad
- Publish and promote a comprehensive festivals and events website
- Agree on a festival friendly events strategy and policy
- Establish and implement systems and procedure improvements so that event organisers are able to work with different council departments more efficiently and effectively.

The increasing pursuit of cultural strategies may be achieved through events and festivals. For example, the Newcastle Gateshead Initiative launched a year of events as the next phase of their culture[10] cultural programme. Built around four themed festivals focusing on music, rivers and the sea, sport and visual arts, the ambitious £12 million programme, 2005 Alive, was used to promote attractions and this region around the world and draw together a range of world-class and community based events. Alan Clarke, Chief Executive of One NorthEast, noted:

This programme of events offers something for everyone; whether they are a resident of the region or a visitor. The scope of the campaign, which will take in events ranging from the Hexham Abbey Music Festival, to the Seve Trophy; the Stockton Riverside Festival to the Great North Run also means the entire region will benefit from the increased marketing activity and give tourists a real reason to stay longer and explore more widely in the North East.

(Newcastle Gateshead Initiative, 2005)

The pursuit of broader outcomes from the conduct of individual events can also be observed. The 2002 Manchester Commonwealth Games, for example, was leveraged by the city's council as a catalyst for educational, skill-building and health improvement programs, as well as a means of creating awareness and understanding of the various communities (from Commonwealth countries) that live in the Manchester area (Carlsen and Millan, 2002). Environmental agenda can also be progressed through events. The London 2012 Olympics are seeking to be the One World Olympics by focusing on sustainability and continuing the positive initiatives started during Sydney 2000 with the 'Green Games'. Among the many achievements of the

Sydney Olympics in this regard was the clean-up of an area (Homebush Bay) that was highly contaminated with industrial waste. This area later became the main Olympic site (Harris and Huyskins, 2002). London 2012 Olympics have also committed to using the event for urban renewal purposes. Its new Olympic Park will act to transform the surrounding east London neighbourhoods, which include some of the poorest and most physically deprived areas of the UK, into a vibrant new urban city quarter (London Organising Committee for the Olympic Games, 2006).

MEASURING PROGRESS TOWARDS EVENT TOURISM GOALS

Whatever the event tourism goals set by a destination, specific benchmarks need to be established to assess progress towards those goals. For example, the Northern Ireland Events Company had the strategic task of supporting −two to three World Class events, −four to six International events and a number of smaller events (NIEC, 2005) − an events remit that has now moved to Northern Ireland Tourist Board.

Other areas of a purely tourist nature, where goals might be set and progress measured, include tourist income generated from events; changes in length of tourist stays; usage levels of tourism services (particularly accommodation); the extent of the geographic spread of tourism flowing from the conduct of events; the volume of event-related media coverage received by a destination and changes in destination market position/image resulting from the conduct of events.

CREATION OF AN EVENT TOURISM ORGANISATIONAL STRUCTURE

To progress a destination's event tourism goals, it is necessary to allocate responsibility for achieving these to one or more organisations. In the case of towns or regions, such responsibilities often lie with the same body charged with overall tourism development. In the case of cities, regions or countries, multiple organisations may be involved, such as bodies responsible for festivals, business tourism, major events and overall tourism development (Figure 4.3). In Belfast, for example, significant organisations with major roles in event tourism development include:

- The *Northern Ireland Tourist Board* (the national tourism organisation) has identified Excellent Events and Business Tourism as two of their winning themes with the potential to deliver competitive advantage for Northern Ireland as part of their tourism *Strategic Framework for Action 2004-2007*. They note for the Excellent Events theme, 'Research confirms that events are an effective tool for changing perceptions and attracting visitors − particularly off-season. Working with key strategic partners (such as the Northern Ireland Events

FIGURE 4.3 Major event tourism organisations

ORGANISATION TYPE	DESCRIPTION
Major event agencies	These bodies are commonly region or country based. Their roles vary depending on their charter. In some instances, they may be involved only in seeking to attract large-scale events through the bidding process. In other instances, they may also have responsibility for creating new events and developing existing events (see the EventScotland case study, pages 148–51). Those agencies with a broader charter may also be charged with overall responsibility for facilitating the development of event tourism in a destination.
Government tourism organisations	These organisations, at local, regional and national levels, can perform a variety of event tourism development roles. In some cases, they may be responsible for developing and implementing a whole destination event tourism strategy. They may also provide a range of services designed to support and develop the sector, such as promotional assistance, grants, the maintenance of event calendars, and the provision of advice and assistance in a variety of areas (for example, marketing, liaising with government departments on behalf of events to obtain relevant permissions/licences etc.).
Specialist event agencies	These often government sponsored bodies act to develop and support specific event forms within a destination. Convention and visitors bureaus, for example, act to promote the development of destinations as locations for meetings, incentives, exhibitions, conventions and special events.

Company and local councils), we will identify new opportunities to showcase excellence and plan investment requirements.' Further, for the Business Tourism theme they note, 'Business tourists spend on average three times more than leisure visitors, making this the most lucrative, high spend, high yield form of tourism.... Our focus here will be on conferences, meetings and incentive travel, to allow more potential for discretionary spend' (NITB, 2003, p. 8). In February 2010, the Department of Enterprise, Trade and Investment commenced a consultation process on a new tourism strategy to 2020, the draft of which continues to recognise the value of events, festivals and business events. Further, in April 2010, the Northern Ireland Tourist Board took over the government's events remit, formerly undertaken by the Northern Ireland Events Company.

- The *Belfast Visitor and Convention Bureau's mission* is, 'to establish Belfast as a world class visitor destination by increasing the contribution that tourism makes to the economy in a way that is customer-focused, delivers a quality solution in a cost-effective way, respects the environment, is acceptable to the local community and offers sustainable growth.' (BVCB, 2010)

- The *Belfast City Council Events Unit,* now amend to "now located within the Development Department at Belfast Waterfront & Ulster Hall and Events Team, has the aim to" 'promote and develop a high quality, sustainable, inclusive programme of public access events, in a safe enjoyable environment, in order to help raise the profile of Belfast in support of regeneration' (Belfast City Council, 2005).

Belfast City Council has also established a unit for promoting sports events in the city (Belfast City Council, 2010).

Type description

The existence of multiple bodies charged with event tourism development at a destination, creates the potential for a loss of focus on its overall event tourism goals as well as a less coordinated approach to their achievement, though this does not appear to have happened in Northern Ireland. For these reasons, there is a strong case for the creation of a single body, either within an existing organisation (see the profile of Event Denmark), or in the form of a new organisation (see the case study on EventScotland, p. 148), with a charter to coordinate, assist and, if necessary, 'push' organisations towards the achievement of broader, 'whole-of-destination' event tourism goals. In the absence of such a body, alternative mechanisms need to be developed to try to produce such an outcome. These mechanisms might include shared board memberships between key event tourism bodies; clearly defined organisational missions to prevent overlapping efforts; regular 'round table' meetings between key organisations and conditions on funding that require broader event tourism goals to be addressed. The Northern Ireland Tourist Board's support for Belfast and Derry Visitor and Convention Bureaus as key partners to help match the winning themes (in this case Business Tourism) with regions able to deliver them successfully, is an excellent example of this (NITB, 2003).

EVENT PROFILE: EVENT DENMARK

At the end of 2003, the Danish Government announced five new steps designed to improve cooperation between business – including the tourism industry – and the nation's cultural life. Following on from this announcement, the Secretary of Culture (Mr Brian Mikkelsen) and the Secretary of Business and Economy (Mr Bendt Bendtsen) agreed on a plan designed to professionalise the development, management, marketing and evaluation of international events in Denmark. In support of seeking such an outcome, they claimed that:

> The staging of many cultural and sports events is positive; it is profitable business, it supports the image of the region and the nation, and it is an asset for tourism, for the local society and commerce, as well as for the national economy (Blicher-Hansen, 2003).

Many other countries (for example, the Netherlands, Scotland and Australia) had made similar observations and subsequently created specialist event agencies as a way of focusing efforts on driving visitation through these means.

Responsibility for progressing this plan fell to the national Danish Tourist Board (DTB), which subsequently developed a strategy embracing both the cultural and tourism aspects of events and created a separate event division within the DTB called Event Denmark. In developing this strategy, the DTB acknowledged that international air travel would continue to grow despite terrorist acts. Additionally, it was believed that in Europe the number of short holiday breaks taken was likely to increase, fuelled in large measure by airline competition. Such competition was making a long weekend city break trip a possible and regular monthly 'habit'. The DTB also acknowledged that since many Europeans were already seasoned travellers, the value of simply promoting a destination might no longer be enough to attract visitors for a second or subsequent time. Events, therefore, and their associated one-off uniqueness had a significant role to play in driving future repeat visitor connection with people. This would be achieved through an association with an individual's cultural interests – whether a Magritte art exhibition in Paris, a unique production of Bizet's *Carmen i Sevilla* in Spain or a performance of Hans Christian Andersen's fairytales in authentic surroundings in Denmark.

With these thoughts in mind and with a desire to attract and develop more international events in Denmark, the DTB developed its event tourism strategy, giving responsibility for its implementation to the newly created Event Denmark. The following are the main aspects of this strategy:

- In the short term, generate a direct tourism effect – measured in terms of the number of visitors and their spending, level of immediate media exposure and awareness of the destination.
- In the medium term, support destination marketing in relation to the branding of Denmark. Branding themes that events could reinforce include the uniqueness of Danish culture (for example, music, ballet, food, design and architecture), sporting opportunities (for example, golf, football, sailing and cycling), historic traditions and the uniqueness of the natural environment.
- In the longer term, enhance the overall profile of Denmark as a unique visitor destination to position the country as a 'must go' destination, – one that is on the cutting edge in many areas and one that offers unique experiences.

In working through its strategy, the DTB sought to identify existing events that embraced its requirements. Key considerations were that such events needed to be:

- open to the public
- unique, not something that could easily be experienced elsewhere
- high quality in content
- appealing to an international audience
- strongly associated with Danish traditions and/or national values
- capable and open to marketing themselves internationally
- accessible via such means as online ticketing facilities
- able to use surplus tourism services (particularly accommodation) during periods of low seasonal demand
- managed in a professional manner
- designed to ensure that they were environmentally sustainable
- preferably conducted on an annual basis.

Once these key considerations were identified, Event Denmark would arrange for these events to be promoted to international markets in a variety of ways – for example, via inbound tour operators, specialised tour operators, overseas travel agents and international online event booking agencies. Additionally, Event Denmark would aid their promotional efforts in such markets by advising them on how to gain exposure on global event listing websites and by conducting public relations efforts through the DTB's overseas tourist offices and Denmark's embassy network around the world.

At the beginning of 2007, a review was conducted of Event Denmark, as it had been funded by a government grant for only three years. As a result of this review, Event Denmark's functions were absorbed into the Ministries of Culture, Business and Economy and Visit Denmark.

For further information about Event Denmark, please visit: www.eventdenmark.dk.
Based on Blichen-Hansen, 2007

DEVELOPMENT OF AN EVENT TOURISM STRATEGY

In terms of general strategic options available to a town, city, county, region or country's event tourism body, several possibilities can be identified. These strategies concern the development of existing events, bidding to attract existing (mobile) events and the creation of new events. These three broad strategic options are not mutually exclusive — for example, event tourism bodies in any one destination may employ composite strategies involving two or all three, of these options to achieve their destination's event tourism goals. Whatever strategy is selected, it needs to reflect the insights gained from the preceding situational analysis.

Existing event development

A range of possible approaches to using existing events to advance a destination's event tourism efforts can be identified. One option is to identify one or several events that have the capacity to be developed as major attractions for an area ('hallmark' events), with a view to using them as the foundation for image-building efforts. The previously cited examples of the Edinburgh Festivals are indicative of how events can be used in this way. A variant on this approach is to develop a single hallmark event that can then be supported by a range of similarly themed events. It may also be possible to merge existing smaller events to create one or several larger events or to incorporate smaller events into larger events to add to their uniqueness and subsequent tourism appeal. Yet another approach is to develop one or several hallmark events, while at the same time maintaining a mix of small-scale events scheduled throughout the year, as a means of generating year-long appeal for a destination.

Event bidding

Many events are mobile in the sense that they move regularly between different destinations. Some sporting events and many business events (for example, association/corporate conferences and exhibitions) fall into this category. Some types of event tourism organisations (namely many national or region-based major event agencies and convention and visitors bureaus) have been specifically established for the purpose of attracting new events to a destination via the bidding process. Bodies of this nature need to be able to identify events of this type — a task that convention and visitor bureaus often undertake by maintaining representatives in other regions and overseas and by directly communicating with meeting, incentive, and exhibition planners. To attract such mobile events, it is necessary to prepare a formal bid (Chapter 4) that makes a persuasive case as to why an event should be conducted in a specific destination. Before doing so, however, it is necessary to ensure that a sound match exists between the event being sought and an area's capacity to host it. In this regard, the Northern Ireland Conference Support Programme (NITB, 2010), administered through Northern Ireland Tourist Board and Belfast and Derry Visitor and Convention Bureaus, note the following criteria for support:

- A minimum of 250 out of state delegates staying in the area for 1 night or 500 bed nights generated from out of state markets.
- Demonstrate a high prestige value, i.e. media coverage, high profile speakers.
- Demonstrate that the conference would not come to Northern Ireland unless support is provided.
- An impact on local businesses by providing opportunities for developing industry links, showcasing local products and using local suppliers.
- The subject area of the conference should relate to local economic strategies or specific priority areas for Northern Ireland (http://www.investni.com/).
- Enhance Northern Ireland's international profile.
- Must promote business extenders/partner programmes to include the rural hinterland areas of Northern Ireland.
- Evidence of strict financial project management, cash flows and projected income will be required.

MeetEngland, based within VisitEngland, is the body responsible for promoting business visits and events in England. It can provide a range of support and services including event ideas, imagery, supplier lists and the latest news on venues and destinations (meetEngland, 2009a). In addition, it can provide support when bidding for conferences, including advice, introductions to venues and suppliers, letters of support from the relevant organisation or ministers where appropriate and a range of other practical assistance (meetEngland, 2009b). ConventionScotland, the business tourism unit of VisitScotland takes forward this role in Scotland.

New event creation

New event creation should be based around the activities and themes identified in a prior situational analysis as providing substantial scope for the development of tourist markets. New events should also be coordinated to bring maximum benefits to the region. The exact nature of the new events created, will vary with the strategic needs of each destination, with the range of generic options including active participant-based events, spectator-based sporting events, religious events, events with environmental/cultural/heritage themes, music-based events, special interest events and business events. As with the development of existing events, event tourism organisations need to be mindful of the need to ensure that new events are adequately resourced if they are to have the best chance of long-term survival. This being the case, it may be desirable for organisations involved in event tourism to limit their support to only a few new events.

General considerations in event tourism strategy selection

In making decisions about what event tourism strategy to pursue, it can be useful to think in terms of what 'portfolio' (or mix) of events (festivals, sporting competitions, business events, etc.) is likely to deliver the required benefits for a destination. A useful first step in this regard is to rate events (existing, new and events for which bids are proposed), — using available data and professional judgement — against established criteria. A simple, 1 (low) to 5 (high) rating system (see Figure 4.4) could be employed for this purpose. If appropriate, weightage could also be applied to each criterion.The final numeric value associated with each event would be a product of the extent to which it meets each criterion, multiplied by the importance of that criterion.

A useful approach to thinking about the 'mix' of events at a destination is to view them from a hierarchical perspective. Using this approach, events with high tourism value and the capacity to progress many of an event tourism body's goals would appear at the top, while those with lower tourism value and limited ability to progress the organisation's goals would be placed at the bottom. Such a hierarchy is commonly represented as a pyramid, as illustrated by the example of Events Tasmania's hierarchical model of events (Figure 4.5). By representing the current stock of events in this way, insights also emerge about 'gaps' in an area's current event portfolio and what possible roles an event tourism body may play in events at different locations within the hierarchy (see the note in Figure 4.5). This model also notes the varying roles that Events Tasmania will play in different types of event.

FIGURE 4.4 Event rating scale

EVENT NAME	CRITERION 1	CRITERION 2	CRITERION 3	CRITERION 4	TOTAL
A	1	2	3	4	10
B	1	4	5	5	15
C	2	4	3	1	10

FIGURE 4.5 Events Tasmania hierarchical model of events

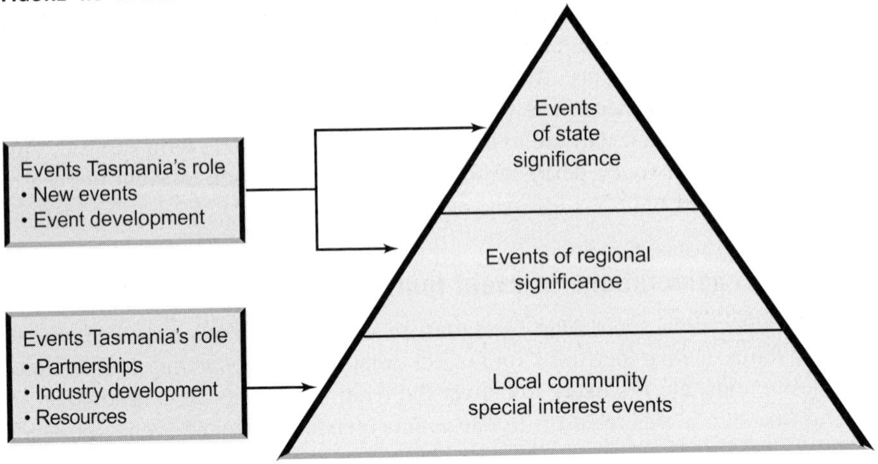

Support for events of state or regional significance includes funding programs, strategic planning and marketing, research and evaluation, targeted funds/grants, event experience design and event programming, resource leverage, and the facilitation of links. Support for local community special interest events includes regional event coordinators, forums and training, resources and website references and research.

(Source: Events Tasmania 2006a, p. 4.)

IMPLEMENTATION OF AN EVENT TOURISM STRATEGY

Once an event strategy has been selected, the next step is for the organisation(s) concerned to implement it by undertaking actions appropriate to its/their charter. This being the case, such actions may vary, from the provision of advice and marketing support up to the actual development and conduct of new events. The following section seeks to identify and broadly categorise the full range of actions that organisations directly involved in event tourism development might engage in.

Financial support

Financial support can be provided in the form of grants, sponsorship and equity.

Grants

Grants are a common means of providing support for events that are deemed to have tourism potential. EventScotland, for example, operates two programmes, focusing on international and national events. The International Events Programme provides funding from one up to three years to support existing events with potential to grow into world-class events; identifies and bids for events that could be staged in

Scotland and helps create events that can take place annually or bi-annually, with the requirement that EventScotland's funding must add value to the event (EventScotland, 2005). The National Events Programme, launched in 2009 to replace the Regional Events Programme, aims to help develop and support sporting and cultural events in towns and cities outside Glasgow and Edinburgh, by providing funds for additional elements to an event or new activities designed to help events to grow. EventScotland's National Events Programme provides grants between £4,000 and £25,000 to events that can:

- Generate economic benefits for specific regions of Scotland
- Attract visitors to specific regions of Scotland from other parts of the country
- Have confirmed financial support of appropriate local agencies
- Enhance the profile and appeal of the host region
- Inspire and involve local communities
- Demonstrate capacity to grow
- Are a good fit with local event strategies
- Display local passion and leadership
- Have a viable budget and realistic planning
- Demonstrate the opportunity to build legacy and sustainability
- Have measurable outcomes

(EventScotland, 2010)

An increasing number of other event support agencies that are emerging across the UK and elsewhere are beginning to have similar schemes in partnership with local councils and regional tourist agencies (for example, with funding from the Leader+ European funding, the Scottish Borders Tourist Board Events Innovation Scheme coordinated support for development of new festivals and events). Some local and city councils and tourist agencies have also moved to create event tourism grant schemes. For example, Wales Tourist Board/Visit Wales developed the Event Marketing Support Scheme (Event Marketing Support Unit, 2005); and the Destination Management Partnership Network Development Fund in Shropshire administers a small grants scheme for tourism related events (Shropshire Council, 2010). These grants are commonly based on a range of criteria, such as those in Figure 4.6.

Grants may also be provided by event tourism bodies in the form of seed money to allow new events to be established or for specific purposes, such as the conduct of a feasibility study to determine the viability of a proposed event. Grants can also be used as a form of incentive to conduct an event in a specific destination. Northern Ireland Tourist Board (NITB), for example, operates a major events grants scheme on behalf of the Northern Ireland Assembly, that supports events where the organisers have secured at least 50% of the funding, the event is likely to achieve significant media coverage in relevant markets and provide significant economic benefits to Northern Ireland (DCAL, 2009). Through Belfast City Council's Sports Events Unit, local government also provides funding support for organisations conducting major sports events that attract high numbers of visiting spectators and participants (Belfast City Council, 2010).

FIGURE 4.6 Common grant selection criteria employed by event tourism organisations

- Potential, or demonstrated capacity, to increase tourist visitation, yield per visitor and length of visitor stay
- Relationship between the event and area's overall tourism development strategy, including its branding efforts
- Level of evident community/local government/business/tourism industry support and associated capacity of event to grow and become self-funding
- Event's current tourism packaging efforts, or potential for tourism packaging
- Timing — does the event occur outside peak visitor seasons when tourism services are already being used at a high level?
- Level and quality of business, financial, operational and marketing planning in evidence
- Media value associated with the event
- Contribution to strategic social, cultural, environmental or economic outcomes sought by the destination
- Existence of processes designed to evaluate the event, particularly its tourism outcomes

Sponsorship

Some event tourism organisations and/or national/local governments act to directly sponsor events as a way of financially assisting them and/or as a way of leveraging the opportunity presented by the event to brand their destination through such means as signage and other visual identification, publicity and advertising. For example, regional development agencies (RDAs) were the principal sponsors of the 2004 Tour of Britain, with North West Development Agency, Yorkshire Forward, East Midlands Development Agency and Welsh Development Agency each investing £150,000 and London Development Agency investing £200,000, to sponsor the event when the race passed through their particular regions (SIRC, 2005).

Equity

To facilitate the conduct of an event, a tourism event organisation may act to directly invest in it. For example, the Manchester International Festival, a major new festival that was launched in 2007 is operated by Manchester International Festival Ltd. With an original budget of £5 million, this event is being funded with £2 million from Manchester City Council, with further funds coming from Northwest Development Agency and the private sector (Higgins, 2004).

Ownership

Some event tourism bodies develop and produce events to stimulate visitation to their destination. They act in this way for a variety of reasons — to ensure that their charter is progressed without the need to rely on the private sector; to address a lack of local event management expertise and to recognise an unwillingness in the private sector to take the financial risk involved in event creation and delivery. This may involve the establishment of a subsidiary company to own and operate the events on the organisation's behalf. For example, Liverpool Culture Company was set up by Liverpool City Council to deliver the European Capital of Culture 2008, including events and the cultural programme before during and after 2008 (Liverpool Culture Company, 2005a). Other event tourism and destination marketing organisations have also acted to establish and develop new events, including Northern Ireland Events Company, EventScotland and NewcastleGateshead.

Bid development and bid support services

As previously noted, bidding is the major focus of some forms of event tourism organisations. Such organisations act to research, develop and make bids, and/or work with bidding bodies (such as sporting bodies or professional associations) to facilitate the making of a bid. Once a bid is won, however, the event tourism organisation commonly plays little, if any, further role other than perhaps assisting to stimulate event attendance or to assist with the creation of an organising committee. Occasionally, however, these bodies will assist with the management and operations of the events they attract.

Event sector development services

Event sector development services include research, training and education and the establishment of partnerships and networks.

Research

Some tourism event organisations commission or undertake research on a range of event-related matters as a way of gaining information that will aid the development of individual events or the sector in general. Matters explored include trends in event visitor markets, developments in competitor destinations, visitor perceptions of the quality of event experiences (particularly those supported by the event organisation concerned), event sector stakeholder viewpoints, event economic impacts, and overall sector management practices. Regarding this last point, research can be insightful in assisting event agencies to develop programs designed to build the events sector. Evidence for this can be found in Goh's (2003) study, which highlighted weaknesses in this area in the context of Irish festivals, specifically:

- 47% of festivals have no data on their audiences
- 59% of festivals do not provide training for their volunteers
- 23% of festivals have no presence on the world wide web
- 58% of festivals have no strategic plan.

Training and education

To promote best practice and continuous improvement and by doing so assist in creating events that are sustainable in the longer term, some event tourism organisations undertake — or commission outside bodies to undertake — training in areas such as event project management, event marketing and general industry best practice. Some also maintain a resource base (electronic and/or print based) on which event organisers can draw for educational/training purposes, while some conduct industry events such as conferences, to facilitate the sharing of event industry-specific knowledge.

Partnerships and networks

A range of opportunities exist for event tourism organisations to establish partnerships and networks both within the events sector and between the events sector and outside bodies. The grants process, for example, can be used to encourage linkages with organisations that have the potential to enhance the attractiveness of events to visitor markets or provide access to these markets. This can be done by explicitly favouring applications that demonstrate links with, for example, tourism bodies and cultural institutions, such as museums, heritage organisations, art galleries and community arts organisations. Other ways in which such links can be established include the purposeful arranging of formal and informal meetings and functions involving members of the events industry, tourism organisations and the general business community. Once networks are established, they can serve a variety of purposes — for example, facilitating the sharing of information and expertise, expanding access to sponsorship opportunities and developing partnerships (both within and external to the event sector) that will assist in the development of tourist markets.

Event tourism organisations may also find they have much to gain by communicating their strategies to a range of public and private sector organisations, thus encouraging dialogue that may lead to the identification of opportunities to progress a common agenda. Government departments associated with the arts, sport and regional development, for example, may all see opportunities to further their goals through an association with one or more event tourism bodies.

Coordination

Event tourism bodies can play a range of coordinating roles. These roles include developing an event calendar to reduce event clashes (see Figure 4.3 on page 134) and providing a 'one-stop shop' at which event organisers can obtain relevant permissions and clarify government policies and procedures of relevance. Given that a range of government bodies may be involved in the delivery of any one event, event tourism organisations can also act to establish coordination and consultation protocols between different government departments and agencies and assist events to 'navigate' their way through legislative and compliance issues. For example, the London

Borough of Hammersmith and Fulham (see chapter 2 for a detailed discussion of its events strategy) in acknowledgement of this function for the development of its events sector, has proposed a range of actions as part of its events strategy:

- Conduct an annual review of events based on informal and formal feedback and neighbourhood consultations.
- Establish the H&F Events Advisory Group to oversee and review large scale events.
- Put in place a policy and selection criteria for hiring out Borough venues for events.
- Improve and extend the use of Council media and other communication channels, including digital, to promote Borough events and venues.
- Signpost to guidelines and standardised procedures for local residents wanting to run successful events

(Hammersmith and Fulham Council, 2009, pp. 4–5).

Event/destination promotion services

To assist organisations (such as sporting bodies and professional associations) in their efforts to stimulate market interest in their events, event tourism organisations, depending on their charter, may provide a range of assistance in the marketing area. Such assistance may extend from the provision of marketing collateral to the creation of comprehensive supporting promotional plans. Such collateral may include brochure shells, giveaways, videos highlighting destination attractions, event facilities and services, and posters. Additionally, such organisations may seek to facilitate the conduct of events by, for example:

- providing information to organisations seeking to conduct events on a destination's event-related facilities and services
- hosting familiarisation tours and site visits (by event organising committees)
- assisting with the preparation of event programs and pre- and post-event tours
- acting as a liaison between government and civic authorities
- assisting in stimulating attendance at events via public relations activities and direct mail.

In the UK context it is noteworthy that VisitBritain (the government statutory authority responsible for international tourism marketing) has established a separate body (eventBritain) to market the UK as a major events destination. Among its aims to achieve its strategy, VisitBritain, as part of its promotional role in relation to business visits and events, seeks to "Improve Britain's ranking as a destination for business and sporting visits and events" and to "maximize the economic benefits for tourism across the UK" through using London 2012 as a platform for securing more events for Britain (VisitBritain, 2010, pp. 9-10). To progress these aims, VisitBritain has developed promotional material for the business visits and events, including the Meeting Britain newsletter, launching EventBritain (www. eventbritain.org) representing business visits and events at major international trade shows and is an active member of the Business Visits & Events Partnership (www.businessvisitsandeventspartnership.com), the organization drawing together the national tourism boards, and main industry associations.

Others

Other roles that event tourism organisations may play include: assisting in the development of business, marketing and risk management plans; providing advice on the negotiation of television rights and merchandising strategies and lobbying on behalf of the sector on matters relating to new infrastructure development.

EVALUATION OF AN EVENT TOURISM STRATEGY

Evaluation is fundamental to the success of any strategy. At the destination level, the broad goals that have been set for event tourism and the objectives associated with those goals, will form the basis of any evaluation that takes place. The collection and interpretation of information is central to this process, with data on visitor flows associated with event tourism being of particular importance. In the context of business tourism in the United Kingdom, for example, data is available from a variety of sources, including STAR UK (drawing together data from VisitBritain and other national tourism bodies), regional tourism agencies/boards and the Business Tourism Partnership. International bodies, such as the International Congress and Convention Association (ICCA), Union of International Associations (UIA) and the Meetings Professionals International (MPI) Foundation also conduct research that relates to the UK's comparative performance in this area. ICCA (2009), for example, provides the following useful data on the UK's recent business tourism performance:

- In terms of association meetings per country, the United Kingdom is fifth in the global rankings in 2008, after occupying 4th position in 2007. The USA is ranked number one, followed by Germany, Spain, France and the United Kingdom — fifth in terms of the number of association meetings held in 2008.
- In terms of market share by continent, Europe remains number one with 55.4% of the market, compared to all other regions. Asia and the Middle East's market share rose from 16% in 2003 to 18.6% in 2008.
- In terms of international association meetings per city, the market is led jointly by Vienna and Paris, followed by Barcelona, Singapore and Berlin. London was in 19th position in the rankings in 2008 with 68 meetings.

In addition to whole-of-destination assessments of event tourism performance in the context of specific types of event or events in general, each organisation involved in an area's event tourism development should have its own goals. To conform to the basic model of event tourism strategic planning used in this chapter, these goals should link directly to the destination's overall event tourism goals. Such individual assessments should also serve to 'build' towards an overall picture of a destination's event tourism performance, which can then be used to form the basis for future strategic decisions regarding event tourism development.

TOURISM EVENTS AND REGIONAL DEVELOPMENT

While the focus of discussion regarding event tourism is often on cities, regions or countries, many regions and towns have acknowledged the benefits that can potentially flow from event tourism and have actively sought to engage in it. Local government in many regional areas is actively showing support for such efforts, being keen for communities to reap the economic and other benefits associated with events. Magherafelt District Council, for example, have community, sport and tourism event grants (Magherafelt District Council, 2010), with a grant system reflected throughout much of Northern Ireland.

SUMMARY

For destinations ranging in size from small towns to countries, event tourism is increasingly becoming a key aspect of their overall tourism development efforts. In this chapter, a basic event tourism strategic planning model has been proposed, that seeks to bring a measure of structure and discipline to this process. This model is based on an understanding of both perspectives — that of event tourism stakeholders and that of a destination's overall tourism goals and strategy. The first step in the model is a detailed situational analysis, which leads to the establishment of event tourism goals. These goals are then progressed through an organisational structure created for this purpose. Ideally, such a structure would involve the establishment of a single organisation with responsibility for the area or the allocation of such responsibility to an existing body. In the absence of such a body, other options — such as regular meetings between key organisations in the area — can be used with similar intent. Once a structure is in place, strategic options need to be considered. Such options centre on using existing events, bidding and/or the creation of new events.

   In pursuit of the selected strategy, a destination may engage in a range of actions including the provision of financial support, promotional assistance and general efforts directed at sector development. How successful these practices are in progressing a destination's event tourism strategy and its associated goals needs to be assessed at both the destination level and the level of those organisations with a major input into the event tourism development process. Information gained from this process can then be used to refine future event tourism development efforts.

QUESTIONS

1. Discuss the value of having a clear understanding of a destination's overall tourism strategy before embarking on the process of creating an event tourism strategy.

2. List and discuss three goals that a destination may seek to progress through the development of an event tourism strategy.

3. What types of non-tourism goals might a destination seek to achieve by expanding its focus on event tourism?

4. In the absence of a single body with responsibility for directing a destination's event tourism efforts, what approaches might be used to ensure a coordinated response to this task?

5. Briefly discuss the three broad strategic options available to destinations seeking to expand visitation through the use of events.

6. Briefly explain the strategic value to destinations of establishing objective criteria upon which to rate their events.

7. What is meant by the term 'destination event portfolio'? What value does this concept have from an event tourism strategy perspective?

8. What types of action might bodies with a major involvement in event tourism consider taking to develop the event sector in their destination?

9. Briefly discuss how events can play a role in branding a destination.

10. Draw a basic event tourism strategic planning model. Briefly describe each step in this model.

11. Discuss the various forms that grants from event tourism bodies can take.

CASE STUDY: EVENTSCOTLAND

Scotland's first strategy, published in 2002, brought EventScotland into existence and has guided the work of the national events agency through its first five years. In that time our events industry has gone from strength to strength and Scotland's portfolio of events now extends to 2014, when both the Commonwealth Games and The Ryder Cup will be staged in our country. It is therefore the right time to extend our vision into the next decade. 'The Perfect Stage' takes account of the new and emerging opportunities for Scotland as a leading destination for major events and as the perfect stage for events of all sizes. It also describes how events can help Scotland rise to some of the challenges it faces in an increasingly competitive global economy. The following extract explains the strategy's background, aims and role of EventScotland in this strategy.

Our 2020 Vision for Scotland
Scotland established as the perfect stage for events.

Our Mission to Deliver This Vision

To develop a portfolio of events that delivers impact and international profile for Scotland.

Strategy for Scotland

Our strategy for delivering the vision and fulfilling our mission is to utilise and develop the assets that Scotland has that make it 'The Perfect Stage' for sporting and cultural events:

- Our cultural identity and heritage
- Our people
- Our natural environment
- Our built facilities
- Our signature events

It is also envisaged that partner organisations and those involved in staging, organising, developing and funding events will use this strategy as an underpinning principle to their own strategies, plans and activities.

Role of EventScotland

Overall Role. EventScotland aims to influence, lead, coordinate, support and bring together people and organisations in order to deliver this events strategy. EventScotland is the lead agency for public sector engagement and investment in events. This lead role is at a national strategy and policy level while other agencies will provide leadership on a geographical or event sector basis.

Priorities. EventScotland will invest the budget allocated by Scottish Government to develop a portfolio of events and as overriding measures will seek:

- A return on investment through estimated economic impact of at least 8:1
- A media index, using its own assessment, of 8, 9 or 10/10 for events where media exposure is the main driver for investment
- A clearly demonstrated level of partners funding for events of at least 1:1

EventScotland will invest in events relative to the levels of all seven of the identified impacts they can bring; however, there will be a greater emphasis on the economic and media benefits in order to reflect the core measures above.

The portfolio of events supported by EventScotland will be those of national and international significance, which will be complemented by other events supported at local level.

Principles. EventScotland works to three core principles which guide all work:

1. Working in partnership both with event organisers and deliverers and with other funding partners as EventScotland is not a deliverer of events and will always seek at least one funding partner.
2. National significance of work undertaken. This has two important consequences. First, support and investment will only be directed to events which have a national significance in their ability to deliver the seven impacts. Second, EventScotland will aim to support events in every local authority area over each four-year period, ensuring that the benefit reaches all of Scotland.
3. Additionality brought by the input of EventScotland. This could be in terms of adding specific value to an event by funding activity which has not taken place previously or could be using funding to secure an event which would not otherwise come to Scotland.

Operational Functions. EventScotland leads work on events in Scotland by:

- Devising and implementing strategy.
- Developing and sharing methodology for measurement.
- Gathering and sharing best practice examples and information.

Continued

CASE STUDY: EVENTSCOTLAND—*CONT'D*

- Assessing, evaluating and publicising the impact of events on other key policy areas.
- Building its international reputation and expertise in relation to events.
- Capitalising on the opportunities presented by Homecoming Scotland 2009 and the Commonwealth Games and The Ryder Cup in 2014, including the development of the new and upgraded facilities.
- Co-ordinating public sector support which is being invested to achieve differing outcomes.
- Identifying legacy opportunities from events and taking action to ensure that resource commitment is made to planning and maximising these legacies.
- Using staff expertise to assess which events will be supported and at what levels.
- Monitoring and evaluating all events supported.
- Working with partners to ensure high quality delivery.

Operational Practice. For every event supported or considered for support, EventScotland will conduct a thorough assessment, including an evaluation of how the event could deliver against the seven impact areas. This will always include a pre-event economic impact assessment and the attribution of a media index to an event. These figures will be reported annually against the portfolio of events supported.

EventScotland will operate programmes of support to deliver against 'The Perfect Stage'. The range and scope of the programmes operated will be regularly reviewed and adjusted to ensure they maximise delivery against the desired impacts. EventScotland will put details of current programmes at any given time on its website. Programmes will always be designed to engage partners in delivering maximum impact.

EventScotland will seek and co-ordinate input from all other public agencies, including local authorities. EventScotland will also look to proactively engage the business community in events. This may involve working with Chambers of Commerce or, where these do not exist, other relevant business-focused groups to fully engage Scottish businesses. The support of this sector is vital to the economic success of events. Many local authorities can also play a key role in supporting this work.

EventScotland will not normally consider support for conferences; the Business Tourism Unit at VisitScotland already covers this function. Exhibitions may be considered as events, but will be required to demonstrate the potential to deliver the same level of impact as other supported events.

Sports Events. Sports events are classified by EventScotland in three categories:

1. Fixed events which happen annually at the same location in perpetuity.
2. Recurring events which happen annually at the same location for a number of years.
3. One-off events which are usually bid for and brought in for a single staging.

EventScotland's approach will be to balance the three different categories, ensuring there is a strong base portfolio of fixed and recurring events, while pursuing opportunities to secure one-off events. EventScotland will look to grow and provide additionality to fixed events, seek to retain and develop recurring events and research, seek and influence the bidding for and allocation of one-off events which will deliver impacts for Scotland. These one-off events must fit with the priorities of the sport at UK and Scottish levels, be winnable and be able to be delivered in our built or natural facilities with resources currently or potentially available.

Sports events being targeted are those that fit with the strategy outlined in section one. EventScotland will work closely with UK Sport as many of the one-off events which will be sought will be bid for by UK governing bodies. This work will align priorities and ensure that, wherever possible, events which are being sought for Scotland are identified as such in UK-level plans.

Cultural Events. Cultural events are in the main either fixed or recurring. There are very few one-off cultural events available to be attracted or bid for in the international market. This necessitates a different approach to supporting and setting objectives for cultural events.

EventScotland will treat many fixed cultural events in the same way as sports events by looking to provide additionality and help them grow. Some events will be specifically identified as having significant growth potential and where the ambition to achieve this growth is shared by event organisers and other partners a longtermand proactive approach will be taken by EventScotland.

EventScotland will also seek to engage with existing cultural events to identify areas where EventScotland could provide additionality and also to identify and possibly exploit growth potential.

EventScotland will also research and proactively seek cultural events which can be attracted to Scotland or bid for.

Summary of Approach

In both cases EventScotland views the role of gathering international intelligence and proactively engaging with international event rights holders prior to any bidding processes as a key role for a national events agency. The diagram below represents EventScotland's role in regard to the three types of event.

EventScotland recognises the needs of partners for more training and development opportunities for those working in the events industry and will take a proactive role in this. EventScotland will also seek to provide opportunities for networking and exchanges between those involved in events. This will include a national events conference.

EventScotland will produce an annual report which will lay out in greater detail its retrospective operation, including details of events supported, case studies and economic impacts.

For further information about EventScotland and Scotland 'The Perfect Stage', please visit: www.eventscotland.org.

Extract from EventScotland (2009). Reproduced with permission of EventScotland.

Questions

1. What was the rationale for the establishment of EventScotland by the Scottish Government?
2. Briefly describe the key roles that EventScotland is charged with performing.
3. Briefly discuss how EventScotland will determine which events it will support.
4. What criteria would you use to measure success of an organisation such as EventScotland? Based on your criteria, how does EventScotland compare? Conduct research to obtain facts and figures to support your answer.

CASE STUDY: THE NOTTING HILL CARNIVAL

The Notting Hill Carnival takes place annually in the streets of Notting Hill, an area in West London. The carnival began in 1964 and provided an opportunity for West Indians to celebrate and commemorate their ancestors' 'freedom from slavery' which is celebrated every year in all parts of the Caribbean.

The first carnival had not been planned as a carnival. In the early 1960s in Notting Hill, there was an event called the Notting Hill Festival, which was a low-key street celebration attended by approximately 200 people, mostly children. In 1964 a Notting Hill social worker, Rhaune Laslett, being aware of the growing number of West Indian children in the area who were not taking part in the festival, decided to add some West Indian culture to the festival as an attraction. She invited a steel band, which was normally present at the Colherne pub in Earls Court, to play at the festival.

Continued

CASE STUDY: THE NOTTING HILL CARNIVAL—*CONT'D*

When the steel band came onto the streets of Notting Hill, nearly every West Indian in the area, adults as well as children, came onto the streets and began to follow the steel band in a processional manner as they did back home, particularly in Trinidad the birthplace of steelpan, playing whatever makeshift instruments (dustbin lids, bottle and spoon, comb and paper) they could lay their hands on.

After that first event, the steel band became a feature of the Notting Hill Festival and the reputation of the festival grew as the only event at which West Indian culture was celebrated. Between 1964 and 1974, no more than 3,000 people attended the festival, which by then, had a change in leadership and became exclusively a forum for West Indian culture, led by West Indians. However, the event was not widely known amongst West Indians from different communities across London. The revellers tended to be exclusively Trinidadian because of the dominance of the steelpan music and its size was due to word-of-mouth transference of information within that community.

The first attempt to market the carnival on a London-wide scale came in 1975 with the advent of a new radio station in London, Capital Radio. That station had a community slot as part of its programming and it announced the fact that there was a West Indian carnival being held in Notting Hill. One hundred and fifty thousand West Indians originating from many different islands in the West Indies – and not just Trinidad – turned up. A wider range of West Indian culture was present; most notably the influence of the Jamaican Sound Systems brought a more contemporary edge to the carnival. Black music was about to invade the English pop charts with Roots, Reggae and the Tamla Motown hits. The Sound Systems played that type of black music and so attracted younger black people to the carnival; and they immediately identified with the ethos of the celebration.

In 1976, 250,000 young black people attended the carnival and the authorities, without warning, decided to stop the event and sent in several thousand police officers. A riot ensued as the young people protested against the suppression of the event, with numerous casualties on both sides. This riot was the first public acknowledgement of the ownership of the event by the West Indian community – the riot united the West Indian community in appreciation of their history and in celebration of their ancestors' 'freedom from slavery'. The riot characterised the event in the eyes of the press and the British public as a violent affair and brought the Notting Hill Carnival to the attention of the press and, so, the world.

Until 2002, the Notting Hill Carnival was organised by the Notting Hill Carnival Trust, a registered charity established some ten years previously, to pursue the development of the carnival and the safety of the people that were in attendance. In 2003 a new organisation, London Notting Hill Carnival Limited was established to organise the carnival. The organisation is assisted by the Metropolitan Police Service, the Royal Borough of Kensington and Chelsea, the City of Westminster, London Underground Limited, the St John Ambulance Service, the London Fire and Civil Defence Authority and the London Ambulance Service.

Today, the Notting Hill Carnival boasts an audience of up to 1.5 million people over the August Bank Holiday Sunday and Monday. It is probably the best known and one of the biggest carnivals in the world, with numerous applications from other carnivals to participate in the event. The carnival has a strong multicultural character and is known for its capacity to cater for all age groups, for the creativity of the designers, artists and communities that create the hugely attractive costumes and the range of music available from top DJs and groups free of charge; hence its attractiveness to young people. Each year an increasing number of visitors and participants from Europe are attracted to the carnival.

The Notting Hill Carnival comprises a range of events that take place over a two-week carnival season:

- *Carnival Press Launch*: two hundred members of the press are invited to the Carnival Press Launch to get a taste of carnival culture and be positively cultivated by the carnival community.
- *Carnival Costume Gala*: this takes place the weekend before the carnival and is the event where the artistry of the Kings, Queens, Male Individuals and Female Individuals are judged. Two hundred 'costumes' perform individually, portraying their themes through costume design and performance. The event is usually held at the Olympia Exhibition Centre and boasts an audience of 500 people.
- *The Calypso Monarch Competition*: this takes place on the Friday of the carnival weekend where ten Calypsonians compete for the title of Calypso Monarch. They compose and sing their own calypsos, which must be based on contemporary issues of politics and life generally.
- *The Steelbands Panorama*: this takes place the evening before the carnival procession and ten steel bands compete for the title of Champions of Steel. Each steel band has up to 100 players who perform innovative musical arrangements of the calypsos of the season. It boasts an audience of 7,000 people.
- *The Two Days of the Carnival*: this comprises a street procession on both days, at which costumes, steel bands, mobile and static sound systems perform in the streets to commemorate the 'freedom to walk the streets' which their ancestors had been denied during the period of slavery. The audience, 'Carnival Revellers', are encouraged to join the procession. The emphasis is on the right of each individual to be part of the celebrations, '*Every spectator is a participant*'.

It would appear that the public has more than just an understanding of the event and identifies with its ethos, ensuring its assimilation into mainstream culture. The carnival has become more than just an event – it has become a way of life. The Notting Hill Carnival is now a major well-publicised event that is important to society on many different levels. While its economic impact has been recently quantified at around £93 million by a study undertaken for London Development Agency (2003) – its societal impact through education and the facilitation of better racial harmony is probably the most valuable outcome of its marketing strategies.

Given the recognised value and role of Notting Hill Carnival, together with its ability to attract a significant number of tourists to the region and the potential impacts and safety issues caused by this number of people, the Mayor of London commissioned a study to evaluate the management, funding and safety of the event (Mayor's Carnival Review Group, 2004), and to make strategic recommendations for the future. The main recommendations from the study were:

- Understanding and documenting the carnival: increase awareness and appreciation of the history of the carnival and develop carnival archives to document this.
- Listening to stakeholders' competing perspectives: draw in the views and build on the support of carnival stakeholders including residents, the Arts Council, Notting Hill Mas Band Association, artistic arenas.
- Achieving an effective communications strategy: drive the news agenda, revise and adopt the Carnival Code for communicating key safety messages, make greater use of directional signage.
- Stewarding and policing: ensure a suitably qualified and sustainable group of stewards to ensure public and participant safety; develop a multi-agency safety group and provide support for St Johns Ambulance.
- Event management: robust event planning and management framework to be adopted; contracts to be introduced for participants to comply with staging and performance protocols.

Continued

CASE STUDY: THE NOTTING HILL CARNIVAL—*CONT'D*

- Waste management and recycling: develop a sustainable carnival waste management and recycling strategy.
- Public safety responsibility and accountability: consider changes to the route and an assessment of the entertainment arena; consider, formalise and document the roles and responsibilities of the organisations involved (for example, local authorities, police); require greater accountability and transparency and consider the role of the Health & Safety Executive.
- Carnival management and leadership: leadership development programmes; limitations on length of service on board; broadening of membership; the inclusion of independent legal, financial, management, marketing, public safety and business personnel with professional skills and experience; the drawing of a distinction between the development of London's carnival industry and event planning and the management and delivery of the Notting Hill Carnival.
- The social, cultural and community value of carnival: study required into educational benefits, including the mapping of carnival arts and education initiatives; good practice in carnival and carnival arts development; contribution of the carnival to development of communication and life skills; the appointment of a Carnival Arts Education Officer; the creation of a Carnival Arts Education network and a potential London Carnival Schools Competition.
- The business of carnival-funding, finance and economic development: potential for the establishment of a Centre for Carnival Arts and Enterprise as a centre for excellence; LDA to consider implementing a Carnival Economic Development Strategy to ensure community benefits from impacts identified in study; the development of a carnival music policy and strategy and a Caribbean-cuisine food and drink strategy.
- Future vision – the way forward: embrace Notting Hill Carnival and support it politically and financially; create a strategic role for Mayor of London, implement London Carnival Development Plan to act as a catalyst for the London carnival industry and focus on priority areas of:

  - Strategic management and leadership
  - Community outreach and development
  - Event operation and management
  - Fundraising and finance
  - Sustainable economic development
  - Marketing, branding and promotion (Mayor's Carnival Review Group, 2004, pp. 20-28)

For further details about Notting Hill Carnival, please visit www.nottinghillcarnival.biz.
Source: adapted from Holder (2001).

Questions

1. The above provides an insight into the development of the Notting Hill Carnival, which has led to the culture and ethos of the event as it appears today. What are the main features of the Notting Hill Carnival? How has history influenced these?
2. Who are the stakeholders in the Notting Hill Carnival? What role do they play?
3. In evaluating the carnival, what are the long-term benefits for London and the host community?
4. How has London used the Notting Hill Carnival to create an identity for the area?
5. The above identified the main recommendations of the Mayor's Carnival Review Group. What implications do the recommendations have on the future of the carnival? Investigate what changes have been made as a result of these recommendations.
6. The case demonstrates the interest of the Mayor of London and other agencies in events. Why do politicians and local authorities taken an interest in the success of Notting Hill Carnival?

Sustainable development and events

5

LEARNING OBJECTIVES

After studying this chapter, you should be able to:

- define the term 'sustainable development'
- discuss key factors that are serving to 'push' events to become more economically, socially and environmentally sustainable
- discuss strategies and practical responses that events have, and can, employ in their efforts to become more sustainable
- source information concerning the management of sustainable events

INTRODUCTION

The concept of sustainable development, 'development that meets the needs of the present without compromising the ability of future generations to meet their own needs' (World Commission on Environment and Development, 1987), emerged in the 1970s and 1980s. Its origins lay in concerns within industrialised nations that patterns of production and consumption were not sustainable in terms of the earth's capacity to support them (Council of the European Union, 2006). Today, the challenge posed by the concept of sustainable development represents, as Kofi Annan, (the immediate past) Secretary of the United Nations, noted, 'our biggest challenge in this new century' (UNESCO, 2005, p. 9).

Events, like most other areas of human endeavour, have increasingly responded to the challenges posed by sustainable development. Indeed, some events, such as the many environment-based festivals and expos, along with a number of large-scale sports events, have themselves become a vehicle for progressing their respective host community's efforts at sustainable development. Over recent years, the events industry has started greening events and festivals and has begun to embrace sustainability issues more broadly, resulting in the growth of sustainable events management and the development and introduction of a dedicated British Standard, BS8901. Research and published best practice are also beginning to emerge to underpin developments in the field and provide best practice approaches, for example, Raj and Musgrave (eds., 2009) explore the foundations of sustainable events through an exploration of their environmental, social and economic impacts and provide case studies of approaches taken, while Jones (2010) provides more detailed practical guidance with examples from leading events and festivals.

Events Management. DOI: 10.1016/B978-1-85617-818-1.10005-2

In this chapter, those forces that have pushed events to engage with the concept of sustainable development are overviewed, along with the events industry's responses to these forces. Examples, including case studies, of both small- and large-scale events that exemplify the matters covered in this chapter are also provided.

FORCES INFLUENCING THE 'GREENING' OF EVENTS

As time moves on, the terms "green events" and "green meetings" have entered the events industry to generally refer to the minimisation of negative environmental impacts of events, including carbon reduction, waste reduction, recycling and other initiatives that event managers can implement. The term also has links to other concerns and initiatives that have grown in prominence within the events industry over recent years, including sustainability, corporate social responsibility and sustainable event management. There are a number of forces influencing the greening of events — some of which are discussed in this section.

Government adoption of the principles of sustainable development

The principles of sustainable development (SD) were adopted by 182 governments on the signing of the Agenda 21 document at the conclusion of the Earth Summit in Rio de Janeiro in 1992. While not legally binding, the adopted principles carry 'a strong moral obligation to ensure their full implementation' (United Nations, 1992, p. 3). Areas covered by this document included solid waste management; the protection of the atmosphere; the protection of the quality and supply of freshwater resources and environmentally sound management of toxic chemicals. Within the UK, in 2006 the government established the Sustainable Development Commission (SDC) as an independent advisory body, which includes a watchdog role, to monitor and report 'Government's performance on sustainable development' (SDC, 2010).

As there is still relatively little published material on the extent to which events of various types have engaged with the principles of SD, it is difficult to be precise about the impact of these principles in the events area in general. Nonetheless, those organisations involved in the creation and conduct of events in signatory countries would be affected by the efforts of their governments (at all levels) to pursue their responsibilities under this agreement. Indeed, the actions by many events in recent years to minimise their use of water, energy and materials can reasonably be argued to be linked, at least in part, to such efforts.

While it is difficult to generalise about how events have approached the challenges posed by the concept of SD, it can nonetheless be observed that a number of individual events have sought to engage directly with it. Of particular note in this regard are recent deliveries of major sports events, the FIFA World Cup, the Commonwealth Games and the Olympic Games. Among the various initiatives in evidence at these events were efforts to reduce or offset greenhouse gases. This has been done by such means as tree planting, use of 'green' energy and building design and the implementation of public transport strategies. With regard to the last point, a number of events both large and small, are now engaging with a range of initiatives designed to encourage communities to use more sustainable modes of transport. The Government Office for the South West (2010) includes reference to transport in various sections of their *Greener Events Guide and Checklist* to demonstrate the importance of this aspect of organising events, as does the Department for Environment, Food and Rural Affairs' (DEFRA, 2007) *Sustainable Events Guide* and Manchester City Council's (2006) *A Guide to Greening Your Event.*

The Olympic Games and sustainable development

Of the major events that take place internationally, it is the Olympic Games (summer and winter) that, arguably, has the most developed approach to the challenges SD poses. This situation is perhaps not surprising given the scale of this event and its associated potential for negative environmental impacts. In seeking insights into how events might respond to SD, it is useful then to overview how the Olympic Games' engagement with SD (flowing from broader international efforts in this area) has evolved over time, the practices that its 'owner' (the International Olympic Committee) employs in seeking to engage with SD and some of the issues it faces in trying to obtain worthwhile SD outcomes in its host cities/countries.

The International Olympic Committee (IOC) was initially slow to acknowledge the need to embrace environmental considerations in the planning and delivery of the summer and winter Olympic Games. Almost 20 years went by from the time (1974) the citizens of Denver, Colorado rejected (by referendum) on environmental grounds, the IOC's offer to conduct the Winter Olympic Games (Lenskyj, 1998, p. 343), well before the environment began to feature as a significant consideration in Games planning and delivery. The first major step in this direction was the signing of the Earth Pledge in 1992. This document emerged out of the Earth Summit in Rio de Janeiro in 1992 and was signed at the Games of that same year (XXV Olympiad in Barcelona, Spain) by all International Sporting Federations, National Olympic Committees and the IOC (Oittinen, 2003). It required that signatories both acknowledge the importance of the environment to humanity's future and committed them to act in ways that would protect it (Planet Drum, 2004a).

The next major environmental step by the IOC occurred after, what had been until that point, the most environmentally friendly Olympic Games, the Winter Games in Lillehammer, Norway, in 1994. It involved the signing by the IOC of a cooperation agreement with the United Nations Environment Programme (UNEP) designed to facilitate the leveraging of future Games for environmental awareness-raising and educational purposes (UNEP, 2004). Under this agreement, the IOC's responsibilities extended to the:

- conduct of regional seminars with the intent of familiarising National Olympic Committees (NOCs) with environmental matters. Additionally, the NOCs were to be encouraged to create their own sport and environment commissions

- creation of specialist and volunteer networks, comprising high-profile sports people to serve as models for responsible conduct vis-a-vis the environment.

(IOC, 2004a, p. 1)

In later years this relationship progressed to the provision of assistance to bidding cities in completing the environmental aspect of their bid documents and memoranda of understanding between the UNEP and Olympic host cities, commencing with Athens in 2004 (G-ForSE, 2004). It should be noted that the Olympics, while the first, is not the only event that the UNEP has signed agreements with. The UNEP worked with the recent 2006 FIFA World Cup, for example, to assist it in its efforts at integrating environmental considerations into its planning and projects (FIFA, 2006; UNEP, 2004, 2006).

The IOC's progress down the path of sustainable development continued with its Centennial Olympic Congress in 1994. At this meeting the environment was proposed as the 'third pillar' of the Olympic Movement — the others being sport and culture'. The topic 'environment and sport' was discussed in a dedicated conference session. This session generated five conclusions and recommendations that subsequently have impacted directly, or indirectly, on the involvement of the Olympic Movement in sustainable development. Specifically, these conclusions and recommendations were the:

- incorporation of concern for the environment as a prominent feature of the Olympic Charter
- extending the Olympic Movement's concern for the environment beyond merely the period of the Games itself. To facilitate this it was recommended that a Sport and Environment Commission be established.
- adoption of an environmental educational policy
- acting to ensure that sport took place in a way consistent with sustainable development practices
- incorporation of the environment as a major criterion in the selection of Olympic Games host cities

(Neeb, 2002, p. 165)

The year after the Centennial Congress, the IOC acted to convene, in association with the UNEP, the first World Conference on Sport and the Environment (WCSE), an event that has been conducted biannually since. At this event a number of actions were taken, including the endorsement of the Congress' decision to make the environment the third pillar of the Olympic Movement and the recommendation to create a Sport and Environment Commission (SEC). The IOC acted to create an SEC that same year, charging it with advising the IOC Executive Board on the policy to be adopted by the IOC and the Olympic Movement with regard to the protection of the environment. The SEC's role also extended to a range of actions/directions, specifically:

- to have the whole Olympic Movement embrace environmental considerations
- to strengthen environmental guidelines for host cities
- to create educational material concerning sport and the environment

- to sponsor conferences and seminars concerning the environment
- to sponsor a national clean-up day with NOCs from around the world
- to work with other sport and environment organisations in promoting environmental issues
- to utilise national and international athletes as environmental ambassadors
- to establish the environment as a major issue for the Olympic Movement by working with the media

(Neeb, 2002, p. 166)

The increased focus of the Olympic Movement on the environment saw its charter amended in 1996 at the 105th IOC Session in Atlanta, USA, to formally acknowledge this change. Rule 2, paragraph 10 was inserted. It states that:

the IOC sees that the Olympic Games are held in conditions which demonstrate a responsible concern for environmental issues and encourages the Olympic Movement to demonstrate a responsible concern for environmental issues, takes measures to reflect such concern in its activities and educates all those connected with the Olympic Movement as to the importance of sustainable development.

(IOC, 2004a, p. 1)

The IOC's next major environment-related action was the decision to alter the criteria for bidding cities to embrace environmental considerations. This resulted in candidates for the 2002 Winter Olympic Games being the first to respond to bid criteria that included environmental considerations. These criteria have been developed and refined over time, with the current version having been developed in 2004.

The Olympic Movement continued to engage with the environment through its SEC and its WCSEs through the late 1990s and into the new millennium. Prior to the third WCSE in 1999, the IOC moved to adopt its own version of Agenda 21. This decision was endorsed at the conference and a statement (the Rio Statement) was made as to how the Olympic Movement and the sports community should pursue this agenda (Athens Environmental Foundation, 2004).

The effort by the IOC to pursue a sustainable development agenda has been aided by the independent desire of some host cities to minimise the environmental impacts of the summer and winter Olympic Games and to generate a positive environmental legacy from it. For example, in the absence of any formal environmental guidelines from the IOC, the organisers of the 1994 Lillehammer Winter Olympic Games undertook a range of actions that resulted in this event being described as the first 'Green' Olympic Games (Neeb, 2002, p.160). While the IOC developed environmental guidelines for bidding cities after these Games, the lead time of seven years involved in the selection process meant that such considerations did not formally come into play until the 2002 Winter Olympic Games (Neeb, 2002). The 1996 Atlanta Olympic Games and the 1998 Winter Nagano Games, therefore, were not under any specific requirement to act in this area, although they did commit to some environmental actions in their bid documents. The subsequent performance of these cities, with regard to the environment, did not approach that of Lillehammer. Indeed, the Nagano Games came in for particularly strong criticism by some environmental groups (Planet Drum, 2004b).

The 2000 Olympic Games in Sydney were also awarded prior to the formal requirement to include an environmental component within the bid document. Nonetheless, the organisers of this event included as part of their successful bid document a set of environmental guidelines based on Agenda 21, a document that had already been embraced in Australia through its National Ecologically Sustainable Development policies. These guidelines primarily focused upon:

- planning and construction of Olympic facilities;
- energy conservation
- water conservation
- avoidance and minimisation of waste
- maintenance of air, water and soil quality
- protection of natural and cultural environments
- merchandising
- ticketing
- catering
- waste management
- transport
- noise control

(Sydney, 2000).

The implementation of these guidelines resulted in the Sydney Olympics being acknowledged by the Chairman of the Earth Council, Maurice Strong, as the 'greenest or most sustainable Games ever' (cited in Campbell, 2001, p. 1).

The Games that followed Sydney, Salt Lake City, Athens, Turin, Beijing and Vancouver, were all subject to a bidding criteria inclusive of an environmental component. However, it appears that most have not yet surpassed Sydney's efforts in this area. For example, Athens 2004 received a score of 0.8 out of a possible 5 from the World Wide Fund for Nature, for its environment program (2004, p. 2); according to Greenpeace, Beijing 2008 achieved and indeed surpassed some of their original environmental goals in relation to transportation infrastructure, energy efficiency and renewable energies but it also missed some opportunities such as the minimisation of use of forestry and water resources, and the initiation of best practice and policies for venues; China also limited engagement with third party assessments of its environmental activities (Zhang, 2008). Vancouver 2010 has, according to some reports, bettered Sydney as the greenest Olympics, due to their commitment to CO_2 offsets, energy efficiency, and recycling (Schwartz, 2010); however, others question how much it achieved, with the David Suzuki Foundation giving it a rating of Bronze in relation to its climate performance (Figure 5.1).

A poor result, as demonstrated in the Athens Games for example, raises several issues for the 'owners' of large-scale 'mobile' events, such as the Olympics, which seek to engage directly with SD, but must rely on the successful bidding city/country for its delivery. These issues relate to an event owner's capacity to control how an

FIGURE 5.1 Summary of the climate performance of the 2010 Vancouver Olympics

CATEGORY	HOW THE VANCOUVER OLYMPICS PERFORMED
1. Goals	Setting goals that are specific, measurable and sufficiently ambitious is a critical first step in developing a successful climate program. The Vancouver Olympic bid set clear goals related to energy efficiency and renewable energy, but was vague in other areas.
2. Transparency	Transparency promotes accountability, and can also provide opportunities for constructive dialogue with stakeholders. VANOC was relatively transparent about its climate program.
3. Measuring climate impact	Measuring its greenhouse gas emissions allows an organization to manage and potentially reduce its climate impact, and VANOC has made improvements over previous Games with a more rigorous and comprehensive approach.
4. Venues	Venues are a visible legacy of all Olympics, and the Vancouver Olympics will leave the region with innovative, energy-efficient buildings that will reduce community greenhouse gas emissions – and save money – for many years into the future.
5. Energy Use	Fossil fuel energy use at venues, including electricity, heating and cooling, is typically a major source of greenhouse gas emissions for winter Olympics. However, the Vancouver Olympics will primarily use clean energy sources.
6. Transportation	Local transportation and shipping are a significant source of greenhouse gas emissions for the Olympics. In Vancouver it appears opportunities to create lasting reductions in transportation emissions in the region have been missed.
7. Overall greenhouse gas emission reductions	The number one priority in managing the climate impact of any large event is to reduce greenhouse gas emissions wherever possible (i.e., before offsetting), and it is estimated that the Vancouver Olympics will have reduced overall emissions by around 15%.
8. Offsetting remaining emissions	Since the Salt Lake City Winter Games in 2002, most Olympics have taken responsibility for some of their climate impact by using carbon offsets. VANOC has so far committed to offset 118,000 tonnes of its emissions, which is substantial, but still represents under half of Games-related emissions.

Continued

FIGURE 5.1 *Continued*

9. Mobilizing sponsors and others	Olympic Games, with their high visibility, have an opportunity to use their own environmental initiatives to leverage action from Olympic sponsors, suppliers and others. The Vancouver Olympics reached out to sponsors and others with several climate-related initiatives.
10. Public Engagement	Environment is one of the three pillars of the Olympic movement, and the Olympic Games are an unparalleled opportunity to reach out to billions of people around the world and inspire them with solutions to climate change. Yet this is the category where VANOC has had the least success.

(Source: © David Suzuki Foundation (2010) www.davidsuzuki.org)

event is delivered once it has been awarded, the linkage between a host city or country's ability to deliver on SD commitments and its overall level of support for and engagement with the concept.

London 2012

The London 2012 Olympic Games, in partnership with World Wildlife Fund (WWF) and BioRegional developed the 'One Planet Olympics' concept based on the ten principles of 'One Planet Living', which has informed the London 2012 Olympics environmental management system. The aim is to achieve the first sustainable Olympic Games (London 2012, WWF and BioRegional, 2005). The five priority themes identified within the Sustainability Plan (London 2012, 2009c) are identified in Figure 5.2.

An independent body, the Commission for a Sustainable London 2012, has been established to monitor the sustainable development of London 2012 and its

FIGURE 5.2 Priority sustainability themes of London 2012

1. Climate change – minimising greenhouse gas emissions and ensuring legacy facilities are able to cope with the impacts of climate change

2. Waste – minimising construction waste and no waste being sent to landfill during Games time, as well as encouraging the development of new waste processing infrastructure in East London

3. Biodiversity – minimising the impact of the Games on the ecology of the Lower Lea Valley, leaving a legacy of enhanced habitats within the Olympic Park

4. Inclusion – promoting inclusion and attitude change, especially towards disability, celebrate the diversity of London and the UK and create new employment, training and business opportunities for the communities living around the Olympic Park site and Lower Lea Valley

5. Healthy Living – the Games will be used to inspire people across the country to take up sport and develop active, healthy and sustainable lifestyles

(Source: London 2012, 2007)

achievement of the legacies set out in its pledge to host the most sustainable Olympics ever (*www.cslondon.org*). The Commission publishes a range of reports based on the outcome of their independent reviews, including focusing on food, procurement, waste and employment.

While the IOC has made a meaningful effort over a more than 10-year period to embrace the concept of sustainable development, other large-scale events have only recently begun to take up the green challenge. The 2006 FIFA World Cup, for example, was the first time this event sought to incorporate environmental considerations into its preparation and staging, setting measurable environmental targets in the areas of water, waste, energy and mobility (FIFA, 2006). The same can be said for the Commonwealth Games, which, while making some efforts in Manchester in 2002 to embrace environmental considerations, engaged more fully with the concept of SD in Melbourne in 2006 where it took place under a sustainable development framework (Office of Commonwealth Games Coordination n.d.). Further advice is provided by Scottish Golf Environment Group Ltd (SGEGL, 2008) who identified five core elements for green sporting events in relation to golf:

- venue and organisers commitment
- establishment of appropriate structures and systems
- identification of all relevant environmental actions
- partnerships
- internal and external communication/Public Relations (PR)

Finally, UK Sport (2002, 2005) has also identified seven steps for 'greening' sporting events. These are:

(UK Sport, 2005, p. 63)

1. adopt a green policy
2. carry out an 'Environmental Scoping Review' of venues and operations
3. establish environmental teams
4. define programmes and set appropriate targets
5. implement programmes
6. monitor and adjust implementation
7. evaluate and accordingly publicise results programmes

The principles identified in this section provide an excellent basis for the staging of major events in the future.

Government waste reduction efforts

While the area of waste management is an aspect of the broader concept of SD discussed previously; its significance from an event perspective is worthy of it being treated here as a separate issue.

With rapid economic and population growth in many countries after World War II and an associated rise in consumerism, came a significant increase in the generation of solid waste. Faced with the increasing volumes of such waste, governments sought to develop strategies aimed at reducing it. It is not surprising that events, which often involve large numbers of people and have the potential to generate significant amounts of waste, have become the targets of such strategies.

A prime example and international exemplar of the response to waste management in the events context is provided by Victoria in Australia and also reflected in most other Australian states. These programs are designed primarily to educate event managers in reducing event-related waste and the recycling of the waste that is collected. The Waste Wise Events Toolkit (see Figure 5.3), developed by EcoRecycle Victoria (now Sustainability Victoria), is one example of an online resource available to event managers seeking to manage their event's waste stream. Noteworthy among the material provided in this toolkit is information on signage, occupational health and safety, approaches to continuously improving waste management practices, bin management, managing caterers and stallholders and promoting and evaluating waste management systems. This document also contains information on a waste-wise certification scheme that has been developed for events in the State of Victoria. This program is currently being broadened to address water and energy consumption issues relating to events.

Australia is not the only country where waste management has become an issue for event managers. In the American state of Wisconsin, for example, recycling laws require event managers to make provisions for the recycling of:

- glass bottles and jars
- aluminium and steel/tin cans
- plastic containers
- newspapers
- corrugated cardboard
- office paper
- other items, depending on the community

To assist event managers in meeting these obligations, the Wisconsin Department of Natural Resources also provides online information (Wisconsin Department of Natural Resources, 2001).

These international developments have also been reflected with initiatives in the UK. For example, as part of the Waste Awareness Wales initiative, the Wales Event Recycling Project (2008) has produced guidelines for implementing successful recycling schemes at events. Although developed in Wales, they note that the advice and information can be used throughout the UK. In order to provide a 'real life' perspective on the issue of waste management at events, Waste Wise Wales has developed a number of case studies of events. Another example from the UK is the previously mentioned Greener Events Guide produced by the Government Office for the South West (2010) — their website provides useful guidelines and checklists for event managers to consider the environmental impact of various aspects of their events, including the choice of venue, CO_2 emissions and a large section on reducing waste. As they note, their checklist can provide a useful starting point for discussions between event organizers, venue owners and suppliers (Figure 5.4). Finally, DEFRA

FIGURE 5.3 Waste Wise Events Toolkit

WASTE WISE EVENTS TOOLKIT
The Waste Wise Events Toolkit helps you gain cooperation of waste contractors and stallholders, educate your patrons to 'do the right thing' and ensure waste management runs smoothly.
- Additional resources for caterers to reduce their waste are provided in the Waste Wise Catering Toolkit.
- Download Sustainability Victoria's preferred Public Place and Event Signage to increase recycling and reduce litter at your event.

Waste Wise certification
There are three levels of Waste Wise certification. Please note, certification is awarded prior to events by the Regional Education Officer (REO) in your local Regional Waste Management Group.
- One star — new events who want to start the program
- Two star — events that have already system [sic] in place and want to improve
- Three star — events that want to adopt continuous improvement and innovative waste reduction.

To start the program, contact your REO who will help you implement the five simple steps and tell you more about certification.

Download the complete toolkit
- Waste Wise Events Toolkit — complete

Download the toolkit by chapter

Step 1: Getting commitment and improving on last year
At this stage, you will be setting key recycling and waste reduction goals for your event.
- *Application form* Complete with details of your event and submit to your Regional Education Officer to apply for certification
- *Guidance on timing* Pre-planning for your event
- *Continuous improvement* Example of how to implement continuous improvement for recycling your waste
- *Caterers' guide* Helpful hints to minimise waste if catering is provided at a permanent venue
- *Occupational health and safety responsibilities* Important contact details to assist your event in meeting its occupational health and safety responsibilities

Step 2: Talking to your contractors about setting up bin systems that work
This step involves the development of bin systems that are appropriately placed, managed front and back-of-house, as well as clearly and consistently signed.
- *Guide to signage* A brief explanation on signage at events
- *Bin cap booking form* Complete and fax to your REO to book the bin caps
- *Equipment management planner* Organise the equipment needed for your waste management system.
- *Bin placement and maintenance guidelines* Where to place bins at your event for maximum effectiveness
- *Setup and maintenance checklist* Onsite checklist for on-the-day equipment
- *Clauses for agreements* Use any of these to assist in developing contracts for waste management at your event
- *Clauses for appointing* caterers Sample agreement clauses to assist in appointing a company to manage food vendors.

Step 3: Talking to your traders about minimising and recycling packaging
The majority of rubbish at an event comes from packaging. Talk to your stallholders or traders about the types of packaging they use as well as encouraging them to use recyclable packaging.

Continued

FIGURE 5.3 *Continued*

- *Stallholder monitoring checklist* Checklist for assessing compliance of stallholders during the event
- *Buying green* A brief explanation of why and how you can help improve the environment
- *Green packaging suppliers* A list of environmentally friendly packaging suppliers
- *Stallholder application form* Use this to gain commitment from your stallholders
- *Stallholder information sheet* Explains the program requirements to stallholders
- *Stallholder letter of confirmation* Confirms commitment and program requirements with stallholders.

Step 4: Promoting your system with patrons

This stage provides tools to ensure that patrons understand the environmental benefits of being Waste Wise, as well as how to put the right item in the right bin. Educating patrons will also reduce contamination costs.

- *Education and promotion ideas activities* Ideas for informing patrons about waste management at your event
- *Media releases and advertisements* Sample media releases and advertisements to use in promotion
- *Public announcements and messages* Sample scripts for public announcements and interesting facts on waste
- *Don't Waste Australia campaign* The Beverage Industry Environment Council (BIEC) Don't Waste Australia campaign is available for organisers of Waste Wise certified events.*

Step 5: Learning to make improvements

After the event, assess the waste and recyclables collected and review the bin system so you can pinpoint opportunities for improvement. Promote your Waste Wise status by notifying local media about how much was recycled.

- *Evaluation questions* How to evaluate waste management at your event
- *Waste volume to weight conversion table* Conversion chart for converting volumes of specific materials to weights
- *Waste assessment form* Template for recording the waste types and volumes of bins
- *Waste audits and assessments information sheet* How to choose between a waste assessment or waste audit
- *Final report template* Fill in basic data to produce a mini case study or event report.

* The Beverage Industry Environment Council (BIEC) has recently changed its name to the Packaging Stewardship Forum

(Source: Sustainability Victoria 2006, Waste Wise Events Toolkit, Melbourne, www.sustainability.vic.gov.au)

(2007) provide useful guidance for event organisers, including transport, catering, venues and preparation.

Cost savings

Increasingly, event organisers and owners and suppliers of event facilities are realising the economic benefits that can result from the adoption of environmental management strategies. Publications such as Chernushenko's (1994) *Greening Our Games: Running Sports Events and Facilities that Won't Cost the Earth* have been

FIGURE 5.4 Greener events checklist

Venue choice (and equipment)	Reducing Waste (and costs)
[ ] Choose a venue that has good access via public transport & for disabled people	**Pre Event:** [ ] Use websites & email lists to promote the event
[ ] Ask potential venues for their in-house environmental policy & priorities	[ ] Use double-sided printing for promotional materials & handouts. Use recycled paper where possible without laminating it
[ ] Choose a venue interested in sustainability issues, and tell them that's why you chose them	[ ] Use easily transportable & reusable display materials
[ ] Venues offering in-house technical equipment & support (e.g. staging, audio-visual) can reduce equipment transportation	[ ] Seek naturally lighted meeting & exhibition areas
[ ] Consider hiring rather than purchasing equipment; specify the most efficient available	[ ] Format any handouts so as to minimise the amount of paper used
[ ] Consider video conferencing and/or recording the event for wider (internet) access	[ ] Where possible, write material in a re-usable format (general rather than event specific)
CO2 Emissions (including travel) (see "Reducing Waste" checklist also)	[ ] Minimise the length of the registration form or use electronic registration where possible & publish the event itinerary on-line
[ ] Take measures to reduce CO2 emissions from delegates travelling to the venue, i.e. provide information about local public transport (with pedestrian routes) and encourage its use. Where appropriate promote car sharing e.g. circulate attendees list in advance	[ ] Ask the venue to recycle paper & cardboard waste etc – and to provide suitable recycling bins [ ] If required, make your own note pads from scrap paper
[ ] Minimise unnecessary lighting, heating / airconditioning	**At the Event:** [ ] If you are providing delegate packs (if in a folder, make it re-usable), give these to delegates when they register on arrival – not beforehand – to avoid duplication
[ ] Offset CO2 emissions arising from the event	
Catering & Locally Produced Food [ ] Plan food requirements carefully to avoid unnecessary waste (e.g. use event registration form to obtain information)	[ ] Avoid mass distribution of handouts - allow attendees to download copies from the internet
[ ] Ensure that dietary requirements are catered for and offer vegetarian choices	[ ] Ensure presenters are aware of electronic presentation facilities & that their presentation will be distributed electronically after the event
[ ] Plan meals using seasonal local produce wherever possible. Consider organic produce	[ ] Provide re-usable name badges (& remember to collect them at the end of the event!)
[ ] If serving fish, use fish from sustainable sources	[ ] Minimise use of accessories that are harmful to the environment (e.g. plastic leaflet wallets)
[ ] Wherever possible ensure fruit is provided as an alternative to sweet desserts	[ ] Feature conference name & date on title slide rather than single use stage set graphics
[ ] Left over food: consider donating to local charity or sending for local composting	[ ] Minimise use of high wattage stage lighting
[ ] Ensure tea/coffee is Fair Trade & provide tap water as an alternative (if you must use bottled water, make sure it is local!)	[ ] Promote energy & water efficiency to participants – e.g. switch off lights when rooms are not in use
[ ] Minimise use of individually packaged food/drink items (e.g. provide milk / cream in jugs rather than individual plastic cartons)	[ ] Use drymark eraser boards rather than paper in workshop presentations [ ] Request that any unused items be collected for use at another event
[ ] Use reusable crockery, glassware & cutlery where possible (to reduce waste)	[ ] Consider including a sustainability activity/session within the conference to raise awareness
	Post Event: [ ] If not issued at the event, send out delegate feedback questionnaire by email [ ] Give any feedback you have to the venue

(Source: © Government Office for the South West, January 2010, p. 2) making the point for some time, that financial savings or avoided costs can flow from the pursuit of environmental programmes and principles. An area of note in this regard is the reduction of disposal fees. Calculations by the Californian Showgrounds in 2000, for example, showed that the venue had realised savings of over US $5.5 million over the previous five years, due to effective environmental management of its waste stream (Strauss, 2000). By recycling 410.44 tonnes of waste at Glastonbury Festival in 2004, organisers saved between £12,313 and £14,364 in waste disposal charges (Waste Awareness Wales, 2005). The SEXI project estimated that the total cost of waste to the exhibitions industry was £40 million per year, with over 60,000 tonnes of waste produced, much of which could be recycled or reduced (Midlands Environmental Business Club Limited, 2002). The decision to purchase reusable items — for example, the use of reusable rather than disposable carpets and cutlery in exhibitions — can also serve to reduce or eliminate disposal charges.

Small-scale events can also benefit from engaging in effective environmental management of their waste. The Wangaratta Jazz Festival in Victoria, Australia, for example, recorded a 26% drop in waste collection, recycling and bin supply costs and a four percent reduction in street cleaning from 2003 to 2004 (Sustainability Victoria, 2007).

The decision to purchase reusable items can also serve to reduce or eliminate disposal charges. The 1999 Pan American Games, for example, eliminated disposable plates and cups from its waste stream by purchasing crockery items. At the completion of the event, these items were sold, resulting in a total saving of an estimated US$30,000 over the alternative of disposal (Crawford, 2000).

Protection by sponsoring companies of their corporate image

The extent to which sponsors influence environmental practices and policies of events is an area that has received little attention; yet sponsor expectations can be an important factor in the uptake of environmental programs by events organisers (Crawford, (2000). Goldblatt (2008), for example, notes that major corporations being sensitive to criticism from consumers, will increasingly require that the events they sponsor meet or exceed certain environmental standards, for example, ISO 14001. He also suggests that companies involved in particular environmental strategies — recycling, for example — are likely to want recycling programs to be in place at the events they sponsor. He is supported in such comments by the Green Meetings Industry Council (2010), a body dedicated to improving the environmental performance of meetings and events. It states that corporations and associations are being pressured by their shareholders and members to be more environmentally responsible, in all areas of their operations, including meetings. In support of this contention it cites a survey by Price Waterhouse Coopers (2002), which found that even as early as 2002, 90% of the 140 largest companies in the United States were adopting environmentally responsible practices in order to enhance or protect their reputation; and 89% of these firms were of the opinion that sustainability as a business issue would continue to grow in importance.

Increasing consumer awareness of environmental issues

The trend towards increasing consumer awareness of environmental issues is well established. In the context of events, however, there is little substantive research to indicate whether people are influenced by environmental concerns in their decisions to participate in or attend them. Nonetheless, Crawford (2000) believes that this influence exists and that event organisers need to ensure they reflect their market's concerns in this area if they are not to experience a consumer 'backlash'. In support of Crawford's contention, it can be observed that many events now have stated environmental policies and/or information concerning how they are managing the environmental impacts included on their websites. An example of such a policy is provided in the Glastonbury Festival case study at the end of this chapter.

The influence of interest groups and event industry bodies

Some events, particularly large-scale events, have from time to time attracted the attention of environmental interest groups due to the potential they possess to negatively impact on a community's physical environment. These groups have included Greenpeace, the World Wide Fund for Nature (WWF), the Earth Council and 'collectives' of environmental groups such as was the case with Green Games Watch 2000 at the Sydney 2000 Olympic Games. These organisations have interacted with events in various ways. Greenpeace, for example, played an environmental advocacy role along with Green Games Watch 2000 in connection with the Sydney 2000 Olympic Games. Additionally, Greenpeace acted to develop environmental guidelines for the Olympic Games in *The Greenpeace Olympic Environmental Guidelines: A Guideline for Sustainable Events* (see Figure 5.5). Organisations such as the WWF *(WWF Environmental Assessment of the Athens Olympic Games),* the Earth Council *(Environmental Performance of the Olympic Coordination Authority)* and the David Suzuki Foundation discussed earlier, have, among other things, critiqued aspects of the environmental performance of Olympic Games' organising bodies.

The interest, or potential interest, of interest groups in events has served to focus the attention of event organisers on environmental issues. Many event organisers have realised that a failure to be proactive in the area of the environment can result in 'bad press' for the event, community protests or pressure on stakeholders — such as government, — to restrict operations in some way. For example, the widely reported World Wide Fund for Nature (WWF) assessment of the Athens Olympic Games was extremely critical of the International Olympic Committee's failure to deliver on its pledges concerning the environmental friendliness of this event. This comprehensive study of the 2004 Summer Olympics' environmental costs and benefits concluded that the IOC had not done enough to ensure the environment would not be damaged by the construction of venues and the conduct of the events, despite incorporating the environment as the third pillar of the Olympic Movement (Environment News Service, 2004). Other initiatives work at the grassroots level; for example, the Every Action Counts initiative led by the Community Development Foundation, has inspired thousands of people to take action to save the planet, with over 2000

FIGURE 5.5 The Greenpeace Olympic Environmental Guidelines: Guiding environmental principles

GUIDING ENVIRONMENTAL PRINCIPLES

If followed carefully, the principles below will ensure that future Olympic Games and other major events have minimal environmental impact.

1. Environmental sustainability

It is vital to ensure that current exploitation of ecosystem resources, including extraction of raw materials, consumption of energy, manufacture and use of chemicals and disposal of wastes, does not compromise the viability of future generations and their access to natural resources and ecosystem services. A truly sustainable project ensures that:

- Substances such as fossil fuels do not systematically increase in the ecosphere
- Synthetic substances do not systematically increase in the ecosphere
- The bases for productivity and diversity of life are not systematically depleted
- Resources are used fairly and efficiently in order to meet human need.

2. Precautionary principle

This should be the overarching guide to decision making even in the absence of certainty regarding the potential impacts of all processes, materials and systems for hosting Olympic Games and other events. In practical terms, the implementation of the precautionary principle implies that:

- Action must be taken to avoid harm, or the threat of harm, before it occurs, even when firm evidence of cause and effect relationships is unavailable.
- Since all processes, materials and systems have environmental impacts they must be regulated accordingly until sufficient evidence becomes available that there is no potential risk to ecosystems or human health.
- High quality scientific information should form a central component of mechanisms for early detection of environmental threats.
- A progressive, ever-improving approach which reduces environmental impacts should be adopted by all Olympic host cities or events.

3. A preventative approach

It is cheaper and more effective to prevent environmental damage than to attempt to manage it. Prevention requires thinking through the development process to prevent environmental impacts. Early planning is critical to a successful integrated environmental approach.

4. Integrated and holistic approach

Establish an approach centred around all potential environmental impacts from the start. This approach recognises that most of our environmental problems — for example, climate change, toxic pollution, loss of biodiversity — are caused by the way and rate at which we produce and consume resources. Adopt an integrated approach to environmental resource use and consumption addressing the full life cycle of the project including all material, water and energy flows, and the economic impact.

5. Specific and measurable environmental goals

Set specific environmental goals to fulfil these environmental guidelines at the outset of Olympic or other projects. Ensure that these goals are real, measurable and achievable and make them publicly available.

6. Community, NGO and public involvement

Consistent and high level consultation with community, environmental and social groups and the public is essential from the start. Establish a clear process for conflict resolution.

FIGURE 5.5 *Continued*

7. Senior environmental management

Place the management of environmental issues at a senior level within the overall management structure of the project. Environmental issues must be an integral part of any large scale event. Environmental teams and input from all levels of the project are vital for success.

8. Environmental reporting and independent auditing

Independent auditing of environmental information on all aspects of a development project is essential to ensure credibility. Make this information available to the public.

9. Public education and training

Plan and budget early to provide public education materials about the environmental aspects of your project. Ensure staff, suppliers, providers, sponsors and media understand the environmental initiatives of the project and why they were undertaken.

(Source: Greenpeace, 2003)

community organisations and 800 community champions signed up so far. They offer useful guidance for organising 'greener' events to the voluntary and community sector, to ensure that organisations are able to achieve their aims while minimising their impact on the planet (EAC, 2008).

Event industry groups with an environmental focus have emerged in recent years that have also served to push events down the sustainability path. AGreenerFestival. com, for example, is an organisation committed to assisting music and arts-based events and festivals in their efforts to green their operations. It does this by providing information and educational resources and by facilitating the sharing of ideas among event managers (A Greener Festival Ltd, 2010). Julie's Bicycle is a not-for-profit organisation dedicated to increasing awareness and reducing greenhouse gas emissions in music related industries. They have developed the Green Music Guide (Julie's Bicycle, 2009) on behalf of the Greater London Authority, which assesses carbon emissions in the music industry and provides case studies demonstrating how organisations have reduced them; they also run the Industry Green Status tool to help the music and creative industries towards lower carbon emissions by, for example, seriously considering how audiences travel to festivals and events and considering how artists tour. The Green Meetings Industry Council, mentioned earlier, and Blue Green Meetings (2010) are other organisations offering guidance, tools and resources to the industry, with a focus more on the conferences and meetings field.

At the level of event industry associations, a stronger emphasis is increasingly being placed on the delivery of green events. The International Festivals and Events Association, for example, have for a number of years acted to acknowledge the environmental achievements of its members through its annual industry awards. Meeting Professional International signed up to the United Nations Global Compact in 2007 as part of their commitment to corporate social responsibility. They have made significant progress on their CSR strategy through thoughtful leadership, developing resources for members and non-members and through leading by example — for example, by holding their conferences according to the BS 8901 specification (see *www.mpiweb.org/sustainability*). National events industry associations have also taken CSR, environmental and sustainability issues seriously, with Eventia leading a range of activities within their One Future initiative, launched in 2007 (Eventia, 2010).

THE EVENTS INDUSTRY APPROACH TO SUSTAINABLE EVENTS

Concern for sustainability and consideration of the environmental impacts of events is increasing, with a number of industry initiatives being developed. Governments are increasingly using public education programmes and legislation to promote the recycling of waste materials and reduce the amount of waste going to landfill sites. Events are targeted as opportunities to demonstrate best practice models in waste management and to change public attitudes and habits. The Commonwealth Games 2002 provided Manchester with sporting facilities to take it well into the twenty-first century, as well as major infrastructure improvements in accommodation, transport and communications. However, the development of facilities for events such as this raises major environmental issues that are magnified by the scale and profile of the project. In order to address these concerns, UK Sport clearly identifies the need for environmental sensitivity in all aspects of bidding for and staging major events. It states:

> *Major events and the environment are inextricably linked, and without due care events can impact adversely on the environment, directly or indirectly. Major events also have a very positive role to play in fostering understanding of environmental issues, raising awareness and generating resources . . . Particular attention will be paid to the environmental issues raised by very large numbers of people coming together for a short period of time, with subsequent problems of safety, congestion, consumption, and waste. Areas of particular attention will include: access; infrastructure; energy consumption; energy renewal; sustainability; minimising resource requirements; the use of natural products; and innovative design and technology that reduces both operating and maintenance costs and greatly extends the lifetime of sports facilities and new event venues.*

(UK Sport, 1999a, p. 10)

For the event manager, incorporating a waste management plan into the overall event plan has become increasingly good policy. Community expectations and the health of our environment require that events demonstrate good waste management principles and provide models for recycling. The environmentally conscious event manager will reap not only economic benefits but also the approval of an increasingly environmentally aware public. For example, Glastonbury Festival effectively reduced their impact on the environment through an effective waste management and recycling strategy, using hundreds of volunteers as part of their dedicated Recycling Crew. Their roles included collecting litter, separating recyclable items, giving out litter bags and working with the 'Reclammator' to help Glastonbury become the greenest festival (Glastonbury Festivals Ltd, 2000). With increasing concern for the atmosphere, events such as the Brit Awards and Glastonbury are also beginning to take part in schemes such as 'Carbon Neutral'. This involves an assessment of the energy used by the event — as a result, sufficient trees are then planted to absorb the carbon dioxide produced.

SEXI (Sustainable Exhibition Industry) was an 18 month project established to research the amount of waste produced by the exhibition industry, identify best practice and make recommendations for reducing this waste in the future. The project resulted in an eight point action plan for the industry:

1. measure, monitor and report
2. raise awareness within the industry and with exhibitors, promulgate best practice and report bad practice
3. improve environmental performance throughout the industry
4. ensure that all areas of the industry are compliant with Duty of Care
5. undertake research on how to improve applied practice, promote outputs and encourage adoption throughout the industry
6. reduce waste to landfill with zero as the ultimate target
7. offset carbon dioxide emissions associated with exhibitions
8. education and training

(Midlands Environmental Business Club Limited, 2002)

Based on experience gained at the 1996 Summer Olympics in Atlanta, the Xerox Corporation (1998) presented an eight-step model for waste reduction and recycling at events, illustrated in Figure 5.6.

BS 8901:2009 — Sustainable event management

Launched in 2007 as an events industry-driven response to the sustainability agenda, BS 8901 is the first worldwide standard for planning and managing sustainable events. BS 801 is the first industry focused standard to emerge from BS 8900 — that focuses on managing sustainable development (BSI, 2006) — and provides the events industry with an opportunity to lead the way on this important issue. BS 8901 has been well received nationally and internationally, with an increasing number of events, venues and events companies applying the principles to their businesses. Based on the first two years of experience in applying BS 901 to events, it was updated in 2009 to make it clearer and to clarify how organisations can claim that their events conform to the standard (BSI, 2009a).

Aimed at event organisers, venues and the supply chain, BS 8901:2009 provides practical guidance for managing environmental, economic and social impacts and risks; and it covers the breadth of the event management process. It will:

- help companies to improve sustainable performance within available budgets
- reduce carbon emissions and waste, improving the resource efficiency of the entire event supply chain
- present opportunities for more efficient planning and encourage the re-use of equipment and infrastructure.

FIGURE 5.6 Eight-stage process for waste reduction and recycling

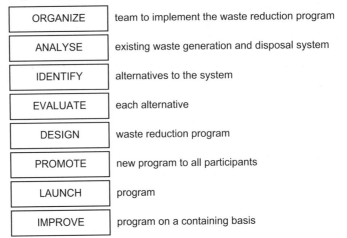

ORGANIZE	team to implement the waste reduction program
ANALYSE	existing waste generation and disposal system
IDENTIFY	alternatives to the system
EVALUATE	each alternative
DESIGN	waste reduction program
PROMOTE	new program to all participants
LAUNCH	program
IMPROVE	program on a containing basis

(Source: Xerox Corporation, 1998, Guide to Waste Reduction and Recycling at Special Events. New York, Xerox Corporation, p. 1)

- reduce environmental impacts such as carbon usage, waste management and effects on biodiversity
- improve social impacts such as community involvement and fair employment
- establish economic impacts such as local investment and long-term viability

(BSI, 2009b)

The key requirements for implementing BS 8901 are summarised in Figure 5.7 (BSI, 2010a). As can be seen, BS 8901 is a full management system that can be

FIGURE 5.7 Key requirements for BS 8901

- Sustainability Policy
- Issue identification and evaluation
- Stakeholder identification and engagement
- Objectives, targets and plans
- Performance against principles of sustainable development
- Operational controls
- Competence and training
- Supply chain management
- Communication
- Monitoring and measurement
- Corrective and preventive action
- Management System audits
- Management Review

(Source: BSI, 2010a)

applied at either event level or throughout the organisation. Embedded in BS 8901 is the continuous improvement principle of PDCA (Plan, Do, Check, Act) — 'Plan' what you are going to do, 'Do' it, 'Check' that you have done it and 'Act' on recommendations to implement improvements, arising from the review.

EVENT PROFILE

London 2012 Sustainability Guidelines. London 2012 has published the first edition of its sustainability guidelines for corporate and public events, underlining its commitment to staging sustainable Games in 2012. The guidelines have been developed primarily for London 2012 events organisers and to encourage interest and the development of sustainability across the events sector.

London 2012 was instrumental in developing the new British Standard for a Sustainable Event Management System (BS 8901), that provides a framework for managing events compliant with sustainability standards. These guidelines form part of London 2012's approach to achieve compliance with BS 8901.

Throughout the period leading up to the Games in 2012, there will be numerous events associated with London 2012, including conferences and seminars, roadshows, cultural events and promotional launches. The guidelines will help ensure that London 2012 events between now and Games-time are organised and staged in a sustainable way.

The guidelines set out a simple framework for improving the sustainability of events and focusing on key topic areas that are most relevant to the types of events, which will be organised in the lead-up to the Games.

London 2012 will continually review how the guidelines are performing in practice and will release updated editions. The experience gained from their application – and from implementing BS 8901 – will reinforce London 2012's efforts to deliver a more sustainable Games in 2012.

London 2012 Head of Sustainability, David Stubbs outlined the importance of the guidelines,

> 'We launched our Sustainability Plans over a year ago now, outlining our overall vision for the Games and since then we have been drilling down into the detail of each different element. Events are a key part of this – between now and 2012, we will be holding any number of events, from press conferences to cultural events and our guidelines will ensure they are arranged and run in the most sustainable way possible. We are fully committed to ensuring that our Games – and everything that happens in the run-up – reaches the highest possible standards in terms of sustainability.'

Anne Hayes, Head of Market Development, Risk and Sustainability BSI British Standards added:

> 'BSI is delighted London 2012 has published its Sustainability Guidelines for individual corporate and public events and will be using BS 8901 to ensure the Olympic Games and Paralympic Games will be as sustainable as possible. This sets a great example for any organisation wishing to reduce the impact of its events. Events organisers who have used the standard since its publication in 2007 have found it useful in enabling a holistic approach to improving the sustainability of their events, combining environmental, economic and social considerations.'

The Games itself in 2012 – including Test Events, Torch Relay, Opening and Closing Ceremonies – will be subject to the full sustainability management system developed by the

London 2012 Organising Committee and therefore go beyond the provision of these guidelines.

For further information on the London 2012 approach to sustainability, please visit: *http://www.london2012.com/making-it-happen/sustainability/index.php*

Source: *London 2012 (2009a).*

The events industry has been quick to embrace BS 8901, with many organisations applying the system to their organisations as a whole as well as to events, with an increasing range of published case studies based on experience. High profile events such as the Meeting Professionals International, the European Meetings and Events Conference, Copenhagen COP15, the United Nations Climate Conference, Manchester International Festival, Lords Cricket Ground, Live Nation and Earls Court Olympia are some of the events, venues and organisers that have successfully applied BS 8901. The case study at the end of this chapter on Google's Zeitgeist event demonstrates the application of BS 8901, while further case studies are also available through *www.bsigroup.com/bs8901*.

There are an increasing number of tools becoming available to help events companies to implement sustainable event management in their organisations which may help to achieve BS 8901, including a number of paid services. For example, Event Berry (*www.eventberry.com*) and Event Sustainability (*www.eventsustainability.com*) provide online tools for assisting organisations who are seeking to conform to BS 8901. As mentioned earlier, Julie's Bicycle has developed the Industry Green Tool' which allows organisations to assess their environmental impact including greenhouse gas reduction (Julie's Bicycle, 2008); while a range of tools allow event managers to measure their carbon footprint, including the Australian Centre for Event Management's Carbon Calculator (calculator.noco2.com.au/acem) and Best Foot Forward's Event Footprinter (*www.footprinter.com*). Finally, Jones (2010) has developed an online Sustainable Event Management Guide to support readers of her publication and the wider events community in the approach to sustainable events.

Building on the successes of BS 8901: 2009, an international project committee is currently working on developing an international standard, ISO 20121, to harmonise the international events industry's efforts for sustainable events and to set benchmarks for best practice. The aim is that this will be available in time for the London 2012 Olympic Games (ISO, 2010). An international group, the Sustainable Events Alliance (2010), has been formed to 'Create a space (virtual), where those currently actively involved in sustainable event management practices can network and exchange ideas,'. These activities include engaging organisations in environmental management systems such as BS 8901 and developing complementary activities alongside BS 8901, such as Sustainable Event Certification. Further, inspired by progress made by delivering the UN COP15 conference as a sustainable event (Bigwood and Luehrs, 2009), a Copenhagen Sustainable Meetings Protocol (CSMP) has been developed by the Copenhagen Sustainable Meetings Coalition (CSMC) as an umbrella framework for developing large sustainable meetings

(Bigwood and Luehrs, 2010). CSMP covers sustainable event management, linking it to a strategic approach to incorporate sustainability into meetings and events, covering the areas of leadership commitment, strategic approach, stakeholder engagement, operational integration and governance.

SUMMARY

This chapter has sought to provide an overview of those forces that have acted to push the events industry down the pathway of Sustainable Development and the growth in sustainable events. These forces are governmental adoption of the principles of sustainable development, government waste reduction efforts, cost savings, protection by sponsoring companies of their corporate image, increasing consumer interest in environmental issues and the influence of environmental interest groups and event industry environmental bodies; that has led to the development of BS 8901:2009 as a British Standard for sustainable events and formed the foundations for ISO 20121 and CSMP to take the sustainable events agenda to an international level. Additionally, this chapter has identified various approaches events have employed in their efforts to engage with the concept of Sustainable Development, along with resources that are available to facilitate this engagement. It is clear that the concept of 'sustainable event management' has developed from specialist organisations focusing on this aspect of events, to mainstream with most events and festivals now considering sustainability.It is therefore important that developments in this field are monitored and acted upon, as there are clear environmental, economic and social benefits in doing so.

QUESTIONS

1. What is meant by the terms sustainable development and sustainable events?

2. Briefly discuss the path followed by the Olympic Games in its efforts to engage with the concept of sustainable development.

3. How has increasing consumer awareness of environmental issues impacted on the conduct of events?

4. What types of cost savings might be available to events that seek to reduce their environmental impact?

5. Briefly discuss, making reference to appropriate examples from industry, how waste associated with food preparation and consumption at events can be minimised.

6. Select an event that has made a significant effort to engage with the concept of sustainable development (for example, the 2006 Melbourne Commonwealth

Games, 2006 FIFA World Cup, 2012 London Olympics, Glastonbury Festival), and identify and discuss the practices it employed/is planning to employ for this purpose.

7. Identify two non-sporting events that have developed sustainable or environmental policies. Briefly indicate the core aspects of these policies.

8. What initiatives is London 2012 taking in order to take forward the sustainable event principles established in Sydney 2000?

9. What role does the United Nations Environment Programme now play in the delivery of environmentally friendly events?

10. Go to the websites *www.agreenerfestival.com* and *www.csmp.dk*. Explore these sites and briefly outline the types of information available on them, which might assist an event manager in producing festivals, meetings and events that are more sustainable.

CASE STUDY – GLASTONBURY FESTIVAL ENVIRONMENTAL POLICY 2008

The Glastonbury Festival of Contemporary Performing Arts (Glastonbury Festival) recognises that running the event at Worthy Farm has a direct impact (both positive and negative) on the environment. The Festival is committed to enhancing the environment through our operations wherever possible and minimising any negative impact.

The Festival also commits to maintaining the rich and diverse environment that has evolved through alternative land usage. Holding a festival once a year in the middle of the growing season, prevents the use of environmentally damaging conventional farming practices that would have a more intrusive impact on the ecology.

This statement will focus on litter management, sewage management, management of the general ecology of the site and environmental messaging to festival goers. The Festival is committed to working with the grain of nature, not against it, and complying with all environmental legal requirements.

Litter Management. Any event with 150,000 attendees will generate significant levels of litter. The Festival is committed to minimising the amount of waste and managing the on-site collection of that waste efficiently. The Festival works to the key environmental management principle of "Reduce, Reuse and Recycle". The Festival is equally committed to quickly and effectively clearing any litter caused by the Festival in the local community.

In 2003, 30% of litter was moved off-site during the event – in itself a 100% increase from 2002. Over the next five years the Festival has set a target of increasing the amount of rubbish moved off-site during the event to 50%. This will be addressed by increasing the numbers of litter bins, tractor teams and dustcarts, while sustaining existing levels of skip clearance and litter clearing staff.

The Festival commits to continuing its policy of reducing waste. Significant reductions have been recorded in the last three years by placing controls on what is brought on-site by staff, contractors, sponsors and traders – and by emphasis on their responsibility to remove items brought on-site.

The Festival is also committed to continuing the composting initiative developed in 2004, to minimise the amount of waste that goes to landfill. It is Festival policy that all disposables provided to food traders by Festival wholesalers will be biodegradable and manufactured in environmental friendly fashion. This is closely monitored and enforced.

The Festival will actively promote recycling to festival goers and will research further recycling options. The Festival achieved twice the 2004 MDC target and commits to exceeding the MDC target of 24% of recycled waste in 2005. This is a demanding target for a one-off event in a field, compared to domestic, industrial or commercial outlets with regular established collection practices. In 2004, in addition to the 110 tonnes of composted organic waste, the Festival recycled 150 tonnes of chipped wood, 26.8 tonnes of cans and plastic bottles, 10.3 tonnes of glass, 100 tonnes scrap metal and 13.3 tonnes of cardboard. The Festival commits to work with the statutory authorities on recycling and litter management issues.

Managing Sewage and Waste Water. The Festival commits to transporting sewage and waste water off-site, with the use of the lagoon as a temporary holding facility, in full consultation with the Environment Agency and Wessex Water.

The Festival undertakes to provide containers for waste water and direct all employees and traders that there should not be any discharge of contaminated water to surface or ground waters. This will continue to be closely monitored. All foul drainage from the market areas and traders premises will be collected and transported to the lagoon for subsequent disposal. The levels of the effluent collection lagoon will be continually monitored, with effluent being transported to approved sewage treatment works during the event. The lagoon will be thoroughly cleansed before it is returned to agricultural use. The Festival undertakes to commit to the standards set by the Environment Agency with regard to sewage disposal; and has an ongoing process of consultation with the Environment Agency and the Mendip District Council with regard to minimising any environmental damage caused by the Festival.

The Festival will protect watercourses to minimise the potential of pollution during the event and undertakes to provide more urinals and toilets than recommended by the Event Safety Guide, siting the additional facilities at potential pollution hot spots. The Festival will also monitor the streams during the event. The Festival also is committed to investigating further developments in technology that may result in minimising the volume that needs to be transported off site, which, in turn, will reduce the impact from carbon emissions caused by tankers. Any developments will only be progressed with the approval of the appropriate authorities.

Managing the Ecology of the Site. The Festival is committed to maintaining the high level of bio-diversity that was found on the festival site by the independent bio-diversity audit carried out by Liz Biron of Somerset Environmental Records Centre in 2003. The Festival aims to further increase this level by continuing its commitment to protecting vulnerable habitats – its new county wildlife sites, badger sets, ponds, streams, hedges and ditches – in nature reserves and non public zones or by fencing them off.

The Festival will continue to try to increase both the abundance and diversity of wildlife by:

- actively enhancing habitats on-site by tree planting, hedge planting, coppicing and hedge laying etc.
- continuing to allow the process of succession from inherited improved grassland to more diverse unimproved grassland
- allowing a significant level of agricultural weed species (docks and nettles etc) to exist on its core site

The Festival will continue to protect individual vulnerable species by establishing new temporary reserves on a need basis. This was successfully achieved in 2003 and 2004 by creating a new reserve within the core site for three deer trapped within the site by the perimeter fence. This temporary reserve was so successful that the deer stayed in this locality long after the fence was removed. Indeed in 2004, the deer moved into the nature reserve of their own accord. This is a good example of area managers/workers and central management working together to resolve serious issues.

Continued

CASE STUDY – GLASTONBURY FESTIVAL ENVIRONMENTAL POLICY 2008—*CONT'D*

The practical reality of this commitment is that the Festival, for the fifth year running, will be enhancing the environment of its core site by more trees and hedge planting at three locations on-site. The planting to date has brought the total number of native tree and hedge plants planted to over four thousand since 2000.

Environmental Messaging. The unique environment of the Festival brings together many Non-Governmental Organisations (NGOs) and environmental groups, and through participation in the Festival, the public are exposed to many positive influences highlighting environmental values – and hopefully, influencing subsequent behaviour. Glastonbury Festival is committed to:

- having a "Green" message central to future marketing campaigns that will dissuade festival goers from urinating in streams, ditches and hedges
- including environmental messages in festival publications such as the Fine Guide, the programme, the daily paper and the Festival website, which have direct links to environmental and humanitarian organisations
- using the screens at the main stages only to promote environmental and humanitarian messages
- employing the services of environmental organisations in the running of the event, increasing the amounts these organisations can raise towards their objectives – and increasing their profile
- maintaining the Greenfields, the largest area of its kind dedicated to environmental awareness. Many different environmental concerns that enhance the fabric of our society, from international organisations such as Greenpeace to small woodland Trusts, place a high value on this facility. The festival is the biggest single regular donor to Greenpeace; it offers Greenpeace fertile ground for the recruitment of members and for promoting environmental campaigns
- continuing to give trading opportunities to green organisations and selecting traders on the basis of green credentials

Additionally the Festival is committed to:

- creating awareness among its employees and subcontractors about the "Reduce, Reuse, Recycle" mantra and the importance of minimising any negative impact on the environment
- employing safe work practices, developing contingencies and implementing measures to prevent, eliminate or reduce pollution
- encouraging festival-goers to use environmentally sound transport options, by promoting the use of public transport and lift share
- continuing to work with Future Forests to be carbon neutral. Future Forests have planted over 6,500 naturally occurring deciduous trees in the woods in the South West of England because of their involvement with the Festival. Since GF pioneered Future Forest's involvement in 1997, many other events have followed this lead. (When the trees planted at Worthy over the last five years are taken into account as well, there is now a significant carbon sink.)
- improving energy efficiency, seeking green alternatives where possible

The Festival will review the effectiveness of the implementation of the above on a regular basis and constantly seek to improve environmental performance according to the above criteria

Although the principles remain largely the same, the statement is revised and updated to reflect current needs and requirements. For further information on many aspects of the planning and management of Glastonbury Festival, including an extensive student information pack, please visit *www.glastonburyfestivals.co.uk*.

By Glastonbury Festival of Contemporary Performing Arts, Worthy Farm, Pilton, Shepton Mallet, Somerset, BA4 4BY.

Questions

1. Summarise the potential environmental impacts of Glastonbury Festival. How do these differ from an event taking place in a purpose-built venue?
2. Based on the case study, identify examples of what you consider to be best practice approaches to environmental management. Discuss why you have chosen these.
3. What other practical measures could the organisers consider to ensure that environmental impacts are minimised?

CASE STUDY: GOOGLE ZEITGEIST CONFERENCE 2009

Zeitgeist – The general intellectual, moral, and cultural climate of an era.

The main objectives of the annual conference Zeitgeist hosted by Google, were to build and create stronger business relationships and to be seen as a thought leader. The focus for the 2009 Zeitgeist conference was to examine the current state of the environmental world; and study how businesses can work together to influence and facilitate change. Given this conference theme, it was natural for Google to run the event in a sustainable manner.

The Zeitgeist conference provides a practical illustration for the implementation of BS 8901.

Self-certification. Google were confident that they had strong evidence of the implementation of *BS 8901 specifications for a sustainability management system for sustainable events* and chose to self-certify. As part of this evidence, Google created and issued documentation that was made available for comment by their stakeholders; these included;

- sustainability development policy
- identification of key issues and objectives
- stakeholder engagement and issue log
- KPIs and targets
- evidence of implementation on site
- summary of achievement made available to stakeholders using an online reporting system *www.eventsustainability.co.uk*

Google Zeitgeist took place on the 17th, 18th and 19th May 2009 at The Grove Hotel, Hertfordshire, UK. It was attended by over 500 guests made up of Google employees, business partners and guest speakers. The event content included guest speakers such as HRH The Prince of Wales and HRH Prince of Asturias, Crown Prince of Spain, with a rainforest themed evening dinner. The sustainability implementation was organised by Organise This Ltd, a sustainable event management company. Steps taken to achieve compliance included benchmarking the event and using the online event tool and the BS 8901 framework, to deliver the objectives.

BS 8901 is a standard for the "specifications for a sustainability management system for sustainable events with guidance for use." This means implementing a way of working that considers environmental, economical, and social impacts. BS 8901 can be self certified, or second- or third-party certified.

The BS 8901 process involves several key stages.

Setting the scope. Before embarking on the implementation of BS 8901, an organisation must first establish the scope of what is to be covered by their sustainability management system. Google set the scope for their management system to cover one event, Zeitgeist. Google can amend and extend their scope in the future and will consider implementation of the standard at the 2010 Zeitgeist conference.

Continued

CASE STUDY: GOOGLE ZEITGEIST CONFERENCE 2009—*CONT'D*

Identifying issues. Google held meetings and workshops with their internal staff and supply chain and they consulted industry best practice to determine and rank their key sustainability issues. The largest issues identified by Google were waste identification and measurement' stakeholder engagement, transportation mileage, internal education and awareness of sustainability.

Setting objectives and targets. From the key issues identified, realistic objectives for Zeitgeist were set; in conjunction with these objectives, measurable targets were set so that performance could be evaluated after the conference. For each of these objectives, numerous Key Performance Indicators (KPIs) were identified and for each of these KPIs a quantifiable target was established. Examples of these for each objective are included in Table 5.1.

Stakeholder engagement. A vital part of the BS 8901 process is to engage all stakeholders with sustainability issues. Google consulted their stakeholders at all stages of the process; Brand Fuel worked to support the implementation of BS 8901 and as a result found their way of work changing to reflect increased sustainability.

'The BS 8901 is the future for event management; we recognised that it was vital to work within the BS 8901to aim to deliver a sustainable event' Kay Pratt, Producer, Brand Fuel

Roles and responsibilities. Vish Patel was identified as the sustainability champion within the Google team and given sustainability as an added area of responsibility. According to the standard, the system requires top management agreement, obtained in this case by Nikesh Arora, President of Global Sales Operations and Development.

Implementation. The implementation stage is where steps must be taken to ensure that the objectives set earlier in the process are met. Examples of steps taken by Google to achieve their objectives included:

- Regular recycling stations including crew areas
- Separate outdoor waste sorting areas
- Mileage recorded for attendees and staff
- Flowers used were given to crew members
- Generators for marquee used anti-idling policy

- 'One' water used which donates profit to African well schemes
- Smaller bulbs used in conference projector which meant less energy used
- Conference stage is reusable for the annual Zeitgeist conference
- Guest passes were made from sustainable resources and were recyclable.

Table 5.1 Examples of measurement objectives and Key Performance Indicators (KPIs)

Item	Measurement Objective	KPI Target
Identify and measure waste generated from the event	Identify waste streams	100%
Educate stakeholders on sustainability	Communication to Zeitgeist supply chain	100%
Measure all transport mileage	Measure overseas flights from travellers who are not already in the UK	90%

Table 5.2 Measurements

Item	Measurement
Linen	7264 pieces travelled 20 miles
Refuse waste (landfill)[1]	0.75 tonnes
Electricity	1595 Kw H
Gas	7640 Kw H
Water	661 cm3
Paper recycling	0.21 tonnes
Aluminium recycling	0.011 tonnes
Plastic recycling	0.028 tonnes
Glass recycling[2]	0.84 tonnes
Overseas delegate travel mileage[3]	840 388 miles
UK delegate mileage[4]	14 474 miles
Speaker mileage	837 miles
Food mileage	1092 miles
On-site mileage	8 082 miles

[1]based on average of 7kg per refuse sack
[2]based on an average of 40kg per bin
[3]based on return flights
[4]based on journey per person via car

Non-conformity. Throughout the process, the Google team reviewed non-conformities; non-conformity is when the team looks at what is working and what is not; and considers actions that can be taken to rectify what is not working, with the aim of achieving their objectives. This was achieved through reviewing documentation such as the sustainability development policy, listing tasks and through communication with the supply chain.

Benchmarking. Part of the benchmarking process included the collection of measurements and evidence of implementation from the conference. Google used an online sustainable event management tool to monitor their measurements. See results in Table 5.2 based over three days of sustainability measurement from *www.eventsustainability.com*.

Management review. Google put in to place an event debrief after the event that identified whether the sustainability objectives were achieved. The results showed that Google achieved the following in relation to objectives:

- waste streams were identified and measured
- mileage was recorded for overseas and UK delegates
- stakeholders were educated on sustainability

Google will use the results of the 2009 Zeitgeist conference as a benchmark for future sustainable events in the UK and Europe, where they aim to set sustainable objectives including:

- easily accessible venue for delegates
- reduction of carbon emissions
- food composting in venues
- reduction in landfill waste

Continued

CASE STUDY: GOOGLE ZEITGEIST CONFERENCE 2009—*CONT'D*

'It's essential that businesses identify areas in which they can be more sustainable, as Zeitgeist this year focuses on the state of the environmental world, we thought it was essential we adhered to the BS 8901 system to deliver a sustainable event.'

Vish Patel, Google

Conclusion. One of the event objectives that Google set out to achieve through the Zeitgeist conference was to be seen as a thought leader. By implementing BS 8901, Google is at the forefront of helping to change the way the events industry plans and implements events.

For further information about Zeitgeist, Google and Organise This, please visit:

Zeitgeist 2009.: www.youtube.com/watch?v=Se-wlHw9XQM Google: *www.google.com/about. html* Organise This: *www.organisethis.co.uk*

For further information and additional case studies demonstrating the implementation of BS 8901, please visit: *www.bsigroup.com/bs8901*

By BSI

Questions

1. What are the implications of BS 8901 for the events industry?
2. What benefits do you believe BS 8901 may bring to an event or events company?
3. Identify and discuss other standards and guidelines that may assist events companies in their approach to sustainability.
4. BS 8901 is currently being developed as an international standard ISO 20121 – what opportunities and challenges do you think that the standard will face when launched on this international stage?

Planning

2

Conceptualising events that will inspire, impart knowledge or achieve any of a myriad of other objectives, is a perpetual challenge for the practising event manager. Whatever concept that is decided upon, then needs to be subjected to a range of planning processes if it is to successfully meet the expectations of its various shareholder groups, such as the attendees, community, sponsors and the event 'owner'.

In this section of the book, the areas of event conceptualisation and planning are discussed, with specific chapters dealing with strategic, financial, human resource, project, marketing and sponsorship planning and event concept development.

The strategic planning function

LEARNING OBJECTIVES

After studying this chapter, you should be able to:

- appreciate the importance of planning to ensure the success of an event
- discuss the nature of the strategic planning process as it applies to events
- identify an appropriate organisational structure through which to conduct an event
- describe the various stages in the event strategic planning process
- construct objectives for an event which are specific, measurable, achievable, realistic and time specific.

INTRODUCTION

This chapter provides an overview of strategic planning as it applies to the conduct of events. It begins by discussing the importance of planning to the overall success of an event and then moves on to describe the strategic event planning process. This process comprises a number of sequential and interrelated steps, beginning with the development of an event concept or intent to bid and ending with event shutdown, evaluation and reporting. The potential for legacy related outcomes flowing from the application of this process is also acknowledged and briefly discussed here. Additionally, this chapter examines the range of organisational structures, from which event managers must select those required to support and implement their planning efforts.

WHAT IS STRATEGIC PLANNING?

In its simplest form, the strategic planning process consists of identifying where an organisation is, deciding where it should be positioned in the market place in order to maximise its chances of progressing its mission and creating strategies and tactics to achieve that position. In other words, the strategic planning process is concerned with end results and the means to achieve those results.

Events Management. DOI: 10.1016/B978-1-85617-818-1.10006-4

Perhaps the value of strategic planning is best summed up by the words of the following conversation between the Cat and Alice in Lewis Carroll's famous children's story *Alice's Adventures in Wonderland* (1865):

> *'Cheshire Puss, . . . Would you tell me, please, which way I ought to go from here?'*
> *'That depends a good deal on where you want to get to,' said the Cat.*
> *'I don't much care where —,' said Alice.*
> *'Then it doesn't matter which way you go,' said the Cat.*
> *'—so long as I get SOMEWHERE,' Alice added as an explanation.*
> *'Oh, you're sure to do that,' said the Cat, 'if you only walk long enough.' (p. 87)*

This quotation, in a somewhat humorous way, makes the point that if you haven't thought about where you wish to go (in our case, your strategic direction), you could end up anywhere. To avoid this situation, an event organisation needs to think through its vision, mission or purpose — concepts that will be discussed later in this chapter. The value of planning is achieved by focusing an organisation (such as an event organising committee) on particular objectives and in the creation of defined pathways by which these objectives can be achieved. Central to the establishment of such pathways is an understanding of internal (for example, available resources) and external (for example, current economic conditions) factors that will condition any decisions that are made. Other benefits associated with the planning process include its capacity to identify and resolve problems, generate a range of potential alternative strategies for consideration and give employees a better understanding of the organisation's strategies and become more committed to achieving them; it clarifies roles and responsibilities and it reduces uncertainty about the future, so that resistance to change is minimised (Hannagan, 2008). While the power of strategic planning in facilitating an organisation's progress towards its vision and mission has been acknowledged by many writers (such as Grant, 2005; Hill, Jones, Galvin and Haidar, 2007; Johnson, Scholes and Whittington, 2008; Lynch, 2009; Pearce and Robinson, 2005; Pitts and Lei, 2006), actual engagement involves a measure of discipline on the part of the event organisation.

Event planning and management has been extensively discussed in an increasing range of texts, including Allen (2009), Getz (2005), Goldblatt (2008), Hall (1997), Mallen and Adams (2008), Masterman (2009), Matthews (2008a, b), Raj, Walters and Rashid (2009), Shone and Parry (2010), Silvers (2004a), Tassiopolous (ed.) (2010),Torkildsen (2005), Tum, Norton and Wright (2005), Van Der Wagen (2008) and Watt (1998); and has also formed the basis of management guides, including UK Sport (2005). Whether taking a planning or production perspective, each author adds an interesting perspective to the professional planning and management of events and adds to the increasing body of knowledge underpinning the educational and professional developments in the field. To engage productively in the planning process, an event manager needs to keep a range of matters in mind. Central among these matters are the need to monitor and evaluate progress, coordinate decisions in all areas so that event objectives are progressed and communicate with, inspire and motivate those responsible for carrying out the various elements of the plan. These matters are discussed in later chapters.

As Sir John Harvey-Jones, a past chairman of ICI in the UK, notes: 'Planning is an unnatural process: it is much more fun to do nothing. The nicest thing about not planning is that failure comes as a complete surprise, rather than being preceded by a period of worry and depression' (Focused Performance, 2006).

Event organisations need to be mindful that plans, as Hannagan (2008) and Thompson with Martin (2005) note, need to be adapted to changing circumstances. Event organisations should also be alert to the fact that occasionally successful strategies might emerge without prior planning (Hill et al. 2007). Such 'emergent' strategies may be due to unforeseen circumstances or might flow from actions taken for non-strategic reasons. For example, a community fair may decide to include a brief music programme at its conclusion as a way of encouraging people to leave the event site progressively and to reduce the big departure rush and subsequent traffic congestion. If this dimension of the programme were to meet with a strong, unexpected positive response from attendees, the event organisers might be prompted to consider changing the event's format to embrace a stronger music component.

PLANNING FOR EVENTS

Where does the event planning process begin? The answer to this question depends on whether the event is being conducted for the first time or if it is a pre-existing event. In the case of a new event, the event manager may be required to first work through the broad concept of the event with key stakeholders and then undertake a feasibility study. If this study shows that the event is likely to meet certain key criteria (such as profitability), they would then move to develop a plan for its creation and delivery. In instances where an event is pre-existing and open to the bidding process (for example, a conference or sporting event), an initial decision needs to be made as to whether (after a preliminary investigation) it is worthwhile making a bid or proposal. If the answer is 'yes', a more detailed feasibility study might be conducted to identify such things as the costs and benefits associated with hosting it before preparing a formal bid. If a bid or proposal is prepared and it is successful, then detailed event planning would commence. The process associated with event planning in the context of new events and events attracted through the bidding process, are shown in Figure 6.1.

ELEMENTS OF THE STRATEGIC EVENT PLANNING PROCESS

The process of strategic planning in an event context involves an event manager moving through a number of sequential and interrelated steps (see Figure 6.1). In this section, each of these steps is identified and briefly overviewed.

FIGURE 6.1 The strategic event planning process

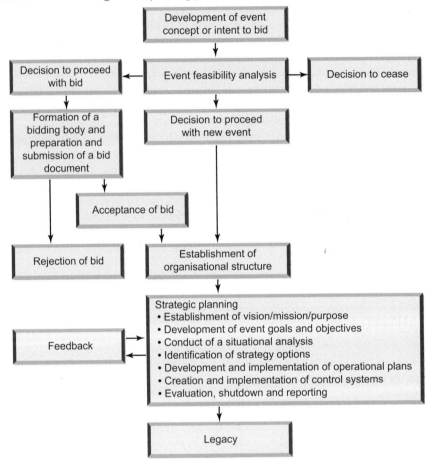

(*Source: adapted from Grant, 2005*)

Concept or intent to bid

In the context of proposed new events, this preliminary stage in the strategic event management process involves making decisions (often after consultation with potential stakeholder groups such as sponsors, telecasters, potential attendees and government departments) that act to refine the initial event concept. These decisions will centre on matters such as the final type/form of the event, duration, location/venue, timing and other key programme elements that will serve to make the event unique or special. Once the event concept is sufficiently developed, it can then be subjected to more detailed analysis. (*Note*: Detailed discussion of developing event concepts can be found in Chapter 7).

In instances where bidding is involved, events for which bids can be made need to be identified. Organisations involved in the identification process may include convention and visitors' bureaus, major event agencies, tourism bodies or local chapters of national or international associations; or it may be as a result of requests for proposals (RFPs).

Once identified, a preliminary assessment can be made as to their 'fit' with the capabilities of the potential event organising body and the hosting destination. Events deemed worthy of further investigation may then be the subject of more detailed scrutiny via a feasibility analysis (see Chapter 4 for a discussion of organisations involved in the event bidding process).

Feasibility analysis

To assess the potential success of an individual event, it is sound practice to objectively (perhaps via the use of an external organisation or consultant) engage in a formal analysis of this potential. There are many considerations that it may be appropriate to take into account in conducting such a study, including (depending on the event) likely budget requirements; managerial skill needs; venue capacities; host community and destination area impacts (both economic and non-economic); availability of volunteers, sponsors and supporting services (for example, equipment hire firms); projected visitation/attendance; infrastructure requirements; availability of public/private sector financial support (for example, grants, sponsorship); level of political support for the event and the track record of the event in terms of matters such as profitability. It should be noted that the level of detail and complexity associated with these studies will vary. An event such as the Olympic Games, for example, is likely to involve a more lengthy and detailed analysis than, say, a regional sporting championship or an association conference.

Given that many events seek public funding to support their creation and delivery, the capacity of an event's organisers to convince granting bodies of the 'feasibility' of their event is often crucial to its proceeding. This being the case, event organisers can benefit from using the criteria employed by granting bodies (see example in Figure 6.2), when evaluating the feasibility of their events.

Decision to proceed or cease

In the case of new events, the outcomes of a feasibility analysis will directly determine if and when the event will proceed. In the case of events involving a formal bid, this decision will depend on whether the bid is accepted or rejected.

Formation of a bidding body and bid preparation

Once it has been decided to proceed with a bid, a body will need to be established to prepare a formal bid document. Often established organisations, such as those noted in connection with intent to bid, will play the central role in this process. Such bids, as noted previously, should only proceed after a formal feasibility analysis.

FIGURE 6.2 Community Festival and Event Fund 2009—10

Introduction

The Community Festival & Event Fund is open to Bristol – based community groups, organisations, companies and charities who are organising free existing, or emerging festivals & events outdoors in Bristol. The fund supports community celebrations that engage communities and enhance local image and identity.

The fund seeks to provide additional financial support to the overall costs of the event.

£20,000 is available for 2009-2010.

Individual funds will be awarded up to a maximum of £2,000 per festival/event.

Objectives:

- To support free festivals and events that are of benefit to Bristol people and creatives.
- Support community celebration outside through festivals and events that engage communities and enhance local image and identity through the arts.
- Encourage good practice in supporting and developing creativity.
- To develop new audiences for, and encourage participation in arts/culture.
- Improve access to and quality of arts/cultural festivals and events.

Priority will be given to festivals/events that:

- Engage communities and enhance local image and identity through the arts.
- Are generated by organisations from within the city, and involve the community in delivery and management.
- Have a proven ability to run successful, safe events.
- Will take place in areas/spaces that have little or no art/cultural activity.
- Are currently not in receipt of funding from Bristol City Council.
- Do not charge entry/sell tickets.

The awarding process and how to apply.

The funding decisions will be advised by a panel with expertise in arts and cultural development and event management. The panel will advise on the granting of funds and awards will depend on the overall demand for grants, the level of priority attached to the event, the proposed use of the grant, and to what extent the stated criteria can be met.

The Funding application deadline for 2009-10 is 4.00pm Wednesday 18th February 2009 and you will be contacted by letter by 9th March 2009. ONLY signed hard copies of the application will be accepted.

Please note late applications will not be considered due to administrative pressures.

Mandatory Criteria.

All applications to The Community Festival & Event Fund MUST meet all of the following criteria before going to the panel:

1. Takes place outdoors
2. Takes place in Bristol between April 1st 2009 and 31st March 2010
3. Demonstrates a commitment to equality of opportunity, celebrating diversity and extending cross-cultural understanding.
4. Supports and develops artists work.
5. Free of charge to enter and accessible to the general public (not restricted to closed groups such as members of an organisation).
6. Describes marketing and publicity activity.
7. Demonstrates a high degree of community involvement & participation
8. Is able to attract partnership funding or in-kind support of 25% of the whole budget.
9. Has enclosed a copy of current bank statement

FIGURE 6.2 *Continued*

10. Has enclosed a photocopy of constitution or articles of association or memorandum & articles to prove they are a constituted organisation/company that has a formal management structure.
11. Application signed and dated
12. Realistic and complete budget

The Fund will not:

- Be the sole source of income.
- Fund research and development activities
- Fund core activities, ongoing arts/workshop projects, touring work.
- Support profit making activities.
- Support national promoters / commercial events and tradefairs
- Support those who aim to raise money for charity.
- Support those who aim to promote religious/political beliefs/interests of an individual or organisation.
- Fund festivals retrospectively.
- Prioritise festivals/organisations who have failed to acknowledge Bristol City Council support/logo in previous funding rounds.
- Support events/organisations who have contravened Bristol City Council Licensing Regulations

Successful recipients of the Fund will be required to:

1. Acknowledge the support of Bristol City Council (including use of (legible) logo) in all relevant publicity and promotional material, as part of a contractual agreement.
2. Submit an evaluation report and final budget statement no later than 3 months after project end date - 20% of the award will be held back until this is submitted. Failure to submit an evaluation form and final budget statement within 3 months will jeopardise any future application to the Fund.
3. Provide free access for BCC arts team and/or their representatives to the event/project for purposes of evaluation/assessment.

(Source: Bristol City Council Arts Festivals and Events Service, 2008)

The bidding process commonly involves a number of steps, specifically:

- identifying resources that can be employed to support the event, for example, venues and government grants
- developing a critical path/timeline for the preparation and presentation of a bid document to the 'owners' of the event
- responding to each of the bid criteria set by the event owners
- developing an understanding of the organisation conducting the event and the exact nature of the event itself
- identifying the key elements of past successful bids to ensure that these elements are dealt with fully in the bid document
- preparing a bid document
- presenting and/or submitting a bid to the 'owners' of the event, such as a sporting body
- lobbying in support of the bid
- evaluating reasons for bid failure (if necessary)

It should be kept in mind that bidding is likely to commence a number of years before the scheduled date of an event. It is also not uncommon for organisations seeking to host an event to go through the bidding process on several occasions before they are successful — if indeed, they do succeed.

In a corporate event context, the bidding process may involve submitting a formal proposal to the potential client (Allen, 2002; O'Toole and Mikolaitis, 2002) in response to the RFP identified earlier, followed by a pitching process — a presentation of the idea to the client against competitors in order to secure the business. Each process and proposal will be developed to the client's specified requirements, and therefore, research will be required into the client organisation. O'Toole (2004) produces a useful checklist for areas generally included in a proposal (Figure 6.3).

Establishment of an organisational structure

Once a decision is made to conduct an event, an organisational structure will need to be established through which the event can be delivered. Research into organisation and structures in events is advancing. For example, Hanlon and Jago (2009) have

FIGURE 6.3 Contents of the event proposal

- CoverLetter
- Title Page
- Proprietary Notice – cautions about unauthorized disclosure
- Table of Contents (TOC)
- List of Abbreviations
- Executive Summary
- Body of Proposal
  - Profile of the Event Company:
    - General: including mission, background, credentials
    - Specific: including previous similar events and resources available
- Project partners and their profiles
- Event Specific information:
  - Objectives
  - Scope of Work
  - Stakeholders
  - Themes, design and ideas
  - Site/venue assessment
  - Resources required : AV, entertainment, catering, staff, suppliers.
  - Marketing and promotional services needed
  - Possible sponsorship
  - Budget – corresponding to functional areas of programme elements
  - Control management – reporting processes,organization structure responsibilities
  - Schedules – planning, transport, running order, promotion
  - Environmental impact – natural environment, traffic, transport.
  - Risk issues including insurance.
- Appendices

(Source: O'Toole, 2004)

advanced the theory relating to 'pulsating organisations'. Many event organisations operate with a small management structure for much of the year and then expand and adapt to incorporate an increased number of management and staff during the period of the event, before contracting post-event. Further, Theodoraki (2007), provides an extensive review of organisation and structures in the context of the Olympics, based on extensive research into host cities and covering phases from bidding through to post-games close down.

Simple structures

As the name suggests, a simple structure has a low level of complexity. As Figure 6.4 illustrates, all decision making is centralised with the event manager, who has total control over all staff activities. This is the most common structure in small event management businesses as it is flexible, adaptable to changing circumstances, easy to understand and has clear accountability — the manager is accountable for all the activities associated with the event. The flexibility of this structure commonly means that staff are expected to be multi-skilled and perform various job functions. This can mean that individual jobs are more satisfying and it can produce higher levels of staff morale. However, this structure has some potential limitations. As staff do not have the opportunity to specialise they may not achieve a high level of expertise in any one area. Additionally, once an event organisation grows beyond a certain size, decision making can become very slow — or even non-existent — as a single executive has to make all decisions and carry out all the management functions. Also, if the manager has an autocratic style of management, staff can become demoralised when their expertise is not fully utilised. There is also an inherent risk in concentrating all event management information in one person — obviously, sickness at an inappropriate time could prove disastrous.

Functional structures

As the name suggests, a functional structure is based upon the main tasks or functions that an organisation needs to perform in order to fulfil its mission. Such tasks commonly emerge from the work breakdown structure process discussed in Chapter 8 and will vary from event to event. The Port Fairy Folk Festival (Victoria, Australia) for example, has identified some 14 key task areas central to its

FIGURE 6.4 A simple organisational structure

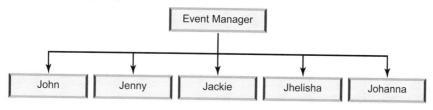

successful conduct, specifically: sponsorship, finance, security, markets, concessions, stalls, community liaison, artist accommodation, ticketing, bars, construction, volunteers, programming and administration. The committee responsible for this event has allocated individuals from within its own ranks to each of these functions (Port Fairy Folk Festival, 2006). By way of contrast and to highlight the fact that each event will customise its functional breakdown of tasks to meet its own specific needs, the Roskilde Festival (a large Danish music festival) has broken its organisational structure into 13 functional areas, each with its own manager (see Figure 6.5).

The more complex an event, the greater the number of tasks that will need to be embraced within a function-based organisational structure. By way of example, Figure 6.6 on page 197 shows the complex organisational structure used to deliver the 2006 Melbourne Commonwealth Games.

This structure also serves to highlight the diversity of tasks associated with large-scale events. In this instance, tasks extended from those of a commercial nature to construction, risk management, overall project management, venue, finance, sport and human resource management, ceremonies and broadcasting.

A number of benefits can be attributed to the use of a function-based organisational structure within an event context. Central among these is that people are able to specialise and so both make use of their pre-existing expertise in a specific area and/or further develop such expertise. This is particularly the case when individuals are placed into functional teams where they can learn from others (Lynch, 2009).

FIGURE 6.5 The functional organisational structure of the Roskilde Festival

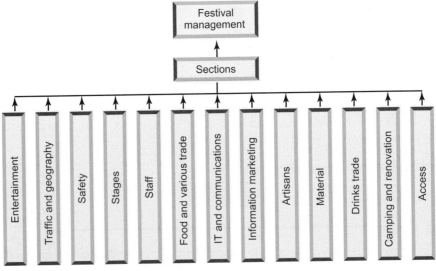

(Source: Roskilde Festival, 2006)

FIGURE 6.6 2006 Melbourne Commonwealth Games organisational structure

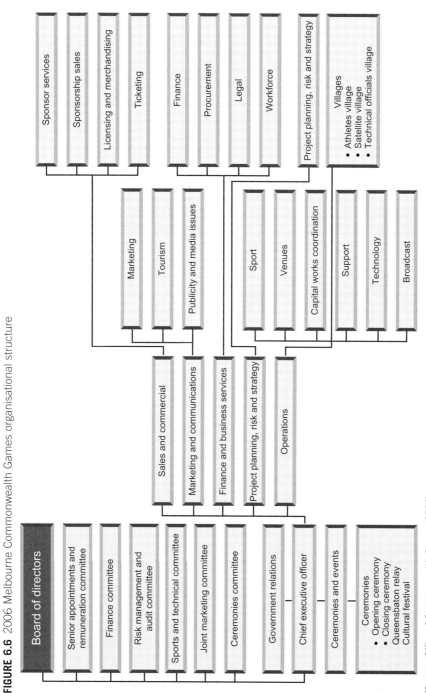

(Source: Office of Commonwealth Games, 2006)

Additionally, when task areas are identified and responsibility given to groups/individuals to carry them out, consideration can be given to the amount of work involved within each task so that it can be realistically performed within the time available. The Philadelphia Folk Festival, for example, uses an organisational structure comprising 30 task-based committees (Philadelphia Folksong Society, 2006). The use of such a large number of committees, it can reasonably be assumed, is in acknowledgement of the event being entirely run by time-constrained volunteers. By breaking down an event into task areas, functional structures also reduce the possibility of inefficiencies resulting from overlapping areas of responsibility.

Finally, as events tend to build their organisational structures quickly and to tear them down even faster, this structure offers event organisations the ability to quickly add, subtract or expand the number of functional areas based on their needs. This capacity is particularly useful when it is necessary to functionally 'evolve' event organisational structures, as an event moves from its planning phase through to its delivery (see the case study on the 2003 Rugby World Cup on pages 219-27).

While a widely used approach to structuring the organisation of an event, there are nonetheless potential limitations to this method. These include problems of coordination due partly to a lack of understanding by staff in individual functional areas of the responsibilities of people in other task areas and the possibility of conflict between functional areas as each seeks to protect what it considers its interests (Hill et al., 2007). Various techniques can be identified that go some way to preventing these problems. These comprise employing multi-skilling strategies that require the rotation of staff through different functional areas, regular meetings between the managers/chairs of all functional areas, general staff meetings and communications (such as newsletters) that aim to keep those engaged on the event aware of matters associated with its current status (for example, budgetary situations or the passing of milestones).

In Chapter 10, activities that are essential elements of the leadership function of the event manager are discussed.

Programme-based matrix structures

Matrix structures group activities by function as well as by project (Hill et al., 2007). What this means is that people working within such a structure commonly have two bosses: a functional boss who is responsible for the particular function to which they have been assigned and a project boss who is responsible for the specific project on which they are working. In an event context, these structures can be seen in operation in large—scale, multi-venue events, such as an Olympic Games. Toohey and Halbwirth (2001) note that the organisational structure of the Sydney Olympic Games, for example, moved from a purely functional structure to that of a venue-based matrix structure as the event approached (see Figure 6.7). The reason for this movement lay in the need to 'push' functional expertise (for example, security, ticketing), which had been developed centrally, out to venues where these tasks needed to be actually undertaken. Additionally, by acting in this way, decision-making bottlenecks and communication problems that might have occurred under

FIGURE 6.7 Sydney 2000 Olympic Games matrix organisational structure

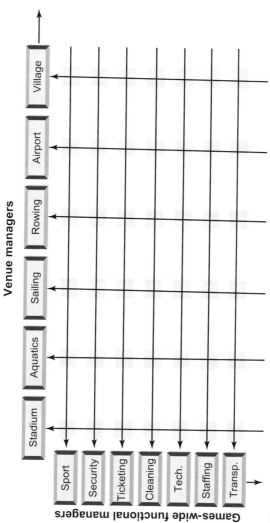

(Source: Sloman, 2006)

a centralised functional structure were largely avoided. While there is much to recommend this structure in large multi-venue events, if the event is to be presented as a unified whole, a high value must be placed on coordination across the various venues by senior management. Additionally, as staff located in venues effectively have two bosses, issues can arise around communication, reporting and lines of authority.

Multi-organisational or network structures

Most specialist event management companies are relatively small in size (fewer than 20 people), yet many conduct quite large and complex events. This is possible because these organisations enlist the services of a variety of other firms (see Figure 6.8). In effect, they create 'virtual' organisations that come together quickly and are disbanded shortly after an event is concluded. Central among the benefits of employing this structure is its ability to allow the event management firm to

FIGURE 6.8 A network structure

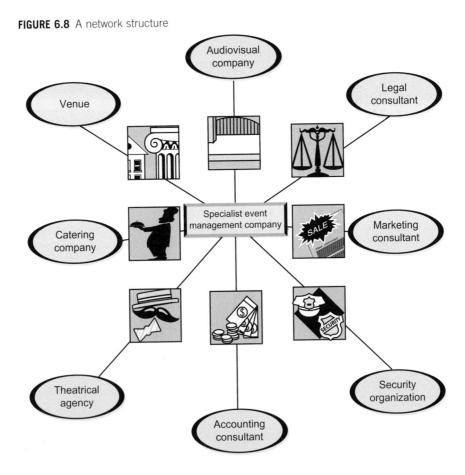

specialise in the 'management' function and so become increasingly capable in this area. This structure also avoids the need to maintain a large staff with multiple skills, which for periods between events would have little or nothing to do.

Other advantages of the network structure include the ability to contract specialist businesses with current expertise and experience; greater accuracy in the event costing process as supplier expenses can be established via the contracting process; and quick decision making as the 'core' management group is made up of only a few people or one individual.

As with the other structures previously discussed, there are also possible disadvantages to be considered. These include concerns over quality control and reliability that arise from the use of outside contractors and the associated potential difficulties involved in developing an integrated event 'team' to deliver the event. Nevertheless, the concept of the network structure is supported by contemporary management thinking on downsizing, sticking to core activities and outsourcing and can be very effective for certain kinds of events.

Strategic plan

Once established, an event organisation's first task is to engage in the formal strategic planning process.

The strategy process, as noted previously, is essentially about identifying the purpose or vision/mission that an event organisation is seeking to fulfil or process through conducting a specific event and creating plans and undertaking actions to achieve that purpose or vision/mission (Lynch, 2009, p. 5). It is a staged process during which an event organisation determines the current situation it faces (strategic analysis/awareness), considers the strategic options available to an event manager (strategic creation and choice) and sets up the mechanisms for implementing and evaluating/monitoring the chosen strategies (strategic implementation), (Thompson with Martin, 2005). Additionally, in the case (particularly) of large-scale events where the creation of legacy outcomes (such as new infrastructure developments) are an aspect of an event's overall strategy, event organisations will need to consider how they will drive this aspect of the overall event programme.

In this section, each of the steps associated with strategic planning in an event organisational context are overviewed.

Purpose, vision and mission statements

At a minimum, a clear statement of purpose and vision should underpin every event. This statement in turn will be conditioned by the needs of the various stakeholder groups with an interest in the event. Such groups may include client organisations, the local community, government at various levels, potential attendees and participants, sponsors and volunteers.

In the case of events with relatively few stakeholders, and/or events which are relatively straightforward in nature, a considered statement of its purpose is all that is really required to provide adequate strategic direction. For example, Brain Awareness Week, an annual international event coordinated by the Dana Alliance (USA), a private philanthropic organisation and the European Dana Alliance for the Brain, a nonprofit organisation that seeks to provide information about the personal and public benefits of brain research, has as its stated purpose:

> *Brain Awareness Week (BAW) is the global campaign to increase public awareness about the progress and benefits of brain research.*
> **(The Dana Foundation, 2010)**

For events that are more complex in nature (such as large public events) that involve a number of stakeholder groups, it can be beneficial to reflect more deeply on purpose, mission and vision. It is evident that many events are now doing this and, as a result, are creating vision and/or mission statements to guide their development and conduct.

A vision statement can be separate from an event's mission or the two may be combined. Vision statements usually describe what the event seeks to become and to achieve in the longer term (Thompson with Martin, 2005). They are also often brief, precise and motivational in nature. The Windsor Festival (2010), for example, states, '… we offer a unique experience, which entertains and enhances the community, linking social, educational and commercial interests… Building on these foundations, we will increase the breadth and variety of the programme, increase accessibility to the arts and encourage wider recognition of the Festival.'

Some events use more expansive vision statements, which are really a combination of both vision and mission. The Liverpool Women's International Music Festival (WIMFEST, 2004), stated their mission was to, 'be a festival that will celebrate diversity, tolerance, tradition, history and story telling; by women, through music and song. It will involve schools, young people, local communities, professional and amateur performers. The festival will encourage both individual and collective endeavour, empowering and enabling women to organise the event, produce, promote and perform.'

It should be noted that vision statements do not necessarily need to be written down (although it is often useful to do so), provided they are shared and understood by those involved with the event. It may be fair to say, for example, that while no formal vision statement may have existed at the time the Notting Hill Carnival began, those involved with it understood clearly that one of its long-term goals was about achieving equality and social acceptance.

A mission statement describes in the broadest terms the task that the event organisation has set for itself. If the event has also established a vision statement, then the mission needs to be viewed in terms of fulfilling this vision. Such statements, at their most advanced, seek to define an event's purpose; identify major beneficiaries and customer groups; indicate the broad nature/characteristics of the event and state the overall operating philosophy or values of the organisation conducting it (for example, to conform to best business practice; to operate within a context of equal opportunity; to adopt environmentally sustainable practices).

Several event mission statements that, to varying degrees, fulfil the previously stated criteria are provided in Table 6.1.

Once established, a mission statement acts as the basis upon which goals and objectives can be set and strategies established. They also serve to provide a short-hand means of conveying to staff (either paid or voluntary), an understanding of the event and what it is trying to achieve. A coherent mission statement can be an invaluable tool for establishing a common direction in a team and promoting unity among its members.

Table 6.1 Sample event mission statements

Event	Mission Statement
Bath Festivals Trust	To enrich people's lives through participation in the arts
Boscombe Arts Festival	Boscombe Arts Festival works to promote participation, enjoyment and creativity for all Bournemouth residents through an annual Boscombe based festival.
Manchester 2002 Commonwealth Games	To deliver an outstanding sporting spectacle of world significance, celebrating athletic excellence, cultural diversity and the unique atmosphere of 'The Friendly Games'. To deliver a successful Games on behalf of all competitors, spectators and stakeholders. To leave a lasting legacy of new sporting facilities and social, physical and economic regeneration. To set a new benchmark for hosting international sporting events in the UK and the lasting benefit they can generate for all those involved.
Salford Film Festival	The Salford Film Festival will promote and raise the profile of Salford as an area of creative excellence in image media. The Salford Film Festival will focus on the community of Salford using moving image, still image and self-image. Through the production and screening of new productions, the festival will encourage the development of links regionally, nationally and internationally and encourage and promote new media work.
Worcester Festival	The Festival is an opportunity for local people to attend and participate in a wide selection of professional and community events and activities or even stage or host their own event. The Festival is for the people of Worcester and the surrounds and is a series of partnerships between large cross sections of the community and an umbrella for a huge range of activities. The Worcester Festival is neither a music festival nor an arts festival (although it has features of both), but is simply a festival for all to enjoy. It is a coming together of people of all ages and backgrounds and is a celebration of life, of Worcester and its people.

(Source: Boscombe Arts Festival (2005); Bath Festivals Trust (2005); Manchester 2002 (2003), p. 3; Salford Film Festival (2010); Worcester Festival (2009))

Goals and objectives

Once an event's mission has been decided, the event manager must then move on to establish the event's goals and/or objectives. Goals are broad statements that seek to provide direction to those engaged in the organisation of the event, as seen in Table 6.2. Objectives in turn are used to quantify progress towards an event's goals and set performance benchmarks that allow event organisations to assess whether the different aspects of their planning have succeeded or failed. It should be noted that the terms 'goals' and 'objectives' are often used interchangeably but they are really distinct concepts. It should also be noted that for some forms of events (particularly those of a corporate nature), the step of creating goals prior to establishing objectives is not usually necessary. The establishment of goals is useful when the event is

Table 6.2 Sample of event goals and objectives

Event	Goals
Salford Film Festival	To present a showcase of past present and future filmmaking in Salford alongside a range of relevant international film productions. To identify and raise the aspirations of emerging filmmakers, primarily in Salford and its environs, by developing sustainable partnerships with key stakeholders and sector champions. To develop pathways into image media partnerships with community groups, educational establishments and professional bodies. To increase the cultural and leisure opportunities and in doing so bring about a positive impact on the lives of young people To utilise culture and leisure to provide more opportunities to develop skills and improve esteem
SeaBritain 2005	To raise awareness of Britain's maritime and coastal heritage To encourage participation in maritime sport and leisure activities To promote the UK coast and its islands as a tourism destination and travel by sea to European visitors To promote an understanding and involvement with the marine environment and marine conservation To raise awareness of the contribution made by the sea and seafaring to the UK economy and culture To develop maritime learning materials designed specifically to link with the National Curriculum To leave a legacy in 2006 and beyond
Windsor Festival	Continue to promote quality performances of music and the arts within the Royal Borough of Windsor and Maidenhead. Increase local access to the arts and music in the unique venues available in Windsor, Eton and Maidenhead. Encourage the development of young musicians and other artists. Provide opportunities for local performers.

(Source: Salford Film Festival (2010), SeaBritain 2005 Press Office (2004), Windsor Festival (2010))

complex in nature and involves a number of stakeholder groups. In such instances, they serve a useful role in building on the event's mission statement to provide direction and focus to the event organisers' activities.

Useful criteria that can be applied to the establishment of objectives are summed up by the acronym SMART, which refers to the fact that objectives should be:

- *specific:* focused on achieving an event goal or, if no goals have been developed, its purpose
- *measurable:* expressed in a way that is quantifiable
- *agreeable:* agreed on by those responsible for achieving them
- *realistic:* in terms of the event organisation having the human, financial and physical resources to achieve them
- *time specific:* to be achieved by a particular time

Each event will obviously vary in terms of the objectives it establishes. Examples of such objectives are as follows:

Economic objectives
- Percentage return on monies invested or overall gross/net profit sought
- Financial value of sponsorship attracted

Percentage of income to be raised from fundraising activities
- Percentage increase in market share (if the event is competing directly with other similar events)

Attendance/participation
- Total attendance/attendance by specific groups (for example, people from outside the area, specific age groups, professions)
- Size of event in terms of stallholders/exhibitors/performers/attendees
- Number of local versus outside artists
- Percentage of an area's cultural groups represented in a programme
- Number of community groups involved with the event

Quality
- Percentage level of attendee/exhibitor/sponsor/volunteer satisfaction
- Number of participants/speakers/performers of international reputation
- Number of complaints from attendees/exhibitors/volunteers.

Awareness/knowledge/attitudes
- Percentage of attendees or others exposed to the event that have changed levels of awareness/knowledge as a result of the event
- Percentage of attendees or others exposed to the event who have altered their attitudes as a result of it

Human resources
- Percentage of staff/volunteer turnover
- Percentage of volunteers retained from previous year.

Wendroff (2004, p. 2) highlights seven goals for non-profit/charity events. These are to raise money, update the mission statement to educate the community, motivate board members and supporters, recruit volunteers and future board members, expand the organisation's network, market the organisation and solicit endorsements.

Situational analysis

Before moving to establish specific strategies for an event, its organisers are well advised to undertake an assessment of its internal environment (for example, financial situation, staff expertise, quality/number of venues, market perception of event) and external environment (for example, the number/type of competing events, legislative changes, community attitude to event or events in general, impact of climate change). One common way of undertaking this task is by employing a strengths, weaknesses, opportunities and threats (SWOT) analysis. Such an analysis will likely involve referring to a range of existing information sources, including data collected previously by the event, census data and general reports/studies on relevant matters such as trends in leisure behaviour. On occasion it may be necessary to commission studies in order to fill information gaps or to update an event organisation on a particular matter. A deeper understanding of the needs, wants, motives and perceptions of current or potential customer groups, for example, may be deemed necessary before dramatically altering an event's programme in an effort to increase attendance. For a more detailed discussion of this aspect of strategic planning see Chapter 11.

The external environment consists of all those factors that surround the event and which can impact on its success. A thorough scanning of the full range of factors that make up the external environment should aid the event manager making decisions on such matters as target market(s) selection, programming, promotional messages, ticket pricing and when to conduct the event. Threats to the event (for example, proposed changes to legislation regarding outdoor consumption of alcohol) or the emergence of new competing events can also be identified through this process.

The external environment is usually assessed first and consists of many factors. The main factors include:

- *Political/legal:* the decisions made by all levels of government become laws or regulations that affect the way in which people live in a society. The laws regulating the consumption of food and alcoholic beverages, for example, have changed radically in the UK since the 1950s, making outdoor food and wine festivals possible.
- *Economic:* economic factors such as unemployment, inflation, interest rates, distribution of wealth and levels of wages and salaries can impact on the demand for events. Declining living standards in a particular region, for example, may require an event to reduce its ticket prices and seek alternative sources of revenue (for example, grants or sponsorship) to subsidise the event costs.

- *Social/cultural:* changes in a population's ethnic/religious make-up or leisure behaviour can act to influence event demand. These changes can provide opportunities (for example, a demand for multicultural events) or pose threats (for example, an increased tendency to engage in home based leisure activities). Existing attitudes among a population towards a particular activity can also be a factor of interest to event managers. The love of sport possessed by many British, for example, was 'tapped' for the successful London 2012 Olympic bid, both to generate demand and to create a climate of tolerance for the various event preparation disruptions. The culture of a particular place can also provide a rich resource on which event managers can draw; for example, the architecture, traditions, beliefs, cuisine and artistic skills associated with a particular area can be embraced, selectively or collectively, by event managers.
- *Technological:* changes in equipment and machines have revolutionised the way people undertake tasks, including aspects of event management (Chapter 14). One example is using the Internet to promote festivals, exhibitions and events. Entering the word 'festival' into an Internet search engine will produce links to a multitude of events in all parts of the globe. Another example is the use of the Internet as a vehicle for conducting events such as conferences. Internet sites that support event professionals, students and educators by providing information, directories, and resources online are also appearing (for example, EPMS.net, TSNN.com, Whitebook.co.uk and WorldofEvents.net).
- *Demographic:* the composition of society in terms of age, gender, education and occupation changes over time. A striking example is the entry of the baby boomers' generation (people born between 1945 and 1960) into middle age. The generation that gave the world rock'n'roll, blue jeans and relaxed sexual morals is, and will continue to be, a large market for event managers and will always have very different needs to the preceding and succeeding generations.
- *Physical/environmental:* concern over such matters as pollution and waste generation within the broader community is affecting the way in which events are conducted. Many councils and sustainable environmental groups are actively encouraging event organisers to 'green' their events (see, for example, Waste Awareness Wales, 2009). Another environmental consideration for event managers is the changing weather patterns caused by the impact of greenhouse gases. Such changes have the potential to impact on outdoor events, particularly when they are conducted.
- *Competitive:* other events that attract a similar audience need to be monitored. In this regard, comparisons relating to such matters as programme and pricing are useful. Events do not necessarily have to be similar in nature to attract a similar audience. A consumer exhibition organiser in a port city, for example, suffered a significant decline in demand for an event they had organised when a visiting aircraft carrier decided to conduct a public open day at the same time.

A thorough scanning of the full range of factors that make up the external environment will reveal the event's target market(s), its range of activities, and opportunities for promotion, sponsorship and fundraising. Similarly, threats to the successful operation of the event can also be identified. Over a period of time, environmental factors can change, sometimes dramatically, necessitating adjustments to an event's objectives or design. For example, the ethnic composition of many areas within the UK has undergone marked change and the resultant shifts in the social and cultural environments of those areas, have affected the demand for festivals celebrating particular cultures. In another example, a predicted reduction in government funding of cultural events is patently a threat to an event organisation dependent on such funding for much of its revenue.

When the analysis of the external environment is complete, the next step in the strategic planning process is to undertake an internal analysis of the event organisation's physical, financial, informational and human resources in order to establish its strengths and weaknesses. Areas of strength or weakness associated with an event may include the level of management or creative expertise on which it can draw, the quality of its supplier relationships, ownership or access to appropriate venues and facilities (for example, stages and sound systems), the quality of event programme elements, access to appropriate technology such as ticketing systems, the level of sophistication of the event management software systems in use, access to financial resources, the event reputation, the size of the volunteer base and the strength of links with potential sponsors.

Identification of strategy options

The environmental scanning process gathers crucial information that can be used by an event organisation to achieve its vision/mission or purpose. Strategies must use strengths, minimise weaknesses, avoid threats and take advantage of opportunities that have been identified. A SWOT analysis is a wasted effort if the material gathered by this analytic process is not used in strategy formulation.

Before examining several generic business strategies that might be adopted by an event organisation, it needs to be noted that some events, specifically those of a public nature, have goals that do not link strongly to concerns such as market share, competitiveness and profit. Goals for events of this nature may be set in any number of areas, such as community building, environmental enhancement and raising community awareness of specific issues. Because of the wide range of potential goals public events might pursue, it is difficult to comment specifically on their strategic choices. Nonetheless, whatever choices they do make must, as with other events, progress their vision and associated mission.

Growth strategy

Many event managers have a fixation on event size and, as such, seek to make their events bigger than previous ones or larger than similar events. Bigger is often thought to be better, particularly by ambitious event managers. Growth can be expressed as more revenue, more event components, more participants or consumers or a bigger share of the event market. It is worth pointing out that bigger is not necessarily better, as some event managers have discovered. An example of this is

Streets Ahead (a Catalan festival which takes place in Manchester). It adopted a growth strategy from 1995 towards a street festival for the millennium, involving ten local authorities in and around Greater Manchester. In the first year, one authority was involved, the following year two, then four, until by 1999, all ten local authorities were taking part (Allen and Shaw, 2000).

It is important to recognise that an event does not necessarily have to grow in size for its participants to feel that it is better than its predecessors – this can be achieved by dedicating attention to the quality of activities, careful positioning and improved planning. However, a growth strategy may be appropriate if historical data suggest there is a growing demand for the type of event planned or a financial imperative necessitates increasing revenue. The annual Reading Festival substantially increased attendance by incorporating contemporary pop acts into the event's line-up, thereby appealing to a market segment with a strong propensity to attend musical events.

Consolidation or stability strategy

In certain circumstances it may be appropriate to adopt a consolidation strategy – that is, maintaining attendance at a given level. Strong demand for tickets to T In The Park, for example, has allowed the event to sell tickets well in advance, cap attendance numbers and further enhance the quality of its programme. By capping ticket sales in a climate of high demand, this event has also created a situation in which it has greater pricing freedom.

Retrenchment strategy

An environmental scan may suggest that an appropriate strategy is to reduce the scale of an event but add value to its existing components. This strategy can be applicable when the operating environment of an event changes. Retrenchment can seem a defeatist or negative strategy, particularly to long-standing members of an event committee, but it can be a necessary response to an unfavourable economic environment or a major change in the sociocultural environment. The management of a community festival, for example, may decide to delete those festival elements that were poorly patronised and focus only on those that have proven to be popular with its target market. Likewise, an exhibition company, which had previously conducted a conference in association with one of its major exhibitions, may cease to do so due to falling registrations. Resources freed in this way could then be used to add value to its exhibition by, for example, offering a free seminar series and introducing a limited entertainment programme.

Combination strategy

As the name suggests, a combination strategy includes elements from more than one of these generic strategies. An event manager could, for example, decide to cut back or even delete some aspects of an event that no longer appeal to their event target market(s), while concurrently growing other aspects.

It should be noted that various marketing strategies (discussed in Chapter 11), are integral to the pursuit of these broad strategies.

Strategy evaluation and selection

In order to determine which strategic option, or options, is likely to be most successful in progressing an event organisation's vision/mission, some form of analysis is necessary. In this regard, Lynch (2009, pp. 374–9), while acknowledging that each organisation will approach this task in their own way, identifies six general criteria that can be used for this purpose:

1. *Consistency with mission and objectives* — if a strategic option does not meet an organisation's mission and objectives there is a strong case for dismissing it.
2. *Suitability* — a strategy needs to be appropriate when viewed within the context of the environment in which an organisation is operating and its available resources.
3. *Validity* — the assumptions (for example, likely future demand for an event) upon which a strategy is based need to be well supported by appropriate research.
4. *Feasibility of options* — a proposed strategy must be able to be carried out. Several areas where possible constraints might arise need to be taken into account.
    (a) *Organisational culture, skills and resources:* will an event organisation have the financial capacity or expertise necessary to pursue a particular strategy?
    (b) *Constraints external to an organisation:* will an event's customer base be accepting of a particular strategy? Will competing events adapt quickly or restrict the ability of an event organisation to pursue a particular strategy? Will government or other regulatory bodies allow the strategy to be progressed?
    (c) *Lack of commitment from management and employees:* while more a potential issue with large-scale events, it is nonetheless the case that there must be an acceptance of a selected strategy by staff, if it is to have a reasonable chance of success.
5. *Business risk* — strategic options bring with them various levels of risk. Such risks need to be identified and assessed in terms of how acceptable they are to an organisation. For example, an exhibition company that is thinking of doubling the size of one of its major exhibitions would need to establish what potential impact such a growth strategy would have on its cash flow and borrowing requirements. As part of this analysis it is likely it would also work through various scenarios around different cost structures, levels of demand and exhibitor and entry fees.
6. *Attractiveness to stakeholders* — The chosen strategy needs to have some appeal to an event organisation's major stakeholders. This may be difficult to achieve at times. For example, the organisers of a major city based festival may wish to pursue a retrenchment strategy due to overcrowding and associated traffic congestion that they view as compromising the experience of attendees, as well as creating problems for residents around the event site. Major sponsors, on the other hand, may be against such a strategy as it might reduce the number of people exposed to their promotional efforts.

Operational planning

Once a strategy has/strategies have been agreed upon, the event organisation needs to develop a series of operational plans in support of it. The application of project management practices and techniques (see Chapter 6) is particularly useful at this point in the strategic planning process.

Operational plans will be needed for all areas central to the achievement of an event's objectives and the implementation of its strategy. Areas for operational planning will likely vary, therefore, across events. It would be common, however, for plans to be developed in areas such as budgeting, marketing, administration, staging, research and evaluation, security and risk management, sponsorship, environmental waste management, programming, transportation, merchandising and staffing (paid and volunteer).

Each area for which an operational plan is developed will require a set of objectives that are linked to the achievement of the overall event organisation's strategy: action plans and schedules; details of individuals responsible for carrying out the various aspects of the plan; monitoring and control systems, including a budget and an allocation of resources (financial, human and supporting equipment/ services).

Given that many festivals, exhibitions and events are not one-off, but occur at regular intervals — yearly, biennially or, in the case of some major sporting events, every four years — standing plans can be used in a number of operational areas. Standing plans are made up of policies, rules and standard procedures and they serve to reduce decision-making time by ensuring that similar situations are handled in a predetermined and consistent way.

Policies can be thought of as guidelines for decision making. An event may, for example, have a policy of only engaging caterers that meet particular criteria. These criteria might be based on licensing and insurance. Policies, in turn, are implemented by following established, detailed instructions known as procedures. In the case of the previous example, procedures may require the person responsible for hiring caterers to inspect their licence and insurance certificates, check that they are current and obtain copies for the event's records. Rules are statements governing organiser action in a particular situation. An event may establish rules, for example, regarding what caterers can and cannot do with the waste they generate on site or on what they can or cannot sell.

In some instances, particularly in the context of large-scale sporting events, the implementation phase may also involve the conduct of test events as a way of identifying any shortcomings in the event's delivery systems. Test events also provide a 'real world' training opportunity for staff and assist in the development of greater coordination between the various 'teams' involved in event delivery.

Control systems

Once operational plans are implemented, mechanisms are required to ensure that actions conform to plans and that adjustments are made for changing circumstances.

These mechanisms take the form of systems that allow performance to constantly be compared to operational objectives. Performance benchmarks and milestones that indicate progress towards these objectives (such as ticket sales over a given period) are particularly useful in this regard. Meetings and reports are generally central to the control process, as are budgets. Budgets allow actual costs and expenditure to be compared with those projected for the various operational areas. A detailed discussion of the budgeting processes appears in Chapter 9.

Event evaluation, shutdown and reporting

For many events, evaluation remains a neglected aspect of their strategic event planning; yet, it is only through evaluation that event managers can determine how successful their efforts have been in achieving whatever goals and/or objectives they have set. As a result of the evaluation process, information is captured and reports prepared for major event stakeholders such as granting agencies and sponsors. Additionally, problems and shortcomings in current event planning and delivery processes are identified and recommendations made for change. A complex area of the strategic event management process, event evaluation is explored further in Chapter 18.

Once an event is concluded, a range of tasks remain that must be undertaken to complete the 'shutdown' phase. The previously cited reporting task is but one of these. To this task can be added a range of others, including returning the site/venue to its original condition; paying suppliers; selling off equipment; grant acquittal (if required); thanking suppliers, government agencies (such as the police), volunteers and other groups associated with event delivery; winding up, or in the case of recurring events, dramatically reducing in size, the event organisation itself and managing the knowledge associated with the event. This last point is significant particularly in the case of recurring events; capturing the systems and processes used in planning and delivery, along with information flowing from the evaluation process, provides a sound base for an event's future conduct. Indeed, the owners of some large-scale events, such as the Olympic Games, have created specific bodies (Event Knowledge Services) for this purpose (Event Knowledge Services, 2010).

Legacy

For some events, particularly large-scale public events, the issue of legacy has become central to the decision to host or create them. Legacy outcomes can span a wide range of areas including infrastructure improvements, increases in tourism visitation, enhanced industry capacities and workforce skills, environmental improvement and improved economic conditions (see Chapter 3).

In order to secure event legacies some writers (such as Kearney, 2006) suggest that a separate legacy programme be created as part of the overall strategic planning process and that a senior level management position be built into the organisational structure of events with this specific responsibility. While few events have yet to act in this way, the issue of legacy is nonetheless a major consideration with many event organisations.

The 2014 Commonwealth Games in Glasgow, for example, identified social, economic and sporting legacies from hosting the games. These ambitions are supported with legacy frameworks within the Scottish Government (2010) and Glasgow City Council (2010). For London 2012 Olympic Games, legacies have been identified by the organisers, the London Assembly and the UK government, with significant research and action plans to underpin this. For example, the Olympics Delivery Authority (ODA), responsible for delivering the venues and infrastructure for 2012 as well as their use after the games, focus on the physical legacy with the redevelopment of the Lower Lea Valley within their Legacy priority; while the Olympic Park Legacy Company has been established to plan, develop and manage the Olympic Park itself after the games. The UK government (DCMS, 2007a) have made five legacy promises:

1. To make the UK a world-leading sporting nation
2. To transform the heart of East London
3. To inspire a generation of young people
4. To make the Olympic Park a blueprint for sustainable living
5. To demonstrate that the UK is a creative, inclusive and welcoming place to live in, visit and for business.

In order to deliver these promises, a Legacy Action Plan has been developed (DCMS, 2008) based on detailed research (e.g. Cragg, Ross and Dawson, 2007; EdComs, 2007) and legacy plans have been developed for the English regions and UK nations (DCMS, 2007a). At a London level, the Mayor of London has stated Five Legacy Commitments (Mayor of London, 2008), committing to:

1. increase opportunities for Londoners to become involved in sport
2. ensure Londoners benefit from new jobs, businesses and volunteering opportunities
3. transform the heart of east London
4. deliver a sustainable Games and develop sustainable communities
5. showcase London as a diverse, creative and welcoming city

Progress towards these commitments is regularly monitored and reviewed by the London Assembly (GLA, 2010), with a programme of research and publications underpinning the commitments, including work relating to skills, sports and disabled people and sports and young people.

STRATEGIC PLANNING FOR EXISTING EVENTS

In addition to events that are attracted through the bidding process and those that are created as 'clean sheet' exercises, some event organisations will be responsible for the conduct of recurring events such as annual festivals or conferences. In such situations, the event organisation concerned would begin with an appraisal of the current situation faced by the event and then move on to review its organisational structure and previous strategic plan. This process is likely to result in minor changes or refinements in its structure, vision/mission statements, goals, objectives and/or strategies, as well as the development of revised operational plans in areas such as marketing, human resources and finance. On occasions, however, such reviews may result in major changes to an existing strategy. Indeed, event managers need to keep in mind, as Mintzberg (2003) points out, the planning process tends to encourage incremental change, when what may be needed is a complete rethink of the current strategy.

SUMMARY

The strategic planning process provides an event organisation with a systematic approach to the challenge of planning and delivering successful events. Its preliminary stages involve the decision to proceed or not to proceed with an event, with this choice being dependent upon the outcome of a feasibility analysis. If an event proceeds, an appropriate organisational structure is needed. The most common of such structures in an event context are function, network or matrix based. Once established, an event organisation following the strategic planning model proposed here would then progress to establish a strategic plan. This plan begins with the creation of a vision, mission or statement of purpose and then proceeds through a cascading series of steps to event evaluation, shutdown and reporting. Flowing from the implementation of this plan and depending on its mission or purpose, will be a range of potential legacies.

QUESTIONS

1. Briefly discuss the value of setting vision/mission/purpose statements for events.

2. Choose a particular event type (for example, festivals); identify four events that have established mission statements and compare these to the criteria given in this chapter.

3. Conduct an interview with the manager of a particular event with a view to identifying the key external environmental factors that are impacting on the event.

4. When might an event employ a retrenchment strategy *or* a growth strategy? Can you identify any specific event where one of these strategies is in evidence?

5. What types of legacy might a large-scale event result in for the city or country in which it takes place?

6.   Select an event with a functional organisation structure and another with a network structure. Describe each of these structures and discuss why you believe each event chose the organisational structure it used.

7.   Explain the difference between a strategic plan and an operational plan.

8.   Briefly discuss the difference between a policy and a procedure.

9.   Explain why stakeholders are significant from the perspective of establishing vision and mission statements.

10. Critically examine the strategic planning process of a particular event in the light of the process discussed in this chapter.

CASE STUDY: THE VODAFONE BALL BY EURO RSCG SKYBRIDGE

An Event with History. Vodafone's continued programme of global acquisition had seen it become the world's largest mobile phone company, incorporating previously independent businesses in local markets under one brand. The company has historically thanked their employees and partners for their hard work and support on an annual basis. The vehicle for this has traditionally manifested itself in the form of a grand-scaled celebratory ball.

Vodafone wanted to find a refreshing way to invigorate the Vodafone Ball concept, whilst maintaining the employee excitement, expectation and enthusiasm that surround the annual ball.

Euro RSCG Skybridge utilised their in depth knowledge of Vodafone as a global company and its employees as individuals, to conceive, create, plan and produce a celebratory ball, designed to be the largest silver-service dinner party in the world and surpassing the previous year's event and the expectations of a global audience.

Initial Aims & Objectives. Euro RSCG Skybridge looked to create a spectacular event to turn attitudes within Vodafone's newly created global corporation on their heads. Where there had been a belief that the business was stuffy and impersonal and that big was bad, the event awakened employees to the personal dynamics reconciling scale with intimacy and demonstrated that anything is possible when you are the biggest.

It was deemed important to understand exactly what fears the new business held for Vodafone employees to ensure that any solution clearly targeted them, transforming negative beliefs into positives.

The Brief. The most impressive non-corporate benefit of being the biggest and a World Record with a place in The Guinness Book of Records combined with the highly interactive and personal nature of a dinner party, was that it was seen as an exciting event at which to participate.

It was also important to move away from the traditional black tie event since the object was to try to create a relaxed and casual environment, which shattered the myth that Vodafone's size made it bureaucratic and unapproachable.

The remit of the brief was therefore to innovatively create, produce and manage a celebratory ball for Vodafone employees and their guests, on a scale and calibre befitting the growing stature of the organisation and its corporate values and beliefs.

The required venue had to safely accommodate the required numbers of attendees, expected to be between 8,000 – 12,000 people.

The brief covered pre-event planning, guest management and the invitation process, total creative treatment including theming and entertainment, production and all logistical considerations relating to the proposed event.

Continued

CASE STUDY: THE VODAFONE BALL BY EURO RSCG SKYBRIDGE—*CONT'D*

For the ball to be a success, it had to exceed the expectations of those guests who had attended in previous years.

Response. The creative response led with the main theme and event identity of a relaxed Beach Party. This was executed across all aspects of the event from the management approach to its tangible assets. The response included all pre-event guest management, overall creative theming and entertainment, production and all logistical considerations relating to the event.

London's Earls Court was selected as the venue of choice due to its size, location, flexibility and reputation as an excellent entertainment venue. Earls Court provided the additional benefit and security of having staged the event previously.

Pre-event Planning: Logistics and Production. The event requirements were assessed, based on the experiences of the previous year's event, the post-event evaluation, de-brief reports and the additional requirements derived from the increase in total guest numbers.

A Project Team was created to manage the complex logistical and production elements of the event. It was necessary to have defined roles and responsibilities across the required key elements of the project that would provide clear channels of communication and allow for areas of speciality to operate for the common stability of the event.

The Project Team developed a project plan complete with a critical path for each functional dynamic. The main functional responsibilities included:

- Overall project, venue and budgetary management
- Entertainment selection and management
- Main stage show production and direction
- Technical production
- Catering
- Health and Safety; including crowd control and security
- Creative execution; including theming, print and communications
- Transportation management
- Database and administrative management

A series of status meetings were established with all stake-holders to continuously monitor and evaluate progress based on SMART principles, both internally within the agency and directly with the client's project coordinators, providing regular budgetary updates, status and contact reports.

The physicality and health and safety aspects of the event were examined in strict Risk Assessments, performed by the Project Team and specially commissioned, professional Risk Assessors. All findings were documented and presented to the client and formed part of the essential event paperwork.

With the physical infrastructure in place, the other tangible elements were planned and executed to plan. Six months prior to the actual event, it was creatively teased to employees through a programme of internal communications, including posters, emails and a website, heightening awareness and expectation.

The Beach Party theme was creatively incorporated into all aspects of the event from printed collateral, a specially designed website with online booking, the hotline, the invitation process through to the theming of the venue and the entertainment.

The logistics management of the event was a huge undertaking involving an invitation process where 6,000 employees around the world were selected at random and invited to apply for two tickets to the event. Guests who accepted were directed to the dedicated website where they inputted required personal details including transport, dietary and medical requirements. A bespoke software tool created in house, provided the power behind every step of the party, including allowing guests to choose their place on the world's largest table plan for 11,500 people. Using a personal login, guests were also able to access all event details including detailed itinerary, up-to-date transport arrangements and even a friendly letter from the Chief Executive, emphasising the personal nature of the initiative.

In total 136 coaches were sourced to transport 8,500 guests. In addition 1,420 car parking spaces were sourced, 300 VIP guests were chauffeured to and from the venue and approximately 700 domestic and international flight movements were booked.

Earls Court itself, was to be metamorphosed into a giant beach party occupying the whole of Halls 1 and 2, with the main hall being transformed into a huge dining and entertainment production arena split across levels one and two. A full sized funfair with side stalls and a 136 vehicle coach park occupied Earls Court 2, whilst most of the complex's satellite rooms were used for such activities as a comedy club, blues club, piano bar, karaoke, a huge gaming and amusement arcade.

The Event: On-site Operation. On the night the guests arrived by coach, car, public transport and foot. Strict marshalling and foot flow was managed around the perimeter of the building as well as dedicated movement channels within the buildings. This movement of people was formulated as part of the Standard Operating Plan derived from the Risk Assessment.

Prior to guests' arrival onsite, all personnel were fully briefed on the Standard Operating Plan and the Emergency Operating Plan by Heads of Departments. The 120 event crew, 150 production crew, 400 security staff, 2 500 catering staff and 150 chefs were all made aware of their responsibilities during these briefings.

With the doors to Earls Court open for arrival, 11,500 guests made their way into the halls to be astounded by scale of their event. The format for the evening event included pre-dinner drinks, a sit down silver-service dinner and entertainment pre, during and post dinner.

Once seated, after a short introductory welcome and vote of thanks from the CEO, 2,500 catering staff served a hot silver-service dinner to guests whilst they watched a full show of entertainment. The stage set was built like a beach bar and the ensuing stage show also included loud, upbeat music of song and dance specifically conceived and choreographed for the event and uniquely performed by a cast of over 100. During "commercial breaks", a specially produced video montage highlighted the different international operating companies within the Vodafone extended family through a series of brand and product commercials.

Post dinner, guests were invited to explore all the entertainment areas within Earls Court, prior to a main stage concert. The main and sub-stages showcased numerous live bands and artistes such as the Corrs, Ronan Keating, Bjorn Again, Right Said Fred, Hear'say, Tony Hadley of Spandau Ballet and an Ibiza meets Handbag disco.

Control of the event was managed via a two-way radio system, with all communications and decisions being run through Event Control – this room contained 4 radio control personnel and the Event Director. The Event Director maintained control by reaching out through all the Functional Section Heads running Catering, Transport, Production, Entertainment and Security & Crowd Control.

Event Challenges and Statistics. The event required a continuous party atmosphere and seamless itinerary with heavy information technology (IT) and logistics support to provide one entertainment act after another, whilst including motivational key messages, faultless hot catering and coping with the various health and safety issues as they arose. Interesting facts from the event include:

- 11,500 people attended
- 136 coaches all arrived and dropped off guests in a 45-minute window in addition to local shuttle buses
- Software was specially created to build a table plan for 11,500 guests
- Transportation was organised for 8,500 guests
- 1,420 car spaces
- 300 VIP guests were chauffeured
- 700 domestic and international flights were booked
- 400 security staff

Continued

CASE STUDY: THE VODAFONE BALL BY EURO RSCG SKYBRIDGE—*CONT'D*

- 2,500 catering staff
- 150 chefs
- 120 event crew
- 150 production crew
- 10 months of planning
- 2 tonnes of chicken
- 3 tonnes of vegetables
- 5,700 bottles of wine
- 2,400 litres of water
- 2,000 litres of coffee
- 3 kilometres of tablecloth
- 65,000 pieces of crockery
- 78,000 pieces of cutlery

Managing such a large number of guests provided an interesting challenge from the point of view of logistics management, crowd control, security, health and safety and subtle 'on-brand' messages.

The Ball became a reason for working at Vodafone and was so popular that it generated a 92% response rate to invitations.

Euro RSCG Skybridge, Vodafone and its employees were awarded the Guinness World Record for the "World's largest silver service dinner party" and the "World's largest table plan", with the Financial Times and Daily Mail giving extensive, positive coverage and a delighted Chief Executive claiming it was "the best party ever".

Post-Event Evaluation and Wrap Up. Post-event evaluation highlighted the absolute appreciation and perception of value by employees. In staff surveys, the event was cited as one of the reasons staff liked to work at Vodafone.

Detailed de-brief reports were written and de-brief meetings were held with the venue owners, key suppliers and importantly, the client, during the post-event period. Great value is gained from the post-event processes, which support increased knowledge, understanding and identify key action points for future events.

For further details about Euro RSCG Skybridge, please visit: www.skybridgegroup.com.

By Randle Stonier, Former Chairman, Euro RSCG Skybridge.

Questions

1. Identify the many stakeholders in the Vodafone ball and list the likely benefits to each.
2. From the event description in the case study, what do you think was the likely process of conceptualising the event?
3. As identified by Skybridge, the event provides two challenges for future years: how to develop the event, while at the same time keeping it aspirational and tightly budgeted. Imagine that you are planning the above event again for next year.
   (a) If the numbers increase above the current level, the existing venue may not accommodate the large audience and the creative interpretation of the brief. Identify the strengths and weaknesses of the current venue. Suggest an alternative venue that could accommodate this event and list the benefits that your choice of venue would bring.
   (b) In order to keep the event aspirational in future, what vision or idea would you develop for this event? How would you conceptualise it? What are the unique elements in your event concept and how would this be expressed in the event?
4. Can you think of any other companies or organisations where a similar event model could be applied? List the potential stakeholders and describe the steps that you would take in conceptualising the event.

CASE STUDY: OPERATIONAL PLANNING AND THE 2003 RUGBY WORLD CUP

Introduction. The hosting rights of arguably the third largest world sporting event, the Rugby World Cup (RWC), were awarded in 1998 by the International Rugby Board (IRB) to the Australian Rugby Union (ARU). The ARU was to co-host the 2003 RWC tournament with the New Zealand Rugby Union (NZRU). However, in March 2002 the ARU was awarded the sole hosting rights. This change occurred because the NZRU was unable to meet certain commercial obligations of the host union agreement with Rugby World Cup Limited (RWCL, a company set up by the IRB to run the RWC every four years).

The Rugby World Cup 2003 involved the planning and ultimate delivery of 48 matches across 11 venues, in six states and one territory in a six-week period. In undertaking this task the ARU began 'ramping up' its organisational capacity from January 2001, more than two and a half years prior to the event which took place from 10 October to 22 November 2003.

Integral to the ramping-up process was the establishment of an RWC unit with responsibility for delivering the event. It is this unit and more specifically the events and operations component of this unit, which is the subject of this case study.

The Rugby World Cup unit. The RWC unit was established in 2001. It reported through the General Manager 2003 RWC, who in turn reported to the ARU managing director and CEO (see Figure 6.9). A tournament organisation committee was also established to provide input into the operational planning aspects of the event. As the event approached, two additional decision-making bodies were created, a tournament commission and a tournament coordination committee. The function of the tournament commission was to meet, as required, to deal with major issues that arose in regard to the event, both operational and public affairs related. The tournament coordination committee met daily throughout the tournament and dealt with the day-to-day matters arising. If required, issues were passed by this body to the tournament commission for final decision making.

Within the RWC unit was located the events and operations department. This department had responsibility for designing and implementing a venue and precinct operational planning strategy designed to ensure the professional delivery of operations supporting the RWC 2003.

Tasks of the events and operations department. The events and operations department was charged with a range of tasks, specifically:

- coordination and integration of all operational planning and delivery by the various departments of the ARU and associated third-party service providers for operations delivered in tournament venues. This included developing planning mechanisms on a month-by-month basis that all departments were to follow, to ensure that the necessary planning tasks were completed.
- procurement of match and training venues, city office spaces and the commercial rights to the 500-metre radius around each venue on favourable commercial terms.
- scoping and delivery of match and training venue specific overlay, including the field of play (such as signage, seating and camera positions).
- development of a computer aided design and drafting (CADD) facility in-house for the preparation of detailed venue drawings and plans.
- delivery of appropriate levels of venue services (for example, catering, cleaning and waste, security) as required under contractual arrangements with each venue.
- ensuring all events and operations team members (paid, volunteer and contractor) were appropriately skilled, experienced and able to receive appropriate training to carry out their assigned roles efficiently and effectively.
- ensuring the event teams were operationally ready to deliver the tournament. This included third party service providers who were part of the team.

Continued

CASE STUDY: OPERATIONAL PLANNING AND THE 2003 RUGBY WORLD CUP—*CONT'D*

FIGURE 6.9 Rugby World Cup unit organisational structure

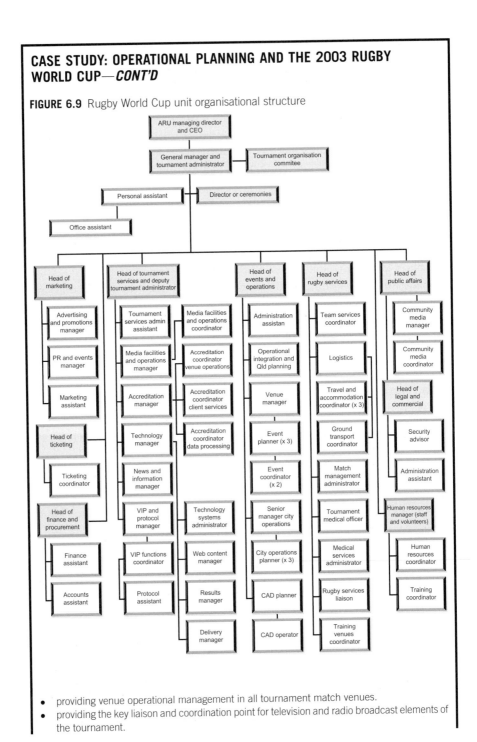

- providing venue operational management in all tournament match venues.
- providing the key liaison and coordination point for television and radio broadcast elements of the tournament.

- management of the media operations and accreditation functions during tournament operations.
- providing a key liaison and coordination point for commercial operations associated with tournament operations as they related to venues and precinct activities, including:

  - acting as the primary operational contact for International Marketing Group (IMG, RWCL's commercial agent for the tournament)
  - coordinating commercial in-stadia activities such as pourage, hospitality requirements including space allocations, signage and imaging implementation
  - coordinating sponsor activities in match venues and precincts
  - ensuring that the overall budget for the events and operations department was appropriately managed and controlled
  - facilitating reporting and issue resolution from tournament locations to World Cup headquarters during operations

In addition to these largely venue and precinct related tasks, the events and operations department was also charged during the planning stage of the event with what was titled the City Operations Program. This programme was moved to report to a different manager (head of tournament services) two months prior to commencement of the tournament. Broadly, the scope of this programme included:

- facilitating the relationships between government agencies and the ARU with respect to the delivery of services by those agencies to the tournament
- establishment of key planning meeting frameworks/committees
- facilitating, where appropriate, the effective flow of information and communication between the ARU, state and local government agencies regarding the provision of government land and/or services to support the Rugby World Cup. This included the creation of key management planning forums incorporating major government service agencies.
- working with all stakeholders (such as marketing, sponsorship, RWCL commercial partners and the government) to develop a strategy and facilitate city festivities/activities
- facilitating and/or coordinating the implementation of local marketing, public affairs and promotional initiatives associated with the RWC in host cities
- coordinating the planning and delivery of precinct activities with landholders and subsequently with IMG in their capacity as coordinator of RWC partners and sponsors.

Integrating planning and operations. As the department responsible for ensuring successful operational delivery across all tournament venues, events and operations coordinated a programme of planning designed to ensure that information was shared between departments at appropriate times and that services would be delivered according to agreed scope. An over-arching planning framework was documented and it sets out the approach that was undertaken to achieve a coordinated planning effort. Importantly, wherever possible, venue owners and operators as well as key third party service providers were included in planning discussions. Under the programme, the events and operations team led initiatives such as:

- developing a concept of operations for a match venue that set out how RWC venues were to be operated, including the role of events and operations. This document was reviewed by all functional departments and represented the common understanding within the host union regarding how tournament match venues would operate.
- undertaking a detailed analysis of venue resource requirements, including those to be provided by the venue operator. This analysis initially resulted in the creation of generic tools in the form of room data sheets, venue overlay and equipment lists, which were later customised by specific venue.

Continued

CASE STUDY: OPERATIONAL PLANNING AND THE 2003 RUGBY WORLD CUP—*CONT'D*

- conducting operational planning group meetings or 'hubs'. These were convened on a need basis, with targeted subject matter based on the detailed planning activities to be undertaken.
- facilitation of workshop sessions to address operational issues.
- leading scenario planning exercises, designed to address operational procedure in both ordinary operations and extraordinary situations. This included detailed table top exercises carried out in each venue just prior to the commencement of tournament operations.
- leading a process to develop and communicate detailed policies covering all aspects of tournament operations. This ensured a level of consistency of operations across the tournament.
- creation of a detailed venue operations plan for each venue. This was a substantial document in each case and set out the key dimensions of all aspects of the operations at the venue, including venue and event profiles and an outline of the operations of each organisational area.

Progression by the events and operations department through these, as well as other planning and operational tasks is shown in Figure 6.10.

Staffing and organisational structure evolution. The staffing model adopted by the events and operations department involved creating a core team of staff who would undertake the planning and coordination task centrally in 2001–02. This group later moved (from early- to mid-2003) to become key venue management and geographic area personnel controlling their own teams. Making this task easier was the fact that a number of senior team members were existing ARU employees and as such, possessed a sound understanding of what was required to plan and create operational venue overlays for rugby-based sporting events.

Volunteers were a major component of the RWC 2003 workforce, filling a number of match day staff positions and providing the 'arms and legs' on event day. To assist volunteers in gaining familiarity with their venue and its procedures, they were, where possible, given roles at

FIGURE 6.10 Planning to operations

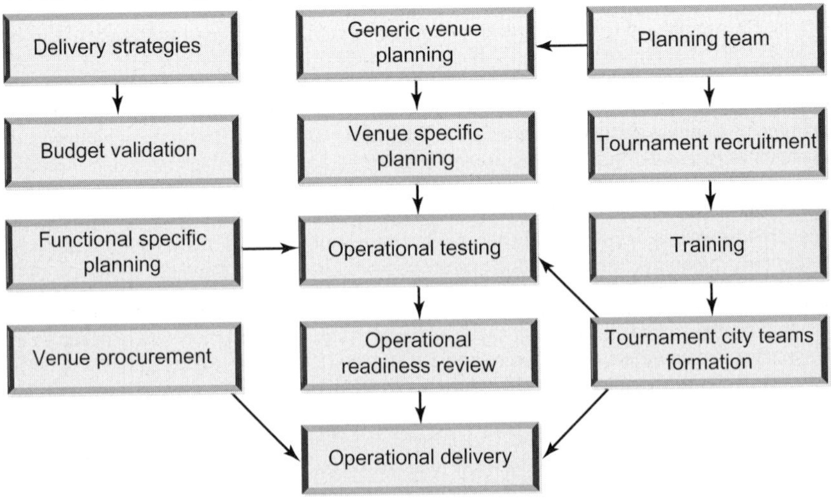

scheduled Rugby test matches in 2003. These 'test' events also allowed management to gauge the suitability of individual volunteers to their RWC 2003 positions.

The 2003 annual domestic test season not only provided an opportunity to further develop the skills of the RWC 2003 volunteer workforce, but also allowed the testing of proposed RWC 2003 policies and procedures. It also enabled some RWC staff to fill operational roles similar to those that they would hold at tournament time. To formalise this latter opportunity, a programme was developed whereby a significant portion of the planning and delivery of annual test events was undertaken by the RWC staff. The evolution of the staffing structure of the events and operations department is shown in Figure 6.11.

The growth in staff from 2002 to 2003 reflected the movement from overall planning to operations, where much greater detailed work was required, including operational testing. Operational integration between departments was also a major concern over this period, as the detailed components of each venue were planned, reviewed and confirmed. Additionally, city operations planning was also key at this time, as city operations planners sought to assist state host unions and their respective state governments in their efforts to maximise benefits from the conduct of RWC matches.

As the tournament date approached, the events and operations department moved to its final tournament time structure (see Figure 6.12 on page 225), reflecting the expanded range of tasks required for event delivery. It was at this time that department staff moved into their key tournament operational roles, which included establishing eight venue teams. Management staff within these teams participated in a week of intense briefing and training, two months before the event. A detailed manual covering all planning carried out to date was produced for each match venue and this formed the basis of a job-specific training week. This week was essential to the overall success of the event as it ensured that all venue and event managers went into their venues with a consistent and common understanding of how the ARU was going to stage the tournament. The manual itself was a valuable resource, enabling the teams to take away documented details of their venue operations planning to date, together with key policies, procedures and operational schedules.

Following the week of training, the venue teams were deployed to their venues/city offices to finalise preparations for their respective matches and further develop their own operational relationships with key external and internal organisations. The tasks they were charged with at this time included:

- overlay implementation/management
- final review of detailed planning, deployment of venue staff, security and access control and timings
- documentation of a detailed event plan specific to the individual matches that was complementary to the venue operations plan
- development of detailed (minute by minute) run sheets for each match
- operations meetings, held weekly, to the day prior to each match
- transition planning, including development of detailed bump in and bump out schedules

At each match venue an organisational structure was required to deliver the event as planned (see Figure 6.13 on page 226). At each venue the events and operations venue manager, guided by an customised run sheet, was ultimately responsible for the delivery of the event on match day, acting to support and direct a particular team as required. The managers were also required to escalate issues, as applicable, to the head of events and operations who was part of the tournament coordination committee.

Conclusion

This case study shows how the tasks, structure and staffing requirements of one department within a large-scale sporting event evolved over a three year period. In doing so it highlights how events move from their planning phase into their operational and delivery phases. Accompanying

Continued

CASE STUDY: OPERATIONAL PLANNING AND THE 2003 RUGBY WORLD CUP—*CONT'D*

FIGURE 6.11 Evolution of the staffing structure of the event and operations department 2002–03

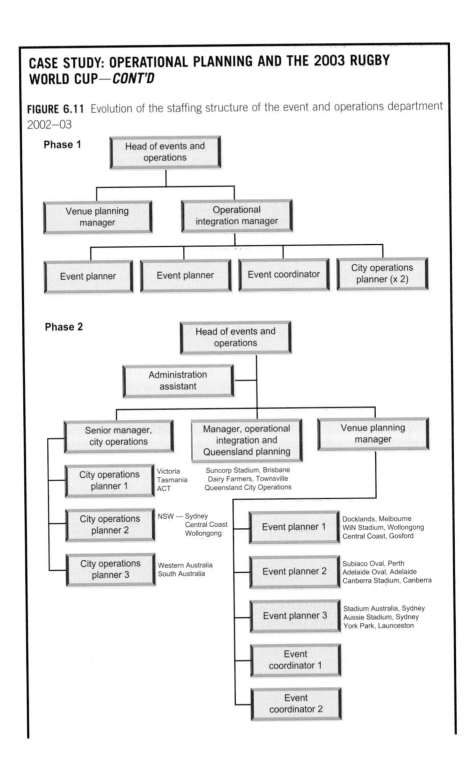

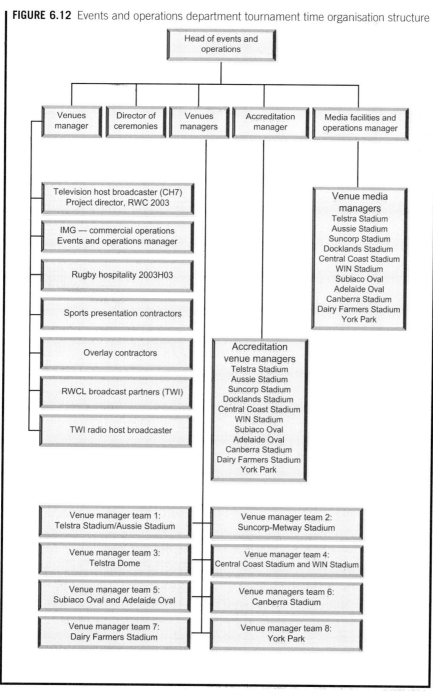

FIGURE 6.12 Events and operations department tournament time organisation structure

Continued

FIGURE 6.13 Generic venue operating team structure

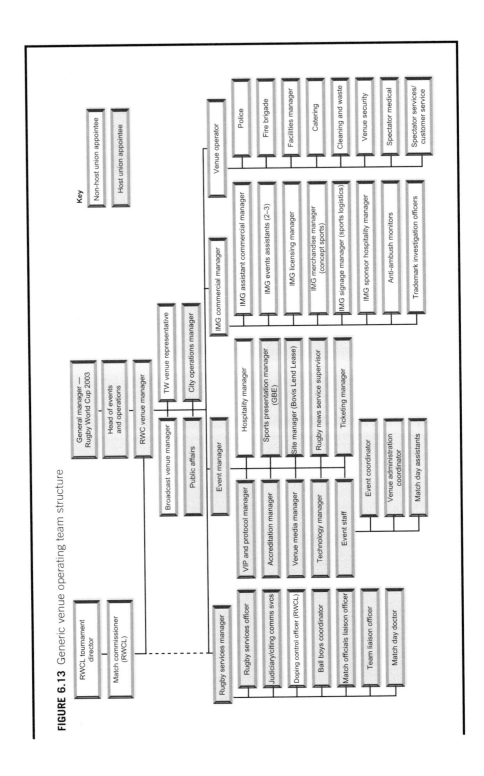

this movement is a range of challenges, including the need to build workable but increasingly complex organisational structures; deal with an expanded and increasingly complex range of tasks; and establish and train integrated 'teams' capable of employing various operational systems and processes.

For further information on the Rugby World Cup, please visit: www.rugbyworldcup.com

By Ian Alker, head of events and venues, Australian Rugby Union

Questions

1. Why do event organisational structures evolve over time?
2. What issues arise as event organisational structures develop?
3. What benefits are there in developing centrally a core team of staff that is later deployed in key venue management and other roles?
4. What function do 'test' events play from an event operations perspective?
5. What function can computer aided design and drafting software play in event operations?
6. What role does staff training play in event operations? What types of training are evident in this case study?
7. What issues might have arisen if the ARU had decided to try to use a centralised organisational structure to conduct the RWC 2003 rather than devolve responsibility to individual venues?
8. What lessons can future Rugby World Cups, and other major events, learn from this case study?

Conceptualising the event

7

LEARNING OBJECTIVES

After studying this chapter, you should be able to:

- identify the range of stakeholders in an event
- describe and balance the overlapping and sometimes conflicting needs of stakeholders
- describe the different types of host organisations for events
- discuss trends and issues that affect events
- understand how to engage sponsors as partners in events
- understand the role of the media in events
- identify the unique elements and resources of an event
- understand the process of developing an event concept
- apply the screening process to evaluate the feasibility of an event concept

INTRODUCTION

A crucial element in the creation of an event is the understanding of the event environment. The context in which the event is to take place will be a major determinant of its success. In order to understand this environment, the event manager must first identify the major players — the stakeholders and the people and organisations likely to be affected by it. The event manager must then examine the objectives of these major players — what each of them expects to gain from the event and how the forces acting on them are likely to affect their response to the event. Once this environment is understood, the event manager is then in the best position to marshal the creative elements of the event and to shape and manage them to achieve the best outcomes for the event. This chapter examines the key stakeholders in events and outlines some of the processes that event managers can use to produce creative and successful events.

STAKEHOLDERS IN EVENTS

As discussed in the previous chapters, events have rapidly become professionalised and are increasingly attracting the involvement and support of governments and the corporate sector. One aspect of this growth is that events are now required to serve a multitude of agenda. It is no longer sufficient for an event to meet just the needs of

Events Management. DOI: 10.1016/B978-1-85617-818-1.10007-6

229

its audience. It must also embrace a plethora of other requirements, including government objectives and regulations, media requirements, sponsors' needs and community expectations.

People and organisations with a legitimate interest in the outcomes of an event are known as stakeholders. The successful event manager must be able to identify the range of stakeholders in an event and manage their individual needs, which will sometimes overlap and conflict (Figure 7.1). As with event impacts, the event will be judged by its success in balancing the competing needs, expectations and interests of a diverse range of stakeholders. For example, UK Sport (1998) identify that a list of key stakeholders for major sporting events would include athletes, the British Olympic Association, broadcasters, coaches, event organisers, the general public, international federations, local authorities, the media, national government, national sports governing bodies, officials, sponsors, sports councils and volunteers.

Mal Hemmerling, architect of the Australian Formula One Grand Prix in Adelaide and former Chief Executive of SOCOG, describes the task of the contemporary event manager as follows (Hemmerling, 1997):

> So when asked the question 'what makes an event successful?', there are now numerous shareholders that are key components of modern major events that are looking at a whole range of different measures of success. What may have been a simple measure for the event organiser of the past, which involved the bottom line, market share, and successful staging of the event are now only basic criteria as the measures by other investors are more aligned with increased tourism, economic activity, tax revenues, promotional success, sustained economic growth, television reach, audience profiles, customer focus, brand image, hospitality, new business opportunities and investment to name but a few.

FIGURE 7.1 The relationship of stakeholders to events

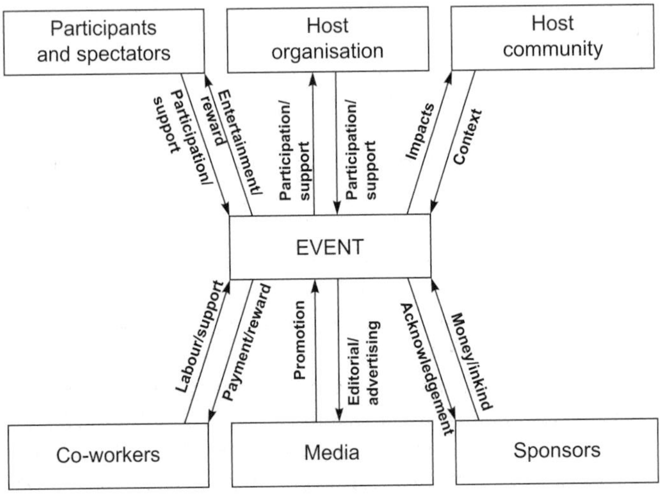

THE HOST ORGANISATION

As we saw in chapter 3, events have become so much a part of our cultural milieu that they can be generated by almost any part of the government, corporate and community sectors (see Table 7.1). Governments create events for a range of reasons, including the social, cultural, tourism and economic benefits generated by events. These events are often characterised by free entry and wide accessibility and form part of the public culture. Government bodies often have a mixed role including not only the generation of events but also their regulation and coordination, as was discussed in detail in chapter 2. The corporate sector is involved in events at a number of levels, including staging their own events, sponsoring events in order to promote their goods and services in the marketplace and partnering with other events that have a common agenda. These events, although they may still offer free entry, are often targeted at specific market segments rather than at the general public.

These sectors often interact, with public events providing opportunities for corporate sponsorships and hosting.

Within the corporate sector, there are also entrepreneurs whose business is the staging or selling of events. These include sports or concert promoters who present ticketed events for profit and conference organisers or industry associations who mount conferences or exhibitions for the trade or public — for example, wine shows, equipment exhibitions or medical conferences. Media organisations often become partners in events organised by other groups but also stage events for their own promotional purposes or to create programme content. Examples are radio stations promoting their identity through concerts, newspapers promoting fun runs or television networks presenting Christmas carol programs live to air.

Other events still emanate from the community sector, serving a wide variety of needs and interests. These may include local sporting events, service club fundraisers, car club gatherings, local art and craft shows — the spectrum is as wide as the field of human interest and endeavour. All of these sources combine to create the wonderful tapestry of events that fill our leisure time and enrich our lives.

Types of host organisation

Whether events emanate from the corporate, government or community sectors will determine the nature of the host organisation. If the host is from the corporate sector, it is likely to be a company, corporation or industry association. The event manager may be employed directly by the host organisation or employed on a contract basis, with the organisation as the client. If the host is from the government sector, the host organisation is likely to be a government or council department. Again the event manager may be a direct employee or a contractor if the event is outsourced. If the host is from the community sector, the host organisation is more likely to be a club, society or committee, with a higher volunteer component in the organisation.

Whatever the host organisation, it is a key stakeholder in the event and the event manager should seek to clarify its goals in staging the event. These goals will often

Table 7.1 Event typology

Event Generators	Types of Events
GOVERNMENT SECTOR Central Government	Civic celebrations and commemorations
Event Corporations	Major events – focus on sporting and cultural events
Public space authorities e.g. National Trust, National Park Authorities	Public entertainment, festivals, leisure and recreation events
Tourism e.g. VisitBritain, VisitScotland, Visit Wales Northern Ireland Tourist Board, regional tourism through Regional Development Agencies	Festivals, special interest and lifestyle events, destination promotions
Visitor & Convention Bureaus	Meetings, incentives, conferences and exhibitions
Arts e.g. Arts Council England, Scottish Arts Council, Arts Council of Northern Ireland, Arts Council of Wales, Regional Arts Councils	Arts festivals, cultural events, touring programs, theatre, themed art exhibitions
Sport e.g. UK Sport, Sport England, Scottish Sports Council, Sports Council for Northern Ireland, Sport Council for Wales	Sporting events, hosting of national and international events
Economic development e.g. EventBritain, EventScotland, Regional Development Agencies	Focus on events with industry development and job creation benefits
Local government e.g. City Councils	Community events, local festivals and fairs
CORPORATE SECTOR Companies and corporate organisations	Promotions, product launches, incentives, corporate hospitality, corporate entertainment, training events and image building sponsorships
Industry associations	Industry promotions, trade fairs/ exhibitions, seminars, training, conferences
Gaming and racing e.g. Racecourse Holdings Trust (owners of Aintree, Epsom, Newmarket)	Race meetings and carnivals
Entrepreneurs	Ticketed sporting events, concerts and exhibitions
Media	Media promotions e.g. concerts, fun runs, appeals
COMMUNITY SECTOR Clubs and societies	Special interest groups e.g. Flower festivals, car shows, traction engine rallies
Charities	Fundraising and profile-building events
Sports organisations	Local sporting events

be presented in a written brief as part of the event manager's job description or contract. Where they are not, it will be worthwhile spending some time to clarify these goals and put them in a written form as a reference point for the organisation of the event and as a guideline for the evaluation of its eventual success.

THE HOST COMMUNITY

Event managers need to have a good grasp and understanding of the broad trends and forces acting on the wider community, as these will determine the operating environment of their events. The mood, needs and aspirations of the community will determine its receptiveness to event styles and fashions. Accurately gauging and interpreting these is a basic factor in the conceptualisation of successful events.

Among the current significant forces acting on the community are globalisation and technology, which are combining to make the world seem both smaller and more complex. These forces are impacting on almost every aspect of our lives, including events. As international travel, trade and communications increase, national boundaries and local differences are increasingly subsumed into the global marketplace.

This process is speeded up by technology and the media, which have the power to bring significant local events to a worldwide audience — overcoming the barriers of national boundaries and cultural differences. This is exemplified by the global television coverage of major sporting events. World championships and mega-events such as the Olympic Games and World Cup Football, calendar events such as the Grand National, The Championships (Wimbledon) and the FA Cup Final, New Year celebrations and even the result of bidding for mega-events are beamed instantly to live audiences throughout the world, giving them previously unimagined coverage and immediacy.

As global networks increasingly bring the world into our living rooms, the question arises of how local cultures can maintain their own uniqueness and identity in the face of global homogenisation. International arts festivals increasingly draw from the same pool of touring companies to produce similar programmes. Local festivals and celebrations must increasingly compete with international products and the raised expectations of audiences accustomed to streamlined television production. The challenge for many events is how to function in this increasingly global environment whilst expressing the uniqueness of local communities and addressing their specific interests and concerns.

Globalisation is also impacting on corporate events as companies increasingly plan their marketing strategies, including their event components, on a global level. This has resulted in some British events companies expanding internationally, for example, WorldEvents; or taking over, merging with or being bought out by overseas companies in an attempt to create networks that can serve the international needs of their clients — for example, Jack Morton Worldwide, Euro RSCG Skybridge Group and MCI. This approach sometimes comes unstuck, as different markets in, say, New York, Sydney and Hong Kong, reflect different event needs and audience responses.

However, the forces of globalisation are likely to lead to an increasing standardisation of the corporate event product and market.

Simultaneously, the all-pervasive Internet and advances in information technology are increasing the availability and technological sophistication of events. For example, live broadcasts from music concerts and dance events are relayed instantly through the Internet to a global market. Madonna's concert at the Brixton Academy in November 2000 had a live audience of only 3,500, but was 'webcast' to millions through the Internet, made possible by a £30 million sponsorship deal with Microsoft's MSN. Basing his forecast on projections by leading futurists and trends in the event management industry, Goldblatt (2000, p. 8) predicts '24 hour, seven day per week event opportunities for guests who desire to forecast, attend and review their participation in an event'. He also predicts that events will eventually become 'totally automated enabling event professionals to significantly expand the number of simultaneous events being produced using fewer human staff' (Goldblatt, 2000, p. 8). As a counter-trend, Goldblatt (2000, p.3) also points out that 'with the advance of technology individuals are seeking more "high touch" experiences to balance the high tech influences in their lives. Events remain the single most effective means of providing a high touch experience'.

Event managers must be aware of these trends and learn to operate in the new global environment. Paradoxically, live events may increasingly become the means by which communities confirm their own sense of place, individuality and cultural uniqueness.

Involving the host community

In addition to the wider general community, events have a specific host community which impacts greatly on the success or failure of the event. This can be the geographical community where the event is located or a community of interest from which the event draws its participants and spectators. Many researchers (Getz, 2005; Goldblatt and Perry, 2002; Jago, Chalip, Brown, Mules and Ali, 2002) have recognised the importance of the host community being involved in and 'owning' the event, which in turn emits positive messages to visitors. For example, the extensive involvement of volunteers during the Sydney Olympics developed community links and harnessed support for the event, which contributed to the positive atmosphere in the city during the games (Jago et al., 2002), with this experience similarly demonstrated at the 2002 Manchester Commonwealth Games (see case study in Chapter 10).

Many community members actively participate in events in their communities and act as advocates on behalf of the event to potential participants. The Pride London (formerly London Mardi Gras) and Manchester Pride — developed for the lesbian, gay, bi-sexual and transgender communities — are both examples of events that are fuelled by social activists committed to the goals of the event. Local participation and ownership of events is perhaps most visible in the many local and regional events that continue to exist only because of the committed input of dedicated volunteers. The host community may also include residents, traders, lobby groups and public authorities such as council, transport, police, fire and ambulance services. The event manager should aim to identify community leaders and to consult them when planning the event. Councils may have certain requirements, such as licences (discussed in Chapter 16). For larger-scale events, the local authorities will generally call a meeting to include emergency services, environmental health, transport and the management team to discuss such matters as street closures, special access and parking arrangements (HSE, 1999).

If the event is large enough to impact significantly beyond the boundaries of the venue, a 'public authorities and residents' briefing may identify innovative ways to minimise the impact and manage the situation. Events held by Leeds City Council at Temple Newsam Park, Leeds, regularly attract upwards of 20,000 people to a wide programme of summer events, for example, Party in the Park (40- to 60,000 people) and Opera in the Park (40,000 people). Consultation with local community groups will ensure that the event is supported and its impacts minimised. With the increasing audience, the events went through a period of receiving much negative publicity due to the impact that these events have on the local community, including traffic disruption, the effect of litter and visitors trampling gardens and damaging the local environment.

Host communities have past experience of different events and event managers can draw on this knowledge to ensure an event's success. In Manchester, local and sporting authorities consciously used major occasions and trial events — such as the Aqua Pura Commonwealth Games Trials and events across other venues — as practice runs for the Commonwealth Games; with event organisers, public transport and public authorities working together to try out operations and venues and refine solutions.

In addition to formal contact with authorities, the event manager should look out for the all-important rumour-mill that can often make or break the host community's attitude to the event, sometimes manifesting itself in commentary within local media. In the summer of 1999, many events established to celebrate the eclipse in and around Cornwall were not as successful as predicted. The two events to be worst hit were the high-profile failure of the Lizard Festival, at a cost of £1.5 million and the Total Eclipse Festival, which led to the subsequent bankruptcy of the event organiser, Harvey Goldsmith's Allied Entertainment Group. These events failed, according to the organisers, due to the negative publicity generated by local authorities that claimed the area would not be able to cope with the anticipated large influx of visitors. This was only heightened by negative reports in the media and, it could be said, a lack of counter-publicity by the promoters. As a result of this and weather forecasts predicting cloud cover for the day, many events were not as successful as planned. Initial information had predicted an influx of 5 million extra visitors to the area; however, only 450,000 eventually arrived (Gartside, 1999).

Another high-profile example of the effect that public opinion can have on events is the Love Parade, hosted in Leeds for the first time in July 2000. The event, originally planned to take place in Leeds City Centre, was at short notice transferred to Roundhay Park due to police concerns over the expected audience being higher than initially predicted. An estimated 250,000 people attended the event which was generally seen as running without major incident. However, many residents did not appreciate the effect of this number of people in the area, with the litter, broken glass and general inconvenience they caused. Campaigning by local politicians and some residents led to the event not returning to Leeds in 2001.

SPONSORS

Recent decades have seen enormous increases in sponsorship and a corresponding change in how events are perceived by sponsors. There has been a shift by many large companies from seeing sponsorship as primarily a public relations tool generating community goodwill, to regarding it as an important part of the marketing mix. Successful major events are now perceived as desirable properties, capable of increasing brand awareness and driving sales. They also provide important opportunities for relationship-building through hosting partners and clients. Major businesses invest large amounts in event sponsorship and devote additional resources to supporting their sponsorships in order to achieve corporate and sales goals.

BDS Sponsorship Ltd (2010), define sponsorship as, 'a business relationship between a provider of funds, resources or services and an individual, event or organisation which offers in return some rights and association that may be used for commercial advantage in return for sponsorship investment'.

In order to attract sponsorships, event managers must offer tangible benefits to sponsors and effective programmes to deliver them. Large companies such as Coca-Cola, Vodafone and Virgin Media will receive hundreds of sponsorship applications each week, and only those events which have a close fit with corporate objectives and demonstrate the ability to deliver benefits will be considered.

Sponsors as partners in events

It is important for event managers to identify exactly what sponsors want from an event and what the event can deliver for them. The sponsors needs may be different from those of the host organisation or the event manager. Attendance numbers at the event, for example, may not be as important to them as the media coverage that it generates. It may be important for their chief executive to officiate or to gain access to public officials in a relaxed atmosphere. They may be seeking mechanisms to drive sales or strengthen client relationships through hosting activities. The event manager should take the opportunity to go beyond the formal sponsorship agreement and treat the sponsors as partners in the event. Some of the best ideas for events can arise from such partnerships. Common agendas may be identified which support the sponsorship and deliver additional benefits to the event.

For the FIFA World Cup in Germany in 2006, German railways provided free domestic rail travel for 6,000 overseas media representatives for the duration of the tournament. The selection of the Escort Kids (McDonalds), the Ball Crew (Coca-Cola) and the Flag Bearers (Adidas) provided further evidence of the commitment of the official partners and suppliers to staging attractive promotions in partnership with the event (Niersbach, 2006).

Barclays Bank was a major sponsor of the Ideal Home Show held at Earls Court, London, in April 2000. The sponsorship was supported with a national advertising campaign in television, radio and print media, and through branches of Barclays' Bank, with customers being offered discounted tickets. The show was retitled 'The Daily Mail Ideal Home Show in Partnership with Barclays Bank', with the logo, all signage, branding, promotional material and main entrance kitted out in Barclays' corporate colour, blue (Litherland, 1997). The sponsorship helped to promote sales of mortgages for Barclays, as well as increasing the profile of the event. Likewise, in 1999, Guinness supported its sponsorship of the Rugby World Cup with a major campaign in pubs and retail outlets, a national advertising campaign through television, print media and the Internet, competitions and street sampling. The sponsorship clearly identified Guinness with the celebrations and provided the event with an additional promotional outlet — so much so, that few can remember other sponsors involved in the event. The role of sponsors in events, along with techniques for identifying, sourcing and managing sponsorships, is treated in more detail in Chapter 13.

MEDIA

The expansion of the media and the proliferation of delivery systems such as cable and satellite television and the Internet, have created a hunger for media products as never before. The global networking of media organisations and the instant electronic transmission of media images and data, has made the global village a media reality. The Olympic Games were first televised on a trial basis during the 1936 Berlin Olympics, when the audience peaked at an estimated 162,000 viewers. When the 1948 London Olympics were televised, the world still relied largely on the physical transfer of film footage to disseminate the images of the Games across the UK and overseas. An estimated 500,000 people watched the 64 hours of coverage, mostly within 50 miles of London. This event proved to be the starting point of what is now seen as a major source of revenue — television rights fees (IOC, 2000). Indeed, Children in Need and Red Nose Day feature multidirectional television link-ups that enable the British to experience the fundraising simultaneously from a diverse range of locations and perspectives. The Opening Ceremony of the Winter Olympic Games in Nagano in 1998, featured a world choir singing together from five different locations on five continents, with 200 singers each in Sydney, New York, Beijing, Berlin and Cape Town, singing along with a 2000-strong choir at the main stadium. Global television networks followed New Year's Eve of the New Millennium around the world, making the world seem smaller and more immediate. When the 2004 Athens Olympic Games began, a simultaneous global audience estimated at 4 billion people was able to watch the event tailored to their own national perspectives, with a variety of cameras covering the event from every possible angle. Events such as the funeral of Diana, Princess of Wales, have become media experiences shared by millions as they are beamed instantly to a global audience. In Britain alone, the Princess's death attracted record media coverage.

Internet companies now regularly partner with events to enhance their presence online, as illustrated by SOHU.COM's five-year agreement with the China Open to supply real-time online wireless Internet information and webcasts of the tennis tournament (Dukes, 2004). Mobile phones allow fans to follow the scores of their favourite teams and to view the highlights of the game. Concerts are webcast globally, and phone owners can participate in short film festivals with selected films downloaded to their phones as with the Portable Film Festival (www. portablefilmfestival.com).

2006 FIFA World Cup organising committee vice-president Wolfgang Niersbach (Niersbach, 2006) summed up the pivotal role that the media played in the World Cup:

> *Laptops and notebooks, the Internet and emails, digital photography and high-definition TV are the symbols of a high-tech FIFA World Cup, with information flashed around the globe in the blink of an eye . . . A total of 21 000 media representatives . . . TV and radio . . . deals with 207 countries . . . the previous record of 28.4 billion viewers, set by Korea/Japan in 2002, will have been significantly exceeded . . . At the end of this mega media World Cup, we must be asking ourselves: how much more? My personal belief is that the limits must be fairly close.*

This revolution in the media has, in turn, revolutionised events. Events now have a virtual existence in the media at least as powerful as reality. The television audience may dwarf the live audience for a sports event or concert. Indeed, the event may be created primarily for the consumption of the television audience — what popular media refer to as 'event television' (Goldblatt, 2000). For example, the London Weekend Television *Audience with . . .* events, which featured a prominent celebrity performing and involving the audience or the more recent trend of music concerts, such as Boyzone and Phil Collins, allowing television audiences to request their favourite songs to be performed. Events have much to gain from this development, including media sponsorships and the payment of media rights. The value of an event to commercial sponsors is often increased greatly by its media coverage and profile. Over recent years, there has been a significant increase in this form of event, with X-Factor, Britain's Got Talent, Dancing on Ice and Strictly Come Dancing, among a number of television programmes that have managed to successfully combine the live event with the television programme. In the case of the former two, this has involved live auditions for competitors in front of live audiences at major event venues across the UK, leading through to live shows in television studios involving television audiences voting for their favourite act, through to a similar format being adopted with the winners from all four programmes, each going on live arena tours following the finale of the television series. The media can often affect directly how events are conceptualised and presented, as in the case of One Day Cricket or Super League, where the competition formats have been modified in order to create a more appealing television product. For example, note the effect on the scheduling of Premier League football matches since the increased involvement of Sky TV. So far sports events have been the main winners (and losers!) from this increased attention by the media. The range of sports covered by television has increased dramatically and some sports, such as basketball, have gone from relative obscurity in the UK to high media profile, largely because of their suitability for television production and programming.

The available media technology influences the way that live spectators experience an event, for example, with instant replays available on large screens at major sporting events. Increasingly, spectators' viewing capabilities are technologically enhanced to parallel those of people watching at home. Media interest in events is likely to continue to grow as their ability to provide community credibility and to attract commercial sponsors is realised. Sporting events, parades, spectacles, concerts and major public celebrations are event areas of strong potential interest to the media and the need to make good television is likely to influence the direction and marketing of events. The role of the media can vary from that of media sponsors to becoming full partners — or even producers — of the event.

Whatever the role of the media, it is important for the event manager to consider the needs of the different media groups and to consult with them as important stakeholders in the event. Once the media are treated as potential partners, they have much to offer the event. The good media representative, like the event manager, is in search of the good idea or unusual angle. Together they might just dream up the unique approach that increases the profile of the event and provides value to the media organisation. The print media might agree to publish the event programme as editorial or as a special insert or might run a series of lead-in stories, competitions or special promotions in tandem with sponsors. Radio or television stations might provide an outside broadcasts or involve their on-air presenters as comperes or special participants in the event. Mobile phone companies and Internet providers might integrate their products with the promotion and delivery of the event. This integration of the event with the media provides greater reach and exposure to the event and, in turn, gives the media organisation a branded association with the event. New media developments and increasingly innovative technologies continue to expand the media dimension of events and to provide additional opportunities for collaboration between event organisers and the media.

CO-WORKERS

The event team that is assembled to implement the event, represents another of the key stakeholders. For any event to be truly effective, the vision and philosophy of the event must be shared by all of the team, from key managers, artists and publicists, right through to the stage manager, crew, stewards and cleaners. No matter how big or small, the event team is the face of the event and each member of the team is a contributor to its success or failure. Goldblatt (1997, p. 129) describes the role of the event manager in this process:

> *The most effective event managers are not merely managers, rather, they are dynamic leaders whose ability to motivate, inspire others, and achieve their goals are admired by their followers. The difference between management and leadership is perhaps best characterised by this simple but effective definition: managers control problems, whereas leaders motivate others to find ways to achieve goals.*

Most people have experienced events that went well overall but were marred by some annoying detail or shortcoming. There are different ways of addressing such problems but team selection and management are always crucial factors in avoiding these problems. The Disney organisation, for example, has a system in which the roles of performer, cleaner and security etc. are merged into the concept of 'one team looking after the space'. The roles tend to ride with the needs of the moment — when the parade comes through the theme park, it is all hands on deck! The daily bulletin issued to all staff members reminds them that customers may only ever visit Disneyland once in their lives and that their impressions will depend forever on what they experience that day. This is a very positive philosophy that can be applied to all events.

PARTICIPANTS AND SPECTATORS

Last but not least are the 'punters' on the day — the participants, spectators, visitors or audience for whom the event is intended and who ultimately vote with their feet for the success or failure of the event. The event manager must be mindful of the needs of the audience. These include their physical needs, as well as their needs for comfort, safety and security. Over and above these basic requirements is the need to make the event special — to connect to the emotions. A skilled event manager strives to make events meaningful, magical and memorable. Hemmerling (1997) describes the criteria by which spectators judge an event:

> *Their main focus is on the content, location, substance and operation of the event itself. For them the ease with which they can see the event activities, the program content, their access to food and drinks, amenities, access and egress etc., are the keys to their enjoyment. Simple factors such as whether or not their team won or lost, or whether they had a good experience at the event will sometimes influence their success measures. Secondary issues, such as mixing with the stars of the show, social opportunities, corporate hospitality and capacity to move up the seating chain from general admission to premium seating are all part of the evaluation of spectator success.*

Current technologies can assist the event manager in involving and servicing event participants, as was discussed above with the use of contemporary stadium technologies to enhance the audience experience and the use of the Internet to extend the reach and access to events.

The Internet now plays a major role in events, with participants using it to research the event before their arrival, keep track during an extended event and re-live the highlights of the event after they have departed. With the advances in technology it is possible to monitor the number of visitors to a website, what pages they have viewed and where they came from. For example, monitoring by WebTrends Ltd revealed that the 2002 Manchester Commonwealth Games web-site received 8.6 million 'hits' on 31 July 2002 (Manchester 2002, 2003), which was perhaps conservative compared to figures reported for the Rugby World Cup (44.5 million hits during the 2003 final)(Kalles, 2003), Olympics (peak traffic of 53 million hits during Athens 2004 Olympics)(Vignette, 2004) and the FIFA World Cup (1.75 billion hits during the 2002 tournament in Korea and Japan, averaging 6.2 million unique visitors per day)(Ayaya, 2002). The growth in the use of the web is perhaps best illustrated by the data reported during the 2008 Beijing Olympics, when a peak of 183 million hits was recorded one week into the games (BOCOG, 2008).

By understanding how the nature and make-up of the event audience influence the event concept, event managers can tailor their events more adequately to meet the needs of participants. As discussed in greater detail in Chapter 9, this under-standing also helps to accurately direct the marketing efforts by using channels specific to the audience — for example, the marketing of National Chess Week to promote the playing of chess in schools and clubs and to raise money for Barnardo's.

EVENT PROFILE

Key stakeholder groups: Manchester 2002 Commonwealth Games. The Manchester 2002 Commonwealth Games Report identified three core-stakeholder groups that worked with the organising committee in the seven years leading up to the Games and the ten days of competition, to create the 'best Commonwealth Games ever'. These core-stakeholder groups were:

- strategic and funding stakeholders
- operational stakeholders
- regional stakeholders (see Figure 7.2)

Strategic and funding stakeholders. When Manchester City Council and the Commonwealth Games Council for England submitted the bid to host the 2002 Commonwealth Games, they were supported by two powerful organisations that stayed true to the vision and the partnership right to the end – The Sports Council (revamped into Sport England in 1997) and the British Government. Funding and support were provided for different elements of the games through this partnership, which had as its objectives:

- *To position the UK as a centre of international sport and to demonstrate the UK's ability to host a major international sporting event. To view the Games as one means to strengthen sports participation at all levels.*
- *To strengthen the economic and social capacity of the Manchester and North West region, recognising the importance of capturing maximum benefits to justify the significant capital investment in facilities.*
- *To advance policies for greater social inclusion, promotion of diversity, access to sport and volunteering.*

FIGURE 7.2 Key stakeholder groups in the XVII Commonwealth Games

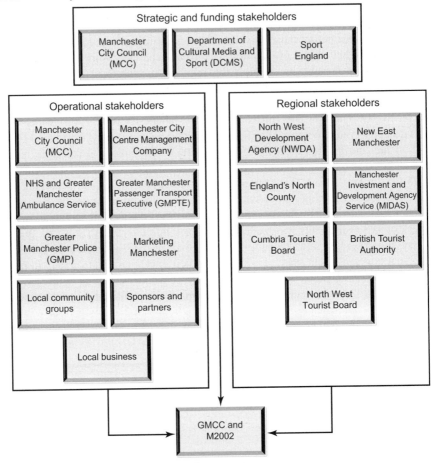

(Source: Adapted from Manchester 2002, 2003)

- *To showcase Britain internationally to raise the profile of the Commonwealth (Manchester 2002).*

Roles and responsibilities. The key roles of the strategic and funding stakeholders were:

- Manchester City Council: to be the host city, to design and procure the venues, to secure the legacy of the city image and venues and to provide an economic, social and sporting legacy to the region
- Sport England: to ensure that the sporting facilities were of world standard and to provide a legacy for elite athletes and the venues after the Games
- Department for Culture, Media and Sport: to promote the UK's ability to provide world class venues and stage major events; and to ensure that the facilities became part of the English Institute of Sport network of facilities and services after the Games (Manchester 2002).

Operational partnerships. A great many partnerships formed with other organisations assisted the Games to run smoothly. The Manchester City Management Group, business groups and local community groups worked together to create a community spirit such as had not been seen in the city for many years. The close relationship between the Games organisers and the Manchester City Police meant that issues were mitigated and dealt with quickly and efficiently; and that the Games and associated events ran smoothly and safely. Through the efforts of the Greater Manchester Passenger Transport Executive and their partners, the Manchester transport system worked effectively to transport thousands of spectators to venues, with more than 75 % of all spectators at Sportcity using public transport. Partnerships with the BBC as host broadcaster, along with other sponsors and partners, ensured the smooth running of many facilities and provided operationally vital valuable in-kind services.

Regional partnerships. Regional partnerships helped Manchester to secure over £600 million of public and private investment. Nearly 30 million people now consider Manchester or the North West as a possible business and visitor destination, because of their improved image and an estimated 300,000 extra visitors are expected to visit the city and the region each year.

The Games generated more than 6,000 permanent jobs in the region, as well as long term cultural programs, such as a Regional Cultural festival, Cultureshock and an annual Commonwealth Film Festival that hope to continue in the region after their inaugural success as part of the Commonwealth Games Spirit of Friendship Festival.

Source: *Adapted from Manchester 2002, 2003.*

SOURCING EVENTS

Events are usually obtained or generated from one of the following sources:

- bidding for events
- franchising events
- developing existing events
- creating new events

Bidding for events

There are many existing events that are 'footloose' in the sense that they are seeking cities or organisations to host them, which may be obtained through the competitive bidding process. This is particularly true of major sporting events and conferences, which typically move between cities on a regular, often annual, basis. These events are usually controlled by a national or international body that is the 'owner' or copyright holder of the event. Permission to stage the event locally must be obtained by successfully bidding for the right to host the event.

There are usually three parties involved in the bid process:

- the local chapter of the event owning body, for example, a sporting or industry association
- a government body that backs and supports the bid, for example, an event agency such as the EventScotland, EventBritain or Northern Ireland Events Company or a convention bureau such as the Scottish Convention Bureau
- tourism and event industry suppliers such as event management companies, hotels and airlines, whose involvement is often coordinated through the event corporation or convention bureau

Considerable research, effort and often cost needs to be committed to the bid process, which is described in more detail in Chapter 6.

Although the basic format of the sporting event or conference will usually already be established, the host city or organisation will contribute greatly to giving the event a local context and creative flair. No two events are ever exactly the same. The Commonwealth Games, for example, will take on a different image and flavour according to whether it is hosted by Manchester, Melbourne or Delhi. An industry conference in London, will vary if it is staged in Cardiff, Glasgow or Belfast, or for that matter, in Singapore, Kuala Lumpur or Hong Kong.

Once the bid has been won and the event obtained, the successful sporting or industry association will appoint a committee and event management team to develop a creative concept and to plan the event.

Franchising events

A variation on bidding for events is franchising, where the core concept of the event is developed by an organisation that then permits or sells the rights for the event to be developed in other locations. An outstanding example is the Rock Eisteddfod Challenge, which began in Australia in 1980 as a New South Wales Arts Council sponsored event featuring a handful of Sydney high schools. In 1988, the New South Wales Health Department came on board, seeing the Rock Eisteddfod as an opportunity for delivering their 'Quit for Life' anti-smoking message to secondary school students in New South Wales (Rock Eisteddfod Challenge, 2010). The event spread rapidly and by 2009, 1,000,000 students in places as far afield as South Africa, New Zealand, the UK and Ireland, Germany, Japan and Dubai United Arab Emirates participated in a drug, alcohol and tobacco free environment. A successful offshoot in 1988 was the Croc Festival, a series of three-day festivals for indigenous and non-indigenous students in rural and remote areas of Australia. The celebration embraces health, education, employment and the performing arts in the spirit of reconciliation. By 2005, more than 18,000 students from 416 schools participated in eight Croc Festival events.

Another successful example of a franchise event is Shootout, a short film festival where films are conceived, shot, edited and shown in competition over the space of a weekend. From humble beginnings in Newcastle, New South Wales, Shootout is now conducted under licence in regional cities as diverse as Geelong in Victoria, Toowoomba in Queensland, Hamilton in New Zealand, Boulder in Colorado and Warwick in the UK.

In each of these instances the creative format and template of the event is supplied to local event organisers and applied by them to create the event under a franchise agreement.

Developing existing events

Some events happen on an annual or regular basis, when a new event manager or team may be given the task of implementing the event. Examples include annual festivals and community events and corporate events such as company annual general meetings, award nights and sales conferences. In such cases the event will have an established history and format and the task of the event manager or team is to update this and to make the event relevant and enjoyable in its current incarnation.

Creating a new event

An event may be entirely new, with the host organisation starting with little more than a need or objective to be fulfilled. Such events may be one-off, as in the celebration of a town anniversary or a corporate milestone. Other events may be intended to become ongoing, with the task of the event manager being to devise a successful concept and format for the new event.

CREATING THE EVENT CONCEPT

In all of the above instances, a core task of the event manager or team will be to create a strong concept for the event or to update an existing concept and apply it to the particular context and circumstances of the event. Deciding on the basic idea or concept of an event creates the foundation on which the whole event creation process will later be built. It is crucial therefore to identify a sound and robust concept, based on a good understanding of the full context of the event and its stakeholders. The concept must be capable of achieving the event's purpose, flexible enough to serve the full range of stakeholders and achievable within the available resources.

Identifying an appropriate event concept will require considerable research, insight and creativity. However, getting the concept right will greatly increase the potential for a successful event outcome.

Defining the purpose of the event

The first step in creating the event concept is to define the purpose of the event, which ideally should be outlined in the event brief supplied by the host organisation. For corporate events, this is sometimes known as the business case or the justification for holding the event. This, in turn, will drive the major decisions regarding the development of the event, including the choice of theme and elements and the key corporate messages that the event needs to deliver.

If the purpose of the event is not clearly expressed in the event brief, then the event manager will need to interact with the client in order to clarify and articulate it. Likewise, for public events, the event manager should clarify with the host organisation the purpose for holding the event. The purpose may be multi-faceted — for example, to provide a leisure activity for residents, to attract visitors and to create economic benefit. Identifying the purpose fully and accurately will provide a sound starting point for determining the event concept.

Identifying the event audience

The next important question is to clarify who will be attending the event. For corporate events, knowledge of factors such as the age and gender of attendees, their levels of seniority in the participating organisation, their experiences and tastes will be of great assistance in tailoring the event concept to the needs of the audience. The event needs and expectations of a group of senior executives and clients will differ greatly from those of younger staff members or middle management. Often, the audience will encompass a wide range of ages and backgrounds, which in turn will influence decisions about the event concept. It will be useful to inquire what previous events the company has conducted and what concepts worked for them. This will provide insights into their corporate culture and help to avoid repeating ideas or themes they have experienced previously.

For public events, it is important to know whether the event is directed at the whole community or to one or more segments within it — for example, teenagers, young singles, couples, families with children or seniors. Their age range, income levels and lifestyle interests will all help to determine the event concept. Studying the history of a repeat event may reveal what has been done before, what was successful and what could be improved. For new events, it may be worth searching the Internet to identify other events that are similar in style or content.

Deciding the timing of the event

Important decisions need to be made about the duration of the event and about the season/time of year, day/s and time/s when the event will be held. For corporate events, the business cycle may influence the timing — for example, the event may seek to avoid a particularly busy time of the year for the company or may seek to coincide with the launch of a new product. A similar logic will determine an appropriate day of the week and time of the day — for example, a product launch may best be held during a week day when clients and the media are available to attend or a company celebration may best be held on a Friday night, isolated from the business week and providing time for recovery.

The timing of public events may be determined by favourable seasons — for example, spring and autumn are likely to provide temperate weather for outdoor events, though this may lead to increased competition with other events in the marketplace. A family event may best be held on the weekend when all family members are available or a seniors' event may best be held on a weekday morning to suit the needs of participants.

Choosing the event venue

The location of the event will be another important factor in developing the event concept. The venue must meet the needs of the event, not only catering for the number of attendees but also contributing to the desired style and atmosphere. A formal event such as an awards night or a black tie ball will have different needs to an informal event such as an office party or a rock concert. The venue must be able to meet the operational needs of the event in terms of access, catering, staging and facilities. It will need to fit inside the budget, including the costs of decoration, theming and the provision of adequate power, water and staging facilities if these are not provided. Lastly, it will need to meet the needs of participants including transport, parking and convenience.

Choosing the event concept

Once the basic parameters of the event have been identified, the task is to choose an event concept that best meets the needs of the event. Firstly, a decision will need to be made about the overall format of the event. If it is a corporate event, should it be a product launch, a training seminar or a media conference? Is a cocktail party appropriate or is a formal sit down dinner required? For a public event, it may be a concert, a festival, an exhibition or a parade. Should it be indoors or outdoors? How large should it be?

A widely used and rewarding technique employed by many event managers for developing event concepts is brainstorming (see Figure 7.3). This involves first bringing a group of people together that may include stakeholders, other work colleagues and interested people. The group should then be briefed on the context and parameters of the event and encouraged to participate in a free and associative flow of suggestions and ideas for the event concept. The only rule is that 'there are no rules', with participants invited to express whatever enters their minds, no matter how outrageous or impractical it may seem. It is useful to record ideas as they are expressed on a whiteboard or on butcher's paper. Often the ideas tend to come in waves, with one person stimulated and inspired by the ideas of another until that particular wave is exhausted. Then after a pause, another idea will start the process again. The brainstorm should be allowed to continue until the waves have subsided and the process is exhausted. Then the ideas can be reviewed and evaluated. At this stage, some ideas may be dismissed as marginal or impractical. Elements of some may be combined with others to form a single concept. If good fortune prevails, one idea may resonate so strongly that it emerges as the chosen event concept. Otherwise, the ideas should be prioritised and carried forward for further consideration and development. In some instances the brainstorming process can be conducted

FIGURE 7.3 The brainstorming process

- Define the parameters of the event
- Form a group of event stakeholders and colleagues
- Brief them on the event context and the parameters of the event
- Brainstorm a wide range of event concepts and ideas
- Identify the ideas that best serve the needs of the event
- Evaluate and prioritise these ideas
- Choose and refine an event concept

over several sessions; or a single session can be used as the basis for identifying ideas that the event manager or team will continue to develop and refine.

Another issue closely related to the event concept is that of the theme. For a corporate event, this may simply be the corporate colours of the company or a smart contemporary look and feel. The message that the event is required to deliver may suggest a theme that amplifies and supports the message. A theme taken from popular culture, such as a current film or musical era, might help to strengthen the event and provide inspiration for the other creative elements and program. Whatever theme is chosen, it is essential that it matches the purpose and needs of the event.

Remember that the event concept is only the basic idea for the event, which will be fleshed out and elaborated later in the event creation process. However, the identification of the event concept is a crucial decision on which the ultimate success of the event will depend.

Summarising the event creation process

Goldblatt (2008) suggests the 'five Ws' as important questions to ask in developing the event concept. These are:

1. *Why* is the event being held? There must be compelling reasons that confirm the importance and viability of holding the event.
2. *Who* will be the stakeholders in the event? These include internal stakeholders, such as the board of directors, committee, staff and audience or guests and external stakeholders such as media and politicians.
3. *When* will the event be held? Is there sufficient time to research and plan the event? Does the timing suit the needs of the audience and, if the event is outdoors, does it take the likely climatic conditions into account?
4. *Where* will the event be staged? The choice of venue must represent the best compromise between the organisational needs of the event, audience comfort, accessibility and cost.
5. *What* is the event content or product? This must match the needs, wants, desires and expectations of the audience and must synergise with the why, who, when and where of the event.

Exploring these key questions thoughtfully and fully will go a long way towards identifying a strong event concept tailored to the specific context and needs of the event, which can then be built upon to create a unique and memorable experience, make the event special and contribute to its image and branding. Millennium event celebrations in 1999 had to be special, particularly with the eyes of the world focused on locations across the globe. In London, celebrations focused along the banks of the River Thames and around Trafalgar Square. At the stroke of midnight and to the chimes of Big Ben, a live audience of over one million, together with a worldwide television audience of millions, watched as the river turned to flames and what was claimed to be the largest firework display ever to take place in the world, illuminated the sky above London.

The elaboration of the event concept and its implications for theming, programming, performance, props and decoration, catering and staging will be discussed in detail in Chapter 14.

EVALUATING THE EVENT CONCEPT

Once the event concept has been decided and an initial scoping of the event completed, it is essential to examine whether the event can be delivered successfully within the available timeframe and resources. This process is known as a feasibility study and may be conducted internally or in the case of larger events, contracted to an external body (see also the section on feasibility analysis in relation to bidding for events on page 92). On the basis of the feasibility study, a decision will be made as to whether or not the event will proceed. Shone and Parry (2010) describe what they refer to as the 'screening process,' to examine the feasibility of the event. This involves using marketing, operations and financial screens to determine the extent to which the event concept matches the needs of the event and the resources available to the event manager to implement it. The basic question is to what degree the event concept serves the purpose or the overall objectives of the event? The three screens are:

1. the marketing screen
2. the operations screen
3. the financial screen

The marketing screen

The marketing screen involves examining how the target audience of the event is likely to respond to the event concept and whether the concept will be inviting and attractive to its audience. To determine this, an environmental scanning process needs to be undertaken. This will help to determine whether the event concept resonates with current tastes and fashions and whether it is likely to be perceived as innovative and popular or as boring, ordinary and predictable. A good barometer will be the media response to the concept. If media representatives consider it to be of current interest, they are likely to become allies in the promotion of the event. If the media response is poor, then it will be difficult to promote interest and engage the audience.

For much of this assessment, event managers will need to rely on their own instincts and on testing the response of friends, co-workers and stakeholders to the concept. An alternative, particularly if a large investment is involved in the event, is to undertake some form of market research. This can be done within the resources of the event management company or by employing marketing professionals to conduct a market survey or focus group research. Such research may reveal not only the likely market acceptance of the concept but also additional information, such as how much the target audience is prepared to pay for the event or how the event concept may be adapted to meet market expectations or requirements.

A further factor in the environmental scan will be to examine the competition provided by other events in the market. This step will examine whether there are other events of a similar type or theme in a similar timeframe or whether major events and public holidays are likely to impact on the target market. An investigation of the competition through a 'What's on' in the city listing, tourism event calendars etc., will assist the event manager to identify and hopefully avoid, head-on collision and competition with other events in the marketplace.

The operations screen

The operations screen will consider the skills and resources needed to stage the event successfully and examine whether the event manager has these skills and resources or can develop them or buy them in for the event. Specialised technical skills, for example, may be needed to implement the event concept. The event manager will need to consider whether event company staff members have these skills or whether an external supplier needs to be engaged to provide them. Special licences, permits or insurance may be needed in order to implement the concept. If the event concept is highly innovative and challenging, the event manager may need to consider the degree of risk involved. It may be desirable to deliver an innovative event, but it can be costly and embarrassing if the event is a failure because the skills and resources available to stage it are inadequate.

Another major consideration that is part of the operations screen, is staffing. This step will examine whether the event company has sufficient staff available with the right mix of skills and at the right time, place and cost, to deliver the event effectively. If the event needs to rely heavily on volunteers, the operations screen will examine whether sufficient numbers are likely to be available and whether the right motivation, training and induction procedures are in place.

The financial screen

The final screen suggested by Shone and Parry (2010) is the financial screen. This screen examines whether the event organisation has sufficient financial commitment, sponsorship and revenue to undertake the event. The first step in this process is to decide whether the event needs only to break even — which may be the case if it is being staged as a corporate promotional event — or whether it is required to make a profit for the host organisation.

The next step will be to undertake a 'ballpark' budget of the anticipated costs and income of the event. Breaking the event down into its component parts will allow an estimate to be formed of the cost of each component. A generous contingency should be included on the cost side of the ledger, as at this stage of the event there are bound to be costs that have been underestimated or not yet identified. Calculating the income may require deciding on the appropriate pricing strategy and identifying the 'breakeven' point of ticket sales. Other key revenue items to take into account may include potential government grants or subsidies, merchandising income and sponsorship support, both in cash and in kind. It is important not to overestimate the sponsorship potential and professional advice or a preliminary approach to the market may be required in order to arrive at a realistic estimate.

Cash flow is an important aspect of the financial screen often overlooked by inexperienced event managers. It is important not only to have sufficient funds to cover the expenses of the event but to have them available when they are required. If, for example, a large part of the revenue is likely to be from ticket sales on the day, then it may be necessary to chart out the anticipated expenditure flow of the event and to consider whether credit arrangements need to be made.

Once the event concept has been screened and evaluated from the marketing, operations and financial aspects, the event manager is in a position to make an informed decision with regard to the conduct of the event. If the result is a 'go' decision, then the process of refining the event concept and developing the all-important event strategies and plans — that are the subject of later chapters of this book — can begin.

THE SYNERGY OF IDEAS

Most good events emerge from a synergistic group process. Such a process was illustrated in 1999, when the Millennium Commission brought together a group of people to devise a programme of celebrations for the millennium.

The brief had some unusual features. The celebrations should capture the mood of the UK population and reflect the multicultural communities within the country. It should provide an opportunity for all people, from all backgrounds, to take part. The Millennium Festival concept was born out of these discussions, with a plan for a whole year of National Lottery funded celebrations across the country. The highest profile element of the Millennium Festival was the Millennium Dome, opened on 31 December 1999. Although much criticised by the press, primarily due to the costs involved and the event not hitting projected attendance targets, it was still visited by over six million people throughout the year, with a high level of customer satisfaction achieved. With the theme 'Time to Make a Difference' and pulling on the creativity of professionals from across the country, the Dome included zones dedicated to mind, body, spirit, learning, skill and play. At the centre, a 10,000-seat auditorium hosted the Millennium Experience — a show developed by Sir Cameron Mackintosh and John Napier as a creative masterpiece, involving artists, circus acts, trapeze artists and stilt-walkers. The overall event experience, it is claimed, was to be a once in a lifetime experience, which people would talk about in years to come. Whether this was achieved, only time will tell; however, Culture, Media and Sport Committee (2000) and The Comptroller and Auditor General (2000) provide useful overviews and reviews of the project.

Although the above may have been its 'highest profile' element, the Millennium Festival also included a wide range of events, from small community events to major city celebrations, on New Year's Eve in 1999 and again in 2000, and throughout 2000. The First Weekend, as the 1999 celebrations were known, enabled 22 towns and cities to develop the scale and creativity of their traditional New Year street parties. Many city councils chose to produce firework and music spectaculars, for example, with Edinburgh's Hogmanay attracting nearly 200,000 people and Liverpool City Centre attracting an audience of around 150,000 people to a laser show highlighting moments from the city's history in the sky.

Perhaps one of the largest initiatives for the evening was the Beacon Millennium Project. Involving communities from across the UK, the project enabled 1,400 beacons to be lit as the focal point of community celebrations, starting in the Scottish islands and moving down the country, taking in Edinburgh, Belfast, Cardiff and London along the way. The event included Her Majesty Queen Elizabeth II lighting the world's largest beacon, in London. With the beacon as the focal point, communities chose to celebrate in their own unique ways. Some celebrated the evening in a traditional manner, focusing on the religious significance of the event with hymns, prayers and reflection; while others developed the evening into a major community occasion, with street parties, fireworks, food and drink and a party atmosphere.

The millennium events served to illustrate festival and community celebrations not seen for some time in the UK, with events ranging from the professionally run council events, to community based, focused and organised events that allowed each community to celebrate in its own unique way. The synergistic process started with funds being made available through the National Lottery funded Millennium Commission and an underlying theme of time. Yet each company, council, committee and community chose to interpret the theme of the event and, as a result, a true sense of community spirit and celebration was developed. Jura Consultants and Gardiner & Theobold (2001) provide an extensive impact study of the Millennium Festival.

SUMMARY

With the increased involvement of governments and the corporate sector, events are required to serve a multitude of agendas. The successful event manager must be able to identify and manage a diverse range of stakeholder expectations. Major stakeholders will include the host organisation staging the event and the host community, including the various public authorities whose support will be needed. Both sponsors and media are important partners and can make important contributions to an event, both in support and resources, beyond their formal sponsorship and media coverage. The vision and philosophy of the event should be shared with co-workers and the contribution of each should be recognised and treated as important. Ultimately, it is the spectators and participants who decide the success or failure of an event and it is crucial to engage their emotions.

Events can be sourced or generated in a number of different ways. However, once the event has been obtained, the creation or updating of the event concept is a crucial step in the event management process. This begins with identifying the objectives of the event and researching its history and participants. Once the unique resources available to it have been identified, the next priority is to brainstorm ideas with stakeholders in order to shape and communicate a shared vision for the event. The screening process then needs to be applied to the chosen concept to determine whether it is achievable within the resources available to the event. No event is created by one person and success will depend on a collective team effort.

QUESTIONS

1. Who are the most important stakeholders in an event and why?

2. Give examples in your region of government, corporate and community involvement in events and their reasons for putting on events

3. Focusing on an event that you have experienced at first hand, list the benefits that the event could offer a sponsor or partner.

4. Using the same event example that you have discussed in the last question, identify suitable media partners and outline how you would approach them to participate in the event.

5. What are the means by which an event creates an emotional relationship with its participants and spectators?

6. What events can you think of that demonstrate a unique vision or idea? What techniques have they used to express that vision or idea and why do you consider them to be unique?

7. Imagine that you are planning an event in the area where you live. What are its unique characteristics and how might these be expressed in an event?

8. Name a major event that you have attended or in which you have been involved and identify the primary stakeholders and their objectives.

CASE STUDY: EDINBURGH INTERNATIONAL BOOK FESTIVAL – FESTIVAL OF IDEAS, JOURNEYING AND IMAGINING

Edinburgh's festivals are a vital part of Edinburgh's life, contributing major cultural, social and economic impacts as well as enhancing the city's civic profile. The economic impact of the festivals is well documented. Recent research by The City of Edinburgh Council and partners revealed that Edinburgh's 2004 summer festivals generated an estimated £127 million and supported up to 2,500 FTE (full-time equivalent) jobs. The study reveals that there were 2.6 million festival attendees last year representing a 63% increase in festival attendance since 1997 (SQW Ltd and TNS Travel and Tourism, 2005). The multiplier effect on tourism businesses in the city is also significant, with hotel occupancy rates typically soaring to 80–90% in the capital during the festival period. Beyond economic impacts, the festivals also play an important role in the cultural life of the city with 36% of festival attendees coming from the local community.

Edinburgh is host to 15 diverse national and international festivals annually, as well as several community and participative festivals. These range from the prominent and internationally known

Continued

CASE STUDY: EDINBURGH INTERNATIONAL BOOK FESTIVAL – FESTIVAL OF IDEAS, JOURNEYING AND IMAGINING—*CONT'D*

Hogmanay and the Edinburgh International Festival (EIF) to lesser known but equally important festivals, such as The Harp Festival and the Scottish International Storytelling Festival. Together with its counterparts, the international Jazz, Fringe and Film festivals, the Edinburgh International Book Festival forms what is now widely regarded as the biggest and best arts festival in the world, during the summer months in Edinburgh.

Background

The Edinburgh International Book Festival began in 1983 and is now a key event in the August festival season, celebrated annually in Scotland's capital city. Biennial at first, the book festival became a yearly celebration in 1997. Throughout its 20-year history, the festival has grown rapidly in size and scope to become the largest and most dynamic festival of its kind in the world. In its first year, the book festival played host to just 30 'Meet the author' events. Today, the festival programs over 600 events, which are enjoyed by people of all ages.

In 2001, Catherine Lockerbie, the Book Festival's fifth director, took the Festival to a new level by developing a high-profile debates and discussions series that is now one of the Festival's hallmarks. Each year, writers from all over the world gather to become part of this unique forum, in which audience and author meet to exchange thoughts and opinions on some of the world's most pressing issues. Catherine also comments on how there appears to be little tension between the commercial and artistic in terms of the programming: 'in fact, we have an experimental and willing audience and they appear willing to buy tickets and books for relatively uncommercial authors'.

Running alongside the general program is the highly regarded Children's Programme, which has grown to become a leading showcase for children's writers and illustrators. Incorporating workshops, storytelling, panel discussions, author events and book signings, the Children's Programme is popular with both the public and schools alike and now ranks as the world's premier books and reading event for young people.

The festival also hosts a Schools Program and a Schools Gala day, exclusively for schools, the day after the mainstream festival. This four-day program of author and arts events is the largest of its kind in the world and is committed to enabling children to engage in 'the wonderful world of books . . . with the focus firmly on participation, imagination and creation' (Karen Mountney, Children's Program Director). The event is non-profit-making, with a key aim being to improve access and contribute to education and lifelong learning for Scotland's school children. To encourage participation, the event is free for teachers and also provides a free bus fund bringing children to the festival from all over Scotland. Key events include the School Gala Day, when the book festival is open to schools only; the 'Outreach Program', which tours some of the authors to libraries in Scotland; focused events for teachers, such as 'Improving Children's Writing Skills' and 'Poetry in Primary Years'.

Since its inception, the Book Festival's home has been the beautiful and historic Charlotte Square Gardens, centrally located in Edinburgh's World Heritage listed Georgian New Town. Each year the gardens are transformed into a magical tented village, which welcomed 207,500 visitors in 2004.

The Book Festival is proud to run its own independent bookselling operation, with a strong publishers' presence. All proceeds from the sale of books are invested back into the running of the book festival, a not-for-profit charity organisation that annually raises 80% of its own funds.

Festival operations. Compared with their peers in the United Kingdom and internationally, Edinburgh's festivals provide extremely good value to the city. Festivals with the turnover of Edinburgh's would expect to receive more in local subsidy. Internationally, public support accounts for approximately 42% of the major European festivals budget, with smaller festivals receiving about 35% (the Edinburgh International Book Festival receives 14.9%). The Book Festival, however, is largely funded privately: Sponsorship and Development 25%, Book Sales 16% and Box Office 41%, with key public funding bodies being the Scottish Arts Council and the

City of Edinburgh Council (18%). The book festival has developed a strong sponsor base, with the inaugural title sponsors being *The Herald/Sunday Herald*, five major sponsors and a series of smaller sponsors and supporters.

In terms of staff structure, the nine senior staff are full-time, year-round staff; everybody below that is on a temporary contract ranging from six months to three weeks. At peak times there will up to 90 staff working on the festival, with 15 in the Box Office and 30 Front of House. The Festival has fought hard to retain its summer seasonal staff by paying them reasonably and offering discounts to the bookshop, catering and entrance to events, in addition to instilling the feeling that they share ownership of the festival. Retention of staff offers the festival security and advancement and increases the level of customer service at the event.

Target markets. Edinburgh residents, particularly those profiled as 'affluent city centre area' or' well off town and city area', represent the largest group of visitors to the book festival (46%). In fact in 2003 79% of visitors were from Scotland, with the remainder from the United Kingdom and a small proportion (11%) of international visitors. Market research has shown that 93% of the audience are ABC1. In terms of demographics, 35% of visitors fall into the 35–54 age category, 24% in the 25–34 age group, 22% in the 55 years plus group and 20% in the 16–24 age category.

Within the local segment, there are several key target markets: the Friends of the Book Festival, who, as well as being keen supporters and lovers of the festival, also have a strong fundraising remit; families, who are avid supporters of the Children's Festival and schools throughout the region.

Key issues

Maximising quality and experience on site. A critical issue facing the book festival is managing capacity and visitor experiences on the site. The temporary nature of the site (which is erected yearly for the festival) can bring a host of problems, because all of the facilities have to be brought in and managed by the book festival. A key issue is obviously climate, because much of the site's ambiance is created through its outdoor nature and location. Extremely high rainfall in 2002 created problems of water logging and flooding. Thankfully, the main events were unaffected because they are held in huge staged tents; and 2003 thankfully experienced a return to sunshine.

Obviously, the site has fixed capacity and in 2004 it experienced visitor numbers of around 11,500 a day; and although over half of the events were sold out, the book festival sold only 63% of its tickets. A further increase in numbers, therefore, would have an effect on the provision of facilities such as toilets and food and drink outlets.

Managing author and customer expectations. Critical to the success of the book festival is the event satisfaction of both authors and customers. Authors are invited to participate in the festival and pay a nominal and, surprisingly, equal fee. Key benefits to them include the exposure to their work that the festival brings, the opportunity to meet with their readers and sign books and have access to international media who are present at the festival. Also, because of the controversial nature of events such as 'East and West' and 'Imprisoned Writers', there are security and political issues around certain authors' presence. Thankfully, due to sound relationships with the police and the presence of a security firm on site, there have been no disruptions to the festival.

Customer expectations also have to be managed. In 2003 tickets could be bought online for the first time and in 2004, 21% of tickets were sold via the Book Festival website; this was seen to be a key improvement in ticket purchasing. Customer feedback is sought from the event in the form of a questionnaire at the information desks and invited e-mail responses. Feedback from key stakeholders, such as the media and the sponsors, is also examined because they are invited to various corporate hospitality events throughout the duration of the festival.

Improving access. A key aim of the Festival is to improve access. Recent research found that the 18–25-year-old market was the most under-represented and as this group would be the future lifeblood of the Festival, research was undertaken in 2003 to examine strategies of how to increase the market share of this key market.

Continued

CASE STUDY: EDINBURGH INTERNATIONAL BOOK FESTIVAL – FESTIVAL OF IDEAS, JOURNEYING AND IMAGINING—*CONT'D*

Another issue is improving access from the more deprived areas of Edinburgh. The Schools Programme is aiming to do this for the family market. The move in 2000 to abolish the entry fee and make the site accessible to all, is another step nearer to social inclusion. The presence of more commercial authors such as Candace Bushnell of 'Sex and the City' fame alongside more radical thinkers such as Susan Sontag, is also instrumental in widening audience participation.

Collaborative working. Pooling and maximising resources has been seen as a critical way forward for Edinburgh's key festivals. Although informal networking and sharing of ideas and practices had commonly been practised, this was formalised in 2001 with the launch of the Edinburgh Festivals Strategy. The strategy recognised the need for a shared vision, which the City of Edinburgh Council, the various festivals and other interested parties could sign up to with a common plan of action. The Strategy Implementation Group holds responsibility for the implementation and monitoring of the Festivals Strategy Action Plan. The Action Plan is critical because it addresses recommendations, implementation partners, timescales and resource implications. Paul Gudgin, Director of the Edinburgh Festival Fringe, comments that 'it is helping to foster closer working relationships across many of their departments and between all the festivals and a number of other key agencies' (Edinburgh Festival Fringe, 2002).

Cross-festival collaboration has resulted in improvements in the following areas:

- the inception of the Association of Edinburgh's Festivals
- joint festivals website www.edinburghfestivals.co.uk
- the appointment of a Tourism Travel Press Officer for Edinburgh's summer festivals
- production of a daily guide to the festivals, sponsored by The Guardian newspaper
- production of an Advocacy document for the festival
- multi-staffing of the festivals.

Conclusion

The Edinburgh International Book Festival is an excellent case study illustrating the process involved in creating and implementing the event concept. The world's largest celebration of the written word in 2004 featured more than 550 authors appearing at over 650 events, with contributors as diverse as Muriel Spark, Irvine Welsh and Michael Buerk. The Book Festival is increasingly being seen as a marketable commodity and there are obvious tensions between artistic programming and commercialisation. However, the continued success of the Book Festival is evident and, as Catherine Lockerbie, Director says, 'The Book Festival is bringing the rest of the world to us to engage in wider debate. A good thing'.

For further information about Edinburgh International Book Festival, please visit *www.edbookfest.co.uk.*

By Jane Ali-Knight, Lecturer in Festival and Leisure Management, Napier University, Edinburgh, based on Edinburgh International Book Festival 2005.

Acknowledgements to Kath Mainland, General Manager, Amanda Barry, Marketing and PR Manager and all the staff at the EIBF for their kind support when putting this case study together

Questions

1. Tension between artistic programming and commercialisation is a critical problem for many festivals and events, particularly those with a strong community base. How can festival and event organisers put in place strategies to counteract this?
2. What kind of activities can the Edinburgh International Book Festival engage in to increase participation from the market segment aged 18–25 years?
3. How can customer experience be measured at a festival and event? Discuss three different techniques that can be used, outlining the strengths and weaknesses of each approach.

Project management for events

8

LEARNING OBJECTIVES

After studying this chapter, you should be able to:

- discuss project management as an approach to the management of festivals and events
- describe the phases of event management
- discuss the knowledge areas involved in conducting an event, using project management techniques
- describe the project manager's place in the event management structure and the competencies they require
- use the fundamental techniques of project management
- comment on the limitations of the project management approach in event management

INTRODUCTION

The production of a festival or event is a project. There are many advantages to using project management techniques to manage the event or festival. Project management oversees the initiation, planning and implementation of the event, in addition to monitoring the event and its shutdown. It aims to integrate management plans from different knowledge areas into a cohesive, workable plan for the entire project.

This chapter examines how the project manager fits into the event management structure. There are specific tools and techniques used by project managers and the most common of these will be overviewed. This will be followed by an examination of how the evaluation of a project can build on the project management knowledge base to improve future project performance. The limitations of the project management approach to event management are also reviewed.

PROJECT MANAGEMENT

According to the leading textbooks on project management, world business is moving towards the accomplishment of business objectives through separate projects. Gray and Larson (2000, p. 3), quoting *Fortune Magazine* and the *Wall Street Journal*, call it 'the wave of the future'. Due to the changing nature of modern

Events Management. DOI: 10.1016/B978-1-85617-818-1.10008-8

business, products and services now have to be managed as projects as a response to this change. A product in the modern world is continually evolving. Software upgrades are an example of this evolution and they create an environment that is constantly evolving. Authors such as Burke (2003), Gardiner (2005), Lock (2007) and Slack, Chambers and Johnston (2010) have extensively discussed project management, while O'Toole and Mikolaitis (2002), Tum, Norton and Wright (2005) and Shone and Parry (2010) have done this specifically within the events context.

O'Toole and Mikolaitis (2002), in their text on corporate event project management, note that the expansion of the event industry is a result of this change. New events are needed to launch products, new conferences and seminars are needed to educate the market and new festivals are needed to re-position towns and regions in the marketplace as the national economy changes. Government departments are not immune from this. The UK Government organised a number of conferences and meetings during the 2005 UK Presidency of the European Union; for example, the UK Presidency Better Regulation Conference was targeted at senior business leaders, ministers of EU countries with an interest in regulation, European Commission representatives and members of the European Parliament.

As project management is used to manage these developments, the event industry appreciates that these techniques can be successfully employed in events. Events and festivals can be seen as a response to a constantly changing business and cultural environment and because they are projects they can import increasingly pervasive management methodology.

WHAT IS A PROJECT?

Gray and Larson (2000, p.4) provide a succinct definition:

> *a project is a complex nonroutine one-time effort limited by time, budget, resources and performance specifications designed to meet customer needs.*

According to this definition, events and festivals are projects. A project produces an asset such as a building, film, software system or even a man on the moon — or an event or festival. The asset is the ultimate deliverable of the project. The management is the planning, organising, leading and controlling of the project.

The project management of events concentrates on the management process to create the event, not just what happens at the event. Many texts and articles confuse the event with its management. The event is the deliverable of a management process. A bridge, for example, is the deliverable of a series of processes called engineering and construction. The event may take place over a period of hours or over days. The event management process may take place over many months or years. Project management is a system that describes the work before the event actually starts, the event itself and finally the shutdown of the event.

Project management is called the 'overlay' as it integrates all the tasks of management. Event management is made up of a number of management areas, including planning, leading, marketing, design, control and budgeting, risk management, logistics, staging and evaluation. Each of the areas continuously affects others over the event project phases. Project management can be regarded as integrating all of these disciplines; thus it covers all the different areas of management and integrates them so that they all work towards the event objectives.

O'Toole and Mikolaitis (2002, p. 23) describe the advantages of using project management for events:

1. It is a systematic approach that can be improved with every event. Project management describes the management system. Once something is described, it can be improved. If it remains hidden there is nothing to improve.
2. It avoids the risk that the event's success relies on one person. By having a system with documentation, filing and manuals as well as clear communication and teams, the event is understood by anyone with the right experience.
3. It uses a common terminology and therefore facilitates clear, timely communication.
4. It ensures accountability to the stakeholders. Stakeholder management is a fundamental knowledge area of project management.
5. It makes the management of the event apparent. Too often the management is hidden by the importance of the event.
6. It helps train staff. Project management provides a framework for step-by-step training of staff.
7. It is used in all other areas of management, not just events. The management methodology used for the event can be transferred to any project. Once the event is over, the staff will find they have learned a useful transferable skill.
8. It is common to other businesses. Many of the event stakeholders will already be familiar with the terminology.

Points 4 and 5 are related to the event itself being mistaken for the management. Clear and timely accountability to numerous event stakeholders is a requirement for event managers. The accountability cannot wait until the event is delivered. Stakeholders, such as the police, sponsors and government, may want a series of reports on the progress of the management. It is too late to find out during the event, that the management company was incompetent. Clients are demanding a work in progress (WIP) reports. A project management system has this reporting facility as a part of the methodology.

Project management comprises basic concepts that are not necessarily found in ongoing management. As described in Gray and Larson's (2000) definition of a project, it has a specific completion date, budget and product. This product or deliverable cannot be improved except by commencing on another project. Unlike ongoing management, such as a company continually producing a product and adapting it, a project has to produce the best product the first time. There is no time for improvement. In the words of the music industry, 'you are only as good as your last gig'. This is important for an event. A yearly festival may improve each year, but the first festival still has to be great.

The management of the project passes through phases. The management has to be aware of the knowledge areas and the way they change over the project life cycle.

EVENT PROFILE

Ramadan Nights, Jordan

Events Aqaba is the events unit of the tourism division at the Aqaba Special Economic Zone Authority (ASEZA), Jordan. The long-term goal of Events Aqaba is to promote Aqaba as a destination to the world. From the need to fulfil that goal, sprang the idea of developing two or three hallmark events for Aqaba. One of these hallmark events was Ramadan Nights in Aqaba.

Ramadan Nights in Aqaba is a street festival that was held in Aqaba in 2005 and 2006 during Ramadan, after Iftar (fasting) hours. The venue for the event was a horseshoe shaped street with many shops and outdoor dining areas and one large hotel. The street is closed during the event. This event took place on Thursday, Friday and Saturday nights during the month of Ramadan 2006. Traditionally these are the nights when families go out into the streets.

Before creating the event plan the SWOT analysis shown below was developed:

Strengths	Weaknesses
• The event is supported by the government (ASEZA) • The event is the first of its kind in the region • The event is for all ages • There is a strong audio/visual marketing plan • The theme of the event has been well chosen. • The event is being held in the low tourism season • It is being held in a tourist city (Aqaba) • The location is in the city centre • There are approximately 20 restaurants and coffee shops in the venue.	• The very limited budget • Weakness of the event managing contracting company • Existence of a mosque close by the venue • Weak security at entrances. • Lack of a main sponsor • The venue becomes too crowded • The local religious community opposes the event • Electrical disconnection.

Event planning

The first item in planning was preparing an event breakdown. An effective timeline for each item with its deliverables was created. Someone was delegated to work on each item or, in a few words, describe a milestone. By using milestones, the event company was able to create the event plan.

The first matter to be planned was the budget. The budget took into consideration the main three categories of the program: kids' theatre and activities, cultural theatre and screenings of movies and plays. As entertainment was a major cost, this was dealt with next. The budget included the cost of accommodation, meals and transportation for all entertainers. Also included in the budget was the cost of service suppliers, such as sound, lighting, staging and documentation, in addition to the cost of the promotion campaign and personnel.

The sponsorship package was next on the list. Events Aqaba worked out with I Aqaba, a sponsorship package that consisted of four categories: platinum, gold, silver and bronze. Each category had different benefits depending on its level.

The third issue to be planned was the media plan. Two media channels were targeted as sponsors to advertise the event: Fan FM and the *Al Ghad* newspaper.

The event program was planned in a way to include the three main sections of the program: kids' activities, cultural activities and movie screenings. All activities had to be synchronised with other activities to keep both adults and children entertained at the same time.

Finally came the planning of the evaluation process. In order to have firm results, Events Aqaba conducted two kinds of evaluations. The first type of evaluation depended on distributing questionnaires to the event attendees during the event and shop owners after the event. The second evaluation was to hold face-to-face meetings with the shop owners.

Nancy Tayyan, Events Aqaba,
Aqaba Special Economic Zone Authority, Jordan

PHASES OF THE PROJECT MANAGEMENT OF EVENTS

A project will pass through a series of phases or stages. Figure 8.1 illustrates these phases.

A project phase is a series of related tasks, performed over a period of time and under a particular configuration of management, to produce a major deliverable. The end of a phase is often characterised by a major decision to begin the next phase. There

FIGURE 8.1 The phases of project management

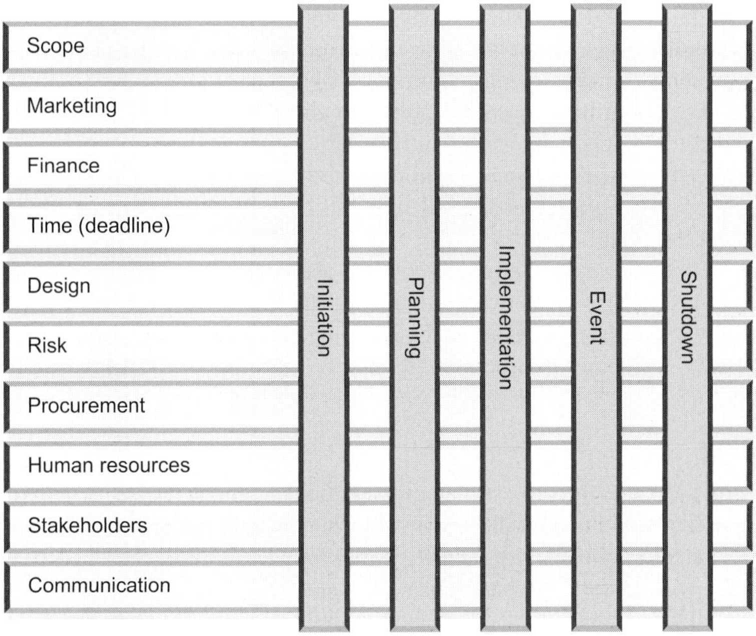

(Source: EPMS, 2006.)

are a number of different views on project phases. Some texts on project management for software development describe up to seven phases. Civil engineering texts have four phases of project management (Project Management Institute, 2008). Event and festival management is accurately portrayed as having five phases, as reflected in the *International Event Management Body of Knowledge* (EMBOK, 2006).

The phase approach to describing the management of an event is purely descriptive — as with any description, it approximates reality. The aim is to provide clarity to the confusing tasks involved in event management. Some project phases overlap — planning and implementation can take place at the same time in different areas of management. The promotion schedule, for example, may be happening at the same time as aspects of the program are being re-designed. This chaos, however, does have a pattern and the five-phase approach is a useful tool to help the reader to understand it.

Initiation

The first phase of project management, initiation, is characterised by the idea of the event being developed and setting its objectives. It may be a vague idea, for example, that a town should organise a heritage festival or that a promoter decides to organise a rainforest concert. As well as this event concept, the initiation phase may include a feasibility study. In corporate events, this stage may be characterised by producing an event proposal and pitching for the client's business. The project feasibility study will report on the viability of the event and the management required to deliver it. It may include site and date suggestions, possible sponsors and supporters, a draft budget, possible risks, required management for the event and event logistics. The feasibility study or proposal may incorporate a number of alternative configurations of the event, so that the sponsor or client can choose the ptions that will suit them best. The initiation phase interfaces and overlaps with the process of conceptualising the event as discussed in chapter 7 and with the strategic planning process as set out in chapter 5. The project objectives will relate to the objectives of the host in sponsoring the event.

The business case for the project is often used as a form of feasibility study. It describes the reason for the event in terms of the return on investment to the host community or company. The end of the initiation phase is characterised by a 'go/no-go' decision — whether to proceed with the event or not.

Planning

The second phase is the project planning. Planning is characterised by working out what is needed and how it will fit together. Chapter 5 discusses this phase in detail from a strategic point of view. Each of the knowledge areas on the left side of Figure 8.1 will produce a separate plan. A major role of project management is to integrate all these plans; that is, to make sure they all work together. For this reason the plans are often called baseline plans. They are regarded as a starting point rather than a finished plan. Once the plans have been formulated, they need to be implemented.

Implementation

Implementation is the third phase. The characteristics of this phase in project managing events are:

- the application of all the plans, such as hiring staff, sending out requests for tender, confirming contractors and carrying out the promotional schedule
- monitoring and controlling — testing the plans and confirming how relevant they are as the organising process progresses
- making decisions based on the comparison between the plans and reality
- work-in-progress reporting to the key stakeholders
- active risk management

The beginning of this phase is a time of high activity with meetings to discuss specific issues, decisions to be made and communication between various parties. The management may need to visit the planning phase when there are major changes and the plans need to be revised. At this time, the team has to be focussed on the project scope and ensure all the plans are compatible with each other and with the overall objectives of the event.

In traditional project management, this third phase is the final phase and involves the handover of the deliverable. Events are not a tangible asset that can be handed over in the same way as a building. For this reason, it is wise to add an extra phase into the project phases and call this 'the event'.

The event

Unlike civil engineering project management, the project event manager is working during the deliverable; that is, the event. Although this is not seen as a separate phase by traditional texts on project management, it fits into the definition above. During the event, the tasks and responsibilities tend to roll on regardless of what the management wants to have happen. The staff numbers during the event, including volunteers, may increase dramatically. The short time period of attendance of the major stakeholders, the audience and the participants, means that the management cannot rely on the same management techniques that were used during the lead-up to the event. This is recognised in all events, when the operations manager, artistic director or the stage manager takes over the running of the event. In the theatre, at an agreed time before the show, the stage manager is regarded as the ultimate authority. At a certain time before the event, the management team will move into 'operations mode', which might mean getting out of the office and into their costumes for the event. The monitoring and controlling at this point will be devolved to other teams and the management will run the event by looking for errors and making on-the-spot decisions. The tools and techniques used by management during this phase are found in Chapter 14 on staging.

Shutdown

The event manager will be responsible for the shutdown of the event. It is the last phase and requires a separate series of tasks and responsibilities. Management will be scaled down and return to their pre-event formation. Chapter 15 describes the processes used in event shutdown. This phase includes the on-site shutdown and the management closure. The shutdown plans will be created during the planning phase and the shutdown ideally is the implementation of these plans. However, in an industry beset by major changes, the shutdown will rarely go exactly to plan. Monitoring and decision making from management will be needed. The shutdown phase can take the event from a seeming success to a failure if the management does not make the right decisions at this time. Shutdown includes preparation for the next event. On-site, this includes packing for the next event; Off-site, the management will be archiving the documents and assessing their management. It is during this phase that the success of the management system is evaluated and the baseline plans or templates created for future events.

In summary, the best way to describe the event management process from a project management perspective is in terms of five phases: initiation, planning, implementation, the event and shutdown. These phases comprise the life cycle of the project. Each of the phases will require different management techniques and tools. Different areas of knowledge will be used. During the event, the event management team will be monitoring the event for any changes, rather than initiating any major new actions.

KNOWLEDGE AREAS

The management of any festival or special event will be concerned with the areas illustrated on the left side of Figure 8.1. The relative importance of each of these management areas will change and evolve over the phases. From this figure, the event itself is seen as a small part of the whole management process.

As mentioned in the planning section, management will produce a number of deliverables in each of these knowledge areas. In the finance area, for example, management will produce a financial plan and a budget. The marketing area will produce a marketing plan and a promotion plan. The design area will produce the site plan and the actual event program. These deliverables are used throughout the management process to organise the event. They focus the staff in each individual area and become the documentation of the event. The areas correspond to the departments of an ongoing business organisation. The project management approach seeks to integrate the plans from each separate knowledge area into a cohesive, workable plan for the project.

PMBOK® (the *project management body of knowledge*) lists nine areas of knowledge for traditional project management: integration, scope, time, cost, quality, human resources, communication, risk and procurement (PMI, 2008). Event management is slightly different. It will also be concerned with marketing and designing the event. In the construction industry, the project manager would rarely be involved in designing the building, finding the money to build it or making decisions on the building's marketability. These are major concerns for the special event and festival manager. These areas of event project management knowledge can be explained as follows:

- *Scope* encompasses all the work, including all the plans, and is defined further in this chapter. The scope, therefore, helps to integrate the many plans. Controlling the scope is a fundamental responsibility of the project manager.
- *Marketing* is a combination of processes that help define the event and, therefore, the scope of the event. Marketing is described in Chapter 9. Marketing is the asset that is not a traditional separate function of project management; however, some of the modern texts on civil engineering and software projects are teaching aspects of marketing. As described in Chapter 11, marketing may be regarded as a feed-forward control mechanism for events and as a risk management tool to minimise uncertainty.
- *Finance* would be called 'cost' in traditional project management. In some industries, the project management would not be concerned with the source of funds. However, in events and festivals, the funding or revenue, — is often a basic responsibility of the event or festival management. These issues are dealt with in Chapters 7, 10 and 11.
- *Time management* in the form of schedules and milestones is primary to all project management. For events and festivals the deadline takes on a higher significance. Project management has developed numerous techniques to manage time.
- *Design* and creation of the asset is found in the project management of software and product development. The event or festival may be changing design right up until the day it starts. Event project management, therefore, must incorporate design under its integration of the event planning. Chapters 5 and 14 describe the processes involved in event design. Within the design area of knowledge resides the PMBOK® heading of 'quality'.
- *Risk management* is seen as one of the knowledge areas of project management. Although it is a recent phenomenon in event management, managing risk is a fundamental function of project management. It covers all the other areas of management and is continuously undertaken and produces up-to-date reports, which is why it has been adapted for the project management of many events. Projects do not see risk management as an arduous exercise. It is regarded as a way to improve the quality of the project and the deliverable. Chapter 18 describes event risk management in detail.
- *Procurement* includes the sourcing and managing of supplies and the management of contracts. This is described in Chapter 17. It is closely linked to sponsorship, finance and risk management.
- *Human resources* could be seen as a part of procurement; but the special conditions of dealing with people, such as team building and leadership, are

indispensable to all projects and so it is considered a separate area of knowledge. Chapter 8 describes this aspect in relation to events in detail.

- *Stakeholder management* is an important responsibility of the event manager. Some large public events will have more than 70 stakeholders; therefore, it is an important area of management for the event team. Finding and servicing sponsors is one of the areas of stakeholder management. Sponsorship will be examined in detail in Chapter 11.
- *Communication* includes external communication with the stakeholders and internal communication with the event team. It changes as the event organising process progresses. The external communication is linked to marketing and stakeholder management. On-site communication is linked to the staging and logistics of events as described in Chapters 14 and 15.

Role of the project manager

Project management can be seen as a collection of skills and knowledge that allows the integration of various contractors to deliver the project. The old term for a project manager was a contract manager. What is the role of the event manager, given that this is also his or her job? There are three solutions to this problem:

1. Expand the skill base of the event manager to include project management
2. Reduce the responsibilities of the event manager and hire a project manager.
3. Train existing project managers in events management

Each of these solutions is being undertaken for different events and festivals. Event managers are being trained in project management at a variety of courses around the world. Project management is now a core subject in these courses. Figure 8.1 illustrates all the areas of responsibility of the event manager trained in project management. Solution 2 is found in public events where the event management is split between the event director and the producer in charge of the creative aspects of the event and the event project manager (who is in charge of the contracts, communication, compliance and other management areas). The event producer and event project manager have equal status in the organisation and report to the client. Originally, for large events, the roles would have been event director and operations or logistics manager; however, the operations manager could not take on the responsibilities of legal compliance, management integration and accountability; hence the pressure to create a new position of event project manager. In Figure 8.1, the event director is mostly concerned with the event design.

Solution 3 is used for very large events such as the Olympics and Grand Prix. Large international project management companies, such as APP and GHD, were involved in events such as the 2006 Melbourne Commonwealth Games and the 2006 Asian Games in Doha, Qatar. In this case, the event is planned and controlled by the project management company, which hires an event director as a contractor. In Figure 8.1, the project company is responsible for all the areas of management. Their primary task is integration and contract management. Most of the areas, such as marketing and finance, would be outsourced.

Key competencies of a project manager in events

Education providers and employers of project managers are moving towards a competency approach to training and employment. Project managers employed by events and festivals are expected to prove their skills in the application of project management to events. This is often expressed in terms of key performance indicators, competency levels or education benchmarking.

An informal survey of recent project management job descriptions for events and festivals has these competencies or skills as essential to the position:

- develop and work in a team and provide leadership
- successfully define and quantify tasks and deliver on time and to quality requirements
- integrate the project plan with the strategic, marketing and artistic plans of the event
- undertake risk management according to the standards of the industry
- use financial controls, indicators and reports effectively
- develop a procurement plan and manage contracts
- demonstrate high level communication skills in presentation and negotiation
- liaise with and manage a wide range of external stakeholders, including public and private organisations
- produce management progress reports for senior management and clients, including project evaluation and project closure
- possess knowledge of the event and similar events in this field
- have the ability to employ and assess project software and management systems related to events

Other areas that may come under the responsibilities of the event project manager are:

- site design and management
- defining client requirements
- sponsorship management
- event concept development

The three areas of event management often missing from the project management areas of responsibility are: the event concept creation, sponsorship development and marketing. In the more traditional application of project management, the finance of the project and the design of the asset are not in the domain of the project manager. In civil engineering, for example, the client will provide the finance and the architect will provide the asset design. However, these are increasingly becoming the roles of project management. Software project management will have a large influence on the design of the product; therefore, event project managers may be required to expand their competencies to include design, marketing and finance.

Many universities offer courses on project management, while providers of events management education, for example, Leeds Metropolitan University, include project management in their events courses.

PROJECT MANAGEMENT TECHNIQUES

Numerous techniques have evolved in project management through live testing in areas as diverse as information technology, product development and engineering. Many techniques originally come from other disciplines such as operations, research and logistics. Most of these techniques are useful to event management. The scope and work breakdown structure are used to delineate the event and provide a management framework for planning and control. The techniques are not used in isolation and they form a process or a series of tasks that overlap. The process is outlined as a cascade model in Figure 8.2. The description of project management as a linear process is only an approximation, as each stage of the process will influence the early stages.

Defining the project and scope of work

The indispensable technique in project management is defining the project and, therefore, defining its scope. Misunderstandings over what is involved in the management of an event are common. Most project management literature stresses

FIGURE 8.2 Project management cascade

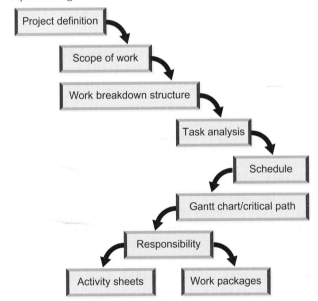

that the time spent on clearly defining a project in the initiation phase, is time well spent. What is involved in the management? Who will do what? What will be the responsibilities of the client and the event company? These are some of the questions that assist project definition. Note that project definition is not the same as defining the event. A simple event may still be a complex project.

The scope — or scope of work — refers to the amount of work required to get the event up and running and then to shut it down; it is all the work. To define the scope is to gain an understanding of the event and its management. Often the event is described in terms of what is happening at the event. The scope definition captures the work necessary to deliver the event, as well as what is going on at the event.

The scope definition may be contained in the brief from the client or primary event sponsor; however, the client brief may be too simple and eventually lead to misunderstandings. Often the brief will only describe the deliverable, that is, the event; and the work required to create it will be hidden. This has been a common problem in project management and the clarity and detail of the brief is identified as essential in the initiation period. For this reason, the event brief may be clarified by an addition of a statement of work (SOW). O'Toole and Mikolaitis (2002) describe the statement of work as 'a document that sets out the event objectives, lists the stakeholders, draft budget, scope, schedule and an outline of responsibilities'.

An important part of defining the scope is the listing and understanding of the requirements of the event stakeholders. In project management, a stakeholder is an organisation or an individual who has an interest in the project. Under this definition, the list will include negative stakeholders, such as competing events and organisations opposed to the event. The primary stakeholders will include sponsors and the organising committee. Secondary stakeholders include organisations that have an interest in the event if some action is not completed or an unexpected incident occurs. For many events the Police and Emergency Services are secondary stakeholders. The deliverable of the stakeholder analysis is the stakeholder management plan. A good example of a stakeholder management plan is the sponsorship plan for an event, as the sponsors are key stakeholders in events. The number of stakeholders in a simple event is large when compared to other projects. For this reason, Figure 8.1 (page 261) and Figure 8.3 (page 270) show stakeholder management as a major function of the event project manager.

Creating a work breakdown structure

The next step in the cascade is the 'work breakdown structure' (WBS). Once the scope has been decided and defined, it needs to be categorised, documented and communicated. The creation of the WBS is a technique that focusses management on the work required to deliver the event. The creation of a visual display of all the work that needs to be done can assist the staff in understanding the scope of the work.

To deliver the event there will be an extensive number of tasks that have to be completed. These tasks can be complex and a long list of them may not be very

FIGURE 8.3 Plans and documents created from the work breakdown structure (WBS)

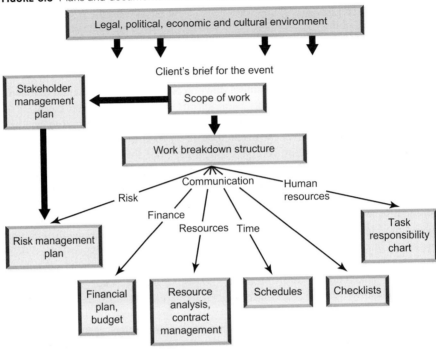

(Source: EPMS, 2006)

helpful. A way to get this under control is to 'aggregate' the tasks under headings. All the tasks concerning the venue, for example, could be grouped under the heading 'venue' or 'on-site'. The tasks that concern finding the money and working out the cost, could be listed under the heading 'finance'. Deciding on task groups and headings should be completed during the initiation phase or at the beginning of the planning phase.

Alternatively, another way to describe task grouping is breaking down all the work required to deliver the event into manageable units. These management units will require common resources and skills. As O'Toole and Mikolaitis (2002) point out, the work breakdown structure often parallels the folder system used on the computer or in the filing cabinet. For a public festival, the work breakdown structure may parallel the sub-committees set up to organise the event. A festival may have four systems: committee, file folders, email folders and paper folders. It makes sense to have them all integrated under the names of the headings in the work-breakdown structure. The committee, the paper folder, the email folder and the file folder should all be called 'venue', for example. It is a simple procedure to standardise the names of folders, but it is often overlooked. A local festival, for example, may have the following sub-committees:

- finance
- marketing (or promotion)
- legal or risk
- human resources (such as volunteers)
- administration

Note that each of these corresponds to the relevant knowledge areas illustrated in Figure 8.1 (page 261). This is an example of the work breakdown structure where the sub-committees represent the work needed to organise the event.

Once the work breakdown structure is created it can be used for the next stage in planning the event. Figure 8.3 illustrates the plans and documents that can be created from the WBS. These plans and documents are often called the deliverables. They are proof that the tasks have been carried out and they are used by other areas of event management; that is, they are delivered to the event management team.

Analysing the resources

The resource list is developed from the WBS. The WBS is fundamental to resource analysis. The resources may be services, such as security, or goods, such as tents and chairs. Resources may also be a mixture of both, such as catering and sound. Resource analysis allows the event management to decide on what services and goods are:

- outsourced to suppliers
- sourced from the client or sponsor
- specially created or constructed for the event

These are major decisions as they will impact on the budget. The resources may be grouped together and given to the one supplier. In project management this is called creating a work package. On large events, the supplier may need to submit a tender to supply these goods or services. An example of this is the supply of sound. From the WBS it appears that sound equipment will be needed in various areas of the event, including the different stages and the entrance. These requirements are grouped together and given to a number of sound companies to supply a quote for the work.

One of the outputs or deliverables of the resource analysis is a list of suppliers. This deliverable is the input into the contract management process. Chapter 18 on risk management explains this process in detail.

Perhaps the most important output of the resource analysis will be the human resource plan. This plan will be linked to the tasks and responsibilities described in the next section. In project management, the tasks are matched to the skills found in the pool of human resources available for the project. This process is outlined in Chapter 8. A straightforward measurement of hours required for the event and the cost per hour can give the overall cost of this resource; however, many events use volunteers. A cost-benefit analysis of volunteers is difficult, as there are so many intangible benefits and hidden costs.

Identifying tasks and responsibilities

The breakdown of event management into the WBS may identify all the tasks that need to be completed to deliver the event; however, this is highly unlikely as there are myriad tasks for even the simplest of events. One only has to think of the many tasks involved in organising a wedding. The WBS will classify the tasks in manageable units. Each manageable unit will have groups of tasks associated with it. A WBS, for example, may have 'promotion' as a heading. Promoting the event will include the tasks of identifying the media, contacting the media, creating a schedule, creating a press release and many more components. Each task has to be completed by a certain time and by a person or group of people; hence the task analysis is the beginning of assigning responsibilities. Chapter 8 on human resources goes into this area in more detail. In a special event and festival environment, a task analysis is deemed more suitable since the activities performed are usually too varied to be adequately captured by a job analysis. Job analyses don't address the question of what needs to be outsourced, and special events and festivals farm out most of the work (for example, catering, advertising and audiovisual).

In project management practice it is common to map the WBS on the organisational structure. Each organisational unit corresponds to an area of the WBS. The management structure of a community event, for example, will be made up of a number of sub-committees. Each will have a clearly defined group of tasks assigned to it. An output of this process, often called task analysis, is the task responsibility chart or document. On this document the tasks are listed — who or what company is responsible for each task, when the tasks should be completed and how the completion of tasks will be communicated. A task/responsibility list can also be put together at the end of meetings. Sometimes these are called action lists. Project managers prefer a task/responsibility list to the minutes of meetings, because they are a 'call to action'. They are direct and the task is not hidden in other information that is not relevant to the required actions.

Scheduling

Project management can be loosely defined as planning the who, what, where and when. The schedule represents the when. Almost all events have a fixed date or a deadline. Completed tasks take on an importance not found in other types of management. The schedule is a vital control tool allowing the project to progress. A mistake in scheduling can have a widespread affect to the other areas of management — leading to blowouts in costs that can compromise quality. The deadline is so important that most event managers work back from the date of the event. The schedule can be clearly represented by a Gantt chart.

Gantt chart

Gantt charts are bar charts named in honour of the management science theorist Henry Gantt, who applied task analysis and scheduling to the construction of Navy ships. The Gantt chart is simple to create and its ability to impart knowledge quickly and clearly has made it a popular tool in project management. The steps in creating a Gantt chart are described as follows:

- *Tasks*: break down the work involved in the area of event management into manageable tasks or activities. One of the tasks of the security team for the event, for example, is the erection of the perimeter fence around the site. This can be further broken down into the arrival of the fencing material, the arrival of volunteers and equipment and the preparation of the ground. As discussed above, this work is usually done as part of identifying tasks and responsibilities.
- *Timelines*: set the time scale for each task. Factors to consider are the starting and completion times. Other considerations in constructing a time scale are availability, hiring costs, possible delivery and pick-up times and costs. A major factor in the arrival time and set-up of large tents/marquees, for example, is the hiring cost. This cost can depend on the day of the week on which they arrive, rather than the amount of time they are hired for. Note that the schedule for many aspects of the event management will work back from the date of the event.
- *Priority*: set the priority of the task. What other tasks need to be completed before this task can start? Completing this priority list will create a hierarchy of tasks and identify the critical tasks.
- *Grid*: draw a grid with the days leading up to the event across the top and a list of the tasks down the left-hand side of the grid. A horizontal bar corresponding to each task is drawn across the grid. The task of preparing the ground for the fencing, for example, depends on the arrival of materials and labour at a certain time and takes one day to complete. The starting time will be when the prior tasks are completed and the length of the timeline will be one day. The horizontal bars, or timelines, are often colour-coded, so that each task may be easily recognised when the chart is completed for all activities.
- *Milestones*: as the chart is used for monitoring the progress of the event, tasks that are of particular importance are designated as milestones and marked on the chart. The completion of the security fence, for example, is a milestone as it acts as a trigger for many of the other event preparation activities.

Figure 8.4 shows an example of a simplified Gantt chart. This chart is common to most small regional festivals.

In his work on project management, Burke (2003) stresses that this display provides an effective presentation which conveys the activities and timing accurately and precisely and can be easily understood by many people; and it provides what Dinsmore (1998) refers to as 'high communication value' to an event. It forestalls unnecessary explanations to the staff and sponsors and gives a visual representation

FIGURE 8.4 Simplified Gantt chart of a small festival

Tasks	F	S	S	M	T	W	T	F	S	S	M	T	W	T	F	S	S
Clear and prepare site		███████████									opening night				◇		
Generators arrive						█											
Lighting on site								█████████████████████									
Tents arrive									████████████								
Stages arrive and set up												██████					
Site security															████████		
Sound system arrives															███		

◆ **Milestone:** start of festival

of the event. Timelines are used in all events, regardless of their size. The on-time arrival of goods and services even at a small event can add significant value.

The advantages of a Gantt chart are that:

- it visually summarises the project or event schedule
- it is an effective communication and control tool (particularly with volunteers)
- it can point out problem areas or clashes of scheduling
- it is readily adaptable to all event areas
- it provides a summary of the history of the event

For the Gantt chart to be an effective tool, the tasks must be arranged and estimated in the most practical and logical sequence. Underestimating the time needed (length of the timeline) can give rise to cost blow-out and render any scheduling ineffective. As Lock (2007) points out, relaxed schedules can lead to budgetary excess.

Network analysis: critical path

One important aspect of any project is the relationship of tasks to each other. This can be difficult to show on a chart. With larger events, the Gantt chart can become very complex and areas where there is a clash of scheduling may be obscured by the detail of bars and colours. A vital part of event management is giving tasks a priority.

Assigning a priority to a task is essential as the event must be delivered on time. The arrival and set-up of the main stage at an event, for example, is more important than finding an extra extension cord. However, on a Gantt chart all of the listed tasks are given equal importance (or weight). The network analysis tool was developed to overcome these problems.

Network analysis was created and developed during defence force projects in the USA and United Kingdom in the 1950s and now has widespread use in many project-based industries. The basis of network analysis is its critical path analysis, which uses circles to represent programmed events and arrows to illustrate the flow of activities, so that the precedence of programmed tasks is established and the diagram can be used to analyse a series of sub-tasks. The most efficient scheduling can be derived from the diagram; this is known as the critical path. Figure 8.5 illustrates a network derived from the Gantt chart shown in Figure 8.4 (page 274). The critical path is shown as an arrow. This means that if the generator did not arrive on time, everything along the critical path would be directly affected. The lights would not be put up and without evening light or electricity to run the pneumatic hammers, the tents could not be erected. Without the protective cover of the tents, the stage could not be constructed and so the sound system could not be set up. The critical path is indeed critical.

FIGURE 8.5 Gantt chart represented as a network

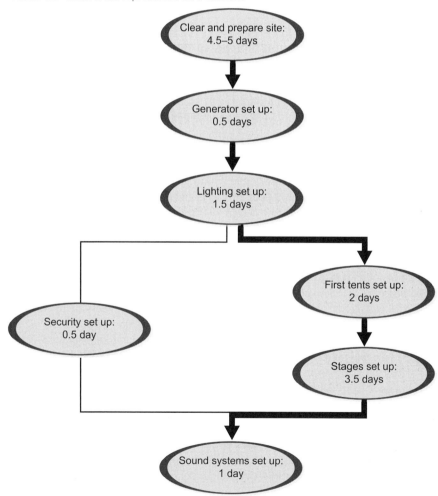

There are a number of software packages available to help create the Gantt chart and critical path. These are project management programs, which are usually used in the construction industry. Unfortunately, most of these packages are based on a variable completion time or completion within a certain time. In the event industry, the completion time (that is, when the event is on) is the most important factor and every task has to relate to this time. The event manager cannot ask for an extension of the time to complete all of the tasks. Time charts and networks are very useful as a control and communication tool; however, like all project management techniques, they have their limitations. Catherwood and Van Kirk (1992) describe how the Los Angeles Olympic Organising Committee gave up on the critical path chart as it became too unwieldy. There were 600 milestones. Rather than assisting with the communication and planning, it only created confusion. The solution was for the committee to return to a more traditional method of weekly meetings.

Responsibilities — from documents to deliverables

In managing a large event, the staff will be made up of various teams, volunteers and sub-contractors. If they are together only for a single event, they may not have a history of working together. This unfamiliarity with each other may lead to confusion in communication. There must be a way of communicating to the management team and stakeholders when tasks are completed, without creating unnecessary data information. The concept of deliverables is one way to control this complexity.

The event itself is the major deliverable of all the tasks that make up the management of the event. A deliverable within the management of the event is the map of the site showing the layout of the event. To create this map the person responsible has to complete the design of the event and consider its logistics; therefore, the map is one of the outputs of the design process. The map is then delivered to other members of the event management team for use in their particular areas. A contract with a supplier is also a deliverable. It is proof that the negotiations have been completed. The deliverable of time planning is the schedule. As seen from these examples, the deliverables are often documents or files. They are developed by one group and passed on to another. After the event, these documents are also used to evaluate the management and may be used to prove the competence of the management. Figure 8.3 (page 270) shows some of the event documentation. Some project management theories suggest that projects should identify all the deliverables and work backwards from these to discover the tasks necessary to create them. This working back from the deliverables allows the construction of the project's WBS.

The deliverables include:

1. *WBS* — a deliverable of the planning scope
2. *task responsibility chart* — a result of analysing all the tasks that need to be completed and assigning them to the relevant people
3. *checklists* — an indispensable tool for the event manager (these are created across all areas of the event)

4. *schedules* — these range from the Gantt charts to production schedules used on the day of the event
5. *resource analysis* — a list of all resources required and the contracts needed
6. *financial plan and budget* — an output of the financial planning process
7. *stakeholder management plan* — includes the sponsorship plan and the various communication plans, such as the promotion plan; as well as the reporting plan for the secondary stakeholders, for example, the local police
8. *risk management plan* — a deliverable of risk management. It may take the form of a risk register and a procedure for updating the register.

The deliverables from points two to eight emanate from the WBS and they help to refine it. There are other documents used in events, including the contact list and site or venue layout map. The event documents can be compiled into an event manual. The manual can then be used for future events, as these documents may be used as templates.

Payback period and return on investment

As mentioned in Chapter 2, a term that is increasingly being used in the event industry is 'return on investment' (ROI). It is a financial measure of the return to the event's key stakeholders as a result of its outcomes. The effects of the event can be multiple and include an increase in sales, community goodwill, increase in tourism and a change of behaviour. These outcomes should relate to the event objectives — and the objectives should be measurable if the ROI is to be quantifiable. In project management, there is a useful term known as the payback period. The payback period is the length of time needed to pay all the costs of the event. After the payback period, the outcomes of the event produce a surplus. A music concert's payback period may occur during or before the concert, as the ticket sales will cover the event costs. The payback period for a local car rally may be measured in years after the event. There are a number of payback problems found only in events — and not in other project-based industries. To establish the payback period, the real costs of the event have to be estimated. Some events, such as those that have in-kind sponsorship or use volunteers, will have difficulty calculating this. The benefits of many events are intangible and difficult to measure in financial terms; however, there are economic tools to assist this process. The most common tool for measuring the intangible benefit of community well-being, is to establish the consumer surplus. The consumer surplus is the amount that the attendee would have paid to attend the event. Using this tool the cost/benefit of an event can be estimated and therefore so can the payback period.

Monitoring the project

Project management is not just a planning tool. It is a method of constructing the plan so that the project can be controlled as it progresses towards the event. This control is dynamic as the project may need to be tweaked or undergo large changes. It means that the event team is comparing the progress of the project to the project plan. The advantage of a project management system is that many of the gaps are visible to the management team. Comparing the Gantt chart to actual progress enables the event team to identify problems. Any gaps that appear will encourage active management to remedy the situation. The budget is another control element as it enables the event team to identify any over-commitment of funds.

Controlling the project is an important responsibility of the event team. The formal process of control involves establishing standards of performance and ensuring that they are realised. This can be a complex process, but consists of three main steps:

1. *establishing standards of performance* — these can come from several sources, including standard practices within the event management industry; guidelines supplied by the board of management of the event; specific requirements of the client and sponsors and audience or guest expectations. Standards must be measurable.
2. *identifying deviations from standards of performance* — this is done by measuring current performance and comparing it with the established standards. Since the event budget is expressed in measurable terms, it provides an important method of highlighting areas that are straying from the plan and that require attention.
3. *correcting deviations* — any performance that does not meet the established standards must be corrected. This can entail the use of many types of problem-solving strategies, including re-negotiating contracts and delegating.

There are numerous informal methods of control that include talking to the staff and volunteers and establishing a conducive team atmosphere, so that any gaps are brought to the attention of senior management.

Reports and meetings

Reports that evaluate the progress of an event are perhaps the most common control method. The reports are presented at management or committee meetings. The frequency of these meetings will depend on the proximity of the event date. Many event management companies hold weekly meetings with reports from the teams (or sub-committees) and individuals responsible for particular areas. The meetings are run using standard meeting rules, such as those described in Renton (1994), with a time for sub-committee reports. The aim of these reports is to assist the meeting in making decisions. Typically, an annual community festival would have monthly meetings throughout the year leading up to the event and increase their frequency to weekly meetings two months before the festival is scheduled to begin. The weekly meetings may alternate between the festival committee and those of the general community (which discusses major decisions by the festival committee). In this way, the public has some control over the planning of the festival. At the committee meetings, the sub-committees dealing with publicity, sponsorship, entertainment, youth and community relations report their actions. The reports expose any gaps so the event coordinator can take action to close them. This is also called management by exception because it assumes everything is flowing well, that routine matters are handled by the subcommittee and that the event coordinator needs to step in only when significant deviations from the plan demand it.

Delegation and self-control

The use of sub-committees at a festival is an example of delegating activities to specialist groups. Part of the responsibility of each sub-committee is to solve problems before they occur. Since it is impossible for the event manager to monitor all the areas of an event, this method is valuable because it allows delegated groups to control their own areas of specialisation. However, the sub-committee must confine its actions to its own event area and the event manager must be aware of possible problems arising across different sub-committees. Solving a problem in the entertainment part of an event, for example, could give rise to problems in the sponsorship areas. The entertainment committee may hire a performer who has a sponsorship deal. The performer's sponsor may be a competitor with the sponsor of part of the festival.

Quality

There are various systems to control the quality of an event and the event company itself. In particular, quality control depends on:

- gaining and responding to customer feedback
- the role played by event personnel in delivering quality service.

Integrating the practical aspects of controlling quality within the overall strategy of an event, is called total quality management (TQM). TQM seeks to create an event company that continually improves the quality of its services. In other words, feedback, change and improvement are integral to the company's structure and operations.

Various techniques of TQM are used by event companies. One technique is finding and rewarding quality champions — volunteer programs often have awards for quality service at an event. Different professional organisations, such as the International Special Events Society (ISES), International Festivals and Events Association (IFEA) and Meeting Professionals International (MPI), share the same aim: to strive to improve the quality of festivals and events. They do this by disseminating information and administering a system of event evaluation and awards for quality. The Meetings Industry Association (MIA) has established AIM (Accredited In Meetings), with the purpose of improving the quality of meetings and services. Originally developed as a requirement for MIA members, AIM has been endorsed by VisitBritain, Visit England, Visit Wales and MPI UK as a universal indicator of quality and is also now available to non-members (MIA, 2009). AIM encourages a continuous improvement approach to improving service standards.

Work in progress report

The client or major sponsor of an event cannot afford to wait until the event happens, to know if it is a success. Often, the sponsor requires a report on how well the management is doing. This status report, commonly known as WIP (work in progress) in the event industry, is a 'snapshot' of the progress of the project. The

WIP report is one of the control mechanisms for event management. Using a project management methodology means that these reports are easily generated. The Gantt chart should give the client an idea of how the tasks are going. The headings often found in a WIP report for a large or complex event include:

- work breakdown structure (WBS) — areas filled in according to their progress
- funds committed — the commitment of funds may be informal (such as by verbal agreement) but will have an effect on the amount of funds available
- risk register — a list of the risks and the status of their remedies
- variances or exceptions — any changes to the original plans.

Part of the WIP report is the risk register (outlined in chapter 18). The register describes the risks that have been identified and the actions taken to treat them. Whereas the WIP is 'static', the actual risk register is a 'live' document regularly reviewed and updated.

Earned value

Earned value is a project technique that places a value on the percentage of the task completed. If the £10,000 promotion campaign for the event is 50% complete at a certain date, for example, it is said to have an earned value of £5,000.

PROJECT EVALUATION

The evaluation of an event is generally concerned with its impact and level of success. Chapter 16 goes into this matter in detail. Project evaluation concerns the evaluation of the management of the event. The term that is common in other areas of project management is the acronym 'PIER' (post implementation evaluation and review). This evaluation process is performed after the project is completed.

One of the attractions of using a project management system is that it enables this type of evaluation and subsequent improvement in management. By setting up a WBS, the management can assess the tasks, responsibilities, schedules and risk management systems and improve upon them.

Project evaluation includes comparing the actual progress of the project against the planned project plan. As a result, the evaluation can suggest areas for improvement in the management. This is different to evaluating the event. It may be part of an event evaluation process; however, it is often forgotten. Figure 8.6 illustrates the project management system used by various events. One essential part of this system is the evaluation and archiving. Whereas PIER occurs after the project is complete, the event plan, archive and review system is a description of the whole project management system from an evaluation point of view. Understanding the way a management system is evaluated creates a system that can be evaluated. The evaluation in this case is evaluating the validity of the system itself. As EPARS — the event, plan, archive and review system — in Figure 8.6 illustrates, one event is used as the baseline plan for the next event.

FIGURE 8.6 The event plan, archive and review system

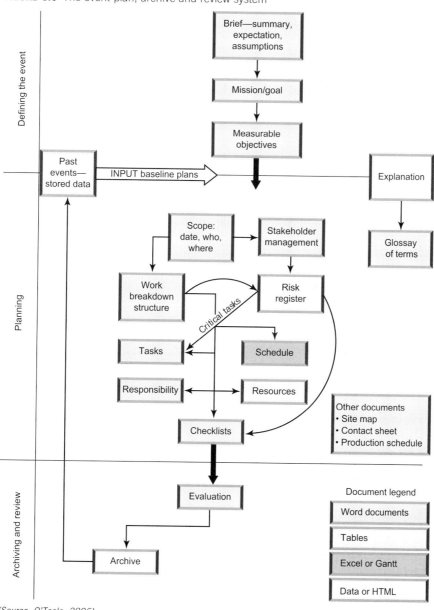

(Source: O'Toole, 2006)

Event project evaluation includes:

- comparing the task descriptions and planned timelines with their actual performance
- assessing the ability of the system to respond to change; that is, its flexibility
- evaluating the timeliness of reports
- assessing the effectiveness of management decisions
- comparing planned milestones with reality

Each of these areas should indicate a fault or success in the management system. This feedback system can be used for each event to improve the management of the events. In this way, the event or festival is far more than a temporary and intangible affair. It is a way to improve the management of events in general. The event or festival can be regarded as a test of the management system.

An interesting offshoot of using such a system as EPARS is that events can be used as a training model. By having a repeatable and improvable management system, a local festival can be used to train people in the skills of project management. Without a describable management system, the skill learned by working on a project cannot be assessed and, therefore, certified. Certification is basic to proving competency. A number of countries, such as South Africa, are seeing this as a way to train their unemployed youth in business and organisational skills. The EMBOK is an attempt by event practitioners and academics to produce an international model of event management that can be used to develop a competency system for training. As events progress towards a worldwide industry, governments need to assess the qualities of an event company. It is too late to find out during the event that the event company is incompetent. Competency standards go hand in hand with industry standards and provide a measure of ability. Standards provide a framework for all parties in the event industry to work within:

> *The work of Janet Landey and her company, Party Design, in Johannesburg is revolutionising the role of events in a developing country. As part of the government's policy of Black Economic Empowerment, her company trains the unemployed through work at events. Even the cleaners become part of the entertainment at the events. Party Design assists in setting up event companies in places like Soweto and in the townships.*

PROJECT MANAGEMENT SYSTEMS AND SOFTWARE

As project management is an integrated system, it is easily translated into a software system. There are a number of project management software systems available to assist the practising project manager. Whether any of these can be directly and simply applied to events is a point for further discussion. Much of the project management software is excellent for planning the event management, as it imposes a discipline on the event team and demands a common language. Each of the systems is similar but due to the fluid nature of event management is limited in its usefulness. The 'Kepner-tregoe Project Cycle Management' and 'Prince 2' are two examples of highly developed and tested project management systems. The event plan, archive and review system shown in Figure 8.6 (page 281), is a visual display of the project management system used to structure the management of an event and, at the same time, assist in knowledge management. By creating templates, the company or organisation can save this information to be fed back into the next event. EPARS represents the adaptation of the traditional project management process, as illustrated in Figure 8.2 (page 268), to the event environment. The inclusion of stakeholder management as a basic function of event management, is an example of this. EPARS includes the use of checklists in the event management process. Checklists are used continually by event managers as they are easy to create and change.

Of the software systems, the most popular in event management is the Microsoft Project. It is easy to buy and is readily set up. It can construct a Gantt chart quickly and is a useful tool for explaining the event to clients. The progress of the event management can be quickly ascertained by the percentage of tasks completed. The limitation of any project management software application to event management is a result of the variability of events themselves. Changes happen all the time. Venue changes, airline cancellations, different performers, more finance, new sponsors and new opportunities to promote the event are just some of the common changes in the event environment. In particular, a special event − that is, one not attempted before − will have a new configuration of suppliers and supplies. In such a situation, current project management software is inadequate to manage the event.

The use of software for event management is limited by its ability to work in a complex, changing and uncertain environment. Most event software currently employed is found in the more predictable and stable parts of the event industry; repeat exhibitions, conferences, meetings and seminars have a wide choice of software − special events and festivals do not have this software choice.

An important aspect of the project management process is that it is scalable. It can be applied to small events or large festivals. It can also be applied to any one area of an event, such as promotion, or to the whole of the event. Chapter 14 on staging an event shows the tools associated with scaling an event. These correspond to the outputs of the project management process. The production schedule is a combination of task/schedule and responsibility documents. Project management software may be successfully applied to a part of the event; for example, a predictable section of the event or a promotion schedule.

LIMITATIONS OF THE PROJECT MANAGEMENT APPROACH TO EVENT MANAGEMENT

The limitations of the direct application of traditional project management have been discussed by O'Toole (2000) and Shone and Parry (2010). Traditional project management depends on a solid definition of the asset during the initiation phase and on a stable management environment. All the management tasks can then be measured against the defined asset. Festivals and special events are not as clearly defined. Often they become more defined as the management of the project progresses, new marketing information comes to hand and new promotion ideas and programming openings arise. A large part of event management lies in taking advantage of new opportunities — which can mean that events can radically change, right up to the morning of the event. Project management, therefore, has to be flexible. Increased documentation, plans, written procedures and rules can easily lead to a management inertia unsuitable to this industry. It can destroy the core characteristic of special events and diminish the 'wow factor', the surprise, the vibe, or the theatre of events — the essence that makes the event 'special'. One solution to this problem used for major events (described in the previous section), is to appoint an artistic director and an event project manager. The former represents the innovative and creative aspects of the event content, while the project manager looks after the management responsibilities. Other areas that limit the use of project management are:

1. *Using volunteers* — the work of volunteers is difficult to quantify and yet, as shown in Chapter 8, they are vital to the success of many festivals. To measure key success factors is an imperative task in a traditional project management system.

2. *Stakeholders number* — more stakeholders mean more objectives that the event has to meet. Given that some stakeholders will change during the lead-up to the event, there is even more uncertainty in these objectives. This leads to a fluid management environment, with the event company continually keeping an eye on any change to the stakeholders. When this is combined with the intangible outcomes of an event, clearly defining stakeholder requirements can be almost impossible. In one sense, each individual audience member may have an array of expectations.

3. *Marketing* — the ability to respond to market changes is a fundamental principle of marketing. This is in opposition to a management system that relies on the definition of the deliverable to stay the same. In project management, thinking about marketing can be regarded as a risk management strategy. The aim of marketing from this point of view is to increase the predictability of management. Using marketing tools such as consumer decision profiling, marketing segmentation, promotion and optimising the market mix can reduce uncertainty.

4. *Finance* — finance may be found right up to the day of the event, during the event and after it is over. Extra sponsors may 'come on board', more tickets may be sold, or, for example, the auction may be a great success. This is another area of uncertainty that makes project planning difficult. Most project management theory assumes a fixed and defined source of funds, therefore, it tends to concentrate on the control of costs.

5. *Event design* — many events are supposed to have a large element of surprise — called the 'wow factor'. This is not an easy element to quantify or describe. At

many events and festivals the right 'wow' can be the difference between success and failure. Traditional project management depends on the asset or deliverable being defined during the initiation phase. The surprise aspect of the event is often difficult, if not impossible, to describe. For some events, describing the 'wow' or surprise (for example, the red London bus during the handover ceremony to London 2012 Olympics at the Beijing 2008 Olympics closing ceremony) may lessen its value. It would be similar to describing the plot of a 'whodunnit' before reading the book.

6. *Infrastructure and resources* – usually of a temporary nature. Events and festivals can have notoriously short timelines. Other projects may take years to complete, whereas the event project may be over in a month. Short-term logistics, temporary structures and short-term contracts do not allow the luxury of detailed analysis that is recommended by many project management books. Overall, event management is under the cloud of the deadline. Every aspect of the management, therefore, must be continually assessed according to its affect on the deadline.

7. *Creativity* – a core element of many events is the creativity of the event team. Special events, in particular, require creative thinking. Some event directors see project management as being at odds with creativity. A system can easily become an end unto itself. It can overpower the artistic basis of an event. Unless these formal tools and techniques are regarded as a support system for the event, they may make the creativity disappear. It is a risk and must be understood by anyone creating and developing an event.

CONVERGENCE

Both event management theory and project management theory are converging. The traditional civil engineering project management is under pressure from the software development project management. In the latter case, software development project management requires softer skills and is considered more of an 'art' than a 'science'. Strict time/cost/quality considerations and tightly planned tasks are giving way to rolling plans and agile systems that are more responsive to change. A new approach to project management, Agile Project Management, attempts to create a different model. This is in response to the enormous number of projects that fail. The Agile approach stresses the human interaction involved in projects and the need to adapt the projects and tasks as the situations demand. It emphasises progress through relatively small tasks, not large plans.

The Project Management Association of Japan describes this development as the second generation of project management. It is characterised by applications well outside the traditional engineering field and stresses organisation, communication and other soft processes. Their third generation project management is characterised by 'not analytical ability, but broad visions, value consciousness and rich insights' (PMAJ, 2005, p. 8). Fortunately, event management is exactly at that position.

Agility in planning, responsiveness to change, leadership, soft skills, understanding values and the art of management are all skills necessary for an event manager. The model for event management has developed independently from the model for software development and other second generation projects, in response to the need for accountability of management and the transferability of the skill across different events, all of which reflects a rapidly growing industry.

SUMMARY

An event or a festival has all the characteristics of a project. The traditional tools of project management can assist the event team in integrating all the areas of management. Each of these areas of management produces deliverables. The deliverables are the result of a number of tasks (proof of good management) and are communicated to the event team. Project management can supply management structure of the event and enable monitoring of the creation, development and organisation of the event. It concentrates on this management, whereas the event itself is often the focus of event studies. Event managers can benefit by using techniques such as scope definition, WBS, scheduling and critical path analysis. The WBS describes the work and generates other plans, such as the tasks, resource analysis and the risk register. By using project management, the event manager can easily produce the progress reports on the management of the event. It provides a professional methodology and the language of modern business adapted to the event management environment. As events grow in scope, the project management becomes the most important aspect of their management. In such cases, an event project manager will be appointed. The event project manager's role is to integrate all the event plans and produce an accountable management system. Although project management is increasingly seen as a solution to compliance and management accountability, it has its limitations. These arise from the intangible nature of the event and the ever-changing event environment.

QUESTIONS

1. Construct a work breakdown structure for these events:

    (a) a rock concert

    (b) a wedding

    (c) a regional festival

    (d) an awards ceremony

2. Construct a schedule of key tasks for the events listed in question 1.

3. List the milestones for the events listed in question 1.

4. What are examples of tasks that can clash? What techniques can be put in place to recognise these clashes in time and enable the event management to fix them?

5. List the types of events and their characteristics that would suit the project management approach.

CASE STUDY: PROJECT MANAGING THE DREAM

On the GamesForce 2000 T-shirts adorning the (debatably) more fashionable staff buzzing around Sydney 2000 headquarters was the slogan, 'Delivering The Dream'. The successful delivery of this dream (the Olympic and Paralympic Games) to the customers and project stakeholders such as the competing athletes, the International Olympic Committee (IOC), national organising committees, spectators, media and the great Australian public depended totally on the seamless integration and project management of the 'big five' Sydney 2000 organisations: the Sydney Organising Committee for the Olympic Games (SOCOG) (including sponsors and service providers), Sydney Olympic Broadcast Organisation (SOBO), Olympic Coordination Authority (OCA), Olympic Roads and Transport Authority (ORTA) and Olympic Security Command Centre (OSCC). SOCOG's Project Management division had the central responsibility for understanding, scoping, integrating, recording and reporting the sub-projects of all four key organisations to the SOCOG Board and executive sub-groups, plus the IOC Executive Board and IOC Coordination Commission. In essence they had the responsibility for coordinating the master project — project managing *The Dream*.

Getting across the Games. Understanding the relationships (or dependencies) between organisational subprojects demands a willingness to work away from your desk; this is essential for building relationships. Initially, many of the venue teams with which I interacted showed a reluctance to share key information and project direction, naturally triggering my suspicion. I felt like a private detective hired by SOCOG to report venue management shortfalls and critical issues (which was not wholly true!) and not their achievements.

The difficulty in translating micro-level detail into macro-level reporting is in maintaining the meaningfulness of summarised information, without misrepresenting the accountable party. For instance, a summary bar may roll up 20 activities – 15 may have been achieved by the deadline and five may be either pending completion or require an extension of time. The summarised status on completion is 75% – in work management terms it may be 99.9% – with five signatures required from a single source on five outstanding documents! It became increasingly important to maintain a regular presence within the venue teams – to be proactive, but not too obtrusive. The key to gaining trust was to provide a range of services that benefited the venue teams (for example, providing user-defined reports, chasing problematic program areas on their behalf, sharing information) – in essence, becoming a part time extension of their teams.

To give you an understanding of the complexity of the SOCOG project management task, you only have to look at the key statistics pertaining to SOCOG's organisational breakdown structure, which are listed below.

- Six 'groups' – for example, games coordination
- Nineteen 'divisions' – for example, project management and special tasks
- Eighty-four 'programs' – for example, project management
- Thirty competition venues
- Five major non-competition venues
- Three villages – Olympic, Media and Technical Officials
- Training venues, hotels, arts festivals and so on
- A Games-time workforce of 110,000 (paid, volunteers and contractors)

Continued

CASE STUDY: PROJECT MANAGING THE DREAM—*CONT'D*

The sheer size of the multi-organisational Sydney 2000 with its multiple projects and multiple dependencies made managing and reporting the status of the master project at varying (hierarchical) levels extremely challenging.

Thoughts into action. There was no blueprint for the Olympic Games (as for many other unique events); although when I joined SOCOG, we had on board many people who had experienced the highs and lows of Olympic Games, World Cups and other large events, the need to speed up the 'conceptual' phase and turn thoughts into structured directives and future actions became the immediate objective. Working hand-in-hand with operational integration program area project management, the concept of the 'Games coordination timeline' was devised to communicate the importance of project managing the events while continually focusing Sydney 2000 on the delivery of the two final stages of the Games project delivery. The strategy behind the two-stage approach was to bring the Games closer in the minds of the organisation ('only two stages to go!') and make the achievement of these stages more tangible to the responsible delivering parties.

The two stages of the Games coordination timeline can be seen in Table 8.1.

Table 8.1 The two stages of the Games coordination timeline

Stage	Name	Dates	Focus
One	Venue project plan	01-01-99–31-01-00	'How we're going to get there', off-site activity planning, documentation and approvals
Two	Day-by-day plan	01-08-00–31-11-00	'What we're going to do when we get there', on-site activity installation, training, rehearsal, operation space-specific — CPA

'Venuisation' – building the team. The promotion of the Games coordination timeline was strategically launched in line with Sydney 2000's arguably most important organisational restructuring. This organisational metamorphosis was referred to as 'Venuisation'.

Venuisation, in basic terms, is the shift of organisational focus from program-based delivery to venue-based delivery. The venue structure was created, multi-organisational venue teams began to develop and Sydney 2000 organisations began to interact with each other on a day-to-day, face-to-face basis in a singular office environment.

Venuisation immediately began to improve communications between formerly remote organisations and instil an empathy in each organisation's individual agenda; an empathy which was previously either unrecognised or, in some cases, not acknowledged.

Project managing the event managers. In my humble and biased opinion SOCOG recruited well. The knowledge, professionalism and dedication of the Games workforce was quite astounding. However, in many organisations positive personal attributes do not always guarantee the possession of project management focus and skills. A good event operations manager, for example, may not necessarily make a good event project manager. The key management issues SOCOG project management had to successfully overcome with the implementation of the Games coordination timeline are briefly outlined in Table 8.2.

Table 8.2 Key management issues

Issue	Definition	Solution	Outcome
Technofear	Fear of the autonomous use of SOCOG's adopted project management software – Primavera P3	Use of a spread-sheet approach – deemed more user-friendly. Facilitated by P3's email-friendly post office system. Centrally managed by SOCOG project management.	Excellent response record to deadlines imposed by the monthly project management cycle; clarity and ownership of information; online ownership and updates
Empathy	Lack of understanding of the dependencies inherent in the delivery of the venue-based project	Pilot project developed before global release – evolution of the 'pilot' communicated to the venue teams.	Consistency in information reported: — level of content — activity descriptions — project structure
Multiple definitions	Key words and project phases that meant different things to different people	Joint OCA and SOCOG definitions of overlay, logistics and operations phases developed by project management/OCA, adopted by Sydney 2000 organisations.	Clear and global understanding of delivery phases, dependencies and project documentation; improved understanding of project management principles
Adoption	Lack of/fear of ownership of the plan – fear of incriminations through transparency and subsequent elevation of information	Venue readiness meetings organised on a monthly basis as part of the project management cycle – chaired by the venue manager. Plan owned by the team.	Venue team ownership of information

E Definition solution outcome

Another 'positive' problem SOCOG project management had to overcome in establishing the Games coordination timeline, was Sydney 2000's focus on test events. Although a distraction from developing the plans, the lessons learnt and the essential team building gained through working on these high-profile, international-standard events added a greater integrity to the information being reported for the Games.

Continued

CASE STUDY: PROJECT MANAGING THE DREAM—*CONT'D*

Managing the software. SOCOG consciously adopted Primavera P3 software as its primary project management tool for controlling the delivery of the Olympic and Paralympic Games. P3 is a high-end software application which is more than capable of managing multiple projects with multilevel, subprojects. In comparison with its off-the-shelf competitors, it has an advanced suite of standard functions, including EVR (earned value report), user-defined reporting, post office and remote data entry. For an experienced project manager, this tool has the flexibility and 'grunt' to generate scenarios and reports reliably and speedily. SOCOG, for example, has extracted information from the core day-by-day project plan to generate the logistics 'bump in' and the site management 'overlay transition' schedules, setting the parameters for program area task-level activity. In my opinion, another plus for P3 is the fact that it is a code-driven application, which encourages the project manager to scope the project and subprojects prior to developing the plan. The work breakdown structure becomes the framework and control mechanism for the project, as shown in Table 8.3.

The drawbacks for P3 as an event project management tool are few, as long as the event manager understands the software and project management principles that drive the creation of the work breakdown structure, coding structure and interdependencies.

For medium-level projects P3 might be considered a bit expensive (about $7,000 off the shelf); but if you believe Primavera is the way to go, there is an offspring of the parent product called Suretrak which has most of the 'whistles and bells' without the sting in the pocket.

You do not have to manage all aspects of a project or multiple projects through a single software application. SOCOG project management did not fully utilise the P3 suite. For instance, cost planning and analysis and resource levelling is owned by the venue manager but controlled via a quantity surveyor/finance manager and venue staffing manager respectively. The quantity surveyor uses specially developed in-house software and the venue staffing manager uses an off-the-shelf spreadsheet package.

Table 8.3 The Games work breakdown structure

Level	Code-Field	Description
1	Master project (1)	The Games coordination timeline
2	Project (2)	Venue project plan and day-by-day plan
3	Event (2)	The Olympic Games and the Paralympic Games
4	Precinct (4)	Geographical areas – for example, Sydney West
5	Venue (30)	Specific venues allocated to precincts – for example, Sydney International Equestrian Centre, Sydney West
6	Space (multiple)	Specific (predominantly) room locations within the venue
7	Cluster (multiple)	Logistical delivery and re-supply area within the venue – cluster of spaces
8	Activity/task	Action description
9	Responsibility	Notification of who is delivering the action and who is receiving the action
10	Reporting	Activities tagged to user-defined reports

Project managing a 'medium-size' event. Many of the principles discussed in this paper can be applied to a medium-sized event. Whatever the scope and budget of your project I would encourage you to do the following:

- Adopt a two-stage (off-site and on-site) focus.
- Project manage space-specific, on-site activities using CPA.
- Use mid-range PM software, such as Primavera Suretrak or MS Project.
- Be proactive – work away from your desk.
- Regular PCGs (Project Coordination Group) are essential – the key players are the event manager, quantity surveyor/finance/commercial manager, architect and local government agencies.
- Establish common project terminology.
- Develop your deployment and recruitment plans early – evolve the plan.
- Use the project plan in a positive way, highlight achievements and incorporate key performance indicators.
- If inexperienced or constrained by time, use the services of an experienced project management consultant to set up and administer the project.

For further information about the Sydney Olympic Games, please visit www.gamesinfo.com.au.
By Neil Timmins, Manager, Programming and Planning, Sydney Olympic Park Common Domain

Questions

1. Construct a lexicon of event terms that may cause confusion at events. This would include terms such as bump-in, shutdown, set-up and staging.
2. Why did the Olympics organisation structure change from program based to venue-based? Was there an alternative way to organise the Olympics?
3. Why did the author use the term 'autonomous' in describing the fear of software?
4. Discuss the constraints of webcasting the Olympics. In your answer, cover technical, political and financial constraints.

CASE STUDY: OPENING AND CLOSING CEREMONIES OF ATHENS 2004 OLYMPICS

With a collective audience of 4 billion television viewers worldwide and 140,000 live attendees, Jack Morton Worldwide delivered breathtaking Opening and Closing Ceremonies for Olympiad XXVIII, working in collaboration with Artistic Director, Dimitris Papaioannou. The Games marked a milestone in Olympic history, as they marked the return of the modern Games to Athens for the first time since their revival there in 1896. This was also the first time a non-indigenous company has produced the ceremonies for a host city. As a result, expectations were high and the pressure to deliver – especially given widely reported skepticism about the Greek hosts' ability to "pull it off" and lingering security concerns – was on. However, Jack Morton was prepared for the challenge, drawing on experience of producing the ceremonies for previous similar events such as the Manchester Commonwealth Games in 2002, the Salt Lake 2002 Paralympic Winter Games and the Hong Kong Handover in 1997. Lois Jacobs, President International at Jack Morton said, "The celebration of the Olympic Games in their ancient place of birth really is an historic event – one that Jack Morton Public Events is honoured to have been asked to produce."

Opening Ceremony. The Olympic Stadium was transformed from a world-class sporting venue into the world's largest theatrical stage. The dynamic Opening Ceremony celebrated the spirit of the Olympics and their homecoming and, at the same time, provided a global branding platform

Continued

CASE STUDY: OPENING AND CLOSING CEREMONIES OF ATHENS 2004 OLYMPICS—*CONT'D*

for Greece itself. The challenge was to create an event that would broadcast a positive image of the country to the entire world, an event that would redress stereotypes and influence perceptions about the country and its people. The ceremonies were held on a world stage and Jack Morton's job was to make Greece its star.

Athens played host to one of the most beautiful and moving Opening Ceremonies in Olympic history. Jack Morton utilised the latest technologies to produce the event including a laser "comet" igniting Olympic rings lying within a 500,000-gallon "sea" on the stadium floor representing the beautiful seas that surround the country; a 60-foot, 22-ton Cycladic head that emerged from the sea's center, rose from its surface and broke apart into Greek statuary and a 370-metre rolling stage and many other magical visual displays. A further feature was a performance by Bjork, who sang an original composition, her "dress" blanketing the entire stadium floor. The audacious performance painted a dramatic picture of a country steeped in pride for its remarkable cultural heritage; a country, which has made an almost incalculable contribution to contemporary civilisation. At the same time, the Ceremony captured the Greek joy of life and the emotional spirit of a newly transformed, modern city and celebrated Olympic ideals.

David Zolkwer of Jack Morton commented, "For us, the greatest achievement has been to bring form to such an intelligent and ambitious creative narrative, with apparent elegant simplicity. Our combined team of production and technical experts has harnessed their talent, innovative thinking, passion and the very latest technology to present to the world a story steeped in ancient culture but which conveys a totally contemporary message that resonates in the hearts and minds of all of us across the world."

Closing Ceremony. Just hours after the conclusion of the much heralded Opening Ceremony and whilst the world became engrossed in the greatest sporting event on the planet, rehearsals for the Closing Ceremony continued apace on the outskirts of Athens. An exuberant celebration of the Games and Greece, the closing ceremony featured a spectacular "ethnic collage" of dance, music and celebration, revelling in the diverse Greek folk culture of dance, music and ritual still very much alive and beloved in Greece today. In yet another incredible transformation of the Olympic stadium, where once a giant lake representing Greece's relationship with the sea that surrounds it took centre stage for the Opening Ceremony, for the Closing a huge beautiful spiral 45,000-stalk wheat field was "planted" to represent the fertility of the earth and Greece's affinity with and dependence on the land.

Drawing on Greek custom and tradition a colourful and vibrant mosaic of dance and celebrations, all of which thrive today and many of them originating from ancient times, punctuated the ceremony. The dance extravaganza included a troupe of men dressed in sheep and goat skins carrying heavy bells to wake nature and frighten away evil spirits; satyrs – wood-dwelling creatures with the head and body of a man and the ears, horns and legs of a goat – gathering grapes and pressing wine; the Tsamikos – a tough dance performed by muscular men; the Tsakonikos – where women dance closely in a row in spiral patterns; Greece's favourite dance the Kalamatianos; table dancing and fire leaping – all culminated in a dance to the famous music of Zorba.

SUMMARY

In January 2003, seventeen days after winning a demanding and competitive bidding process that took over a year to complete, just three Jack Morton staff members opened the doors to a small Athens office to begin work on the ceremonies. Jack Morton's UK office led the ceremony production with a team of over 850 in Athens as well as international expertise drawn from its London, Los Angeles, Sydney and Hong Kong offices. To bring this enormous undertaking to life required Jack Morton to recruit and manage an army of over 8,500 volunteers both performing and supporting the backstage effort. The vast majority were Greek, but the volunteer team also included ceremonies' "enthusiasts" representing 15 other countries working alongside Jack Morton's technical crew. To produce and execute the ceremonies required a significant level of project planning including over 50,000 telephone calls to recruit volunteer performers, 6,600 cast bus trips to and from rehearsal sites, five miles of audio and data cable, 7,000 in-ear audio monitors, 11,000 yards of costume fabric and hundreds of hours of music recording. By the time both ceremonies were over, more than 700,000 bottles of water had been consumed by cast and crew.

The Opening and Closing Ceremonies and Jack Morton's work received extensive major media coverage worldwide. In September 2004, a nationwide survey conducted in Greece showed that the public majority believes that the success of the Olympic Games enhanced the perception of their country on an international level; they identified the Ceremonies as the top two most memorable moments of the entire Olympics experience. In June 2005, the Independent reported that tourism to Greece had increased 10% in the ten months following the Olympics; the National Bank of Greece estimated 13.5 million tourists in 2005 and 14 million in 2006 as a result of the games' popularity – in no small part due to the flawless execution of the Opening and Closing Ceremonies.

For further information about Jack Morton Worldwide, please visit www.jackmorton.co.uk.
By Jack Morton Worldwide.

Questions
1. What was the scope of the project for the events identified in this case study?
2. What challenges were faced by the organisers?
3. What project management tools and techniques could the organisers use to help manage these challenges?
4. Conduct further research into the 2004 Athens Olympic Games and identify other examples of project management in practice.

Financial management and events

LEARNING OBJECTIVES

After studying this chapter, you should be able to:

- understand the role of financial management in the overall management of an event
- create an event budget
- understand the methods of event costing and ticket pricing
- monitor and control the event spending and incoming finances
- identify the key elements of budgetary control and explain the relationship between them
- understand the advantages and shortcomings of using a budget

INTRODUCTION

Financial management is defined as the decisions that are made in respect of the sourcing, planning, allocation, monitoring and evaluation of the money resource. In the event environment, financial decisions take place within the overall objectives of the event or festival. This chapter concerns the financial tools and techniques that are used in the process of delivering an event and the management of a port-folio of events. Many of these tools and techniques are taken from the financial management of ongoing companies and from project management. Although these tools are the same, the event environment will place a different emphasis and priority in their employment. As well as the well-known general financial management tools, tools and techniques have been developed specifically for the event industry.

Money is one of the resources of event management. If an event is run for profit, the sourcing and allocation of money will be very important. This is because the primary objective of the for-profit event is to have income greater than expenditures. Other events and festivals, however, regard profit as a lesser objective. They may have a combination of aims, such as community development, tourism, business networking and public awareness. For some events and festivals, a financial surplus can be a problem. Their aim is to break even. They may just want to meet their

Events Management. DOI: 10.1016/B978-1-85617-818-1.10009-X

budget and no more. Figure 9.1 provides an insight into the commercial realities of some events. As Sonder (2004, p. 137) writes:

'Even if money is not the issue, your event will have to meet or exceed certain financial performance objectives. All events must have responsible financial management.'

Mismanagement of finance can lead to unforeseen operational risks, such as safety, crowd control and legal problems. So it behoves all event managers to know about financial management. There are legal obligations on an event team to ensure the event finance is managed in a proper and correct manner. Tax obligations, such as VAT, require an event to have systems to record all transactions. A client or major sponsor may want to see the financial statements. In some cases, if there is any problem, the client may want to audit the books of the event company.

It is therefore a necessity that the event organisation set up a management system that can control the flow of money to the various management areas, such as marketing, insurance, venue costs and design. At the same time, the event team may be looking for extra inflow by seeking new sponsors and re-examining contracts, while also looking for cost savings. Unforeseen costs can quickly arise. The client can also change requirements; for example, there was a 40% budget reduction for the 2004 Athens Olympics opening ceremony. External influences, such as an airline strike or a supplier going bankrupt,can impinge on finance.

The fluidity of the event environment is illustrated by Ric Birch in his insightful book *Master of ceremonies* (2004, pp. 281−2). He describes the numerous meetings leading up to the 2000 Sydney Olympics:

By late 1999, the content of the opening and closing ceremonies was more or less settled. There were still changes to come, but they could now be made within the framework of a budget that was much more accurate. The SOCOG group around the table, however, could only see that the budget had increased from A$43 to A$54 million.

I pointed out that over a five-year period, the budget had increased only eight percent from my original estimate, which was less than inflation. I also pointed out that SOCOG had made a windfall profit of more than $20 million from the extra seats that had become available when the athletes were removed from the stands for the opening ceremony . . . But no one around the table was interested.

In this quote Ric Birch illustrates a number of characteristics of financial management for events:

- Although there was a framework for the budget, its accuracy changed over time
- Unexpected income and costs arise, even for a major event such as the Olympics
- Financial management is a high-level responsibility
- The event manager is expected to defend the spending
- There are mutual dependencies between the different areas of event management (in this case between finance, operations and the program)

FIGURE 9.1 Profit or perish

Successful events are big business, requiring leaders who understand the importance of profit making. Consumers demand innovation and quality. Innovation and quality cost big bucks. If you don't offer what your customers want then your competitor will. Profits mean success, confidence and influence. Leisure and the arts are not immune to such market trends.

Money will always get in the way, but the more money you have, the less painful your problem is! It's easier to manage the threat of compromising your artistic integrity for commercial imperatives than explaining to your investors that you've planned for their demise.

Producing events is a serious business. If your strength is about inspiring and creating, then you may find yourself too busy and (most probably) by nature unable to focus on maintaining the level of discipline, attention to detail and tough decision making that the business of events requires. Don't try to do it all, play to your strengths and weaknesses by developing the team around you. A call to the best accountancy firm in town may prove to be your best investment!

Step one of the business of any event is to appoint, befriend and learn to trust your chief financial officer or treasurer. Build a working relationship of respect that actively engages those with the discipline and expertise of money management in your decision making. Step two is to underpin your relationship with your financial adviser with the belief that one of the primary aims of operating a business is to make money, to make as large a profit as possible while balancing your need to achieve your event's primary goals. It is more than appropriate that you measure your event's overall success in terms of other less tangible goals, among which you may list the celebration of a moment, community development, attendee satisfaction, challenging your audience, delivering an intended message or the like. Such claims of success belong in the introductory section of your annual report to excite and engage your event constituents. However, these words will stand for little if your financial statement records an undisciplined budget result. When

seeking sound financial advice, be sure to maintain the responsibility of making the final decisions on the artistic and strategic directions of your event. Such decisions can then be made with the confidence that you have proactively sought the financial implications and therefore clearly understand and can articulate the implications of these decisions. After all, you will ultimately be held accountable for the areas of your responsibility.

So long as you understand that profit equals success, continuity and strength, then you'll be on the right track. With money in the bank you have options and opportunities. The alternative of operating at a loss is that your event will struggle, your ability to influence your financiers will be eroded and if the problem persists, your position and your event, or both, will perish. Some of your peers may wish to challenge your decision making with cries of 'too commercial' or 'sold out for the almighty dollar', but at least you'll be around to take heed of such criticism and reassess the balance of your business, artistic and strategic intent.

No matter how engaging, wholesome and humanistic your ideology or creativity may be, if you don't possess a robust business plan centred on the discipline of good decision making and wise investment of your available resources — including meticulous assessment of the risk elements of your adventurous plan — then your position or your event will be short-lived. All that you stood for, sought to achieve, your artistic endeavour and uncompromised beliefs and, perhaps more tragically, the countless hours you and your loyal followers invested will result in nothing but heartache. You owe it to yourself, your investors, your followers and believers, including financial backers, staff, volunteers, sponsors and attending public, to make as much money as you can to enable the business of your event to grow and prosper.

Please disregard all of the above if money grows on trees in your neck of the eventing woods.

John Aitken, General Manager, Events and Marketing, Sydney Royal Easter Show

(Source: Aitken, 2006)

Even with all these changes, the event must go on. The cloud that hangs over every financial decision is the deadline. Figure 9.2 illustrates the financial management process from the project management point of view.

The management of event finance is a process, a series of steps that starts with forecasting and setting up, to monitor the event finances. As illustrated in Figure 9.2, there are inputs to this process. The primary inputs come from the management areas of scope, stakeholder and marketing. Each of these management areas directly influences the finance. Stakeholders, for example, can increase funding through sponsorship, ticket sales or legislation. Although the process is illustrated as being step by step, the reality is that many of the tools are used concurrently.

Cost benefit analysis and cost analysis go hand in hand. The budget can be developed as a draft budget and then refined, as the cash flow management and the cost control planning becomes more detailed. At all times the event manager has to be aware of external trends that will affect the event finance. As with every aspect of special event and festival management, there will be developments. Management of finance is not just observing the flow of money according to how it is set out in the budget. It is active management. It is decision making that concerns the reallocation of funds, the finding of new sources of income and reduction of new costs. All of these decisions sit under the cloud of the deadline. Every financial decision in the event environment must take into account the variable time as well as the constant — the deadline.

FORECASTING FINANCE AND ROI

Financial management begins during the initiation phase of event management. It takes place when deciding on the feasibility of the event. The question of 'Will it work?' generally implies 'Are there enough funds?'. The case presented for the event will have 'Finance' as a heading; in other words, 'Where will the money come from'. In this text there is a chapter on sponsorship and many events depend heavily on sponsorship for their finance. Other events, such as corporate events and council events, are given a fixed amount. Events such as concerts and some conferences will depend on ticket sales for their main source of income. Some event organisations will have all the money up-front and, therefore have the financial certainty that many other event companies would envy. Other events are expected to earn the money over the period leading up to the event. Others may only make their money on the day of the event. Finally, there are events that will make some of their income after the event has finished. In the case of product launches, all of the finance is generated post-event. Timing — when the finance comes in and when the bills have to be paid — is an important part of financial management for events.

Return on investment (ROI) is the measure of the financial return for the investment in the event. The ROI will be different for each of the stakeholders. The host of a major event, such as the government or a large corporation, will expect

FIGURE 9.2 The financial management process from the project management point of view

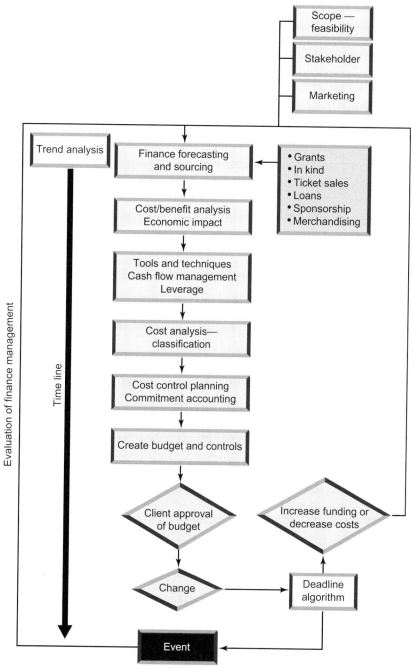

(Source: O'Toole, 2006)

a complex return on their investment. It may not be easily expressed in financial terms. In this context, the complexity stems from the degree of risk caused by a number of variables. An event such as the Olympics provides many returns on the government's investment. A number of the Olympic stakeholders have not agreed on the value of this return. For small events the ROI may be simply worked out in terms of ticket sales or incoming registration payments.

Currently there is a trend to express all of the complex returns in financial terms and therefore give a more realistic assessment of the event. This is to enable the event to be compared to other investment projects. However, the jury is still out on whether this can be achieved. How can 'community happiness', for example, be expressed in financial terms? The ROI (or lack thereof) for many events may not actualise until years after the event.

These are complex issues and involve cost-benefit analysis, input-output analysis and other economic tools (see economic impact studies in Chapter 3). It should be noted that not all economists agree on the tools or the conclusions reached, when applying them to events and festivals. As outlined in Chapter 6, another measure of the financial success of a special event or festival, is the time it takes the event to pay off its expenses, — 'the payback period'. The Victorian Auditor-General's 2007 report on major events, illustrates this with the comparison of two very different economic benefit studies of the 2005 Melbourne Grand Prix (Victorian Auditor-General, 2007).

THE BUDGET

A budget can be described as a quantified statement of plans (in other words, the plan is expressed in numerical terms). The budget process includes costing and estimating income and the allocation of financial resources. The budget of an event is used to compare actual costs and revenues with projected costs and revenues. In particular, maximum expenditure for each area of the event's operation is estimated. To achieve this efficiently, a budget can take many forms. For instance, it may be broken into sub-budgets that apply to specific areas of a complex or large event, such as the staging, logistics, merchandising and human resources. Budgets are of particular importance to the management of events because most aspects of the event incur costs requiring payment before the revenue is obtained. Cash flow needs special attention. Most funding or sponsorship bodies need to see a budget of the proposed event, before they will commit their resources.

The second part of this chapter expands on these points and provides an example to illustrate them. A number of examples will illustrate the form of an event budget and its use.

Constructing the budget

Two types of budget processes can be used in event management. The master budget, as the name suggests, focuses on each cost and revenue item of the total event (or event company) and the functional budget is constructed for a specific programme element, costs centre or department (Dyson, 2007). An example of the latter is a budget devised for a festival, which concerns only the activities of one of the performance areas or stages. Such a budget effectively isolates this area of the event from the general festival finance. In this way, individual budgets can be used to compare all the performance areas or stages. The line items are performers' fees and so on.

An example of the master budget is illustrated in Figure 9.3. It includes box office, marketing, artist fees and staging.

The creation of a budget has the advantage of forcing management to establish a financial plan for the event and to allocate resources accordingly. It imposes a necessary financial discipline, regardless of how informally an event may be

FIGURE 9.3 Festival Trust 2010-13 — Financial Plan

**Festival Trust Financial Plan
2010/11 - 2012/13**

	Year 1 2010-11	Year 2 2011-12	Year 3 2012-13
INCOME	£	£	£
Ticket Sales	297 330	311 080	322 190
Other Sales	92 290	100 650	103 180
Private Sector Fundraising	345 840	372 020	381 260
Council Grant	347 600	345 290	331 870
Arts Board Grant	150 700	155 430	159 280
Other public sector fundraising	69 630	72 600	73 370
TOTAL	1 303 390	1 357 070	1 371 150
EXPENDITURE			
Artists & Staging	606 980	621 500	622 820
Marketing	125 950	123 200	126 280
Merchandising	24 860	25 520	26 180
Box Office	29 150	29 920	30 690
Salaries	349 030	360 470	369 490
Overheads	134 090	137 280	140 690
Contingency	33 110	37 070	37 950
TOTAL	1 303 170	1 334 960	1 354 100
SURPLUS/(DEFICIT)	220	22 110	17 050

FIGURE 9.4 The budget process

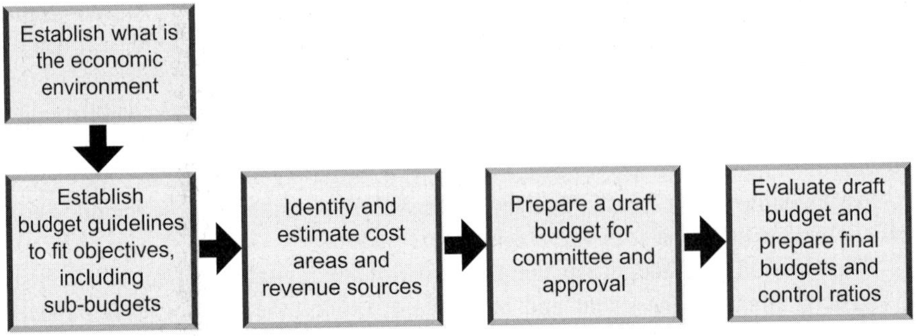

organised. In a similar way to the Gantt chart, it can be used for review long after the event is over.

Preparing a budget is illustrated by Figure 9.4. The process begins by establishing the economic environment of the event. The economy of the region and the country (or even European or world economy), may impinge on the event and significantly change the budget. For example, the effects of the fall in value of sterling against other world currencies, in particular those in the European Union using the Euro, has made it more expensive for UK companies to run events overseas and made it more difficult to sell events within other countries. However, the benefit is that it has made it cheaper for overseas delegates to come to UK events. To determine the economic environment, it is useful to ask the following questions. What similar events can be used as a guide? Will changes in the local or national economy affect the budget in any way? If the event involves international performers or hiring equipment from overseas, will there be a change in the currency exchange rates? These, and many more, questions need to be answered before constructing a budget that will result in reasonable projections of costs and revenue.

The next step is to obtain the guidelines from the client, sponsors or event committee. For example, a client may request that only a certain percentage of their sponsorship be allocated to entertainment, with the rest to be allocated to hospitality. Guidelines must fit with the overall objectives of the event and may require the construction of sub-budgets or programme budgets. This is both an *instructive phase*, in that the committee, for example, will instruct the event manager on the content of the budget and also a *consultative phase*, as the event manager would ask the advice of other event specialists and the subcontractors.

The third step is to identify, categorise and estimate the cost areas and revenue sources. The categories become the items in the budget. A sample of the categories is given in Figure 9.5. This is a summary or a first-level budget, of the cost and revenue areas. The next level down expands each of these main items, as shown in Figures 9.6 and 9.7. The use of computer-generated spreadsheets enables a number

FIGURE 9.5 Generic budget — first level

Income	£	Expenditure	£
Grants		Administration	
Donations		Publicity	
Sponsorship		Venue costs	
Ticket sales		Equipment	
Fees		Salaries	
Special programmes		Insurance	
Concession		Permits	
Security			
TOTAL		Accounting	
		Cleaning	
		Travel	
		Accommodation	
		Documentation	
		Hospitality	
		Community groups	
		Volunteers	
		Contingencies	
		TOTAL	

of levels in the budget to be created on separate sheets and linked to the first level budget. Cost items take up the most room on a budget and are described below.

Once the costs and possible revenue sources and amounts are estimated, a *draft budget* is prepared and submitted for approval to the controlling committee. This may be the finance subcommittee of a large festival. The draft budget is also used in grant submissions and sponsorships. The funding bodies, for example, UK Sport, Arts Council England, Scottish Arts Council, Arts Council of Northern Ireland, Arts Council of Wales and Awards for All, have budget guidelines and forms that need to be filled out and included in the grant application.

A major problem associated with a budget, particularly for special events, may involve blind adherence to it. It is a tool of control and not an end in itself. The

FIGURE 9.6 Generic budget – second level

		£			£
Administration	Office rental		Insurance		Public liability
	Fax/photocopy				Workers comp.
	Computers				Rain
	Printers				Other
	Telephone				**SUB-TOTAL**
	Stationery		Permits		Liquor
	Postage				Food
	Office staff				Council
	SUB-TOTAL				Parking
Publicity	Art work				Children
	Printing				**SUB-TOTAL**
	Poster leaflet distribution		Security		Security check
	Press kit				Equipment
	Press ads				Staff
	Radio ads				**SUB-TOTAL**
	Programmes		Accounting		Cash and cheque
	SUB-TOTAL				During
Equipment	Stage				After
	Sound				**SUB-TOTAL**
	Lights		Travel		Artists
	Transport				Freight
	Personnel				**SUB-TOTAL**
	Toilets		Accom.		
	Extra equipment				**SUB-TOTAL**
	Communication		Documentation		Photo/video
	First aid				**SUB-TOTAL**
	Tents		Hospitality		Tent
	Tables and chairs				Food
	Wind breaks				Beverage
	Generators				Staff
	Technicians				Invitations
	Parking needs				**SUB-TOTAL**
	Uniforms		Community		Donations
	SUB-TOTAL				**SUB-TOTAL**
Salaries	Co-ordinator		Volunteers		Food and drink
	Artists				Party
	Labourers				Awards and prizes
	Consultants				**SUB-TOTAL**
	Other		Contingencies		
	SUB-TOTAL				**SUB-TOTAL**

FIGURE 9.7 Generic budget — third level

Income	£	Ticket sales	£
Grants	Local government	Ticket sales	Box office
	Central government		Retail outlets
	Millennium Fund		Admissions
	Arts Council		**SUB-TOTAL**
	Other	Merchandise	T-shirts
	SUB-TOTAL		Programmes
Donations	Foundations		Posters
	Other		Badges
	SUB-TOTAL		Videos
Sponsorship	In kind		**SUB-TOTAL**
	Cash	Fees	Stalls
	SUB-TOTAL		Licences
Individual contributions			Broadcast
	SUB-TOTAL		**SUB-TOTAL**
Special programmes	Raffle	Advert sales	Programme
	Auction		Event site
	Games		**SUB-TOTAL**
	SUB-TOTAL	Concessions	
			SUB-TOTAL

elegance of a well laid-out budget and its mathematical certainty can obscure the fact that it should be slave to the event's objectives; and should not be their master. A budget is based on reasonable projections made within an economic framework. Small changes in the framework can cause large changes in the event's finances. For instance, extra sponsorship may be found if the right products are added to the event portfolio. A complicated, highly detailed budget may consume far more time than is necessary to make the event a success. However, this may be required by the client and the time and cost to create such a budget needs to be factored into the overall project plan.

Time is a crucial factor in special event management. Keeping rigidly within budgetary standards can take up too much of the time and energy of the event management, thus limiting time available for other areas.

Finally, a budget that is constructed by the event management may be imposed on staff without adequate consultation. This can lead to losing valuable specialist staff, if they find themselves having to work to unreasonable budgetary standards. In particular, an innovative event requires the creative input of all the staff and subcontractors. At such events, informal financial control using a draft budget is often far more conducive to quality work than strict budgetary control.

It needs to be remembered that a budget is only an approximation of reality; it is a plan for what should be done and not reality itself. It will need to be adjusted as the event changes and new information comes to hand. However, it is a vital part of the financial management of events.

The final step involves preparation of the budget and financial ratios that can indicate deviations from the initial plan. An operating business has a variety of budgets including capital expenditure, sales, overheads and production. Most events will only require an operation budget or a cash budget.

Note the similarity between the classification system used for the budget (see Figure 9.5) and the WBS described in Chapter 6 ('Project management for events'). The WBS is often used as a basis of a budget. The costs of the lower levels are added to give the overall costs — called 'rolling up'. This means many aspects of the event can be coded. A simple coding system can be used to link the WBS, the budget, the task sheets and risk analysis — for example, the artwork (A) and the publicity (P) can use the code PA. The coding system can be cross-referenced to the company, person who is responsible, possible risks or the amount budgeted.

With regard to estimating amounts within the budget, Watt (1998, p. 45) suggests that although it must be, 'as accurate as possible . . . it is always advisable to *overestimate expenditure* and *underestimate income*. To do the opposite is a recipe for disaster'.

CONTROL AND FINANCIAL RATIOS

Once a plan has been developed and agreed to, the next step is to monitor and control its implementation. For large events, such as the 2012 London Olympics, the control mechanisms are set up when the management plan is created. The budget is a control mechanism as it enables the event management to identify when the event is drifting away from the forecast.

As described in Chapter 6, the process of control involves the following steps.

- Establishing standards of performance: this is the budget itself, indicator ratios, success factors and milestones
- Identifying deviations from standards of performance by comparing the budget to the actual spend. Often this can be difficult as the spend can be spread over time. Therefore the ratios and milestones become important as a method to indicate if there are problems
- Correcting deviations — this may involve cutting costs, finding more money or shifting resources

The breakeven chart

This simple graphic tool can highlight problems by finding the intersection of costs and revenue. Figure 9.8 shows a simple but effective breakeven chart for an

FIGURE 9.8 The breakeven chart

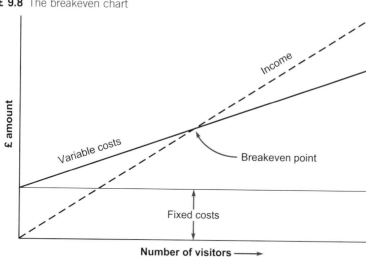

event that is dependent on ticket sales. For example, the Proms in the Park in Birmingham would have fixed costs of stage, pyrotechnics and administration costs. However, the greater the attendance, the larger are the costs of security, seating, cleaning, toilets and so forth. However, at one point the revenue from ticket sales exceeds the costs. At this point, the breakeven point, the event would be making a profit. If a fixed cost such as venue hire is increased, the extra number of people needed 'through the door' can quickly be calculated. How would the organisers attract the extra people to the event? One means might be increased promotion.

Ratio analysis

There are several ratios that can be used to identify any problems in the management of an event. These can also be used for predictive control, as in the earlier example. Their main function is as the indicator of the health of the event organisation. Dyson (2007) identifies two simple ratios as a useful starting point — known as liquidity ratios, they measure the extent to which assets can be turned into cash. The current assets ratio is calculated as:

$$\frac{\text{Current assets}}{\text{Current liabilities}}$$

It indicates the financial strength of the event company or organisation. The second liquidity ratio is known as the acid test ratio. Based on the premise that stock cannot always be turned into cash in the short term or that it may be unwise to do so, this removes stocks out of the equation. The acid test ratio is calculated as:

$$\frac{\text{Current assets} - \text{Stocks}}{\text{Current liabilities}}$$

However, calculation of assets can be difficult, since events by their nature have few current assets except those intangible qualities: goodwill and experience. In a similar way to a film production company, an event company may be formed to create and manage a one-off festival where every asset is hired for the duration of the event.

Return on capital employed (ROCE), sometimes referred to as return on investment (ROI), is a significant ratio for any sponsors or investors in an event, as it assesses the profitability of an event. This is expressed as:

$$\frac{\text{Net profit}}{\text{Capital}} \times 100 = \text{X\%}$$

The net profit for a sponsor may be expressed in advertising pounds. For example, media exposure can be measured by column centimetres for newspapers, or time on air for television/radio, and approximated to the equivalent cost in advertising. This ratio is most often used for events that are staged solely for financial gain. An entrepreneur of a major concert performance must demonstrate a favourable ROCE to potential investors to secure financial backing.

Other ratios can provide valuable data. As Brody and Goodman (1988) explain in their text on fundraising events, the ratio between net and gross profit is important in deciding the efficiency of the event for fundraising and in comparing one event to another. This ratio is called the percentage of profit or the profit margin. Another example of an effective ratio is that of free publicity to paid advertising, particularly for concert promoters.

By performing a series of appropriate ratio analyses, an event management company can obtain a clear picture of the viability of the organisation and identify areas requiring more stringent control.

Perceived value/cost pax

A ratio that is common to event financial management is the perceived value compared to the cost per head (pax). It is employed in corporate special events, festivals and conferences. The perceived value is an estimate of the value the attendees regard as gained from attending the event. It is what they would expect to pay for the event, if they had to purchase a ticket. The 'cost per head' is the total cost of the event divided by the number of attendees. A jazz festival, for example, may attract 5,000 attendees. The total cost of the festival is estimated as £100,000. The cost per head is therefore £20. The question then becomes: does a member of the audience get £20 worth of value from the event? This ratio is particularly important at high-level corporate events. If the ratio is greater than one, the event management may consider if they are giving too much value for the cost. If it is less than one, the event management may be in trouble!

Cash flow

The special nature of events, exhibitions, conferences, and festivals, requires close attention to the flow of cash. Catherwood and Van Kirk (1992), Getz (2005) Goldblatt (2008) and O'Toole and Mikolaitas (2002), all emphasise the importance of the control of cash to an event, which Goldblatt (2008) goes on to stress, is imperative for the goodwill of suppliers. Without prompt payment the event company faces immediate difficulties. Payment terms and conditions have to be fully and equitably negotiated. These payment terms can ruin an event if they are not given careful consideration beforehand. To obtain the best terms from a supplier, Goldblatt, (2008) suggests the following:

- Learn as much as possible about the suppliers and subcontractors and the nature of their businesses. Do they own the equipment? What are the normal payment terms in their business? Artists, for instance, expect to be paid immediately, whereas some information technology suppliers will wait for thirty days.
- Be flexible with what can be offered in exchange − including sponsorship. Try to negotiate a contract that stipulates a small deposit before the event and full payment after it is over
- Suggest a line of credit, with payment at a set time in the future
- Closely control the purchasing
- Ensure that all purchases are made through a purchase order that is authorised by the event manager or the appropriate finance personnel. A purchase order is a written record of the agreement to supply a product at a prearranged price. All suppliers, contractors and event staff should be informed that no purchase can be made without an authorised form. This ensures that spending is confined to what is permitted by the budget.
- Obtain a full description of the product or service and the quantities required. Itemise the price to a per unit cost
- Calculate any taxes or extra charges
- Determine payment terms
- Clarify delivery details
- Consider imposing penalties if the product or service delivered is not as described

As Figure 9.9 shows, the ability of an event co-ordinator to affect any change diminishes rapidly as the event draws closer. The supply of goods and services may, of necessity, take place close to or on the actual date of the event. This does not allow organisers the luxury of reminding a supplier of the terms set out in the purchase order. Without a full written description of the goods, the event manager is open to all kinds of exploitation by suppliers and, as the day of the event comes up, there may be no choice but to accept delivery.

FIGURE 9.9 Control, cost and time

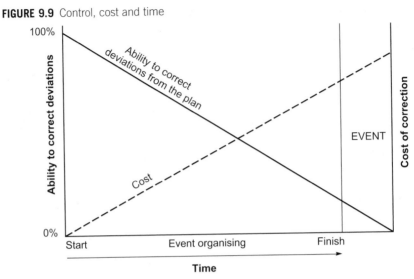

(Source: adapted from Burke, 2003)

When considering cash flow, the advantage of the ticketing strategies of events such as the Glastonbury Festival is obvious. As tickets are sold months before the event, the management is able to concentrate on other areas of planning. Event companies that specialise in the corporate area obtain a similar advantage. Generally they are paid upfront. This allows the event manager or producer the freedom to negotiate terms and conditions with the suppliers without having to worry about the cash flow. A cash flow timing chart similar to the Gantt chart is often helpful in planning events. This shows the names of the suppliers and their payment requirements. It includes deposit dates, payment stages, payment on purchase, monthly fixed cost payments and thirty-, sixty- or ninety-day credit payments.

COSTING AND ESTIMATING

The cash flow at an event is heavily dependent on the cost of goods and services. These are estimated for the construction of the budget. The prediction, categorisation and allocation of costs is called the costing. In relation to the break-even chart (see Figure 9.8), two types of costs have been identified. These are described in the following text.

Fixed costs or overheads are costs associated with the event that occur no matter how many people come to the event. They include the unchanging expenses concerned with the operation of the event management company, for example, rent, staff salaries, telephone and other office expenses. At a large festival these expenses may include rates and interest on loans. When deciding on a budget, these costs need to be apportioned reasonably to the various event areas. This process is called absorption of the overheads by the cost centres. Cost centres, for example, include entertainment, catering, staging or travel. If the fixed costs are incorrectly absorbed, the cost centre will be wrongly described. For a correct financial picture of the future event, the overheads have to be reasonably spread to all areas. The aim of an event company is to reduce the fixed costs without affecting the quality of the event.

Variable costs are expenses that purely concern the event and are directly related to the number of people who attend the event. Food and beverage costs are related directly to the number of people attending an event. When more people attend an event, more tickets need to be printed, possibly more staff may need to be hired and certainly, more food has to be provided

This division of costs is not as clear-cut in the event industry as in other industries. It is sometimes clearer, instead, to talk in terms of *direct costs* (the costs directly associated with the event, whether variable or fixed) and *overheads* (costs associated with the running of the event company). In this case, the direct costs are the major costs − and the aim of the event company is to control these costs. Figure 9.6 lists the detailed budgeted costs of a one-off event.

Catherwood and Van Kirk (1992) divide the costs of an event into four main categories:

1. operational or production costs, including hiring of event staff, construction, insurance and administration
2. venue/site rental
3. promotion − advertising, public relations, sales promotion
4. talent − costs associated with the entertainment.

To obtain the correct cost of each of the elements contained in the budget categories (sometimes called cost centres) there is a common costing process involved. According to O'Toole and Mikolaitis (2002), the tools of project management can be used to estimate event costs. These include:

1. *top-down estimating:* the event management arrives at a figure based on their experience and a comparison to events of a similar type and size. It can also be called a conceptual estimate or 'ballpark figure'. It is used in the early development stage of the event to give management an idea of what costs are involved. Generally, this would have an accuracy of plus or minus 25%.
2. *bottom-up estimating*: the event is divided into its components and the costs are estimated for each component. If the event company employs a project management approach, this is easily accomplished using the work breakdown structure as a guide. During the feasibility study only the major costs may be identified and estimated. The cost of headline speakers, for example, varies according to their popularity and type of career. Asking other event managers what was paid for the speaker, gives the event producer a basis for negotiating a fair price and for a more realistic budget estimation. A more accurate estimate is obtained by getting quotes from the suppliers. The larger festivals will put out

to tender many of the elements of the event including sound, lights and security. A near correct estimate can be made on this basis. For small events, the quote may be obtained by ringing a selection of suppliers and comparing the costs. However, it is rarely the case that the costs are comparable, as there are so many unusual features or special conditions. Once an event company has built up a relationship with a supplier, it tends to stay with that supplier.

3. *parametric estimating*: parametric estimating is where 'the overall cost of the event is assumed to be related to one element, a parameter of the event' (O'Toole and Mikolaitas, 2002, p. 226). The cost of a single person at an event is one such parameter. If the cost of one person is multiplied by the number of people, the cost of the whole event can be estimated. Parametric estimating is common in conferences and exhibitions. The latter uses 'floor space' or 'cost per square metre' as the parameter. Note that this is related to the perceived value ratio explained earlier in this chapter.

Costing time

It would not be a complete chapter on finance without a mention of how the event company costs its time. A private event company will generally charge at least 20% of the total amount to organise the event. It can be a percentage of the overall event budget, a fixed fee as a lump sum or a per hour rate, an incentive fee or a mixture of the three. If the event income is dependent on ticket sales or registrations and the event company owns the event, its fee will be the profit that is left after all expenses are paid. An event unit within a government or a major company may have to demonstrate it has produced a surplus. Most of these event units are a cost to the organisation and the event unit will be expected to 'cost its time'.

The most common problem in an event is the cost blow-out. Special event planners often encounter unforeseen circumstances that can cost dearly. The subcontractor who supplies the sound system, for example, can go bankrupt; the replacement subcontractor may prove far more expensive. One of the unwritten laws of project management is that the closer the project is to completion, the more expensive any changes become. Appropriate remedial action may be to use cheaper catering services or to find extra funding. This could take the form of a raffle to cover the extra costs. Figure 9.9 (page 310) graphically shows how the cost of any changes to the organisation of an event, escalate as the event date nears.

Sensitivity analysis

The degree of influence that the changes in the costs have on the event and its management, is called sensitivity. It is almost certain that there will be changes over the time the event is organised. The change could be external, such as political or economic; or internal, such as staff or the event program. The wise event company is aware of the effect of any changes. The examples of the Athens Olympics and the Sydney Olympics outlined earlier in this chapter, provided two instances. Some costs will remain constant and others will vary. Some real examples of unpredictably changing costs are airline ticket prices, exchange rates, sponsor withdrawal and extraneous artists' expenses. There will be other changes that can be a result of the event being developed and responsive to opportunities. The marketing team, for example, may find better promotional channels causing an increase of interest in the event, which flows on to an increase in demand for the press release and complimentary tickets to the event.

The contingency amount is the expected change in the budget estimation. It reflects the uncertainty in event finance. This will be different according to how the budget is estimated, the expertise of the estimator and the type of event. However the contingency can also be given by the client. Some event companies add a 10–15% contingency in their budgets.

Tips on reducing costs

With careful and imaginative planning, costs can be reduced in a number of areas:

- *Publicity*: an innovative event may need a large publicity budget that is based on revenue from ticket sales. The event manager's aim should be to reduce this wherever possible. Established festivals may need very little publicity as 'word of mouth' will do all the necessary work. For example, Bradford Festival 2000, with a budget of £684 511, spent relatively little on publicity (8% of total expenditure) because it had built up such a reputation with its target audience and had developed an extensive collection of media partners for the event (Bradford Festival, 2000). The more innovative the event, then the greater is the possibility for free publicity. The 1999 Rugby World Cup, for example, gained an enormous amount of free publicity due to the efforts of one of the main sponsors, Guinness.
- *Equipment and suppliers*: suppliers of products to events have down times during the year when their products may be hired cheaply. In particular, theatrical productions at the end of their run are a ready source of decoration and scenery. Annual events like the summer festivals may have equipment in storage that can be hired.
- *In-kind gifts*: many organisations will assist events to achieve cross-promotional advantages. Entertainment can be inexpensive if there is a chance that they can promote a performance or product at the event. For example, a supplier may agree to supply their beer free to the party for the media and guests prior to the event, in exchange for the rights to sell it at the concert.
- *Hiring charges*: hire charges of large infrastructure components, such as tents and generators and headline acts, can be reduced by offering work at other festivals and events. The large cultural festivals around the UK, including the Edinburgh International Festival and the Harrogate International Festival, can offer a festival circuit to any overseas performer. Costs can therefore be amortised over all the festivals.
- *Prioritise cost centres*: at some time it will be necessary to cut costs. This must be planned by knowing beforehand the effect on the overall event if one area or part of it is significantly changed or eliminated. In project management this is called

sensitivity analysis (Burke, 2003). Estimates are made of the influence of cost changes on the event and the cost centres are placed in a priority list according to the significance of the effect. For example, a sensitivity analysis could be applied to the effect of imposing a charge on a programme that was previously available free. While this could significantly increase revenue, it may produce a negative effect in sponsorship and audience satisfaction, which may well be translated into the reduction of revenue.

- *Volunteers*: costs can be reduced by using volunteers instead of paid staff. It is important that all of the skills of the volunteers are fully utilised. These skills should be continually under review as new skills may be required as the event planning progresses. For charitable functions, volunteers will often absorb many of the costs as tax deductible donations.

Revenue

Anticipating potential sources of revenue should be given as much attention as projecting expenses. The source of the revenue will often define the type of event, the event objectives and the planning. A company product launch has only one source of revenue — the client. Company staff parties, for example, are paid for by the client with no other source of revenue. The budget then has only one entry on the left-hand side. A major festival, on the other hand, has to find and service a variety of revenue sources, such as sponsors and participants. This constitutes a major part of festival planning.

Revenue can come from the following sources:

- ticket sales — most common in entrepreneurial events
- sponsorship — common in cultural and sports events
- merchandising
- advertising
- in-kind broadcast rights — an increasingly important source of revenue in sport events
- grants — local government, national government, Arts Councils, UK Sport
- fundraising — common in community events
- the client — the major source for corporate events

Figure 9.7 features an expanded list of revenue sources. For many events, admission fees and ticket prices need careful consideration. The revenue they generate will impact on the cash flow and the break-even point. One or more of three methods can decide the ticket price:

1. *Covering costs*: all the costs are estimated and added to the projected profit. To give the ticket price, this figure is then divided by the expected number of people that will attend the event. The method is quick, simple and based on knowing the break-even point. It gives a 'rule of thumb' figure that can be used as a starting point for further investigations in setting the price.

2. *Market demand*: the ticket price is decided by the prevailing ticket prices for similar or competing events. In other words, it is the 'going rate' for an event. Concert ticket prices are decided in this way. In deciding on the ticket price, consider elasticity of demand. For instance, if the ticket price is increased slightly will this affect the number of tickets sold?

3. *Perceived value*: the event may have special features that do not allow a price comparison to other events. For instance, for an innovative event the ticket price must be carefully considered. By its nature, this kind of event has no comparison. There can be variations in the ticket price for different entertainment packages at the event (at many multi-venue events the ticket will include admission only to certain events), for extra hospitality or for special seating. Knowing how to grade the tickets is an important skill in maximising revenue. There are market segments that will not tolerate differences in pricing, whereas others expect it. It can be a culturally based decision and may be part of the design of the event. As Gaur and Saggere succinctly write, 'will the event be able to make them (the customers) happy at (the) end?' (2004, p. 108).

Tips for increasing projected income

Income can be increased using a number of methods, a number of which are discussed below.

Ticket scaling

There are many ticketing strategies that strive to obtain the best value from ticket sales. The most common strategy is to vary the pricing, according to seat position, number of tickets sold and time of sale. Early-bird discounts and subscriptions series are two examples of the latter. Another strategy involves creating a special category of attendees. This could include patrons, special clubs, 'friends of the event', people for whom the theme of the event has a special meaning or those who have attended many similar events in the past. For example, for a higher ticket price, patrons are offered extra hospitality, such as a separate viewing area, valet parking and a cocktail party.

In-kind support and bartering

One way to increase income is to scrutinise the event cost centres for areas that could be covered by an exchange with the supplier or bartering. For example, the advertising can be expanded for an event with a programme of 'give-aways'. These are free tickets to the event, given away through the press. Due to the amount of goodwill surrounding a fundraising event, bartering should be explored as a method of obtaining supplies. Bartering may have tax implications. It should not be undertaken without close scrutiny of this risk.

Merchandising

The staging of an event offers many opportunities for merchandising. The first consideration is, 'Does the sale of goods enhance the theme of the event?' The problems of cash flow at an event, as stated earlier in this chapter, can give the sale of goods an unrealistically high priority in event management. It is easy to cheapen a 'boutique' special event with the sale of 'trinkets'. However, the attendees may want to buy a souvenir. For example, a large choir performing at a one-off spectacular event may welcome the opportunity to sell a video, CD or DVD of their performance at the event. This could be arranged with the choir beforehand and result in a guaranteed income. As a spin-off, the video CD or DVD could be incorporated into promotional material for use by the event management in bidding for future events.

Broadcast rights

An increasingly important source of revenue, particularly in sports events, is the payment for the right to broadcast. A live television broadcast of an event is a lucrative area for potential income — but it comes at a price. The broadcast, rather than the needs and expectations of the live audience, becomes master of the event. Often the live audience becomes merely one element in the television entertainment. As a result, the audience may include 'fillers' — people who fill any empty seats so that the camera will always show a capacity audience.

If the entire event is recorded by high-quality video equipment, future broadcast rights should also be investigated. For example, in many countries there is a constant demand for worthwhile content for pay television (cable or satellite). At the time of writing, Internet broadcast is still in its infancy. There have been a number of music and image broadcasts over the Internet but they have been limited by the size of the bandwidth. There can be no doubt that this will become an important medium for the event industry. Pod casting is an interesting alternative to web casting. Pod casting involves recording aspects of the event and uploading these to the event website. These can be downloaded at anytime and viewed or listened to on the computer or a portable digital device. Pod casts of literary discussions and debates at festivals have been used to generate interest in the next event.

Sponsorship leverage and activation

Leverage is the current term for using the event sponsorship to gain further support from other sponsors. Very few companies or organisations want to be the first to sponsor a one-off event. However, once the event has one sponsor's support, sufficient credibility is gained to enable an approach to other sponsors. For example, gaining the support of a major newspaper or radio station allows the event manager to approach other sponsors. The sponsors realise that they can obtain free publicity. Activation refers to adding to the sponsor's benefits through extra services and innovative ideas. Innovation can create a deeper involvement by the sponsor in the event.

Special features

When an event is linked to a large population base, there are many opportunities for generating income. Raffles, for example, are frequently used to raise income. At a concert-dance in Bath, all patrons brought along a prize for a raffle drawn on the night. Each received a ticket in the raffle, as part of the entry fee to the event. The prizes ranged from old ties to overseas air tickets. The raffle took two hours to get through, but every person received a prize and it became part of the entertainment of the evening.

Holding an auction at an event is also an entertaining way to increase event income. For example, the Childline Next St Clements Ball (held in October 2000), included auction items such as a trip on a Sunseeker powerboat, a football signed by the England team and a pair of British Airways Club Class return tickets. The sale of the football shirts after a major match, complete with the mud stains, has been a lucrative way of raising revenue.

FINANCIAL REPORTING

The importance of general reporting on the progress of the event planning has been described in this chapter. The budget report is the means to highlight problems and suggest solutions. It is an efficient way to communicate this to the event committee and staff and should be readily understood. It is important that appropriate action is taken in response to the report's suggestions. Figure 9.10 is a list of guidelines for a straightforward report.

For many events, financial reports may need to be sent to interested parties. The client may need ongoing financial reports. The budget can be revisited with a new column called 'Actuals'. This lists the actual amount spent. At the end of the event, a profit and loss statement may need to be prepared and sent to the host organisation. All these activities must be placed on the management timeline. If the event management opens a special bank account for the event, the reporting can be simplified as the bank will have a statement of the account.

A tool used in project management and one that is common in the event industry is the commitment account. One of the problems met by events is that they are unlike most other continuous businesses. They have a short timeframe. Therefore the most common accounting methods can miss the financial action.

FIGURE 9.10 Reporting guidelines

- The report should relate directly to the event management area to which it is addressed.
- It should not contain extraneous information that can only obscure its function. Brevity and clarity are key objectives.
- The figures in the report must be of the same magnitude and they should be comparable.
- The report should describe how to take remedial action if there is a significant problem.

An example will illustrate this statement. Consider an event with a budget of £50,000; the event manager contacts a sound company and agrees over the phone to a fee of £12,000. This means that there is £38,000 left to spend. It is obvious. However, according to accounting rules, there is nothing to record. There have been no goods or services delivered. Therefore event and project managers often have a commitment account where they note these 'transactions' or commitments. The short timeframe for many events means that many of these decisions are made 'on the run' and based on trust. Having a record of commitments is a safe way to ensure that the trust between the event management and its suppliers is maintained.

SUMMARY

There is little point in expending effort in creating a plan for an event if there is no way to closely monitor it. The event plan is a prerequisite for success. The control mechanisms to keep the project aligned to the plan, need to be well thought out and easily understood by the management team. When the event strays from the plan there need to be ways to bring it back into line or to change the plan.

An estimate of the costs and revenues of an event is called the budget and it acts as the master control of an event. With a well-reasoned budget in place, all sections of an event know their spending limits and can work together. The cash flow of an event needs special consideration. When is the cash coming in? Moreover, when does it need to go out? An event that does not have control mechanisms, including a well-thought-out budget, is not going to satisfy its stakeholders. Not only will it fail but also the organisations involved will never know the reason for its failure. A sound budget gives management a solid foundation on which to build a successful event.

QUESTIONS

1. The budget is often perceived as the most important part of event management. What are the limitations of running an event by the budget? Do many events such as the arts festivals always come in under budget? What can lead to drastic changes in the budget?

2. The benefits of events are many and varied. What are the financial benefits to each of the event stakeholders?

3. Identify the cost centres and revenue sources for:

    a. a celebrity poetry reading for a charity

    b. a rural car auction with antique cars

    c.   a corporate Christmas party

    d.   a hot-air balloon festival

4.   Why is cash flow of such importance to event management? Can an event be run on credit?

CASE STUDY: EDINBURGH INTERNATIONAL FESTIVAL

Introduction. The Edinburgh International Festival as was founded in 1947 in the aftermath of a devastating World War. The founders believed that the Festival should enliven and enrich the cultural life of Europe, Britain and Scotland and provide a platform for the flowering of the human spirit. The programmes were intended to be of the highest possible standard, presented by the best artists in the world. The achievement of many of those aims over the years, has ensured that the Edinburgh International Festival is now one of the most important cultural celebrations in the world.

    Both the political world and the world of the arts are now very different from the immediate post-war years and the Festival has developed significantly in the interim. However, the founders' original intentions are closely reflected in the current mission and objectives of the Festival. The mission is 'to be the most exciting, innovative and accessible Festival of the performing arts in the world, and thus promote the cultural, educational and economic well-being of the people of Edinburgh and Scotland' through:

- Presenting arts of the highest possible international standard to the widest possible audience
- Reflecting international culture to audiences from Scotland, the rest of the UK and the world
- Offering an international showcase for Scottish culture
- Presenting events which cannot easily be achieved by any other UK arts organisation through innovative programming and a commitment to new work
- Actively ensuring equal opportunities for all sections of the Scottish and the wider public to experience and enjoy the Festival
- Encouraging public participation in the arts throughout the year by collaborating with other arts and festival organisations
- Ensuring that the Festival has adequate core funding to fulfil its mission and address its sustainability

    The Festival brings to Edinburgh some of the best in international theatre, music, dance and opera and presents the arts in Scotland to the world. Around the International Festival, a number of other festivals have grown – the largest of which is the Fringe. There is also the Military Tattoo, a Jazz & Blues Festival, a Film Festival, Mela, a Science Festival, a Children's Festival and a Book Festival. All of these are administered separately from the International Festival. A survey in 2004/5 showed that the summer festivals generate £135 million for the economy of Edinburgh and sustain nearly 2,900 jobs across Scotland.

    A team of 30 permanent staff work year round to make the Festival possible. In the run up to and during the three weeks of the Festival itself, this core team is joined by a significant number of additional paid staff who work as drivers, technicians and in the ticketing and press offices.

Festival Finances. All artists and companies in the annual three-week event appear at the invitation of the Festival Director. The Festival's budget covers all of the costs associated with delivering the programme including artists' fees, travel, venue hire and promotion of the event. In return, the Festival retains all income from ticket sales. The Festival is responsible for funding all its activities. As a not-for-profit organisation and a registered charity, its budget is a carefully balanced mix of income raised from ticket sales, fundraising and sponsorship, along with public sector grants.

Continued

CASE STUDY: EDINBURGH INTERNATIONAL FESTIVAL—*CONT'D*

- The total income of the 2009 Festival was approximately £9.6 million. Forty seven percent of the Festival's total income was generated through earned income, including ticket sales, sponsorship and donations, with 53% coming from public sector grants.
- Ticket sales: The Festival raised £2.25 million of income through the sale of tickets through the box office, representing 23% of total income. 2009 saw a substantial increase (7.4%) in the number of students and young people, and an increase from 2008 of 9.4% in the number of people taking advantage of the discount scheme for disabled people. Interestingly, 45% of tickets are now purchased through the website.
- Sponsorship and donations: The Festival is Scotland's most successful arts organisation at generating income from this area. The total of £2.03 million raised in 2009 represents 21% of the Festival's total income and continues to be a strength. Income from trusts, foundations and individual donors is playing an increasingly important role, with income from the corporate sector declining in recent years..
- Public sector grants: In 2009, revenue grants from The City of Edinburgh Council and the Scottish Arts Council and project grants from the Scottish Government's Festivals Expo Fund and Homecoming 09, amounted to £5.1 million, representing 53% of total income.

The development of The Hub, the home for the Edinburgh International Festival, means that there is potential for growth. However, given that The Hub is not a purely commercial resource but has an educational and artistic remit, it is expected to cover running costs from commercial income, thus enabling a year round programme of education activities. The total income and expenditure are summarised in Figure 9.11.

Revenue grants from the local authority and from central government have been at the core of the Festival's finances since 1947. This public subsidy helps define the style and tone of the Festival presented, enabling a subsidised ticket pricing policy that ensures access to the widest possible audience.

Seventy five percent of the Festival's expenditure was allocated directly to meeting the costs of presenting performances: artists' fees and travel, hiring the venues and paying the technical costs involved with staging events. The remaining 25% of the budget was spent on marketing, selling the tickets, fundraising and administration.

In summary, as a result of stabilising public sector grants and increasing earned income by 4% since 2008, the Edinburgh International Festival has managed to maintain income levels in an increasingly challenging economic environment. Expenditure is tightly controlled and savings are being made where possible. The Festival continues to offer an extensive programme of events that are proving increasingly attractive to young people and students and the overseas market. All of the various stakeholders in the Festival face hard choices about how much money they are prepared to invest in its future and what kind of Festival they want. It is only through maintaining funding levels, that the Edinburgh International Festival will continue to maintain and develop its role in Scotland's cultural future.

For further information about Edinburgh International Festival, please visit www.eif.co.uk.

By Edinburgh International Festival, The Hub, Castlehill, Royal Mile, Edinburgh, EH1 2NE Tel: 0131 473 2001.

Questions

1. Edinburgh International Festival is one of the largest internationally known festivals in Britain. What factors do you think have led to its growth and success?
2. Edinburgh International Festival is reliant on public funding for over 50% of its funds. From what you have been told in the case study and your wider reading, what challenges may exist for maintaining this level of public funding?

FIGURE 9.11 Edinburgh international festival company statement of financial activities

	Unrestricted general funds	Restricted funds	Total funds year ended 31 October 2009	Total funds year ended 31 October 2008
	£000s	£000s	£000s	£000s
Incoming resources				
Incoming resources from generated funds				
▸ grant income	5,118	-	5,118	4,713
▸ sponsorship and donations	2,030	-	2,030	1,782
▸ activities for generating funds				
▸ investment income	10	-	10	94
Incoming resources from charitable activities				
▸ ticket sales	2,255	-	2,255	2,246
▸ publications and other earned income	204	-	204	219
Total incoming resources	**9,617**	**-**	**9,617**	**9,054**
Resources expended				
Costs of generating funds				
▸ fundraising	(353)	-	(353)	(320)
▸ support costs	(218)	(7)	(225)	(234)
Charitable expenditure				
▸ productions and performances	(7,084)	-	(7,084)	(5,857)
▸ marketing & public affairs	(1,157)	-	(1,157)	(1,128)
▸ support costs	(651)	(23)	(674)	(702)
Governance costs	(36)	-	(36)	(37)
Total outgoing resources	**(9,499)**	**(30)**	**(9,529)**	**(8,278)**
Net incoming/(outgoing) resources	118	(30)	88	776
Defined benefit scheme actuarial losses	(760)	-	(760)	(74)
Net movement in funds	(642)	(30)	(672)	702
Total funds brought forward at 1 Nov 2008	612	152	764	62
Total funds carried forward at 31 Oct 2009	(30)	122	92	764

(Source: Edinburgh International Festival Society (2010), p. 27)

Continued

CASE STUDY: EDINBURGH INTERNATIONAL FESTIVAL—*CONT'D*

3. In the long-term, various options exist for the organisers, including a shift in income streams to other areas, such as corporate sponsorship, or a reduction in the size of the event.

   a. Evaluate the stated alternatives in the light of what is known from the case study. What other options could be considered?

   b. How would a shift in income stream change the style of the festival and programming?

   c. What effect would this change have on the image portrayed by the festival?

Human resource management and events

10

LEARNING OBJECTIVES

After studying this chapter, you should be able to:

- describe the human resource management challenges posed by events
- list and describe the key steps in the human resource planning process for events
- discuss approaches that can be employed to motivate event staff and volunteers
- describe techniques that can be used for event staff and volunteer team-building
- state general legal considerations associated with human resource management in an event context

INTRODUCTION

Effective planning and management of human resources is at the core of any successful event. Ensuring that an event is adequately staffed with the right people who are appropriately trained and motivated to meet its objectives, is fundamental to the event management process. Human resources related to events have been explored by a number of authors, including Baum, Deery, Hanlon, Lockstone and Smith (eds.) (2009) and Van Der Wagen (2007), with Holmes and Smith (2009) focusing on the management of volunteers. This chapter seeks to provide an overview of the key aspects of human resource planning and management that an event manager should be familiar with. It begins by examining considerations associated with human resource management in the context of events. It then moves on to propose a model of the human resource management process for events and to discuss each of the major steps in this model. Selected theories associated with employee/volunteer motivation are then described, followed by a brief examination of techniques for staff and volunteer team building. The final part of this chapter deals with legal considerations associated with human resource management.

CONSIDERATIONS ASSOCIATED WITH HUMAN RESOURCE PLANNING FOR EVENTS

The context in which human resource planning takes place for events can be said to be unique for two major reasons. First, and perhaps most significantly, many events

Events Management. DOI: 10.1016/B978-1-85617-818-1.10010-6

FIGURE 10.1 Manchester Commonwealth Games 2002, growth in full-time workforce (cumulative)

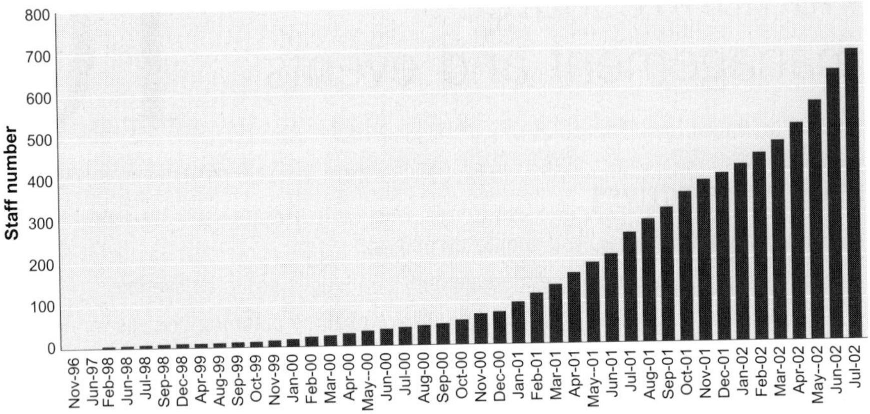

(Source: Commonwealth Games Legacy Manchester, 2002)

have a 'pulsating' organisational structure (Hanlon and Jago, 2000, 2009; Hanlon and Cuskelly, 2002; Hanlon and Jago, 2002, 2009). This means they grow in terms of personnel as the event approaches (Figure 10.1), but quickly contract when it ends.

From a human resource perspective, this creates a number of challenges including that of obtaining paid staff given the short-term nature of the employment offered; working to short timelines to hire and select staff and develop and implement staff training; and needing to shed staff quickly. Also, volunteers, as opposed to paid staff, often make up the bulk of people involved in delivering an event. In some instances, events are run entirely by volunteers. The challenges presented by this situation are many and relate to such matters as sourcing volunteers, quality control, supervision, training and motivation. Later parts of this chapter suggest responses to these challenges.

THE HUMAN RESOURCE PLANNING PROCESS FOR EVENTS

Human resource planning for events should not be viewed simply in terms of a number of isolated tasks but as a series of sequential, interrelated processes and practices that take their lead from an event's vision/mission, objectives and strategy. If an event seeks to grow in size and attendance, for example, it will need a human resource strategy to support this growth through such means as increased staff recruitment (paid and/or volunteer) and expanded (and perhaps more sophisticated) training programmes. If these supporting human resource management actions are not in place, problems such as high staff/volunteer turnover due to overwork, poor quality delivery and an associated declining marketplace image may result, jeopardising the event's future.

Events will obviously differ in terms of the level of sophistication they display in the human resources area, given factors such as their access to resources in terms of money and expertise. For example, contrast a local community festival that struggles to put together an organising committee and attract sufficient volunteers, with a mega-event such as the Olympic Games. Nonetheless, it is appropriate that the 'ideal' situation is examined here — that is, the complete series of steps through which an event manager should proceed for human resource planning. By understanding these steps and their relationships to one another, event managers will give themselves the best chance of managing human resources in a way that will achieve their event's goals and objectives. The case study ('Beijing 2008 — training to deliver the "best games ever"') in this chapter, introduces the application of various aspects of this process to an event.

While a number of general models of the human resource management process can be identified, the one chosen to serve as the basis of discussion in this chapter is based on that proposed by Getz (2005). This model (Figure 10.2) represents an attempt to display how this process works within an event context.

FIGURE 10.2 The human resource planning process for events

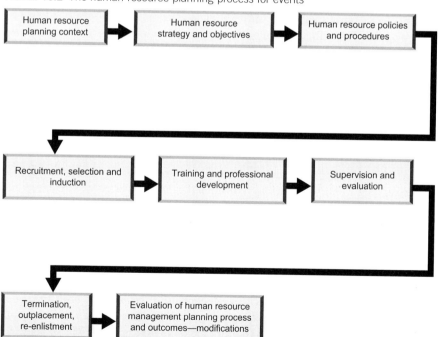

(*Source: adapted from Getz, 2005, p. 221*)

Human resource strategy and objectives

This stage in the human resource management process for events involves a variety of activities, including establishing guiding strategies and objectives, determining staffing needs (paid and volunteer) and undertaking a job analysis and producing job descriptions and specifications. Each of these tasks is discussed in turn in this section.

Strategy

An event's human resource strategy seeks to support its overall mission and objectives. This link can be demonstrated by reference to the following examples that identify a few selected areas in which an organisation might set objectives and subsequently focus on supporting human resource management objectives and activities:

- *Cost containment* — improved staff/volunteer productivity, reduced absenteeism and decreased staff numbers.
- *Improved quality* — better recruitment and selection, expanded employee and volunteer training, increased staff and volunteer numbers and improved financial rewards and volunteer benefits.
- *Improved organisational effectiveness* — better job design, changes to organisational structure and improved relations with employees and volunteers.
- *Enhanced performance regarding social and legal responsibilities* — improved compliance through training in relevant legislation, such as those relating to occupational health and safety, antidiscrimination and equal employment opportunity.

Whatever the human resource management objectives that are set for an event, they need to meet the SMART criteria discussed in Chapter 6.

Staffing

Staffing is the main strategic decision area for event managers in the area of human resources, because without staff there is nothing really to 'strategise' about! Event managers need to make decisions concerning how many staff/volunteers are needed to deliver the event, what mix of skills/qualifications/experience is required and when in the event planning process these staff/volunteers will be needed (e.g. at the event shutdown stage only). The starting point for these decisions should be an event's work breakdown structure (WBS) (see Chapter 8). As an event's WBS serves to identify the tasks associated with its creation, delivery and shutdown, an event manager can use this document as the basis for: determining the number of people needed to deliver the event; identifying the skills and knowledge needed by them and establishing the level of managerial/supervisory staff required in each task area. Additionally, once event tasks have been identified, decisions about work to be contracted out or done in-house by event staff and/or volunteers, can begin to be made. Also, by placing the tasks identified in the WBS into a Gantt chart (see Chapter 8), the event manager is able to identify when various components of the event's workforce will be needed.

Perhaps the most difficult task in the previously outlined process is that of determining exactly how many people will be needed to perform the various identified tasks, particularly if the event is new. Armstrong (2006) claims that managerial judgement is the most common approach used in business to answer this question. Such an observation is also likely to apply to the world of events. The event manager or various functional managers if the event is large enough, will estimate how many and what type of human resources are needed to meet their objectives. In doing so, they are likely to base their decisions on factors such as their own prior experience, demand forecasts for the event, the number of venues/sites involved, skill/expertise requirements of the event workforce, previous instances of similar (or the same) events, the degree of outsourcing possible, the availability of volunteers and the human resource strategies adopted by the event. It should be noted that it is not uncommon in the context of large-scale events for initial estimates of workforce size to grow as an event's delivery date draws closer. The Manchester Commonwealth Games, for example, first estimated (via a consultant's report) its core workforce requirements at 262. This number was revised upwards to 660 as the organising committee gained first-hand experience of other major sports events and their workforce requirements (Manchester 2002, 2003).

In the case of some tasks associated with the conduct of events, it is possible to estimate staffing needs by engaging in some basic arithmetic. The number of people who can pass through a turnstile per hour, for example, can be easily calculated by dividing the processing time of individual spectators in 60 minutes. Assume the figure generated in this way is 240 — that is, 240 spectators can be processed in an hour through one turnstile. Next, an estimate of event attendance (including peaks and troughs in arrivals) is required. Now assume total attendance for the event has been fairly consistent at 5000 over the past three years, with 80% (4000) of people arriving between 9.00 a.m. and 11.00 a.m. If this number of people is to be processed over a two-hour period, about eight turnstiles would need to be open (4000 attendees divided by two hours = 2000 per hour; divided by 240 transactions per hour per turnstile). Based on these calculations, eight turnstile operators would be required for the first two hours; after this time, the number of operators could be dramatically decreased. Calculations such as this could also be used in other areas of event delivery. For example, it should be possible to estimate with a fair degree of accuracy the number of staff required to prepare, plate and serve a given number of meals within a particular time period or the number required to process a given number of on-site registrations at a conference/exhibition. However, care should be taken to ensure that sufficient members of staff are available at the event, particularly when considering stewards and security staff. The Health and Safety Executive (HSE, 1999) advise that the number of stewards should be based on the risk assessment, rather than precise mathematical formulas, in order to take into account the unique circumstances of the event.

Job analysis

Job analysis, sometimes referred to as job evaluation, is an important aspect of this stage of the human resource planning process. It involves defining a job in terms of specific tasks and responsibilities and identifying the abilities, skills and qualifications needed to perform that job successfully. According to Stone (2007), questions answered by this process include:

- What tasks should be grouped together to create a job or position?
- What should be looked for in individuals applying for identified jobs?
- What should an organisational structure look like and what are the inter-relationships that should exist between jobs?
- What tasks should form the basis of performance appraisal for an individual in a specific job?
- What training and development programmes are required to ensure staff/volunteers possess the needed skills/knowledge?

The level of sophistication evident in the application of the job analysis process differs between events. Some small-scale events that depend exclusively, or almost exclusively, on volunteers may simply attempt to match people to the tasks in which they have expressed an interest. Even under such circumstances, however, some consideration probably should be given to factors such as experience, skills and physical abilities.

Job descriptions

Position, or job descriptions are another outcome of the job analysis process with which event managers need some measure of familiarity if they are to effectively match people (both employees and volunteers) to jobs. Specifically, a job description is a statement identifying why a job has come into existence, what the holder of the job will do and under what conditions the job is to be conducted (Stone, 2007). The value of this part of the planning exercise is well documented in management literature. Beardwell, Holden and Claydon (2004) contend that position descriptions are helpful to managers in recruiting and selecting staff. In addition, they may be drawn upon for inducting and training new employees, and in development, job evaluation and performance appraisal of existing employees. Mullins (2005, p. 802) states that job analysis, leading to the job description and person specification is 'Central to a planned and systematic approach' in human resource planning. He goes on to stress that although valuable, it is important not to write job descriptions in a bureaucratic manner, which would imply 'a lack of flexibility, imagination or initiative on the part of the job holder'. Mullins highlighted criticism of job descriptions by Townsend, who described them as straitjackets; and Belbin, who suggested that they were obstacles to progress in organisations, as they lead to a lack of co-operation, claims for additional payment based on additional responsibilities or inflexibility in taking on team roles. Beardwell, Holden and Claydon (2004), report that problems can arise if job descriptions are not regularly updated and this may be the detrimental to the development of the staff and organisation. In order to try to begin clarifying roles and develop career paths, MPI have developed a collection of standard job descriptions for positions at different levels in the Meetings Industry as part of their MPI Professional Pathways project.

Job descriptions commonly include the following information:

- Job title and commitment required — this information locates the paid or voluntary position within the organisation, indicates the functional area where the job is to be based (e g. marketing coordinator), and states the job duration/time commitment (e.g. one- year, part-time contract involving two days a week).
- Salary/rewards/incentives associated with position — for paid positions, a salary, wage or hourly rate needs to be stated, along with any other rewards such as bonuses. With regard to bonuses, it is not uncommon for large-scale events to make payments of this nature conditional on completion of the contract through to the end. In this way the number of staff, particularly senior staff, leaving at crucial times in the event's delivery cycle is reduced. In the case of voluntary positions, consideration should be given to identifying benefits such as free merchandise (e.g. T-shirts and limited edition souvenir programmes), free or discounted meals, free tickets and end-of-event parties, all of which can serve to increase interest in working at an event.
- Job summary — this brief statement describes the primary purpose of the job. The job summary for an event operations manager, for example, may read: 'Under the direction of the event director, prepare and implement detailed operational plans in all areas associated with the successful delivery of the event'.
- Duties and responsibilities — this information lists major tasks and responsibilities associated with the job. It should not be overly detailed and should identify only those duties/responsibilities that are central to the performance of the position. Additionally, it is useful to express these in terms of the most important outcomes of the work. For an event operations manager, for example, one key responsibility expressed in outcome terms would be the preparation of plans encompassing all operational dimensions of the event, such as site set-up and breakdown, security, parking, waste management, staging and risk management.
- Relationships with other positions within and outside the event organisation — what positions and service suppliers report to the job? (An event operations manager, for example, may have all site staff/volunteers/suppliers associated with security, parking, staging, waste management, utilities and so on reporting to him/her.) To what position(s) does the job report? (An event operations manager may report only to the event director/manager.) What outside organisations will the position need to liaise with to satisfactorily perform the job? (An event operations manager may need to liaise with, for example, local councils, police, roads and traffic authorities, and local emergency service providers.)
- Know-how/skills/knowledge/experience/qualifications/personal attributes required by the position — in some instances, particularly with basic jobs, training may

quickly overcome most deficiencies in these areas. However, for more complex jobs (voluntary or paid), such as those of a managerial or supervisory nature, individuals may need to possess experience, skills or knowledge before applying. Often, a distinction is drawn between these elements, with some attributes being essential while others are desirable. Specific qualifications may also be required. Increasingly, job advertisements for event managers, for example, are listing formal qualifications in event management as desirable. Personal attributes — such as the ability to work as part of a team, to be creative, to work to deadlines and to represent the event positively to stakeholder groups — may also be relevant considerations.

- Authority vested in the position — what decisions can be made without reference to a superior? What are the expenditure limits on decision making?
- Performance standards associated with the position — criteria by which performance in the position will be assessed are required. While such standards apply more to paid staff than to voluntary positions, they should still be considered for the latter. This is particularly the case if volunteers hold significant management or supervisory positions, where substandard performance could jeopardise one or more aspects of the event. If duties and responsibilities have been written in output terms, then these can be used as the basis of evaluation.
- Trade union/association membership required with position.
- Special circumstances associated with the position — does the job require heavy, sustained lifting, for example?
- Problem solving — what types of problems will commonly be encountered on the job and whether they would be routine and repetitive problems or complex and varied issues?

While job descriptions for paid positions often involve most, if not all, of the information noted previously, voluntary positions are often described in far more general terms. This is because they often (but not always) involve fairly basic tasks. This is evident from Figure 10.3, which illustrates a job description for the volunteer steward position at the Harrogate International Festival.

Job specification

A job specification is derived from the job description and seeks to identify the experience, formal qualifications, skills, abilities, knowledge, motivation, and personal characteristics needed to perform a given job (Crompton, Morrissey and Nankervis, 2002). As Mullins (2005) notes, care must be taken to ensure that legal requirements are considered. In essence, it identifies the types of people that should be recruited and how they should be appraised. The essential and desirable/preferred criteria shown in Figure 10.3 provide an example of how job specifications can be used in the recruitment process, with these elements also used in job advertisements to attract appropriate applicants.

FIGURE 10.3 Extract from Volunteer Event Steward job description and person specification

Volunteer Event Stewards promote and are ambassadors for the Festival; they are the first point of contact for members of the public when buying programme books, event merchandise and requesting general information. Volunteer Event Stewards are responsible to the Admin and Marketing Assistant.

The role of the Volunteer Event Steward is critical to the success of the Festival; stewards are advocates for our work, and support what we do. They are responsible for looking after, and being of service to, our most valued asset – our audience.

Responsibilities:
- Selling Festival programmes at all events pre-performance, during the interval, and post-performance
- Providing good customer service to all audience members
- Cash handling during events
- To promote the work of the Festival and support Festival staff during events
- To carry out other duties, including merchandise sales, as required by Festival staff from time to time

Person Specification:

Essential: - Committed to the aims and objectives of the Festival
- Cash handling experience
- Ability to work as part of a team
- Smart appearance
- Ability to sell effectively
- Knowledge of and enthusiasm for the arts

Preferred: - Previous customer service experience
- Previous sales training or experience
- Knowledge of health and safety procedures

Personal Characteristics:
- Reliable, punctual
- Enthusiastic
- Hard-working
- Friendly and approachable
- Flexible attitude

(Source: Harrogate International Festival, 2004)

Policies and procedures

Policies and procedures are needed to provide the framework in which the remaining tasks in the human resource planning process take place: recruitment and selection; training and professional development; supervision and evaluation; termination, outplacement, re-employment; and evaluation. According to Thompson with Martin (2005, p. 758), 'Policies are designed to guide the behaviour of managers in relation to the pursuit and achievement of strategies and objectives'. He notes that they:

- Guide thoughts and actions — for example, an event manager who declines to consider an application from a brother of an existing employee, may point to a policy on employing relatives of existing personnel if there is a dispute.
- Establish a routine and consistent approach — for example, seniority will be the determining factor in requests by volunteers to fill job vacancies.

- Establish how certain tasks should be carried out and place constraints on management decision making — for example, rather than a manager having to think about the process of terminating the employment of a staff member or volunteer, he can simply follow the process already prescribed.

Human resource practices and procedures for events are often conditioned or determined by those public or private sector organisations with ultimate authority for them. A local council responsible for conducting an annual festival, for example, would probably already have in place a range of policies and procedures regarding the use of volunteers. These policies and procedures would then be applied to the event. Additionally, a range of laws influence the degree of freedom that the management of an event has in the human resource area. Laws regarding occupational health and safety, privacy, holiday and long service leave, maternity and paternity, working hours, minimum wages, discrimination, dismissal and compensation all need to become integrated into the practices and policies that an event adopts. Figure 10.4 provides an example of the approach to employee privacy at the Melbourne 2006 Commonwealth Games - although the laws will differ internationally, for example with the Data Protection Act applying in the UK, the general approach remains.

If an event manager takes the time and effort to develop policies and procedures, he or she also needs to ensure these are communicated and applied to all staff. Additionally, resources need to be allocated to this area so the 'paperwork' generated by those policies and procedures can be stored, accessed and updated or modified, as required. Such paperwork may include various policy/procedure manuals and staff records such as performance evaluations and employment contracts.

Again, the larger (in terms of number of staff and volunteers) and more sophisticated (in terms of management) the event, the more likely it is that the event managers would have thought more deeply about policy and procedural concerns. Nonetheless, even smaller events will benefit in terms of the quality of their overall human resources management, if some attempt is made to set basic policies and procedures to guide actions.

RECRUITMENT, SELECTION AND INDUCTION

The recruitment of paid and volunteer employees is essentially about attracting the 'right' potential candidates to the 'right' job openings. Successful recruitment is based on how well previous stages in the human resource planning process have been conducted and involves determining where qualified applicants can be found and how they can be attracted to the event organisation. It is a two-way process, in that the event is looking to meet its human resource needs at the same time as potential applicants are trying to assess whether they meet the job requirements, wish to apply for the position and perceive value in joining the organisation. Figure 10.5 is a diagram representing the recruitment process.

How event managers approach the recruitment process depends on the financial resources they have available to them. It may be appropriate, depending

FIGURE 10.4 Melbourne Commonwealth Games workforce privacy policy

Introduction

Melbourne 2006 Commonwealth Games Corporation has been appointed by the Commonwealth Games Federation to organise and stage the XVIII Commonwealth Games to be held in Melbourne and surrounding areas in March 2006.

Melbourne 2006 Commonwealth Games Corporation has created this workforce privacy policy in order to demonstrate our firm commitment to protecting the personal and health information (referred to collectively in this document as personal information) of job applicants and all members of the Melbourne 2006 Commonwealth Games Corporation workforce. We are bound by the *Privacy Act 1998* (Cwlth), the *Information Privacy Act 2000 (Vic) and the Health Records Act 2001 (Vic).*

We have adopted the Information Privacy Principles and Health Privacy Principles as minimum standards in relation to handling personal information.

What we collect and how

Personal information

Melbourne 2006 Commonwealth Games Corporation collects personal information about you when you apply for a position or during your employment. The personal information which may be collected includes your name; date of birth; address; referee names; tax file number; banking details; superannuation details; qualifications; performance appraisals; details of paid outside work/directorship; referee reports; and other information collected from various sources. This information can be voluntarily provided when you apply for employment or from information contained in Melbourne 2006 Commonwealth Games Corporation employment forms. Your supervisor and nominated referees will also provide Melbourne 2006 Commonwealth Games Corporation with information about yourself. If you are on secondment from another organisation the Melbourne 2006 Commonwealth Games Corporation may gather information from your employer.

Health information

Health information may be collected as part of the employment application process or when the candidate commences employment with Melbourne 2006 Commonwealth Games Corporation.

Use of personal information

Melbourne 2006 Commonwealth Games Corporation may collect your personal information for the purpose of processing and assessing your employment application. If you are employed by Melbourne 2006 Commonwealth Games Corporation, the primary purpose for collecting personal information is to maintain your records and to administer the employment contract, salary, superannuation and other related human resource policies. Your personal information may also be used in an aggregate (non-identifying) form to report on workforce profiles.

Disclosure of personal information

Melbourne 2006 Commonwealth Games Corporation does not use or disclose personal information about an individual for a purpose other than that for which it was collected, unless such use or disclosure would be reasonably expected or consent from you has been obtained. Please note that if at any time Melbourne 2006 Commonwealth Games Corporation is required by law to release information about you or your organisation, Melbourne 2006 Commonwealth Games Corporation must fully cooperate.

Information provided by you is used primarily for the purpose of recruitment. The information is disclosed only to our staff who are on the selection panel and any recruitment agency used in the recruitment process. Melbourne 2006 Commonwealth Games Corporation may keep an electronic copy of your application to be considered for future employment. This information is confidential.

Continued

FIGURE 10.4 *Continued*

Accuracy, security and storage of personal information
Melbourne 2006 Commonwealth Games Corporation stores personal information in computer and paper based record management systems. Melbourne 2006 Commonwealth Games Corporation has designed security measures to protect against the loss, misuse and/or alteration of the information under its control. These security measures include restricted access, password protection on databases and clauses in employee agreements requiring confidentiality.

Melbourne 2006 Commonwealth Games Corporation takes reasonable steps to ensure the personal information it stores is accurate, complete and up to date. Where Melbourne 2006 Commonwealth Games Corporation shares your personal information with any third party (such as a recruitment agency), Melbourne 2006 Commonwealth Games Corporation seeks a commitment from such parties to protect the information in accordance with our policy.

Access to personal information
As is reasonable in the circumstances and subject to any limitation required by law, you may gain access to your personal information at any time. You can also contact us to update your details when necessary.

Updates to this policy
Melbourne 2006 Commonwealth Games Corporation will update the workforce privacy policy as required. Any changes will be posted on this website.

(Source: Melbourne Commonwealth Games, 2006)

FIGURE 10.5 The recruitment and selection process for paid and voluntary employees

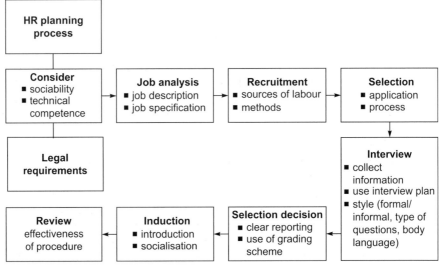

(Source: adapted from Mullins, 2005)

on the types of positions that need filling, to use recruitment agencies — for example, Anne Ellington Associates, Chess Partnership, Dragonfly, Eligo, Ellis Fairbank, ESP Recruitment, JB Event Recruitment or Regan and Dean, for full-time staff; or the local job centre or employment agencies (e.g. Adecco, Event-Staff Co. UK) to meet temporary staffing needs. With large events, a budget is likely to be set aside for this purpose, designed to cover costs such as recruitment agency fees (including online recruitment firms), advertising, the travel expenses of non-local applicants and search fees for executive placement companies. However, because of the perceived attractiveness of working on events, it may be cheaper to recruit using advertisements in appropriate newspapers or trade journals; for example, *The Guardian* (national), *Manchester Evening News* (local) or *Event* (trade). In addition, there are an increasing number of internet-based general recruitment services, for example, Stepstone (www.stepstone.co.uk), Topjobs.co.uk (www.topjobs.co.uk) and Monster.co.uk (www.monster.co.uk), or events-industry-specific sites, such as Event-Jobs.net, JobsUpdata (www.meetpie.com/jobs), or Eventjobsearch (www.eventjobsearch.co.uk — which draws together vacancies advertised in Conference & Incentive Travel, Event and AV magazines). Nevertheless, it must be recognised that the time spent by managers on this quite time-consuming process is also a cost and therefore it may be more efficient to outsource to an agency. For links to event recruitment agencies and other resources, please visit WorldofEvents.net.

The reality for most events — particularly those relying heavily on volunteers — is that they will have few resources to allocate to the recruitment process. Nonetheless, they can still successfully engage in this process by:

- Using stakeholders (e.g. local councils, community groups, sponsors and event suppliers) to communicate the event's staffing needs (volunteer and paid) to their respective networks. McCurley and Lynch (1998), in the context of volunteers, call this approach 'concentric circle recruitment' because it involves starting with the groups of people who are already connected to the event or organisation and working outwards. It is based on the premise that volunteers are recruited by someone they know — for example, friends or family, clients or colleagues, staff, employers, neighbours or acquaintances, such as members from the same clubs and societies.
- Writing sponsorship agreements in a way that requires the sponsor, as part of the agreement with the event, to provide temporary workers with particular skills, such as marketing staff.
- Identifying and liaising with potential sources of volunteers/casual staff, including universities and colleges (projects and work placements/internships may be specially created for these groups, particularly if they are studying festival, exhibition and events management or a related area such as film), religious groups, service clubs (such as Lions and Rotary), community service programmes, senior citizen centres and retirement homes, chambers of commerce and community centres. The International Festival and Events Association maintains an internship/ employment 'bank' on its website (www.ifea.com).

- Seconding staff from associated organisations, such as state and local government.
- Utilising existing programmes for the unemployed.
- Determining the make-up (e.g. age, sex, occupations) and motivations of existing volunteers and using this information as the basis of further targeted recruitment.
- Gaining the assistance of local and specialist media (e.g. radio, television, newspapers, specialist magazines) in communicating the event's human resource needs. This process is greatly assisted if one or more media organisations are in some way (such as through sponsorship) associated with the event.
- Targeting specific individuals within a community who have specialist skills to sit on boards or undertake specific tasks, such as those tasks associated with the legal and accounting aspects of conducting an event.
- Registering with a volunteer programme. In UK, these include Manchester Event Volunteer Programme (see case study at the end of this chapter), London Active Partnership, TimeBank, Community Service Volunteers and Volunteer to Win (programme for London 2012 and events before it).
- Conducting social functions at which, for example, existing volunteers or staff might be encouraged to bring potential candidates or to which particular groups/ targeted individuals are invited.

Once an appropriate pool of applicants has been identified, the next step is to select from among them, those applicants that best fit the identified available positions. It is important to approach this process systematically, employing appropriate tools, to avoid the costs (financial and otherwise) that come from poor selection (increased training time, high turnover of staff/volunteers, absenteeism, job dissatisfaction and poor performance).

A useful starting point in the selection process is a selection policy. This policy should have been developed earlier in the policy and procedures stage of the human resource planning process. In constructing such a policy, thought needs to be given to:

- outlining how the event organisation intends to comply with equal employment opportunity legislation.
- approaches to measuring the suitability of candidates — for example, simple rating scales based on set criteria.
- the sourcing of people — for example, will the event organisation promote from within where possible?
- the decision makers — that is, who will have the final decision on whom to engage?
- selection techniques — for example, will tests be employed? Will decisions be made after one interview or several?
- the organisation's business objectives — for example, do the candidates selected have the qualities and qualifications to progress the event's objectives?
- how the event organisation intends to comply with equal employment opportunity legislation.

The application process will vary based on the needs of the position, the number of applications anticipated and the resources of the event organisation. In cases where a large number of applications are anticipated, it may be appropriate to consider the preliminary screening of applicants by telephone by asking a few key questions central to the position's requirements — for example, 'Do you have a qualification in event management'? Those individuals who answer these questions appropriately can then be sent an application form. In the case of volunteers, applicants for positions in small-scale events may be asked to simply send in a brief note indicating what skills/qualifications they have, any relevant experience and the tasks they would be interested in doing. For larger events, volunteers may be asked to complete an application or registration form, (increasingly online), such as that developed by for the Harrogate International Festival (Figure 10.6).

However basic, application forms for paid employees generally seek information on educational qualifications, previous employment and other details deemed relevant to the position by the applicant. The names and contact details of referees who can supply written and/or verbal references are also normally required. Additionally, a curriculum vitae (CV) is generally appended to these forms. Once received, applications allow unsuitable applicants to be culled; those applicants thought to be suitable for short-listing can be invited to attend an interview. It is often the case with volunteers that selection is based only on the information supplied on their application/registration form, with successful applicants being contacted and asked to attend a briefing session.

When selecting among applicants, Robertson and Makin (1986) (cited in Beardwell and Holden, 2001) suggest taking into account the following factors:

- **Past behaviour**: Past behaviour records can be employed to predict future behaviour. That is, the manner in which a person completed a task in the past is the best predictor of the way that person will complete a task in the future. Biographical data (obtained from the curriculum vitae or application form), references and supervisor/peer group ratings are commonly the major sources of such information.
- **Present behaviour**: A range of techniques can be used to assess present behaviour, including: — tests, which may be designed to measure aptitude, intelligence, personality and basic core skill levels (e.g. typing speed).
    - interviews,(see later discussion).
    - assessment centres, which conduct a series of tests, exercises and feedback sessions over a one- to five-day period to assess individual strengths and weaknesses.
    - portfolios/examples of work, which are used to indicate the quality/type of recent job-related outputs. An applicant for the position of a set designer for a theatrical event, for example, may be asked to supply photographs of previous work.
- **Future behaviour**: If appropriate, interview information can be supplemented with observations from simulations to predict future behaviour. If the position is for a sponsorship manager, for example, applicants can be asked to develop sponsorship proposals and demonstrate how they would present these proposals

FIGURE 10.6 Volunteer application form

HARROGATE INTERNATIONAL FESTIVAL

VOLUNTEER APPLICATION

Title .... **Full name** ....

Address ....

....

Telephone number (daytime) .... **Telephone number** (evening) ....

The Festival is staffed by a full time team of four and one part time member of staff. However, as a registered charity (no. 244861) we rely on the help of volunteers to assist with various areas of work at different times of the year. Please indicate below which areas of work you would be able to assist with, and an outline of your availability.

I would be happy to help with the following (please tick all that apply):
- ☐ Distribution of Festival print material in Harrogate
- ☐ Distribution of Festival print material in Knaresborough
- ☐ Distribution of Festival print material in Ripon
- ☐ Distribution of Festival print material elsewhere (please specify) ....
- ☐ Stewarding at Harrogate International Festival events (21 July - 5 August 2005)
  Stewarding at Harrogate International Sunday Series events (dates tbc -
- ☐ February - April 2005)
- ☐ Assisting with sticking and stuffing envelopes for Festival mailings
- ☐ Other (please specify) ....

I am available to help at the following times (please tick all that apply):
- ☐ Evenings
- ☐ Day time
- ☐ Weekends
- ☐ Weekdays
- ☐ Other (please specify) ....

Are you available for the period of this year's Festival, 21 July - 5 August 2005?
- ☐ Yes - throughout
- ☐ Partially (please specify) ....
- ☐ No - not at all

Do you have any cash handling experience?
- ☐ Yes: if so, please give details: ....
- ☐ No

Do you have any basic First Aid knowledge?
- ☐ Yes: if so, please give details:.......................................
- ☐ No

Where did you hear about volunteering opportunities at the Festival?
....

Please give details of two referees:

Name	Name ....
Address	Address ....
....	....
....	....
Phone number	Phone number ....
Relationship to you	Relationship to you ....

Thank you for your time. Please return this to us at the following address:

Harrogate International Festival, 1 Victoria Avenue, Harrogate HG1 1EQ
If you have any queries, please telephone 01423 562303

(Source: Harrogate International Festival, 2004a)

to potential sponsors. Another common approach, according to Noe et al. (2003), is to ask, in the context of managerial appointments, for applicants to respond to memos that typify problems that they are likely to encounter.

Interviews are likely to be the most common means of selection used by event organisations, so it is worthwhile spending some time looking at how best to employ this approach.

Interviews

According to Noe et al. (2002), research clearly indicates that the interviewing process should be undertaken using a structured approach, so that all relevant information can be covered and candidates can be directly compared. Mullins (2005), suggests using a checklist of key matters to be covered in the interviews. A sample checklist for a paid position associated with an event is shown in Figure 10.7. Checklists should also be used if interviews are to be conducted for volunteers. In such instances, answers might be sought to questions regarding the relationship between the volunteer's background/experience and the position sought, the reasons for seeking to become involved with the event and the level of understanding about

FIGURE 10.7 Sample interviewer's checklist

INTERVIEWER'S CHECKLIST

Position title: _____ Candidate's name: _____

Date: _____

Interviewees: _____

Interview
1. Qualifications held
2. Employment history
3. Extent to which applicant meets essential criteria for the position
4. Extent to which applicant meets desirable criteria for the position
5. Organisational fit
   (a) To what extent will the position result in personal satisfaction for the applicant?
   (b) To what extent does the applicant identify with the organisation's values and culture?
   (c) Can the applicant's remuneration expectations be met?

Assessment
Summary rating of applicant based on the above criteria. A simple scale of 'all, most, some, none' may be used for criteria 3 and 4. Additionally, some relevant summary comments may be made on each applicant.

Action
Follow-up action to be taken with applicant — for example:
- Advise if successful/unsuccessful.
- Place on eligibility list.
- Check references.
- Arrange pre-employment medical check.

the demands/requirements of the position (such as time and training); another area for consideration is whether an applicant has a physical or medical condition that may have an impact on the type of position applied for (keeping equal employment opportunity legislation in mind).

Applicant responses flowing from the interview process need to be assessed in some way against the key criteria for the position. One common means of doing this is a rating scale (e.g. on a scale of 1 − 5). When viewed collectively, the ratings given to individual items lead to an overall assessment of how the applicant fits with the job, the event organisation and its future directions.

Interviews may be conducted on a one-on-one basis or via a panel of two or more interviewers. The latter has some advantages in that it assists in overcoming any idiosyncratic biases that individual interviewers might have, allows all interviewers to evaluate the applicant at the same time and on the same questions and answers and facilitates discussion of the pros and cons of individual applicants.

Once the preferred applicant has been identified, the next step is to make a formal offer of appointment, by mail or otherwise. In the case of paid event staff, the short-term nature of many events means that any offer of employment is for a specific contracted period. The employment contract generally states the activities that are to be performed, salary/wage levels and the rights and obligations of the employer and employee.

Under the Employment Rights Act 1996, employees are entitled to receive a contract of employment within eight weeks of commencing employment. The legislation ensures that minimum conditions of employment are established in the contract. Armstrong (2006, p. 859), identifies the following areas typically to be included − details may either be discussed or referred to in separate documents (e.g. grievance procedure):

- a statement of job title and duties
- the date on which continuous employment commenced
- rate of pay, allowances, overtime, bonuses (and any associated conditions), method and timing of payment
- hours of work including breaks
- holiday arrangements/entitlement
- sickness procedure (including sick pay, notification of illness)
- length of notice due to and from the employee
- grievance procedure
- disciplinary procedure
- work rules
- arrangements for terminating employment
- arrangements for union membership (if applicable)
- special terms relating to confidentiality, rights to patents and designs, exclusivity of service and restrictions on trade after termination of employment (e.g. cannot work for a direct competitor within six months)
- employer's right to vary terms and conditions, subject to proper notification

If large numbers of employees are used in an event, an enterprise agreement negotiated with employees can engender an atmosphere of trust and working together to achieve a commonly sought objective.

In the case of volunteers, a simple letter of appointment accompanied by details regarding the position may be all that is necessary. It is also appropriate to consider supplying volunteers with a statement about their rights and those of the event organisation, regarding their involvement in the event (Figure 10.8). Once an offer has been made and accepted, unsuccessful applicants should be informed as soon as possible.

Records of paid employees must also be kept. These should include:

- name, address and telephone number
- employment classification/employee number and national insurance number

FIGURE 10.8 Rights and responsibilities of volunteers and voluntary organisations

Both the volunteer and the organisation have responsibilities to each other. The volunteer contracts to perform a specific job and the organisation contracts to provide the volunteer with a worthwhile and rewarding experience. In return, each has the right to some basic expectations of the other.

Volunteers have the right to:
- be treated as co-workers. This includes job descriptions, equal employment opportunity, occupational health and safety, anti-discrimination legislation and organisational grievance processes.
- be asked for their permission before any job-related reference, police or prohibited person checks are conducted
- a task or job worthwhile to them, for no more than 16 hours a week on a regular basis
- know the purpose and 'ground rules' of the organisation
- appropriate orientation and training for the job
- be kept informed of organisation changes and the reasons for such changes
- a place to work and suitable tools
- reimbursement of agreed expenses
- be heard and make suggestions
- personal accident insurance in place of workers compensation insurance
- a verbal reference or statement of service, if appropriate.

Organisations have the right to:
- receive as much effort and service from a volunteer worker as a paid worker, even on a short-term basis
- select the best volunteer for the job by interviewing and screening all applicants. This might include reference and police checks and, where appropriate, prohibited person checks for roles that involve working directly with children.
- expect volunteers to adhere to their job descriptions/outlines and the organisation's code of practice
- expect volunteers to undertake training provided for them and observe safety rules
- make the decision regarding the best placement of a volunteer
- express opinions about poor volunteer effort in a diplomatic way
- expect loyalty to the organisation and only constructive criticism
- expect clear and open communication from the volunteer
- negotiate work assignments
- release volunteers under certain circumstances.

(Source: School of Volunteer Management, 2001)

- whether full-time or part-time
- whether permanent, temporary or casual
- whether an apprentice or trainee
- date when first employed
- date when terminated
- remuneration and hours worked
- leave records
- superannuating contributions

McCurley and Lynch (1998) advise that it is also sound practice to keep records of volunteers. These may based on employee records but will include as a minimum:

- contract
- job description
- application/interview forms
- name and address
- role in the event and training received
- skills and expertise
- performance appraisal
- access to special equipment
- willingness to volunteer again

This type of information facilitates human resource planning for future events.

Induction

Once appointees (paid or voluntary) commence work with an event organisation, a structured induction programme designed to begin the process of 'bonding' the individual to the event organisation, needs to be conducted. Getz (2005, p. 226), suggests that a range of actions be taken as part of an effective induction programme:

- provide basic information about the event (mission, objectives, stakeholders, budget, locations, programme details)
- conduct tours of venues, suppliers, offices and any other relevant locations
- make introductions to other staff and volunteers
- give an introduction to the organisational culture, history and working arrangements
- overview training programmes (both general and position-specific)

In addition to these actions, it is sound practice to discuss the job description with the individual to ensure that he or she has a clear understanding of matters such as responsibilities, performance expectations, approaches to performance evaluation and reporting relationships. At this time other matters associated with the terms and conditions of employment should also be discussed/reiterated, including proba-tionary periods, grievance procedures, absenteeism, sickness, dress code, security, holiday/leave benefits, superannuation, salary and overtime rates, and other benefits, such as car parking and meals. One means of ensuring mutual understanding of these matters is to have the staff member/volunteer read and sign their position description. Figure 10.9 gives an example of a position description that could be used for this purpose for volunteers.

The induction process can also be facilitated by the development of an induction kit for distribution to each new staff member or volunteer. Such a kit might contain:

- an annual report
- a message from the organising committee chairperson/chief executive officer welcoming staff and volunteers
- a statement of event mission/vision, goals and objectives
- an organisational chart
- a name badge
- a staff list (including contact details)
- a uniform (whether a T-shirt or something more formal)
- a list of sponsors
- a list of stakeholders
- any other appropriate items — for example, occupational, health and safety information

FIGURE 10.9 Example of a job description and contract for a volunteer

Job title: _____

Supervisor: _____

Location: _____

Objective (Why is this job necessary? What will it accomplish?):
_____

Responsibilities (What specifically will the volunteer do?):
_____

Qualifications (What special skills, education, or age group is necessary to do this job?): _____

Training provided: _____

Benefits (parking, transportation, uniforms, food and beverage, expenses):
_____

Trial period (probation, if required): _____

References required (yes or no): _____

Any other information: _____

Date: _____

Signature of volunteer (to be added at time of mutual agreement):
_____

Signature of supervisor: _____

(Source: Bradner, 1997, p. 75)

A central outcome of the induction process should be a group of volunteers and staff who are committed to the event, enthusiastic and knowledgeable about their roles in it and aware of the part their jobs play in the totality of the event.

Training and professional development

According to Armstrong (2006), learning, training and professional development should be considered in terms of meeting business needs and strategies. Training focuses on providing specific job skills/knowledge that will allow people to perform a job or to improve their performance in it. Professional development, on the other hand, is concerned with the acquisition of new skills, knowledge and attitudes that will prepare individuals for future job responsibilities.

Both training and professional development are significant in driving the success of an event, acting to underpin its effective delivery. For small and mid-sized events, much training is on-the-job, with existing staff and experienced volunteers acting as advice givers. This approach, while cheap and largely effective, has limitations. The major one is that it is not often preceded by an assessment of the event's precise training needs and how best to meet them within resource limitations.

A formal approach to training needs assessment — it serves to determine whether the training taking place is adequate and whether any training needs are not being met. Additionally, such an assessment generates suggestions about how to improve the training provided by the event. These suggestions might include:

- Sending or requesting stakeholder/government support to send staff/volunteers on training programmes dealing with specific areas or identified training needs, (e.g. risk management, event marketing and sponsorship).
- Identifying individuals associated with the event who would be willing to volunteer to conduct training sessions.
- Commissioning consultants/external bodies to undertake specific training.
- Encouraging staff/volunteers to undertake event-specific training programmes, now provided by some public and private colleges, universities and event industry associations (see Figure 10.10), in return for certain benefits (e.g. higher salaries, appointment to positions of greater responsibility/satisfaction).

When trying to identify what training is required to facilitate the effective delivery of an event, the central consideration is to determine the gap between the current performance of staff and volunteers and their desired performance. This can be achieved by:

- performance appraisals of existing staff/volunteers (what training do staff identify as being required to make them more effective?)
- analysis of job requirements (what skills are identified in the job description?)
- survey of personnel (what skills staff state they need?)

The types of training provided by events will vary; however it is not uncommon for them to provide a level of general training for all staff in areas such as health and

FIGURE 10.10 Example of training programme offered by the UK centre for events management, Leeds Metropolitan University: certificate in creating and managing events

> The Certificate in Creating and Managing Events covers the fundamentals of events management as well as engaging participants in more strategic thinking around event support, sponsorship and marketing to maximise the impact of their events. The programme also includes training for the National Certificate for Personal Licence Holders which is a nationally recognised level 2 qualification designed to provide the knowledge and information required by anyone wishing to apply to their local authority for a personal licence.
>
> The course will be delivered over six 2 day workshops. The workshops will cover creative thinking and risk management, motivating teams and volunteers, innovative marketing and sponsorship in events, National Certificate for Personal License Holders, event planning and production and financial and data management in events

(Source: Leeds Metropolitan University, 2010)

safety and first aid, as well as training designed to provide position-specific skills and knowledge. Because of the infrequent nature and short duration of events, training of event volunteers usually takes place on the job under the direction of the event manager or a supervisor. For this to be effective it should be structured to include:

- Defined learning objectives: these outline what the trainee should be able to do at the end of the training.
  Appropriate curriculum: the content of the training should be appropriate to the learning outcomes.
- Appropriate instructional strategies: these can take the form of discussion groups, lectures, lectures/discussions, case studies, role-playing, demonstrations or on-the-job training.
- Well-conducted training: the trainer should not be an expert handing down instructions from on high but a facilitator who can identify, explain and model the skills, observe trainees' attempts and correct their errors.
- Evaluation: this is to assess whether the trainees have acquired the appropriate skills.

Buckler (1998, pp. 18–19), developed a simple model of learning from his research into learning organisations. The model is based on the premise that the involvement of leaders in the learning process is crucial for success, as learning cannot be effective if the manager does not understand the process. Buckler goes on to argue that effective learning requires interaction between managers (the teacher) and staff (pupils), in order to develop a shared vision of what is to be achieved, remove barriers to learning and encourage innovation/try new ideas in a safe environment. This process of learning can be modeled as shown in Figure 10.11. As can be seen from the typical comments made by learners, essential elements of the training process are reflection and feedback — trainees think deeply about the connections

FIGURE 10.11 A simple model of the learning process

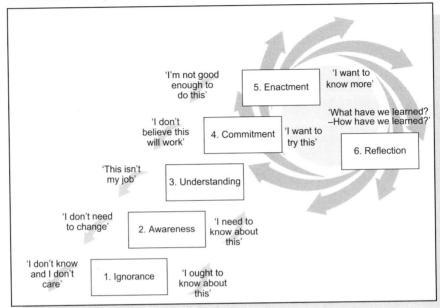

'I'm not good enough to do this'

5. Enactment

'I want to know more'

'I don't believe this will work'

4. Commitment

'I want to try this'

'What have we learned? –How have we learned?'

6. Reflection

'This isn't my job'

3. Understanding

'I don't need to change'

2. Awareness

'I need to know about this'

'I don't know and I don't care'

1. Ignorance

'I ought to know about this'

(Source: Buckler, 1998)

between what they already know about the topic and the new data they receive, by relating new knowledge to experience and using theory to extend experience. Feedback, from trainer, supervisor or peers or their own reflection, enables trainees to adjust their actions to enable the task to be correctly completed. It is unlikely that anyone has learnt any new skill without this process of reflection and feedback.

Supervision and evaluation

As a general rule, the bigger and more complex the event, the greater is the need for staff and volunteers to perform a supervisory function. This function may be exercised through a variety of means, including having would-be supervisors understudy an existing supervisor, developing a mentoring system or encouraging staff to undertake appropriate professional development programmes.

One of the key tasks of supervisors and managers is that of performance appraisal. This task involves evaluating performance, communicating that evaluation and establishing a plan for improvement. The ultimate outcomes of this process are a better event and more competent staff and volunteers. Stone (2007), proposes a dynamic performance appraisal programme (see Figure 10.12) based on goal establishment, performance feedback and performance improvement.

According to Stone (2007), goals should be mutually arrived at by a supervisor and a volunteer or staff member. These goals, while specific to the particular job, are

FIGURE 10.12 Dynamic performance appraisal system

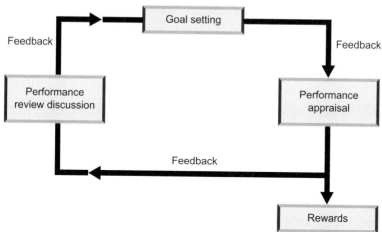

(Source: Stone, 2007)

likely to relate to matters such as technical skills and knowledge, problem solving/ creativity, planning and organising, interpersonal skills, decision making, commitment to quality and safety, the achievement of designated results, attitudes and personality traits, reliability/punctuality and professional development. It is important that measurements of progress towards goals are established, otherwise there is little point in setting goals in the first place. A person charged with overseeing waste management for an event, for example, may be assessed in terms of the percentage of material recycled from the event, levels of contamination in waste, the percentage of attendees (as determined by survey) that understood directions regarding the placement of waste in containers and the level of complaints regarding matters such as full bins. Other areas for assessment might include those associated with personal development (enrolment and completion of a specific course), interpersonal relationships (opinions of supervisors/co-workers) and problem solving/creativity (approaches employed in response to the unexpected).

Performance, in terms of progress towards the established goals, can be assessed in a variety of ways, including performance scales. According to Wood, Chapman, Fromholtz, Morrison, Wallace, Zeffrane, Schermerhorn, Hunt and Osborn (2004), irrespective of what assessment measures are used, responses to the following questions must underpin any efforts in this area:

- what does the job require?
- what does the employee/volunteer need to do to perform effectively in this position?
- what evidence (from work undertaken) would indicate effective performance?
- what does the assessment of evidence of performance indicate about future actions required?

Once an appraisal has been conducted, there should be a follow-up review discussion in which the supervisor/manager and the staff member/volunteer mutually review job responsibilities, examine how these responsibilities have been performed, explore how performance can be improved and review and revise the staff members/volunteers short-term and long-term goals. The interview process should be a positive experience for both parties. To this end, it is worthwhile considering the provision of training to the managers/supervisors involved in this process so that they adhere to certain basic practices such as preparing for the interview by reviewing job descriptions, reviewing previous assessments, being constructive not destructive and encouraging discussion.

Integral to the appraisal system are rewards that paid staff receives in the form of salaries, bonuses, profit sharing and promotion to other jobs or other events; and benefits such as the use of cars and other equipment (e.g. laptop computers). Options also exist to reward volunteers for their efforts. These include:

- training in new skills
- free merchandise (e.g. clothing, badges, event posters)
- hospitality in the form of opening and closing parties, free meals/drinks
- certificates of appreciation
- gifts of sponsor products
- opportunities to meet with celebrities, sporting stars and other VIPs
- promotion to more interesting volunteer positions with each year of service
- public acknowledgement through the media and at the event
- certificates of appreciation
- free tickets to the event
- event commencement and concluding parties

The 'flip side' to rewards — that is, discipline — also requires managerial consideration. It is useful to have in place, specific policies and practices that reflect the seriousness of different behaviour/actions, and these should be communicated to all staff (paid and voluntary). These policies and practices are likely to begin with some form of admonishment and end with dismissal. Many of the approaches to disciplining paid employees (such as removing access to overtime) are not applicable to volunteers. Instead, approaches that may be applied to volunteers include re-assignment, withholding of rewards/benefits and suspension from holding a position as a volunteer.

Termination, outplacement and re-enlistment

Whether employing staff on contract or as permanent employees, event managers are occasionally faced with the need to terminate the services of an individual. This action may be necessary in instances where an employee breaches the employment contract (e.g. repeatedly arriving at the workplace intoxicated) or continually exhibits unsatisfactory performance. This need may also arise when the economic or commercial circumstances of the organisation conducting the event, require it to shed staff (such as when there is insufficient revenue due to poor ticket sales).

Various legal issues surrounding termination need to be understood by those involved in event management. In the UK, these issues relate to unfair or unlawful dismissal/termination and are spelt out in employment legislation. Essentially, employers are required to give employees an opportunity to defend themselves against allegations associated with their conduct; in cases of unsatisfactory performance, they must warn and counsel the employee before terminating his or her service. These requirements do not apply to contracted or casual employees or to staff on probation. A need can also arise to dismiss volunteers; for this purpose, Getz (2005), suggests a variety of approaches. These include making all volunteer appointments for fixed terms (with volunteers needing to re-apply and be subjected to screening each time the event is conducted) and using job descriptions and performance appraisals to underpin appropriate action.

Outplacement is the process of assisting terminated employees (or indeed volunteers) or even those who choose to leave the event organisation voluntarily, to find other employment. By performing this function the event organisation is providing a benefit to employees for past service, as well as maintaining and enhancing its image as a responsible employer. In the case of an event organising company that decides to downsize, as many did after the 11 September 2001 (9/11) terrorist attacks and again during the economic downturn in 2009, this process could lead to staff being aided to take up positions with, for example, other companies operating their own event divisions or large events that maintain a full-time staff year round. Even volunteers who are no longer needed can be helped into other positions by being put in contact with volunteer agencies or other events.

With recurring events, such as annual festivals, opportunities often exist to re-enlist for paid or voluntary positions. Many staff from the Sydney and Athens Summer Olympic Games, for example, took up positions within the organisation responsible for the Beijing Olympics. To maintain contact with potential volunteers and past staff between events, a variety of approaches can be employed including newsletters (see the Manchester Event Volunteers website, www.mev.org.uk), social events, the offer of benefits for re-enlistment and personal contact by telephone between events.

Event managers should also keep in mind that staff will often leave of their own accord. The involvement of such staff in exit interviews can provide valuable information that could be used to fine-tune one or more aspects of an event's human resource management process. A study of volunteers at a jazz festival (Elstad, 2003), found the main reasons that volunteers quit were (in order): (1) their overall workload, (2) a lack of appreciation of their contribution, (3) problems with how the festival was organised, (4) disagreement with changing goals or ideology, (5) wanting more free time for other activities, (6) a lack of a 'sense of community' among volunteers, (7) family responsibilities, (8) the festival becoming too large, (9) the inability to make decisions regarding their own position, (10) a dislike for some of their responsibilities, (11) lack of remuneration, (12) moving out of the festival's geographic area.

Evaluation of process and outcomes

As with all management processes, a periodic review is necessary to determine how well, or otherwise, the human resource management process is working. To conduct such a review, it is necessary to obtain feedback from relevant supervisory/ management staff, organising committee members and paid and voluntary staff. As part of its review process, the California Traditional Music Society, for example, uses a questionnaire to obtain feedback from volunteers (Figure 10.13). A specific time should then be set aside, perhaps as part of a larger review of the event, to examine the extent to which the human resource management process as a whole (and its various elements) achieved its original objectives. Once the review is complete, revisions can be made to the process for subsequent events.

MOTIVATING STAFF AND VOLUNTEERS

Motivation is a key, if implicit, component of the human resource management process. It commits people to a course of action, enthuses and energises them and enables them to achieve goals, whether the goals are corporate or their own. The ability to motivate other staff members is a fundamental component of the event manager's repertoire of skills. Without appropriate motivation, paid employees and volunteers can lack enthusiasm for achieving the event's corporate goals and delivering quality service; or they can show a lack of concern for the welfare of their coworkers or event participants.

In the context of volunteers, pure altruism (an unselfish regard for, or devotion to, the welfare of others) may be an important motive for seeking to assist in the delivery of events. Although this proposition is supported by Flashman and Quick (1985), the great bulk of work done on motivation, stresses that people, while they may assert they are acting for altruistic reasons, are actually motivated by a combination of external and internal factors, most of which have little to do with altruism. As McCurley and Lynch (1998, pp. 11–12, 13), point out: 'Motivation for the long-term volunteer is a matter of both achievement and affiliation, and often recognition is best expressed as an opportunity for greater involvement or advancement in the cause or the organisation.' Further, short-term volunteers are motivated by recognition of their personal achievement, which can be achieved by simply thanking them for their contribution. The parameters of reward are discussed in this section.

Researchers from a variety of disciplines have done much work over many years on what motivates people, particularly in the workplace. Perhaps the most relevant and useful of these studies within the context of festivals and events are content theories and process theories.

Content theories

Content theories concentrate on what initially motivates people to act in a certain way. As Mullins (2005, p. 480), points out, they 'are concerned with identifying

FIGURE 10.13 Example of a volunteer survey

Name: _____ Job: _____

CTMS VOLUNTEER SURVEY   Year _____

As in past years, we ask that you help by responding to these questions about your volunteer duties, so that we can continue to improve your entire volunteer experience. Please fill out this questionnaire and mail it back to CTMS in the return envelope provided. If you have any further comments or suggestions, please feel free to write or type your comments separately. Thanks again, and we look forward to seeing you again next year!

The Volunteer Coordination Committee

What shift(s) did you work?

Did you clearly understand, before the festival, what you were supposed to do, what **time** you were expected to work, and **where** you were going to work?

Was the printed training information you received at the training meetings thorough and complete? What would you change or add to it?

Do you think there were enough volunteers assigned to your job? Were you kept so busy that you could not do your job properly?

Do you think there were too many volunteers assigned to the same job as you were? Were you bored?

Was your job too difficult or strenuous for you in any way? Please explain.

Was there an extremely busy time during your shift? When was it? Do you feel you needed more help during this time?

Was there an extremely quiet time during your shift? When was it?

Did you run into any difficulties or situations that you didn't expect or didn't know how to handle? What were they? What did you do?

Is there anything you think CTMS should have provided or advised you to bring with you that would have made your job easier, more comfortable, or more efficient?

Were you able to get away during your shift to use a restroom if you needed one? If you were alone at your position, did someone come around and offer to relieve you temporarily so you could use a restroom?

Were there any problems that you were aware of that need correction for next year?

Would you volunteer for next year? If not, why not?

Thank you very much for completing and returning this questionnaire. Please write any comments specific to your volunteer job on a sheet of paper. Please write any other comments relative to the festival in general on a separate sheet of paper. Return both to CTMS.

(Source: California Traditional Music Society, 2003)

people's needs and their relative strengths, and the goals they pursue in order to satisfy these needs'. Figure 10.14 represents the essential nature of theories of this type.

Content theories assert that a person has a need — a feeling of deprivation — which then drives the person towards an action that can satisfy that need. Maslow's (1954) hierarchy of needs, illustrated in Figure 10.15, popularised the idea that needs are the basis of motivation.

In essence, Maslow's theory proposes that lower order needs must be satisfied before people are motivated to satisfy the next, higher need. That is, people who are trying to satisfy physiological needs of hunger and thirst have no interest in satisfying the need for safety until their physiological needs are satisfied. The first three needs are perceived as deficiencies; they must be satisfied to fulfill a lack of something. In contrast, satisfaction of the two higher needs is necessary for an individual to grow emotionally and psychologically.

Although little empirical evidence exists to support Maslow's theory, it can give insights into the needs people may be seeking to fulfill through employment. Some research, for example, indicates a tendency for higher level needs to dominate as individuals move up the managerial hierarchy.

Another researcher who falls within the ambit of content theory is Hertzberg (1968). He argues that some elements, which he calls hygiene factors, do not of themselves motivate or satisfy people. Among these factors are pay levels, policies and procedures, working conditions and job security. However, the absence or perceived reduction in these items can stimulate hostility or dissatisfaction towards an organisation. Hertzberg further argues that other factors, which he calls motivators, of themselves lead to goal-directed behaviour. These elements include achievement, recognition and interesting work. Hertzberg's theory is illustrated in Figure 10.16.

Hertzberg's theory suggests event managers can motivate staff and volunteers by:

- instituting processes of recognising achievement
- empowering staff to take responsibility for the outcomes of their part of the event
- providing opportunities for them to grow in skills, experience and expertise

FIGURE 10.14 Basis of content theories of motivation

(Source: Peach and Murrell, 1995)

FIGURE 10.15 Maslow's hierarchy of needs

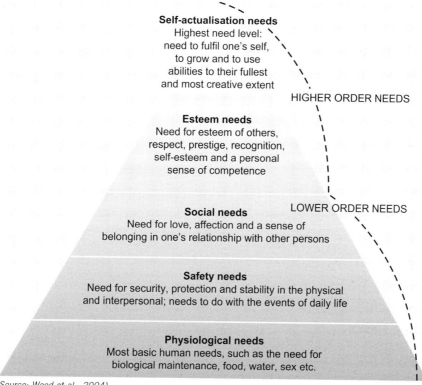

Self-actualisation needs
Highest need level:
need to fulfil one's self,
to grow and to use
abilities to their fullest
and most creative extent

HIGHER ORDER NEEDS

Esteem needs
Need for esteem of others,
respect, prestige, recognition,
self-esteem and a personal
sense of competence

Social needs   LOWER ORDER NEEDS
Need for love, affection and a sense of
belonging in one's relationship with other persons

Safety needs
Need for security, protection and stability in the physical
and interpersonal; needs to do with the events of daily life

Physiological needs
Most basic human needs, such as the need for
biological maintenance, food, water, sex etc.

(Source: Wood et al., 2004)

It also suggests event managers need to be conscious of certain hygiene factors that can act as de-motivators. These might include attitudes of supervisors, working conditions such as the length of meal/coffee breaks and hours of work, quality of food provided, the status of one job compared with another (e.g. waste management officer versus publicity coordinator) and policies such as the type/quality of uniforms provided to staff versus volunteers.

Content theories, such as those of Hertzberg and Maslow, provide event managers with some understanding of work-related factors that initiate motivation; they also focus attention on the importance of employee needs and their satisfaction. They do not, however, explain particularly well why a person chooses certain types of behaviour to satisfy their needs (Wood et al., 2004). Process theories, the subject of the next section, take up this challenge.

Process theories

Representative of process theories of motivation are Adams' (1965), Equity Theory and Vroom's (1964), Expectancy Theory.

FIGURE 10.16 Herzberg's two-factor theory of motivation

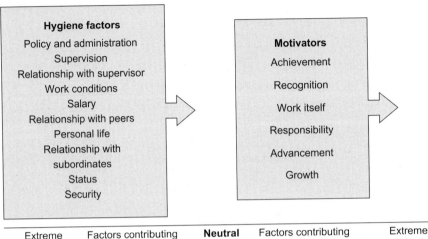

(Source: Adapted and Reprinted by permission of Harvard Business Review. [Exhibit]. From "One More Time: How Do You Motivate Employees?" by F. Herzberg, 01/03, p. 90. Copyright © 2003 by Harvard Business School Publishing Corporation; all rights reserved)

Equity Theory

Equity Theory is based on the reasonable premise that all employees (or, for that matter, volunteers) expect to be treated fairly. This being the case, if one employee or volunteer perceives a discrepancy in the outcomes that he or she receives (e.g. pay or type of work allocated) compared with those of other employees or volunteers, that employee or volunteer will be motivated to do more (or less) work (Wood et al., 2004). This situation is represented in the equation below:

$$\frac{\text{Individual rewards}}{\text{Individual inputs}} \xleftrightarrow{\text{comparison}} \frac{\text{Others' rewards}}{\text{Others' inputs}}$$

What an employee or volunteer perceives as fair in terms of compensation (monetary or non-monetary) is subjective. The best way of maintaining an awareness of what an individual is thinking in this regard, is to develop and maintain open lines of communication. If in-equity is perceived and goes unnoticed, a number of outcomes are possible, including:

- a reduction in effort
- pressure to increase remuneration
- exit from the organisation

Expectancy Theory

Expectancy theory holds that an individual's motivation to act in a particular way comes from a belief that a particular outcome will result from doing something (expectancy). This outcome will result in a reward (instrumentality). The rewards for accomplishing this outcome are sufficiently attractive/desirable to justify the effort put into doing it (valence). Motivation, under this theory (in its most simplistic form), can therefore be expressed as:

$$\text{Motivation} = \text{Expectancy} \times \text{Instrumentality} \times \text{Valence}.$$

This being the case, whenever one of the elements in this equation approaches zero, the motivational value of a particular decision is dramatically reduced. Event managers need to be aware of this and, therefore, try to maximise all three motivational components. In other words, there must be a clear payoff if employees and volunteers are to perform at a high level. To understand what this payoff needs to be for each staff member and volunteer is difficult; however, the chances of doing so are greatly increased if lines of communication are kept open and if a genuine effort is made to understand each individual.

As an example of how the Expectancy Theory works, take the situation of people who decide to work voluntarily in their local community festival. They may have certain expectations:

- An expectation that by working on the event they will gain certain new skills.
- An expectation that these new skills in turn will enhance their future employability, thus creating an instrumentality.
- An expectation that the jobs for which they will be able to apply with these new skills are ones that they would find extremely rewarding, adding a strong degree of value to the volunteer positions on offer.

While the focus in this section has been on the individual, it should not be forgotten that as events often involve a number of functional areas, 'team rewards' for collective performance need also to be considered.

If all three factors are strongly positive, then motivation will be high. It is from this theoretical framework that Peach and Murrell (1995, pp. 238–9), derive their reward and recognition techniques, which are shown in Table 10.1.

BUILDING EFFECTIVE STAFF AND VOLUNTEER TEAMS

As noted at the outset of the chapter, event organisations often come together quickly and exist only for relatively short periods of time. This being the case, one of the greatest challenges faced by an event manager is creating effective 'team(s)' capable of achieving an event's objectives. In the case of small-scale events, such as corporate product launches or hospitality-based events, the event manager will often create a single team comprising members of their own company's staff and those of a range of suppliers (the venue, A/V hire firms, caterers, etc.). To develop a sense of 'team' within such a group, the event manager will often rely solely upon one or more 'team' briefings/meetings, supported by detailed event production schedules indicating the roles to be performed by all involved. What simplifies this process in

Table 10.1 Reward and recognition techniques

Reward Systems that Work.	Recognition Techniques that Work.
Rewards that integrate the needs of the individual and the organisation in a win-win understanding.	Carefully constructed systems that are built on the motives needs of volunteers – individualised need recognition for each person.
Rewards based on deep appreciation of the individual as a unique person.	Recognition integrated into task performance, where clear performance objectives are established.
Rewards based on job content, not conditions – rewards intrinsic to the job work best. Assignment of the tasks that can be performed effectively, leading to intrinsic need satisfaction. Consistent reward policies that build a sense of trust that effort will receive the proper reward.	Corporate growth and development objectives also become opportunities for recognition. Longevity and special contributions recognised frequently, not just every ten years. Recognition grounded deeply on the core values of the organisation; what is recognised helps as a role model.
Rewards that can be shared by teams so that winning is a collective and collaborative experience	

(Source: Peach and Murrell, 1995)

many instances is the ongoing (as opposed to one-off) use by event managers of a given set of contractors, who over time, come to understand increasingly how best to integrate their activities with those of the event production firm. In the case of larger events where there are many function-based teams, and where the teams that are created exist for longer periods, creating effective teams becomes a more complex issue. In this regard, event managers need to give significant thought to such matters as:

- Clearly establishing team tasks.
- Choosing team members with due regard to personality traits, skills/knowledge and availability (for the period of the event).
- Providing adequate support in the form of training, information, resources, opportunities for team building and designing processes, to monitor team performance and provide feedback (Mullins, 2005).

Most events are conscious of the significance of the creation of effective teams to their success, with some developing creative responses to facilitate their formation. The Manchester Commonwealth Games, for example, in their efforts to integrate volunteers and paid staff, conducted a pre-event 'celebration'. This event, attended by The Earl and Countess of Wessex and hosted by a well-known television presenter, included motivational videos, live sketches, singing and other entertainment. Staff and volunteers attending this function were seated as venue teams and were greeted by their respective venue's management, as part of the event's overall effort to strengthen team bonds. Among other things, this event also sought to:

- inspire and motivate staff
- transfer key messages about what to expect and what was expected of staff and volunteers
- educate staff and volunteers about the global nature of the event and participating nations

Writing in the context of volunteers in general, Nancy McDuff (1995, pp. 208–10), proposes a 14-point formula for effective team building and maintenance. Many of these points (noted below) can be said to apply equally to teams of paid staff.

1. Teams must be of a manageable size. Most effective teams are between 2 and 25 people, with the majority fewer than 10.
2. People should be appropriately selected to serve on a team. Care and attention should be paid to selecting people with the right combination of skills, personality, communication styles and ability to perform, thereby improving the chances of the team being successful.
3. Team leaders should be trained. Leaders who find it difficult to delegate and want to do everything themselves make poor leaders. Team leaders must have training in supervision skills.
4. Teams should be trained to execute their tasks. It is unrealistic to expect teams to perform effectively without appropriate training. The training should include an appraisal of the team's role in the activity and how this role contributes to the activity's overall success.
5. Volunteers and staff should be supported by the organisation. Teams must feel that the administration is there to support their endeavours, not to hinder them.
6. Teams must have objectives. The purpose of the team must be spelt out in measurable objectives. Having a plan to achieve those objectives helps build trust.
7. Volunteers and staff should trust and support one another. People trust each other when they share positive experiences. When each team is aware of the organisation's objectives and how its role helps to achieve those objectives, it trusts co-workers and supports their efforts.
8. Communication between volunteers and the event organisation should be both vertical and horizontal. Communication, which means sending 'meanings' and understandings between people, is a process involving an active and continuous use of active listening, the use of feedback to clarify meaning, the reading of body language and the use of symbols that communicate meaning. Communication travels in all directions — up and down the reporting line and between teams and work groups. Working together is facilitated by good communication.
9. The organisational structure should promote communication between volunteers and staff. The organisation's structure, policies and operating programmes

permit and encourage all members of the organisation to communicate with their co-workers, their managers and members of other departments. This helps build an atmosphere of cooperation and harmony in the pursuit of common objectives.

10. Volunteers and staff should have real responsibility. A currently fashionable concept in management is 'empowerment'. This means giving staff the authority to make decisions about their work and its outcomes. Take, for example, a group of volunteers having the somewhat mundane task of making sandwiches. If they are empowered with the authority to decide what sandwiches to make, how to make them and what to charge, their enthusiasm for the task will probably be enhanced and there will be a corresponding improvement in outcomes.

11. Volunteers and staff must have fun while accomplishing tasks. Managers should strive to engender an atmosphere of humour, fun and affection among co-workers within the culture of the organisation. Such actions as ceremonies to acknowledge exemplary contributions to the event, wrap-up parties and load-in celebrations can facilitate this atmosphere.

12. There must be recognition of the contributions of volunteers and staff. Paid staff should express formal and informal appreciation of the work of volunteers and volunteers should publicly recognise and appreciate the work of the paid staff. This mutual appreciation should be consistent, public and visible.

13. Volunteers and staff should celebrate their success. Spontaneous celebrations with food, drink, friendship and frivolity should be encouraged by the management of the event, to celebrate achievement of objectives. The event manager should allocate a budgeted amount for these occasions.

14. The entire organisation should promote and encourage the wellbeing of volunteer teams. Everyone in the organisation should be a member of a partnership and actively promote such relationships.

Once teams are in place and operating effectively, the event manager should monitor their performance and productivity by observing their activities and maintaining appropriate communication with team leaders and members. If deficiencies are noticed during the monitoring procedure, then appropriate action can be taken in terms of training, team structure changes or the refinement of operating procedures in a climate of mutual trust.

LEGAL OBLIGATIONS

Employment law regulates how employers deal with their employees in terms of pay and conditions and prevents discrimination in relation to race, sex or disability. This legislation generally sets out minimum rates of pay and conditions such as annual leave and working hours. Of course, there is nothing to stop an event manager from paying more than the minimum wage, as the labour market is not controlled, except by minimum conditions that must be met. Traditionally, the market has been based on the concept of free collective bargaining; however, in recent years, there have been increasing levels of legislation, including the impact of European Union directives. To ensure compliance with appropriate legislation, event managers who employ paid labour should consult the Department for Business, Innovation and Skills (www.bis.gov.uk), which undoubtedly can supply details of current labour legislation.

Many paid employees of events are employed as casual workers. To compensate for the irregular nature of their work, these employees may be paid rates above the normal full-time hourly rate. It is the responsibility, and in the best interests, of the event manager to ensure these employees are paid appropriately, particularly during the summer event season when there is increased competition for their services.

Event managers should also remember there are common law requirements regarding the duties of the parties to an employment relationship. In the context of volunteers, common law precedents also provide rights to damages if negligence can be shown on behalf of an event organiser.

SUMMARY

Event managers should approach the task of human resource management not as a series of separate activities but as an integrated process involving a number of related steps, taking the event organisation's mission, strategy and goals as their starting points. These steps have been identified in this chapter as: (1) the human resource strategy and objectives; (2) policies and procedures; (3) recruitment; (4) training and professional development; (5) supervision and evaluation; (6) termination, outplacement and re-enlistment; and (7) evaluation and feedback. Each of these stages in the human resource management process, it has been argued here, have application to the employment of both paid and volunteer staff, as well as to events of varying size and type. This chapter has also dealt with the issue of motivation, examining two broad theoretical perspectives on the matter, process and content theories. The final sections of this chapter dealt with mechanisms for developing task teams to conduct events and the legal considerations associated with human resource management.

QUESTIONS

1. Interview the organiser of an event of your choice and ask him or her what legal/statutory requirements have an impact on human resource management processes and practices.

2. In the context of a specific event, identify the policies and procedures regarding human resource management. Collect examples of forms and other material that support them.

3. Develop a job specification for a management position within an event of your choice.

4 Construct an interview checklist for candidates seeking a management position within a special event of your choice.

5 Discuss two theories of motivation and indicate how an event manager might draw on these theories to motivate their paid and volunteer staff.

6 Identify an event that makes significant use of volunteers and critically assess its approach to recruiting, selecting, managing and motivating this component of its workforce.

7 Propose an induction programme for paid staff entering into the employment of a large-scale sports event.

8 Critically review one stage in the human resource management process (as proposed in this chapter) employed by an event of your choice.

9 In general terms, what responsibilities does an event organisation have to its employees under occupational health and safety legislation?

10 Construct a post-event evaluation questionnaire for volunteers involved in an event of your choice.

CASE STUDY BEIJING 2008 – TRAINING TO DELIVER THE 'BEST GAMES EVER'

Introduction

For any Olympic Games organiser faced with the task of training a Games workforce comprising paid staff, contractors and volunteers, a range of key questions need to be answered:

- how will training needs be determined?
- when should training take place?
- how will training be delivered?
- how will the task of volunteer recruitment be managed?

This brief case study attempts to answer these questions from the perspective of the Beijing Olympic Games (BOG), drawing in part on how other such major events have approached this challenge and also upon the limited information available about training from the Beijing Olympic Games Organising Committee (BOGOC) before the games.

Training needs analysis. For any major event, such as BOG, a training needs analysis is necessary to determine specific workforce requirements in terms of knowledge, skills and attitudes. Groups covered by such an analysis should include not only paid staff and volunteers but also other event stakeholders such as emergency service personnel, contractors, tourism/hospitality personnel and transport service providers. While the nature of any such analysis so far undertaken in the context of BOG is not yet publicly available, it can reasonably be assumed that the organisers would have drawn upon approaches used at past Games and other large-scale events, as well as consultants with expertise in this area. It is also likely that primary research (using such means as focus groups and questionnaires) of major stakeholder groups would have been conducted to establish exact training requirements.

When should training take place?. Training in the context of an Olympic Games commonly commences 3–5 years out and is initially directed primarily at management and administrative staff who are engaged in the 'start up' phase of the event. As the event approaches and staff numbers rise quickly, the training task becomes more complex and extensive, as well as being continuous in nature.

In terms of timing, training can be viewed as falling into two categories: pre-Games and Games. The former will commonly include an orientation programme (which will continue until shortly before the event begins) that ensures that all staff, volunteers and (often) contractors have a clear understanding of what the event is about, along with certain basic knowledge and skills. In the case of the BOG, this training should provide:

- basic Olympic Games knowledge
- an introduction to the Beijing Olympic and Paralympic Games
- an overview of Chinese history and traditional culture
- coverage of the history and cultural life in Beijing
- knowledge and skills necessary to serve the disabled
- etiquette
- medical knowledge
- first-aid skills

In addition to an orientation programme, the training needs analysis referred to earlier is likely to identify a range of more specific skills/knowledge training requirements needed in the early stages of building an event workforce. In the case of the Sydney 2000 Olympic Games, for example, these included information technology, budgeting, presentation skills, management development and project management.

In the Games period (up to 6 months out from the event), training needs greatly expand as the event's workforce grows quickly in order to deliver the event. To cope with this expanded need for training, various training modules are commonly developed and rolled out across the various functional areas. These modules address both common training needs, such as customer service, radio protocols and procedures and job specific requirements associated with, for example, venue management and operations, staff supervision and approaches to staff training.

In addition to the training of paid staff is the major task of training volunteers. As with paid staff, volunteers will be required to attend an orientation session. They will also require specific job skills and knowledge to prepare them for the task(s) they have been assigned. If they have been attached to a venue, for example, they will need an understanding of its specific layout and services, the sporting programme held at the venue, revenue policies, and procedures such as those associated with emergencies and crowd control.

How will training be delivered?. As communication technologies develop, the potential delivery options for training in an event context increase. In the case of the Sydney Olympic Games in 2000, only a limited amount of training information was available on the Internet. This situation changed dramatically by the time of the Athens Olympic Games in 2004 when the e-learning project developed for staff and volunteers at this event became the largest such project to be attempted in Greece. Among the various capacities of the technology used in this project, was the ability to record and distribute live presentations to the event's 6500 team leaders as part of their training.

While BOG will certainly employ the Internet as one training delivery mode, issues associated with the distribution and level of usage of this technology will mean that a range of delivery approaches will need to be used. These approaches, which Chinese Government press releases call 'the way of training', will include the use of television broadcasts (a world first for an event), correspondence programmes and face-to-face training in classroom/lecture theatre environments. Valuable practical experience will also be gained at special events and test events, for example, at the 'Good Luck Beijing' test event to be held in November 2007, which will involve some 34 Olympic sports and the use of 46 training venues.

Continued

CASE STUDY BEIJING 2008 – TRAINING TO DELIVER THE 'BEST GAMES EVER'—*CONT'D*

Who will deliver the training?. It is unclear at present who will be responsible for Games time training programmes. BOGOC has the option of keeping the provision of such services in-house or outsourcing them to a training related organisation. In the case of the Sydney 2000 Olympic Games, for example, the official training services supporter was TAFE NSW (the New South Wales government's technical and further education training body). This organisation provided both management and volunteer training programmes as part of a sponsorship arrangement. While acknowledging the lack of certainty in this area at the moment, there would nonetheless appear to be an intent, in the context of volunteers, by BOGOC to use Beijing-based educational institutions (universities, colleges, schools), from which the vast majority of volunteers are expected to come, as training providers. Each institution would be responsible for undertaking training programmes, under BOGOC's directions, for those volunteers sourced from them.

How will volunteer recruitment be managed?. While most volunteers will be drawn from Beijing's colleges, schools and universities, some will come from other sources. These sources will include the general populace, foreigners residing in the city and people from outside Beijing, including:

- co-host cities such as Shanghai and Qingdao
- other Chinese provinces, municipalities and autonomous regions
- Hong Kong
- Macao
- Taiwan
- overseas-based Chinese
- foreign nationals

To attract the required number of volunteers (approximately 70,000), a communications plan has been developed. The first phase of this plan (from July 2005 to July 2006) involved creating interest in volunteering for the Games. It sought to 'sell' the concept of volunteering and its personal and community benefits. The next phase (April 2006–April 2008) is designed to drive Games-time volunteer recruitment. It provides information on volunteer positions, qualification requirements and the application process. Given that as of March 2007 BOGOC had received approximately 379,000 applications from potential volunteers, this stage can be said to have been extremely successful. The final phase will largely involve reporting on the successful efforts of Games volunteers.

Conclusion

As the Beijing Olympics moved into its final planning phase, its organisers must ensure they have thought through a number of key questions that surround the area of training. While there is limited information available as to how BOGOC has answered these questions, the information that is available indicates that it has learnt from prior Games and is developing its own unique approach to ensuring the successful integration of the training function into its overall planning efforts.

Questions

1. What were the key questions BOGOC needed to successfully answer, in order to ensure the success of its staff/volunteer training efforts?
2. Why didn't BOGOC make greater use of technologies such as the Internet in rolling out its Games-time training programme?
3. What specific function does a training needs analysis perform?
4. What are some of the different approaches to training ('the way of training') BOGOC employed?

5. How has BOGOC managed the recruitment and training of the many thousands of volunteers it required?
6. What is the value of undertaking orientation training for both paid and volunteer staff?
7. How did BOGOC cope with the vastly expanded need for training as the Games period approached?

CASE STUDY: THE XVII COMMONWEALTH GAMES 2002 MANCHESTER – A VOLUNTEERING LEGACY

Introduction

In May 2001 a major recruitment programme was launched to fill the 10,000 volunteering roles needed to underpin the delivery of the 2002 Commonwealth Games in Manchester. In order to qualify, applicants had to be available to work for at least 10 days, attend interview and training sessions and have reached 16 years of age by 1 December 2001. In return they would have the opportunity to play an important role at the third largest sporting event in the world, an event which would occupy a unique place in the city's history.

Facing the challenge. Initially there was some concern expressed as to whether it would be possible to fill all the positions. A volunteer programme on this scale was unprecedented in peacetime Britain. Many predicted that the recruitment of 10,000 unpaid workers would prove difficult in a country in which the profile of volunteering was seen primarily in terms of charity shop workers and not part of the nation's wider cultural identity. However, these reservations proved to be totally unfounded as there was a tremendous response from the people of Manchester and the North West (around 80% of those whose applications were successful originated from the North West of England).

In total 22,346 people applied for the 10,311 Games-time roles of which 53% were women and 47% men. Over 56% of applications were received over the Internet, with 70% of people aged 20–24 filling in their forms on-line. Older people preferred the more traditional method of sending their application (around 80% of people 65 and over applied by post). The oldest volunteer was 87 year old Desmond Pastore from Northenden Manchester, who worked as an assistant on the statistics desk at the Rugby 7s tournament.

Aim of the programme. One of the aims of the volunteer programme was to encourage applications from the long term unemployed, ethnic minorities, people from disadvantaged areas and those with disabilities and special needs.

A Pre Volunteer Programme (PVP), part of the NW 2002 Social and Economic Legacy programme, had already been in operation in 23 regeneration areas around the North West since early 2000. The programme offered training, the chance to achieve a qualification in event volunteering and enhanced opportunities for volunteering for the Games itself. During 2001, events and road shows were held across Manchester and the North West to recruit volunteers from the targeted groups.

Once appointed, all volunteers were issued with the Crew 2002 Games uniform which was designed to be distinctive and easily identifiable. The uniform with its purple shell suit and northern style flat cap initially attracted negative comments, but the resulting national media attention, combined with the fact that Coronation Street's Norris Cole regularly donned his outfit during the popular TV show, helped to raise awareness of the Games across Britain.

By the end of the Games, the volunteer uniform became a symbol of the huge contribution made to the event's success by the purple army.

Volunteer roles. The volunteers were perhaps most visible when directing spectators around the city centre or acting as stewards for the sports venues. However, they were involved in many different aspects of the running of the Games in fields as diverse as logistics, medical services, catering and marketing.

Continued

CASE STUDY: THE XVII COMMONWEALTH GAMES 2002 MANCHESTER – A VOLUNTEERING LEGACY—*CONT'D*

The venue which employed the most volunteers was the Games Village (1247), followed by Sports City Plaza (1096) and the City of Manchester Stadium (967). In terms of the supporting infrastructure, transport required the most voluntary staff (2234), with event services next (1314) and security third (940).

City guides provided 281 volunteers to provide a warm welcome, signpost walking routes to the stadium and deliver front line visitor information. Road Events had the largest number of sports event volunteers (just over 200) followed by Athletics (just under 150) and Lawn Bowls (around 80).

The volunteer programme was certainly one of the major success stories of the Commonwealth Games. The friendliness and enthusiasm of the volunteers earned them high praise from athletes, spectators and national media alike; and there is no doubt that they can also claim some credit for the more positive image of Manchester that emerged from the Games.

Volunteer feedback. It is also clear from the testimony of the volunteers themselves that they found their time at the Games to be a most enjoyable and rewarding experience. Indeed comments such as 'the best time of my life' and 'amazing experience' are frequently repeated in their descriptions of how they felt to be part of 'Crew 2002'. For a few volunteers their Games experience proved to be the passport to longer term employment, whilst others were happy just to have been taken part in such a prestigious event. However the closing event at the City of Manchester stadium did not signify the end of the volunteer programme but rather the beginning.

Post Games Volunteer Programme. After the games were over, volunteers from the North West and participants in the PVP scheme were given the opportunity to take part in the Post Games Volunteer Programme (PGVP). This project ran from January 2003 until March 2005.

The aim of this project was to respond to the upsurge in interest and the positive experience of volunteering. Games volunteers became involved in community projects as well as major events including the Salford Triathlon and Great Manchester Run. The project also offered support to volunteers who were seeking to gain new skills and experience or looking for a route back into employment. The summer of 2003 saw the volunteers back on the streets as city guides providing a very northern welcome to the 70,000 Italians in Manchester for the UEFA Champions League Final at Old Trafford. More than 150 events across the region including the London Triathlon in 2004 and the World Paralympics in 2005 have benefitted from the volunteers' continuing commitment.

In April 2005 the volunteering legacy continued to run as the project was mainstreamed into Manchester City Council's structure as Manchester Event Volunteers. Over 2500 volunteers are now registered on the database. Manchester Event Volunteering is open to both Commonwealth Games volunteers and new members.

For further details about the 2002 Manchester Commonwealth Games legacy, please visit web.archive.org/web/20071022064134/www.gameslegacy.com. The Manchester Event Volunteer programme can be contacted on enquiry@mev.org.uk. The M2002 records and archive are now held at Central Library Manchester.

By Manchester City Council's Games Xchange, the information legacy programme.

Questions

1. How can the success of the Manchester 2002 Commonwealth Games Volunteer Programme be measured?
2. What role does recognition play in the success of the events volunteer programme?
3. What functions does a volunteer training manual perform?
4. Can you suggest any additional means by which the legacy of the volunteer programme can be continued?

Marketing planning for events

11

LEARNING OBJECTIVES

After studying this chapter, you should be able to:

- describe how the marketing concept can be applied to festivals and events,
- understand how event consumers can be segmented into markets,
- understand the consumer decision process for festivals and events,
- apply the principles of services marketing in creating strategies and tactics for events and festivals,
- plan the event 'service–product' experience, including its programming and packaging,
- develop event pricing strategies or other entry options for events,
- create strategies for place/distribution, physical setting and event processes that respond to consumer needs and
- apply the knowledge generated into an effective and efficient marketing plan.

INTRODUCTION

This chapter examines a strategic approach to festival and event marketing planning, and how the event manager carries out all the marketing planning activities necessary to achieve the event's objectives, as set out in the event's strategic plan. Over the past few years, an increasing number of authors have demonstrated the importance of understanding the marketing domain applied to events (Allen, 2004; Davidson and Rogers, 2006; Hoyle, 2002; Masterman and Wood, 2005) in addition to the established marketing body of knowledge (Blythe, 2009; Brassington and Pettitt, 2006; Dibb, Simkin, Pride and Ferrel, 2006; Hoffman, Bateson, Wood and Kenyon, 2009; Jobber, 2007; Kotler, Wong, Saunders and Armstrong, 2008; Kotler, Bowen and Makens, 2010; Kotler and Armstrong, 2010). To begin, it is useful to explore the concept of marketing as an event management function.

WHAT IS MARKETING?

Marketing is a term often used, yet there is no standard universal definition. The Chartered Institute of Marketing (CIM, 2005) defines marketing as 'the management process responsible for identifying, anticipating and satisfying customer

Events Management. DOI: 10.1016/B978-1-85617-818-1.10011-8

requirements profitably'. In simple terms, marketing is concerned with satisfying consumer needs and wants by exchanging goods, services or ideas for something of value. More often, we are not just purchasing products, we are buying experiences (as we do with events and festivals) or adopting new ideas — for example, participation in extreme sports or new theatre forms. We might offer our money in exchange for a concert experience, but for some types of marketing exchanges — for example, community festivals — the time of the consumer to attend may be the only exchange.

Kotler et al. (2008, p. 7) suggest that marketing is 'A social and managerial process by which individuals and groups obtain what they need and want through creating and exchanging products and value with others'. In effect, marketing has evolved well beyond early views of the marketing concept (Perrault, Cannon, McCarthy, 2008) as meeting customer needs through decisions about the four Ps — product, place, price and promotion.

While it is agreed that the consumer is the primary focus of marketing, changes over time have reshaped the marketing function for events. These include:

- growth in the number and diversity of leisure and business-related services (including events) that require different marketing approaches from those for goods;
- recognition of the unique marketing requirements of not-for-profit organisations (typical of many festivals);
- the increasing importance of stakeholders — for example, the community, government, investors/sponsors, media and suppliers of public services, such as the police and the ambulance service, who can be as influential as consumers in affecting the success and organisational survival;
- advances in technology such as the Internet, the linking of information and communication technologies and other innovations that affect the marketing of services, including events, and
- internationalisation, which has created global opportunities to enter new markets — for example, the touring and staging of events in offshore locations and the ability to distribute event services to an international market.

As a result of these changes, marketers of events and festivals have the benefit of new knowledge in services marketing, stakeholder management, customer relationship management (CRM) and e-marketing to help shape their strategies.

There is another definition of the phrase 'event marketing' that could confuse readers, which is the use of events to promote a product or service to a defined target market. An example of this common occurrence is mobile communications companies using music events to promote their products. This chapter, however, is concerned with the actions taken by the event manager to achieve the event's marketing objectives, such as attendee satisfaction, revenue or participation numbers. Therefore, event marketing can be defined as the process by which event managers and marketers gain an understanding of their potential consumers' characteristics and needs in order to produce, price, promote and distribute an event experience that meets these needs, and the objectives of the event.

Increasingly, this knowledge helps the event or festival marketer to perform the marketing role defined by Hall (1997, p. 136):

> *that function of event management that can keep in touch with the event's participants and visitors (consumers), read their needs and motivations, develop products that meet these needs, and build a communication program which expresses the event's purpose and objectives.*

At a practical level, the following list shows the marketing activities that an event marketing manager may undertake to produce a successful festival or event:

- Analyse the needs of the target market to establish the design of the event experience and the way in which it will be delivered.
- Predict how many people will attend the event and the times that different groups or market segments will attend.
- Research any competing events that could satisfy similar needs, to devise a unique selling proposition (USP) for the event that enables it to be differentiated from similar leisure activities.
- Estimate the price or value that visitors are willing to exchange to attend an event — for example, ticket price or donation.
- Decide on the type and quantity of promotional activity (otherwise known as marketing communication), including the media mix and messages that will reach the audiences of the event.
- Consider how the choice and design of venue(s) and the methods of ticket distribution fit with the needs of attendees.
- Establish the metrics to judge the degree of success of the event in achieving its marketing objectives.

All these activities, vital for a successful event, are part of the marketing function. This chapter explores how event marketing managers seek insights into consumers of their festival/event and the event marketing environment before developing their marketing strategies and plans. We discuss ways in which event managers can apply theories of marketing, including services marketing theories and CRM, to develop their event marketing approach.

THE NEED FOR MARKETING

Some critics of marketing argue that some cultural festivals and events should not be concerned with target markets and satisfying market needs, but should simply focus on innovation, creativity and dissemination of new art forms. The argument is that consumers' needs are based on what they know, so consumers are less likely to embrace innovative or avant-garde cultural experiences. Dickman (1997, p. 685) highlights the reluctance of some administrators 'to even use the word [marketing], believing that it suggested "selling out" artistic principles in favour of finding the lowest common denominator'.

Erroneously, this view assumes that marketers, by adopting a consumer focus, respond only to the expressed needs of event visitors. In reality, sound marketing research can unveil the latent needs of consumers that only innovative events can satisfy. Often, a distrust of marketing is based on a misunderstanding of marketing principles and techniques. This attitude can be self-defeating for the following reasons:

- The use of marketing principles and techniques gives event managers a framework for decision making that should result in events that not only reflect innovation and creativity but also cater for market segments that seek novelty or the excitement of something new.
- Sponsoring bodies need reassurance that their sponsorship is linking their brand with their target markets. Sound marketing practices give marketers the ability to convince sponsors that a festival or event is the right marketing investment for them.
- Local and national government financially assist many festivals and events. Governments usually fund only those events whose management can demonstrate some expertise in marketing planning and management.
- Event stakeholders, such as the community, environmentalists, and providers of public services, such as the police, political leaders, and consumers, are critical in today's societal marketing approach. A societal marketing approach (Kotler et al., 2008) emphasises the importance of society's well-being alongside satisfaction of the needs and wants of event or festival markets.
- Consumers, particularly those who reside in major cities, have an enormous range of leisure activities on which they spend their disposable income. This means that a festival or event, which, by definition, can be categorised as a leisure activity, will attract only those who expect to satisfy at least one of their perceived needs. Therefore, any festival or event needs to be designed to satisfy identified needs of its target market. Failure to do this usually results in an event that is irrelevant to the needs of its target market and does not meet its objectives.

All festivals and events, therefore, can benefit from understanding marketing techniques and having some experience in applying those techniques to satisfy the identified needs of a target market. Failure to understand the role of marketing, including its societal perspective, can lead to dissatisfied consumers and a weak relationship with stakeholders who can strongly influence an event's long-term survival.

Events as 'service experiences'

The marketing concept is just as applicable to a leisure service such as an event as it is to any other product. In fact, it could be even more so, as a leisure service, like other services, is intangible, variable, perishable and inseparable. Pine and Gilmour (1999) argued that we have moved beyond simply products or services into engaging or immersing customers in experiences, while Berridge (2007) explored how experiences can be controlled by design. We are exposed to many well-known brand names in leisure services that have been marketing success stories, and some of these are events — for example, the Moscow State Circus, the Edinburgh Tattoo, the Aintree Grand National and the Glastonbury Festival.

Events as services differ from products in a number of ways. What is different about services is that we must experience them to consume them — delivery and consumption of an event are inseparable, happening simultaneously in most cases. Given this immediacy of service consumption, the way in which an event is experienced can vary daily or each year the event or festival is staged. The challenge for event managers and marketers is to try to manage these, smooth out any variations in quality and ensure that there is an immediate recovery where poor service occurs. Because people are central to the delivery of most services (including the staff or vendors at an event, as well as its visitors), managing the quality of an event experience depends on managing its human delivery and the behaviour of its consumers — that is, people who attend an event affect the level of enjoyment of other visitors.

Other key differences of services like events are that they are intangible and, unlike a product, cannot be owned — that is, we do not take the experience home with us. While a skateboard has physical qualities (we can examine it for its style, shape, texture and colour), events or festivals have only experiential qualities. There is nothing tangible for us to pick up, touch, feel or try before purchasing tickets or after the event (other than event merchandise or mementos that can jog the memory of the event experience). Event marketers add some tangibility via promotional posters, event programmes or compact discs of the artist's work, but the primary purchase is an intangible experience. The marketer has the challenge, therefore, of providing potential visitors with advance clues about the nature of the event experience.

It is generally agreed (see, for example, Lovelock and Wirtz, 2011) that the intangibility of services makes them much harder to evaluate than goods, and this is also true for events. Many special events also have some credence qualities — characteristics that we, as consumers, do not have enough knowledge or experience to understand or evaluate. For certain types of events, real-time interpretation (subtitles at the opera or expert commentary at a sports game) and post-purchase interpretation (views expressed by commentators or critics) enhance the consumer's total experience.

For marketers, a further challenge is the perishability of the event experience — for example, seats unsold at today's football game or tonight's concert will not be available for sale again. While we can store an unsold product on the shelf, we cannot store today's unused opportunities for festival attendance until tomorrow or another date. Events are delivered in real time. If the weather is poor on the day of the festival, unsold tickets cannot be retrieved, and food and beverage sales for that day are lost. This means that event demand and supply and the factors that may affect it must be well understood, so that seating, food and beverage, and other vital supplies to an event are not wasted.

The five key characteristics of services discussed here — inseparability, variations in quality, intangibility, lack of ownership and perishability — each have implications for an event's services marketing mix discussed later in this chapter.

THE NEXUS BETWEEN EVENT MARKETING AND MANAGEMENT

Given the differences between services and goods, there is a need to understand the tight links between an event's marketing, its people management (human skills and expertise) and its operations management (for example, site layout, ticketing, queuing, sound and lighting, and other functions). While Chapters 10, 14 and 15 explore these topics, it is important to grasp just how closely the event's marketer needs to work with other managers to ensure consumer needs and expectations are fully met.

When we attend an event, our entire experience can be enhanced by the spectacle of stage design or lighting, special sound effects or ways in which the venue is designed to bring the performance to the audience. Our experience can also be marred by poor acoustics or incorrect advice from venue staff about parking or entry to the event. In their study of theatre event satisfaction, Hede et al. (2003) used an expert panel to identify event attributes that consumers evaluate — for example, vision from the seats, theatre ambience, quality of acting and singing, costumes and service at the theatre.

An event's management plan must be congruent with its marketing plan and vice versa. All plans have one function — to achieve the event's objectives by focusing on its target market's needs. It is important, therefore, to create a synergy between marketing, human resource and operations management — a relationship called the services trinity (Figure 11.1).

THE ROLE OF STRATEGIC MARKETING PLANNING

Before describing the strategic marketing planning process, it is useful to think about what 'strategy' means. In the world of business and in event management and marketing, strategy can be interpreted as how an organisation (or event) marshals and uses its resources to achieve its business objectives within its ever changing political, economic, sociocultural and technological environment. Chapter 4 on event planning outlined this process. In this chapter, the strategy process is linked to the marketing function to show the framework in which event managers develop marketing objectives and strategies to satisfy consumer needs.

Some key points about strategy are that it is:

- long term, rather than short term — once a marketing strategy is decided, it can be wasteful of resources and disruptive to an event to change the strategic direction.

FIGURE 11.1 The event services trinity

Careful thought is required before deciding on what marketing strategies should be used to achieve event objectives.

- not another word for tactics — strategy is the broad overall direction that an event takes to achieve its objectives, while tactics are the detailed manoeuvres or programmes that carry out the strategy. Tactics can be changed as market conditions change, but the overall direction — the strategy — remains constant (at least for the planning period).
- based on careful analysis of internal resources and external environments — it is not a hasty reaction to changes in the market.
- essential to survival — well-considered thought out marketing strategies enable event managers to achieve the objectives of their event.

While the logic of deciding on a long-term strategy appears sound, festivals and events, like other organisations, vary in the extent to which their strategies are deliberate or emergent processes (Mintzberg, 1994). In particular, festivals that begin their life as community celebrations run by local volunteers are less likely to have a deliberate strategy selection process. It is unlikely that the Glastonbury Festival, for example, commenced with a formal marketing vision and process that led to the strong brand image that the event enjoys today. It can be wrong, therefore, to assume failure will result from implicit (rather than explicit) strategies or those that simply emerge from the hundreds of decisions made by organisers in staging an event. However, a holistic vision of an event's direction and the fit between the marketing strategy and vision is a desirable starting point. The following definition reflects the essence of the strategy concept for the practising event marketer: 'Strategic event marketing is the process by which an event organisation aligns business and marketing resources available to the event organisation with the environments in which they occur, in order to fulfil the needs of event consumers and to achieve the event's objectives.'

Based on this definition, the starting points for any strategic marketing process should be the long-term objective and mission or vision of the event organisers, which is usually arrived at during an event's corporate strategic planning process. Figure 11.2 shows the forces that influence these platforms of the strategic marketing process.

The mission is defined, according to Johnson et al. (2005, p. 13) as 'the overall purpose of the organisation, which … is in line with the values and expectations of major stakeholders, and concerned with the scope and boundaries of the organisation'. It answers the question of 'what are we here for?', and it is the starting point for all planning activities.

As Figure 11.2 demonstrates, both the stakeholders of the event and the personal values of its organisers are critical influences. For example, Bath Festivals Trust was created in 1993 in order to develop Bath as a Festival City. The overall mission of the Trust is 'to contribute to the development of Bath as a European Festivals City by providing an accessible arts programme of the highest quality, encouraging participation and offering entertainment, challenging and enriching experiences to the people of Bath and North East Somerset and visitors to the area' (Bath Festivals Trust, 2005). The vision and values of festival organisers Imaginate have had a profound effect on all aspects of the Bank of Scotland Imaginate Festival, a theatre festival for children. Imaginate's aim is, 'that children and young people, aged up to 18, have regular access to a diverse range of high quality performing arts activity, from home and abroad, that will entertain, enrich, teach and inspire them' (Imaginate, 2010). The festival in May 2010 attracted over 15,000 children aged 3 to 18 years, their teachers and their families and is the largest performing arts festival for

FIGURE 11.2 Constructing the mission

children and young people in the UK (Events Edinburgh, 2010). Other events present more of an event-focused mission — for example, the Scottish Traditional Boat Festival 2010 'has set its sights on helping bring the great traditional skills of the past into the future for folk of all ages, the young in particular (The Scottish Traditional Boat Festival, 2005). Some events and festivals also state the philosophical principles that underpin their mission and guide event management and marketing. Clapham Festival of Music and the Arts organisers express philosophies that recognise the role of arts in education, the prevention of violence, racism and social exclusion (The Clapham Festival of Music and the Arts, 2010). In effect, an event's philosophies and mission statement are the important foundation for determining the marketing approach that best reflects the interests of its stakeholders and achieves its marketing objectives. Vision and mission have been discussed in detail in Chapter 6.

Stages in the strategic marketing planning process for events include research and analysis of the macro- and micro-environment, including the competitive, political, economic, sociocultural and technological (C-PEST) forces; research into the psychology of event consumers; segmentation, targeting and positioning; setting of marketing objectives; and decision making about generic marketing strategies and the event's services marketing mix. Figure 11.3 shows a recommended framework for developing the event marketing strategy.

EVENT MARKETING RESEARCH

Before the marketing strategy is developed, research is usually conducted at (1) the macro-level, to understand external forces affecting the event and its markets, and (2) the micro-level, to gain insight into the event's existing and potential consumers and any strategies previously used by the organisers. A range of event marketing information can be obtained from primary and secondary sources to guide the strategy process.

To begin, a search of secondary data on macro-level trends affecting leisure consumption and the competitive environment for events can be drawn from on-line and off-line sources. Some useful information sources are:

- government statistics and reports (national and region statistics on the consumption of festivals and events, arts and sports);
- media coverage (about the events sector and particular events or festivals in the region);
- industry magazines, such as Conference & Incentive Travel (www.citmagazine. co.uk), Conference News (www.conference-news.co.uk), Event (www. eventmagazine.co.uk) and Meetings & Incentive Travel (www.meetpie.com), and
- historical and current data from other events, festivals and event organisers. A content analysis of the websites of festivals, events and event production agencies can be a valuable research technique. Jack Morton, which directed the opening

FIGURE 11.3 The strategic event marketing process

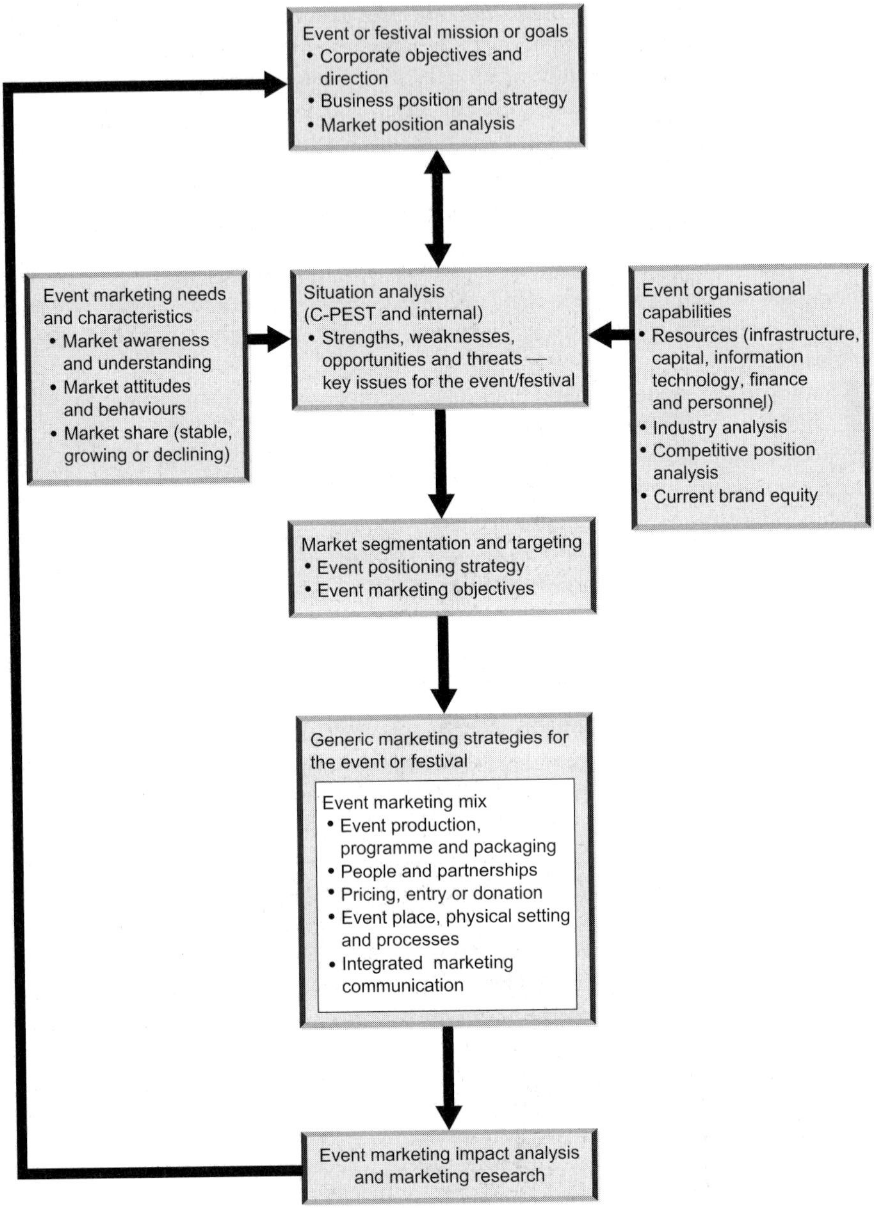

```
                    ┌─────────────────────────────────┐
                    │ Event or festival mission or goals│
                    │ • Corporate objectives and        │
                    │   direction                       │
                    │ • Business position and strategy  │
                    │ • Market position analysis        │
                    └─────────────────────────────────┘
                                    ↕
┌──────────────────────┐  ┌─────────────────────┐  ┌──────────────────────────┐
│ Event marketing needs│  │ Situation analysis  │  │ Event organisational     │
│ and characteristics  │  │ (C-PEST and internal)│ │ capabilities             │
│ • Market awareness   │→ │ • Strengths,        │← │ • Resources (infrastructure,│
│   and understanding  │  │   weaknesses,       │  │   capital, information    │
│ • Market attitudes   │  │   opportunities and │  │   technology, finance     │
│   and behaviours     │  │   threats —         │  │   and personnel)         │
│ • Market share (stable,│ │   key issues for the│  │ • Industry analysis      │
│   growing or declining)│ │   event/festival    │  │ • Competitive position   │
└──────────────────────┘  └─────────────────────┘  │   analysis               │
                                    ↓               │ • Current brand equity   │
                    ┌─────────────────────────────┐ └──────────────────────────┘
                    │ Market segmentation and     │
                    │ targeting                   │
                    │ • Event positioning strategy│
                    │ • Event marketing objectives│
                    └─────────────────────────────┘
                                    ↓
                    ┌─────────────────────────────┐
                    │ Generic marketing strategies for│
                    │ the event or festival       │
                    │  ┌────────────────────────┐ │
                    │  │ Event marketing mix     │ │
                    │  │ • Event production,     │ │
                    │  │   programme and packaging│ │
                    │  │ • People and partnerships│ │
                    │  │ • Pricing, entry or donation│ │
                    │  │ • Event place, physical setting│
                    │  │   and processes         │ │
                    │  │ • Integrated marketing  │ │
                    │  │   communication         │ │
                    │  └────────────────────────┘ │
                    └─────────────────────────────┘
                                    ↓
                    ┌─────────────────────────────┐
                    │ Event marketing impact analysis│
                    │ and marketing research      │
                    └─────────────────────────────┘
```

and closing ceremonies of the 2004 Athens Olympics, Imagination and Euro RSCG Skybridge, the subject of case studies elsewhere in this book, are among many event companies whose websites offer a window to new and innovative event types.

A greater depth of understanding of macro-level issues, such as event funding by national or local government and the sponsorship environment, the seasonal saturation of events, the potential for oversupply of particular types of event, and new technologies for event delivery, can also be obtained through in-depth interviews with opinion leaders — for example, long-standing event directors or producers, public sector event agencies and academics — if they are willing to talk. Careful observation of the marketing of other events can give useful insights into these topics.

At the micro-level, event marketers can use a mix of research techniques to gain insights into consumer segmentation and targeting. Past event reports that show vendor participation, event visitation, situational issues influencing past attendance and event satisfaction are desired resources, but are not always available. Often, established members of the event organising body (including volunteers) become a rich source of informal advice about the event's consumption trends. Furthermore, more specific insights into existing event consumers can reliably be obtained from a mix of qualitative research (either in-depth interviews or a series of focus groups with 8–10 people across different segments of the market) and quantitative research (on-site intercept surveys or post-event research). For intercept surveys that are commonly undertaken at entry or exit points of the event, to be statistically valid a randomly selected sample of at least 200 attendees (Getz, 2005) is recommended to obtain meaningful marketing information. In this context, 'random' means all event attendees have an equal chance of being selected for the survey. As customers exit the event, for example, every tenth customer could be asked to participate.

Data related to the visitors' demographics, motives, satisfaction and intention to revisit the event (where applicable) are generally sought. The data analysis can be manually performed for a small-scale survey that seeks only descriptive data about event consumers, but a statistical software package such as PASW Statistics (formerly known as SPSS) offers a deeper understanding of relationships between variables such as attendance motives and satisfaction. Data mining (analysis of data already stored by the event organisation from previous events) is another useful tool to establish demographics and motivations of consumers. However, do not succumb to paralysis through analysis. Market research is an aid to competent event marketing, it does not replace it.

Analysing event environments

Strategic marketing is a planning tool that emphasises on thorough analyses. The marketer's own sense of judgement is not enough to make good strategic decisions (Rao and Steckel, 1998). Astute marketing decisions emerge from a thorough analysis of competitor activities, the political, economic, sociocultural and technological (C-PEST) environments in which the event occurs and a rigorous analysis of the event organisation's internal resources to establish the organisation's strategic capability, in other words, what the event organisation is capable of with its available resources.

The C-PEST analysis

Figure 11.4 depicts each of the analyses contained in the C-PEST framework. Note that the global entertainment environment is included because changes in the world of artistic or sporting endeavour need careful monitoring by event and festival managers. Such trend analyses are done for a good reason: to establish opportunities and threats for the festival/event and its management. Using this process, organisers can shape marketing strategies to capitalise on emerging entertainment opportunities and neutralise threats.

In conducting environmental analyses, it is easy to become overwhelmed by potential influences on the effective marketing of the event or festival. Stick to what is most critical to the event or festival in developing its marketing strategy in the

FIGURE 11.4 Components of the environment analysis

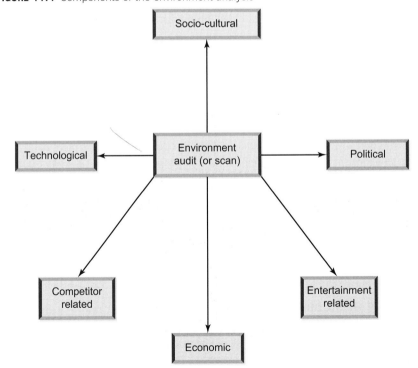

current environment. To illustrate the C-PEST framework, the situation of the Edinburgh International Festival is considered. Being over 60 years old, the Edinburgh International Festival is a 3-week celebration of dance, theatre, visual arts, opera and music, which energises the city each summer.

Competitive analysis

In describing competitor analysis and strategy, Porter's (1990) seminal work identified four elements that affect competition within an industry (Figure 11.5). This analytic tool is used to understand both industry-level and company-level competition, and it can also guide festival and event managers in their marketing decision making.

To begin, festival or event suppliers include the venues, artists and physical resources (such as lighting and staging) needed to produce an event. Unless other artistic festivals occurring at the same time depend on these suppliers, no major difficulties usually emerge with event supply. However, given that the mission of the Edinburgh International Festival is to be the most exciting, accessible and innovative performing arts festival in the world, the organisers will liaise with suppliers of highly valued artists who have the power to increase talent costs or specify the conditions under which the artists will perform. Here, a relational strategy of building long-term alliances with agents and other festivals is important to ensure a continuity of supply at reasonable prices. This relational strategy could also be

FIGURE 11.5 The four competitive forces

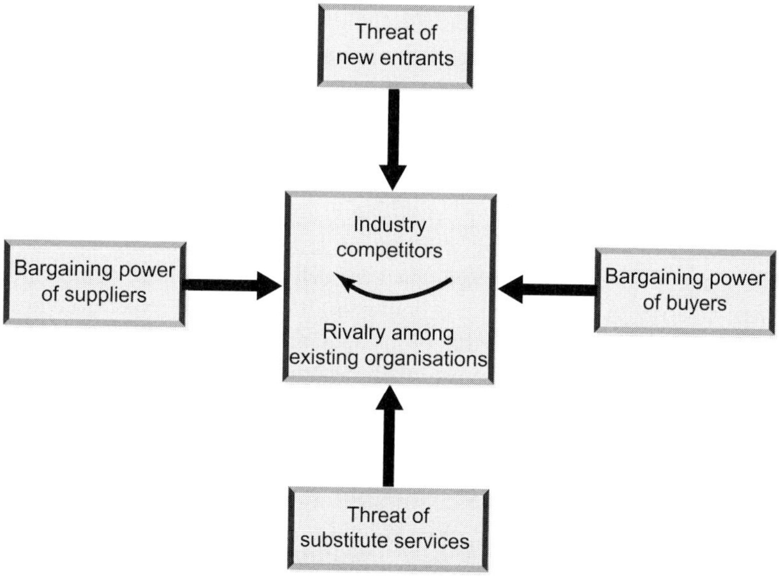

(Source: Porter, 1990)

applied in forging close ties with venues such as King's Theatre, so that the best venues for the festival's events are available and affordable. While some event suppliers such as venues and entertainment agents can wield considerable power, relationship marketing strategies help to address this power imbalance.

Because the buyers of the Edinburgh International Festival are large in number, little power is concentrated in their hands. Their only power is their price sensitivity to the festival's offerings. Given the festival's objective of providing arts of the highest possible standard, an end result could be higher ticket prices. If consumers decide that a particular offering does not give value for money, and they stay away in droves, the festival organisers and sponsors could suffer embarrassment and a loss of money. Consequently, the role of the marketer is to carefully identify (through observation, experience and market research) the price level at which this sensitivity could arise. In addition, with the mission of increasing accessibility, initiatives are also in place to encourage new audiences through tickets available at lower prices, for example, with tickets available at 50% off for under 18 years and students and with customers under 26 years able to access £8 on-the-day tickets.

A threat of new entrants exists if there is some potential for market share to be lost to another festival or event offering similar experiences. The history of events within the UK is littered with examples of once hugely popular festivals or events that now no longer exist or have been rejuvenated. For example, 1998 saw the end of the once popular Phoenix due to lack of ticket sales, and Reading Festival (established as an alternative to mainstream music events) has over the years broadened its musical appeal to incorporate mainstream music (Mintel, 2000). If there are few barriers to new entrants, this can be a real threat to the festival's viability. However, festivals such as the Edinburgh International Festival depend on grants and sponsors for much of their funding, so the barriers to entry are quite high. These entry barriers remain high while major sponsors (including government and corporate partners) are satisfied with the results of the festival — that is, so long as the funding agencies' objectives are met and the organisers' strategy for sponsorship management (Chapter 12) ensures their business results are achieved.

The notion of substitutes for an event or festival is based on the marketing premise that consumers are purchasing not a service but a package of benefits — in this case, an array of stimulating entertainment. If a substitute experience provides entertainment that is more satisfying or just as satisfying in the same time frame at a lower cost, then the threat of substitution becomes very real. A commonly cited strategy to avoid this threat is to offer a unique event experience to a well-defined target market that is not readily substituted. For the Edinburgh International Festival, the scale and sophistication of festival programming, together with the history and reputation of the festival, mean that it would not be easily or quickly replaced by another event on the city's calendar. Yet, the ongoing proliferation of events and festivals, and the 'copy cating' that typifies services (including events), is a growing challenge for event marketers. 'Me too' events occurring on a smaller scale at other times of the year may have little short-term effect on attendance, but a gradual dilution of the existing event's USP (the aspect that best distinguishes it in the marketplace) is one potential outcome of new entrants with similar event offerings.

Political environment

All levels of government can be active players in producing and sponsoring events and offering event development grants. For the Edinburgh International Festival, both the Scottish Parliament and the City of Edinburgh Council, together with EventScotland and other agencies, have played an active role in funding/sponsorship and venue supply. Strategies to maintain this involvement are necessary, especially if a change of government or minister occurs. As well as identifying the nature of government support, organisers need to take steps to understand new legislation or changes in the regulatory environment that affect event delivery — for example, rising public liability costs and regulations related to licensing, racing, gaming, lotteries and so on.

Economic environment

Some issues that have an impact on event marketing strategies are the buoyancy of the economy, foreign exchange rates, interest rates, employment rates, growth/reduction in household disposable incomes, and the government's fiscal policy (taxation, for example). The value of the pound compared to the currency of other nations, for example, can rise or lower the cost of attracting foreign artists to the Edinburgh International Festival. Methods of combating economic challenges that affect the festival's mission are subject to continual review by the event management. For example, if the pound suddenly devalued (as happened in the latter years of the past decade), the cost of international artists would increase. Therefore, the product strategy might change to focus on more UK-based artists, yet the UK would also potentially be more appealing for international travellers.

Sociocultural environment

Factors of a social or cultural nature that affect event marketing strategies include the size and variety of cultural/subcultural groups in the event's target market; changes in lifestyle, including work–leisure patterns; changes in demography; changes in entertainment demand; and changes in education levels and household structures. For example, during the late 1980s/early 1990s, the increase in popularity of dance music and its related culture led to an increased demand for illegal dance events, commonly known as 'raves'. Interest in these illegal gatherings diminished after the mainstream nightclubs organised events to cater for this new market, including high-profile venues, such as the late Hacienda in Manchester, that went on to enter the folklore and legend of dance music. These early developments led to the branded dance events and clubs, such as Ministry of Sound in London, Cream in Liverpool, Gatecrasher in Sheffield and the Back to

Basics concept in Leeds. Organisers of arts festivals might observe that women aged 18–30 years are more outwardly mobile, are less tied to child rearing than ever before and have more time and income to participate in events. A slightly higher proportion of females than males has been seen among attendees at various festivals — for example, research undertaken for Arts Council Northern Ireland (Stephenson, 2005) found that 56% of attendees at arts or cultural events were female. At The Town & Country Festival 2004 at Stoneleigh Park, the split was even more pronounced with 62% female visitors (Haymarket Land Events LLP, 2005). A concentration of women in the workforce and increased travel by retirees has also contributed to a declining volunteer base for events and festivals (Cordingly, 1999).

Technological environment

Changes in technology present both opportunities and challenges for event organisers. In particular, the use of the World Wide Web, e-mail marketing (including e-newsletters), mobile phone-based web browsing, social media (Web 2.0) and a mix of on-line and off-line event participation is now prevalent and is discussed in depth in Chapter 12. The event website serves as a diverse branding tool for festivals and events, with opportunities for consumer interaction with event performers/players, up-to-the-minute event results and replays, and on-line recognition of event sponsors. For the Harrogate International Festival, organisers use web pages to provide previews of the events; promote major sponsors; provide news updates, local information and details about the education programme; and give current news about recruitment for event volunteers. On analysing the technological environment, event marketers should evaluate the advantages and disadvantages of all forms of technology. Direct marketing via SMS messaging on mobile phones, for example, has become a popular event marketing tool, both before and during events. For those events with few resources and no permanent staff, the ability to build and maintain an effective website and stay abreast of new technology can be daunting. Yet, the failure to update a festival website on a regular basis or respond to on-line enquiries in a timely fashion can devalue the brand in the eyes of event visitors and sponsors. Marketers analysing their technological environment should note any opportunities for low-cost, technical support that could be available to their event or festival. And of course, the Internet provides much efficiency by using electronic distribution of tickets to an event.

Other, more esoteric uses of the Internet include 'buzz tracking'. For a fee, a company monitors blogs to ascertain how and in what way a product such as an event is being discussed. With more than 30 million blogs now in existence and numbers doubling each year (McDermott, 2006), this form of communication can create a positive or negative buzz about an event of which an event manager should be aware. Another is the concept of co-creation (Rice, 2007), where consumers communicate electronically with event management to help create the event product by means of their input. It is not commonly used now, but it might have a major influence on future events.

Entertainment environment

Entertainment is characterised by constant change as new ways of expression are developed, through new artistic forms or new types of sporting endeavour. The festival or event director generally tries to offer new experiences to consumers, to balance the familiar and novel event components. Trend analysis in the entertainment environment can be done via desk research and travel to centres of artistic innovation or places where emerging sports are practised (certainly a fun part of the job). While most events and festival organisers do not take an annual 'ideas tour' to exotic places to construct their marketing plan, they actively observe entertainment trends all year around. A good understanding of event innovations is also gained from reading professional and popular journals, networking with industry colleagues and travelling to trade fairs and exhibitions. Again, a key purpose of this analysis is to align the event's marketing strategies with opportunities and strengths, and to minimise the impacts of any threats and weaknesses.

Marketing internal resource analysis

Another vital step in developing the marketing strategy is an assessment of the event's internal resources. Classic economists categorise the resources available to an entrepreneur as land, labour and capital. In event or festival organisations, the resources needed are human resources, physical resources and financial resources.

Human resources

The event marketer analyses the number and type of staff and volunteers available, the particular skill sets required to produce the event, the costs of employing people, and innovative ways in which people can contribute to the event's success. An analysis of the Edinburgh International Festival would show that the festival's directors have been individuals with a high profile since the festival's inception. As a result, a lynchpin of the marketing communication strategy is the use of the director as the public face of the festival who features strongly in media releases and interviews. Promoting a festival through its senior producers/directors and organising through word of mouth by staff and volunteers can also minimise the cost of an event's marketing communication campaign. The Edinburgh Festival Fringe is an example of a festival that has capitalised on word-of-mouth marketing over the years through its participants and audiences. This was taken a stage further in 2005 by tapping into word of mouth of the loyal body of event-goers through implementing a show rating system using mobile phone texts, based on a unique number allocated to each of the 1800 shows (Ferguson, 2005).

Physical resources

For an event, physical resources can include ownership of a venue (although this is rare). More often, they include computer hardware and software, desktop publishing equipment, access to venues at competitive rates and use of conference rooms in buildings of some significance. For example, the use of event management software capable of supplying timely data on all aspects of the festival would be a physical resource strength. A far less tangible resource is the festival's brand equity (public awareness and attitudes towards the event built over a longer period). It is fair to assume that community goodwill towards the Edinburgh International Festival has become a valued resource.

Financial resources

Without access to suitable finance, no event marketing strategy can be put into place. Current access to funds or a demonstrated ability to acquire capital is an obvious strength for any event. This access includes the ongoing involvement of government and corporate sponsorship funds. With the direct involvement of the local government through City of Edinburgh Council and the Scottish Arts Council, the patronage of Her Majesty the Queen, the inclusion of representatives of the City of Edinburgh Council on the festival board, and its corporate sponsors, the Edinburgh International Festival relies on a well-established resource base, though this is not taken for granted as noted in the case study in Chapter 9. Adequate financial resources or backing for events and festivals often simultaneously depends on the strengths of its partnerships (a key reason for this element featuring in the event marketing mix). The adequacy or otherwise of financial resources has a significant impact on the marketing strategies and tactics available to the marketer.

The SWOT analysis

Once the C-PEST and the internal resource audit are completed, an analysis of strengths, weaknesses, opportunities and threats (SWOT) can be conducted. This summary of the critical issues identified through the C-PEST and internal resources analyses (Johnson et al., 2008) enables the event marketer to take advantage of the event's opportunities and strengths, improve weaknesses, negate threats and, just as importantly, have a sound basis for establishing marketing objectives and strategies for the event. This task is made easier if all the data collected are summarised into no more than 10 points for each section of the SWOT analysis.

THE EVENT CONSUMER'S DECISION-MAKING PROCESS

Understanding the consumer's decision-making process for events and festivals is aided by the following PIECE acronym:

- problem recognition – the difference between someone's existing state and his/her desired state relative to leisure consumption,
- information search – an internal and/or external search; limited or extensive search processes for leisure (including event) solutions,
- evaluation and selection of leisure alternatives,
- choosing whether to attend an event and which optional purchases to make at the event or festival and
- evaluation of the post-event experience.

Reflecting this PIECE process, the consumer identifies a need that may be satisfied by attending an event or other leisure experiences, searches for information about such an experience in different media (the Internet, entertainment section of newspapers, the radio, magazines, friends and relatives) and then evaluates the alternatives available. Potential consumers examine how the leisure experience compares with a list of the attributes they most desire. Event-goers may want to improve family ties, so they attend a local community festival that all members of the family can enjoy. Alternatively, they may be looking for a novel or innovative event to satisfy their curiosity. After experiencing (or 'consuming') the event, they re-evaluate the experience for its quality of service and its capacity to satisfy their needs.

Problem recognition

For would-be event or festival consumers, problem recognition means that a difference exists between what they would like to experience and what they have to satisfy that need (Neal, Quester and Hawkins, 2002). The central starting point for this problem recognition is the existence of one or more needs that may be satisfied by attending a festival or event. Events and festivals fulfil physiological needs (exercise, relaxation, sexual engagement), interpersonal needs (social interaction) and/or personal needs (enhanced knowledge, new experiences, fulfilment of fantasies) (Getz, 1991, 2005). How quickly consumers decide whether to attend an event partly depends on their event purchase involvement – that is, the level of interest in the purchase process, once it has been triggered (Neal et al., 2002). Some events are spontaneous, low-involvement decisions, such as when we visit a local park on a weekend, notice a small, cultural festival in progress, and wander over to join in. In contrast, attending events such as the World Cup in South Africa in 2010 or visiting New Zealand to follow the British Lions tour are high-involvement decisions.

Information search

In looking for information, most consumers try to determine (1) the relevant criteria on which to base their decision – the nature of event performers, the location, other attractions in the area, the ticket price and so on – and (2) the extent to which the event will satisfy their needs. As they compare different leisure experiences, event consumers engage in both external and internal searches for information.

External influences

Among the external influences on the potential event-goer are various social factors. These factors are described below in the context of event participation.

- *Family and household influences*, such as the desires of children, often influence the leisure behaviour of parents. The need for family cohesion and building family ties is a strong leisure motivator for many people. It explains the large numbers of children and exhausted parents who congregate at agricultural shows around the UK, for example, the Great Yorkshire Show. Many festivals focus on children's entertainment for this reason.

- *Reference groups* are those groups that influence the behaviour of individuals. Groups in close contact with individuals (peers, family, colleagues and neighbours) are called primary reference groups. Those who have less frequent contact are called secondary reference groups. Most people tend to seek the approval of members of their reference groups. If attendance at a particular festival is perceived to be acceptable and desirable, then group members are more likely to attend. Showing examples of a typical reference group (for example, a nuclear family or a group of young people) enjoying themselves at a festival can be a persuasive communication strategy when those groups represent the festival's target market.
- *Opinion formers or opinion leaders* are those people within any group whose views about events and leisure experiences are sought and widely accepted. These opinion leaders are often media, theatrical or sports personalities (including critics and commentators), who are highly rewarded for their endorsement of products and leisure services. Often, the views of critics and commentators have a strong impact on attendance in sports and the arts.

  The adoption of new leisure services tends to follow a normal distribution curve. Innovators (generally opinion leaders within a group) are the first to try the experience. Early adopters, who are a little more careful about adopting the innovation, follow them and act as opinion leaders for the majority. Laggards are the last to try something new; some may be loyal attendees of very mature events or events that are close to decline. It is logical that the marketing of new festivals or events begins by targeting the opinion formers or innovators within the market.
- *Culture* includes the 'knowledge, beliefs, art, morals, laws, customs and any other capabilities and habits acquired as a member of society' (Neal et al., 2002, p. 22). The UK is an example of a culturally diverse country in which indigenous people and various ethnic groups with different patterns of living co-exist. Our culture can affect our buying habits, leisure needs, attitudes and values.

  Culture has a profound influence on the design, marketing and consumption of events and festivals. In effect, events are simultaneously a celebration and a consumption experience that reflect our way of life. A growth of interest in events as diverse as London's Notting Hill Carnival, the Bradford Mela and the Eisteddfod, demonstrates the influence of, and interest in, culture.

An external search involving reference groups or other sources becomes especially important when event or festival attendance requires an extended decision-making process. Going to the Football World Cup, for example, is a high-involvement, extended decision, and event-goers will seek advice from websites, travel agents and other sources. Participating in some cultural events, such as the Shetland Folk Festival, could involve extended decision making because it requires travelling by airplane or ferry to the island.

Internal influences

A range of internal influences also affect consumer decision making about events. These influences include perception (how we select and process information), learning and memory, motives, personality traits and consumer attitudes. If, for example, consumers have an existing preference (attitude) that steers them towards a classical music event, then they would deliberately select information about such events. Similarly, if consumers have information stored in their memory that helps to resolve a need (a mental picture of spectacular fireworks at The Riverside Festival in Nottingham), then that event could quickly become the single, most satisfactory solution to their entertainment needs on a given weekend in August in Nottingham.

Personality, or an individual's characteristic traits that affect behaviour (Brassington and Pettitt, 2006), is another influence on event or festival decisions. People can be introvert/extrovert, shy/self-confident, aggressive/retiring and dynamic/sluggish. Although the effects of personality on consumer choice are difficult to measure, it can be assumed that festivals that celebrate adventure or sporting prowess will attract participants with 'outgoing' personalities. An awareness of particular personality characteristics among event consumers can help marketers to fine-tune their strategies.

Among all the internal influences, 'in developed economies, most consumer behaviour is guided by psychological motives' (Neal et al., 2002, p. 19). A body of empirical research on motives for event and festival attendance has emerged since the 1990s. Three theories of event motives, as summarised by Axelsen and Arcodia (2004), are:

1. *the needs achievement hierarchy*: a theory based on Maslow's original hierarchy, whereby motives change as each level of need − from the physiological through to self-actualisation − is satisfied.
2. *'push' and 'pull' motives*: a theory in which push factors (for example, social interaction, escapism, novelty, curiosity) propel consumers towards an event, while pull factors (for example, aspects of events, such as a style of music, wine and gourmet food) draw consumers to an event.
3. *intrinsic motives for leisure*: a theory related to 'push' and 'pull' motives that consumers seek change from routine (escape) and intrinsic personal and inter-personal rewards from visiting/travelling to other environments. Examples of these rewards might be the increased sense of endurance and friendships formed during a historic horse-riding event (as described by Mannell and Iso-Ahola, 1987).

A set of common motives (or need satisfiers) for attending festivals has been cited in a wide range of studies (see, for example, Backman, Backman, Muzaffer and Sunshine, 1995; Crompton and McKay, 1997; Uysal, Ghan and Martin, 1993). A summary of motives for festival attendance that consistently emerge are:

- socialisation or external interaction: meeting new people, being with friends and socialising in a known group,

- family togetherness: seeking the opportunity to be with friends and relatives and doing things together to create greater family cohesion,
- escape from everyday life, as well as recover equilibrium: getting away from the usual demands of life, having a change from daily routine and recovering from life's stresses,
- learn about or explore other cultures: gaining knowledge about different cultural practices and celebrations,
- excitement/thrills: doing something because it is stimulating and exciting, and
- event novelty/ability to regress: experiencing new and different things and/or attending a festival that is unique.

The above list tends to reflect the earlier three theories of event motives (Axelsen and Arcodia, 2004). These motives have been found in most festival studies and also among visitors to events and exhibitions. Both special event and gallery visitors during the Ilkley Autumn Arts Festival (staged at the King's Hall and various venues around Ilkley each autumn), for example, may seek social interaction, novelty and relaxation, entertainment, education and a variety of other motives through their attendance at the different events. The order of importance given to the different motives appears to vary according to the type of festival or event. Visitors to a specialised festival, such as a hot air balloon festival, have been shown to be highly motivated by a desire to socialise with people sharing the same interest (Mohr, Backman, Gahan and Backman, 1993), while people attending a community festival have been shown to be motivated by 'escape' from day-to-day life (Uysal et al., 1993).

Evaluating alternatives and making event choices

It is fair to assume that consumers rarely weigh up whether they will attend more than one or two events on a given day. Instead, they are likely to choose among an event/festival, a cinema, a private party or an entirely different leisure activity. For everyday products and services, evaluative criteria are often price, brand image and the contents of the market offer.

Services such as events that consumers have not previously attended are quite hard to evaluate, and they experience some uncertainty due to the financial, social, psychological, sensory, performance-related and time-related risks involved (Lovelock and Wirtz, 2011). Even if a festival has free entry, there are travel costs, childcare and other costs involved. Socially, consumers may think about the types of people they will encounter at an event, and the psychological costs and benefits of those encounters. They also evaluate the time that it will take to attend the event, and sensory risks such as their ability to see the stage or hear the music with clarity. The choice of whether to attend sports events can be linked to the stadium atmosphere, layout and facilities, and the fans of the other team, rather than team performance. For example, Robertson and Pope (1999) found that the atmosphere, the live action, stadium cleanliness and ease of getting seats were quite influential in the decision to attend Brisbane Lions (Australia Football League) games, while in the study of

Minor League Baseball, Lee et al. (2003) found that cleanliness of facilities followed by quantity and convenience of facilities and parking were the three leading environmental motivation factors.

Any number of values may be applied in making different event consumption choices. Functional values, such as perception of an event's price–quality relationship and ease of access, may dominate. Alternatively, emotional values may be more influential (the likely effects of a festival experience on mood). Other conditional values for a festival may be whether there is convenient transport, acceptable food and beverage, good quality classical music or nearby suitable accommodation that suits our tastes.

Post-event evaluation

Once consumers have attended an event, they start to compare what they expected with what they experienced. Consumer expectations arise from a combination of marketing communications (promotional activities) planned by the event or festival organiser, word of mouth from friends and family, previous experience with this or similar events and the event's brand image. The exercise of comparing consumer's expectations with actual experiences of services is now commonplace. However, even when markets are tightly segmented into a group of people with a common characteristic, members of the same group can have different perceptions of the benefits they receive. Two close friends may attend City of Derry Jazz Festival: one may rate all the event services very highly, yet the other may not be as enthusiastic, despite having experienced the same service. The relationship between event-goers' satisfaction, their perceptions of service quality and their intentions to revisit is very important to marketers who want to build a loyal visitor market.

EVENT SATISFACTION, SERVICE QUALITY AND REPEAT VISITS

Because leisure services are intangible, inseparable, variable and perishable, defining and maintaining service quality is difficult, as is identifying and recovering from services failures. From the viewpoint of a festival or event consumer, quality service occurs when expectations of the event match perceptions of the service experienced. Understanding perceived service quality is thus a primary goal of marketers. Both existing and potential attendees can have a perception of event quality (formed from experience of the event, word of mouth and/or other marketing communication). However, perceptions of the event itself are based on the technical (performance outcomes) and functional (process related) qualities of the experience (Gronroos, 1990). Other external factors – for example, wet weather and personal factors such as an argument with a partner during the event – also affect consumer perceptions.

Because it is harder to evaluate 'technical' quality (such as the musical performance at the festival or the performance of a sporting team), much of the focus in measuring perceived service quality is on functional aspects, or ways in which service is delivered. For this reason, the five main dimensions of service quality in the commonly used SERVQUAL questionnaire (Parasuraman et al., 1988) mostly reflect functional service aspects. These dimensions are:

- *assurance:* staff and/or volunteers give the appearance of being knowledgeable, helpful and courteous, and event consumers are assured of their well-being,
- *empathy:* the event staff and/or volunteers seem to understand consumers' needs and deliver caring attention,
- *responsiveness:* the staff and volunteers are responsive to the needs of the consumer,
- *reliability:* everything happens at the event in the way the marketing communication has promised, and
- *tangibles:* the physical appearance of the event equipment, artists' costumes/ presentation and the physical setting meet the visitor's expectations.

Using these five dimensions, the SERVQUAL questionnaire measures the difference between visitors' expectations and perceptions of a festival or event. When visitors' perceptions of their event experience match or exceed their expectations, a quality experience has been delivered, and the outcome is satisfied attendees who could decide to go to the event next time it is held. The SERVQUAL instrument has also been used in a number of other event-related studies. For example, Robinson and Callan (2001, 2002a,b, 2005) explored service quality in relation to venue choice of conference organisers, while O'Neill, Getz and Carlsen (1999) and Getz, O'Neill and Carlsen (2001) investigated service quality at a surfing event, Thrane (2002) in the context of a jazz festival and Jung (2006) in exhibitions.

Event satisfaction is related to perceived service quality, but it is experience dependent. Satisfaction can be measured only among existing visitors to the event. Because the event experience is heterogeneous, not every customer will be satisfied all the time; to maintain a competitive position, however, the event marketer should aim to achieve more than a basic level of satisfaction. A sense of delight or extreme satisfaction among event visitors is the ideal outcome (Lovelock and Wirtz, 2011). To this end, one objective in an event's strategic marketing should involve visitor satisfaction — for example, '95% of event participants will give a satisfied or higher rating of the event'. Figure 11.6 shows how consumer dissatisfaction can occur based on some perceived gap in festival or event quality.

Given the difficulty in understanding consumer expectations (with there being no clear set of expectations for each service setting), it is often argued that a 'perceptions only' measure of satisfaction (one that excludes expectations) is more useful. For festivals, various writers suggest that consumer 'perceptions' are better indicators of the link between quality, visitor satisfaction and intentions to revisit (see, for example, Baker and Crompton, 2000; Thrane, 2002). Because musical performance has been highlighted as an important determinant of quality at a music festival (Saleh and Ryan, 1993; Thrane, 2002), the use of the SERVQUAL approach

FIGURE 11.6 Quality – the fit between customer expectations and perceptions

(*Source: Marketing for Leisure and Tourism by Michael Morgan, Pearson Education Limited. Copyright © Pearson Hall Europe 1996*)

alone is probably not the marketer's best approach to research. Thrane (2002), however, also notes that aspects of quality measured by SERVQUAL do contribute to jazz festival patrons' satisfaction and intentions to revisit. A research instrument that adequately investigates both festival 'performance' and 'process' should be considered, therefore, in creating and evaluating festival and event marketing strategies.

Table 11.1 summarises the mental process that potential event attendees go through when deciding to attend an event and their satisfaction with the experience, and then provides what marketing strategic decisions need to be made. These steps are discussed in depth in the next section.

STEPS IN THE STRATEGIC MARKETING PROCESS

Marketing planning involves distinct steps that event managers must understand to create a successful marketing plan. These steps include segmenting the market,

Table 11.1 Event consumer decision-making process and the implications for strategic marketing planning

Stage in the Decision-Making Process	Implications for Marketing Strategies	Marketing Decisions
Recognition of the need, such as novelty, social interaction, excitement	Selection of appropriate target market segments – marketer must know what needs can be satisfied	Target market – mass or focused
Search for information	Marketing communications options	Internet, direct e-mail, paid advertising, publicity, posters
Evaluation of alternatives	Event product, promotional messages – does the event product satisfy the needs of the target market?	Product development? Promotion messages?
Choice of place of purchase	Ease of purchase	Internet, ticketing agency, at venue, post office mail, e-mail
Evaluation of leisure experience	Service quality standards	Measurement of consumer satisfaction – how experience will be rigorously evaluated

targeting and positioning, setting measurable marketing objectives, choosing generic marketing strategies, and designing an effective marketing mix.

Segmenting and targeting the event market

Most events do not appeal to everybody, so it is essential to identify those consumer segments whose needs most closely match the event experience. The market segments chosen should be:

- measurable — that is, the characteristics of the segment (socioeconomic status, gender, age and so on) must be accessible to the event marketer,
- substantial enough in size to be worth targeting,
- accessible by normal marketing communication channels and
- actionable by the event organiser, given the marketing budget and other resources (Morgan, 1996).

The segmentation process uses the concept of the buyer's decision-making process as a guide. The process of identifying appropriate target markets is known as market segmentation. Segmentation can occur by geography, demography or lifestyle (psychography). The Pembroke Festival 2004, for example, had an extensive product range, categorised into arts, drama, music, dance, food, family and youth (Pembroke Festival, 2004). Each of these categories has different offerings, appealing to the buyer's behaviour of different submarkets. The music category alone featured about 22 different offerings. By thinking about the potential visitors to the music programme the festival organisers can develop a mental snapshot of the overall target market for the music category and events within it. Actual segmentation of the markets could be based on geography, demography (including visitors' life-cycle phase) and/or behaviour (lifestyles, benefits sought and attendance profile — that is, first-timers or repeat visitors).

Geographic segmentation based on the place of residence of event visitors is a commonly used method. Many community festivals are dominated by local visitors or day-trippers from the immediate county or region. For this reason, managers of community festivals often decide to focus on local residents as their major geographic segment. A key determinant of geographic segmentation is the potential 'drawing power' of the event as a tourist attraction. An event such as a capital city agricultural show (for example, the Great Yorkshire Show in Harrogate) would have a regional geographic segmentation and probably a national market segment for its more specialised event experiences. Although many event organisers have visions of creating tourist demand, few events develop the brand equity and 'pull' characteristics to succeed as independent tourist attractions. Many more events could succeed in attracting tourists if organisers improved their skills in packaging and marketing the event alongside other regional tourist experiences. If an event demonstrates its ability to attract geographically dispersed markets — for example, Notting Hill Carnival — then the potential geographic spread could be:

- local residents of the area,
- day visitors from outside the immediate area,
- regional domestic tourists and
- international inbound tourists.

However, it is a rare event that can attract such widely dispersed market segments. Major international sports events are probably the only events that have such a widespread pulling power.

Demographic segmentation concerns the measurable characteristics of people, such as age, gender, occupation, income, education and cultural group. A demographic segmentation tool often used by marketers is a socioeconomic scale based on occupation (usually the head of the household, in family units). The traditional JICNARS classification, or social status/class, used by British marketers, used five categories based on occupation. These are summarised in Table 11.2 which details this scale in an events context.

Although developed for the UK, these classifications are relevant to other developed countries. Media buyers in advertising agencies first used this method of classification, as the system is a very good predictor of reading and viewing habits. For example, ABC1 adults make up the majority of the readership for 'broadsheet' newspapers, such as *Financial Times* (92%), *The Guardian* (90%), *Daily Telegraph* (89%), *The Times* (87%), and *The Independent* (84%), whereas they account for a minority of the tabloids readership (for example, *The Daily Star*, 33%; *The Sun*, 38%; and *Daily Mirror*, 40%) (National Readership Surveys Limited, 2009).

Table 11.2 A classification of socioeconomic market segments for events

Group	Social Status	Social Grade	Head of Household's Occupation	Types of Events Group is Likely to Attend	England/Wales Population (approx. %)
A	Upper middle class	Higher managerial, administrative or professional	Professional people, very senior managers in business or commerce or top-level civil servants, retired people (previously grade A) and their widows	Cultural events such as fundraisers for the opera, classical music festivals	4
B	Middle class	Intermediate managerial, administrative or professional	Middle management executives in large organisations (with appropriate qualifications), principal officers in local government and civil service, top management or owners of small businesses, educational and service establishments, retired people (previously grade B) and their widows	Cultural events (but purchasing cheaper seats), food and beverage festivals, historical festivals, arts and crafts festivals, community festivals	23
C1	Lower middle class	Supervisory or clerical and junior managerial, administrative or professional	Junior management, owners of small establishments, all others in non-manual positions. Jobs in this group have very varied responsibilities and educational requirements. It also includes retired people (previously grade C1) and their widows.	Most popular cultural events, some sporting events, community festivals	29

C2	Skilled working class	Skilled manual workers, and those manual workers with responsibility for other people, retired people (previously grade C2) with pensions from their job and widows (if receiving pensions from their late husband's job)	Motor vehicle festivals/shows, sporting events, community festivals	21
D	Working class	Semi-skilled and unskilled manual workers, and apprentices and trainees to skilled workers, retired people (previously grade D) with pensions from their job and their widows (if receiving a pension from their late husband's job)	Some sporting events, ethnic festivals	15
E	Those at lowest level of subsistence	State pensioners, widows (no other earner), on benefit/ unemployed, casual or lowest grade workers	Those entirely dependent on the state long term, through sickness, unemployment, old age or other reasons, those unemployed for a period exceeding 6 months (otherwise classify on previous occupation), casual workers, those without a regular income. Only households without a chief income earner will be coded in this group.	Very little, except occasionally free events	8

(*Source: adapted from Morgan, 1996, National Readership Surveys Limited, 2008 and ONS, 2003*)

However, these classifications are not always an accurate guide to income. For example, many Cs earn considerable incomes. The essential difference among As, Bs, C1s and the other categories is in the level of education. Research suggests that the higher the level of education, the higher the propensity of a person to participate in cultural activities including arts and community festivals (Torkildsen, 2005). Morgan observes that the age at which individuals terminate their formal education (16 years, 18 years or after higher education at 21 years or more) can indicate their ambition, intelligence and, importantly for event managers, their curiosity about the world in which they live (Morgan, 1996, p. 103). For directors of festivals and events that include cultural elements, their target market is usually an educated one.

From 2001, new National Statistics Socio-Economic Classifications (NS-SEC) were adopted for the purposes of official statistics. This breaks the population down into 17 operational categories based on occupation, size of employing organisation, type of contract, benefits and job security. These may enable more clearly defined groups, particularly considering the trend towards the 'middle classes' within the UK population (Rose and O'Reilley, 1998). Depending on data analysis requirements, eight-, five- and three-class versions may be used, though the analytic version using eight overall classes is used for most analyses, with the 'Not Classified' including students, occupations not stated or inadequately described, and not classifiable for other reasons (Office for National Statistics, 2005) (see Table 11.3).

Table 11.3 Socioeconomic classification classes

Analytic Class	Operational Category	Percentage of Population
1	Higher managerial and professional occupations	10.8
	1.1 Large employers and higher managerial occupations	
	1.2 Higher professional occupations	
2	Lower managerial and professional occupations	22.2
3	Intermediate occupations	10.3
4	Small employers and own account workers	7.7
5	Lower supervisory and technical occupations	9.4
6	Semi-routine occupations	13.3
7	Routine occupations	9.8
8	Never worked and long-term unemployed	16.5

(Source: Labour Market Survey and ONS, 2004)

Other demographic variables are gender and age. The baby boomers, born between 1946 and 1960, are the largest and most affluent of the age demographics. Many are in the empty nester part of the family life cycle and most have reduced their mortgage repayments to negligible amounts. They therefore usually have considerable disposable income to spend on leisure experiences. Generation X, born between 1961 and 1980, is a growing market segment, among which food and wine festivals have become a popular leisure experience (with women marginally out-numbering men). Targeting the media-savvy, Generation X market, which is not at all homogeneous (singles, couples with and without children), requires a different approach, as does Generation Y, or the so-called Digital Natives. Women and men occasionally have different needs and some events cater for these different needs. The years in which people are born can affect their outlook on life, their attitudes and values and their interests. Depending on the event, one or several of these generations may be targeted, with event programme elements designed to cater for each age segment. Table 11.4 shows the different generations born in the twentieth and twenty-first centuries.

Another method of age segmentation is by life cycle. This relies on the proposition that peoples' leisure habits vary according to their position in the life cycle. Wells and Gubar (1966) developed the original life-cycle model that reflected the life stages of the time (that is, bachelor, newly married, full nester, empty nester and solitary survivors); however, due to changes in society this has now become outdated (Brassington and Pettit, 2006). The family life cycle, illustrated in Figure 11.7, is reflective of the modern family.

Table 11.4 The generations born in the twentieth and twenty-first centuries

Generation	Born	Age in 2011 (years)	Formative Years
World War I	Pre-1924	88+	Pre-1936
Depression	1924–1934	76–87	1936–1946
World War II	1935–1945	65–76	1947–1957
Early boomers	1946–1954	56–65	1958–1966
Late boomers	1955–1964	46–56	1967–1976
Generation X	1965–1976	34–46	1977–1988
Generation Y/Echo boom/Net Generation/Generation Me	1977–1997	14–34	1989–2009
Generation Z/Digital Natives/Generation Next	1998–2009	2–13	2010–2021
Generation Alpha/Generation I (Internet)	2010–	0–	2022–

(Source: adapted from US Travel Data Centre, 1989, cited in Getz, 2005, p. 92, McCrindle with Wolfinger, 2009 and Tapscott, 2009)

FIGURE 11.7 Modern family life-cycle model

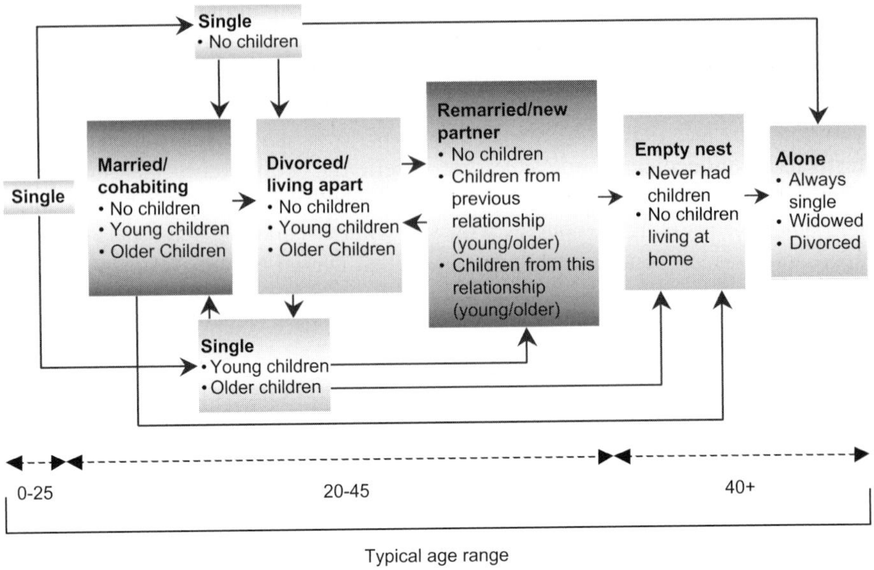

Typical age range

(Source: Brassington and Pettitt, 2006, p. 134)

Marketers sometimes employ a combination of age and lifestyle segmentation. 'Full nesters' are the target market for events that feature entertainment for both children and adults, for example, whereas 'AB empty nesters' are the perfect market for cultural festivals featuring quality food and drink, and arias from well-loved operas. However, care should be taken not to resort to age stereotypes. Many early baby boomers, in or approaching their fifties, are fit, active and interested in all types of culture, popular and contemporary, as well as high-culture festivals such as classical music or theatre. It could be argued that the most successful community festivals are those which are inclusive of all age groups, rather than focusing on just one age group, but of course most baby boomers would feel positively ill at ease at a dance music concert.

Geodemographics is segmenting residential areas according to variables from population census data and additional sources including lifestyle databases. One of the best-known classifications is ACORN (A Classification of Residential Neighbourhoods) (Blythe, 2009, pp. 182–185). ACORN classifies residential areas into six main categories (see Table 11.5) with 17 subgroups and 55 types (including Unclassified), thus allowing areas to be linked to buying behaviour and lifestyle for more effective marketing. The new ACORN incorporates 2001 Census data and has been extensively revised to be more robust and not only classify postcodes but geographic areas to allow better discrimination. Registering on the CACI website (www.caci.co.uk) allows access to further information about ACORN and the ability to search specific postcodes.

Table 11.5 ACORN classification

Category	% UK Pop	Group		% UK Pop
Wealthy Achievers 1	25.4%	A	Wealthy Executives	8.6
		B	Affluent Greys	7.9
		C	Flourishing Families	9.0
Urban Prosperity 2	11.5%	D	Prosperous Professionals	2.1
		E	Educated Urbanites	5.5
		F	Aspiring Singles	3.8
Comfortably Off 3	27.4%	G	Starting Out	3.1
		H	Secure Families	15.5
		I	Settled Suburbia	6.1
		J	Prudent Pensioners	2.7
Moderate Means 4	13.8%	K	Asian Communities	1.5
		L	Post-Industrial Families	4.7
		M	Blue-collar Roots	7.5
Hard-Pressed 5	21.2%	N	Struggling Families	13.3
		O	Burdened Singles	4.2
		P	High-Rise Hardship	1.6
		Q	Inner City Adversity	2.1
		U	Unclassified	

(Source: CACI, 2006, p. 8)

The Office for National Statistics (ONS) publishes a great deal of data taken from each census that categorises residential areas according to the demographics of the residents of that area. This information was traditionally published as paper-based documents, with a separate edition published for every region throughout the UK. However, it is now available in a range of other formats and is a valuable store of demographic information categorised by geographic area. Data shown include the demographic variables of sex, age, marital status, household membership and relationships, cultural characteristics, qualifications, employment, workplace and household accommodation. The launch of National Statistics in 2000 illustrated a shift towards more accessible official statistics, which includes census, other data and publications being freely available on-line for not-for-profit end users (see www.statistics.gov.uk for further information). Directors of community festivals and other event managers should find these data very useful for product planning.

Psychographic segmentation is dividing a market according to its lifestyle and values and is another useful marketing planning technique. This method involves measuring AIO (activities, interests, opinions) dimensions and demographics (Blythe, 2009; Brassington and Pettitt, 2006; Kotler et al., 2008). Table 11.6 illustrates the primary lifestyle dimensions. Based on consumer research, classifications have been developed by various organisations.

However, like personality segmentation, psychographic segmentation of a market has some serious limitations for an event marketer:

The main problem ... is that psychographic segments are very difficult and expensive to define and measure. Relevant information is much less likely to

Table 11.6 Lifestyle dimensions

Activities	Interest
Work	Family
Shopping	Home
Holidays	Work
Social life	Community
Hobbies	Leisure and recreation
Entertainment	Fashion
Spots interests	Food
Club memberships	Media
Community	

Opinions	Demographics
Themselves	Age
Social and cultural issues	Education
Politics	Income
Educations	Occupation
Economics	Family size
Business	Life-cycle stage
Products	Geographic location
Future	

(Source: adapted from Brassington and Pettitt, 2006, pp. 204–205)

exist already in the public domain. It is also very easy to get the implementation wrong. For example, the organisation that tries to portray lifestyle elements within advertisements is dependent on the audience's ability to interpret the symbols used in the desired way and to reach the desired conclusions from them.

(Brassington and Pettitt, 2006, p. 206)

However, like personality segmentation, psychographic market segmentation has serious limitations for an event marketer. It is difficult to accurately measure the size of lifestyle segments in a quantitative manner, which breaks one of the cardinal rules for market segmentation — that segments must be measurable in order to judge if it is worthwhile to target that segment. Nevertheless, this type of segmentation offers, however, a better understanding of the types of experiences and benefits that different 'lifestyle' groups seek from their leisure experience. For example, the 'surfer' lifestyle segment is attracted to events sharing their ethos and perspective on life. Any event sponsored by Billabong is sure to be designed to appeal to this lifestyle segment.

Positioning the event

How to position an event in the mindset of the market is an important strategic decision. Positioning represents the way in which the event is defined by consumers, or 'the place the product occupies in consumers' minds relative to competing products' (Kotler and Armstrong, 2010, p. 233). Event positioning can be achieved in at least 10 different ways, as shown below:

1. the existing reputation or image of the event — for example, the Olympic Games and other long-standing events such as a Football World Cup or the Edinburgh Tattoo;
2. the charisma of a director or leader — for example, the Belfast Festival's director, currently Graeme Farrow, part of whose role is to generate positive publicity about the event to position the event in the perceptions of its consumers;
3. a focus on event programming — for example, Trafalgar Square Festival 2008, which was a 3-week festival programmed and positioned around three themes linking to the Olympics hand over from Beijing 2008 to London 2012;
4. a focus on performers — for example, major sports (such as football and golf) and theatre that highlight the players/performers;
5. an emphasis on location or facilities — for example, Wimbledon, which is now synonymous with world-standard tennis, or Wembley Stadium, which is strongly associated with football;
6. event users — for example, Bank of Scotland Imaginate Fesitival, a theatre festival targeted at children;
7. price or quality — for example, a free concert series such as those that are part of the Lancaster City Council's annual lunch-time concert series versus an operatic performance by the world's three best tenors;

8. the purpose or application of the event — for example, health awareness of SIDs or diabetes, or celebrations such as the UK's Trafalgar Weekend as the centrepiece of SeaBritain 2005;
9. the event category or 'product' class — for example, fashion events, food and wine festivals, and concerts, and
10. multiple attributes — for example, the London Fashion Week, which is positioned on its designers, reputation and image, as well as its purpose of bringing new fashion designers into the public eye.

Once decisions have been made about the event's segmentation, targeting and positioning, a platform is available to decide on event marketing objectives, strategies and tactics.

Developing event marketing objectives

Any successful development of a marketing plan is based on sound marketing objectives. Cravens, Merrilees and Walker, (2000, p. 272) made this important point: 'For marketing to be a beneficial business discipline, its expected results must be defined and measurable.' Event marketing objectives can be profit oriented where the objective of the event is to maximise the return on investment in the event. Alternatively, an event marketer may want to use market-oriented objectives, such as increase market share of the leisure/festival market or increase the geographic scope of attendees. Other types of event marketing objectives are to attract more participants, to improve the consumer satisfaction rating, to decrease the number of complaints from stakeholders or to increase revenues from food and beverage sales. What is essential is that the marketing objective is measurable — that is the achievement or otherwise of the objective can be empirically measured (Strauss and Frost, 2009). Hypothetical examples of marketing objectives for an event such as the Cheltenham International Music Festival might be to

- increase box office receipts in 2010 by 10% (market share growth objective),
- increase the number of acts by 10% (event growth objective),
- increase the percentage of seats sold in all ticketed events to 80% in 2010 (efficiency objective),
- retain 90% of sponsors for 2010 (effectiveness objective) and
- increase publicity generated in print and electronic media by a further 10% from 2010 (efficiency objective).

It is important to stress again how marketing objectives, like all objectives, must be measurable and not expressed in vague terms that make measurement impossible. While many managers are tempted to state general aims rather than set objectives (making it harder to be accountable for whether event objectives have been achieved), this temptation must be resisted. Clearly defined and measurable objectives give the marketer the ends, while strategies and their supporting tactics are the means to those ends.

The dimensions of the marketing objective thus have an impact on the choice of marketing strategies. Consider the hypothetical objective for the Cheltenham International Music Festival of increasing box office receipts by 10% in 2010. This increase is a substantial amount, much higher than the inflation rate, which implies that a business objective of the festival is to grow substantially each year to satisfy the entertainment and cultural demands of a more diverse audience base. The objective and the strategies to achieve are chosen, therefore, only after careful analysis of the market needs, organisational capabilities and opportunities.

Choosing generic marketing strategies and tactics for events

Before event marketers begin the more precise task of deciding on marketing elements such as the programme, the ticket price and other variables, they should reflect on their overall strategies for the event's future. Is there a plan to grow or expand the event and/or its markets? Or is there a plan to consolidate the current programme and further penetrate existing markets? Any number of strategic options is available to the event/festival, depending on its resources, its competition and its objectives. (Chapter 4 explains a range of these strategies.)

The following discusses the application of Porter's (1990) generic strategies and the potential use of growth strategies including diversification or integration (Kotler et al., 2010) as they affect event marketing. First, Porter (1990) suggested that most organisations have a choice of strategies of differentiation, focus or cost leadership. For the event marketer, decisions on these strategies are based on whether the aim is for the event to hold a leadership position in a region or city's leisure market or to have a narrower, yet well-defined market scope. The Henry Wood Promenade Concerts at the Royal Albert Hall appear to have established a cost leadership position with Day Prommers places available for those queuing on the day at £5, with brand equity in diverse market segments and some economies of scale and efficiency in its management (including its branding and communication strategies). In contrast, the Greenbelt Festival at Cheltenham Racecourse draws a more specialised audience with a focused strategy, servicing a particular segment — that is, Christian music lovers — with a high-quality performance. A differentiation strategy means creating something that is perceived to be quite unique across the event/festival sector. Interesting examples of events that employed this strategy could include Beautiful Night, a concert that took place in Belfast and Dublin in 2004 using live broadcasting from BBC and RTE to link the two sites together to form one concert and broadcast on television. It also formed the finale to the 11-day BBC Music Live festival (BBC, 2004).

Other marketing strategy options arise from the overall event strategies of intensive growth, integration and diversification. Perhaps the most commonly cited tool in deciding on growth strategies is the product–market expansion grid (Ansoff, 1957, cited in Kotler et al., 2010) shown in Figure 11.8.

An event that has a well-designed programme, but is not yet drawing large numbers, could consider a market penetration strategy — that is, concentrating on attracting more people from the same target market. If organisers consider that the event could reach a different target market without changing its programme, a market development strategy could be used. Finally, if consumer satisfaction studies show that the event is not satisfying its current visitor needs, new and different programme elements could be needed. The arena spectacular Global-Gathering represents a good example of a new event being used to better satisfy the needs of contemporary visitors. Furthermore, Barclays Cheltenham Jazz Festival's introduction of the Budvar Stage in central Cheltenham, as a feature of Jazz on the Square, is an example of market development, in that it took the existing product of a jazz festival to a new market in Cheltenham.

Integration strategies also present marketing opportunities for events. An event producer may decide to formally integrate with a venue provider (a festival that goes under the wing of a cultural centre) or integrate with other events or festivals. More commonly, international acts may tour to other parts of the UK or Europe, thereby reducing the overhead costs of the acts. It has been suggested that integration strategies have become more common in recent years among those events unable to cover excessive public liability fees. However, integration is also an opportunistic strategy: finding an event that complements the existing programme and bringing new partnerships to a larger festival can be very attractive.

Diversification strategies can lead the marketer to add new events or support services to its stable of activities, or go into complementary businesses. A festival may develop an innovative range of merchandise for its existing market or it may market its software for visitor relationship management to other festivals. Such

FIGURE 11.8 Ansoff's product–market matrix

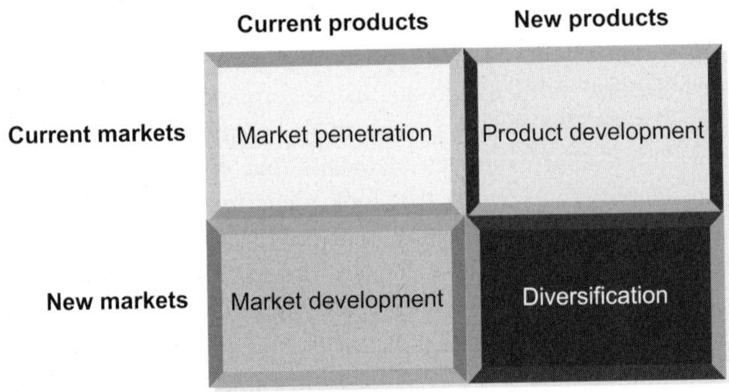

(Source: Ansoff, 1957)

strategic options represent an important framework for deciding on the event's marketing mix, which is discussed next.

Selecting the event's 'services marketing' mix

Variations in the marketing mix have been made since the original four Ps of marketing were proposed by Professor EJ McCarthy in 1960. This chapter uses an adaptation of Getz's (2005) event marketing mix to present nine closely related components of event marketing. While each element is of considerable strategic and planning importance, it is relatively easy to group them, as shown below:

- the event product experience (the core service), its programming (different event components, their quality or style) and its packaging (a mix of opportunities within the event or marketing of the event with other external attractions, accommodation and transport to the event);
- the place (location where the event is held and how its tickets are distributed), its physical setting (the venue layout relative to consumer needs) and on-site event processes (queuing and so on);
- people (cast, audience, hosts and guests) and partnerships (stakeholders such as sponsors and media);
- price, or the exchange of value to experience the event, and
- integrated marketing communication (media and messages employed to build relationships with the event markets and audiences) (Getz, 2005), which is discussed in some depth in the next chapter.

PLANNING EVENT 'PRODUCT' EXPERIENCES

Festivals and events, as service product experiences, contain three elements (Lovelock and Wirtz, 2011):

1. the core service and benefits that the customer experiences — for example, a performing arts or sports event;
2. supplementary features/augmented services that differentiate an event from its competitors — for example, its artists, service quality, the type of visitors, different modes of transport and merchandise, and
3. the delivery process — for example, the role of the customer in the experience, length of event, level and style of event.

As suggested earlier, an important characteristic of the marketing of leisure services is that people are also part of the product. In other words, much of visitors' satisfaction comes from their interactions with other people attending the event. This means event marketers need to ensure (1) visitor segments within their audience are compatible and (2) there is an ease of interaction among people on-site.

Developing the event

The 'product' of an event is the set of intangible leisure experiences and tangible goods designed to satisfy the needs of the event market. The development of an event or festival can be easily modelled on the processes used to plan, create and deliver services (Figure 11.9).

The product life-cycle concept suggests that most events travel through the stages of introduction, growth and maturity to eventual decline or rejuvenation in a new form. Although there is no predictable pattern of life-cycle transition for most products and services, we can find many examples of events that appear to have experienced all life-cycle phases. Attendance at Notting Hill Carnival, for example,

FIGURE 11.9 The process of creating an event 'product'

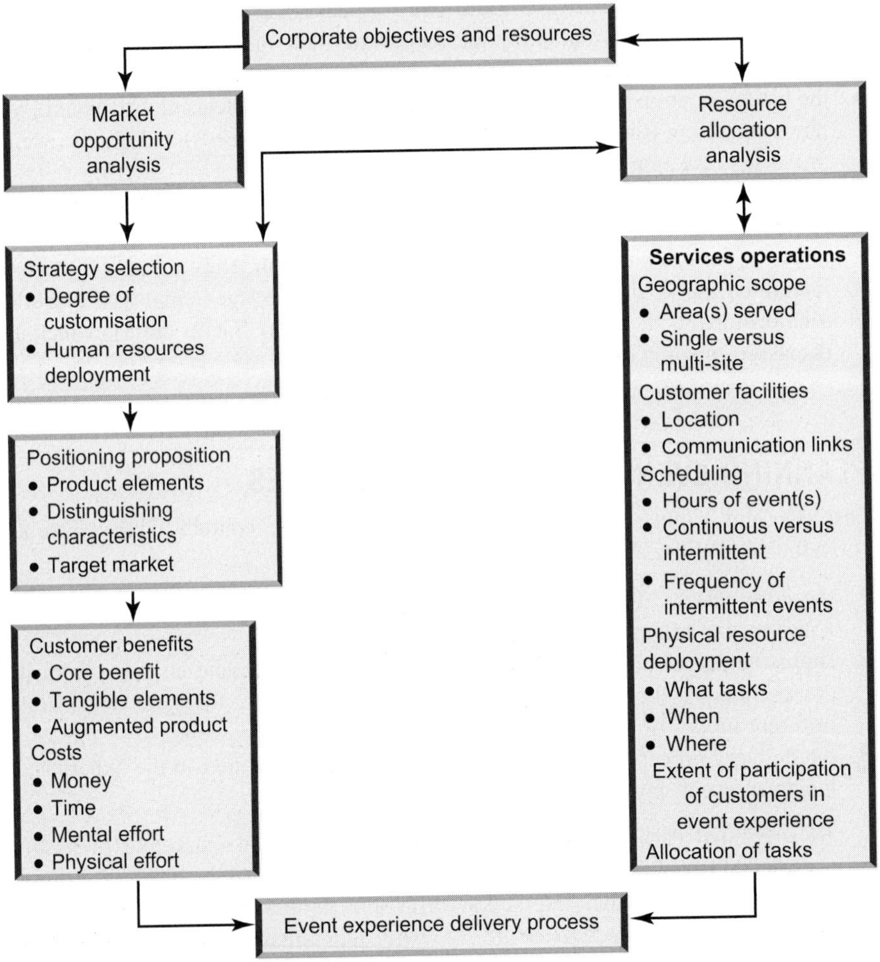

(Source: adapted from Lovelock and Wirtz, 2004)

has waxed and waned over a number of years as the 'product' has been changed to reflect changing community, organiser and stakeholder needs and in no small part due to the weather and other external forces. Based on police estimates, in recent years attendances peaked at an estimated 1.4 million in 2000 and declined to hit a low of 500,000 in 2001 (Cook and Morse, 2004), with attendances fluctuating again to an estimated 720,000 in 2009. To avoid the decline, event managers need to closely monitor public acceptance of the content of their event product, to ensure it is still congruent with the leisure needs of contemporary society.

The creation of new service experiences usually ranges from major service innovations through to simple changes in the style of service delivery (Lovelock and Wirtz, 2011). These are evident in the event and festival sector:

- Major 'event' innovations — producing new events or festivals for previously undefined markets. Extreme sports events may represent one such innovation that emerged in the 1990s. In the first decade of the twenty-first century, major sports events captured the imagination of the British people with the success of the Manchester Commonwealth Games in 2002, the bid to host the 2012 Olympics in London and 2014 Commonwealth Games in Glasgow among other major events, and the Football Association is currently bidding to host the Football World Cup in 2018. However, major 'event' innovations are extremely hard to identify in an already crowded and innovative events sector, in which a wide variety of events serve existing, rather than new, leisure segments.
- Major process innovations — use of new processes to deliver events in new ways with added consumer benefits. The Internet has played a central role in innovating event marketing delivery — for example, tickets for virtually all events can now be purchased on-line. More significantly, the use of the Internet for promotion and distribution of events has produced considerable efficiencies for event marketers, and simplified the process for the event consumer. Live 8 gave people the chance to attend, watch on television, listen on radio and/or log on through the Internet (through the sponsorship by AOL) to participate in this major world event.
- Product (event) line extensions — additions to the current event programmes of existing events or festivals. This form of product development is very common. The Education & Community Programme, for example, is an initiative of the Harrogate International Festival which extends the festival's programme to include events year-round into the surrounding community.
- Process (event delivery) extensions — adjustments to the way in which existing events or festivals are delivered. The use of Internet ticketing agencies and on-line booking of festival space by food and beverage vendors, for example, has enhanced event delivery processes.
- Supplementary service innovations — extra services that build on the event or festival experience. Examples are on-site childcare facilities, automatic teller machines and wireless hot spots at event sites or conference venues.

- Service improvements — modest changes that improve the event performance or the way in which it is delivered. Examples are a fashion festival featuring the work of a wider array of designers, easier access to the event venue by public transport or more outlets being provided for ticket purchase.
- Style changes — simple forms of product development for an event. Examples are improved seating arrangements, a new festival logo and improved costumes.

For any event, the decision to undertake any of the 'product' development strategies proposed must be based on market research. Although it is not possible to pre-test events as market offerings, new concepts or style changes (such as a new festival logo) are readily tested in the target market using qualitative research techniques such as focus groups. Some form of event concept testing is desirable before major changes are made.

Programming the event

A critical aspect of the event product that is not widely discussed is the development of an attractive event programme. For event managers, it is important to have an event portfolio that reflects (1) the mission, (2) the desired level of quality that satisfies artistic and market criteria and (3) the revenue or profit objectives of event managers. The nature and range of market segments and the ability to create thematic links between programme elements are further considerations. Often, organisers need to balance the personal or artistic vision of event directors with the realities of market success criteria and the costs involved. The event programme may also reflect media broadcasting requirements, the availability of desired performers or players, and the practicalities of staging the event concept. In addition, the event manager must consider the programming of competing events, the event's life-cycle phase (for example, more mature events may require some innovative programming to survive) and the duration of the event. An excellent example of event programming is the Trafalgar Square Festival 2005. Taking the theme 'city rites', the festival explored energy, diversity, aspirations and dreams making full use of the square with a range of commissions, performances by artists and visiting companies over 3 weeks (Mayor of London, 2005).

Reflecting on their event programming experience at a Dublin discussion forum (The Theatre Shop Conference, 2002), Archer and several other producers pointed to at least four key elements in programming success:

1. The need for a distinguishing core concept in the programme — what is it that you're presenting that actually has meaning to the audience? The Leeds and Notting Hill Carnivals celebrate Caribbean culture through music and dance, as a link back to the communities spiritual homeland (see case study in Chapter 2).
2. The need to marry the event programme with its physical environment or site —what kinds of performances will really be spectacular in this setting? What kinds of performers and stage structures (existing and created) will shine in this environment? The Leeds Shakespeare Festival, which takes place annually in the

ancient outdoor setting of Kirkstall Abbey Cloisters, or the Sheffield Shakespeare Festival taking place in Sheffield's Botanical Gardens, demonstrates contrasting unique venues for the same event.

3. The role and operational approach of the artistic director/producer — the producers are both programme gatekeepers (selecting event participants from proposals submitted by performers) and poachers (travelling around to pick the best performers, just as sports clubs send out their talent scouts to sign talented athletes).

4. Established criteria for programme content — criteria include the compatibility of performers to a festival's market, the history of this type of performance at other events and a performance's technical quality. Some producers of bigger festivals have a rule about (1) how many times an overseas act has been performed within the country and (2) a desired ratio of innovation and tradition in their event portfolio.

Programming is both an art and a science. The event manager considers the artistic, entertainment, educational or sports-related criteria that an event should achieve, as well as its marketing criteria. However, as with all successful entertainment, an intangible 'wow' factor also differentiates the truly successful event programme.

Packaging the event

Packaging is perhaps one of the most underdeveloped elements of the event marketing mix. Avenues for packaging include the opportunity to package different types of entertainment, food and beverage and merchandise as a single market offer (a service bundle), and the opportunity to package the event with accommodation, transport and other attractions in the nearby region (a holiday package). Some events fail to exploit packaging opportunities that can be an effective means of better positioning the festival in its current markets and to engage in market development by attracting tourists. In contrast, motor racing events such as the FIA British Grand Prix at Silverstone draw national and overseas tourists, demonstrating some sophistication with packaging. For example, packages are available including flights, hotel accommodation, grandstand tickets, return coach transfers, VIP parking, full hospitality and much more depending on the price the customer is willing to pay. The ability to package an event goes back to its 'drawing power' discussed earlier. However, in performing arts and sports, special package deals for existing subscribers or members represent another viable marketing use for the package concept. Academic or professional conferences usually package the conference, accommodation, entertainment, and post- and pre-conference tours into one easy-to-book package.

PEOPLE AND PARTNERSHIPS

The principles of relationship marketing and management of key stakeholders and consumers now pervade the marketing literature. Many festivals and events start their lives on the basis of 'relationships and goodwill' between a dedicated group of people, so it is not unusual to find that successful events have solid partnerships and strong links with loyal supporters (attendees, volunteers, government and corporate representatives). For many festivals and events, a 'sense of sharing a common vision' often pervades the atmosphere, with a loose alliance between the types of people who produce the event and those who enjoy it. With large-scale events, it is hard to create that same sense of belonging, but strategies dedicated to building relationships with volunteers, sponsors and visitors are common. Partnerships are critical in attracting the resources to plan, manage and evaluate the event's marketing strategies.

Stakeholders are not just event staff and volunteers (Chapter 7) and event attendees, but also the wider residential community and providers of public services to the event such as the police service. Community consultation and relationship building should be marketing concerns for an event from its inception. While organisers of the Glastonbury Festival worked to overcome negative reactions by local residents, local newspapers and other media annually reflect coverage of events that retain protestors. From a brand equity perspective, events need ambassadors internally and externally to fully capitalise on their competitive potential.

PRICING

Given the diversity of leisure experiences offered to consumers, price can be a key influence on event demand. Contrasts in pricing strategy exist according to the type of event and its target markets. A mass-market event such as a lifestyle consumer show must keep its price at a level of affordability for its customers — middle income, middle Britain. On the other hand, a fundraising event such as the Barnardo's Firecracker Ball can ask a much higher price as its target market is much smaller (socioeconomic group AB who are supporters of the Barnardo's) but wealthier, and therefore willing to pay for a perceived quality experience. However, the high price can represent quality (or 'value for money') to the potential consumer and influence the decision to purchase.

While many special events are ticketed, a large number of festivals do not charge an entrance fee, and some simply seek a gold coin donation. However, a 'free' event still presents costs to the consumer, such as:

- time and costs (opportunity to do other things with that leisure time),
- psychic costs (social and emotional costs of attendance, mental effort to engage in the social interaction required),
- physical costs (the effort to travel to and then consume the leisure experience) and
- sensory costs (unpleasant environment and unnecessary loud noise).

The production of the event usually has costs associated with it and these must be covered by some means other than an admission fee.

Other key influences on ticket price or entry fees are competing leisure opportunities and perceived value. The concept of 'net value' or the sum of all perceived benefits (gross value) minus the sum of all perceived costs (monetary and otherwise) is useful for event marketers. The greater the positive difference between perceived benefits and costs, the greater the net value to the consumer.

With special events such as the NSPCC fundraiser example, potential consumers compare the perceived benefits — dinner, drinks, entertainment, parking, opportunities to socialise, prestige and the novelty of an unusual night out — with the perceived costs. These costs could include money, time, the physical effort involved in getting to the venue, psychic costs (related to social interaction) and sensory costs (such as going out on a rainy night). If the organiser has adequately positioned the event and communicated its benefits, the target market is likely to perceive a positive net value and purchase tickets.

In establishing the pricing strategy for an event, an organiser will account for two cost categories:

1. Fixed costs — costs that do not vary with the volume of visitors (for example, venue rental, interest charged on loans, lighting and power costs, promotion, the cost of volunteers' uniforms and artists' fees).
2. Variable costs — costs that vary with the number of visitors to the event (for example, the cost of plastic wine glasses at a festival, catering costs at a product launch and the cost of staff needed to serve attendees).

As well as analysing the above costs, the event manager should investigate the price of competing leisure experiences. If a similar leisure experience has a price of £x, the choices are to (1) match and charge the price £x, (2) adopt a cost leadership strategy and charge £x minus 25% or (3) adopt a differentiation strategy and use a price of £x plus 50%, and use marketing communications to promote the exceptional value of the event.

Pricing strategies used to achieve event objectives may be revenue oriented, operations oriented or market based. A revenue-oriented strategy is designed to maximise revenue by charging the highest price that the target market will pay. The Barnardo's Firecracker Ball is an example of a revenue-oriented pricing strategy. An operations-oriented pricing strategy seeks to balance supply and demand by introducing cheaper prices for times of low demand and higher prices at times of higher demand. Agricultural shows often use an operations-oriented pricing strategy. Finally, a market-oriented strategy uses differential pricing, which may be linked to alternate event packages. A clear link between packaging and pricing exists where a 3-day music festival charges one price for those who participate for all 3 days (the fanatics), a day price to capture the first-timers or 'dabblers' and another price to see the headline act and enjoy a gourmet dinner package.

Key questions that the event marketer must resolve in determining the pricing strategy relate to both pricing levels and methods of payment. Figure 11.10 summarises the decisions to be made by the marketer, along with some of the strategic options available.

FIGURE 11.10 Pricing decisions for event marketers

How much should be charged?
- What costs must be covered?
- How sensitive are customers to different prices?
- What are leisure competitors' prices?
- What levels of discounts to selected target markets are appropriate?
- Should psychological pricing (for example, £10.95 instead of £11) be used?

What should be the basis of pricing?
- Should each element be billed separately?
- Should one admission fee be charged?
- Should consumers be charged for resources consumed?
- Should a single price for a bundled package be charged?

Who shall collect payment?
- The event organisation?
- A ticketing intermediary?

- Direct to event's bank account via a debit/credit card when tickets booked online?

Where should payment be made?
- At the event?
- At a ticketing organisation?
- At the customer's home or office by using the Internet or telephone?

When should payment be made?
- When tickets are given out?
- On the day of the event?

How should payment be made?
- Cash — exact change?
- Credit card – via the Internet?
- Credit card – via the telephone?
- Using PayPal (www.paypal.com/), which simplifies accepting credit cards online
- Electronic point of sale (EPOS)?
- Token donation?

(Source: adapted from Lovelock and Wirtz, 2004, p. 173)

EVENT 'PLACE', PHYSICAL SETTING AND PROCESSES

'Place' refers to both the site where the event takes place (the venue) and the place at which consumers can purchase their tickets to the event. Other decisions with marketing implications are (1) the design of the event setting and (2) the processes used to deliver and experience the event.

The choice of a single venue or multiple sites for sports or cultural events should be made in the context of the event's overall strategy — for example, a strategy of market penetration or expansion. Increasingly, event marketers are recognising that market expansion can be achieved by taking their events to new locations. For example, Euro RSCG Skybridge worked with Endemol, producers of Big Brother reality television programme, to use the Big Brother House for corporate hospitality packages — an example of an innovative use of 'place'.

The physical setting, as noted in the discussion of programming, is crucial to the satisfaction of the event consumer. Most services marketers include it as a key element in the marketing mix, alongside processes of service delivery. As a result, you are encouraged to review the consumer implications of all facets of event design (see Chapter 14).

In deciding the most appropriate place(s) for ticket distribution, organisers usually question whether to use a ticketing agency. Ticketing agencies widen the distribution network, ease the consumer's purchase process and speed up the entry of customers to a venue. While they also facilitate credit card purchases and telephone bookings, charges are incurred by both the event organiser and the customer, which can be costly to both. The benefits of using a ticket agency depend on the type of event, the availability of other ticket distribution options (such as the box office of a small theatre company and/or direct mail), the willingness of the target market to pay for a ticketing service and the service's relative affordability.

Selling tickets via a ticketing agency or another distribution network such as the Internet has some advantages for the event producer. Ticket sales can be monitored, and the data collected can guide decisions on the level of marketing communication expenditure needed to attract the targeted visitor numbers. The security problems inherent in accepting cash at the door or gate are also alleviated. Because customers pay in advance, the cash flow to the event producer occurs well before the staging of the event, with obvious financial advantages for the event organiser.

The use of the Internet as a distribution medium for events is now widespread, with the key advantages of on-line ticket sales being:

- speed — consumers can purchase tickets without leaving their home, queuing or waiting for a phone operator to become available;
- consumer ease — consumers can view the different experiences offered by the event or festival in their own time, selecting the events or shows that best suit their pocket and time constraints;
- revenue — ticket revenue comes from the buyer's credit card, which facilitates security and ease of collection;
- up-to-date technology — more and more consumers expect leisure services to be available for purchase on the Internet. An on-line presence is critical in establishing an event or festival brand.
- cost — the event only pays a small merchant fee to the credit card company or to PayPal, and the consumer pays no fee at all, and
- distribution — the tickets are sent as an e-mail to the consumer at practically no cost, but very conveniently for the consumer.

Leeds and Reading festivals (members of the Festival Republic stable — www.festivalrepublic.com) use an on-line ticketing system (see combining Really Useful Theatre ticketing, Ticketselect and Way Ahead — www.seetickets.com) to provide an on-line booking system to support retail sales through HMV, official ticket agencies and telephone ticket hotline/Ticketmaster. Consumers have a choice of booking on-line, by telephone or from a box office or retail outlet. However, the booking fee remains even if the consumer chooses the on-line medium, with tickets available at face value if paid in cash at Reading Arts & Venues Box Office (for Reading Festival) or Leeds Visitor Centre (for Leeds Festival).

Events and festivals rarely have their own on-line booking system that can accept bookings and credit card details electronically at no charge to the consumer. However, advances in technology such as PayPal are likely to result in increased efficiencies in on-line distribution over time. In 2006, the Melbourne Commonwealth Games used an on-line booking facility from their website, as do many sports events. It is interesting to note, however, that some festivals still stick with the old technology of snail mail. An example of a festival that has commenced using its website to distribute its tickets to its consumers is the Edinburgh International Festival (www.eif.co.uk). It is also significant that many other aspects of festival production such as registering to perform, to sell merchandise and to become a volunteer may also migrate to websites.

Apart from ticketing, other operational processes have an immediate impact on the experience of event consumers. Visitors evaluate security checks on entry to the event, queuing for food and beverages, and the speed of access to services such as the car park and toilets. While later chapters address many of these event 'processes', the marketing implications of a smooth integration of 'front stage' and 'backstage' happenings at an event cannot be underestimated. The physical environment and processes that happen in that physical space directly contribute to the event's brand image — for example, mosh pits and crowd surfing at youth concerts are a logistical issue with significant implications for these events' ongoing market acceptance.

THE MARKETING PLAN

The final step in the marketing planning process is to put all the thinking as outlined in this chapter into a coherent plan that is the basis for the revenue and marketing expenditure budget. Marketing plans can come in various construction formats, but the simplest and most effective is that proposed by McDonald (2002). It would usually include all the steps and content shown in Figure 11.11 and gives guidance to how the marketing of the event is articulated to other stakeholders.

SUMMARY

A common misconception of many in the festival and event area is that marketing means nothing more than 'event promotion'. As this chapter has shown, marketing is a structured and coherent way of thinking about managing an event or festival to achieve objectives related to market/stakeholder awareness, event attendance, satisfaction and either profits or increased understanding of a cause.

The core of event marketing is the focus on existing and potential leisure consumers — in this case, the event attendees. Successful marketing flows from a complete understanding of these consumers — who they are, where they live and the leisure needs they seek to satisfy. This understanding comes from primary and secondary market research and two-way communication with event stakeholders and consumers. From this knowledge, event organisers can develop strategies and tactics that span the event product (including its programming and packaging), its place (venues, the physical setting and ticket outlets), its delivery processes, its people and partnerships, and integrated marketing communication.

FIGURE 11.11 The marketing plan

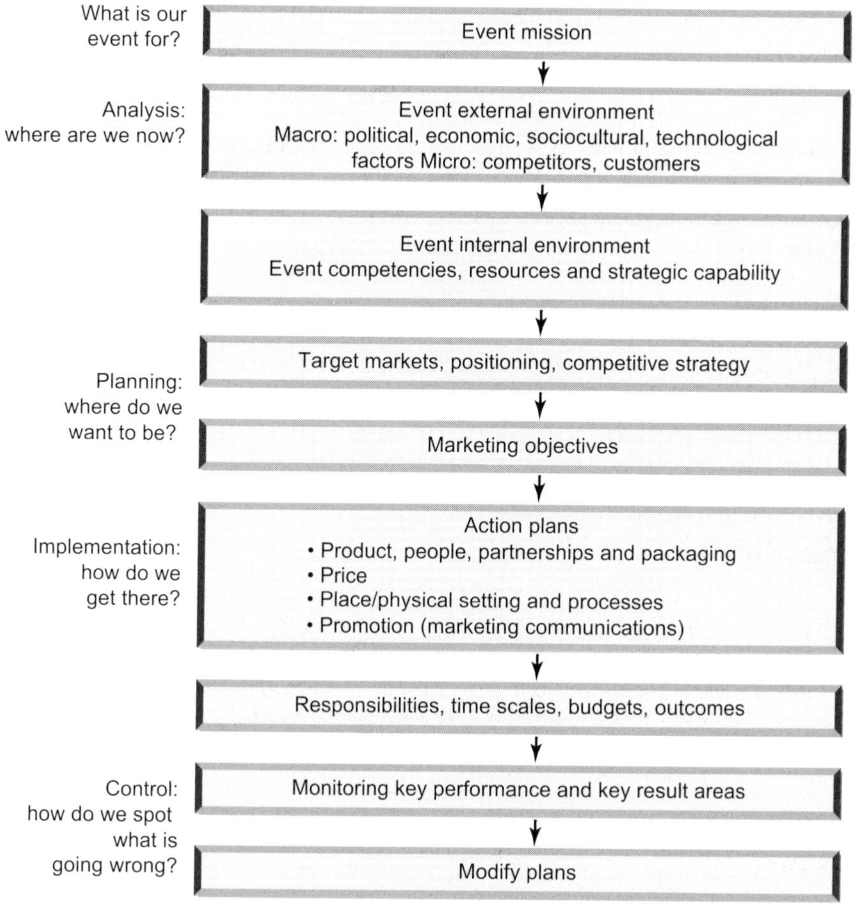

What is our event for? → Event mission

Analysis: where are we now? → Event external environment
Macro: political, economic, sociocultural, technological factors Micro: competitors, customers

Event internal environment
Event competencies, resources and strategic capability

Planning: where do we want to be? → Target markets, positioning, competitive strategy

Marketing objectives

Implementation: how do we get there? → Action plans
• Product, people, partnerships and packaging
• Price
• Place/physical setting and processes
• Promotion (marketing communications)

Responsibilities, time scales, budgets, outcomes

Control: how do we spot what is going wrong? → Monitoring key performance and key result areas

Modify plans

QUESTIONS

1. Why should event managers focus on the needs of their consumers, rather than the needs of the event organisers?

2. Why should an event manager segment a market? What are the advantages?

3. Outline five key motives for attending a community festival attendance.

4. Identify the key steps in the consumer decision-making process. Offer examples of how each step affects the event consumer.

5. What considerations (other than monetary costs) influence decisions on pricing an event?

6. What are the advantages of conducting research into event consumers? Are there any negatives in this process?

7. Provide examples of three forms of product development in the event or festival context.

8. Find an event that uses its website for the sale and distribution of tickets. What are the advantages and disadvantages of this to the event?

CASE STUDY: FORD THUNDERBIRDS BY IMAGINATION

Background

Having agreed to take responsibility for the main design execution of Lady Penelope Creighton-Ward's FAB 1, a 27-feet, pink, six-wheeled Thunderbirds car (as well as the provision of other vehicles, where required), Ford treated their association with the 'Thunderbirds' movie as more than just a 'product placement' opportunity. With this in mind, Ford invited design and communications company Imagination to think about ways to create an entertaining and engaging 'Thunderbirds' experience that would leverage their target family audience. Like FAB 1, it needed to be big, bold and larger than life, as well as make sure the essence of Ford came across – creativity, emotion and excitement...

The solution

So, when it was announced that The Sunday Times Motor Show in 2004 was to move to a slot in late May/June at Birmingham NEC, Imagination saw an opportunity to do something quite spectacular. The tagline 'Thunderbirds Powered by Ford' enabled Imagination to provide a good theme to direct and support Ford's technologies and, with this in mind, Imagination set to work designing a 'best in show' experience for the 7400-m^2 motor show stand, the largest European stand that Imagination had produced for Ford over its 30-year relationship together. The team worked on the interactive stand and live event performance for over 10 months with over 200 staff involved.

An entire themed experience was created, including the Ford design process (linking the original Ford Thunderbird to FAB 1), Brains' Lab (as a test bed for innovative futuristic ideas from Ford), and a style studio for Lady Penelope's pink StreetKa. The stand, nearly the size of a football pitch, was a recreation of International Rescue base, Tracy Island, complete with an 840-m^2 'lake', a 5-tonne sandy beach, a 16-m long model of Thunderbird 2 (suspended from above the stand) along with a huge array of ground-breaking lighting and sound equipment. Props used in the Universal Pictures film 'Thunderbirds', which was to be released to the UK in July 2004, were also incorporated. The stand was divided into over 11 different areas, including a VIP upper deck, an International Rescue Vehicle Hanger and even a submerged Thunderbirds Submarine which appears within the live show. The Ford range of cars, including the FAB 1, Lady Penelope Creighton-Ward's stunning pink, six-wheel, bubble canopy limousine, was also on full display to the public until the end of the motor show. Designed to create a 'family friendly' atmosphere, visitors could interact with the experience as well as be entertained. In addition to the core stand, Imagination created a fun, live-action show featuring audience participation, as well as a brand film, aimed directly at a family audience, that made the most of Ford's link with 'Thunderbirds'. This 'experiential' approach involving the whole audience is something which both The Ford Motor Company and the Birmingham Motor Show organisers, the Society of Motor Manufacturers and Traders, were keen to establish at the 2004 show.

Ford's Public Affairs Department also took advantage of the experience by asking Imagination to organise its eve-of-show press event, where invitees included design, TV, film and lifestyle press, as well as the core automotive media, together with writing, designing and producing a limited edition Press Pack about the making of FAB 1.

Results

Overall, the dramatic stand architecture, controlled walk-through experience, live show and merchandise helped to draw visitors through the entire product display. The whole experience was considered a huge success by public, press and clients alike and was visited by approximately 250,000–300,000 visitors over the course of the 9-day show.

Its success was also demonstrated in the sheer volume of press interest that it attracted. Ford's involvement in the show itself attracted column inches in local and national papers including *The Sunday Times*, *Daily Telegraph*, *Birmingham Evening Mail* and *The Mirror*, as well as TV and media coverage from ITV, BBC, Five and Sky News. In addition, a host of industry and design magazines – including *FX Magazine*, *Design Week* and *Events Magazine* – were keen to concentrate on Imagination's role on the project. 'Thunderbirds Powered By Ford' received a certificate of High Commendation in the 'Automotive' category and was short-listed in the 'Best Brand Experience' category of the 2004 Marketing Brand Design Awards.

Acknowledging the project as an important part of their strategy to appeal to a wider family audience, Ford achieved its goal to deliver a compelling, exciting and fantastic visitor experience. Mark Cameron, Sponsorship and Events Manager, Ford of Britain noted:

> *Ford's Thunderbirds partnership with Universal Pictures provided an exciting and challenging project brief for Imagination to work with. The results are nothing short of amazing; providing a vibrant, engaging and unique experience for the huge numbers of expected visitors at the Ford stand. We want our customers to discover how fun and innovative the Ford brand is by creating much more than simply a display of the latest hot metal.*

Imagination's Chris Marsh, Group Account Director, added,

> *Experiential design is all about developing a positive lasting customer engagement and to create an exhibition experience with this theme has been a design dream. The biggest challenge was not where to start, but where to stop in terms of letting the imagination run on the project. Creating the best ways to communicate, inform and have fun has allowed us at Imagination to become kids again and in the process deliver a win-win for Ford, Universal and the audiences directly in the 'live' spirit of this whole event.*

SUMMARY

It is clear that developing a live event, which reflected the ethos of Ford and engaged visitors in an interactive brand experience, was key to the success of the Thunderbird concept. Increasingly with the way that shows are developing, organisers, exhibitors and their designers have to be increasingly creative in order to capture the imagination of visitors. The partnership with Universal Pictures, and the Thunderbirds film, provided a clear opportunity for the Imagination designers to use their talents to bring the brand alive and provided visitors with a memorable event.

For further information about The Imagination Group, please visit www.imagination.co.uk.

By Imagination, 25 Store Street, South Crescent, London WC1E 7BL.

Questions

1. How does Ford Thunderbirds outlined above meet the definition of an event? How would you classify this type of event?
2. The case study discusses the concept of experiential design. What do you understand by this term? How is this applied in the Ford Thunderbirds event?
3. Identify the 'five Ws' of the Ford Thunderbirds event. What do you consider to be the prime 'wow' factor of the event?
4. Effective theming can add an additional dimension of attractiveness and impact to an event. Discuss this statement with reference to the above Ford Thunderbirds event.

CASE STUDY: IDEAL HOME SHOW

Background

Maintaining a market leading position for a major exhibition may be a challenge for many organisers, but achieving this for a show that has been the biggest home event since 1908 is all the more remarkable. The Ideal Home Show, now organised by Media 10 Limited at Earls Court in London, has reflected changes in society and home living since those early days, and continues to innovate in order to meet the needs of visitors.

The target audience for the show is homeowners and new home buyers who are in the market to refurnish their home, seeking products and services, advice and inspiring ideas in DIY, gardening and the lifestyles they provide to their families. Research undertaken after the 2009 show on behalf of the organisers identified that 83% of the visitors were from ABC1 social grades and over 30% above the national average, with 67% of the total visitors female. Over the duration of the show, a total of £100,000,000 was spent, an average of £475 per visitor. As can be appreciated from these figures, the show presents an excellent opportunity for exhibitors to showcase innovative new products, services and design ideas, and also to sell directly to a clearly defined target market. The Ideal Home Show attracts the highest audited attendance of all consumer exhibitions in the UK, with the 2009 show drawing over 200,000 visitors and the 2010 show aiming to break through 300,000 visitors across 17 days.

Innovations for 2010

The 2010 Ideal Home Show (in association with npower) has been developed to have a brand new look and feel following the new ownership by Media 10. The organisers recruited a panel of celebrities to advise on content and features, including Gregg Wallace, Linda Barker, Monty Don, Fiona Phillips and George Clarke. The celebrity guests offered expert advice on everything from home improvement and interior design to gardens, gadgets and the latest innovations. The new-look Ideal Home Show explores the world of home interiors and style with a fresh, new, inspiring and entertaining show format that includes eight exciting shows in one, offering Ideal Interiors, Ideal Home Improvements, Ideal Food, Ideal Gardens, Ideal Home Gadgets, Ideal Shopping, Ideal Woman and Ideal Village.

Ideal Interiors. Ideal homes reflect the personality and personal style, and there will be plenty of inspiration on offer in the Ideal Interiors area of the Ideal Home Show. Whatever visitors' tastes, they will find plenty of choice for every room in the house, from clever storage and impressive furniture to innovative design and decorating solutions. Visitors are able to take inspiration from professionally designed room sets, which will fire their imagination and help them find the perfect look for their ideal home. Features include:

- The Central Marina – The focal point of the show this year is the stunning Central Marina, where visitors can take time out from the bustling aisles by getting on the water. Three decked bridges lead to the superb Floating Cafe, where you can soak in the view of the Ideal Village over a light bite. There will be a sumptuous Sunseeker boat to explore, plus a unique Floating Office pod, on this exciting feature for 2010. Complete with four 15-m screens broadcasting live show news every day, this stunning central spectacle offers a fantastic Marina experience, right at the heart of UK's biggest home show!

Ideal Home Improvements. Ideal Home Improvement provides the very best in innovations, from making best use of the space you have with clever storage solutions to planning or converting new living spaces. Visitors can discover the latest eco-solutions to help save energy and improve your carbon footprint in your home. Ideal Home Improvements features an array of top brands and ideas. Features include:

- How to Theatre – The theatre is home to live seminars and demonstrations presented by leading experts and TV celebrities offering the latest advice and ideas for DIY, home improvements, exterior design and much, much more! Hosted by an expert compere, each 15- to 20-min session offers practical tips as well as new ideas and information.

- Ideal Home of the Future sponsored by Virgin Media – The Ideal Home of the Future showcases the latest in technology, design and innovation for the home.
- Ideal Home Magazine Roomsets – Ideal Home Magazine is once again presenting its fabulous room sets at the Ideal Home Show this year, presenting a range of contemporary, attainable designs and ideas for across the home. The rooms will include a bedroom, kitchen, bathroom and children's room, and showcase the latest trends and clever design solutions that visitors can be transfer into their own living space. This year the rooms have a 'Luxe for Less' theme, with colours, patterns and textures that show how to create a dream boudoir, or a spa-style bathroom at home, plus living room storage ideas and schemes to give the kids what they want too – all without breaking the bank!

Ideal Food. Ideal Food features the ever-popular Chef's Kitchen Theatre, showcasing the top culinary names preparing some delectable dishes live at the Ideal Home Show. Sit, watch and listen to the world's best chefs giving you the best seat in the house whilst they work their magic. Features include:

- Celebrity Chef Theatre – The Celebrity Chef Theatre, situated in Ideal Food, provides the opportunity for visitors to gain first-hand inspiration from their cooking heroes.
- Zilli Cafe – Located on the upper level, 'Taste of Zilli' will offer visitors café style eating, with Italian street food, in a relaxed, stylish and quiet setting away from the hustle and bustle of the main show.

Ideal Gardens. Ideal Gardens brings together all the latest innovations for outdoor living. If visitors are planning a new patio, looking for the perfect furniture set or planning to turn their garden into that extra 'outdoor room' to relax and enjoy, then this area will provide inspiration. Features include:

- Show Gardens – The Show Gardens at this year's Ideal Home Show will strive to entertain and educate all who visit. Designed by top TV Gardener David Domoney, the gardens will feature a tribute to Alice in Wonderland, a section dedicated to 'sexy plants', as well as introducing visitors to a series of brand new plants, never seen before. The centrepiece of these gardens, however, will appeal to the sweet toothed, a pure chocoholics dream, with a garden completely made of chocolate.
- Lodge & Garden Café – Holiday homes in the UK are growing in popularity and are now more affordable than ever. At the Leisure Lodge feature, visitors will see how much luxury they can get for less in a brand new lodge home, The Woodland Oak, which has features they would be thrilled to have in their permanent home. It comes fully furnished with features, such as a beautiful open-plan kitchen complete with an American-style fridge freezer, a walk-in wardrobe with a dressing area and a 32-inch LCD flat-screen TV in the lounge. Outside, the lodge has a decking area with a hot tub and is set within a landscape of mature trees and plants to really set the scene and feel of peaceful, relaxing holidays.

Ideal Home Gadgets. Ideal Home Gadgets is the place to find the very best in labour saving devices at the Ideal Home Show. Visitors can watch demonstrations of the latest innovations in homewares to help prepare food or clean your home, see if there is a better or more economical way of doing an everyday task or discover the latest models of one's most loved items at home that may need replacing.

Ideal Shopping. Upstairs at Earls Court visitors will find a wealth of gifts and gadgets in the popular Ideal Shopping area of the Ideal Home Show. Must-have items and good ideas are everywhere, some which visitors might not even realise that they need until they have seen them demonstrated at the show.

Continued

CASE STUDY: IDEAL HOME SHOW—*CONT'D*

Ideal Woman. Ideal Woman at the Ideal Home Show sees the return of the Beauty Bar where visitors can take time out and indulge themselves with a manicure or make-up lesson and escape the bustle of the Ideal Home Show. They can also shop here for unique and stylish accessories, or fashion and hair products, pick up health and fitness advice and test fitness equipment and health products. Features include:

- The Beauty Bar – With an air of a spa, visitors will be able to book in treatments or take some refreshments in this calm and relaxing area.
- The Catwalk – Visitors will be able to see what's in store for 2010 with two daily fashion shows (three on weekends and Thursdays). Models will be showing off a variety of stylish fashions.

Ideal Village. There are not two or even three fabulous houses at the show in 2010 but five amazing homes! At the Ideal Village, sponsored by Anglian Home Improvements, visitors see some very different houses, each of which meets the needs of a different part of the housing sector. Two houses, a single-storey property and a two-storey home called 'Cube Living', cover affordable, yet high tech living for the first-time buyer. A three-bedroom executive home features open-plan living and a traditional town house provides accommodation for a family of four. The fifth property looks at how you can update an existing home and reduce your running costs, and of course all have stunning interiors designed to give you plenty of decorating ideas and inspiration!

Ideal Homes for Heroes Appeal 2010

The Ideal Home Show 2010 is supporting ABF The Soldiers' Charity to raise £100,000 for 'Ideal Homes for Heroes'. This ground-breaking partnership will fund grants and home improvements for soldiers, including those returning from current and recent conflicts in Afghanistan and Iraq. The scale and scope of the appeal work will be vast but, in particular, will help with vital home adaptations, home improvements, general housing needs and homelessness of those who served in the armed forces. The appeal will also offer funds to support older veterans who need assistance with home adaptations so that they can stay in their own homes, as well as support those coping with other issues, such as homelessness, debt and unemployment and those suffering post-traumatic stress disorder. To meet this £100,000 target, the Ideal Home Show is donating 50p of every ticket sold to this appeal. In addition, there will be a special Troops Day on 22 March, the first Monday of the show, as a tribute to the Armed Forces. This will include military-themed events and performances, with hundreds of troops attending to officially launch this fantastic appeal.

SUMMARY

The organisers of the Ideal Home Show, Media 10, have maintained its position as the leading home lifestyle consumer show through continuous innovation. Working effectively with exhibitors, sponsors, celebrity designers and the media ensures that creative new features are added each year, while incorporating interactive elements to the show ensures that visitors have an enjoyable experience. This is clearly appropriate given the aim of the event and has proven to be a winning formula since 1908. Extensive research before, during and after the event, conducted with visitors, exhibitors and the wider target market, ensures that the show reflects trends and styles in society and continues to meet the needs of attendees by delivering quality events, strong market opportunities for exhibitors and the best visitor experiences. Media 10 subscribe to Audit Bureau of Circulations (ABC) auditing of the show attendance data, which ensures that data are comparable with other exhibitions. In 2009, these data indicated that the show was the largest consumer show in the UK.

For further information on the Ideal Home Show, please visit www.idealhomeshow.co.uk.
By Media 10.

Questions

1. What is the purpose of constructing a visitor profile? What other details could this include?
2. What needs does this exhibition try to meet?
3. What constitutes the exhibition product?
4. How has the Ideal Home Show developed over the years?
5. Who are the stakeholders of the Ideal Home Show?

Promotion: integrated marketing communication for events

12

LEARNING OBJECTIVES

After studying this chapter, you should be able to:

- describe the purpose of integrated marketing communications for event management,
- describe the constituent elements of these communications,
- apply these concepts to the integrated marketing of events.

INTRODUCTION

Where 'promotion' was once the primary term for the communication element in the marketing mix, the use of 'integrated marketing communication' (IMC) has all but overtaken it. With diverse changes in media technology, market expectations and competition, the traditional idea of promoting 'to' a market has been replaced by the need to form relationships 'with' the market. The term integrated marketing communications has long been found in the marketing literature (see, for example, James, 1972; Shaw, Seminik and Williams, 1981; Barry, 1986; Linton and Morely, 1995; Belch and Belch, 2004; Pickton and Broderick, 2005). Its first use in the area of a leisure activity (tourism) was probably that of McDonnell (1999) who used the case of Australian leisure travel to Fiji and Bali to demonstrate how IMCs help achieve a tourist destination's marketing objectives. He proposed the intefrag marketing continuum, which posited that the closer an organisation's marketing was to the integrated end of the continuum (and further away from the fragmented end, hence 'intefrag') the more effective it would be. As with tourism products and other leisure services, so with festivals and special events. The more integrated the marketing communication, the more effective it will be in achieving an event's marketing objectives because potential consumers see and hear consistent messages, imagery and activities produced to satisfy needs that motivate them to attend the event.

Events Management. DOI: 10.1016/B978-1-85617-818-1.10012-X

Smith and Taylor (2004) define the communications mix as consisting of the following:

- personal selling
- advertising
- sales promotion
- direct mail

- publicity
- sponsorship
- exhibitions
- packaging

- merchandising
- word of mouth
- corporate identity

With the possible exception of exhibitions, all these elements can be effectively used by marketers of special events. They state that integrated simply means that a *unified* message is consistently reinforced, when any or all these communication techniques are used.

From another viewpoint, the American Marketing Association (AMA, 2010) defined IMCs as:

> *A planning process designed to assure that all brand contacts received by a customer or prospect for a product, service, or organization are relevant to that person and consistent over time.*

Moreover, Shimp (2010, p. 10) defines IMC as:

> *A communications process that entails the planning, creation, integration and implementation of diverse forms of marcom (advertisements, sales promotions, publicity, releases, events, etc.) that are delivered over time to a brand's targeted customers and prospects.*

Another view of IMC provided by Shimp (2010, p. 7) is that IMC 'considers all touch points, or sources of contact, that a customer/prospect has with the brand [event] as potential delivery channels for messages and makes use of all communication methods that are relevant to customers/prospects'. The underlying premise of Shimp's view is of course that all sources of contact are consistent messages, constantly reinforced with similar meanings.

From these definitions it can be seen that, for marketing communications to be properly integrated, they must have the qualities of being unified and consistent with all aspects of the event's marketing mix and clear in their message, which results from a coordinated management process. This is reinforced by Linton and Morley's (1995) claim that the advantages of integration (IMC) are consistency of message, more effective use of media, improved marketing precision, cost savings, creative integrity and operational efficiency.

APPLICATION OF IMC

As with all marketing techniques, IMC strategies for events and festivals are based on knowledge about their consumers and potential consumers, that is, the target market. How an event manages its consumer relationships drives its brand value

(Duncan, 2002). When we think about an event brand such as Glastonbury Festival, we think of 'an integrated bundle of information and experiences that distinguish [it]' (Duncan, 2002, p. 13) from competing leisure experiences. Figure 12.1 offers an insight into the IMC process for an event, and the range of traditional and non-traditional media that help to create its brand relationships.

Branding for an event is much more than a physical identity, such as the five interlocking rings of the Olympics. The Olympics brand is based on consumer perceptions, how they relate to that event and what it promises, as well as the physical logo and symbols (for example, the Olympic torch). However, clever integrated and consistent use of the brand helps the event manager to make an intangible phenomenon more tangible for event consumers, as the 100 years of use of the Olympic symbols and imagery have exemplified.

In developing an IMC strategy, an event manager should understand four sources of brand messages, or marketing communications, as in this case they are synonymous (Duncan, 2002):

1. planned messages (media releases, personal selling by the box office and/or ticket agency, advertising, e-newsletters, websites — in other words, all the planned promotional activities)

FIGURE 12.1 The IMC process model for events

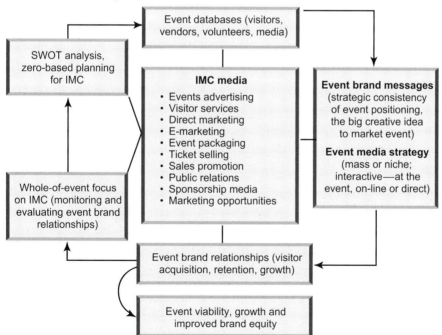

(Source: adapted from Duncan, 2002, p. 9)

2. unplanned messages (unexpected positive or negative impressions formed by word of mouth, media coverage, complaints)
3. product messages (implied messages of information about the event — programme, pricing, venue)
4. service messages (the nature of contact with festival or event staff or volunteers, the quality of event transport and other support services)

Given these message types, the event brand is shaped by more than its planned promotional tools; instead, there are many influences on the brand, some of which are more controllable than others.

Mirroring the strategy process, the development of an IMC plan hinges on an effective SWOT/C-PEST analysis, plus competitor, consumer and stakeholder research. The information from the analysis and research provides the platform for deciding whether objectives and strategies for the IMC campaign should be informational, transformational (attitudinal), behavioural or relational in their focus. Figure 12.2 shows how these different approaches correspond with the 'think, feel, act' model of consumer behaviour. However, for most community and social events, the majority of messages will be informational.

FIGURE 12.2 Event message objectives and strategies

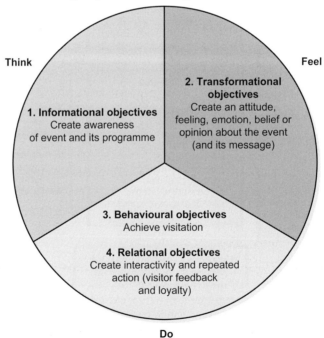

Think

Feel

1. Informational objectives
Create awareness
of event and its programme

2. Transformational objectives
Create an attitude,
feeling, emotion, belief or
opinion about the event
(and its message)

3. Behavioural objectives
Achieve visitation

4. Relational objectives
Create interactivity and repeated
action (visitor feedback
and loyalty)

Do

(Source: adapted from Duncan, 2002, p. 320)

ESTABLISHING THE IMC BUDGET

The quip 'I know that half of my advertising is wasted, but I don't know which half' is usually attributed to Lord Leverhume, the English industrialist and soap manufacturer, and the addition of 'and I don't know if that is half enough or twice too much' is attributed to the American department store magnate John Wanamaker (Kotler et al., 2010). So it can be seen that allocating the most efficient amount of resources for an IMC plan is no easy task. Kotler et al. (2010) advised four methods to establish a budget for this activity:

1. top down — what the event can afford
2. top down — percentage of sales method
3. top down — competitive parity method
4. objective and task method

The first three methods are referred to as top down because management fixes an amount to be spent on promotion without considering what its outcomes are to be and imposes the budget.

What the event can afford

Most community festivals and amateur sports events have limited resources to produce the event, and the amount to spend on IMC can be rigorously debated among the executive. Such debate transpires probably because most people consider themselves to be experts on 'advertising' and therefore assert that they know how much should or should not be spent. A figure is then decided on what is thought can be afforded, not on what is needed to achieve the event's marketing objectives. If an event is new or is being relaunched it will need more resources (financial and human) than an event that is well established in a target market. In this case what is thought can be afforded may well be far short of the resources required to communicate the event's need-satisfying properties to its target market. This method is what Belch and Belch (2004) referred to as the top-down method, where the board or top management sets a spending limit and the event marketer then constructs an IMC plan that may or may not achieve the event's marketing objectives using the resources allocated. It also applies to smaller community festivals and events where the board or festival coordinator makes a decision on the spend when constructing a budget.

Percentage of sales method

This method is commonly used in the marketing of fast-moving consumer goods, where the budget for promotion is set at x% of the forecast revenue. It has the claimed advantage of providing stability to the event as the resources allocated to promotion should be commensurate with the return. However, it is clear that this method is based on the false premise of sales cause promotion rather than promotion causes sales.

Competitive parity method

This method establishes what other similar events spend on IMC and then bases the promotional spend on this figure; it is based on the premise that, if the norm for that sector is used, the event is adhering to the collective wisdom of the sector. This of course begs the question of whether the collective wisdom is correct. Every event has different characteristics and the IMC resources required can differ greatly. The disadvantage of the three top-down approaches (affordable, percentage of sales and competitive parity) is that they are not linked to any promotional objectives and the ways in which these objectives are achieved.

Objective and task method

The objective and task method consists of three sequential steps (Belch and Belch, 2004):

- establish IMC objectives
- determine specific tasks to achieve these objectives
- calculate approximate cost of tasks

It is the most rational of the four methods.

The budget then is the total of these costs, which is the method of budget construction that can help achieve an event's overall objectives. Figure 12.3 shows how this is done for a local community festival — Pittwater Festival in Manly (Sydney, Australia). Figure 12.3 shows that by using this rational and logical method, the marketing communication objectives of an event can be met at reasonable cost.

ELEMENTS OF IMC

Importantly, consumers do not react to marketing messages in any set order — they may feel, then act (local festival attendance) and later reflect on the experience, or they may go through a sequential processing of 'think, feel and act' (such as a decision to visit France to attend the next Rugby World Cup, a decision that has financial implications and therefore takes a great deal of thought, discussion and reflection). It is important to consider these different decision-making patterns of market segments when deciding how to set out the objectives of a campaign.

The IMC strategy reflects the thrust of the chosen objectives and uses both message and media strategies to fulfil them. To illustrate, the Leeds Carnegie rugby union team may have a behavioural objective of 'achieving a 10% increase in attendance at home games at Headingley Carnegie Stadium in 2010'. Their message strategy would be developed with reference to the psychological appeal — for example, motivators such as the responsibility of locals to support the home side and the atmosphere and nostalgia attached to Headingley as a rugby venue.

FIGURE 12.3 Objective and task budget setting for the Pittwater Festival

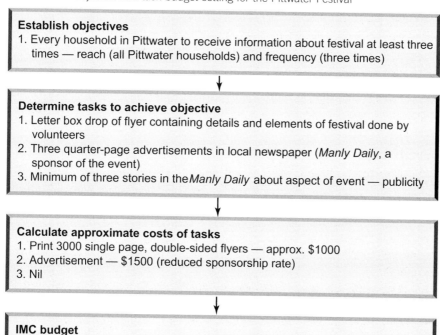

Establish objectives
1. Every household in Pittwater to receive information about festival at least three times — reach (all Pittwater households) and frequency (three times)

Determine tasks to achieve objective
1. Letter box drop of flyer containing details and elements of festival done by volunteers
2. Three quarter-page advertisements in local newspaper (*Manly Daily*, a sponsor of the event)
3. Minimum of three stories in the *Manly Daily* about aspect of event — publicity

Calculate approximate costs of tasks
1. Print 3000 single page, double-sided flyers — approx. $1000
2. Advertisement — $1500 (reduced sponsorship rate)
3. Nil

IMC budget
$2500

Planning the IMC campaign requires 'one voice, one look' (Duncan, 2002) — that is, all direct marketing, advertising, publicity and event packaging must convey the same message and look in its communication. At a national level, the 2002 Manchester Commonwealth Games successfully achieved 'one voice, one look' with its campaign for the games.

For the RBS 6 Nations Series for rugby union, the media strategy could involve choosing how the mix of planned advertising, e-marketing, publicity and/or other media will be used to best convey the message about packages to the games. As shown in Figure 12.1, the IMC mix can include a wide range of marketing communication functions. Public relations may involve the use of a celebrity spokesperson in the campaign — for example, rugby legend Martin Johnston could be used to boost interest in the games. A direct mail campaign and an e-mail newsletter to a database of corporate executives (a key market for rugby) could also feature Martin Johnston and give further strategic consistency to the campaign. Sales promotion in the form of a competition directed at the national supporters clubs might also bolster demand for the attendees at rugby games, which could include participation at a dinner hosted by Martin Johnston that continues the integrated marketing theme.

Given the numerous marketing communication tools to include in an IMC mix, the event marketer needs to be familiar with their strengths and weaknesses, including their budgetary implications. An event with a mass market (for example, the Great Yorkshire Show or a major sporting event) may use television advertising as a promotional device, whereas planned IMC for a community festival is more likely to concentrate on organised word of mouth, local media publicity and community service announcements, or indeed increasingly social networking sites. A brief review of the more commonly used marketing communication media is offered here.

Advertising

Advertising is any form of non-personal promotion paid for by the event organisation. Radio, television, newspapers, magazines, the Internet, outdoor advertising (billboards, bus shelters and toilets) and mobile platforms such as buses and taxis are all channels for advertising. For most events and festivals, the expense of mainstream media (television, newspapers and radio) cannot be justified. Media partnerships (such as Cambridge Festival's sponsorship by BBC Radio 2 or Channel 4 and Virgin Radio's partnerships/sponsorships at V Festival) can help to resolve this issue. However, the creative process of producing the messages can also be expensive, especially if done by an advertising agency. In creating advertising campaigns for events and festivals, it is vital to:

- provide tangible clues to counteract the intangible nature of the event — that is, show the artistic event or sports players in action, the event logo and the spectacle of the fireworks;
- seek continuity over time by using recognisable symbols, spokespersons, trademarks or music — for example, football codes often use the tunes of famous artists, such as 'We are the champions' by Queen;
- promise what is possible to foster realistic expectations — for example, show real-time action (it is necessary to take care with promises about ticket availability because they can become contentious), and
- make the service more tangible and recognisable by showing members of the target market enjoying the event — for example, the roar and spectacle of a grand final crowd at the football can be very persuasive to the target market of a football event.

The metric usually applied to advertising effectiveness is reach and frequency — the number of people in the target market that the promotional message has reached and how many times they have received the promotional message. Farris et al. (2006) consider as a general rule that four exposures (frequency) to a message are necessary for it to be effective.

Public relations

Public relations (PR) is used to build mutually beneficial relationships with stakeholders and consumers. It uses a wide range of tools, including publicity, special promotional events, community consultation, e-publications and traditional newsletters. While all activities incur costs, media publicity is often favoured by festival organisers because it provides unpaid space in the media that reaches the event's market. An advantage to festival and event directors is that people generally enjoy reading about sports, arts and entertainment. However, marketers must be aware that the media will use a story only if it has news value (a unique angle or item of information of interest to readers, viewers or listeners). Journalists also carefully assess the structure and style of media releases, and the credibility of their source. The event profile demonstrates the advantages of this promotional method.

An interesting example of the use of publicity was the handing out of 1000 free tickets to a Blackburn Rovers games against Birmingham City through Blackburn with Darwen Council. The aim of the football club was to attract people from a town that had not been to a match before. This action received coverage in the local newspaper, the *Lancashire Telegraph*, and gained the club excellent publicity (Moseley, 2010).

Sales promotion

Sales promotion consists of those activities that use incentives or discounts to increase sales or attendance. Examples of sales promotion are family days at city shows or exhibitions and offering group discounts or a free ticket for one child. Alternatively, consumers may be offered free merchandise (T-shirts and posters) when purchasing several tickets or more. An example is the Real Food Festival offering discounted VIP tickets, through the http://30daysoffoodanddrink.co.uk website, for £9.50 instead of the normal £15 advance/£20 on the door price.

Direct marketing

Direct marketing communicates one-on-one with existing festival or event-goers via postal mail, telephone, e-mail or Internet. It relies on organisers developing a list of people who previously attended the event (or similar events) and obtaining information about their demographic profile and preferences. Incentives for consumers to provide information may include entry in a competition and the receipt of next year's event programme. Organisers can purchase lists of potential event consumers — those who fit the demographic profile — from direct marketing agencies. However, a key consideration in collecting information to build a database is the need to gain consumer permission and to respect their privacy. An understanding of current regulations about direct marketing (including the use of e-newsletters) is now mandatory. With the now almost total penetration of home computers, the use of e-mail for these direct marketing activities is far more efficient. For example, Strauss and Frost (2009) showed, in Table 12.1, that cost efficiencies gained by using e-mail, rather than postal mail. The task for the event marketer is to assemble a reliable e-mail list of the target

Table 12.1 Metrics for electronic and postal mail

Activity	E-mail	Postal Mail
Delivery cost per thousand	$30	$500
Creative costs to develop	$1,000	$17,000
Click through rate	10%	N/A
Customer conversion rate	5%	3%
Execution time	3 weeks	3 months
Response time	48 hours	3 weeks

(Source: Jupiter Communications in Strauss and Frost, 2009)

market, which is generally built up over time by collecting these data from existing event-goers.

Another effective method of collecting these data is to have a 'contact us' section on the event's website, or an e-newsletter. The event can build a database of all who made an enquiry by e-mail, which means that they are part of its target market. This then gives an event a most efficient resource that can be used to transmit IMCs, as Table 12.1 shows.

On-line presence

The event website is another IMC resource that, if used successfully, is a most effective and efficient method of communicating with its target market. The event website construction is usually best outsourced to a professional website designer; however, the event manager must know how to brief the web designer. Figure 12.4 shows the steps involved in website construction that form the basis of the brief to be given to the designer.

Planning consists of establishing the purpose or function of the site, which can be to:

- offer information about the event to potential consumers, that is, to have an on-line brochure — brochureware;
- provide a forum where potential consumers can interact with the site by asking questions of event staff via a 'contact us' page, provision of a frequently asked questions page, provision of a full calendar of event elements — interact;
- provide a platform where consumers can make transactions by purchasing tickets using a credit card and then have the tickets e-mailed to them — transact, and
- have all aspects of the event management, marketing and production integrated into the website — integration.

Figure 12.5 shows the choices and the nexus between investment and Internet-based interaction.

The function of the website depends on the type of event. For example, a simple community cultural event needs only a brochure website. A larger community

FIGURE 12.4 A model of the website construction process

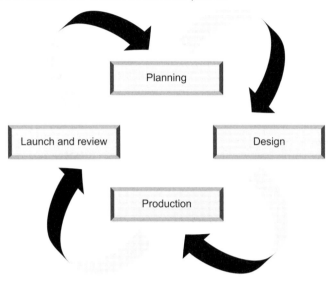

FIGURE 12.5 Types of internet-based marketing for events

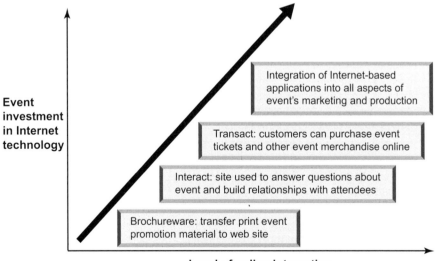

(Source: adapted from O'Connor and Galvin, 1998)

festival may decide on an interactive site. A large music festival could decide on a transaction site. An academic or professional conference may choose an integration style, where site delegates can register and pay for the conference, book accommodation and travel, submit academic papers and plan their programme.

Once the website's function and objectives have been agreed on, the next step is to decide on content and look, which of course has to be integrated and consistent with all other marketing communications that the event uses.

Website design

The key to the success of a website, no matter what function is chosen, is to ensure that the site is simple and easy to use — in other words, that it is user-friendly. After the function is chosen, the design or look of the web pages containing the text graphics and other media are selected. They have to be consistent and integrated with all other marketing communications used by the event. While a site might need only a low-level interactivity to suit an event's needs, it still needs to be integrated with the other non-on-line communications.

An on-line search for advice on web design for the novice designer will produce millions of hits. In addition, there are thousands of published texts available on the subject of web design and creation. Sites may be professionally produced by an external web design company or depending on skills (and budget) may be produced internally. Two sites that specialise in sites for events are http://www.eventware.co.uk and http://www.aspevents.net.

The basic website design principles are:

- determine the basic layout of the site so that the various pages are linked in a coherent manner;
- ensure that the content imagery is consistent with and integrated with any off-line marketing communications and consistent throughout the site;
- make sure that the site is easy to read by using an appropriate font and lots of white space, use dot points rather than continuous text and use simple colour schemes rather than complex and garish ones;
- use an easy to understand navigation system (framed or unframed), use either a side bar or navigation system along the top or bottom of the page, so that viewers know where they are and how to get to the pages they want;
- determine the copy and supporting graphics before posting to the site to ensure that they can achieve the site's objectives;
- do not make the text too complex or dense — no viewer enjoys ploughing through hectares of text, except perhaps academics, lots of white space is easy on the eye and attractive to the viewer;
- do not use capital text in the copy as it implies SHOUTING;
- while many texts suggest the use of thumbnail graphics linked to a larger version of the image, the speed of most browsers makes this usually unnecessary for most event websites, especially with the trend of users towards a broadband connection. However, if a site contains many graphics, the page will certainly load faster

with thumbnails. The spread of broadband connections means that many sites now effectively utilise flash animation.

- ensure that the home page (the first page in the site) can load quickly and is displayed on one or a maximum of two pages;
- provide a clearly signposted 'contact us' page;
- give details of the site's privacy policy to engender confidence in users;
- for transaction sites, provide details of the security system used to ensure that users feel confident about using a credit card for purchases and
- use the web page production programme's default colours unless there is an aesthetic reason to vary them. For example, web surfers are used to and comfortable with blue for unvisited links, which then change to a darker colour such as purple to indicate a visited link.

Given the advancement in web development, it may be appropriate to implement a content management system (CMS). This is a database-driven website that once fully implemented will allow relatively quick updates using a WYSIWYG (What you see is what you Get) text editor. This type of website is particularly useful for sites that will require constant updates, for example, with regular news to keep the website alive and the target market informed. Content management systems need not be expensive — there are a range of Open Source programs available, for example, Joomla or Drupal, some of which include a range of free add-ons (for example, directories, event booking systems, etc.).

Once the site has been produced it is then launched into cyberspace. The launch process is relatively simple: a URL (uniform resource locater) is obtained from a domain name registrar such as http://www.123-reg.co.uk and then loaded onto a hosting package on a web server. Hosting packages can be obtained at competitive prices, with a number offering free software pre-installed, including Joomla and Drupal mentioned earlier. The site can then be submitted to search engines (such as Google, Bing or Yahoo) so that users will be able to locate it.

Search Engine Optimisation is an area that event and festival managers should be aware of. In essence, this means reviewing the website to ensure that the site overall, and individual pages, include descriptions, keywords (in meta-tags and the page) and rich content, together with page names that are clear (Search Engine Friendly), so that the site has the best chance possible of appearing on the first pages of search results in search engines such as Google and Bing. It is also useful to consider implementing some form of tracking, for example, the free service Google Analytics, to see where people who look at your website are coming from, what search terms they used to find you, and how long they stay on your site.

Part of the IMC for an event that uses a website is to promote the site at every opportunity. For example, all off-line marketing communications, such as advertisements, flyers, posters, press releases, directory entries and event stationery, need to highlight the web address (URL) of the site. Arrange for the event site to be linked with complementary sites that can encourage visitors to the site. Other possible sites to link would be national bodies of the particular artistic or sporting endeavour with which the event is involved and banner advertisements from event sponsors. In addition, ensure that the website details are included in appropriate directories, particularly where free entries are available, in order to maximise the chances of potential customers finding the site.

Social Media and Networking

Over recent years, a new communications tool has taken off that has the potential to revolutionise communications, on-line social media. The area is evolving at a rapid pace and the opportunities arising from it for events are only now becoming apparent. Sometimes referred to as Web 2.0, social media is defined by Formic Media (2009) as: 'An umbrella term that defines the various activities that integrate technology, social interaction, and the construction of words and pictures.' Brian Solis (2010), a recognised thought leader and author on the subject, notes that although discussion continues on the definition, a short working definition has been agreed as, 'Any tool or service that uses the Internet to facilitate conversations', with a long version proposed as, 'Social Media is the democratization of information, transforming people from content readers into publishers. It is the shift from a broadcast mechanism, one-to-many, to a many-to-many model, rooted in conversations between authors, people, and peers.'

Social media includes discussion groups, Internet blogs, forums, microblogging, podcasts, social bookmarking, social networking, videos and wikis. In this form, the terms may not be familiar. However, by highlighting a few of the well-known sites, such as Blogger or WordPress (blogging), Facebook (social networking), Flickr (sharing photographs), LinkedIn (social/professional networking), Twitter (micro-blogging), Wikipedia (wiki) and YouTube (video), it is clear that social media is already part of our lives.

Social media offers the opportunity, as the definitions suggest, for anyone to write or produce material and publish this on-line — this may be personal conversation (for example, letting people know what you are currently doing) or professional material (for example, announcing the programme for an event), short (limited to 160 text characters for Twitter or profile updates) or long (length of blog may be limited only by any restrictions placed by the service provider) one. This material may then be communicated through their social network (an on-line group with shared interests) of 'contacts' (LinkedIn), 'friends' (Facebook) or 'followers' (Twitter). One of the key benefits of social media is that it is using one of the oldest forms of communication, word of mouth, and utilising the power of the Internet and the latest mobile technologies to provide the (usually free) tools to connect people together quickly.

Opportunities

Social networking is a phenomenon that has significantly increased in recent years, particularly but not exclusively with the younger market who have grown with it and embraced it during their school, college and university years. As a result, there are major opportunities (and potentially some negative implications) for event managers. With the new tech-savvy audience, a positive or negative experience may be communicated to their network or the on-line community instantly, through services such as Twitter or status updates on Facebook or LinkedIn, and longer reviews of the event may appear on forums or blogs. Likewise, when harnessed with advanced technologies on web-enabled mobile phones, photographs or video footage of the event experience (positive or negative) may also be communicated to the world before the audience has even left the venue. Peter Kerwood, Head of Events at Merlin Entertainment Group, who is an events industry advocate of power of social media, has identified a range of business benefits from social networking for events (Figure 12.6).

As Kerwood (2009) demonstrates, event and festival managers can exploit social media for their events to build an ongoing relationship between the event/organisation and its customers and to ensure that the existing and potential audience receives positive and up-to-date communications about the event. For relatively little cost, beyond the time required to keep updating information and professional development to understand the range, realise the potential, and learn how to use the tools available, event managers can enhance their on-line presence to great effect. In addition, monitoring the on-line chatter informally, or integrating social media monitoring formally within the evaluation plan, can ensure that a rich understanding is gained of what the customer likes about the event, or indeed, where the event could be improved.

SUMMARY

With the addition of the web, social media and networking to the event marketer's toolkit, it is possible to have a fully IMC programme that satisfies an event's marketing objectives at a relatively limited cost, provided that all marketing communications are consistent, integrated with all other communications from the event so that they are unified and consistent with all aspects of the event's marketing mix, and clear in their message. This outcome results from a coordinated management process that ensures that the event's marketing communications are at the integrated end of the intefrag continuum, rather than the fragmented undesirable end.

This chapter has shown why IMC is a significant aspect of event marketing, the methods that can be used to achieve IMCs and the advantages of using Internet-based marketing communications. Without effective IMCs an event will struggle to achieve its objectives, so the techniques discussed in this chapter make up an essential part of the event manager's toolkit. Social media is expanding at a rapid pace, and therefore it is imperative for the event professional of the future to understand how to use this effectively in the digital future.

FIGURE 12.6 Business benefits of social media for events

Information
- Got a question? It's very likely someone somewhere has the answer
- Share your ideas with others, see what they think and gain valuable feedback
- Find what others are saying about a product or article you are interested in
- Teach, learn and interact with likeminded people
- Research information on a company or product
- Brainstorm and collaborate (crowdsource)
- Use Twitter as a tool to stay current on breaking news and events

Customer service
- Use Twitter and Facebook to communicate events and special offers
- Use Twitter to update customers and provide solutions or information in real time
- Develop one-on-one relationships with customers
- Use Twitter and Facebook to conduct polls and surveys to help you offer a better service
- Use social networking to humanize your business

Traffic
- Use social networking sites to send traffic between other social networking platforms that directs traffic to your website or blog
- Interesting or helpful content can be easily passed on to others using social media which helps your content go viral
- User driven content sites such as Digg, and StumbleUpon provide huge increases in traffic to your website or blog

Networking
- Build personal relationships with customers as people are more likely to buy from someone they know and trust
- Connect with peers and like minded people
- Participate in conversations, help out others and become an active participant
- By helping others you create 'social currency' which can be used to leverage your brand from one platform to another
- Ning.com allows you to create your own social groups – there are 4.062 listed under events including EventCrowd
- Professional networking sites include LinkedIn, Xing and Ziggs
- Directories allow you to find and connect with people on social networking sites for events try eventweeps.com

Business Management
- Utilize social networking sites as a tool to see who is talking about your business
- Track positive and negative experiences to improve business performance
- Utilise social networking sites to update or make announcements
- Use sites such as Twitter and Facebook as an intranet system to remind colleagues of meetings and make announcements

(Source: Peter Kerwood, cited in Quainton, 2009)

QUESTIONS

1. Give an example of an event's marketing communications. Place it on the intefrag continuum and explain why it is at that position.

2. Identify an example of an event that uses an integrated website in its operations. What are the advantages of this to the event?

3. Outline an example of an event's IMC. Explain why you consider it to be both effective and efficient from the information available to you.

4. Most UK cities have a programme of events and festivals organised by the local authority or council. Select one event or festival and analyse its marketing communications – establish if they can be made more effective or efficient or both.

5. The potential value of social media and social networking are now beginning to be understood for events and festivals.

    a. Identify an event or festival that has effectively used social media. Why do you believe that their approach is effective?

    b. Evaluate what software/services they have used and discuss how each of these has been integrated with the other aspects of their marketing communications efforts.

    c. What other software/services could they utilise and what other benefits would it bring to their event?

CASE STUDY – INTERNATIONAL CONFEX

Background

Now in its twenty-seventh year, International Confex – the biggest event for people organising events worldwide, organised by Confex Group (a division of United Business Media Information Ltd) – is recognised as Europe's leading annual forum for the meetings, events and corporate hospitality industries and support services. For exhibitors, it is a dedicated forum to showcase brands, products and services. For the visitor, it is more than just a trade show – it is the essential industry forum, where they can meet and network with key decision makers face to face.

The event

International Confex is split into five specialist areas:

1. *UK Venues and Destinations* – visitors planning to organise events within the UK recognise International Confex as the event where they can source the widest range of destination ideas, hotels, conference and exhibition centres, from breathtaking unusual venues to the most popular multi-use venues.
2. *International Venues, Destinations and Travel*: presenting worldwide destinations from the contemporary to the well established, this area includes venues and resorts, business solutions and international travel inspiration.
3. *Corporate Events and Parties*: visitors to International Confex are fully aware of the benefits of corporate events and parties. They visit the show to source all those finishing touches and corporate event services, including incentives, corporate gifts, marquees, caterers, flowers, entertainers, team building events and the most glamorous party venues.

Continued

CASE STUDY – INTERNATIONAL CONFEX—*CONT'D*

4. *Exhibitions and Events Live*: Support services help with the essential elements of any event. From building an exhibition stand for an event to technological support for a conference, this area includes contractors, stand builders insurance, lighting specialists, AV products, technology providers, security, signage, merchandise/gift suppliers and much more.
5. *London Area*: Complementing the UK sector, the London Area flaunts its fabulous offering of venues throughout one of the world's greatest capital cities, including elite and boutique hotels, famous conference and exhibition centres, traditional offerings and tourist favourites.

In total, there were over 400 stands, with around 1000 companies represented across the five areas – filling the ground floor of Earls Court 1. The exhibitors are drawn from over 50 countries, presenting their venues, products and services to UK- and overseas-based visitors.

International Confex is committed to support the events industry. This means assisting, informing, advising and inspiring visitors so that they can hold captivating and inspirational events as well as those that require cost efficiency or involve complicated logistics. Whatever type of event visitors organise, International Confex aims to help them to make it the best it can be. Beyond this the show aims to provide visitors with the tools to help them enhance and further their career.

Confex Knowledge has been introduced to achieve this, through offering a huge variety of seminars and high-level **keynote speeches** which are free to attend on a first-come first-serve basis. Speakers are experts in their field and present a programme of speeches and seminars and take part in panel debates on all aspects of conference organising, incentive travel, corporate hospitality and events. Alongside the educational features, there is a free **Advice Centre** including a **CV Clinic** where specific queries can be addressed, from career advice to finding a venue for unusual requirements.

Visitor marketing programme

Visitors to International Confex can essentially be broken down into two key groups – specialists and generalists.

1. Specialists: visitors whose core job function is an event organiser. These specialist visitors represent blue chip companies, major professional conference organisers, exhibition organisers, agencies and incentive motivation houses.
2. Generalists: these visitors are responsible for meetings and events as part of a wider job remit. This group encompasses visitors including sales and marketing managers, PR executives, training and personnel managers, executive PAs and association executives.

International Confex is known as the one show in the meetings and events industry that delivers. To ensure the quantity and quality of visitors at the show, Confex Group undertakes a comprehensive marketing campaign. This includes advertising, inserts, direct mail, e-mail, PR and joint exhibitor promotions.

- Advertisements and inserts are placed in leading UK industry trade titles, such as Conference & Incentive Travel, Event and Meetings & Incentive Travel, and generalist titles, such as Marketing and Executive PA, as well as key specialist trade titles across Europe.
- The direct mail campaign starts about 4 months before the show. Using Confex Group's extensive databases and external lists, tickets and inserts are sent to carefully targeted individuals. The direct mail campaign reinforces the advertising campaign to ensure the right messages reach the right people, at the right time.
- Marketing by e-mail has increased over the last few years, with regular e-mail news bulletins being sent to both the visitor and exhibitor databases. This is a cost-effective and quick way of communicating regularly with an audience that attends International Confex on an annual basis.

- PR for the event is achieved through editorial in over 60 worldwide publications. Around 20 industry magazines run previews of the event, detailing who is exhibiting and what they will be promoting at the show.
- Promotional opportunities offered to exhibitors include sponsorship to reinforce the exhibitor's message at the show, such as branding of the visitor badges, carrier bags, etc. Exhibitors are issued with visitor invitations and can request visitors to be qualified via an HTML e-mail as a VIP (very important person), to identify key buyers to the show.
- The International Confex website offers exhibitors the opportunity to promote their company on the Web. Each exhibitor may include up to 50 words free of charge, and has the opportunity to add a hyperlink to their own website, or place a banner advertisement to promote their product.
- A training day called Confex Consults, takes place every year with advice for exhibitors to get the most from the show.

With large international trade shows like International Confex, it is increasingly important to ensure that a relationship is built between visitors and exhibitors beyond the show itself. Confex Group is harnessing the power of social media, with visitors and exhibitors now able to follow us on Twitter, and join our groups on Facebook or LinkedIn. This enables us to build the relationship before, during and after the show and keep people updated on show developments for International Confex and other shows within our portfolio.

Evaluation

International Confex is evaluated each year from a variety of perspectives, including extensive on-site visitor evaluation. The statistics from this provides useful information for the organisers and exhibitors and also proves the success of the show for potential exhibitors and visitors. The show itself is ABC audited to ensure that the data produced are authentic, reliable and verified by an external organisation. ABC-audited figures confirmed that International Confex 2010 was a highly successful event, with a total attendance of 14,109, made up of 10,896 registered visitor attendance (an increase on 2009) and 3213 other attendance (press, exhibitor personnel, etc.).

In exhibitions, the number of visitors is important. However, it is the quality of these visitors that will continue to attract the leading companies to exhibit and as such the evaluation gathers these data. The ABC audit in 2010 showed that:

- Confex visitors organise over 100,000 events per year,
- 92% of the events organised are to be held in the UK,
- 83% were looking for conference/meetings venues,
- 1 in 5 visitors' companies spend £1m+ on events,
- 1 in 3 visitors' companies spend more than £0.5m on events,
- 92% of visitors said they would definitely or possibly do business with Confex exhibitors,
- 72% of Confex visitors approve, recommend or influence purchasing decisions,
- 50% of visitors organise over 11 events/annum and
- 215% increase in PAs attending PA Day.

Finally, from the organisers perspective, one of the ultimate measures of an events success is whether exhibitors book for the following year's event – International Confex 2010 exhibitors valued the show so highly that on-site nearly 70% of the show rebooked a stand for International Confex 2011, which in itself is a record.

SUMMARY

As 'the perfect event for any event', International Confex is in the spotlight of fellow industry professionals and the industry media. Confex Group uses the results of visitors, exhibitors and other sources of evaluation to develop the exhibition on an annual basis to increase the quality

Continued

CASE STUDY – INTERNATIONAL CONFEX—*CONT'D*

and quantity of exhibitors and visitors. Through using the social media tools at our disposal, face-to-face networks and relationships can continue on-line all year round. It is only through developing and refining the exhibition in the light of evaluation and the external environment that the International Confex will continue to be the leading annual forum for the events industry.

For further details about International Confex, please visit www.international-confex.com.

By Confex Group

Questions

1. What are the advantages and disadvantages of the marketing campaign used by International Confex?
2. What visitor's needs and wants do International Confex fulfil?
3. What alternative distribution strategies could International Confex utilise?
4. International Confex product includes the opportunity to access Confex Knowledge which includes an educational seminar programme. What other elements could be included in International Confex to develop the exhibition for the future?
5. Why do you think International Confex is successful in attracting the quality and quantity of visitors? What other strategies could be implemented to ensure that this quality is maintained and developed in the future?

Sponsorship of events

13

LEARNING OBJECTIVES

After studying this chapter, you should be able to:

- understand the use of sponsorship in the context of festivals and events,
- discuss trends that have led to the growth of sponsorship as a marketing communication medium in the private and public sectors,
- recognise the benefits that event managers can attract from reciprocal partnerships with sponsors,
- identify the key sponsorship benefits sought by events and sponsoring bodies,
- discuss the importance of sponsorship 'leveraging',
- understand the need for sponsorship policies to guide decision making by events and their sponsors,
- outline the sequential stages in developing and implementing an event sponsorship strategy,
- develop strategies and tactics to manage event—sponsor relationships and achieve positive and enduring relationships with sponsors.

INTRODUCTION

Sponsorship, either provided as cash or in-kind support such as products or services (often called 'contra'), is central to the revenue and resources of new and continuing events. Event managers and marketers are usually actively engaged in tasks such as identifying potential sponsors, preparing sponsorship proposals and managing their ongoing relationships with sponsors, as event sponsorship is a large part of modern event management.

Over the past decade, there has been a significant increase in the number of texts offering guidance related to sponsorship (Amis and Cornwall, 2005; Geldard and Sinclair, 2003; Grey and Skildum, 2003; Jeffries-Fox, 2005; Lagae, 2005; Masterman, 2007; Skinner and Rukavina, 2002). This chapter begins with a discussion of the role and growth of sponsorship as a marketing communication medium. It also explores the benefits that events and their sponsors seek, before explaining the policies, strategies and actions needed for successful event and festival sponsorship.

Interestingly, it is certainly not a modern concept as probably the first recorded instance of sponsorship was undertaken by the Medici family who ruled Florence from 1434 to 1637. Cosimo the Elder (1389—1464) and particularly his grandson Lorenzo the Magnificent (1449—1492) sponsored graphic artists, sculptors and poets

Events Management. DOI: 10.1016/B978-1-85617-818-1.10013-1

such as da Vinci, Donatello and Botticelli, who helped Florence to be at the centre of the artistic Renaissance period. It is reasonable to assume that they sponsored these artists for the same reason that Walker Morris sponsored the inaugural exhibition at the Saatchi Gallery in London — to generate goodwill towards them from a target market, to generate awareness and acceptance of their business and to entertain their clients with hospitality centred on these artistic endeavours.

WHAT IS SPONSORSHIP?

Sponsorship has become a critical element in the integrated marketing communication mix (discussed in Chapter 10) of many private and public sector organisations. Among the different types of marketing communications (for example, public relations, advertising, personal selling, sales promotions and direct marketing), sponsorship is said to be one of the most powerful media now used to communicate and form relationships with stakeholders and target markets (Grey and Skildum-Reid, 2003).

Although sponsorship may be attached to social causes and broadcast media such as television programmes as well as special events (De Pelsmacker, Geuens and Van den Bergh, 2004), just about every public event is now sponsored in some way (Kover, 2001). With the emphasis now on 'connecting with' rather than 'talking at' the marketplace, event and festival sponsorship can be an ideal way for marketers to create brand interaction with consumers and stakeholders. For example, the Co-operative Cambridge Folk Festival engages folk music-loving listeners through their media sponsor BBC Radio 2. In contrast, Chevron or their Texaco brand has sponsored a range of events in the Pembroke areas to build good relationships with the local community where one of their refineries has been based for over 40 years.

The well-known American sponsorship consultancy IEG defines sponsorship as 'a cash and/or in-kind fee paid to a property (typically a sport, entertainment, event, or organisation) in return for the exploitable commercial potential associated with that property' (in Cornwell, Weeks and Roy, 2005). The following definition from the International Chamber of Commerce *International Code on Sponsorship* (ICC, 2003, p. 2) also explains the concept:

> *any commercial agreement by which a sponsor, for the mutual benefit of the sponsor and sponsored party, contractually provides financing or other support in order to establish an association between the sponsor's image, brands or products and a sponsorship property in return for rights to promote this association and/or for the granting of certain agreed direct or indirect benefits.*

Globally, expenditure on event sponsorship has been escalating each year — from £18.1 billion in 2001 to an estimated £29.1 billion in 2005 according to research by consultant SponsorClick (Day, 2002). By 2008, according to Arts & Business, it was estimated to have reached £43.5 billion, although this was a reduction on the previous year due to the global recession (Mermiri and South, 2009). It is difficult to put an accurate value on the market overall, however, overall sponsorship spending in the UK each year is estimated to be around £934 million, made up of sports (51%), arts and business (18%), broadcasting (20%) and others (10%) (Mermiri and South, 2009). Importantly, most spending estimates only take into account the sponsorship purchase itself, but it is generally accepted that many sponsors will spend at least equal to the cost of the event property itself on leveraging or maximising investment impacts (Meenaghan, 2001a). Importantly, sponsorship is a strategic marketing investment, not a donation (philanthropy) or a grant (a one-off type of assistance), which means events and festivals managers must view sponsorships as working business partnerships. Most sponsors are investors who expect to see a direct impact on their brand equity (enhanced awareness and imagery) as well as the potential for increased sales and profits. In the case of public sector sponsors, some kind of social marketing result is usually sought (for example, a greater awareness of water conservation or the dangers of drink driving). Tetley sought to maximise their image as 'The Beer' of Rugby League following their 5-year sponsorship of Tetley's Rugby Super League with signing up as 'Official Beer' partners of many of the league's clubs (Anon, 2005b), while in 2004 THINK! (the road safety campaign of the Department of Transport) boosted the awareness of their 'Save Racing for the Track' message to motorcyclists through sponsoring the British Superbikes Championship.

While long-term cash sponsors are highly sought after by events and festivals (for example, Coca-Cola's continuing long-term sponsorship of the Olympics), a mix of private sector cash and in-kind sponsorship, plus grants, can be vital for festivals. As discussed in the case study in Chapter 9, Edinburgh International Festival secured revenue from three main revenue streams: ticket sales (£2.25 million), sponsorship and donations (£2.03 million) and public sector grants (£5.1 million). Sponsorship may also take the form of in-kind sponsorship, for example, through a media partner in radio or television, promoting the event or festival effectively rather than providing direct funds. Hence, creating a successful event or gaining festival sponsorship means establishing a reciprocal relationship between the organisation providing the sponsorship (corporate, media and/or government) and the event. However, it also means an emotional connection must be made with those consumers targeted by both the event and its sponsors. This three-way relationship, which underpins the success of sponsorship, is illustrated in Figure 13.1. Sponsors use events to emotionally tie their product or service to a market segment that identifies with the event and consequently identifies with the sponsor's product.

Bank of Scotland's sponsorship of Edinburgh International Festival's Connecting to Music Workshops was a good example of the interplay between the event itself, its sponsors and the needs of the target market. The challenging and appealing workshops introduce 1000 children to a creative way of listening to classical music, culminating in live performance by a professional musician. For the sponsor and organiser, the workshops achieve their aims by increasing access to and enjoyment of the arts and inspiring children to learn about their responses to music. At the end of the sponsorship in 2007, Bank of Scotland's sponsorship continued with the sponsorship of the Connecting to Music website as a legacy resource for teachers,

FIGURE 13.1 The trinity of sponsor, event and audiences

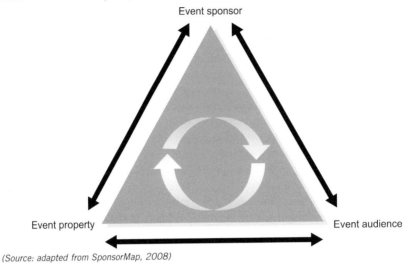

(Source: adapted from SponsorMap, 2008)

while their sponsorship continues with the Bank of Scotland Connecting to Culture project (Edinburgh International Festival, 2010b). This type of sponsorship illustrates how a mutually beneficial relationship can emerge when an event initiates opportunities that closely fit the sponsor's corporate or marketing objectives (Geldard and Sinclair, 2003). This chapter now discusses a number of trends, including the need for more innovative and flexible marketing media, which underpin the rising popularity of sponsorship.

TRENDS INFLUENCING THE GROWTH IN SPONSORSHIP

The worldwide interest in sponsorship as a form of integrated marketing communication originates from a range of sociocultural and business (including marketing and media) trends. Firstly, a growth in the popularity of events and festivals as leisure experiences has paralleled recognition that festivals and events offer unique social environments (at the event and on-line) to tap into discrete market segments. Creative sponsorship can reach consumers in environments in which they are having a good time and so they are more likely to accept a well-considered marketing message. It is no surprise that marketers are keen to tap into the kind of loyalty that festival-goers display — such as enduring primitive hygiene and severe sleep deprivation to see their favourite bands live (Blyth, 2003). There is also evidence (Crimmins and Horn, 1996; McDaniel, 1999; Schrieber, 1994) that committed and loyal fans of a musical group or sport will attach themselves to those brands that support their interest; for example, Barclays, Coca-Cola and Vodafone are companies that have gained significant brand equity from UK sports sponsorships.

Similarly, Virgin Mobile, as a major festival sponsor in the UK, considers that 'festivals offer a fantastic opportunity for brands to get close to consumers when they are excited and passionate. It's by harnessing that passion and adding to that experience that you benefit' (Blyth, 2003), and O_2 have capitalised on their association with music, developed through sponsorship of events such as The O_2 Wireless Festival and Party in the Parks, with taking naming rights of music/live entertainment venues, including O_2 Academies in Leeds, Sheffield, Glasgow and across the UK and The O_2 in London (formerly known as the Millennium Dome).

While sports have dominated event sponsorships, accounting for 75–80% of sponsorship expenditure (Harrison, 2004), there is evidence to suggest that the corporate sector is seeking a greater balance of investment across the arts and sports. Despite Heineken's extensive involvement with the Rugby World Cup (RWC) and the Heineken Cup, one of European rugby's leading events, it was reported in late 2003 that the company was shifting its global focus towards cultural events (Pearce, 2003). Most large brands now use a sponsorship mix within a wide-ranging brand marketing strategy. The Royal Bank of Scotland Group (RBS), for example, has over the years attached its brand names to the RBS 6 Nations rugby tournament and NatWest Series of 1-day international cricket, but also sponsors The Royal Bank of Scotland/Scottish Economic Society Annual Lecture and the Royal Highland Show.

International companies operating in the UK also view sponsorship as an effective method to connect with their British and international markets. For example, renowned British events such as The Open golf tournament were sponsored in 2010 by a Japanese photographic company, a Swiss watch manufacturer, a global professional services company, a Japanese prestige car brand and a Scottish bank. All must believe that their target market both watches golf and will feel emotionally closer to the product as a result of their sponsorship.

Other influential trends on sponsorship are evident in the arenas of business, marketing and media. Companies expanding into international markets have harnessed the value of event sponsorship to create brand awareness in their new markets. An example is FxPro, a leading foreign exchange broker, sponsoring the FIA World Rally Championships and the Virgin F1 Racing Team as Official Forex Trading Partner to raise awareness of its brand in international markets (FxPro, 2010). Financial group AEGON, through their sponsorship as a lead partner of British Tennis, have used international events, such as the AEGON Championships at The Queen's Club and sponsorship of Ajax in The Netherlands, to raise awareness of their brand in the UK and overseas. Sports sponsorship has become a multi-billion dollar business in Asia, with companies, such as Samsung, becoming global brands and leveraging investment in global sports. Samsung, for example, made a $4.6 million sponsorship investment in a historic, 1-day cricket contest between India and Pakistan (Sudhaman, 2004).

The growth of sponsorship can also be attributed to changes in marketing itself – with the shift away from simple transactions to relationships (Gronroos, 1994). New trends in marketing communication media give event sponsors the chance to interact directly with their markets to create a brand relationship. Simultaneous brand exposure can be achieved through a range of on-site communication and alternative media. Sponsors are getting extra exposure, for example, as a result of live streaming events on the Internet, text messages, sponsorship of live sites away from the event and giant screens at festivals that display text and photo messages from the crowd responding to billboard advertisements. Events such as the V Festival and the Rip Curl Newquay Boardmasters Festival used Jumbotrons (giant text screens) and posters inviting text responses for instant-win opportunities such as VIP access to the backstage area and free product samples (Blyth, 2003).

Sponsorship is also gaining leadership in most marketers' 'toolkits' because consumers are more cynical about traditional advertising — sponsorship is perceived to be a more effective and efficient promotional method. When sponsorship is perceived to be a commercial activity with some benefit to society, consumers view advertising as being more manipulative with far less social value (Meenaghan, 2001b). The involvement in traditional media for event sponsorship by marketers has also shifted as a result of:

- the rising costs of media space and the perceived reduced effectiveness of advertising — many consumers now simultaneously use multiple media, such as television, the Internet, mobiles and text messaging (Duncan, 2002).
- a growth in the overall number of media outlets (including pay television channels, radio stations, specialist magazines, direct mail pieces, and the Internet) with media advertising becoming extremely cluttered (De Pelsmacker et al., 2004; Duncan, 2002).
- the expansion of pay television channels (satellite and cable) and their subsequent need for programme material. Events, especially sports events, have thus had more opportunity to be televised, enhancing exposure opportunities available to event sponsors (Lieberman, 2002).
- the globalisation and commercialisation of sports (Hinch and Higham, 2004) as both amateur and professional sports offer more opportunities for organisations to engage in sponsorship of events that have huge television audiences.
- a proliferation of brands, products and services offered by fewer manufacturers/ providers (Duncan, 2002). Companies, therefore, choose to improve their distributors' relationships with event-related entertainment and hospitality.
- the relative inability of mass media to target a desired particular market segment, making the promotion not as effective as more tightly targeted promotions.

Sponsorship, especially through events and festivals, has been able to exploit these trends because it communicates in experiential environments, rather than via static media. Yet some events are also becoming cluttered with the diverse brands of multiple sponsors. As a result, sponsors must work closely with event organisers to achieve 'cut-through' with their own brands. Research by MEC MediaLab across 20 countries suggests that over 40% of respondents believed sports events have become too heavily sponsored (Sudhaman, 2004). In this context, the event manager's task of making strategic decisions about an event's portfolio of sponsors (discussed later in this chapter) will become even more critical as sponsorship matures as a marketing medium.

The state of the economy will also influence the sponsorship environment, as generally a firm's promotional budget is reduced during periods of reduced economic activity. Also, the number of events and individuals seeking sponsorship compared with the sponsorship pounds available in the UK's corporate sector challenges the event manager's access to new, 'big money' partnerships. A number of other potential influences on the event manager's ability to attract sponsorship (De Pelsmacker et al., 2004) that should be considered are:

- the changing expenditure patterns among marketers; for example, increased interest in radio and television programme sponsorship (Dolphin, 2003) and cause-related projects;
- an increased diversity in the types of industries, firms and agencies using sponsorship (ranging from local florist shops to national financial institutions);
- a demand for more sophisticated (and innovative) sponsorships, tailored to a sponsor's needs, which produce a behavioural result (sponsorships that 'make the phones ring'), and
- the growing attachment of sponsors to events with broadcast coverage — events that are not televised or streamed to the audience via other channels are less attractive to corporate sponsors because the sponsors receive less exposure.

All these environmental trends underline the need for event managers to ensure that their preliminary research and SWOT and PEST analyses include a comprehensive analysis of the sponsorship environment. Part of ensuring the success of the event's sponsorship strategy is in knowing the range of benefits available to sponsor partners — not just the benefits to be accrued by the event or festival.

SPONSORSHIP BENEFITS FOR EVENTS AND SPONSORS

Sponsorships are pursued by events and festivals and purchased by corporations, media and government based on a thorough assessment of the benefits to be derived. Event managers must therefore obtain a good understanding of the full suite of potential benefits that a sponsorship will bring to their event/festival and their sponsors so they can customise their strategies. Figure 13.2 shows the exchange relationship between events/festivals and the sponsorship partners first identified by Crompton (1994).

Before embarking on a sponsorship strategy, the event manager should consider the sponsor-partnering benefits for the event and whether the event or festival is 'sponsorship ready'. That is, the event manager must be in a position to be able to supply appropriate benefits to the sponsor.

How events can benefit from sponsorship

For many events and festivals, sponsorship through cash and/or contra (sponsorship paid for in services supplied by the sponsor, such as air travel or hotel rooms if the

FIGURE 13.2 Exchange relationship in event sponsorship

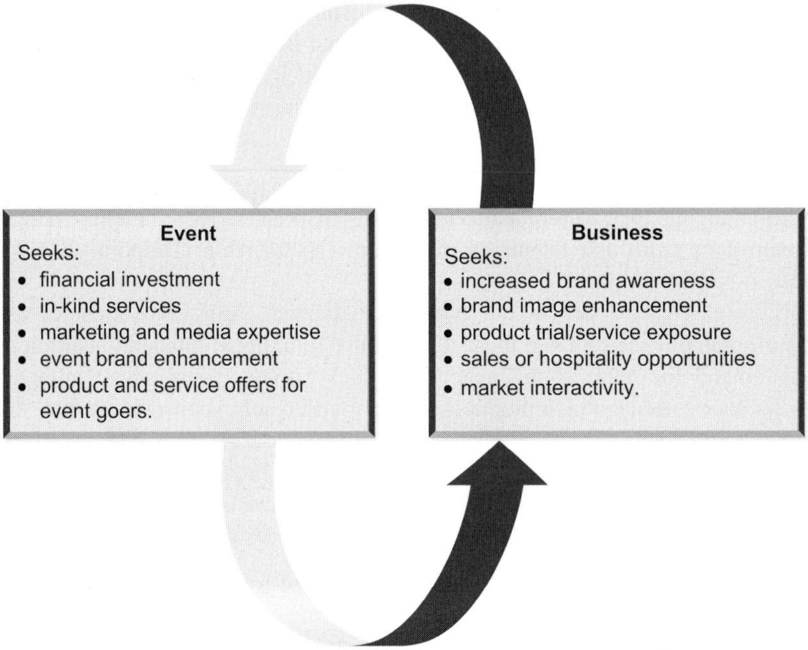

| Event
Seeks:
• financial investment
• in-kind services
• marketing and media expertise
• event brand enhancement
• product and service offers for
  event goers. | Business
Seeks:
• increased brand awareness
• brand image enhancement
• product trial/service exposure
• sales or hospitality opportunities
• market interactivity. |

(Source: Crompton, 1994)

sponsor is an airline or hotel chain) brings a valuable opportunity for long-term business partnerships that assist in growing not only the event but also the audience numbers of a particular art form or sport. In the UK, Virgin Mobile's long-running sponsorship of the successful V Festival not only improved the brand equity of the festival, but it became a platform for Virgin Mobile to take 'ownership' of the festival audience and associate the Virgin Mobile brand with the youth market and music with the sponsorship selling a lifestyle and an image (Matheson, 2005). Virgin Mobile capitalises on the sponsorship at the event with a number of initiatives, including festival-goers being able to 'text the fest' to get their messages on the big screens, free kebabs and beer for their customers and angels on-site to help put up tents or direct people back there at the end of the evening (Cake, 2005). For the event or festival, sponsorship is therefore much more than a means of boosting revenues, but must also meet the needs and objectives of its sponsors. Wider objectives for having sponsor partners at an event could include sustaining an art form or developing a new sport (for example, note the growth in snowboarding over recent years), achieving issues-related objectives such as a sustainable environment or ensuring the survival of not-for-profit agencies; for example, the Air Ambulance Service.

Despite the obvious advantages of sponsorship, not all events and festivals understand the management implications of attracting business partners. Many event managers assume that sponsorship is an appropriate source of income for their event, but confuse it with philanthropy and set about seeking to obtain it — later running into difficulties — not the least of which is being unable to attract any sponsors. Geldard and Sinclair (2003) identified a number of questions that an event manager should ask before seeking sponsorship as a revenue stream. These questions are as follows:

- *Does the event have sufficient rights or benefits that can be offered to sponsors?* Organisations must be able to recognise the potential of the event to achieve their marketing objectives, such as image enhancement or the development of stronger relationships with suppliers/buyers. If the desired benefits are not present, an event manager would be wasting his or her time in seeking income from this source. A better alternative in some instances may be to seek a donation which, by its nature, does not require strategic marketing benefits to be given in return. It is not uncommon for corporations, particularly large corporations, to provide a philanthropic allocation of funds specifically for this purpose. Commonly, these funds are made available to events of a community or charitable nature.
- *Are the event's stakeholders likely to approve of commercial sponsorship?* It is not hard to imagine situations where some members of a particular association or the potential event audience might view commercial sponsorship negatively. A conservation body seeking sponsorship for its annual conference, for example, could find that its membership is against commercial involvement and at best, extremely selective about the companies with whom they will associate. In effect, broad support among the event's internal stakeholders is essential for sponsorship to be successful.
- *Is the target market of the event congruent with the target market of the sponsor?* In order for the sponsorship to be able to deliver benefits to a sponsor, the target markets must be congruent. For example, Kellogg's confirmation as the Official Cereal of the FINA World Swimming Championships, a sponsorship that included training 3 female lifeguards and 48 youngsters to get their Swimming Helpers Certificate (FINA, 2007), and the competition's markets were congruent, which meant that Kellogg's brand received the important marketing benefit of association with a respected event, and strengthened their association with swimming and investing in legacies for the future.
- *Are there some companies that are simply not suitable as sponsors?* Event managers need to identify organisations that are inappropriate as sponsorship partners. For example, a charity event aimed at raising funds for a children's hospital or another health-related cause, is unlikely to accept sponsorship from fast food or tobacco companies or breweries. As another example, in the past tobacco has been accepted as a major source of sponsorship, particularly for sports events such as motor racing, snooker and darts. However, due to implementation of the Tobacco Advertising and Promotion Bill events have been forced to identify other sources of sponsorship.
- *Does the event have the resources to market and manage sponsorship?* A considerable amount of time and effort is required to research, develop and

market sponsorships to potential sponsor targets. Furthermore, sponsorship must be managed after the contract is finalised to ensure all promises made in the proposal are fulfilled. This involves allocating staff and other resources to building and sustaining the sponsor relationship.

Sponsors' benefits — links with the consumer response

An appreciation of the effects of sponsorship on event consumers helps to understand the engagement of corporate and government bodies with events and festivals. Knowledge and familiarity with a corporate or product brand, as well as attitudinal and behavioural effects have been linked with event sponsorship. The sponsor's investment assisting a sport or art form is believed to create goodwill among attendees, which in turn influences their attitude and behaviour towards the sponsor's brand (Crimmins and Horn, 1996; Meenaghan, 2001a).

Although there is still a great deal of research to be conducted on sponsorship effects (most data have been gathered by private firms), it appears that sponsorship does stimulate goodwill (a positive attitude), which in turn influences consumer relationships with sponsors' brands.

According to Meenaghan (2001a, p. 102), the goodwill is generated for sponsors at three levels: the generic level (consumer feelings about their engagement in sponsorship as an activity), the category level (within sports or arts audiences) and the individual activity level (fans of the England cricket 1-day series team develop goodwill towards its sponsor, Vodafone). Clearly, goodwill effects are achieved intensely for sponsors at an event category level (art or sport) and the individual event/activity level. Underlining the importance of fan/audience involvement with an event category in getting a sponsorship result, Performance Research (2001) has reported that over half of those with an interest in the arts said that they would almost always buy a product that sponsored cultural events (Dolphin, 2003). Figure 13.3 shows how sponsorship effects narrow at an individual event/activity level. It also demonstrates how the intensity of goodwill towards the sponsor moves in parallel with the intensity of fan or event consumer involvement.

Clearly, some additional benefits can be gained from leveraging a sponsorship in target markets with higher levels of event knowledge — 'involved' or 'highly active' event consumers are more likely to make an effort to process a sponsor's message (Roy and Cornwell, 2004). The more actively engaged a person is with what is being sponsored, the stronger the carry-over effect and the link between the sponsor's brand and the event (De Pelsmacker et al., 2004). However, this is not always the case. Euro 2000 was noted as being one of the most successful tournaments ever, however, only half the fans were able to identify any of the sponsors involved, and only 18% reported that they would choose the sponsor's product over others. The reasons for this lack of engagement are not known, but it was believed that television coverage on BBC meant that fans avoided many of the sponsor's messages. This illustrates that even high-profile, big-budget sponsorships need to be managed effectively to gain return on investment (Performance Research, 2000).This is

FIGURE 13.3 The sponsorship effects process

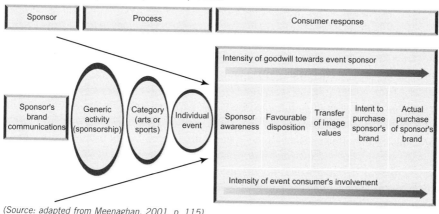

(Source: adapted from Meenaghan, 2001, p. 115)

a good reason why many companies try to sponsor festivals or events that have loyal and dedicated audiences.

The translation of a passion for the event itself into customer gratitude/goodwill and a commitment to use the sponsor's services or products is of interest to all existing and would-be sponsors. Emphasis is placed on consumers being in a positive environment at events as sponsoring brands are perceived in a favourable light. However, products that gain a stronger link to the event and its audience are often those that are demonstrated creatively in some way during the event (Cornwell et al., 2001). For the 2010 V Festival, Virgin Media, the headline sponsors, capitalised on Virgin's fifteenth year of sponsorship in a number of ways including urging the 165,000 festival-goers to 'text the fest' to get their messages shown on large screens around the event (Matheson, 2005) and aimed to make the festival experience the best possible for visitors, including a Hidden Garden where those lucky enough to find it will be rewarded with complimentary beer and other benefits.

Based on consumer behaviour theories, various writers on sponsorship (De Pelsmacker et al., 2004; Geldard and Sinclair, 2003; Meenaghan, 2001b) highlight an array of marketing benefits of event and festival sponsorship gained by corporate sponsors. These benefits include the following:

- *Access to specific niche/target markets*: Mobile phone operators are using event sponsorship as a means of targeting potential customers in specific age brackets. For example, O_2 sponsored music concerts to appeal to a youth market and establish itself as the biggest mobile network in the youth market (Carter, 2004), while Virgin Mobile sponsors V Festival as discussed elsewhere.
- *Corporate brand image creation/enhancement*: For major service providers like banks, the lack of a tangible product complicates the task of brand imaging. Sponsorship of festivals and events is therefore a valuable form of corporate

image enhancement, illustrated by The Royal Bank of Scotland's sponsorship of the Royal Bank Lates at Edinburgh International Festival — a series of 30 late-night events over 20 days in six venues with a ticket price of only £5. Royal Bank of Scotland's rationale for the sponsorship is that they see this as an opportunity to raise their profile in their home city to locals and visitors, while continuing their support for the arts and Edinburgh International Festival (Royal Bank of Scotland, 2004). Renault sponsored Cirque du Soleil's Saltimbanco Season at the Royal Albert Hall in London in 2003. The partnership was seen as offering 'the perfect fit for two companies who insist on innovation in their own respective fields' while offering Renault the opportunity to promote their premium range of cars to an audience that met the profile of their target market (Renault, 2003).

- *Building brand awareness for an organisation and its services/products*: CreditExpert, the on-line credit-monitoring service from Experian, sponsored stand-up comic Bennett Aarron's show, 'It Wasn't Me, It Was Bennett Arron' at The Edinburgh Festival. The show focused on what it is like to become a victim of identity theft and how to prevent it and was therefore seen as a good opportunity to promote the on-line service which can notify subscribers of unusual activity on their accounts (Bond, 2005).

- *Influencing consumer attitudes about a product or service brand*: Some companies use sponsorship as a strategy to change consumer perceptions about a long-standing brand. For example, Scottish Courage sought to change attitudes towards their Strongbow Cider brand as although this product had 63% of the on-trade cider market, cider was seen as an uncool drink with a poor image. Recognising music as a powerful medium with their target market of 18- to 35-year-olds, and having been involved in festivals since 1999, they developed the Strongbow Rooms concept to add value to the festival experience. The programme of festival sponsorship includes a spectacular Strongbow Rooms arena at 7 leading UK music festivals, exclusive tie-ins with world-class DJs, pre-event promotions in 450 pubs and 75 Students Unions, exclusive media partnerships with MTV and NME including a dedicated website, an extensive PR campaign and post-event loyalty programme (Scottish Courage, 2005).

- *Associating a product or service with a particular lifestyle*: Makers of alcoholic beverages, for example, often sponsor or directly support youth-oriented events, such as rock music festivals, to develop an association between their product and a demographic that is young, fun seeking and keen to experiment. Bacardi Martini toured the 2003 summer festival circuit in the UK with BBar, a marquee that held up to 1000 people and featured 65 DJs and a small army of cocktail mixers. The aim was to create a memorable experience that tied in with Bacardi's brand values — an association with the party spirit (Wallis, 2003). Nokia took up headline sponsorship of the Prince's Trust event, Nokia Urban Music Festival, taking place at Earls Court. The festival for a crowd of 16,000 featured high-profile acts including Will Smith and Craig David. Aligning themselves with an 'edgy urban culture', Nokia was seen as a strong fit for the event as the brand

(and therefore the event) appeals to the young people (which was the Prince's Trust aim) and for Nokia it was an opportunity to showcase latest handsets and technology (Bond, 2005).

- *Improving relationships with distribution channel members*: A corporation may be seeking to develop stronger relationships with agents or firms that currently distribute its products or services or to establish new distribution outlets. For example, Barclays sponsorship of the 2002 Scottish Open at Loch Lomond allowed the Barclay's and Barclays Capital to treat clients to a range of experiences at the event including hospitality, meeting players and participating in golf clinics, in addition to the brand awareness opportunities offered by the event. Bob Diamond, head of Barclays Capital notes, 'We view our sponsorship relationships in the same way as client relationships. There is an incredible sense of partnership and working together towards a common goal' (Barclays Capital, 2005)

- *Achieving product sales and merchandising opportunities*: For companies with a product (rather than an intangible service), high sales targets can be set for an exclusive in-game presence at sporting events − for example, Heineken at the RWC in 1995, 2003, 2007 and 2011 − or through having exclusive rights in their product category at a festival. Tiger Beer, for example, has targeted the Tartan Asian Extreme Festival for cult films. Their headline sponsorship included rolling out sampling of their beer as part of an integrated marketing campaign which also included the launch of The Tigers' awards to celebrate Asian films in the UK (Anon, 2005c). The Scottish Courage Strongbow Rooms concept resulted in an estimated increase in 12% monthly sales gain, or 232,320 pints per annum, from those exposed to the brand at the seven festivals (Scottish Courage, 2005). Strongbow is continuing its established involvement in music festivals with the Bowtime Bar concept. Delivered by experiential marketing agency RPM, the concept includes hidden VIP areas, 'the fastest coldest serves on site', masseurs and a selection of acts in purpose-built arenas (Thorley, 2009).

- *Demonstrating product attributes*: Many festivals and events are primarily used by sponsors to demonstrate new products or technology. Through its sponsorship of events such as the Edinburgh International Festival and Brisbane's International Film Festival, the mobile phone distributor Nokia has showcased the functionality of its handsets and educated people about new technologies such as MMS. Similarly, the telecommunications giant Orange uses its sponsorship of the Glastonbury Festival in the UK to offer free recharge points, to provide e-top-ups and phone cards and to get people to experiment with technology like text alerts (Wallis, 2003).

- *Providing employee rewards and recognition*: Organisations often perceive the sponsorship of a sporting or cultural event as a way of giving their employees access to a corporate box and/or tickets to reward or motivate them. For example, following on from their sponsorship, Royal Bank of Scotland's and Edinburgh International Festival secured New Partnership funding from Arts & Business which enabled the bank's staff to take part in 'Royal Bank Turn Up and Try It' workshops. Using arts for development purposes, the workshops focused on drama, theatre and music while linking in with festival events. The bank was keen to see a number of results from staff, including more creative thinking, dealing effectively with customers or colleagues and looking at situations more laterally, while also involving staff in the arts sponsorship (Royal Bank of Scotland, 2003).

- *Creating goodwill and a climate of consent for an organisation's activities*: Companies as diverse as mining organisations, energy providers, banks and pharmaceutical manufacturers all support charity events to create an image in the community of being good corporate citizens. For example, npower became headline sponsor for Macmillan Cancer Relief's flagship fundraising event, World's Biggest Coffee Morning, in 2004 (Anon, 2004). Gwinner (2005) points out that if, without the sponsor, a sports event may not happen, or the standard of the athletes may not be as high or that ticket prices may be more expensive, considerable goodwill is generated for the sponsor from the attendees of the event.
- *Entertaining key clients with corporate hospitality*: Corporate hospitality is an important drawcard for sponsors, especially those with business-to-business clients. Every major sport or cultural event is replete with corporate boxes, where the sponsoring organisation has opportunities to entertain key clients in an informal and enjoyable environment. Where working relationships are quite intense, corporate hospitality events can break down the barriers and create social bonds that forge a better relationship between suppliers and clients. As Ellery (2004) notes, 'There is nothing quite like strawberries and cream washed down with chilled champagne at the Wimbledon Tennis Championships to woo potential business.'

In looking at the many benefits derived by sponsors, it should also be remembered that public sector bodies (for example, local councils, regional development agencies, authorities/commissions and agencies) engage in sponsorship as a marketing communications tool. Many of the benefits illustrated in the corporate context are equally applicable to them. Most public sector agencies now employ marketing strategies to generate awareness of their products/services or issues and to influence community behaviour. For example, Glasgow City Marketing Bureau and Clyde Waterfront fund Glasgow River Festival, supported by Glasgow City Council, Strathclyde Partnership for Transport, the Royal Navy, Clydeport and Radio Clyde, with the aim of supporting the regeneration of the Clyde Waterfront and attracting people back to the river (Glasgow City Marketing Bureau, 2009)

As noted in Chapters 3 and 7, local or national government or regional development agencies will normally support events through sponsorships, grants or contributions towards constructing the infrastructure needed to stage events because of the community benefits they bring. Events and festivals can also stimulate economic development in an area (for example, the 2002 Commonwealth Games in

Manchester), create a greater sense of identity or cohesion and enhance the facilities available to local residents. To attract sponsorship, event organisers must think about how they can provide at least several of the benefits identified here.

Sponsorship leveraging — adding value to the investment

To fully capitalise on a sponsorship investment, most corporate and government agencies develop a leveraging strategy or a range of marketing activities that extend the sponsorship benefits well beyond the event's or festival's promised offer. The 2009 IEG/Performance Research Sponsorship Decision Makers Survey of 110 corporate marketers found that sponsors are now spending at a ratio of around 1.4:1 on leveraging their sponsorships, though this was down on previous years, with a peak of 1.9:1 in 2007 (Performance Research, 2009). Adidas, as an official sponsor of the FIFA 2002 World Cup, reportedly budgeted around $88 million to exploit their sponsorship, with the cost of official sponsorships being somewhere between $20 million and $28 million (Pickett, 2002).

For example, for Suncorp's RWC 2003 sponsorship, the leveraging ratio was closer to 3:1, but the firm achieved quantifiable results with enhanced brand equity (awareness and favourability) and sales (Ferguson, 2004). As part of their overall sponsorship package, Suncorp invested in broadcast sponsorship for the first time which included exposure through a 15-s in-game commercial, sponsorship of GIO Player of the Match and opening and closing billboards. The success of RWC sponsorship paved the way for Suncorp's 4-year sponsorship of the Australian Wallabies team. It also served to reverse (alongside state government public relations) the previously low recognition and name use of Suncorp Stadium (built on the site of Lang Park) in the Brisbane media and marketplace (following RWC 2003, 95% media recognition and use of the name was evident).

A number of factors contributed to Suncorp's successful leveraging of the RWC sponsorship. These are:

- a careful analysis of the fit between the event property and the sponsor's market — Suncorp established that the rugby audience was both its existing and aspirational audience (a good basis for a leverage investment) as is shown in the section on fit below.
- a dedicated internal marketing strategy — RWC was a property that needed to be adopted by all business areas within the company. Marketing and sales personnel were briefed on how the RWC could be leveraged with a 50/50 buy-in between the sponsorship unit and a business unit on specific marketing activities. Staff were also directly engaged with the sponsorship.
- an intensive consumer-branding campaign themed on the RWC — for example, television campaigns, outdoor advertising in transit hubs, branch office imagery, live sites at Brisbane's South Bank and in regional towns with extensive branding and giveaways, direct mail offers, website incentives and merchandise prizes, and the use of rugby ambassadors such as Nick Farr-Jones on Suncorp's recorded telephone messages.

- a dedicated business-to-business marketing campaign centred on 31 corporate hospitality events staged throughout Australia either in the stadia or close to the stadia where RWC games were held. Suncorp's business banking managers each injected funds from their budgets towards the corporate entertainment of clients, and all managers achieved measurable results in sales and referrals.

For Suncorp, like most other event and festival sponsors, effective leveraging relies on establishing multiple opportunities for consumers to engage with their brand and their personnel (on-site, off-site and on-line).

When sponsors already have a high level of corporate brand awareness, leveraging is best focused on activities that achieve two-way communication with the market — for example, business-to-business customer hospitality or specific consumer offers either during the event or on-line. The need for sponsors to offer event consumers something they cannot obtain elsewhere is gaining importance. Beverage marketer Red Bull, for example, has set up a branded skate ramp at festivals in the UK, while the Wall's company created a unique ice-cream beach to engage visitors at the 2003 V Festival in England (Wallis, 2003). In effect, the need to think of leveraging strategies that achieve 'cut-through' to a media-savvy market without irritating them is the sponsor's challenge and also the event marketer's concern in order to add value for their sponsors.

The fit between sponsor and sponsee

Cornwell et al.'s (2006) work shows that the greater the fit between sponsor and sponsee (the event) the more effective the sponsorship will be for both parties. Fit has been defined as relevance, complementality or compatibility in the sponsorship literature (Rifon et al., 2004; Johar and Pham, 1999), but another definition is the extent of the congruence between the sponsor's products and markets and the event's. Figure 13.4 shows the different elements and results of the 'fit' phenomenon.

- *Brand cohesiveness*: brands that have a clear and distinct image. British Airways is an example in the UK marketplace.
- *Event identification*: how essential and important is the event to its audience. For the 18- to 25-year-old music-loving demographic, the Wireless in London's Hyde Park is an event with which it identifies strongly.
- *Sponsor fit*: how relevant to and compatible with the event market are the sponsor's products. Virgin's long-running sponsorship of the V Festival over the past 15 years is an example of fit.
- *Attitude towards the sponsor*: this is the favourable disposition that the event market has to the sponsor's products. Pay television, broadband, landline and mobile telephone group Virgin Media's sponsorship of the V Festival would increase the favourable disposition towards this provider from the event's audience.

FIGURE 13.4 The effect of excellent sponsor fit

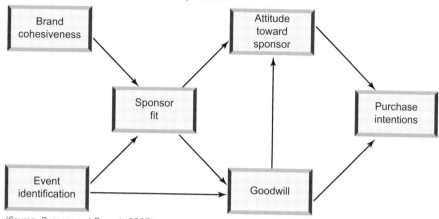

(Source: Gwinner and Bennet, 2007)

- *Goodwill*: when a sponsor takes actions that facilitate the event market's enjoyment of the event, goodwill is generated towards the sponsor. Radio station Kiss FM's sponsorship of Wireless 2010 as radio partner, alongside Barclaycard as headline sponsor, caused the audience to consider the station partly responsible for enabling the event to occur with the line-up of artists, which generated goodwill to the sponsor.
- *Purchase intentions*: the primary reason that business sponsors invest in events. If purchase intention changes, the sponsorship is effective. Tennent's sponsorship of 'T In The Park' includes an initiative, the Be Chilled service, which enables festival-goers to pre-order Tennent's Lager for their stay at the festival, which will be delivered chilled to the campsite for collection.

Gwinner and Bennet's (2007) study of the audience of an action sports event in the US showed that 'those who perceive fit between an event's image and the sponsoring brand exhibit a significantly better attitude toward the sponsoring brand than those who perceive less fit between the two properties'. They also found that goodwill to the sponsor's brands is influenced by fit. Another of their study's findings was that perceived fit positively impacted on purchase intentions through both the attitude towards the sponsor and goodwill elements shown in Figure 13.4. However, in their study of sponsorship of music festivals, Rowley and Williams (2008, p. 789) found that, 'evidence to suggest that brand sponsorship of music festivals has an impact on brand recall, awareness and attitude to the brand, but little evidence of impact on brand use'.

The lesson for event managers is to approach those organisations whose products have congruence with the perceptions of the event's market. In this way the benefits of the sponsorship are enhanced for the sponsor, which ensures that both parties to the sponsorship achieve their objectives – the classic win–win situation.

THE VALUE OF SPONSORSHIP POLICY

Just as most corporate and government agencies will establish a sponsorship policy to guide their decision making, Grey and Skildum-Reid (2003) strongly recommend that all events seeking sponsorship design a policy to guide their actions. They suggest that a sponsorship policy should state:

- the event's history of sponsorship and its approach to it, including some definition of what constitutes sponsorship versus grants and donations;
- the event's objectives, processes and procedures for seeking sponsorship;
- the rules for entering into sponsorship and the kinds of companies that 'fit' the event;
- the uniform approach adopted in seeking sponsorship, including whether all proposals are to follow a particular format and whether each sponsorship is required to have a management plan developed for it (see later discussion);
- the levels of accountability and responsibility, such as who in the organisation can approve the sponsorship, who is responsible for its outcome and who is the sponsor liaison person in the organisation and
- the time at which the policy will be subject to review and evaluation.

For most events and festivals, involving the senior management of the event as well as staff and lead volunteers in the drafting of the sponsorship policy is a wise idea. Having a sense of ownership of the sponsorship policy becomes important if there are conflicts or disputes over decisions about sponsors. For larger events and festivals, the policy would also be presented to and approved by a board of directors.

STAGES IN DEVELOPING THE EVENT SPONSORSHIP STRATEGY

Developing an event sponsorship strategy is a distinct task. Remember that it will have an interactive relationship with the event's marketing strategy because, whether it is venue design, ticketing, integrated marketing communications or even the programme itself, you will need to be creative about how you can integrate the sponsor's brand with the event's marketing plans. Accenture sponsored Total Meltdown, a concert featured as part of the London South Bank Centre's 50th anniversary celebrations in 2001 (Sponsorship Consulting Limited, 2005). Total Meltdown, a concert of contemporary music, was based on the concept of a well-known personality, such as Elvis Costello, programming their fantasy festival. The aims for Accenture's sponsorship were:

- to create awareness of the new Accenture name and to achieve the transfer of values (youthful, dynamic, expressive) from the concert to Accenture;
- to deepen the Accenture impact on potential graduate recruits;

- to offer access to the event for existing staff and excite and motivate staff in the 22- to 44-year age bracket and
- to offer corporate hospitality for existing and potential clients.

To capitalise on the sponsorship, Sponsorship Consulting Limited worked with Accenture and South Bank Centre to create:

- an eye-catching visual identity for the sponsorship, which was used throughout the leveraging campaign
- FreeCard promotions in restaurants, which achieved a 93% pick-up rate
- London Underground 6 – sheet poster campaign across 62 stations
- exciting private party room at the Royal Festival Hall
- a successful and memorable event
- press advertising campaign and web banners
- Time Out ticket promotions
- impactful venue signage
- Dramatic sponsorship of the lighting of the Royal Festival Hall for 2 weeks (Sponsorship Consulting Limited, 2005)

A strategy means knowing the direction in which you are headed, which also applies to your event's sponsorship. For event managers, this involves thinking about event/festival visitors and the fit they might have with corporate brands. It also involves thinking about the attributes and values of the event and companies that might share those values, the mix of sponsors who together might create a close-knit sponsor family and brainstorming the kinds of partnerships that will grow the event – in other words, enhancing the fit.

Profiling the event audience

The first step in sponsorship strategy development is to consider again the target markets of your event or festival. By adopting the market segmentation strategies outlined in Chapter 11, you will have a sound basis for establishing fit between potential sponsors and the consumers who frequent your event. Like all forms of integrated marketing communication, event sponsorship is most successful as a marketing medium when there is a solid database that profiles existing visitors and members/subscribers and their preferences. Sponsors will look for a reliable picture (demographics, socioeconomic status, psychographics) of the event audience to ensure there is market congruence and that an investment in the event will help achieve their own marketing objectives efficiently.

In the case of T In The Park, research undertaken in 2003 by Hall & Partners showed that 98% of consumers recognised Tennent's Lager as sponsor, with 35% believing that it was a perfect fit, 48% believing that Tennent's Lager was supporting the Scottish music scene through this sponsorship and 23% believing that the event would not happen without Tennent's support (Material Marketing & Communications Ltd, 2005) (for further information on T In The Park, please see the case study in Chapter 14). However, even for smaller events and festivals, steps to identify the market and demonstrate a fit between the event and sponsors' markets must be taken. This may be a more straightforward task for smaller festivals where links can be logically made with small to medium brands in their local market (Harrison, 2004). To obtain detailed market information to assist with sponsorship planning, some of the research tools noted in Chapter 7 (for example, on-site surveys and focus groups) can be especially useful.

Establishing what the event can offer

Despite the variation in the size and scope of different events and festivals, some common assets (defined as benefits that the event can offer the sponsor) include the agreement to purchase product/services from a sponsor (for example, alcohol, transport, food), event naming rights, exclusivity (the capacity to lock out competition within a brand category), business and sponsor networking opportunities, merchandising rights, media exposure, including advertising opportunities during the event, venue signage, joint advertising with sponsors, the capacity to demonstrate their product or technology at the event, corporate hospitality services and a volume of tickets for the sponsor's use.

In building their asset register, a sports team such as the Leeds Rhinos or Leeds Carnegie, may take steps to group their assets (for example, in-game media exposure, player clothing), record the quantities and current availability of those assets (for example, 15 s of remaining in-game advertising) and build the sale value and cost of sales into the pricing of their marketable assets (Allsop, 2004). On a practical level, their website lists a number of opportunities including Main Club Sponsor, Official Kit Sponsor and Associate Sponsors (Leeds Rugby, 2010). An overall asset register can serve to tabulate the profits (the value minus the cost) for each of the individual sponsorships.

For a smaller event or festival, the process will be much less complex. Where the Leeds Rhinos could have a list of 100 saleable assets or more (over a series of games), a local festival staged annually has an inventory that is much easier to manage. Yet, with a little creativity, the festival or event marketer can also create new sponsor benefits. Apart from identifying benefits like signage not previously used for branding within the festival (for example, brand exposure at the front of a concert stage), some tailor-made assets for sponsors can be devised. Sponsorship of the Brit Awards, for example, paved the way for Mastercard to run a promotional campaign with British Airways. A video, 'A History of the Brit Awards' was shown on all in-bound UK flights with more than 500,000 passengers given the opportunity to enter a postcard into a competition to win tickets to the award show at Earls Court in London in February (Anon, 2004). It is safe to assume that many small- to medium-sized events and festivals with few if any sponsorship management staff will have untapped resources. However, in identifying and expanding the event's sponsor benefit register, careful consideration must also be given to the time and personnel needed to effectively manage and market those sponsor benefits.

Building the event sponsorship list

In designing a sponsorship strategy, event managers will usually work out how a list of potential sponsors can be established, given the bundles of festival or event assets that are available for purchase. Geldard and Sinclair (2003) identify strategies for this, such as sole sponsorship, hierarchical packages (for example, tiers of gold, silver, bronze), a pyramid structure (whereby each sponsor level below the principal sponsor jointly spends the amount invested by the top sponsor with proportional benefits), a level playing field (all sponsors negotiate and leverage their own benefits) and an ad hoc approach. For example, The Guardian Hay Festival, Wales, has four levels of sponsorship, media, event, venue and project sponsors:

- The festival was branded as The Guardian Hay Festival, with Sky Arts also appearing alongside the logo recognising *The Guardian* and Sky Arts as media and broadcast sponsors, respectively.
- Event, project and venue sponsorship was available between £1000 and £50,000 for which sponsors received benefits, including credit in on the website and in the programme, on sponsored event tickets and in the sponsors directory (The Guardian Hay Festival, 2010).

Although sole sponsorship of a festival may have the advantage of 'keeping it simple', the festival's survival is threatened if the sole sponsor is lost. For this reason, many events and festivals with a limited array of assets choose the tiered approach (different levels of investment for set benefit packages). However, as Grey and Skildum-Reid (2004, p. 97) pointed out, 'most events/festivals end up formulating their packages so that all of the levels get access to the best benefits, with the lower levels simply getting less of the supporting benefits'. For this reason, many events now tailor their benefit packages for each sponsor using only broad categories, such as major media, corporate and support sponsors. Using this approach, the sponsors are usually grouped according to their *type* (for example, naming rights; presenting sponsorship of a section, event, entry, team or particular day; preferred suppliers; etc.) and their *exclusivity* (among sponsors at any level, among sponsors at or below a given level, as a supplier or seller at the event or within event-driven marketing collateral) (Grey and Skildum-Reid, 2004). The purchase of other event assets, such as merchandising rights, licences and endorsements, hospitality, signage and database access by sponsors, to name just a few, can serve to further differentiate the event sponsor packages. The use of tailor-made sponsorship packages is recommended for a number of reasons (Welsh, 2003):

- Packaged event properties are rarely a perfect fit for potential sponsors — most are either too broad or too narrow in their consumer reach and the rights available may be either more or less than those the sponsor wants.
- Sponsors are often seeking more control over their sponsorship and its potential leveraging than packaged strategies offer — the simple transactional nature of buyer–seller arrangements is being replaced by partnerships and in some cases, the sponsor clearly has leadership in driving the relationship.

- Poor sponsorship packaging by events and festivals can lead to a greater instance of *ambush marketing* in certain industry/product categories (for example, banking and finance) or attempts by non-sponsoring companies to capitalise on an event's image and prestige by implying that they are sponsors (www. uksponsorship.com, 2002).
- Multiple layers of sponsorship introduced by events can cause confusion among audiences and sponsors — as the different sponsorship categories become more prolific, there is more potential for a loss of control by event organisers and sponsor conflicts (Shani and Sandler, 1998).

In light of these challenges, the appeal of determining sponsor partnerships on a case-by-case basis (with all sponsors informed of this practice) is growing. Cheltenham Festivals, discussed in the case study at the end of this chapter, is just one of many events shifting towards tailor-made sponsorships. Although an indication is given of the different levels of sponsorship that are typical and the potential costs associated with this, the opportunity is available for potential sponsors to discuss their specific requirements and how they support or partner one or more of the Cheltenham Festivals.

Matching event benefits with potential sponsors

Once the approach to building a potential sponsorship list is determined, the process of identifying the right sponsor(s) begins. As noted, a first criterion is to find those organisations that want to communicate with the same audience (or a significant component of it), or who have a specific issue (market, image or penetration of a segment, for example) that sponsorship of the event may assist in solving. Sponsorship managers for events use various research techniques to identify potential sponsors. By keeping track of business developments through industry associations, business and financial media and the web, a great deal of information can be gathered on the marketing direction of firms to guide sponsorship targeting. Which organisations are looking to enter new markets in the event's region? Which companies appear to have attributes and values that match those of the event/festival? The Reading and Leeds Festivals, until 2007 branded as The Carling Weekend, were seen as an opportunity to attract young males aged 25–34 years to the Carling brand, as evidence suggests that people would then grow with the brand. The V Festivals were originally launched to promote Virgin Cola but more recently have been sponsored by another Virgin brand, Virgin Media, as they believe that the lifestyle and image associated with the brand matches the image portrayed by the festival (Matheson, 2005).

An appropriate example of an event offering potential sponsors a list of event benefits is the M&IT Industry Awards 2010, organised by Meetings & Incentive Travel Magazine (Conference & Travel Publications Ltd, 2010). The gala presentation dinner, established in 1988 and held in February each year, brings together the various sectors of the events industry to reward excellence and to enjoy excellent food, wine and entertainment while raising money for Save the Children, which to date totals over £700,000. According to the organisers, 'M&IT Industry Awards provides a unique opportunity for any organisation associated with the events industry to achieve outstanding exposure to a captive audience of corporate, association and agency decision makers. It is also an opportunity for superb networking and entertaining clients.' With four levels of sponsorship, Platinum (£5500 + VAT), Gold (£3750 + VAT), Silver (£1950 + VAT) and Bronze (£1250 + VAT), the sponsorship packages offer a range of benefits. For examples, the organisers list the following benefits for the Platinum package:

- five-minute DVD presentation with music to be played
- during dinner course
- area in foyer for display of promotional literature
- full page colour advertisement in event programme (worth £2500)
- half page colour advertisement in April issue of Meetings & Incentive Travel (worth £2590)
- logo credits on screen during event
- verbal name check by Master of Ceremonies during event
- name credit on awards advertisements appearing in Meetings & Incentive Travel
- logo, name credit and promotional paragraph in event programme
- name credits in February preview and April report issues of Meetings & Incentive Travel
- name credit on meetpie.com web site at www.meetpie.com/awards/awards.asp
- name or logo credits on e-mails (plain text and html) promoting the event

(CAT Publications Ltd, 2010)

By a process of monitoring the business environment, an event manager can actively identify any government agencies or firms that are seeking to reposition themselves, regain market acceptance or introduce new products or services. Once identified, and depending on the nature of the event, such organisations can become a sponsorship target. An organiser of a garden festival, for example, may notice that a horticultural company has just launched a new range of fertilisers. This development could be a sponsorship opportunity if the company can be convinced that the event draws the right consumer audience to increase awareness and sales of its new product line. Event managers can also obtain insights into potential sponsors by reading their annual reports or viewing their websites. These sources often provide a good picture of the broad strategies the organisation is pursuing. They also indicate the types of sponsorship they already have in place and whether they have any specific requirements for sponsorships. Another means of finding potential sponsors is to simply identify who has sponsored similar events or festivals in the past. This can be done by examining programmes/promotional material/websites of these other events, or directly contacting the event organisers (many festivals and events now see the value in some productive networking and information sharing). Finally, it is unlikely that you will be looking for all of your sponsors simultaneously, unless you are managing a brand new event. Therefore, the existing sponsors of the event or festival can be a very useful source of referral to other potential sponsors. This method of finding sponsors can be highly successful because the existing sponsor is presenting its company as a satisfied partner of the event in 'opening the door' and endorsing the event as a sponsorship property.

As Cowan (2005) pointed out, sponsorship of arts events has the following benefits for sponsors.

- It has the ability to attract key decision makers to the event. Many people in executive positions are interested in the arts and women executives are more likely to accept an invitation.
- The arts and the organisations that sponsor them find favour with politicians, as government support for artistic endeavours attests.
- Research by Brown and Dancin (1997) supports Cowan's claim that the goodwill created is much greater if the audience believes that the sponsor is making a particular contribution that enables the event to occur rather than merely supporting an event that would have happened without the sponsorship.
- Many events, particularly creative arts events, generate media attention because they fulfil the first criterion for news — they are new, so a sponsor can be associated with good news stories.
- The twenty-first century will see companies valued because of their innovation and creativity; therefore, associating via sponsorship with innovative and creative arts events may help give them an image of innovation and being a leading edge in technological innovation.

Once potential sponsors are identified, a more detailed examination of their business and marketing objectives and the types of asset that will meet their needs can be completed. Additional information that might be sought includes the types of event the organisation is willing to sponsor, whether the organisation is tied to particular causes (for example, charities) and the time in their planning cycle when they allocate their sponsorship budget (sponsorship proposals should be submitted to them some months before this time). Information such as this last item is likely to require direct enquiry to the company's marketing personnel.

The sponsorship pitch

Once the potential sponsors have been listed, the next challenge for the event manager is to determine the marketing or management person who will be the sponsorship decision maker within the targeted company. In small companies, this person is likely to be the chief executive officer or managing director. In companies of moderate size, the marketing or public relations manager may make such decisions, while in large corporations a dedicated sponsorship section could exist within the marketing, public relations or corporate affairs areas, as exists for Vodafone, Royal Bank of Scotland and other major sponsors of UK events.

Before developing any written proposal, it is customary to write a brief introductory letter to profile your event and the sponsorship opportunity. However, some sponsorship managers make direct contact by e-mail or telephone, especially if they have been referred by another sponsor or have some informal rapport with the company's personnel (which may be the case for a sports sponsorship property such as Leeds Rhinos or an arts opportunity such as the Harrogate International Festival).

There are many benefits in becoming acquainted with the company before preparing a proposal, simply because of the need to fully understand their product/ brand attributes, their business objectives, their competition, how they use their current sponsorships and the ways in which sponsorship proposals need to be structured to satisfy their needs. If you can develop some preliminary rapport with those deciding on the value of your proposed partnership, you will have a better grasp of why they may be interested in sponsoring the event/festival and how the proposal should be written to attract their investment. However, the ability to personally discuss your interest in a partnership may depend on the company's policy about written or verbal communication in the first instance. Most major companies are inundated with sponsorship offers, so generally a request will be made for the sponsorship proposal to be in writing.

The most successful sponsorship approach is one where the event has put a lot of effort into planning before approaching the sponsor (much like applying for a job). Certainly, you should start to think about how you can marry the event with the company's culture and explore some innovative ways in which to address the company's marketing objectives before you commence your final proposal (Harrison, 2004).

Preparing and presenting sponsorship proposals

A formal proposal document is commonly how sponsorship is negotiated and partnerships are formed. In broad terms, Geldard and Sinclair (2003) suggest that the sponsorship proposal should address the following questions:

- What is the organisation being asked to sponsor?
- What will the organisation receive for its sponsorship?
- What is it going to cost?

The length and level of detail a proposal uses to answer these questions depends on the value and cost of the sponsor partnership. However, a comprehensive treatment of these areas would mean the proposal would include:

- an overview of the event, including (as applicable) its mission/goals, history, location, current and past sponsors, programme/duration, staff, past or anticipated level of media coverage, past or predicted attendance levels, and actual or pre-dicted attendee profile (for example, age, income, sex and occupation).

- the sponsorship package on offer and its associated cost. In pricing the spon-sorship, it should be remembered that marketers have a range of alternative promotional media, such as advertising, direct marketing and other tools, that could achieve similar outcomes (depending on the sponsor's marketing objec-tives), so the sponsorship should not cost more than other types of promotion, reaching a similar volume of their target market.
- the proposed duration of the sponsorship agreement.
- the strategic fit between the proposal and the business and marketing needs of the organisation. Discussion here will be based on research conducted using the sources noted earlier.
- the event's contact details for the company's response and follow-up negotiation.

Many large corporations, to assist sponsorship seekers, have developed specific proposal guidelines or criteria. In Figure 13.5, an example of the criteria and areas required by the request form is provided for Saga. Consideration is required for the time frame for sponsorship as time is required not only for the company to consider the application but also for any successful sponsor to be able to capitalise on their involvement. Although for smaller-scale sponsorships, a few months may be suffi-cient, most sponsors require at least a 12-month time frame to maximise their sponsorship and around 2 years for a major sponsorship — for example, an RWC. Sponsorships for events scheduled less than 6 months from the time of the initial approach have far less opportunity to be successfully leveraged by marketing personnel.

From the points discussed, it is possible to gain an insight into what makes a successful proposal. However, the failure rate with sponsorship proposals suggests that much more needs to be understood by event managers about their preparation. According to Ukman (1995), there are six attributes of a successful proposal:

1. *Sell benefits, not features*: Many proposals describe the features of the event, such as the artistic merit of the festival, rather than the event's marketing assets and sponsor benefits. Sponsors buy marketing communication platforms so that they can reach their stakeholders and market(s) to form relationships or sell products/services.

2. *Address the sponsor's needs, not those of the event*: Many proposals emphasise the event's need for money, rather than the sponsor's needs such as market access, corporate hospitality or a better understanding of a new brand. Remember, event sponsorships should be seen as partnerships, not a means to patch holes in the event budget (Harrison, 2004).

3. *Tailor the proposal to the business category*: As noted, each of the event's benefits will have a different level of importance to each potential sponsor. An insurance company, for example, might be interested in an event's database, while a soft-drink marketer is likely to be more concerned with on-site sales opportunities. A tailored strategy should be worked out based on some research

FIGURE 13.5 Saga sponsorship strategy and proposal requirements

Saga is proud of its achievements in the field of sponsorship. Our past activity has included the Chelsea Flower Show 2006, Sir Robin Knox-Johnston's participation in the Velux 5 round the world yacht race and the Masters Snooker.

Our main objectives are to create awareness of the Saga brand among today's over 50s and to demonstrate we are a company which likes to do things properly.

Saga regularly receives invitations to participate as a sponsor for a variety of events. Naturally we expect a return on our investment and have therefore developed a sponsorship strategy, where the following criteria must be adhered to:

Awareness
- Will the event be featured in the National Press or on TV?
- Can Saga be featured as part of this coverage? Saga has a preference for events that have a wide audience reach.

Appeal and brand fit
- Does the event appeal to today's over 50s market?
- Will people over 50 play an integral role in the sponsored activity?
- Is the theme of the activity of genuine interest to the over 50s audience?
- Does it fit with our brand values of genuine and authentic, reliable and honest and supportive and dedicated?

Geographic reach
- How many people will be aware of the event?
- In which parts of the UK will it have a presence?
- How widespread is its media coverage likely to be by region? The wider the audience, the greater the opportunity.

Data capture
- At our events, we often like to run competitions to increase our customer base. Would this be possible? The more new customers the activity introduces us to the better.

Product showcase
- Will there be an opportunity at the event for us to promote our insurances, magazine, cruise and holiday products?

If the sponsorship package for your proposed event fulfils the majority of the above criteria, please send your sponsorship proposal including the following details:
- Name of event
- Date(s)
- Synopsis of event
- Audience reach
- Where the event will be advertised
- Data capture
- Brand fit with Saga
- Cost

To: **Events Manager, Saga Building, Enbrook Park, Folkestone, Kent CT20 3SE**

Please note that we cannot consider sponsorship requests within less than six months of the occurrence of the event. We prefer to have a year to plan the activity to ensure we can present our involvement as well as possible.

Exhibitions

Please note Saga will only attend exhibitions with an attendance rate of more than 10,000 visitors.

(Source: Saga Group Ltd, 2010)

and discussions among interested event personnel before constructing the sponsorship proposal.

4. *Include promotional extensions*: The two major sources of sponsor benefits are addressed here. First, there are the benefits being purchased; for example, identification in marketing material and on-site signage that come with the sponsorship and only require action on the part of the event manager. The second set of benefits emerges from the sponsor's event leveraging discussed earlier — for example, trade, retail and sales extensions. Particular leveraging activities might include competitions, redemption offers (for example, free ticket offers for the customers of a sponsor's wholesalers) and hospitality. It is not enough to give sponsors a checklist of the direct benefits of the assets being purchased — a proposal should include the 'exploitation or leveraging menu' showing them how to leverage their investment.

5. *Minimise risk*: Risk can be reduced through indicating some guaranteed marketing activities (including media space reach and frequency) in the package, listing reputable co-sponsors and showing the steps that will be taken to minimise the risk of ambush marketing by other companies. A clear indication of how the event/festival will service the sponsorship should also be given prominence in the proposal.

6. *Include added value*: The proposal should be presented in terms of its total impact on achieving results for the sponsor, rather than focusing on one aspect such as media. Generally, sponsors will be looking for an array of those benefits highlighted earlier in the chapter — how the sponsorship will build relationships internally with staff, ways in which it will facilitate networking with other sponsors or potential business partners and how it can build sales among consumer and business audiences.

Given that many of the organisations targeted by events as potential sponsors receive large numbers of proposals each week, an effort should be made to ensure the proposal provides sufficient information on which a decision can be made. If the organisation has published guidelines for sponsorship seekers to follow, it should be evident from the contents page and a quick scan of the proposal that these matters have been addressed. Some attempt to make a proposal stand out can also be useful. A food and wine festival might print a brief version of the proposal on a good bottle of wine, for example, as well as submitting the fuller version. But be aware that glossy, printed proposals and presentations are usually not well accepted, because they do not suggest that the event is offering a customised partnership (Grey and Skildum-Reid, 2004).

Time is increasingly crucial in business. If a proposal is too long, has not been based on sound research, does not contain adequate information or it leaves out key elements (such as event contact details), the chances of the proposal being discarded are high. As a general rule, the length of a sponsorship proposal should be commensurate with the amount of money sought and must be as succinct as possible. If the value of the sponsorship is substantial and the proposal is over five pages (more than 10 pages could be too long), an executive summary should give a snapshot of its key elements along with a contents page.

Undertaking the sponsorship screening process

Commonly, organisations apply a screening process to sponsorship proposals as they seek to determine which relevant benefits are present. An understanding of this screening process is useful to the event manager as it assists in crafting sponsorship proposals. The framework for understanding the screening process developed by Crompton (1993) remains one of the most comprehensive developed to date. The framework adopts the acronym CEDAREEE to identify the major elements of the sponsorship screening process employed by corporations. The acronym is derived from:

- **C**ustomer audience
- **E**xposure potential
- **D**istribution channel audience
- **A**dvantage over competitors
- **R**esource investment involvement required
- **E**vent's characteristics
- **E**vent organisation's reputation
- **E**ntertainment and hospitality opportunities

These criteria are expanded in Figure 13.6.

While not all these criteria are applicable to every sponsorship proposal, it is a most effective checklist for the sponsorship proposer to evaluate the sponsorship offer to ensure that all aspects of sponsorship have been thought of and that all the benefits of the sponsorship offer have been developed and described to the potential sponsor.

An organisation that has received a sponsorship proposal will act in several possible ways. After scanning the proposal, its management and/or marketing personnel may:

- dispose of it,
- request further information,
- seek to negotiate in an attempt to have the sponsorship offering,
- improve to meet its needs and
- accept the proposal as presented (it is more likely though that some adaptations will occur through negotiation).

Once sent, it is a useful practice to follow up sponsorship proposals within a reasonable period (for example, 2 weeks afterwards) to determine their status (for example, yet to be considered, under review or rejected). On occasions, the proposed sponsorship package may be of interest to the organisation, but they may wish to 'customise' it further. If this is the case, both the event and potential sponsor can negotiate to move the sponsorship towards a more mutually beneficial offer. Event managers should have a clear understanding of the minimum payment

FIGURE 13.6 Screening criteria used by businesses to determine sponsorship

1. Customer audience
- Is the demographic, attitude and lifestyle profile of the target audience congruent with the product's target market?
- What is the on-site audience?
- Is sponsorship of this event the best way to communicate the product/service to this target audience?

2. Exposure potential
- What is the inherent news value of the event?
- What extended print and broadcast coverage of the sponsorship is likely?
- Will the extended coverage be local, regional or national? Is the geographical scope of this media audience consistent with the product's sales area?
- Can the event be tied into other media advertising?
- Can the company's products/services be sold at the event?
- What is the life of the event?
- Are banners and signage included in the sponsorship? How many and what size? Will they be visible during television broadcasts?
- Will the product's name and logo be identified on promotional material for the activity?
- Event posters — how many, where placed?
- Press releases — how many?
- Point-of-sale displays — how many, where placed?
- Television advertisements — how many and on what stations?
- Radio advertisements — how many and on what stations?
- Print advertisements — how many and in what print media?
- Internet advertisements (on the event website, banner advertisements) — how many and on what sites?
- Links to sponsor's websites?
- Where will the product name appear in the event program? Front or back cover? Number and site of program advertisements? How many programs?
- Will the product's name be mentioned on the public address system? How many times?
- Can the sponsor have display booths? Where will they be located? Will they be visible during television broadcasts?

3. Distribution channel audience
- Are the sponsorship's advantages apparent to wholesalers, retailers or franchisers? Will they participate in promotions associated with the sponsorship?

4. Advantages over competitors
- Is the event unique or otherwise distinctive?
- Has the event previously had sponsors? If so, how successful has it been in delivering the desired benefits to them? Is it strongly associated with other sponsors? Will clutter be a problem?
- Does the event need co-sponsors? Are other sponsors of the event compatible with the company's product? Does the company want to be associated with them? Will the product stand out and be recognised among them?
- If there is co-sponsorship, will the product have category and advertising exclusivity?
- Will competitors have access to signage, hospitality or event advertising? Will competition be allowed to sell the product on site?
- If the company does not sponsor it, will the competitor? Is that a concern?

FIGURE 13.6 *Continued*

5. Resource investment involvement required
- How much is the total sponsorship cost, including such items as related promotional investment, staff time and administrative and implementation, effort?
- Will the sponsorship investment be unwieldy and difficult to manage?
- What are the levels of barter, in-kind and cash investment?
- Does the event guarantee a minimum level of benefits to the company?

6. Event's characteristics
- What is the perceived stature of the event? Is it the best of its kind? Will involvement with it enhance the product's image?
- Does it have a 'clean' image? Is there any chance that it will be controversial?
- Does it have continuity or is it a one-off?

7. Event organisation's reputation
- Does the organisation have a proven track record in staging this or other events?
- Does it have the expertise to help the product achieve its sponsorship goals?
- Does the organisation have a reputation and an image with which the company desires to be associated?
- Does it have a history of honouring its obligations?
- Has the company worked with this organisation before? Was it a positive experience?
- Does it have undisputed control and authority over the activities it sanctions?
- How close to its forecasts has the organisation been in delivering benefits to its sponsors?
- How responsive is the organisation's staff to sponsors' requests? Are they readily accessible?
- Is there insurance and what are the company's potential liabilities?

8. Entertainment and hospitality opportunities
- Are there opportunities for direct sales of product and related merchandise, or for inducing product trial?
- Will celebrities be available to serve as spokespeople for the product? Will they make personal appearances on its behalf at the event, in other markets, or in the media? At what cost?
- Are tickets to the event included in the sponsorship? How many? Which sessions? Where are the seats located?
- Will there be access to VIP hospitality areas for the company's guests? How many will be authorised? Will celebrities appear?
- Will there be clinics, parties or playing opportunities at which the company's guests will be able to interact with the celebrities?

(Source: adapted from Crompton, 1993)

they are prepared to accept for the event sponsorship benefits on offer — to what extent can the event move in its negotiations to create a 'win—win' situation (particularly if multiple sponsors are being sought)? At this stage, it is vitally important not to undervalue the event's benefits — a sponsorship sold below its potential market value will eventually need a price correction, which creates tension with event partners.

An effective method of calculating the worth of an event sponsorship is to calculate the cost of communicating with the target market using other media, such as print. If the cost of newspaper advertisements that reach a target market of 10,000, with a frequency of three times is £x, the value of an event sponsorship that reaches the same size target market should not be less than £x, given all the other advantages that come to a sponsor with a good 'fit' with an event.

Organisers also need to consider the time, effort and pounds that they devote to seeking sponsorship in determining their final 'price'. Harrison (2004, p. 8) suggested that 'the amount of money, or its equivalent value to you, that you raise in sponsorship should be (at least) double the amount that it has cost you to get it, otherwise you are going backwards'. When it is clear that both the event and sponsor have a sponsorship arrangement that offers the best possible outcomes for both partners, it is then usual for a written contract to be developed.

Negotiating event sponsorship contracts

It is standard business practice to commit the sponsorship agreement to paper to avoid misunderstandings about the event assets and benefits being offered, their costs, payment terms and the responsibilities of both parties. Where the contract was once just a reference for event organisers and sponsors, in the case of major sponsorship deals, the contract now establishes the ground rules for the ongoing working relationship between the sponsorship partners. Chapter 17 offers some more general guidelines about event contracts. With large-scale events, a contract is essential to ensure that the obligations of both the event organiser and sponsor are met and that category exclusivity for the sponsor is protected to discourage ambushers. Closer event–sponsor relationships may technically be easier to establish in smaller-scale events and festivals, but the business practicalities of having a contract (approved by the lawyers of both parties) makes a lot of sense. If a prolonged period of negotiation is needed for a sponsorship (this is usual for a very large event sponsorship property), having a legal letter of agreement to confirm that the sponsorship will go ahead is important.

To help plan the content of an event sponsorship contract, various sponsorship agreement pro formas are available, which can help draft the document for discussion with the sponsor and legal advisors. Some community organisations may offer sponsorship pro formas on their websites. Entering the words sponsorship agreement into a Google search engine provides event managers of smaller festivals and special events with many examples of sponsorship agreements that can be adapted to suit their needs. Grey and Skildum-Reid (2003) offered excellent support materials of this nature in their toolkit. The content of contracts would usually include the objectives and responsibilities of both parties, benefits to be obtained by the event and the sponsor, termination conditions, ambush marketing protection, details of media, branding and leveraging, the promised exclusivity, marketing and sponsor servicing, and insurance and indemnity requirements.

For small events and festivals, the scope and depth of the contract will be reduced (and the cost of legal advice is a key consideration), but often some in-kind (contra) support from a legal service can be obtained by a local community festival.

MANAGING SPONSORSHIPS

Once sponsorship has been secured, it must be effectively managed in order to ensure that the benefits that were promised are delivered. Indeed, this is usually a requirement that is spelt out in some depth in sponsorship contracts for large events. However, a sponsorship management plan is essential for successful events and festivals. This allows the event to successfully manage the sponsor's marketing needs listed in the sponsorship agreement and to build a quality, long-lasting relationship with its sponsors.

Effective management of sponsorship agreements involves everything from maintaining harmonious relationships between a sponsor's staff and people within the event/festival to ensuring sponsor's signage is kept in pristine condition. Some festivals and events also tailor their servicing approach to the sponsor's needs. For example, as discussed in the Cheltenham Festivals case study, although there are a range of options available to potential sponsors, further benefits and approaches can be explored to maximise the sponsorship benefits for the sponsor (and the event). However, there should be no doubt about the level of servicing that a sponsor likes or expects if front-end negotiations have been well managed. Allsop (2004) suggested that at least 10% (but preferably up to 50%) of the sponsorship revenue should be set aside for actively servicing the sponsorship and this management budget needs to be spent wisely.

Effective relationships between events and sponsors, like any other relationship, are built on a strong foundation of communication, commitment and trust. If a sponsor believes that its sponsorship has been effective — that is, achieved the marketing and business objectives of the sponsorship — there is every likelihood that it will renew the sponsorship for another year. As has been stated before, the longer a sponsorship lasts, the better it is for both parties. Flora's former long-term sponsorship of the London Marathon is an example of how a sponsor's name can become synonymous with the event itself, thereby delivering branding benefits to the sponsor. Farrelly and Quester's (2003) research showed a link between having a market orientation (a customer-focused approach to doing business) and building commitment, satisfaction and trust between the sponsor partners.

It appears that sponsors who do not see their event partner as being particularly 'market/consumer-oriented' often engage in less joint marketing activities with that event. As a result, it is important to establish effective communication with sponsors so that they see the event manager as a serious marketer who will look for joint leveraging opportunities. Both the sponsor and the event need to have a reasonably equal input to how the sponsorship can be used to achieve its full potential. Perceptions by the sponsor of an equitable contribution to the relationship could lead it to look for a more customer-oriented event (Farrelly and Quester, 2003) in its next sponsorship round.

Techniques for effective sponsorship management

A number of suggestions and techniques (based on Geldard and Sinclair, 2003) can be adopted to ensure positive and enduring relations are developed with sponsors:

- *One contact*: One person from the event organisation needs to be appointed as the contact point for the sponsor. That person must be readily available (a mobile phone number helps), have the authority to make decisions regarding the event and be able to forge harmonious relationships with the sponsor's staff.
- *Understand the sponsor*: A method of maintaining harmonious relationships is to get to know the sponsor's organisation, its mission, its staff, its products and its marketing strategies. By doing this, it becomes easier to understand the needs of the sponsor and how those needs can be satisfied.
- *Motivate an event organisation's staff about the sponsorship*: Keeping staff informed of the sponsorship contract, the objectives of the sponsorship and how the sponsor's needs are to be satisfied will help ensure the sponsorship will work smoothly and to the benefit of both parties.
- *Use of celebrities associated with the event*: If the event includes the use of artistic, sporting or theatrical celebrities, ensure sponsors have an opportunity to meet them in a social setting. Most people enjoy immensely the opportunity to tell anecdotes about their brush with the famous!
- *Acknowledge the sponsor at every opportunity*: Use all available media to acknowledge the sponsor's assistance. Media that can be used include the public address system at a local festival, newsletters, media releases, the annual report and staff briefings.
- *Sponsorship launch*: Have a sponsorship launch to tell the target market about the organisations and agencies that will sponsor the event or festival. The style of the launch depends on the type of sponsorship and the creativity of the event director. Finding an innovative angle to draw media coverage is valuable.
- *Media monitoring*: Monitor the media for all stories and commentary about the event or festival that include mention of the sponsor (a media-monitoring firm may be contracted to perform this task). This shows the sponsor that the event takes a serious interest in the sponsorship and is alert to the benefits the sponsor is receiving.
- *Principal sponsor*: If the event has many sponsors, ensure the logo of the principal sponsor (that is, the sponsor who has paid the most) is seen on everything to do with the event, including stationery, uniforms, flags, newsletters, stages and so on. Usually, this requirement will be spelt out in legal agreements, but it is important to add value for the principal sponsor wherever it is possible.
- *Naming rights*: If the event has given naming rights to a sponsor (for example, John Smiths Grand National and Ricoh Women's British Open), it has an

obligation to ensure these rights are used in all communications employed by the event organisation. This includes making every endeavour to ensure the media are aware of, and adhere to, the sponsored name of the event. Sometimes this is difficult, but it must be attempted so that the event holds up its side of the deal.

- *Professionalism*: Even though volunteers may be involved in the management of many events, this does not mean that staff can act like amateurs. Sponsors expect to be treated efficiently and effectively, with their reasonable demands met in a speedy manner. Sponsorship is a partnership and loyalty to that partnership is often repaid with an ongoing investment.
- *Undersell and overdeliver*: Do not promise what cannot be delivered. Be cautious in formulating your proposal and then ensure the expectations raised by the sponsorship agreement are met and, ideally, exceeded.

There is plenty of evidence of events that have found innovative ways to 'go that extra mile' with their sponsorship relationships. For example, the Wall's Beach at V Festival 2004, partnering Wall's and Virgin Radio, was designed as the 'ultimate festival experience' including sand, palm trees and deck chairs. It was billed as, 'the perfect place to chill in the day and soak up the festival vibe, and as the sun sets let yourself go at the coolest beach party this side of Ibiza!' (Virgin Radio, 2004). Often, it takes only a little imagination to think of ways in which to prove to sponsors that the event or festival is an active business and marketing partner.

Sponsorship management plans to service sponsors

Once the sponsorship contract has been signed, it is good practice to construct a sponsorship management plan (or action plan) to operationalise the agreement. At its most basic, this plan should identify what objectives the sponsorship will achieve for the sponsor, the benefits that have been promised, costs associated with providing specified benefits, review and evaluation approaches, and the timeline for activities that need to be conducted to deliver on the sponsorship. These activities are discussed below.

'Objectives' associated with any given event sponsorship will be tailored to the needs of that partnership, but they should be specific to the sponsorship, measurable in that the success or otherwise of the sponsorship can be established and agreed to by the person responsible for carrying out the plan, while perhaps challenging the objectives can be achieved under normal circumstances and remain realistic, and have a time frame in which the objectives have to be achieved. Lloyds TSB Scotland sponsored the children's programme at the Edinburgh International Book Festival from 1999 to 2004 (Lloyds TSB Scotland, 2005, p. 9). The rationale for the sponsorship was that they were supporting the premier event of its kind in the world for children bringing literature, language and ideas to a wide and diverse audience, while providing the opportunity to penetrate an audience which is difficult to reach. The key objectives were to provide product placement for the

Young Savers account and continue Lloyds TSB Scotland's commitment to education by increasing the number and range of events. The event and sponsor set out some specific performance measures for evaluation. The outcomes from the sponsorship included:

- achieving 77% sponsor's recognition,
- increasing sales of the Young Savers account,
- doubling ticket sales since the start of the sponsorship,
- increasing exposure of visitors to the brand as visitor numbers to Edinburgh International Book Festival increased from 70,000 in 1999 to 207,000 in 2004,
- the 2004 Lloyds TSB Children's Programme included 185 events with 110 authors, over 40 workshops and 30 storytelling sessions,
- increasing the percentage of schools attending from outside Edinburgh from 15% in 2002 to 60% in 2003,
- attracting Arts & Business funding of £37,500 for Bus Fund and Schools Gala Day in 2002–2003 and
- involving Lloyds TSB staff — assisting with the Bus and Schools Gala Day, staffing the Activity Corner and making more than 250 tickets available for hospitality and family use (Lloyds TSB Scotland, 2005, pp. 9–10).

Stakeholders affected by the sponsorship also need to be addressed in the management plan — these groups would include attendees, members of the broader community in which the event is taking place, staff of the sponsoring organisation and media. All 'benefits and associated actions' need to be clearly identified, along with the target group(s) to be reached and 'costs' (financial or otherwise) that are associated with them. These costs might include signage manufacture and erection, supporting advertisements, promotional material, prize money, sponsor hospitality costs, professional fees, labour costs associated with hosting sponsors on-site, tickets, postage and preparation of an evaluation report. A budget needs to present all costs and show those costs in the context of the overall value of the sponsorship. Figure 13.7 provides a checklist of items to be included in a sponsorship budget (see Chapter 9 for more information on preparing budgets). It should also be remembered that sponsorship (both in-kind and cash) attracts tax, and this tax must be factored into any bottom-line calculations. However, in many cases, particularly smaller events such as conferences or community festivals, the benefits that accrue to the sponsor cost the event virtually nothing, except for the management time of ensuring what was promised is delivered. The sponsor supplies the promotional material, such as banners, signage and artwork for advertisements and other costs are absorbed into the administration of the event. Nevertheless, it is good practice to isolate costs associated with the sponsorship to establish the net benefit to the event the sponsorship generates.

A list of the 'actions' necessary to fulfil the sponsorship should be made, specifying what is to be done, when it is to be completed and who is responsible. Mapping out all the management and marketing activities on a spreadsheet or other form of graphic display such as a Gantt chart is a useful management aid.

FIGURE 13.7 Items that can be included in a sponsorship budget

ITEMS THAT WILL INCUR CASH OUTLAYS OR PERSON HOURS TO SUPPORT THE SPONSORSHIP	COST (£)
☐ Event programs	
☐ Additional printing	
☐ Signage production	
☐ Signage erection	
☐ Support advertising	
☐ Hospitality — food and beverage	
☐ Telephone, Internet and fax	
☐ Public relations support	
☐ Tickets for sponsors	
☐ VIP parking passes	
☐ Cost of selling sponsorship (staff time at £ per hour)	
☐ Cost of servicing sponsorship (staff time at £ per hour)	
☐ Legal costs	
☐ Travel costs	
☐ Taxis and other transport	
☐ Evaluation research/report	
☐ Media monitoring	
Total costs	
Profit margin	
Minimum sponsorship sale price	

An 'evaluation and review' process needs to be built into the sponsorship management plan. The review process should be ongoing and act to identify and address any problems that could affect sponsorship outcomes. Evaluation is concerned with providing a clear understanding of how the sponsorship performed against the objectives that were set for it. Evaluation seeks to answer questions such as: Did the promised media coverage eventuate? Did the attendee profile of the event reflect the market profile described in the sponsorship proposal? What was the overall quality of the sponsorship's delivery and management? Evaluation also gives the partners the chance to fine-tune the sponsorship arrangements, so that both parties are well placed to renew the partnership in subsequent years. In general terms, the development of the sponsorship action plan can be a creative and rewarding task that simply serves to communicate to the sponsor that its investment is being managed professionally.

MEASURING AND EVALUATING THE SPONSORSHIP

A shared responsibility of the event or festival and its sponsor is the measurement of the overall impact of the partnership. There are two components to measurement and evaluation: first, the evaluation of the effectiveness of the partnership and how the sponsor and event have contributed to it and, second, the measurement of the consumer-related marketing objectives set by the sponsor. While most events seek some feedback from their sponsors about the effectiveness of their sponsorship management, much more effort needs to be devoted to measuring the consumer effects of sponsorship. Many events have limited budgets for conducting sophisticated market research (and should consider some of the techniques suggested in Chapter 7), but many sponsors also do surprisingly little research to determine whether their investment in an event was warranted in terms of value for money. The 2009 IEG/Performance Research Sponsorship Decision Makers Survey found that 29% of participating companies did not currently undertake any measurement of their sponsorships and 38% spent 1% or less of the rights fee on evaluation (Performance Research, 2009). This contrasts with advertising campaigns where pre- and post-testing of consumer effects is commonplace. Jeffries-Fox (2005) observed that only a small proportion of public relations companies evaluated their involvement in event sponsorships and as a result produced *A Guide to Measuring Event Sponsorships* for the Institute for Public Relations.

Some of the factors that complicate the measurement of sponsorship are that brand marketers often use a number of media, including sponsorship, to create brand relationships and there are often carry-over effects of previous media and marketing expenditure on brand awareness and image (De Pelsmacker et al., 2004). Of particular importance in sponsorship measurement is the use of audience research that measures unaided and aided recognition of the event sponsor's name (sponsor awareness), attitudes towards the sponsor and any actions/behaviours that the sponsorship has caused in its target audience (this could be a signed contract on an important deal for a business-to-business bank client or a driver who has reduced their driving speed as a result of the sponsor's event messages).

While there is a need for more formal research (and publicly available findings) about the effects of sponsorship, it is clear that some sponsors of high-value event properties are becoming very rigorous about their measurement of the value of sponsorship. The event profile below details Suncorp's approach in evaluating its sponsorship of the 2003 RWC.

EVENT PROFILE

2003 Rugby World Cup sponsorship

Suncorp conducted brand recall surveys, attitude tracking and focus groups in its Queensland and interstate markets to understand the consumer response to its sponsorship of the 2003 RWC. From May to December 2003, the company interviewed 100 people per month asking them to name the RWC sponsors. Commuters at Wynyard Station in Sydney were involved in exit surveys to track attitudes towards the GIO sub-brand and the effectiveness of an outdoor campaign. Studies were also conducted to understand brand awareness and whether goodwill continued after the event.

As a preface to the Wallabies sponsorship, Suncorp also used focus groups during the RWC's quarter finals among customers and non-customers, and rugby fanatics and non-fanatics to find out what they thought about the Suncorp and GIO brands and also what they thought about the Wallabies team. (The timing of this research before the Wallabies made it into the finals was important to avoid bias.) This was the sponsor's way of discovering that there was a strong fit between the perceived brand values of Suncorp and the Wallabies team. Media tracking was also used to assess the value of Suncorp's expenditure, which determined a media value of between $4 million and $5 million in unpaid media space during the RWC sponsorship.

T Ferguson, Sponsorship Manager, Suncorp 2004

Given the ubiquity of e-marketing, Cohen (2005) suggests these opportune techniques for the measurement of e-activity generated by sponsorship of an event:

- Provided the sponsor has an e-mail address database of its customers (as it should), it can survey a sample of them pre- and post-event to measure changes in brand awareness, sponsorship association, brand favourability and intent to purchase.
- If the sponsorship includes an advertisement on the event's website (as it should) the click-through rate can easily be measured by the event. This is the ratio between the number of visitors to the event's website and the number of those who clicked on the sponsor's advertisement, which would take them to the sponsor's website. Obviously the higher the ratio, the better for the sponsor.
- If a viral marketing campaign is used as part of the sponsorship leverage strategy (forward to a friend links that incorporate some aspect of the event sponsorship), the number of times this occurs can be measured.
- Count visits to web pages in the sponsor's website that feature event-related activities, such as contests, opportunities to win tickets and chances to meet the event celebrities.

Overall, it is clear that there is a marked contrast in the effort and expenditure devoted to measuring sponsorship effects across different events and festivals and among sponsors themselves. What is clear is that marketing budgets and sponsorship expenditure are subject to tighter scrutiny as competition for funds increases — it is timely, therefore, for all events and festivals and sponsorship managers (who also compete for budgets in their companies) to review their measurement tools.

SUMMARY

Sponsorship is now an often used component of the marketing communication media of many corporations and public sector organisations. Influences on sponsorship growth worldwide can be found in the business and marketing environment and in the diversity of consumer and stakeholder benefits that sponsorships create.

From an event's perspective, sponsorship often (but not always) represents a significant potential revenue stream. Yet, sponsorships are fast becoming business partnerships that offer resources beyond money. To succeed in attracting and keeping the sponsorship stakes, event organisers must thoughtfully develop policies and strategies, providing a clear framework for both events/festivals and sponsors to decide on the value and suitability of potential partnerships. Having an inventory of the event or festival benefits available for sale is an important starting point for those seeking sponsorship.

The sponsorship proposal must be based on comprehensive research of the benefits that the event generates for sponsors and the potential sponsor. Event managers need to formalise and manage their agreements so that commitments made to sponsors are met.

QUESTIONS

1. What is the difference between looking at event sponsorships as philanthropy rather than as a business relationship?

2. Explain in your own words the significance of Crompton's exchange relationship model.

3. Describe why in many circumstances a sponsorship can be a much more effective promotional spend than other forms of promotion for an organisation.

4. Name an event or festival for which sponsorship may be inappropriate (a conference may be a good place to start your inquiry) and discuss why you have formed this conclusion.

5. List the various methods of describing an audience for an event and explain why this is an essential part of constructing a sponsorship proposal.

6. Identify a festival or event of interest to you and state the steps that you would follow in identifying potential sponsors for this event.

7. What is one effective method of establishing the price asked for in a sponsor-ship proposal?

8. Select an event and establish the actions it takes to manage the sponsorships associated with the event.

CASE STUDY: MICROSOFT UK'S SPONSORSHIP OF THE 2002 COMMONWEALTH GAMES

Introduction

At the end of 2000, Microsoft UK was approached by the Manchester 2002 Commonwealth Games Organising Committee, M2002 Limited, to become a sponsor following the demise of Atlantic Telecom which had been signed up previously. Prior to the approach, Microsoft UK had never undertaken sponsorship before of any kind. Sarah Fasey, the Commonwealth Games project director for Microsoft UK, takes up the story, 'Our local office supplied software to the original M2002 organising committee as a community giving project. What became clear was that it was a much bigger and more complex project and after a series of meetings we saw it as a fantastic opportunity for Microsoft UK and that we should be there.'

The activity was weighed up against other marketing activities and it was considered that the Games gave Microsoft a broader opportunity not only to support image and reputation objectives but to showcase technology and entertain customers. Microsoft UK, therefore, became the official software and technology partner of the 2002 Commonwealth Games. Susan Hunt, who was general manager of sponsorship for M2002 Limited, is clear in defining the objectives from the event perspective at that time, 'We wanted a leading edge approach but not a bleeding edge approach. The Games are very risk adverse so we needed be sure we could absolutely deliver what was the minimum standard excellently. So we wanted solidity and a company that could make it happen.' She continues, 'We had to have delivery. We also sought companies that could pick up our brand values and run with them as well. We were lucky in Microsoft that we could deliver the two. But the priority in this instance was being able to deliver.'

Objectives and target audiences

Microsoft UK provided the first-ever single technology platform for a major multi-venue sports event. Fasey explains, 'M2002 wanted the simplicity of one single platform. In the past, such as in previous Olympics, you had lots of different IT companies involved and then you had to spend a bunch of money on systems integration because of the different systems and then you needed a whole bunch of people to help you integrate them all. They [M2002] didn't want to be forced down the road of having to involve lots of different consultants to make the system work.' M2002's Hunt expands, 'To be able to deal with one partner with the size, clout and capacity of Microsoft UK was a definite advantage. There is no better IT company that we could have worked with.'

Financial details

So did any money change hands or did Microsoft UK just supply peoplepower and kit? According to Betty Maitland, who is a sponsorship consultant to Microsoft UK and was involved in the M2002 sponsorship, 'The majority was in value in kind. However, it is generally known that top tier sponsors paid $3million.' Microsoft UK's Fasey adds, 'They needed comprehensive infrastructure to run the games on, multiple sports, athlete tracking, managing the athletes' village, media centre etc. They needed a lot of support from the hardware and software perspective so it was largely a value in kind deal.'

Continued

CASE STUDY: MICROSOFT UK'S SPONSORSHIP OF THE 2002 COMMONWEALTH GAMES—*CONT'D*

Marketing

According to Microsoft UK's Fasey, the company wanted to get three things out of the Games. 'One was to showcase our technology which we did. It was the first ever single multisports event to run on one platform – in this case Windows – and it was very successful. Secondly we wanted to exploit hospitality and we got fantastic feedback. We took 1400 customers during the course of the 10 days.' Post-event research carried out by the event marketing team showed 89% gave top scores for the experience and 100% would attend similar hospitality. 'The third thing was to demonstrate that we were good guys really and that we are a business in the UK and contribute to the UK', adds Fasey.

Fasey feels that prior to the Games, 'the general public was quite cynical I think and the Games didn't have a lot of noise around them. But the minute they started everyone got behind them and we got good feedback internally largely due to the fact that we'd done something visible that our employees could be proud of.'

Execution and exploitation

Technology. The technology platform involved a team from Microsoft UK working as a partner to M2002 during the 18-month build up to the Games. Fasey explained, 'We had some of our people there helping design, build and make sure it was working. Then there were support people on site to sort out any bugs or faults so that there weren't any problems from the users' perspective. So we had a team of around 20 support staff there during the Games on site 24/7.' And further help was never far away if needed adds Fasey, 'We had our people on site but if something had happened that they couldn't fix then they would have been calling on the bigger teams in Reading, London and the US. They would have had access to whatever resources were needed to fix it.'

Awareness/image and reputation. Awareness of the sponsorship was promoted to achieve several image and reputation objectives. Microsoft supported UK athletics events in the build up to the Games which gave opportunities to promote Microsoft's involvement in the Commonwealth Games to the TV audience and also to gain a greater understanding of the way major sports events worked out. In terms of internal promotion Microsoft UK had great fun according to Fasey. 'We had a relationship with Tanni Grey Thompson as part of our marketing programme and she came to our head office a few times, she came to our charity day and sports day which got people engaged. She also spoke at our company conference which was very inspiring. We also had competitions to win tickets to go to the event and looked for volunteers to be involved on site. We also put an Internet Cafe into the athletes village and we had our own people there to show people how to use e-mail and Xboxes etc.'

Managing the sponsorship process. According to M2002's Hunt, the event's modus operandi was inspired by the Olympics and was aimed at teaching sponsors to leverage an involvement 'without the branding and the easy stuff such as signage and hospitality. It's more about what are the things that are going to help you fulfil your marketing objectives through this property. It's more of a marketing proposition.'

Regular sponsor workshops were held in the build-up to the Games. Hunt says, 'In retrospect we would have made them less process-driven and more inspirational/ideas-driven. The problem was that there were so many first time sponsors that we had to make the workshops very prescriptive in terms of timing, ticket applications etc, the basic stuff. That took up so much time that we didn't have enough time to inspire them on how they could leverage their sponsorships. We did provide case studies and encourage them to do various things and most of them did.'

The workshops were combined rather than aimed at individual sponsors explains Hunt, 'For example, Cadbury spoke about what they did during the Olympics in Sydney and we had various speakers in from time to time to inspire all the sponsors. Regular work in progresses ended up being held monthly.'

There were two camps of sponsors according to Hunt, 'Those involved from a marketing perspective and those who were also suppliers such as Asda supplying food and Microsoft providing IT. There were therefore dual work in progresses – ones where we treating them as a client and ones where we treating them as a supplier. Contact reports were all circulated so everyone knew where everyone was up to. There was regular phone contact too.'

Outcome and evaluation

M2002 and Microsoft UK are proud that a single technology platform was achieved. Says Microsoft UK's Fasey, 'It [the single platform] made it a much simpler process. In terms of cost it was 10 times cheaper than the previous Winter Olympics at Salt Lake City which is a comparable size.'

In terms of measuring the success of the sponsorship Hunt believes there are lessons to be learnt: 'Because Microsoft and many of the sponsors came on relatively late in the piece, there was a scramble towards the end in terms of measurement. There could have been more benchmarking and we did try and encourage them but there wasn't much time. We did everything we could to facilitate that but it something we could have done better.'

Research of Games spectators by Intrepid showed that 32% perceived Microsoft much more positively and 48% slightly more positively. Microsoft's involvement was positively received as respondents did not expect a large US company to be a sponsor. Overall, there was a 13% shift in attitude with 84% of this positive.

Microsoft's infrastructure successfully demonstrated scalability to major enterprise customers and provided a valuable case study. Xbox became the official console and provided an on-site consumer experience resulting in 45,000 trials. Xboxes were also well received in the athletes' villages, resulting in 13,000 visits. An MSN-dedicated Games channel received 240,000 hits and 6000 competition entries.

Lessons to be learned

According to Microsoft UK's sponsorship consultant Maitland, 'As a first time sponsor, valuable lessons were learnt about the amount of budget needed to support any future sponsorship; the commitment by all parts of the company and the need for technology partners to fully exploit the technology category.'

M2002's Hunt believes the sponsorship could not have gone more smoothly as far as the operations were concerned. 'The biggest success was that the Games imposed a personality on Microsoft and showed people the fun side through hospitality and gaming. It wasn't all clinical IT stuff, it was showing how technology can impact people in day to day life and put a relaxed informality on everything they did.' Nothing was ever a problem with Microsoft UK adds Hunt, 'They were terrific friends and neighbours. We were amazed how friendly an organisation they are and that they really are a separate company to the US one and driven by the values of this country [the UK]. They proved themselves to be relaxed and competent. It was a really good partnership.'

Maitland comments, 'The Commonwealth Games provided the first sponsorship to really work as integrated marketing. Sport was seen to be a highly visual way of demonstrating Microsoft's products.'

But would Microsoft UK do it all again? Fasey would not rule it out, 'We are certain that we would do something similar again. It was a new experience and a lot of hard work but we are glad that we did it and learned a lot.' Microsoft UK has no other sponsorships planned at the moment, but according to Fasey, 'We are feeling our way through a couple of proposals at the moment.' And one cannot help but think that an Olympics hosted by London in 2012 would be high up on Microsoft UK's wish list.

By Rachael Church, Editor, Sport and Technology.

Continued

CASE STUDY: MICROSOFT UK'S SPONSORSHIP OF THE 2002 COMMONWEALTH GAMES—*CONT'D*

Questions

1. Discuss how well Microsoft's evaluation of its sponsorship reflects the sponsorship effects process shown in Figure 13.3.
2. Select five key benefits of event sponsorship and briefly explain how Microsoft achieved those benefits from its sponsorship of the 2002 Manchester Commonwealth Games.
3. Using Ansoff's product–market matrix, discuss the strategies that Microsoft appeared to achieve from its sponsorship. In your discussion, use examples from the above case study.

CASE STUDY: CHELTENHAM ARTS FESTIVALS

Background

Cheltenham Festivals is a not-for-profit organisation registered both as a charity and as a company limited by guarantee. It is responsible for the annual Cheltenham Jazz, Science, Music and Literature Festivals. It also runs extensive education and outreach programmes, many to local schools and communities.

Since the launch of the Music Festival in 1945, Literature Festival in 1949, Jazz Festival in 1996 and Science Festival in 2002, their development continues to rely heavily on the generosity of donations, grants and sponsorship.

In 2006, the four festivals started to work more closely together under the umbrella brand of Cheltenham Festivals and Donna Renney was appointed as the first chief executive of the new organisation. The anvil-shaped marque of the organisation embodies both the tradition of the festivals which stretches back over 60 years with the point of the anvil symbolising the festivals' desire to challenge perceptions and produce programmes with 'edge' and 'bite'.

Today, Cheltenham Festivals is one of the leading cultural organisations in the country with the four festivals boasting combined ticket sales of over 150,000 and enjoying enviable international reputations as leaders in their own fields.

Each festival features the most up-and-coming, controversial and entertaining performers, showcasing new works, young artists and unique performances, ensuring Cheltenham an exceptionally high profile with audiences and performers around the world.

The Cheltenham Festival of Science with *The Times* as headline sponsor in 2010 in association with Pfizer is the newcomer among the festivals – launched in 2002, this 5-day festival includes topical debates, talks, workshops, an interactive science space (the Discover Zone) and a mix of live art installations, experiments and cinema. Since 2002, the festival has attracted over 10,000 to the Discover Zone and sold over 23,000 tickets annually.

The Cheltenham Jazz Festival with Barclays as headline sponsor in 2010 in association with BBC Radio 2 – since starting in 1996 the festival now attracts an audience of over 17,000. A 5-day event, the festival hosts an array of popular international jazz stars alongside the best, new and more adventurous artists. With a varied and adventurous programme, the Festival has successfully made its mark in the UK music calendar, challenging the stylistic boundaries set by other festivals and developing new audiences in jazz.

The Cheltenham Music Festival with HSBC as headline sponsor in 2010 is the longest running of the festivals and was also the first of the post-war festivals in the UK. Beginning in 1945 as a showcase for British contemporary music, in recent times Michael Berkeley (Artistic Director until 2004) expanded the festival's repertoire to include contemporary music from across Europe. In addition to presenting orchestral, chamber, choral and solo music alongside contemporary music-theatre and opera, the 17-day festival boasts an afternoon series, which features the very best in young and local musical talent, as well as a late-night strand of programming, commencing at ten in the evening. The new director, Meurig Bowen, has succeeded in making the event even more accessible, with increasing attendances at the family events. The 2009 festival was a huge success, with ticket sales reaching 17,000 and hundreds more taking advantage of the free events programmed throughout the Festival, 19 events completely sold out and an impressive 15 world premieres and 8 UK premieres performed.

The Cheltenham Literature Festival, with *The Times* as headline sponsor in 2010 in association with Waterstone's, began in 1949 when Gloucestershire writer John Moore organised a gathering of writers to celebrate the written word in Cheltenham. Over the last decade the festival has grown rapidly, with ticket sales in 2009 reaching 115,000, over 650 authors and 440 events. At the heart of the festival is the love of literature and the art of the book, with additional strands including *Book It!*, all taking place in venues all over Cheltenham. The established 10-day Autumn Festival is complemented by a 3-day Spring Events Weekend in April.

Sponsorship

The festivals seek funding for strands, venue, events sponsorship community and education programmes from a wide range of sources including public funding bodies, commercial organisations, foundations and trusts and sponsorship. Sponsorship of the festivals offers:

- a partnership with an important international brand
- a method of increasing brand awareness and raising company profile
- an opportunity for corporate hospitality and client entertainment
- an association with excellence and creativity
- a way of demonstrating commitment to the community

Benefits

There are a range of benefits to be gained through sponsorship of each of the festivals. These are tailored to suit individual requirements but can include the following:

- profile – branding and product promotion initiatives, for example, accreditation in 100,000 colour brochures, the main print vehicle; on-site sampling; website links
- events and corporate hospitality with, for example, an opportunity to meet artists, complimentary tickets in prime seat locations, priority booking and staff discount schemes
- networking and business development opportunities

Each of the Cheltenham Festivals also offers its own unique benefits to sponsors:

- *Jazz*: Barclays Cheltenham Jazz Festival is acclaimed as one of the leading festivals of its kind. The audience, largely young professionals, enjoys its leisure time and the Jazz Festival offers excellent opportunities for highly targeted reach with brand promotions and product sampling.
- *Science*: The phenomenally successful The Times Cheltenham Science Festival is winning praise from the science community for its innovation and pioneering ethos. The festival features many exclusive benefits for its sponsors, including opportunities for business-to-business marketing, brand promotion and corporate entertainment. The festival achieves a perfect balance between accessibility and integrity, featuring debates, lectures, interactive family events, schools workshops and more.
- *Music*: The HSBC Cheltenham Music Festival is renowned for showcasing the very best of international contemporary music alongside a well-established traditional programme. The core audience is extremely loyal – over half are mature professionals with high levels of disposable income. The festival provides exceptional opportunities for corporate hospitality, so why not entertain your clients with a champagne lunch after a morning recital or dinner after a concert?

Continued

CASE STUDY: CHELTENHAM ARTS FESTIVALS—*CONT'D*

- *Literature*: The Times Cheltenham Literature Festival is not only one of the oldest and largest literary events in Europe, it is also one of the most accessible, offering a rare chance to listen to debates and lectures, meet authors and see beyond the written word. The audience is diverse and sponsors can be carefully matched to individual events, providing companies with excellent opportunities for both niche marketing and relationship building.

Types of Sponsorship

There are six types of sponsorship associated with Cheltenham Festivals:

1. *Association*: An association with the Cheltenham Festivals brand is sure to raise the profile of any organisation, and above all we are interested in working with our sponsors to build mutually rewarding, long-term relationships.
2. *Fees*: The sponsorship fees reflect the status of the performers, profile of the event, place in the programme, how much visibility the sponsoring organisation requires and organisational costs. Shared sponsorship packages between two or more sponsors are available by arrangement. Fee levels vary between festivals based on specific sponsorship opportunities, but the following gives a general indication:

   - Title Sponsorship: £50,000–£60,000
   - Principal Sponsors: £15,000–£35,000
   - Major Sponsors: £8000 and above
   - Festival Partners: £3000 and above
   - Festival Sponsors: £1000 and above
   - In-Kind and Co-sponsoring are also considered

3. *Title Sponsorship*: Title Sponsorship packages are built around the sponsoring organisation's requirements, but a key benefit is the profile achieved by incorporating the company logo within the festival logo on all literature and banners erected at festival venues and throughout Cheltenham prior to and during the festival.
4. *Principal Sponsors*: Principal Sponsorship is most suited to organisations requiring high-level exposure and a flexible package. At this level we provide ideal opportunities for product and brand promotion, such as named sponsorship and full branding of a key venue like the Festival Marquee and Arena or branding of the Festival Bags (5000–10,000 units per festival). Further brand awareness can be generated by being named sponsor of a series of headline events, or even a series co-programmed with the sponsor, for example, the Swan Hellenic's Better to Travel series at the 2004 Literature Festival.

   A sponsorship launch is held in advance of each festival with the purpose of releasing programme information to potential sponsors and supporters. A sponsorship pack is collated for the launch, containing an overview of the festival themes, an outline of the benefits to be gained through sponsorship and full details of all events, print sponsorship opportunities and education and outreach projects available. Packs are also distributed to those unable to attend the launch. The Cheltenham Festivals also produces a corporate sponsorship brochure, intended for distribution to potential new, and predominantly national, commercial sponsors, and a quarterly newsletter, which contains news and information about the festivals with particular emphasis on sponsorship and the benefits it brings. This newsletter is targeted mainly at a local and regional audience in the business sector.

Other ways of giving

Leaving a Legacy: Individuals can make a positive contribution to the arts by leaving a legacy to the Cheltenham Festivals. This could be used in a number of ways including sponsorship of a concert/event, supporting the education strands or commissioning new works in your name. A will is a chance to help the organisations that have been important in their lifetime.

Patrons of the Festivals: The support of Patrons makes a real difference to the quality of the festival programme. Benefits of the Gold and Festival Patrons' scheme include a dedicated booking line, information about festival events from the festival directors in advance and invitations to festival parties and receptions throughout the year.

SUMMARY

Sponsorship provides a source of funding and offers a range of other benefits. As a result, a professional team is in place to attract and manage the sponsorship, which currently comprises 13 members of staff including a fundraising manager for each festival. In August 2005, the website was re-launched in order to provide a clearer image for the Cheltenham Festivals brand, increase access to information about the festivals including news, sponsorship, and education and outreach. The programme of festivals and events in Cheltenham has developed over the years to gain an enviable reputation for some of the most prestigious cultural events which bring significant benefits to Cheltenham and the surrounding region, including an estimated economic impact of £34 million (Brookes and Landry, 2002). The challenge for the team is in attracting appropriate sponsors for the Cheltenham Festivals brand which will continue to provide some of the funds necessary for the festivals to develop now and in the future.

For more details about the Cheltenham Festivals, please visit www.cheltenhamfestivals.com.
By Cheltenham Festivals Ltd.

Questions

1. Focusing on one of the festivals, describe the target market in demographic and socioeconomic terms.
2. What factors would a potential sponsor look for when considering whether to sponsor the festival identified in question 1?
3. How would you break down the festival in order to maximise income from sponsorship for the festival, and the benefits gained by the sponsor?
4. Based on what you have read within the case study, and your identified target markets, what companies would find sponsorship of the festival a worthwhile investment of their marketing resources? Briefly explain the appropriateness of each sponsor to the festival.
5. Construct a sponsorship pack for the sponsorship launch.
6. Design a corporate sponsorship brochure.

Event Operations and Evaluation

3

This part of the book looks at how choice of venue, theme and elements such as safety have a bearing on the successful staging of events. The following chapters relate to how the science of logistics can be adopted to manage events, the legal factors that event managers need to be aware of, and how to identify, minimise and manage the risks inherent in an event. The final chapter in this section describes the critical role of evaluation in the event management process and the range of techniques available to effectively conduct this.

Staging events

14

LEARNING OBJECTIVES

After studying this chapter, you should be able to:

- analyse the staging of an event according to its constituent elements,
- demonstrate how these elements relate to each other and to the theme of the event,
- understand the safety elements of each aspect of staging,
- identify the relative importance of the staging elements for different types of events,
- use the tools of staging.

INTRODUCTION

The term 'staging' originates from the presentation of plays at the theatre. It refers to bringing together all the elements of a theatrical production for its presentation on a stage. Most events that use this term take place at a single venue and require similar organisation to that of a theatrical production. However, whereas a play can take place over a season, an event may take place in one day or night. Examples of this type of event are product launches, company parties and celebrations, award ceremonies, conference events, concerts, large weddings, corporate dinners, and opening and closing events.

Staging can also refer to the organisation of a venue within a much larger event. A large festival may have performance areas positioned around the site. Each of these venues may have a range of events with a distinct theme. At Glastonbury Festival of Contemporary Performing Arts (Pilton, Somerset), there are five main stages and a total of 80 stages or performance spaces, each with its own style. Because it is part of a much larger event, one performance area or event has to fit in with the overall planning of the complete event and has to fit in with programming and logistics. However, each performance area is to some extent its own kingdom, with its own micro-logistics, management, staff and individual character. On a larger scale, BBC Music Live 2000 involved concerts the length and breadth of the UK, each with its own event manager, stage manager, and light and sound crew members, together with the involvement of television production crew members to broadcast a live performance of Lou Reed's song 'Perfect Day' synchronised from

Events Management. DOI: 10.1016/B978-1-85617-818-1.10014-3

491

38 locations. This perfectly illustrated the interaction of event staging and television broadcast skills (Ball, 2000).

The main concerns of staging are as follows:

- theming and event design
- programming
- choice of venue
- audience and guests
- stage
- power, lights and sound
- audiovisuals and special effects
- decoration and props
- catering
- performers
- crew
- hospitality
- the production schedule
- recording the event
- contingencies

Of course there are other areas of event management that are part of staging, such as risk, logistics and finance. Silvers (2004a) referred to the six dimensions of an event experience which lead from the first impressions before arrival through to the last perception on departure, the dimensions being marketing materials, transport and entrance, atmosphere and decor, food and beverage, entertainment, and amenities and souvenirs. This chapter analyses the staging of an event according to these elements. It demonstrates how these elements revolve around a central event theme. The type of event will determine how important each of these elements is to the others. However, common to the staging of different events are the tools: the stage plan, the contact and responsibility list and the production schedule. Silvers (2004a, p. 2) used the term professional event coordination to cover 'the integrated implementation of all the operational and logistic requirements of an event, based on the scope of event elements included in the event design'.

THEMING AND EVENT DESIGN

When staging an event, the major artistic and creative decision to be made is that of determining what the theme is to be. The theme of an event differentiates it from other events. In the corporate area, the client may give the theme of the event. For example, the client holding a corporate party or product launch may want medieval Europe as the theme, or Hollywood, complete with actors and film set. Outside the corporate area, the theme for one of the stages at a festival may be blues music, debating or a children's circus. Whatever the nature of the event, once the theme is established, the elements of the event must be designed to fit in with the theme. This is straightforward when it comes to deciding on the entertainment and catering. With the medieval corporate party, the entertainment may include jongleurs and jugglers, and the catering may be spit roasts and wine. However, audiovisuals may need a lot of thought in order to enhance the theme. The sound and lights must complement the entertainment, as they do not fit in with the period theme. In his insightful work on event design and experience, Berridge (2007) noted that there is limited insight and analysis of the designed environment for events, with many people relating design only to the theme when it should influence all elements of the experience and be embedded in all aspects of the event planning process. This view is supported by EMBOK (Silvers et al., 2006) where design was identified as a clear knowledge domain. Figure 14.1 illustrates the elements of staging, and it emphasises the central role of the theme of the event. However, it should be remembered that, within events, these areas are not so clearly defined. For example, there is generally a close working relationship between audiovisual, special effects, light and sound staff in order to produce the event.

Theme Traders express the importance of staging in the following way:

At Theme Traders our mission is to create unique and unforgettable events. Funnily enough, meticulous planning and staging are crucial when trying to create a spontaneous and vibrant atmosphere. This can be understood in terms of 'staging' because things like lighting, space, noise and furniture are tools of 'mood' to be manipulated. Bad lighting, unwanted noise or bad use of space and access can make or break a party by affecting the response of guests to their environment. Similarly, responses to event features such as lighting and

FIGURE 14.1 The elements of staging revolve around the theme

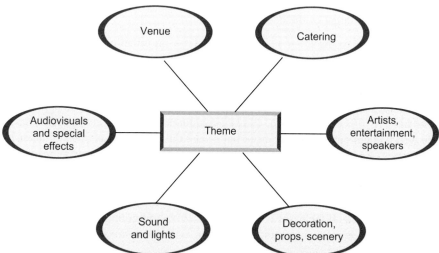

entertainment can help steer guests around a venue without them being aware of it. Stage managing their environment can often ensure that the guests do not have to be 'ferried' around and will 'naturally' go home at the right time! It is interesting that the most tightly staged environment will often inspire guests to feel a natural part of a very exciting party.

PROGRAMMING

The programme of the event is the flow of the performers, speakers, catering and the other elements of the event over time. It is the 'what's on' of the event. The programme creates the event experience for the attendee. Ultimately, the event experience for the attendee and the sponsors rests on the success of the programme. Silvers (2004b, p. 271) described its importance as follows:

> *An event experience must be choreographed and blocked out as carefully as any dance or play. The professional event coordinator crafts a plan that takes the attendee or guest through a structured progression of various sights, sounds, tastes, textures, smells, highs, lows, climaxes, diversions, and discoveries that delivers the intended impact and message of the event.*

The programme contains the schedule of performance. As with all the elements of staging, programming is both an art and a science. The programme of the event depends on:

- the expectations of the audience,
- the constraints of the venue and infrastructure,
- the culture of the client and main sponsors,
- the availability of elements of the staging, and their relationship to each other,
- the logistics and
- the creative intent of the event team.

It is similar to the order in a street parade — the timeline or schedule of the programme is set out in a linear fashion. Far from this being a simple example, a parade is multi-faceted, and there is little the event manager can do to change it once it starts moving. Consider the music: the brass band cannot be performing near the highland pipe band; they perform at slightly different beats. An event programme also has a rhythm of its own. The mix of entertainment, catering and speeches has to be well thought out so that the event builds and the audience has times of intensity and times of rest. A New Year's Eve programme, for example, gradually lifts the audience to the moment before midnight.

A large festival's programme is a complex of activities. Many festivals use a form of a Gantt chart to map the various attractions and to help the audience navigate the event programme. If the event is broadcast, the event programme may have to be in sync with the television programming. This is a major consideration for sports events.

CHOICE OF VENUE

The choice of venue is a crucial decision that will ultimately determine many of the elements of staging. Figure 14.2 lists the major factors in the choice of a venue. The venue may be an obvious part of the theme of the event. A corporate party that takes place in a zoo is using the venue as part of the event experience. However, many events take place within 'four walls and a roof', the venue being chosen for other factors. It can be regarded as an empty canvas on which the event is 'painted'. Events can be staged in a variety of spaces, as demonstrated in Figure 14.3.

The list illustrates that almost any area can be the site of an event, though as Matthews (2008a) note, this does not necessarily impact the internal operation or management of the event. In some of these cases, such as extinct volcanoes and caves, the uniqueness of the venue adds to the 'specialness' of the event. The event manager must be aware of the advantages and disadvantages of using purpose-built sites such as conference centres or a hotel function room. The main advantage of such sites is that they allow control of a greater number of environmental variables such as the temperature of the room, audience entrances and exits, and the light and sound. This control enables the event team to compel the audience to completely focus on the stage. The layout of most function rooms follows a similar pattern, thereby giving event staff familiarity with the type and use of the facilities. The familiarity, however, can be a disadvantage as the attendees may be tired with the same type of venue. The advantages of an unusual (or non-purpose) site are its uniqueness and the surprise this gives to the attendees. The site becomes part of the event.

The event manager can exploit the surroundings and characteristics of the venue to enhance the event experience. When the audience and the performers mix

FIGURE 14.2 Factors to consider in venue selection

- Location
- Matching the venue with the theme of the event
- Matching the size of the venue to the size of the event
- Venue configuration, including sight lines and seating configuration
- History of events at that venue, including the venue's reputation
- Availability
- What the venue can provide
- Transport to, from and around the venue; parking
- Access for audience, equipment, performers, VIPs, staff and the disabled
- Toilets and other amenities
- Catering equipment and preferred caterers
- Power (amount available and outlets) and lights
- Communication, including telephone
- Climate, including microclimate and ventilation
- Emergency plans and exits

FIGURE 14.3 Variety of event sites

Wetlands, caves, extinct volcanoes, beaches, forest clearings, parkland
School halls, town halls, shopping centres
Theatres, picture theatres, art galleries
Factory floors, empty factories, disused mines, current mines
Harbours, boats, ships, islands, foreshores
Avenues, streets, roads, bridges
Rooftops, car parks, railway sheds
Shearing sheds, vineyards, farmyards
Back yards, front yards, the whole house
Foyers, stages, loading docks
Churches, both consecrated and deconsecrated
Conference centres, entertainment centres, community centres and sports centres.

together and where they and the venue become the entertainment package, the delineation between stage and auditorium is no longer appropriate. In these situations, the traditional roles of stage manager and event manager become blurred.

An event that uses a purpose-built venue, for example, an arena or exhibition centre, will find that much of the infrastructure will be in place. However, because so many factors in an event depend on the venue or site, an inspection is absolutely necessary. If time permits, the event manager should attend a function at the venue to observe how the facilities are used during an event. There are many tips to testing a facility while on site, such as placing a long-distance telephone call, trying the food and staying in the approved accommodation.

Two documents that are a good starting point for making an informed choice about the venue are the venue plan/map and the list of facilities. It is good practice for the event manager to meet the venue management before committing to hire the venue. The principal purpose of this meeting is to check the accuracy of the two documents, because the plan/map, the list of facilities and the photographs can be out-of-date or aimed at promoting the venue rather than imparting detailed information. The photograph of the venue, for example, may be taken with a wide-angle lens so that all the facilities are included. Such a photograph may not give a realistic view of the site if it is being used for event design. Also, these meetings are part of the occupational health and safety consultation process and proper notes need to be kept. Chapter 18 describes the importance of consultation with the suppliers and other stakeholders of the event risk management. However, because there are so many factors in an event that are dependent on the venue or site, an inspection is absolutely necessary. For music events, the HSE (1999) suggests that main considerations for the site visit are available space for the audience, temporary structures, backstage facilities, parking, camping and rendezvous points, together with some idea of proposed capacity, concept for the entertainment and rough calculations of space requirements. For conference events, Shone (1998) identified that location will be the key consideration, with the venue needing to be close to a main motorway and within an hour's travelling time of a major city and airport (if international delegates are expected). Furthermore, Owen and Holliday (1993) recommended that the event manager makes a preliminary unannounced visit to the venue to check the ambience and courtesy of staff before making arrangements. Lyon (2004, p. 2) noted that a site inspection or familiarisation (Fam) trip provides you with the opportunity to sample the destination or potential venue, with the aim of you being able to sell this back to your organisation and recapture the experience for your delegates. He provides a useful handbook to assist this process.

Rogers (1998) suggested that there are a number of points to consider when short-listing conference venues. These include:

- the type of venue (hotel, conference centre, university, football stadia or stately homes),
- the conference rooms and facilities available (including combination of room sizes and style of seating for the requirements of the event),
- accommodation and leisure options (depending on residential requirements and opportunities for social activities) and
- an identifiable point of contact.

As with many aspects of supplier selection, the Internet has had a significant effect on venue choice. Using a search engine is often the first action in the investigation of a suitable venue. Some websites display a choice of venues once certain information (such as size of audience, approximate location and type of event) has been entered. The major hotels, conventions and exhibition centres, universities and purpose-built venues have websites to enable the matching of event requirements to venue characteristics. However, this method has the same limitations as those of using photographs and brochures to assess a venue. The websites are a tool for selling the venue, not a technical description. In addition, many suitable venues may not have an Internet presence. An Internet search will show only venues that expect to host events. If the event is truly special, the event venue may be part of that theme. A car park or a rainforest, for example, will not appear in a search for event venues.

The final consideration when choosing an event is whether it requires a physical location at all. With the ongoing development of video conferencing, and the extensive developments in the Internet, events can take place in 'cyberspace'. With some events, for example, music concerts, the event takes place live in the venue in the traditional manner, however, with the introduction of webcasting, a worldwide audience can view or experience the event simultaneously. In this instance, access to technological support and facilities, for example, a large bandwidth telephone line, will be a consideration. In other areas, for example, exhibitions and conferences, technology has been deployed in such a way that it may support the live event experience, through the website hosting supporting materials for visitors to view and in some cases interact with. Relatively recent advances in Internet technology, together with faster telecommunication infrastructure, have enabled conferences to take place solely on-line, with delegates interacting, either visually through video conferencing or through text with instant messaging. Exhibitions can take place at virtual exhibition venues, which can either be modelled on the live exhibition venue as a means of supporting the event experience or can take place solely in the virtual world without the boundaries of traditional venues and limited only by imagination and the available technology. The value of such developments is only just beginning to be realised, with some commentators predicting the death of live events, while other, more enlightened, observers view these developments as a further medium to support or enhance the live event experience.

AUDIENCE/GUESTS

The larger issues of audience (customer) logistics are described in Chapter 15. The event-staging considerations concerning the audience are:

- position of entrances and exits
- arrival times — dump or trickle
- seating and sight lines
- facilities

Goldblatt (2008) emphasised the importance of the entrance and reception area of an event in establishing the event theme, and suggested that the organiser should look at it from the guest's point of view. It is in this area that appropriate signage and meeting and greeting become important to the flow of 'traffic' and to the well-being of the guests. An example of a carefully planned entrance was the launch of Virgin Atlantic's service to Shanghai, where Terminal 3 of Heathrow Airport was transformed into a mini-Shanghai, with passengers leaving the departure lounge through a giant dragon's mouth (de Smet, 1999).

Once the guests have entered the event area, problems can occur that are specific to the type of event. In the case of conferences, audiences immediately head for the back rows. Interestingly, the HSE (1999) mentioned the opposite problem at non-ticketed music events, where the area in front of the stage is rushed as soon as the gates are open. Graham, Neirotti and Goldblatt (2001) noted a similar occurrence at sports events. The solutions, therefore, is in the type of admission. For example, organisers can adopt reserved seating methods, by using ticket numbers or roping off sections, and using a designated seating plan. This will allow the crowd to be evenly distributed in the venue. The style of seating can be chosen to suit the event; theatre-, classroom- and banquet-type seating are three examples. Ultimately, the seating plan has to take into consideration:

- type of seating — fixed or movable,
- standing room, if necessary,
- the size of the audience,
- the method of audience arrival,
- safety factors including emergency exits and fire regulations,

- the placement and size of the aisles,
- sight lines to the performances, speakers or audiovisual displays,
- disabled access and
- catering needs.

The facilities provided for the guests will depend on the type of event. Referring to Figure 14.4, the corporate event will focus on particular audience facilities as they relate to hospitality and catering, whereas a festival event will concentrate on audience facilities as they relate to entertainment. For example, there are no chairs for the audience at the BBC Proms in the Park (Hyde Park, London), but because of the theme of the event, spectators are happy to bring their own or to sit on the ground on picnic blankets. At the other end of the spectrum, The Mistletoe Ball at The Dorchester Hotel (London) has high-quality furnishings and facilities.

THE STAGE

A stage at an event is rarely the same as the theatrical stage complete with the proscenium arch and auditorium. It can range from the back of a truck to a barge in a harbour. It is important to note that, in event management, the term 'stage' can also be applied to the general staging area and not just to a purpose-built stage. However, all stages require a stage map called the stage plan. The stage plan is simply a bird's-eye view of the performance area, showing the infrastructure such as lighting fixtures, entrances, exits and power outlets. The stage plan is one of the staging tools (Figure 14.4) and a communication device that enables the event to run smoothly. For large events, the stage plan is drawn in different ways for different people, and supplied on a 'need-to-know basis'. For example, a stage plan for the lighting technician would look different to the plan for the performers. A master stage plan would contain a number of layers of these different plans, each drawn on a separate layer of transparent paper. Other plans that are used in event design are the front elevation and side elevation. In contrast to the bird's-eye view that the stage plan gives, these plans show the staging area as a ground-level view from the front and side. They assist in establishing the audience's sight lines — that is, the audience's view of the staging area and the performers.

Catherine Sterry, Art Director at Theme Traders, described the value of clear stage plans:

> To create successful and memorable events it is absolutely essential to be both imaginative and have a precise understanding of planning techniques. Site visits to venues are essential as you need to create accurate technical plans which are both clear and easily understood by members of the installation and production team. This is imperative as members of the team may not have had the opportunity of a site visit and need clear visual and technical instructions.

FIGURE 14.4 An example of a stage plan

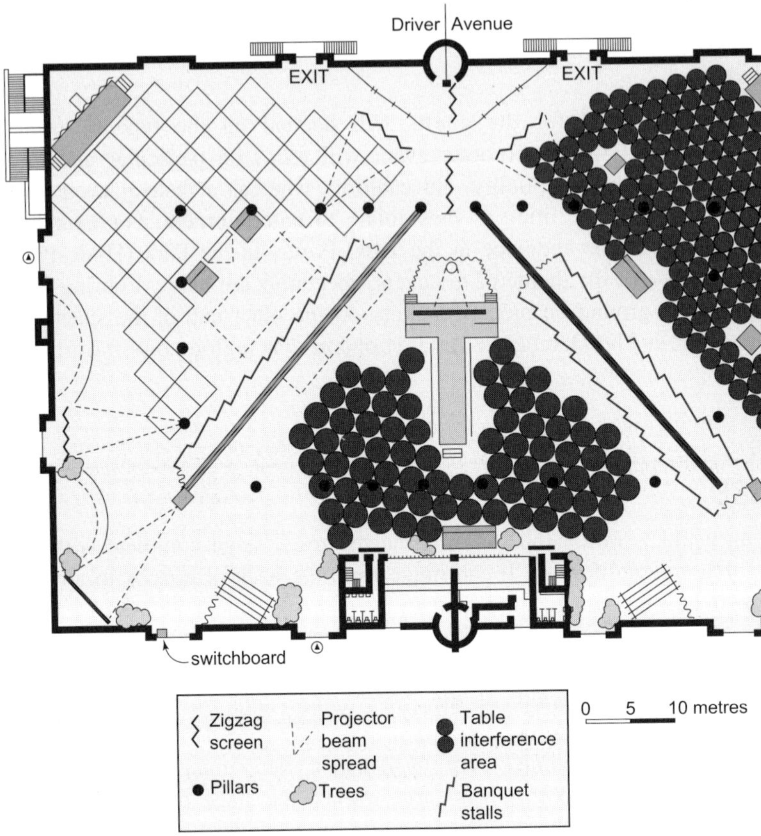

(Source: Roger Foley, Fogg Productions www.fogg.com.au)

An example of when a large stage plan for a special event was used was for the Vodafone Ball at Earls Court, London (see case study in Chapter 6). The 11,500 guests were treated to a choice from zones of entertainment that reflected the theme, 'Beach Party', including a comedy club, a blues club, an arcade and a full-scale fairground.

Where the staging of an event includes a large catering component, the stage plan is referred to as the venue layout, seating plan or floor plan. This occurs in many corporate and conference events where hospitality and catering become a major part of the staging. Figure 14.5 illustrates how the focus on the elements of staging changes according to the style of the event.

The stage manager is the person in control of the performance and responsible for signalling the cues that coordinate the work of the performers. The scheduling of the event on a particular stage is generally the responsibility of the event manager. The stage manager makes sure that this happens according to the plan. The public face of the event may be called the master of ceremonies (MC) or compere. The

FIGURE 14.5 The relationship between types of event and the relative importance of the staging elements

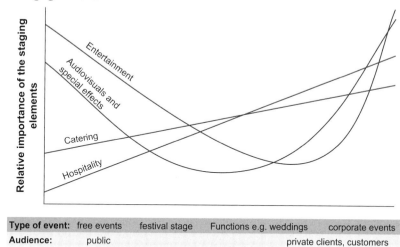

Type of event:	free events	festival stage	Functions e.g. weddings	corporate events
Audience:	public			private clients, customers

compere and the stage manager work closely together to ensure that all goes according to the plan. The compere may also make the public announcements, such as those about lost children and programme changes.

The combination of electric wiring, hot lights, special effects and the fast movement of performers and staff in a small space that is perhaps 2 m above ground level makes the risk management of the stage area particularly important. At the event, stage safety is generally the responsibility of the stage manager. Figure 14.6 lists a selection of safety considerations.

The backstage area is a private room or tent/marquee near the performance area set aside for the performers and staff. It provides the crew with a place to relax and the performers with a place to prepare for the performance and to wind down

FIGURE 14.6 Factors to consider in stage safety

- There must be a well-constructed stage done professionally by a company with adequate insurance.
- There must be clear, well-lit access points to the stage.
- All protrusions and steps should be secured and clearly marked.
- Equipment and boxes should be placed out of the way and well marked.
- There should be work lights that provide white lighting before and after the event.
- All electric cabling must be secured and tagged.
- A first-aid kit and other emergency equipment should be at hand.
- There must be clear guidelines on who is in charge during an emergency and an evacuation plan.
- A list of all relevant contact numbers should be made.

afterwards. It can be used for storage of equipment and for communication between the stage manager and performers, and it is where the food and drink are kept.

POWER

Staging of any event involves large numbers of people, and to service this crowd, electricity is indispensable. It should never be taken for granted. Factors that need to be considered concerning power are as follows:

- type of power — three phase or single phase,
- amount of power needed, particularly at peak times,
- emergency power,
- position and number of power outlets,
- types of leads and distance from power source to device,
- the correct wiring of the venue, because old venues could be improperly earthed,
- the incoming equipment's volt/amp rating,
- safety factors, including the covering of leads and the possibility of electricity earth,
- leakage as a result of rain and
- regulations regarding power.

LIGHTS

Lighting at a venue has two functions. Pragmatically, lights allow everyone to see what is happening; artistically, they are central to the design of the event. The general venue or site lighting is important in that it allows all the other aspects of the staging to take place. For this reason, it is usually the first item on the checklist when deciding on a venue. Indoor lights include signage lights (exit, toilets, etc.) as well as lighting specific areas for catering and ticket collection. Outside the venue, lighting is required for venue identification, safety, security and sponsor signs.

Once the general venue or site lighting is confirmed, lighting design needs to be considered. The questions to ask when considering lighting are both practical and aesthetic. They include the following:

- Does it fit in with and enhance the overall event theme?
- Can it be used for ambient lighting as well as performance lighting?
- Is there a backup?
- What are the power requirements (lights can draw far more power than the sound system)?
- Will it interfere with the electrics of other systems? For example, a dimmer board can create an audible buzz in the sound system.
- Does it come with a light operator, that is, the person responsible for the planning of the lighting with the lighting board?

- What light effects are needed (strobe, cross-fading) and can the available lights do this?
- What equipment is needed (for example, trees and cans), and is there a place on the site or in the venue to erect it?
- Does the building have permanent trusses available for rigging lighting?
- How can the lighting assist in the safety and security of the event?

The lighting plot or lighting plan is a map of the venue that shows the type and position of the lighting. As Reid (2001) pointed out, the decisions that the event manager has to make when creating a lighting plan are:

- placement of the lights,
- the type of lights, including floods and follow spots,
- where the light should be pointed and
- what colours to use.

SOUND

The principal reason for having sound equipment at an event is so that all the audience can clearly hear the music, speeches and audio effects. The sound system is also used to:

- communicate between the sound engineer and the stage manager (talkback or intercom),
- monitor the sound,
- create a sound recording of the event and
- broadcast the sound to other venues or through other media, including television, radio and the Internet.

This means that the type of equipment used needs to be designed according to:

- the type of sound to be amplified including spoken word and music;
- the size and make-up of the audience, for example, an older audience may like the music at a different volume from that preferred by a younger audience;
- acoustic properties of the room, for example, some venues have a bad echo problem, so attaching drapes or material to the walls may alleviate this, and
- the theme of the event, for example, a bright silver sound system may look out of place at a black tie dinner.

The choice of size, type and location of the sound speakers at an event can make a difference to the guests' experience of the sound. Figure 14.7 shows two simplified plans for speaker positions at a venue. The speakers may all be next to the stage, which is common at music concerts, or distributed around the site. They may also be flown from supports above the audience. At a large site, with speakers widely distributed, the sound engineers need to take into account the natural delay of sound

FIGURE 14.7 Two examples of audio speaker layout

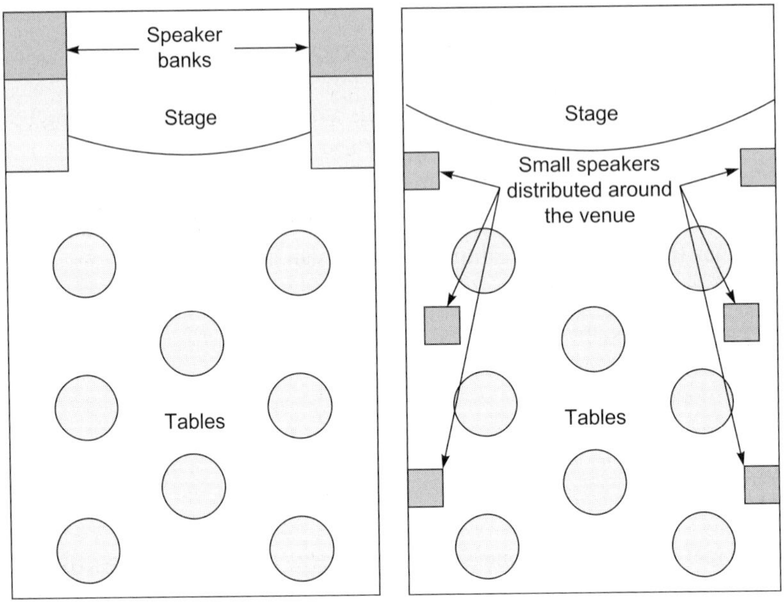

travelling from the various speakers to the members of the audience. A ducting system could also be installed above audience height to avoid tripping hazards caused by trailing cables.

For small events, a simple public address (PA) system may be used. This consists of a microphone and microphone stand and one or two speakers. It is basically the same as a home stereo system with a microphone added, and generally only has enough power to reach a small audience. The quality of sound produced makes them only suitable for speeches.

For larger events that have more complex sound requirements, a larger sound system is needed. This system would incorporate:

- microphones, which may include lapel microphones and radio microphones;
- microphone stands;
- cabling, from microphones to the mixing desk;
- a mixing desk, which adjusts the quality and level of the sound coming from the microphones before it goes out of the speakers;
- an amplifier;
- speakers, which can vary in size from bass speakers to treble speakers that enhance the quality of the sound within a certain sound spectrum;
- a sound engineer;
- sound technician, or front of house engineer, who looks after all aspects of the sound, in particular the sound quality that is heard by the audience, and
- backup equipment including spare leads and microphones.

FIGURE 14.8 A simple flow chart for a sound system

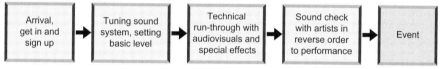

The next step up from this type of system includes all the above plus:

- monitor speakers (also called wedge monitors) that channel the sound back to the speaker or performer so they can hear themselves over the background sound,
- monitor control/mixing desk and
- monitor engineer, who is responsible for the quality of sound going through the monitors.

If an event needs a sound system managed by a sound engineer, time must be allocated to tune the sound system. This means that acoustic qualities of the venue are taken into account by trying out the effect of various sound frequencies within the venue. This is the reason for the often heard 'testing, one, two, one, two' as a sound system is being prepared. The sound engineer is also looking for any sound feedback problems. Feedback is an unwanted, often high-pitched sound that occurs when the sound coming out of the speakers is picked up by the microphones and comes out of the speakers again, thereby building on the original sound. To avoid the problem of feedback, microphones are positioned so that they face away from sound speakers. The tuning of a large sound system is one of the main reasons for having a sound check or a run through before an event. Figure 14.8 shows a simplified sound run through prior to an event.

Volume and sound leakage during an event can become a major problem. Local councils can close an event if there are too many complaints from residents. At some venues, for example, there are volume switches that automatically turn off the power if the sound level is too high. At multi-venue events, sound leakage between stages can be minimised by:

- thoughtful placement of the stages,
- careful positioning of all sound speakers (including the monitors),
- constant monitoring of the volume level and
- careful programming of the events on each stage in a way that avoids interference.

AUDIOVISUAL AND SPECIAL EFFECTS

Many event managers hire lighting and sound from separate companies and integrate their services into the overall design of the event. However, some suppliers provide both lighting and sound equipment and act as consultants prior to the event. These audiovisual companies can supply a fully integrated system of film, video, slides and often special effects. However, most audiovisual companies are specialists in flat-screen presentations and the special effects area is often best left to specialists in this field. For example, pyrotechnicians require different skills and licences from ice sculptors. Complex events that use a variety of special effects and audiovisuals require a coordinator who is familiar with the event theme and knows how to link all the specialist areas to each other. This coordinator is called the event producer. Although the terms 'event manager', 'stage manager' and 'event producer' are confusing, they are terms that are used in the industry. The position of event producer is created when there are many different specialists involved in the event. Organisers of corporate events, including product launches and conferences, often subcontract the audiovisual elements, because the specialist knowledge requirement means an expert is needed to operate these systems effectively. The decision to use an audiovisual company for an event depends on:

- how the audiovisual presentation fits in with the overall event design,
- the budget allocated to the event,
- the skills of the audiovisual company, including its technical hardware and software, and
- the abilities of the audiovisual producer and writer.

For large-budget events, the audiovisual company will act as a consultant, with the producer and writer researching and creating a detailed audiovisual script.

According to Goldblatt (2008), special effects at an event are used to 'attract attention, generate excitement and sustain interest as well as startle, shock or even amuse'. In larger events, for example, the Millennium Eve celebrations along the River Thames in London, the pyrotechnics become part of the overall logistics planning. Event managers and planners must fully realise the importance of event decoration, scenery and appropriate props as an enhancing tool for the staging of any event.

Because much of the audiovisual and special effects technology is highly complex, it is often 'preprogrammed'. This means that all lighting, audiovisual and sound 'presets' (technical elements positioned prior to the event), including the changing of light and sound levels and the cueing of video or slide presentations, can be programmed into the controlling computer. The computer control of much of the audiovisuals means that the whole presentation can be fully integrated and set up well in advance. Because these aspects are pre-arranged, including all the cue times, the advantage is that few technicians are needed to control these operations during the event. The disadvantages, however, are that spontaneity can be taken from the event and, the more complex the technology, the more things can go wrong. Moreover, the technology becomes the master of the cue times and it is nearly impossible to take advantage of any unforeseen opportunities.

PROPS AND DECORATION

Some events are similar to operatic productions in their use of scenery, stage properties (props) and decoration. Skilled use of these elements can make the attendees feel as though they are in an imaginary world. The audience can often enhance this by dressing the part and becoming part of the entertainment. Themed parties, festivals and dinners are a significant part of the event industry. The way in which these staging elements are combined and their relative emphasis at the event often reflects the personal style of the event company. Malouf (1999) devoted more than two-thirds of her book to theming in events, particularly the use of flowers, lights and colour to create a sense of wonder. The South African company Party Design regards decor as the key to their success. They have a dedicated factory with more than 1000 employees devoted to the creation, design, manufacture, delivery, set-up and return of event decor.

The large sports events are now famous for their props. Some of these props have been auctioned after the event to become sculptures in parks and offices.

CATERING

Catering can be the major element in staging, depending on the theme and nature of an event. Most purpose-built venues already have catering. For example, the Wembley Exhibition and Conference Centre has a contract with a catering company. The dinners that take place in the conference centre can only use the in-house caterers. Figure 14.9 illustrates some of the many factors to be considered in catering.

There are general principles that can be followed when planning the catering for events. For example, at a corporate function or formal dinner, a ratio of 1:10 (one member of staff to serve 10 customers) is appropriate, whereas at a Christmas party, a ratio of 2:30 (two members of staff to serve three tables of 10 customers) may suffice. Staffing numbers will be varied depending on the style of service being adopted, for example, whether silver served or plated, the complexity of the menu, the requirements of the client and the speed of service required. For example, a formal dinner, where the top table dictates the serving of all other guests, may require more staff than if a rolling service can be operated, with tables cleared and the next course served as each table finishes. In this way, teams of staff can work together in order to ensure that all elements of the meal arrive in front of the guest at the same time. Theatre can play a large part in formal meals, for example, using an MC to call guests into the dining area, the top table entering to the synchronised clapping of all other guests and tight coordination of waiting staff. For example, having all waiting staff entering the room in a formal line before 'breaking off' to take up their positions; upon the signal of the banqueting manager, usually involving the raising of an arm, the top table is served, followed immediately by all the other tables. In this way, the status of VIP guests on the top table is maintained.

As Graham et al. (2001) stressed, the consumption of alcoholic beverages at an event gives rise to many concerns for the event manager. These include the special training of staff, which party holds the licence (venue, event manager or client) and

FIGURE 14.9 Issues to be considered when arranging catering for an event

In-house or contracted out?
The advantage of in-house catering is the knowledge of the venue. The advantage of contract catering is that the event manager may have a special arrangement with the caterer that has been built up overtime; the event manager can choose all aspects of the catering; and the catering can be tendered out and a competitive bid sought.

Quality control factors to consider
- Appropriateness and enhancement of the event theme.
- Menu selection and design, including special diets and food displays.
- Quality of staff and supervision.
- Equipment, including style and quantity, and selection of in-house or hired.
- Cleanliness.
- Culturally appropriateness - a major consideration in a culturally diverse society.
- Staff to guest ratio.

Costs
- Are there any guarantees, including those against loss and breakage?
- What are the payment terms?
- Who is responsible for licences and permits: the caterer, the venue or event management?
- What deposits and up front fees are there?
- What is the per capita expenditure? Is each guest getting value commensurate with client's expenditure?

Waste management
- Must occur before, during and after the event.
- Must conforming to food hygiene and food safety regulations and environmental concerns.
- Must be appropriate to the event theme.

the legal age for consumption. The possible problems that arise from the sale of alcoholic beverages, for example, increased audience noise at the end of the event and general behavioural problems, can affect almost all aspects of the event. The decision whether to allow the sale or consumption of alcoholic beverages can be crucial to the success of an event and needs careful thought.

There are a variety of ways that the serving of alcohol can be negotiated with a caterer. The drinks service can be from the bar or may be served at the table by the glass, bottle or jug. A caterer may offer a 'drinks package', which means that the drinks are free for, say, the first hour of the catered event. A subtle result of this type of deal is that the guest can find it hard to find a drinks waiter in the first hour.

PERFORMERS

The 'talent' (as performers are often called) at an event can range from music groups to motivational speakers to specially commissioned shows. A performing group can form a major part of an event's design. As well as the cost of the performer, the major factors to consider when employing artists are:

- *Contact*: The event's entertainment coordinator needs to establish contact only with the person responsible for the employment of the artist or artists. This could be the artist, an agent representing the artist or the manager of a group. It is important to establish this line of authority at the beginning when working with the artists.
- *Staging requirements*: A rock band, for example, will have more complex sound requirements than those of a folk singer. These requirements are usually listed on a document called the spec (specification) sheet. Many groups will also have their own stage plan illustrating the area needed and their preferred configuration of the performance area.
- *Availability for rehearsal, media attention and performance*: The available times given by the artists' management should include the time needed for the artists to set up on stage as well as the time needed to vacate the stage or performance area. These times need to be considered carefully when, for example, scheduling a series of rehearsals with a number of performing groups. These are referred to as the time needed for 'set-up' (load in) and 'breakdown' (load out).
- *Accompanying personnel*: Many artists travel with an entourage that can include technicians, cooks, stylists and bodyguards. It is important to establish their numbers, and what their roles and needs are.
- *Contracts and legal requirements*: The agreement between the event manager and the performers is described in Chapter 17. Of particular importance to the staging are minimum rates and conditions, the legal structure of the artists and issues such as workers' compensation and public liability. Copyright is also important as its ownership can affect the use of the performance for broadcast and future promotions. The rider must be costed and understood. This aspect of contracts is covered in Chapter 17.
- *Payment*: Most performing groups work on the understanding that they will be paid immediately for their services. Except for 'headline' acts that have a company structure, the 30-, 60- or 90-day invoicing cycle is not appropriate for most performers, who rarely have the financial resources necessary to wait for payment.

Performers come from a variety of performance cultural backgrounds. This means that different performers have different expectations about the facilities available for them and how they are to be treated. Theatre performers and concert musicians, for example, expect direct performance guidelines – conducting, scripting or a musical score. Street and outdoor festival performers, on the other hand, are used to less formal conditions and to improvising.

Supervision of performers in a small theatre is generally left to the assistant stage manager, whereas a festival stage may not have this luxury and it may be the stage manager's responsibility. Regardless of who undertakes the supervision, it cannot be overlooked. The person responsible needs to make contact with the artists on arrival, give them the appropriate run sheets, introduce them to the relevant crew members and show them the location of the green room (the room in which performers and invited guests are entertained). At the end of the performance, the artists' supervisor needs to assist them in leaving the area.

THE CREW

The chapter on leadership and human resources (Chapter 8) discussed the role of staff and volunteers at an event. While a large festival or sporting event will usually rely on the work of volunteers, staging tends to be handled by professionals. Dealing with cueing, working with complex and potentially dangerous equipment and handling professional performers leave little room for indecision and inexperience. Professionalism is essential when staging an event. For example, the staging of a concert performance will need skilled sound engineers, roadies, security staff, stage crew, ticket sellers and even ushers (the roadies are the skilled labourers that assist with the set-up and breakdown of the sound and lights). The crew is selected by matching the tasks involved with their skills and ability to work together.

The briefing is the meeting, before the event, at which the crew members are given their briefs, or roles, that match their skills. The name and jobs of the crew members are then kept on a contact and responsibility sheet. The briefing tends to be more informal than the later production meeting. The event producer should also not forget that the crew comes with an enormous amount of experience in the staging of events. They can provide valuable input into the creation and design of the event.

It is also interesting to note that the changes in the events industry, particularly in the audiovisual area, are reflected in the make-up and number of crew members. As the industry developed, the event crew was often sourced from the casual labour available in the music industry, called the roadies. However, with the sophistication of the events, the modern crew is more likely to be specially trained and have trade and information technology skills. As Lisa Proto, Operations Director at Theme Traders, points out:

> In recent years development of new technology has eased the way for highly intelligent sound and lighting. This has resulted in a better use of resources and manpower as you will need less crew to run a highly technical console. Effects can be designed and programmed prior to the event, yet be flexible enough to adapt at the push of a button. Well programmed intelligent lighting and effects add to the drama and consistently create impact if planned effectively.

HOSPITALITY

A major part of the package offered to sponsors is hospitality (Catherwood and Kirk, 1992). What will the sponsors expect event management to provide for them and their guests? They may require tickets, food and beverages, souvenirs and gifts.

As well as the sponsors, the event may benefit in the long term by offering hospitality to other stakeholders and VIPs. They can include politicians, media units, media personalities, clients of the sponsor, potential sponsors, partners and local opinion formers. They are all referred to as the guests of the event.

The invitation may be the first impression that the potential guest receives, and it therefore needs to convey the theme of the event. It should create a desire to attend, as well as impart information. Figure 14.10 is a checklist for making sure that the various elements of hospitality are covered.

In their informative work on sports events, Graham et al. (2001, pp. 85–92) describe 10 strategies to achieve success in the provision of hospitality to guests:

1. Know the guests' needs and expectations.
2. Plan what the sporting event is expected to achieve for the guest, for example, networking, incentive and promotional activity.

FIGURE 14.10 Looking after corporate sponsors – a hospitality checklist

HOSPITALITY CHECKLIST

Invitations
- Is the design of a high quality and is it innovative?
- Does the method of delivery allow time to reply? Would hand delivery or email be appropriate?
- Does the content of the invitation include time, date, name of event, how to RSVP, directions and parking?
- Should promotional material be included with the invitation?

Arrival
- Has timing been planned so guests arrive at the best moment?
- What are the parking arrangements?
- Who will do the meeting and greeting? Will there be someone to welcome them to the event?
- Have waiting times been reduced? Will guests receive a welcome cocktail while waiting to be booked into the accommodation, for example?

Amenities
- Is there to be a separate area for guests? This can be a marquee, corporate box (at a sports event) or a club room.
- What food and beverages will be provided? Is there a need for a special menu and personal service?
- Is there a separate, high-quality viewing area of the performance with good views and facilities?
- Has special communication, such as signage or an information desk, been provided?

Gifts
- Have tickets to the event, especially for clients, been organised?
- What souvenirs (programs, pins, T-shirts, compact discs) will there be?
- Will there be a chance for guests to meet the 'stars'?

Departure
- Has guest departure been timed so guests do not leave at the same time as the rest of the audience?

3. Understand arrival patterns of guests in order to plan, for example, staffing requirements.
4. Plan according to what has preceded or will follow the guests arrival, for example, meal requirements.
5. Create appealing invitations to capture the prospective guests attention.
6. Understand the protocol for the specific sport event, as most have specific guidelines.
7. Focus on first and last impressions to gain maximum impact.
8. Exceed the guest's expectations, particularly through providing extra amenities, for example, parking, welcome signs, and information desk in the hotel lobby.
9. Be responsive to changes in the guests' needs during the event.
10. Evaluate the event so that it can be improved next time.

Corporate sponsors may have a variety of reasons to attend the event and these reasons have to be taken into account in hospitality planning. Research conducted for Sodexho Prestige (2004) suggested that the main drivers for corporate hospitality, from a host perspective, are to keep client happy/generate goodwill, build relationships, find an opportunity to meet with potential customers, raise the profile of company, allow clients to relax/enjoy themselves, say thank you, aid client loyalty/retention and boost staff morale; clients expect it and it is an informal occasion to discuss business.

The hospitality experience is of particular importance at the corporate events. In one sense such an event is centred around hospitality (Figure 14.4). As it is a private function, there is no public and the members of the audience are the guests. Most of the items on the hospitality checklist, from the invitations to the personal service, are applicable to staging these events. For the guests, the hospitality experience is fundamental to the event experience.

There are a number of systems to assist the event manager develop a quality hospitality experience for the guests. Getz (2005, p. 179) defines the dimensions of service as:

• tangibles — time, cleanliness
• reliability — such as consistency
• responsiveness — such as promptness
• assurance — such as courteousness
• empathy — such as individual attention

Both Getz (2005) and Tum et al. (2006) describe the event or festival from the service perspective. The event team can use the tools of service mapping. The attendee's or customer's on-site experience is described in the form of a flow chart. Each of the customer's actions, such as parking, buying the tickets and finding their sets, is assessed from the customer's point of view as a series of service experiences (see Chapter 9). This enables the event to be audited and improved from the perspective of the attendee.

THE PRODUCTION SCHEDULE

The terms used in the staging of events come from both the theatre and film production. A rehearsal of the event is a run through of the event, reproducing as closely as possible the actual event. For the sake of 'getting it right on the night', there may also need to be a technical rehearsal and a dress rehearsal. A production meeting, on the other hand, is a get-together of those responsible for producing the event. It involves the stage manager and the event producer, representatives of the lighting and sound crew or audiovisual specialists, representatives of the performers and the MC. It is held at the performance site or on stage as near to the time of the event as possible. At this crucial meeting:

- final production schedule notes are compared,
- possible last-minute production problems are brought up,
- the flow of the event is summarised,
- emergency procedures are reviewed,
- the compere is introduced and familiarised with the production staff and
- the communication system for the event is tested

(**Neighbourhood Arts Unit, 1991, p. 50**).

The production schedule is the main document for staging. It is the master document from which various other schedules, including the cue or prompt sheet and the run sheets, are created. Goldblatt (2008, p. 208) refers to it as the minute-by-minute running order for the event, reflecting set-up of the event's equipment (also known as load in) through to the eventual removal of all the equipment (breakdown or load out). It is often a written form of the Gantt chart (see Chapter 8) with four columns: time, activity, location and responsibility. Production schedules can also contain a description of the relevant elements of the event. In hotel venues it is also called the 'event order'. The more the event programme relies on tight programming and the use of entertainers and audiovisuals, the more detailed is the production schedule. For highly produced events, such as national day celebrations with large budgets spread over a few hours, the operations manual is often called the production book.

Two particularly limited times on the schedule are the 'load-in' and 'load-out' times. The load in refers to the time when the necessary infrastructure can be brought in, unloaded and set up. The load-out time refers to the time when the equipment can be dismantled and removed. Although the venue or site may be available to receive the equipment at any time, there are many other factors that set the load-in time. The hiring cost and availability of equipment are two important limiting factors. In most cases, the larger items must arrive first. These may include fencing, tents, stage, food vans and extra toilets. Next could come the audiovisual equipment and, finally, the various decorations. Supervision of the arrival and set-up of the equipment can be crucial for minimising problems during the event. The contractor who delivers and assembles the equipment often is not the operator of the equipment. This can mean that once it is set up, it is impossible to change it without recalling the contractor.

Load out can be the most difficult time of an event, because the excitement is over, the staff are often tired and everyone is in a hurry to leave. Nevertheless, these are just the times when security and safety are important. The correct order of load out needs to be on a detailed schedule. This is often the reverse of the load-in schedule. The last item on the checklist for the load out is the 'idiot check'. This refers to the check that is done after everything is cleared from the performance area, and some of the staff do a search for anything that may be left.

The run sheets are lists of the order for specific jobs at an event. The entertainers, for example, would have one run sheet while the caterers would have another. Often the production schedule is a loose-leaf folder that includes all the run sheets. The cue sheets are a list of times that initiate a change of any kind during the event and describe what happens on that change. The stage manager and audiovisual controller use them.

EVENT PROFILE

TSUNAMI RELIEF CARDIFF

When Britain awoke to the news of the South Asia tsunami disaster on Boxing Day 2004, people quickly looked for ways to help. Some had more at their disposal than others. With the pitch at Cardiff's Millennium Stadium out in preparation for a New Year's Eve event, general manager Paul Sergeant saw an opportunity, and along with Pablo Janczur, Director of Cardiff-based production company Push4, began to consider the feasibility of holding a 'Live Aid-style' fundraiser at the stadium.

Short lead time

With the pitch scheduled to go back on 24 January 2005 ahead of the first Six Nations Rugby international on 5 February, time was tight. Ignoring received wisdom that such an undertaking might be impossible in the time frame available, a small team began making calls to record labels and tour managers, while discussing crewing and equipment availability with contractors for a prospective date of 22 January. 'For the first week we were like coiled springs', Push4's technical project coordinator, Matt Wordley, explains, 'One of the most frustrating things was having to ask so many people to be on standby for an event that might not even happen.'

Amid mounting speculation in the press, enough artists were able to confirm their support for the event in time for the team to meet a last-chance deadline with the local authorities 2 weeks ahead of the show date. Regular Nine Yards collaborators John Armstrong and Jane Kelly were production manager and site manager, respectively, allowing Claire Sampson to effectively take on the role of event producer, and assist the venue and Push4 with various activities usually tackled by the promoter. 'I'm doing a lot of things I wouldn't as production manager', she agrees, before reeling off a variety of examples, not least the hours spent compiling last-minute video messages that morning, her role cuing presenters and VT clips during the show to allow stage manager Julian Lavender to focus entirely on the enormous movement of kit between change-overs and the need to manage the breadth of broadcast crew members on site, not least a BBC documentary team.

Broadcast schedule

Balancing television requirements with the demands of running a smooth live show was an involved process despite the tight timescale. Agreeing times during sound check when the front of house PA would be turned down to allow various news anchors to deliver their pieces to camera a case in point. Flexibility, co-operation and goodwill were required from all involved. 'We've had wonderful support from the venue, the licensing team, police and fire services', Sampson continues. 'Everybody has listened and been realistic about the timescales. Because of the speed this has been put together we haven't had all the usual meetings in advance. The running order was still being finalised right up to the show and we're grateful to crew and artists alike for their co-operation.'

Production schedule

The need to minimise changeover times between the 21 acts on what remained a taut 7-hour live broadcast meant guitar bands were strewn among acoustic sets and vocals to track throughout an unashamedly eclectic line-up, with Stereophonics frontman Kelly Jones, Goldie Lookin' Chain, Aled Jones, Charlotte Church and show-opener Katherine Jenkins among considerable local presence. Physical turnarounds were aided by a substantial upstage production area, with as much kit as possible staying set up on risers following sound checks, while Brit Row operated a double-desk system alternating between Yamaha PM1Ds for the live acts and PM5Ds for the presenters, video playback and vocals to track. Success was rooted in thorough pre-production, with both sets of desks programmed in advance to speed up the line checks. A final massive changeover for Jools Holland's Rhythm & Blues Orchestra took just 9 minutes.

'Brit Row knows the acoustics of the venue very well and had enough first division engineers as well as the kit to do it', Sampson reflects, while acknowledging the wealth of choice she had across the board following an outpouring of production support. In the end, a combination of experience at the venue, of working for live broadcast, and a familiarity with Nine Yards and each other, coupled in some cases with sheer speed out of the blocks, won through. Most organisations worked at cost, with others going further: McGuinness supplied free trucking, Energyst Cat Rental Power donated the 455 kVA and 250 kVA Twinpacks that enabled Power Logistics to supplement mains supply in order to run the PA, lighting and video screens, while Showsec and Imaginators were among companies whose employees donated wages.

Despite the venue's many plus points, notably the ability to unload articulated lorries directly onto the stage from the arena floor, it remains a sporting venue that requires significant augmentation for the handful of music events staged each year. Logistically, Tsunami Relief upped the ante even further, with any spare space hijacked for the cause, while in-house caterer Letheby & Christopher extended its remit to include artist and VIP hospitality. Eat To The Beat served 185 media representatives from its kitchen truck parked among the outside broadcast vehicles and took over facilities at the adjoining Cardiff Arms Park social club to cater for the 250 crew members.

SUMMARY

Tsunami Relief Cardiff demonstrates how a successful large-scale event can be achieved at short notice. However, the event would not have been possible without the skills, experience and determination of a strong team of professional venue managers, event managers, producers, technicians, broadcasters, artists and other logistics organisations, together with support and co-operation of the appropriate authorities. Public response to the event was beyond expectations, with live Internet streaming and interest from international broadcasters extending its reach. James Dean Bradfield of crowd favourites Manic Street Preachers captured its essence, 'You've got three minutes to get your gear on and that's it. We got on stage, saw the people in the crowd and knew everybody had made the right decision.'

For further information on the organisations discussed in this case study, please visit www. millenniumstadium.com (Millennium Stadium), www.push4.com (Push4), www.britanniarow.com (Britannia Row), www.energyst.co.uk (Energyst), www.powerlog.co.uk (Power Logistics), www. crowd-management.com (Showsec), www.imaginators.co.uk (Imaginators), www.compass-group. co.uk/outdoor-catering.htm (Letheby & Christopher) and www.eattothebeat.com (Eat To The Beat).

Source: *Lisa Gudge, Deputy Editor, Access All Areas, www.access-aa.co.uk.*

RECORDING THE EVENT

By their very nature, events are ephemeral. A good-quality recording of the event is essential for most event companies, as it demonstrates the ability of the organisation and it can be used to promote the event company. It can also help in evaluating the event and, if necessary, in settling later disputes, whether of a legal or other nature. The method of recording the event can be on video, sound recording or as photographs. Making a sound recording can be just a matter of putting a cassette in the sound system and pressing the record button. With digital cameras now available at low prices, extensive photographs can be taken at minimal cost, which can then be used on the company website to provide cases of successful events. However, any visual recording of the event will require planning. In particular, the correct lighting is needed for depth of field. Factors that need to be considered for video recording are:

- What is it for — promotion, legal purposes or for sale to the participants?
- What are the costs in terms of time and money?
- How will it affect the event? Will the video cameras be a nuisance? Will they need white lighting?
- What are the best vantage points?

Recording the event is not a decision that should be left to the last minute; it needs to be factored into the planning of the event. Copyright clearance, for example, can be an issue long after the event. Once an event is played out there is no going back.

CONTINGENCIES

As with large festivals and hallmark events, the staging of any event has to make allowances for what might go wrong. 'What if' sessions need to be implemented with the staff. A stage at a festival may face an electricity blackout, performers may not arrive or trouble may arrive instead. Therefore, micro-contingency plans need to be in place. All these must fit in with the overall event risk management and emergency plans. At corporate events in well-known venues, the venue will have its own emergency plan that needs to be given to everyone involved.

SUMMARY

The staging of an event can range from presenting a show of multi-cultural dancers and musicians at a stage in a local park to the launch of the latest software product at the most expensive hotel in town. All events share common staging elements, including sound, lights, food and beverage, performers and special effects. All these elements need to create and enhance the event theme and overall event experience. The importance of each element depends on the type of event. To stage an event successfully a number of tools are used: the production schedule, the stage plan and the contact and responsibility list, all of which are shown in Figure 14.11.

FIGURE 14.11 A summary of the tools necessary for staging an event

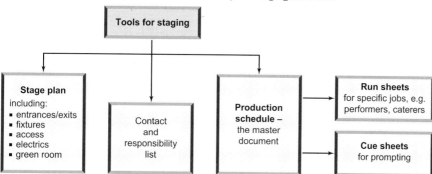

QUESTIONS

1. Break an event into its staging elements and discuss the relationship between each element.

2. Choose a theme for a company's staff party. How would you relate all the elements of staging to the theme?

3. Compile a stage plan, contact responsibility list and production schedule with the relevant run sheets for:

    a. a corporate party for the clients, staff and customers of a company;

    b. a fun run with entertainment;

    c. a large wedding, and

    d. one of the stages for a city arts festival.

4. Discuss the constraints on programming the following events:

    a. a large musical concert in a disused open-cut mine,

    b. an association award dinner,

    c. a multi-stage arts festival,

    d. a surfing event,

    e. a mining exhibition conference,

    f. an air show and

    g. a tax seminar for accountants.

5. What is the case for contracting one supplier for all the staging elements? What are the disadvantages?

CASE STUDY: THEMING – A MARKETING TOOL

Theming, styling, designing, creating, setting the scene and building an atmosphere are all areas covered on a day-to-day basis by Theme Traders – a specialist event management company based in Cricklewood, London.

Theming is similar to marketing. When a company plans the launch of a new product or service, all the Ps have to be considered – presentation, product, positioning and price. These are all areas that have to be taken into account when planning and theming an event.

Through the 1980s and early 1990s, themes such as 'Wild West Ho Downs', 'Hawaiian Beach Parties', 'Arabian Nights', 'Science Fiction' and 'Bond Parties' were all the rage and these perennial 'themes' will never die. However, what event managers should always ask their clients is what they want to achieve – in a budget-driven world, objectives are the name of the game. Heaven forbid that someone should have a party just for fun!

When a city bank asks for a party for 1300 people to be designed, the questions are endless – other than the standard issues (for example, age of guests, sex, venue and type of food), the most important enquiry for the event manager concerns what the client wants to achieve. In order to choose the 'style' and put a creative team to work, the event manager needs to know if this is a 'thank you' party, a celebration or perhaps an event to 'schmooze' their top 10 clients? Is there a need to create a moody mysterious scene or a fun and funky setting, or is it to be a full on 'party party' with games and entertainment for the staff?

When one of those lovely 'ladies who lunch' comes to Theme Traders and asks them to arrange a top-notch summer party to celebrate her husband's 50th birthday, they might suggest a retro 1960s and 1970s evening, Austin Powers style – this could include bubble columns and lava lamps, animal print draping, a circular bed covered in fluffy pink material, psychedelic colours and glitter boots – or a night of rock 'n' roll where the birthday boy can go back to his teens, air guitar in hand and play to the strains of Pink Floyd and Deep Purple! But without asking the right questions the event manager could easily get it all horribly wrong – as the chief executive of a major blue chip company, he wants a sophisticated stylish party with a string quartet and a harpist!

Theme Traders were asked to design the launch party for a new Internet company, cooldiamonds.com – now a highly successful Internet site where you can buy the best diamonds in the world or, alternatively, a cheeky diamond stud for your belly button! The brief was a mix of sophistication and fun. The directors wanted to invite a young sector of the press, trendy designers from Bond Street, clients from Knightsbridge and city business associates – including their bank manager!

It had to be somewhere central, so Theme Traders chose a beautiful room overlooking the Thames in a top London hotel. In essence, the event had to ooze sophistication but they wanted the youngsters to be able to party, the designers to be able to 'chill' and the Knightsbridge and city set to be able to enjoy deluxe dining in exclusive surroundings. The evening was to be special, unique, inviting and rich. After all, they were launching a luxury item!

One of the Theme Traders creative teams brainstormed the proposal, appointed an art director to the project and one of their senior event managers was assigned to make it all happen. At this stage, an illustration is often produced, which helps the client to focus on the creative team's ideas. Through experience, there is rarely any point in providing more than one illustration as the creative team would have usually made a critical decision on how the party will appear through extensive brainstorming, therefore eliminating other second-rate ideas along the way. A crew from the showroom was assigned to the project and all the different departments worked together on the event. All events and parties at Theme Traders are the result of teamwork. Everyone employed is creative, not necessarily through his or her qualifications, but as people. It is essential for Theme Traders to be able to 'paint' a picture for their clients, and to bring that picture to life.

The result? The room was divided into two main areas blending one 'atmosphere' into the other. Using rich midnight blue velvet the entire area was draped with custom-made star cloths through which peeped twinkling silver white lights. At one end, low fluffy cloud-like tables were laid out with enormous soft pastel coloured cushions and beanbags around a starry dance floor. Lit with different shades of blue and white beams and gobos, the cooldiamonds.com logo shimmered everywhere! Over the dance floor hung rotating mirror balls that threw tiny diamond-like specs all around the room. In the 'champagne' area the tables were dressed to the floor with the same rich velvet material. In every centrepiece was a waterfall gently cascading over silver stones around the flicker of tiny tea-lights.

The mood of the whole room was changed as the evening progressed with creative use of lighting. Lighting designers had set the tone of the evening adding shades of blue and indigo which highlighted and brightened the 'diamond' effect around the room as the evening progressed. All in all a cool but rich atmosphere was produced swimming in dreams and desires. The client was delighted!

What the client actually said after the event was that Theme Traders had solved their problem. They thought they would have to have two events, use different venues, incur double the expenses and basically could not see a way through their dilemma. Providing two very distinct arenas for two audiences in the same venue and at the same time could be considered a dilemma, but dilemmas like this are second nature to Theme Traders and they thrive on the challenge. Carefully mixing colours, fabrics and lighting to enhance moods, change atmospheres and make dreams come true – that is Theme Traders' speciality!

For further details about Theme Traders, and to view their website, image and event database, please visit www.themetraders.com.

By David Jamilly, Director, Theme Traders, The Stadium, Oaklands Road, London NW2 6XN.

Questions

1. What process is involved in developing the theme for the event?
2. What benefit does theming bring to an event?
3. How do the elements of staging relate to the theme for the cooldiamonds.com event?
4. Based on the brief given, brainstorm alternative themes for the cooldiamonds.com event.
5. From the results of question 4, choose one theme for further development.

   a. How will this theme deliver the client's requirements.

   b. Referring to the elements of staging, describe how you would conceptualise and implement this theme. You may wish to illustrate your answer to focus your idea.

CASE STUDY: LIVE 8

Introduction

The Live 8 show on Saturday, 2 July 2005, to help publicise the campaign to 'make poverty history' in Africa, was the biggest event in Hyde Park's history and the biggest ticketed event ever in the UK. Among those artists taking part were Coldplay, Elton John, Madonna, Paul McCartney, Robbie Williams, U2 and Pink Floyd.

Supplying the a-v for these shows was an enormous job, and four main contractors were assigned – Britannia Row Productions, which supplied the sound; Creative Technology (CT), which supplied 12 giant LED screens; PRG, which brought in six articulated truck loads of lighting equipment; and Star Events Group, which provided the staging. The site and production areas for the Live 8 concert were constructed and operated by a crew of over 2000 and managed by Clear Channel Entertainment Group. The event overall was produced internationally by a number of people, including Richard Curtis, Sir Bob Geldorf, Harvey Goldsmith, John Kennedy and Kevin Wall with Ken Ehrlich, Larry Magid, Tim Sexton, Greg Sills and Russell Simmons (Live 8, 2005).

Continued

CASE STUDY: LIVE 8—*CONT'D*

Screen Technology

Due to the sheer numbers attending Hyde Park, over 200,000, the Live 8 concert in Hyde Park on 2 July was always going to rely heavily on large screen video technology. It will come as no surprise that the show saw the biggest ever concentration of screens for an outdoor concert anywhere in Europe, with the equipment for both front stage and backstage supplied by Avesco companies, CT and MCL. The screen aspects of the production also included:

- Five LED screens positioned on stage; the main screen comprised 8×6 modules of Lighthouse 19 mm measuring 9.76×5.25 m. Flanking it were two 6.4×4.8 m, 25-mm Unitek screens, which were divided into four equal columns and arranged in a 90° arc on either side of the main screen to visually 'wrap round' the performers. On each of the PA wings were 8.54×6.44 m Lighthouse 19 mm screens.

- Two relay screens 100 m from the stage, these were 44 m^2 CT/Screenco mobiles with Saco 15-mm screens, one of which is based in the UK and the other from CT's Dutch sister company JVR, which also supplied four Barco D-Lite 7 LED screens, each measuring 4.48×2.69 m, to Screen Visions for the Berlin production. These were used as relay screens along Berlin's 'Straßeder 17 Juni', while two Barco G5 projectors with 300×225 projection screens and three 42-inch plasma screens were supplied to one of Dutch national television's studios for their broadcast of the event.

- Three further mobiles towards the back of the Hyde Park arena, two 40-m^2 Lighthouse 25 mm and one 30 m^2 Panasonic, subcontracted by CT from Sweden's Massteknik. All the mobile screens were fed via digital video delays, allowing the timing on the video signal to be adjusted, to sync with the sound.

- Unitek modules (25 mm) were deployed as a giant 1.2×35 m LED banner panel across the top of the stage, a configuration more commonly seen at the side of football pitches. Driven by a dedicated text system, it was used to display slogans from Comic Relief, which provided much of the supporting visual material. The control system was operated by score board company Technographics.

- Video gear for the backstage area, supplied by CT and MCL – a Lighthouse 10-mm screen in the artist's garden and two of the new stand-alone Lighthouse Pop Vision screens in the main hospitality area, as well as a number of plasma screens put in by MCL.

Avesco also had the massive logistical task of controlling the entire on-screen video production and programming at Hyde Park. Outside broadcast supplier Bow Tie – which facilitated the main BBC system – provided a dedicated outside broadcast truck for screen production equipped with its own dedicated cameras and multi-channel VT record/playback facilities. Much of this equipment was supplied by another Avesco subsidiary, Presteigne Broadcast Hire. Graphic content for the main screens was managed using three Doremis and two channels of Arkaos. Further graphics-related services were provided for the SMS and MMS messaging facilities, which were available to the audience via sponsors AOL and Nokia. This enabled audience members to send images from camera phones via MMS. Montages of those pictures were then collated live on site and put onto the screens during breaks between acts, alongside the SMS messages.

Lighthouse screens were also in use at the Berlin Live 8 concert, where two 5×4 R16 16-mm pixel pitch screens helped relay the action to another huge audience. Meanwhile, 500 miles from Hyde Park in Gleneagles, Scotland, Lighthouse screens were also a key part of the G8 conference itself, where the leaders of the world's richest eight countries were meeting. Two 8×8 panel R16 screens were used to relay the conference to the gathered crowd supplied by Massteknik.

Sound

With 26 major artists, a scheduled turnaround time between bands of less than 5 minutes and a large audience in Hyde Park, Britannia Row Productions, which provided the full PA system for the Live 8 show, certainly had its work cut out. Eighteen technicians and 25 sound engineers operated the PA system including:

- two hundred Electrovoice (EV) X-Line loudspeaker cabinets, all powered by EV's Precision Series P3000RL remote controlled amplifiers;
- six towers of EV X-Line, also powered by EV's Precision Series P3000RL, used as delays with additional L Acoustic V DOSC towers to ensure full coverage for the crowd;
- the entire sound system controlled by IRIS (Intelligent Remote Integrated Supervision), the software program remotely controlling the P3000RL amplifiers from front of house;
- stage monitors were Turbosound TFM-450 wedges with Turbosound Flashlight side fills and Turbosound TQ-440/TQ-425 drum fills powered by Pulse amplifiers;
- several computers used to control and monitor the loudspeakers over 3 km of signal cable and
- over 500 Sennheiser microphones and 8000 m of microphone cable used in order to keep the show running quickly from band to band. As well as providing a generic wireless radio and in-ear monitoring system, Sennheiser also added its experienced technical support staff to Britannia's stage team.

Britannia enlisted both the assistance of the DiGiCo team and its D5 Live digital mixing console. In Hyde Park, three DiGiCo D5 Live digital mixing consoles were positioned at front of house, with a further three D5s at the monitor position. At front of house, one console was used for prepping, while the other two sat at the mix positions with the same arrangement for monitors.

Audio-Technica microphones were used extensively at Live 8 concerts around the world, in particular at the Philadelphia Museum of Art, in America, and at Live 8 Africa Calling at the Eden Centre, in Cornwall. The Philadelphia event in front of the Museum of Art, featured performances by leading artists such as Jay-Z, Linkin Park and Def Leppard, all using Audio-Technica's Artist Elite 5000 Series UHF Wireless Systems. The Tokyo Live 8 concert featured Good Charlotte, performing on the Audio-Technica Artist Elite 5000 Series UHF Wireless System, and the Artist Elite AE6100 dynamic vocal microphone.

Lighting

PRG Europe supplied the lighting rig for the Hyde Park Live 8 event. The statistics for the event illustrate what a huge job it was to light such a show: six articulated truck loads of lighting equipment, 15 miles of cable, 47 tonnes of lights, suspended up to 10 m above the stage from almost 180 m of truss, 150 state-of-the-art moving lights, plus a further 120 other lights, six follow-spots, a total of 295,000 kW of light and 16 crew members.

The lights had been on site since 22 June in preparation for the 2 July event. Pete Barnes, UK lighting designer for Live 8, whose designs were also adapted as the basis for the Paris event, said: 'The challenge for this particular event is to provide lighting effects that meet the artistic values of a huge range of musicians, and at the same time make sure that the 150,000 people there can see what's happening as well as the billions watching on television.' James Thomas Pixel Fixtures were in use at Live 8. Peter decided on using high-impact LED fixtures to do this, and chose 120 PixelLine 1044s and 14 of the new PixelLine 110ecs. LED borders along the onstage trusses used 721044s units.

Staging

To give an idea of the size of the stage the Star Events Group had to provide for Hyde Park, it was as high as five London double-decker buses stacked on top of each other and as wide as six buses lined up nose to tail, with an additional backstage area to accommodate equipment for the 26 bands that could have housed 29 London buses.

Continued

CASE STUDY: LIVE 8—*CONT'D*

The stage for Live 8 had a 25-m span by 20-m-deep main floor and the same area again as wing space. A raised floor area was built at the back, protected by a marquee and used for rolling risers to enable quick band changeovers. This was almost 5 m above ground due to the slope on the site and was as big as the stage again. Another aid to the fast changeovers was a revolving stage, split into two so one band could be setting up while the previous one was playing. It was hired in from the Revolving Stage Company.

The major challenge for the Star Events team was time. Whereas Party In The Park was due to happen on Sunday, 3 July (it was postponed to make way for Live 8), Live 8 took place a day earlier.

Production

The Live 8 shows saw the first ever relay of High Definition (HD) footage to the UK public by the BBC. The transmission was carried on satellite direct from Hyde Park to a BT downlink in the grounds of Cardiff Castle in Wales to a crowd of several thousand people. The BBC worked in partnership on the event with Shooting Partners.

The huge HDTV-compatible LED display was supplied by Anna Valley Displays, which also provided a full HDTV projected picture on site. The HD screen was made up of 112 modules of Toshiba's 6-mm LED display in 16×9 format. For this project Anna Valley chose the Sanyo PLV-HD10 projector, capable of 5500 ANSI lumens, with a contrast ratio of 1000:1.

The entire concert footage was filmed in HD, by 19 different HD cameras near the stage. Anna Valley's screen had to cope with changes in the footage from HD to Standard Definition footage, and to the text message services the Live 8 organisers were putting out. Blitz Charter Group (BCG) supplied a fully functional, true HD camera channel for BBC's coverage of Live 8. It was UK's first transmission from an HD source camera. BCG supplied a camera channel, which included a Sony 750 HD Camera and a J11 HD lens, as well as a specially designed transmitter backpack for the cameraman who was out among the crowd, and a receiver desk, which was also designed by Charter.

SUMMARY

Concerts of the size of the one at Live 8 happen all too rarely, the only comparable event in the UK was the original Live Aid event held 20 years ago at Wembley Stadium. This case study has detailed the staging and audiovisual aspects of the event. It is testimony to the dedication of those involved that the Hyde Park show ran as smoothly as it did.

For further information about Live 8, please visit www.live8live.com. For further details about the suppliers discussed in this case study, please visit: www.audio-technica.com (Audio-Technica), www.avesco.com (Avesco), www.britanniarow.com (Britannia Row), www.presteignecharter.com (Charter Broadcast, now merged into Presteigne Charter), www.clearchanneleurope.co.uk (Clear Channel), www.digiconsoles.com (DiGiCo), www.lighthouse-tech.com (Lighthouse Technologies), www.pixelpar.com (Pixel), www.productionresource group.co.uk (Production Resource Group, PRG), www.shooting-partners.co.uk (Shooting Partners) and www.stareventsgroup.com (Star Events).

By Paul Milligan, Assistant Editor, AV magazine, www.avinteractive.co.uk.

Questions

1. What key elements of staging are identified within the case study?
2. Identify the challenges faced by organisers of the Live 8 events. How may these differ between venues and countries?
3. Discuss what tools and techniques would be available to Live 8 producers to ensure the smooth running of the events?
4. Selecting one of the concerts, what skills would be required to organise this event?
5. From your understanding, what were the objectives of Live 8? How would success be measured for the Live 8 events?

Logistics

15

LEARNING OBJECTIVES

After studying this chapter, you should be able to:

- define logistics management and describe its evolution,
- understand the concept of logistics management and its place in event management,
- construct a logistics plan for the supply of customers, event products and event facilities
- use event logistics techniques and tools.

INTRODUCTION

This chapter adapts the science of business and military logistics to events. The management of an event is divided into supply, setting up and running the event on site, and the shutdown process of the event. Communication, transport, flow and supply, and linking the logistics with the overall event plan are the elements of event logistics treated in this chapter. Various checklists that can assist in the management of event logistics are outlined.

WHAT IS LOGISTICS?

The management science of logistics assists the event manager to identify the elements of event and festival operations. Although the term 'operations' is often used for events, the temporary nature of festival and event operations gives the sourcing and movement of its elements a priority not found in day-to-day operations of a business. Movement of people and material is essential to all special event operations. Logistics is an analysis tool to manage an aspect of an event by sub-dividing the work into categories. Many people regard event management as what is happening during the event. This ignores the event set-up and shutdown. Logistics concerns the whole operation. Unlike business logistics, event logistics takes place over a comparatively short time and there is rarely the time to improve it. The logistics has to be right the first time. The tools and techniques of logistics fit into a project approach to event management.

Events Management. DOI: 10.1016/B978-1-85617-818-1.10015-5

Placing the word 'logistics' into its historical context provides an understanding of its use in present event management. Logistics stems from the Greek word *logistikos*, 'skilled in calculating'. The ancient Romans used the term for the administration of its armies. The term evolved to refer to the practical art of the relocation of armies. Given the complexity of modern warfare, logistics became a science that included speed of operations, communications and maintenance of the armed forces. After the Second World War, modern business applied the experience and theory of logistics as they faced problems with transport and supply similar to those faced by the military.

The efficient movement of products has become a specialised study in the management discipline. Within large companies, especially international companies, a section can be devoted to coordinating the logistics requirements of each department. Logistics has become a discipline in its own right. This has led to consolidation into a separate independent function in companies, often called integrated logistics management. The Chartered Institute of Logistics and Transport (UK) defines logistics as, 'The time-related positioning of resources to meet user requirements', where resources may be transport, storage or information (Supply Chain Inventory Management Forum, 2003). Canadine (2001) notes that logistics is generally being used to operate the supply chains in order to satisfy a customer. He also highlights that an alternative definition of logistics is, 'The detailed organization and implementation of a plan or operation', where the plan or operation is to satisfy customer needs. The benefit of efficient coordination of logistics in the event company is that a company's product value can be improved.

For a complete understanding of event logistics, this chapter is divided into sections dealing with the tasks of event logistics and the role of the logistics manager.

THE ELEMENTS OF EVENT LOGISTICS

The various elements of event logistics can be organised into the logistics system, illustrated in Figure 15.1. This system is used to organise the logistics elements of an event.

Whereas most logistics theory concerns the supply of products to the customers, event logistics includes the efficient supply of the customer to the product, and the supply of facilities to and from the event site. In this sense, it has more in common with military logistics than modern business logistics. Business logistics is an ongoing activity and is part of the continual management of a company. Military and event logistics often concern a specific project or campaign rather than the continuing management. There is a definite preparation, lead-up, execution and shutdown. Also, issues such as inventory control and warehousing, which are the basis of business logistics, are not as important to a one-off event.

FIGURE 15.1 Elements of the logistics system

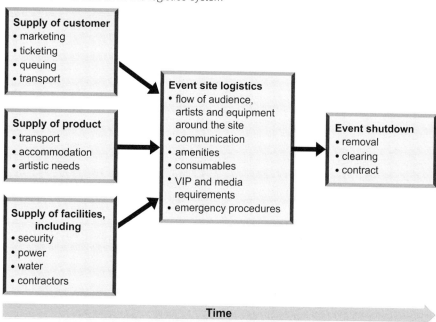

The areas of importance to event logistics can be categorised as follows:

- *Supply*: This is divided into the three areas of customer, product and facilities. Supply also includes the procurement of the goods and services.
- *Transport*: The transport of these goods and services can be a major cost to an event and requires special consideration.
- *Linking*: Logistics is part of the overall planning of an event and is linked to all other areas. Logistics allows the event operations to be part of an integrated approach to event management. Logistics must be linked with marketing as marketing is a tool that sources and creates the flow of the attendees. Figure 15.2 illustrates a risk when logistics and marketing are not closely linked. With large multi-venue events, the logistics becomes so complex that an operations or logistics manager is often appointed. The logistics manager functions as part of the overall network management structure outlined in this chapter.
- *Flow control*: This refers to the flow of products, services and customers during the event.
- *Information networks*: The efficient flow of information during the event is generally a result of efficient planning of the information network. This concept is expanded in the section about on-site logistics.

FIGURE 15.2 Marketing versus logistics

THREE DIE IN IKEA STAMPEDE

Three people were killed and 16 injured when thousands of people stampeded to claim cash vouchers at the opening of an Ikea furniture showroom in Jeddah (western Saudi Arabia).

Many men, women and children fainted and some of them were trampled upon as the crowd of shoppers swelled just before the opening. Red Crescent emergency services rushed some of the victims to the nearby King Fahd Hospital. Sixteen people received hospital treatment for their injuries and were later discharged.

The Swedish furniture showroom had mounted a big pre-opening ad campaign with the offer of SR500 (£81) vouchers to the first 50 shoppers and SR100 (£16) vouchers to the next 200 as part of its normal free gift scheme. Prior to the scheduled 10.00 am opening, the three-metre entrance gate was opened. Several thousand people who had converged on the scene surged forward to be among the first 250 to claim the vouchers. While police sources said they would investigate any security lapse on the part of Ikea, one of Ikea's senior executives said the establishment had taken 'full security measures anticipating a big turnout of shoppers'.

Looking at the crowd, we anticipated trouble and decided to open the main entrance around 9.00 am. We kept the door slightly open, just enough for one person to enter at a time, and distributed vouchers to the first 50 and the next 200 people as per our ad campaign', a spokesperson said.

'The trouble was outside the showroom and everything inside was smooth.'

Ikea said it had worked closely with emergency services in planning for the opening and that the store would not reopen until safety issues had been considered.

(Source: based on information from Ramkumar and Hassan, 2004 and BBC News, 2004)

All these areas need to be considered when creating a logistics plan. Even for small events, such as a wedding or a small product launch, a logistics plan needs to be incorporated in the overall event plan. For these sorts of events, logistics comes under the title 'Staging', which is described in Chapter 14.

Given that the major elements of logistics are supply and movement, logistics plays a large role in some types of event, including:

- events that have a large international component, such as major conferences, sporting events and overseas corporate incentive programmes;
- complex events in foreign countries, such as trade exhibitions and conferences. An example is the importance of logistics to the 2006 Asian Games in Doha, Qatar. The Asian Games required a large number of the facilities to be built, including new hotels and roads. At the same time the ability to import, store and finally export the required equipment and personnel had to be worked out in a city that had little in the way of facilities. Three years before the Games, a visitor needed to queue at the airport at a single desk to obtain local currency and then queue at another desk to buy a visa. The government of Qatar was quick to change these impediments to allow the logistics of the Games to proceed.

- events that occur in remote locations and need most of the supporting resources transported to the site;
- exhibitions of large or complex products, such as mining or agricultural exhibitions, and
- events that are moving, such as travelling exhibitions and races.

Supply of the customer

The customers of the event are those who pay for it. They can be the audience (concerts and festivals), spectators (sports), visitors (exhibitions), delegates (conferences) and the sponsors or the client (corporate events). The customers have expectations, which include logistical aspects, that have to be met for a successful outcome. The way in which the event is promoted will particularly influence their expectations. In addition, there are legal requirements under Disability Discrimination Act (as discussed in Chapter 16) to ensure that events are accessible to people with disabilities. These expectations for all customers will include aspects of logistics.

Linking with marketing and promotion

The supply of customers is ultimately the responsibility of marketing activities. The numbers, geographical spread and expectations of the customers will affect the logistics planning. The targeting of specialist markets or widespread publicity of an event will require a logistics plan with very different priorities. For example, the transport requirements of the customers will vary according to the distance travelled. The majority of the audience of Party in the Park either drives from the surrounding area or uses the shuttle bus service. Therefore, vehicle access, parking and the availability of an effective bus service are priorities at the event site. The British International Motor Show, until 2004 in Birmingham and in 2006 and 2008 at ExCel, London, used a nationwide publicity campaign which attracted a large audience from all corners of the UK. This offered opportunities for special negotiations with coach operators, train companies and hotels. If the publicity of an event is spread nationwide, the logistics will be different to a product launch that only concerns the staff and customers of a company. In this way, the logistics are closely linked to the marketing of an event.

Figure 15.2 illustrates the link between marketing and logistics. Unfortunately, this may only become obvious when there is a problem at the event.

Ticketing

Ticketing is important to events whose primary income is from the entrance fee. Most corporate events, including office parties and product launches, and many public events are free. However, for other events, such as sports events, the extent of ticket sales can determine success or failure (Graham et al., 2001). Ticket distribution is regarded as the first major decision in event logistics.

The pricing and printing of the tickets is generally not a logistics area. However, the distribution, collection and security are of concern, and with free events, form an effective means of controlling numbers. In the UK, tickets for events can be sold through various distributors like Ticketmaster for a fee, or they can be sold by mail or through the Internet, for example, through Aloud.com. Glastonbury Festival has always traditionally sold out tickets months in advance, however, in recent years they have sold out within hours of going on sale. Selling tickets at the gate gives rise to security problems in the collection, accounting and depositing of funds. The ticket collectors need training to deal with the public, as well as efficiently moving the public through the entrance. The honesty of the staff may also be a security concern. Events that have successfully managed this include The Open Championship, which each year has support through sponsorship from The Royal Bank of Scotland to provide cashiers/ticket staff. In larger venues, an admission loss-prevention plan is used to minimise the possibility of theft.

It is not unusual to sell tickets through retail outlets. The Millennium Dome (now the O2 in London) attempted this on a grand scale by using National Lottery outlets as a distribution channel to sell tickets. Inventory control and cash receipts are two areas that require special attention when using retail outlets for ticket distribution. Numbering of the tickets and individual letters of agreement with each outlet are the most efficient methods of control. The letter of agreement would include the range of ticket numbers, level of the tickets (discount or full price) and the method of payment. Depending on the size of the event, the ticketing can be crucial to the event's success and take up a significant amount of the event director's time. Figure 15.3 is a checklist of the logistics of ticketing an event.

An innovative method of ticketing for festivals is to use the hospital-style wristbands, called crowd control bands. These are colour coded to indicate the level of the ticket — a day ticket, a weekend ticket or a special performer's ticket. The use of these wristbands introduces a visual method of control during a large event, as the sale of food and drinks is only allowed if the wristband is shown. In this way, the food vendors become part of the security for the event.

The Internet is increasingly used for the distribution of tickets for large events, concerts and conferences. This use of the Internet illustrates the linking of logistics and marketing, as discussed in Chapter 7. Originally the World Wide Web was used in the marketing of events by means of advertising them through a website. The introduction of encrypted data enabled the increase in the privacy and security of payment methods and the sale of tickets from a site. The site collaborates with the existing ticketing system, and can be connected to travel agencies, hotels, transport companies and a whole host of other related services. The Internet has introduced some unique risks in the sale of tickets. Aside from the obvious risk of security of the payment method, the on-line resale or touting of tickets on eBay and other on-line websites is a risk. The UK government has become so concerned about the issue that the Department for Culture, Media and Sport held a consultation on the issue in 2009

FIGURE 15.3 Ticketing – logistics checklist

Does the artwork on the ticket contain the following?
- Number of the ticket Tamworth, Made-Up Textiles Association.
- Name of the event
- Date and time of the event
- Price and level of the ticket (discount, complimentary, full price, early bird)
- Seating number or designated area (ticket colour coding can be used to show seating area)
- Disclaimer (in particular, this should list the responsibilities of the event promoter)
- Event information, such as a map, warnings and what to bring/not to bring
- Artwork so that the ticket could be used as a souvenir (part of the ticket could be kept by the patron)
- Contact details for information
- Security considerations, such as holograms to prevent copying
- Colour scheme, font and size suitable for reading and downloading from the event website

Printing schedule
- When will the tickets be ready?
- Will the tickets be delivered or do they have to be collected?
- If there is an error or a large demand for the tickets, will there be time for more to be printed?

Distribution
- What outlets will be used - retail, Ticketmaster, Internet, mail or at the gate?
- Has a letter of agreement with all distributors, setting out terms and conditions, been signed?
- What method of payment will be used (by both the ticket buyer to the distributor and in the final reconciliation) - credit card, cash, direct deposit?
- Are schedule of payment and reconciliation forms available?
- Does the schedule of communications refer to ticket sales indicate sales progress and if more tickets are needed?

Collection of tickets
- How will the tickets be collected at the gates and transferred to a pass-out?
- How experienced are the personnel and how many will there be? When will they arrive and leave?
- Is a separate desk for complimentary tickets needed site of ticket collection site?
- What security arrangements are in place for cash and personnel?
- How will the tickets be disposed of?

Reconciliation of number of tickets with revenue received
- What method of reconciliation will be used? Is an accountant being used?
- Is the reconciliation ongoing, at the conclusion of the event, or at the end of the month?
- Is the system robust to allow for independent auditing, such as ABC auditing of exhibition visitor numbers?
- Has a separate account been set up just for the one event to assist the accountancy procedure?

(DCMS, 2009), following a Select Committee investigation and report in 2008 (Culture, Media and Sport Committee, 2008) with a view to encouraging the ticketing industry to develop a voluntary code of practice. If this does not succeed, legislation has not been ruled out.

Tickets can be sent to the purchaser's mobile phone via short message service (SMS). The use of bar-coding enables events, such as exhibitions, to track their attendees via their mobile phone or portable digital assistant (PDA). The bar code is downloaded to the PDA or phone as an image file and scanned at the entrance and booths.

Queuing

Often, the first experience a customer has at an event is the queue for tickets or parking. This was illustrated in 2003 by the queues of traffic making their way to Knebworth for Robbie Williams' sell out concerts. With an estimated 375,000 fans attending the shows over three consecutive days, the largest in UK music history (BBC News, 2003), the concert will be remembered not only for the scale of the event but also the traffic and parking issues that made press head-lines and led to a number of fans not seeing the concert due to being stuck in traffic.

Once inside the event, customers may be confronted with queues for food, toilets and seating. An important aspect of queue theory is the 'perceived waiting time'. This is the subjective time that the customers feel that they have waited. There are many rules of thumb about diminishing the customer's perceived waiting time. In the catering industry, the queuing for food can affect the event experience. An informal rule is one food or beverage line for every 75—100 people. Figure 15.4 lists some of the factors to consider in the logistics of queuing.

The Atlanta Olympics and the Millennium Dome successfully used enter-tainers to reduce the perceived waiting time at the entrance and exhibit queues. Exit queuing can be the last experience for the customer at an event and needs the close attention of the event manager. At London's New Year's Eve celebrations, the authorities planned to use 'staggered entertainment' to spread the exit time of the crowds and avoid overcrowding on the London Underground. Within football stadia it is common practice to keep fans of one team within the ground until the opposing team's fans have dispersed, to avoid confrontation. Nightclubs may employ similar tactics, by raising lights shortly before the end of the evening and circulating security staff to avoid customers all waiting until the final record has played.

The oversupply of customers at a commercial event can give rise to a number of security and public safety problems that should be anticipated in the logistics plan. Equally, free events can attract too many customers if not

FIGURE 15.4 Queuing — factors to consider

- How many queues and possible bottlenecks will there be?
- Has an adequate number of personnel greeters, crowd controllers, ticket collectors and security staff been allocated?
- Is signage (including the estimated waiting time) in place?
- When will the queues form? Will they form at once or over a period of time?
- How can the perceived waiting time be reduced (for example, queue entertainers)?
- What first aid, access and emergency procedures are in place?
- Are the lighting and sun and rain protection adequate?
- Are crowd-friendly barricades and partitions in place?

carefully controlled. Only pre-sale tickets, and ticketing free events, will indicate the exact number of the expected audience. When tickets are sold at the entrance to an event, the logistics plan has to include the possibility of too many people turning up on the day. Oversubscription may be pleasing for the event promoter, but can produce a logistical nightmare of what to do with the excess crowd.

Customer transport

Transport to a site is often the first physical commitment by the audience to an event. The method and timing of arrival — public or private transport — is important to the overall logistics plan. The terms used by event managers are *dump*, when the audience arrives almost at once, and *trickle*, when they come and go over a longer period of time. Each of these needs a different logistics strategy. This first impression of the event by the audience can influence all subsequent experiences at the event. For this reason, it is the most visible side of logistics for customers. Graham et al. (2001) commented on the importance of spectator arrivals and departures at sports events. They stressed that arrival and departure is a part of the event hospitality experience. The first and last impression of an event will be the parking facility and the traffic control.

The organisation of transport for conferences takes on a special importance. Shone (1998) emphasised the linking of transport and the selection of the venue. The selection of the conference venue or site has to take into account the availability and cost of transport to and from the site. Also, the transport to other facilities has to be considered. A venue that involves a 'long haul' will increase overall costs of a conference or event as well as add to the organisational confusion. It can also make the event seem less attractive to the delegates and, therefore, have an impact on attendee numbers.

For large events, festivals and parades, further logistics elements are introduced to the transport of the customer to the event. In particular, permission (council, highways department, police) and road closures need to be part of the logistics plan. Another requirement would be to plan sufficient signage to the event to ensure that customers, and equipment, arrive quickly and with the minimum of disruption to the local community. Events such as The Open Championship have signage commencing on main routes miles from the site as part of a coordinated transport plan to ensure that people are directed to the appropriate car parks. A leaflet, The Provision of Temporary Traffic Signs to Special Events, is available from the Department of the Environment, Transport and Regions to assist event managers in planning this aspect of the event. Guidance can also be gained from professional signage companies such as Royal Automobile Club signs service or Automobile Association signs. Figure 15.5 lists the elements of customer transport that need to be considered for an event.

The significance of transport to the event stakeholders such as local authorities is illustrated by the publication of *Traffic Management for Special Events* by the New

FIGURE 15.5 Customer transport checklist

- Have the relevant authorities (e.g. local council, police) been contacted for information and permission?
- Has adequate signage to the site been implemented?
- What public transport is available? Are timetables available?
- Has a back-up transport system been organized? (in case the original transport system fails)?
- Is the taxi service adequate and has it been informed of the event? (Informing the local taxi service is also a way of promoting the event).
- What quality is the access area? Do weight and access restrictions apply? Are there any special conditions that must be considered (e.g. underground sprinkler systems under the access area).

- Is there adequate provision for private buses, including an area large enough for their turning circle, driver hospitality and parking?
- Is there a parking area and will it be staffed by trained personnel?
- Is a towing and emergency service available if required?
- Has transport to and from drop-off point been organized (e.g. from the car park to the site or venue entrance and back to the car park)?
- At what rate are customers estimated to arrive (dump or trickle)?
- Is there adequate access and are there parking facilities for disabled customers?
- Are the drop-off and pick-up points adequately lit and signposted?

South Wales government (RTA, 2001) and *Managing Travel for Planned Special Events* by the US Department of Transportation (2003). The New South Wales document defines events in terms of their impact on traffic:

> *A special event (in traffic management terms) is any planned activity that is wholly or partly conducted on a road, requires multiple agency involvement, requires special traffic management arrangements, and usually involves large numbers of participants and/or spectators. Examples are marathons, fun runs, cycling events, parades, marches and the like.*

(RTA, 2001, p. 2)

Solving logistics problems (for example, transport and parking) can become a significant issue for event organisers and will form part of the licence requirements for the event. For example, for Glastonbury Festival 2000, wheel-wash and road-sweeping facilities were put in place as a contingency against poor weather, to ensure that mud was not deposited on the roads, which would cause a safety hazard.

SUPPLY OF PRODUCT — PRODUCT PORTFOLIO

Any event can be seen as the presentation of a product. Most events have a variety of products and services — a product portfolio — all of which go to create the event experience for the customer. The individual logistics requirements of the various products need to be integrated into a logistics plan.

For a large festival, the product portfolio may include over 200 performing groups coming from around the UK and from overseas. For a small conference, the product may be a speaker and video material. For an exhibition the product may include not only relevant exhibition stands focused on the theme of the event but also displays and an educational seminar programme. It should be remembered that the product could also include the venue facilities. This is why the term 'the event experience' is used to cover all the aspects of the customer's experience. It can include, for example, the audience itself and just catching up with friends, in which case, the people become part of the product portfolio.

Transport

If the product portfolio includes products coming from overseas, the logistics problems can include issues such as carnet and customs clearance. A licence allows the movement of goods across an international border with an ATA Carnet, issued by Chamber of Commerce for exporting goods temporarily, or a TIR Carnet, issued by the Road Hauliers Association or Freight Transport Association for importing goods temporarily. A performing artist group coming into the UK is required to have clearance for all its equipment, and needs to pay any taxes on goods that may be sold at the event, for example, videos, DVDs or compact discs (CDs).

A large account with an airline company can allow the event manager an area of negotiation. In exchange for being the 'preferred airline' of the event, an airline company can grant savings, discounts, free seats or free excess charges.

The artistic director would forward the transport requirements for the performers to the logistics manager well before the event. This one aspect of logistics illustrates the linking of the various functional areas of a large event.

In his text on event production, Sonder (2004) listed five cost items of transport issues under the revealing heading 'The high cost of entertainment'. One of these issues is the transport of the artists to the venue. Birch (2004, p. 191), in his informative description of his life in events, related many stories of transporting artists. He described one opera diva's refusal to take the artist shuttle bus to the performance at the opening of the Olympics as she was expecting a private limousine.

Importing groups from overseas provides the logistics manager with an opportunity to communicate with these groups. The 'meet and greet' at the airport and the journey to the site can be used to familiarise the talent (that is, the artists) with the event. Such things as site map, rehearsal times, accommodation, dressing room location, equipment storage and transport out can be included in the artist's event or festival kit.

Accommodation

The accommodation requirements of the artists (such as performers, keynote speakers or competitors) must be treated separately from the accommodation of the audience. The aim of the event manager is to get the best out of the 'product'. Given that entertainers are there to work, their accommodation has to be treated as a way of increasing the value of the investment in entertainment. Substandard accommodation and long trips to the site are certain ways of reducing this value. Often these requirements are not stated and need to be anticipated by the logistics manager.

Artists' needs on site

A range of artists' needs must be catered for, including transport on site, storage and movement of equipment, stage and backstage facilities, food and drink (often contained in the contract rider), sound and lights. All these have a logistics element and are described in detail in Chapter 14.

As with accommodation, an efficient event manager will anticipate the on-site needs of the artists. Often, this can only be learned from experience. In multicultural Britain, the manager needs to be sensitive to requirements that are culturally based, such as food, dressing rooms (separate) and appropriate staff to assist the performer. The artist's requirements on site have a very strong sense of urgency. Often there is not a lot of time to adjust the food, costumes, dressing rooms or on-site transport if the artists are dissatisfied. These last-minute changes can impinge on the production time of the event. Therefore, understanding the artists' needs should be regarded as a critical task. The term 'artist' used in this section refers to speakers, MCs and sports personalities, as well as cultural artists such as musicians. They are also referred to as the 'talent'.

SUPPLY OF FACILITIES

The supply of the infrastructure to an event site introduces many of the concepts of business logistics. The storage of consumables (food and drink) and equipment and the maintenance of equipment become particularly significant. For a small event taking place over an evening, or conferences and exhibitions in permanent venues, most of the facilities will be supplied by the venue. The catering, toilets and power, for example, can all be part of the hiring of the venue.

Figure 15.6 illustrates a common spreadsheet system for planning and monitoring the sourcing and payment of suppliers. Such a system enables the event team to simply display their good governance. As the event or festival grows, this spreadsheet can be scaled up.

Larger or more innovative events require the sourcing of many of the facilities. Some of these facilities are discussed in detail in Chapter 14. An inaugural outdoor festival will need to source just about all the facilities. To find the best

FIGURE 15.6 List of suppliers for a jazz festival

**Register of suppliers and purchase order status
2011 Festival**

ITEM	STATUS	QUOTES SOUGHT	QUOTATION RECEIVED	SUPPLIER	CONTACT DETAILS	SERVICES/GOODS TO BE SUPPLIED	COST	ORDER NUMBER	ISSUED	INVOICES	AMOUNT
Copyright											
Catering for performers	Confirmed										
Children's rides											
Clean-up staff											
Entertainment	Confirmed										
Fireworks	Confirmed										
First aid											
Food stalls											
Garbage bins											
Generator	Confirmed										
Lighting towers	Confirmed										
Marquees etc.											
Parking	Contacted										
Portaloos											
Security											
Sound system	Confirmed										
Staging	Call for quotes										
Venue	Confirmed										

information about the availability and cost of the facilities, the event manager should look for a project in the area that required similar facilities. For example, toilets, generators, fencing, earth moving equipment and security are also used by construction and mining companies. Some facilities can be sourced through film production companies. Many of the other facilities, such as the marquees and stages, travel with the various festivals. Large tents and sound systems need to be booked in advance. The Made-Up Textiles Association (2009) provides useful guidance on marquee hire including a code of practice for hiring, use and operation.

Innovative events, like a company-themed Christmas party in an abandoned car park, will require a long lead time to source the facilities. For example, it may take months to source unusual and rare props and venues for an event. These lead times can significantly affect the way in which the event is scheduled.

ON-SITE LOGISTICS

The site of an event may vary from an old warehouse for a dance event to an underground car park for a Christmas party, to a 50-acre site for a festival. Logistics considerations during the event become more complex with the size of the event. The flow of materials and people around the site and communication networks become the most important areas of logistics.

Flow

With larger festivals and events, the movement of the audience, volunteers, artists and equipment can take a larger part of the time and effort of the logistics manager than does the lead-up to the event. This is especially so when the site is physically complex or multi-venue and there is a large audience. A mistake made by people unfamiliar with events is to disregard what happens at various times on the event site or venue. For some events, the site is in constant motion, although this may not be obvious to the audience. During the lead-up time to an event, the subcontractors can take care of many of the elements of logistics. For example, the movement of the electricity generators to the site would be the responsibility of the hire company. However, once the facilities are on site, it becomes the responsibility of the logistics manager for their positioning, movement and operation.

Something is being moved around on most events sites. The logistics must take into account the potential for flow of equipment and people during an emergency.

The access roads through a large festival and during the event would have to accommodate:

- artist and equipment transport,
- waste removal,
- emergency fire and first aid access and checking,
- stall set-up, continual supply and removal,

- security,
- food and drink supplies,
- staging equipment set-up, maintenance and removal, and
- site communication.

As illustrated in Figure 15.7, even during a straightforward event, many factors of the traffic flow must be considered. The performers for an event will need transport from their accommodation to the stage. Often, the performers will go via the equipment storage area to the rehearsal rooms, then to the stage. At the conclusion of the performance, the performers will return their equipment to storage, then retire for a well-earned rest in the green room. For a community festival with four stages, this to-ing and fro-ing can be quite complex.

At the same time as the performers are transported around the site, the media, audience and VIPs are on the move. Consideration also has to be given to accessibility for people with disabilities. Figure 15.7 does not show the movement of the food vendors' supplies, water, security, ambulances and many more. When any one of the major venues empties there is further movement around the site by the audience. This results in peak flow times when it may be impossible, or unsafe, to move anything around the venue except the audience. These peaks and lows all have to be anticipated in the overall event plan. For example, movement of catering from the main production kitchens to the various hospitality units around Lord's Cricket Ground could only take place before spectators arrived and at set times when crowd density would be lighter, for example, avoiding morning coffee, lunch and afternoon tea service. Getting the timing wrong could lead to a 30-minute journey, from what would normally take 10 minutes.

Each event contains surprising factors in traffic flow. For the Brit Awards, taking place at Earls Court, for example, coordinating thousands of limousines, mostly containing celebrities, together with taxis and other traffic, could cause significant logistical problems on this main route through London. However, getting the limousines to set down customers at local hotels solves this. The case study of the Vodafone Ball, organised by Euro RSCG Skybridge Group, also illustrates the point as it requires meticulous planning, with 11,500 guests sitting down to a silver-service meal at the same time, and 2500 catering staff to coordinate. This earned a place in the Guinness Book of Records for the largest silver-served sit-down meal in the world, which recognised the success of the planning involved.

FIGURE 15.7 Some traffic patterns to be considered when planning a multi-staged music festival

```
0  Performers' accommodation  → equipment storage area → rehearsal area →
   stage → equipment storage area → social (green room)
1  Media accommodation  → media centre → stages → social area
2  VIP accommodation → stages → special requests
3  Audience pick-up points → specific venue
```

Communication

On-site communication for the staff at a small event can be via the mobile phone or the loud-hailer of the event manager. With the complexity of larger events, however, the logistics plan must contain an on-site communications plan (Figure 15.8). The size of the communications plan and detail included will depend on the size of event — at one end of the scale, this may simply be a list of names, positions and mobile telephone numbers; at the other, it may also include PDA and landline extension numbers, fax, two-way radios, pagers, on-site locations and lines of responsibility illustrating who is responsible to whom in the organisation structure. Contractor contact details may be included on the main plan, however, on larger or more complex events, each contractor or service area (for example, security, stewarding and catering) may be assigned a separate radio channel. It may be preferable for all communications to be directed through a main communications control centre, rather than via mobile phones, to ensure that operational issues are not confused and lines of communication remain clear. Policies should be implemented on radio usage to guarantee professionalism is maintained at all times.

The communication of information during an event has to work seamlessly with the other functions of event management. In particular, the immediacy of the information is important. The information has to be highly targeted and timely enough for people to act on it. This immediacy of information is unique to events because they must meet a deadline and generally involve large numbers of people. For this reason, event management tends to involve a variety of communication methods and devices, including:

- *two-way radios*: very common at large events, where the channels are reserved for emergency and police.
- *mobile phones and text messages*: although limited by capacity, possibly becoming overloaded in an emergency. For this reason, some large venues acquire additional coverage.

FIGURE 15.8 Simple communication plan

Name	Position	Location/ Base	Contact Mobile Number	Radio Number	Reporting to	Responsible for
Jane Green	Event Director	Roving	07771 XXX XXX	001	Board	Event Manager
Jackie Brown	Event Manager	Main Office	07771 XXX XXX	002	Event Director	Overall
Alan White	Assistant Event Manager	Area 1	07771 XXX XXX	003	Event Manager	All staff in area 1
Caroline Black	Assistant Event Manager	Area 2	07771 XXX XXX	004	Event Manager	All staff in area 2

- *signage*: a common form of communication. Its placement and clarity are important issues (dealt with later in this chapter).
- *runners*: people whose job is to physically take the information to the receiver. Runners are indispensable if there is a power failure. Some large public events have bicycles ready for this purpose.
- *news sheets*: paper news sheets used to inform the exhibitors of daily programme changes and updates on the attendee numbers and types.
- *loud-hailer*: surprisingly useful devices at some events such as parades.
- *a sound system*: useful for announcements. The event team should know how to use it correctly.
- *flags*: often used at sports events such as car racing.
- *visual and audio cues*: used to communicate the start or finish of an action. Whistles, horns and flashing lights can all be used in this way. Artistic lighting can be used to move an audience around a venue.
- *closed circuit television and webcams*: used in venues such as exhibition and entertainment centres.
- *short-range FM radios*: used to broadcast information during the event.
- *WiFi and bluetooth*: two more recent technologies that are employed at some conferences and exhibitions to send and receive information such as last-minute news and attendee numbers. These can provide a comprehensive mobile network for immediate data transfer.
- *bulletin boards*: a humble and often effective way of contacting the volunteers and performers on site.

The movement around the event site or venue of equipment, suppliers and people — that is, the logistics during the event — needs an efficient communication system. For this reason, events often have levels of redundancy or backups for any one type of communication. The test of good communication planning is a power failure or emergency when the system will stop or be overloaded, and the event management team will be swamped with decisions to be made. Communication planning has to account for such a situation, so it must be a fundamental part of the project management and undergo a thorough risk assessment. A common experience is the lack of mobile phone connections over the New Year's Eve event celebrations when lines are swamped with calls of congratulations.

Signage

On-site signage is an important part of communicating to all the attendees of the event. It may be as simple as messages on a whiteboard in the volunteers' dining area, or it may involve large on-site maps showing the public the locations of facilities. Two important issues of on-site signage are position and clarity. A direction sign that is obscured by such things as sponsors' messages diminishes its value to the event.

For large events, the signage may need a detailed plan. The issues to consider are:

- overall site placement of signs — at decision points and at danger spots, so that they are integrated into the event;
- types of signs needed, such as directional, statutory (for example, legal and warning signs), operational, facility and sponsor;
- sign literacy of attendees — what sort of signs are they used to reading?
- actual placement of signs — entrance, down the road, height;
- accessibility of signs — are they accessible to people with disabilities?
- orientation of signs (that is, when a customer is looking at the sign does it reflect the direction that they are facing?) (Nightingale, 2009);
- supply of signs, their physical maintenance and their removal, and
- maintaining the credibility of the signs — if a facility is moved, then the signs may need to be changed.

The most effective way of communicating with the audience at an event is to have the necessary information in the programme. Figure 15.9 shows the type of essential information that can be included in the programme for the audience, spectator or visitor.

FIGURE 15.9 Event programme information

Accommodation – whether accommodation is provided onsite or available nearby? May include contact details
Banking facilities – where are the nearest banking facilities? Are these onsite?
Cameras – are there any restrictions on camera usage? For example, some events may ban all cameras, others only commercial cameras.
Catering/bar facilities – what catering/bar facilities are available onsite? Where are they located?
Clothing – is there a compulsory or suggested dress code?
Directions – where is the event situated? Are there any special routes for getting there?
Disabilities – what extra facilities/services are provided for people with disabilities?
First aid – where are these situated? Assistance from the St Johns Ambulance or Red Cross may be acknowledged.
Information/meeting point – is there an area onsite where people can arrange to meet or have any queries answered?
Lost and found – where is office located for lost and found children or items of value?
Organiser/security – where are the organiser and security offices located?
Rules – are there any rules that visitors, spectators or the audience must observe?
Telephones – where are the nearest telephones located?
Tickets – remind visitors/audience of the requirement to bring their ticket to the event and of any restrictions (for example, is access restricted to certain areas?)
Toilets – where are toilets located?
Video/viewing screens – for sporting events and festivals, where are video screens located? For greenfield sports (e.g. golf), where will scores be posted?
Website – what is the address of the event website? What type of information may be found there?

Amenities and solid waste management

For large festivals, events and exhibitions, the layout of the amenities is always included in the logistics site map. Figure 15.10 is an example of a large festival logistics site map that shows the layout of amenities.

The site map is an indispensable tool for the event manager, and is described in more detail later in this chapter. The schedules for the maintenance and cleaning of the amenities are part of the plan. For smaller events, these areas may be the sole responsibility of the venue management and part of the hiring contract.

Responsibility for cleaning the site and restoring it to its original condition is of particular importance to an event manager, as it is generally tied to the

FIGURE 15.10 Creamfields 2000 site map

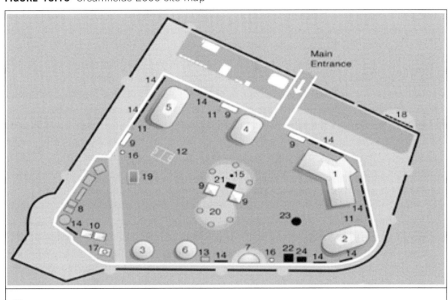

Key

1 Arena One: Cream	9 Bars	17 Hospital
2 Arena Two: Golden	10 Cloak room	18 Box Office
3 Arena Three: Cream-House US	11 Water Point	19 Evian Swimming Pool
4 Arena Four: Big Beat Boutique	12 Football Pitch	20 Picnic Area/Food Stalls
5 Arena Five: Bugged Out!	13 Ladies Powder Room	21 Information/Welfare
6 Arena Six: Metalheadz	14 Toilets	22 Internet Cafe
7 Radio One: Outdoor stage	15 Meeting Point	23 The Smirnoff SCAD jump
8 Fun Fair	16 First Aid	24 Chill Out

(Source: Slice, 2000)

nature of the event. For example, Leeds Festival at Temple Newsam in Leeds attracted a huge audience to a delicate area. Merely the movement of the audience destroyed the grass and resulted in local residents being wary of any further events in their area. However, violence at the 2002 event, following trouble at previous years events, caused over £250,000 of damage and injuries. As a result, the event moved to Bramham Park near Wetherby from 2003, where the festival can be better managed to avoid disruption to local residents and the infrastructure can be invested in for the festival's long-term future. If an event takes place in the countryside, such as an open-air concert, a motor sport event, a cross-country race or a corporate team challenge, extra care must be taken by the event manager to minimise the impact on the environment, particularly in protected areas such as National Parks. An environmental impact assessment may generally assist the event manager in managing this. However, the National Parks may have their own specific guidelines and rules for such events. Lake District National Park Authority (1999) noted that, although the impact of large events can be significant, for example, the Three Peaks Race, even small events can raise concerns and therefore size is not the major issue. They observe that, 'It is more important that the organisers of any event have taken account of the potential problems, and made every effort to avoid them, or reduce them to an acceptable level' (Lake District National Park Authority, 1999, p. 50). In order to be able to manage the events effectively, it is advised that the event manager effectively liaise with local bodies and local communities, and include areas such as transport, parking, toilet provision, marshalling (for sporting events) and safety within the plan. Guidelines and codes of practice provided by sporting or professional bodies and user groups, for example, those developed by the Institute of Fundraising (2002), can be a useful source of advice to event organisers, based on years of experience. Motor sport events are highlighted as causing particular concerns, and as a result, specific criteria have been developed to minimise the impact of this type of event. These relate to when the events can take place, which routes are allowed, restrictions placed on vehicle numbers and that all houses along the route are notified. Overall, the principles to consider when planning events in Greenfield sites may form part of the licence conditions and include the following:

- traffic arrangements (for example, planning effective routes to minimise traffic on narrow lanes, unsuitable routes, or local villages/towns, protecting verges and keeping routes clear),
- parking management (for example, solid ground, plan for if vehicles get stuck, road cleaning),
- waste management (for example, collection and minimisation of litter inside and outside the site),
- drainage considerations for the site (including effective road surfaces for vehicle access),

- safety (for example, uneven surfaces for audience/spectators) and
- noise control.

Well-maintained toilets can be a very important issue with the audience, in particular, their number, accessibility and cleanliness. The HSE (1999) provides useful guidance in this respect. Requirements for minimum number of toilets for public entertainment buildings are outlined in BS6465: Part 1 1994, however, for licensed entertainment, the location and number of toilets should be agreed with the local authority and may be a term within the licence. The number of units required will depend on the type of event, for example, those with higher fluid intake or where camping will take place. However, a general rule of thumb for a music event opening 6 hours or more is one toilet for every 100 females, and one toilet per 500 males plus one urinal per 150 males. Hand-washing facilities should be provided with no less than one per 10 toilets, together with suitable hand-drying provision. The HSE (1999) also reminds organisers of their responsibilities for people with special needs, for example, those requiring wheelchair access, and suggests a minimum of one toilet with hand-washing facilities per 75 people, although this should relate to anticipated numbers. One need only look at the press coverage of the summer festivals in the mid- to late-1990s in order to recognise the importance to customers of clean toilets, which resulted in significant improvements over the past couple of years. The logistics manager has to be aware of 'peak flows' during an event and of the consequences for vehicle transport of the waste and opening times of treatment plants.

The collection of solid waste can range from making sure that the venue manager has enough bins to calling for a tender and subcontracting the work. The number of bins and workers, shifts, timelines for collection and removal of skips should all be contained in the logistics plan as it interrelates with all the other event functional areas. This is a further example of linking the elements of logistics. A plan for primary recycling — recycling at collection point — would include both the education of the public (signage) and specialist bins for different types of waste (aluminium, glass, paper). Effective management of the event, for example, by banning the audience from bringing in glass bottles, can not only reduce the physical impact on the environment and reduce clear-up costs but also increase safety.

Consumables: food and beverage

The logistics aspects of food and beverage on a large, multi-venue site primarily concern its storage and distribution. Food stalls may be under the management of a stall manager as there are regulations that need to be followed. The needs of the operators of food stalls, including transport, gas, electricity and plumbing, are then sent on to the logistics manager. In particular, the sale of alcoholic beverages can present the logistics manager with specific security issues.

At a wine and food fair, or beer festival, the 'consumables' are the attraction. The collection of cash is often solved by the use of pre-sale tickets that are exchanged for

FIGURE 15.11 Food and beverage — factors to consider

- Has a liquor license been granted?
- What selection criteria for stall applicants (including design of stall and menu requirements) will be used?
- What infrastructure will be needed (including plumbing, electrical, gas)?
- Does the contract include provisions for health and safety regulations, gas supplies, insurance, and workers payment?
- What position on the site will the stalls occupy?
- Have arrival, set up, breakdown and leaving times been set?
- What cleaning arrangements have been made?
- Do stallholders understand the need for ongoing inspections, such as health, electricity, plumbing, waste (including liquids) disposal and gas inspection?
- Are there any special security needs that must be catered for?
- How and when will payment for the stall be made?
- Will the stallholder provide in-kind support for the event (including catering for VIPs, media and performers)?

the food, wine or beer 'samples'. The tickets are bought at one place on the site, which reduces possible problems with security, cash collection and accounting. Figure 15.11 lists some of the main factors to consider when including food and beverage outlets at an event.

Due to the temporary nature of events and festivals and the large number of inexperienced volunteers, food can be a high-risk item in the event. In the UK it is recommended that the event organisers follow the advice of the Food Standards Agency and their local environmental health officers. The importance of good food hygiene was illustrated in 2010 when 1200 athletes at a sports festival in the Dominican Republic were treated for suspected food poisoning (Anon, 2010). The methodology of hazard analysis critical control point is being applied to large events. The hazards are identified in the preparation and delivery of food. Critical control points are instances in this process when the risk can be controlled. It is part of the general risk management methodology described in Chapter 18.

Figure 15.12 illustrates the importance of food handling education for volunteers or staff working with food. Checklists such as this illustrate the micro-management needed in events, particularly when it comes to food.

As well as feeding and watering the public, logistics includes the requirements of the staff, volunteers and performers. This catering area, often called the green room, provides an opportunity to disseminate information to the event staff. A strategically placed large whiteboard in the green room may prove to be an effective means of communicating with volunteers.

Last, but not the least, is the catering for sponsors and VIPs. This generally requires a separate plan to the general catering. At some festivals a 'hospitality tent' is set up for the 'special guests'. This aspect of events is covered in Chapter 13 on staging.

FIGURE 15.12 Quick food safety checklist

We have provided the checklist below to help you. This is specifically designed for caterers attending outdoor events.

Food Safety Management

Do you have any documentation on the food safety controls you adopt to ensure the food you prepare is safe to eat?	☐ Yes	☐ No
Do you keep monitoring record sheets, training records, etc.?	☐ Yes	☐ No
Are these available for inspection on your trailer/stall?	☐ Yes	☐ No

Storage

Are all food/ equipment storage areas under cover and protected from contamination? Are they clean and free from pests?	☐ Yes	☐ No
Do you have enough refrigeration? Does it work properly?	☐ Yes	☐ No
If you use raw and cooked foods are they adequately separated during storage?	☐ Yes	☐ No
Are high-risk foods (e.g. cooked rice) stored under refrigeration below 8°C?	☐ Yes	☐ No

Food Preparation and Service Areas

Have you got enough proper washable floor coverings for the food preparation areas? What precautions have you to keep mud out of the stall in wet weather?	☐ Yes	☐ No
Are all worktops and tables sealed or covered with a impervious, washable material? Have you got enough preparation worktop space?	☐ Yes	☐ No
Have you got enough wash hand basins? Are they supplied with hot and cold water, soap and paper towels?	☐ Yes	☐ No
Are your staff washing their hands regularly?	☐ Yes	☐ No
Have you got sinks large enough to wash food and equipment in (including bulky items)? Are they supplied with hot and cold water?	☐ Yes	☐ No
Have you got detergent and clean cloths? Have you got any sanitizer, e.g. anti-bacterial sprays?	☐ Yes	☐ No
Have you got enough water containers? Are they clean and have they got caps?	☐ Yes	☐ No
Have you got a supply of hot water reserved for washing up and hand washing?	☐ Yes	☐ No
Have you got adequate lighting and ventilation?	☐ Yes	☐ No

Continued

FIGURE 15.12 *Continued*

After cooking

Is food cooked and served straight away? ☐ Yes ☐ No

If 'no' is it held at 63°C or above until served? ☐ Yes ☐ No

Once cooked, is food protected from contact with raw food and foreign bodies? ☐ Yes ☐ No

Cleaning

Is your stall/vehicle clean? Can it be kept clean? Have you allowed time for thorough cleaning of the vehicle/ stall equipment between events? ☐ Yes ☐ No

Do you have a cleaning schedule to ensure all areas are kept clean? ☐ Yes ☐ No

Do you use clean cloths and a 'food-safe' disinfectant to clean food contact surfaces? ☐ Yes ☐ No

Do you ensure that cleaning chemicals are kept away from food? ☐ Yes ☐ No

Contamination

Can food be protected from contamination at all times? Is food being stored directly on the ground? ☐ Yes ☐ No

Is the unit free from pests, and is open food protected from flying insects ☐ Yes ☐ No

Food waste

Have you got proper bins for rubbish? Where will this be disposed of? ☐ Yes ☐ No

If there is no mains drainage have you made hygienic provision for the disposal of wastewater? ☐ Yes ☐ No

Staff

Have your staff had food hygiene training? Have you any untrained casual staff carrying out high risk food preparation? ☐ Yes ☐ No

Have you got a good supply of clean overalls or aprons hygiene and wear clean over-clothing? ☐ Yes ☐ No

Are food handlers aware that they should not work if suffering from certain illnesses? ☐ Yes ☐ No

Is there a first aid box with blue waterproof plasters? ☐ Yes ☐ No

Remember that food poisoning is preventable, and we can all help avoid it by following good hygiene practices.

(Source: Wiltshire Council www.wiltshire.gov.uk/foodsafety.htm, 2009)

The VIP and media requirements

The effect on event logistics by media coverage of the event cannot be over-estimated. Even direct radio broadcasts can disrupt the live performance of a show — both in the setting up and the actual broadcast. The recording or broadcasting of speeches or music often requires separate microphones or a line from the mixing desk and these arrangements. This cannot be left until just before the performance. Television cameras require special lighting, which often shines directly into the eyes of the audience. The movement of a production crew and television power requirements can be distracting to a live performance, and need to be assessed before the event.

Media organisations work on very short timelines and may upset the well-planned tempo of the event. However, the rewards in terms of promotion and event finance are so large that the media logistics can take precedence over most other aspects of the event. The event manager in consultation with event promotions and sponsors often makes these decisions. This is an area that illustrates the need for flexible negotiations and assessment by the logistics/operations manager.

The VIP requirements can include special security arrangements. Once again it is a matter of weighing up the benefits of having VIPs with the amount of extra resources that are needed. This, however, is not the logistics manager's area of concern; the event manager or event committee should deal with it. Once the VIPs have been invited, their needs have to take precedence over the publics'.

Emergency procedures

Emergency procedures at an event can range from staff qualified in first aid to using the St John Ambulance or Red Cross service, to the compilation of a comprehensive major incident or disaster plan. The location of first aid facilities should be indicated on the site map and all the event staff should be aware of this location. The number of first-aiders, medical staff and ambulance provision will depend on the nature and size of the event. HSE (1999) recommends that a ratio of 2:1000 (for the first 3000 attending) may be appropriate for smaller events, with no less than two first-aiders on site. However, exact requirements should be established as part of the risk assessment process and included within the event plan. HSE (1999) provided a method of estimating these. Large events require an emergency access road that has to be kept clear. These issues are so important that a local council may immediately close down an event that does not comply with the regulations for emergencies. Festivals in the countryside can be at the mercy of natural disasters, including fires, storms and floods.

HSE (1999) and Home Office (2000) offer guidance in the preparation of a major incident plan. HSE (1999, p. 32) defined a major incident as one 'that requires the implementation of special arrangements by one or more of the emergency services, the NHS or local authority' for treatment, rescue and transport of a large number of people, and associated issues, such as dealing with enquiries and the media. Figure 15.13 suggests the areas that should be considered when planning the major incident plan.

The emergency plan must be developed for major incidents, with further plans covering minor incidents. The above provides a useful starting point for areas to consider, but you are strongly advised to obtain a copy of *The Event Safety Guide* (HSE, 1999) or other appropriate guidance notes currently available for exhibitions, outdoor events and sporting grounds (see references). The on-site emergency procedures are an example of the two functions of event management — risk and logistics — working together to formulate a plan. Overall, they come under the project plan. They are now mandatory for many events.

Considerations for creating the plan include: Under whose authority is the plan being prepared? And what are the plan's aims and objectives? The emergency plan will influence the design of the site, particularly for large public events. Local councils require emergency access to all parts of the event, and the access route must be the correct width for an emergency vehicle and kept clear at all times. A mistake in this area can result in the event being closed immediately.

Emergencies can occur at any time during the event and the planning has an effect on the evacuation procedures. For major emergencies when the site needs to be cleared, these procedures should be different:

- while the audience is arriving, before they have entered the venue or site. The logistics involved are concerned with stopping the inflow.
- while some of the audience is already in the venue and others are arriving. This is a complex period of two directions of flow: people who are arriving

FIGURE 15.13 Areas for consideration in a major incident plan

- Identify the key decision-making workers
- Stopping the event
- Identify emergency routes and access for emergency services
- Requirements of people with special needs
- Identify holding areas for performers, workers and the audience
- The script of coded messages to inform staff and announcements for the audience
- Alert/communication procedures, including public warning
- Procedure for evacuation and containment
- Identify rendezvous points for emergency services and ambulance loading points
- Locate nearest hospitals and traffic routes
- Identify temporary mortuary facilities
- Identify roles, contact list and communications plan
- Location of emergency equipment and availability
- Documentation and message pads.

(Source: HSE, 1999, p. 32)

and have not heard that the event has been cancelled, and those who are eager to leave.

- during the event, when most of the audience is on-site.

The disaster plan stresses the lines of authority and necessary procedures. These procedures include the partial evacuation of the festival site in the event of a disaster (particularly prolonged heavy rain). It notes that rescuers should concentrate on personnel in immediate danger when conducting an evacuation.

SHUTDOWN

As Pagonis (1992) pointed out, military logistics is divided into three phases: deployment, combat and redeployment.

Redeployment, the complete movement of military forces and equipment to a different area, often takes the most effort and time. Similarly, the exiting of the people and removal and return of equipment that take place during an event can take a considerable amount of time and effort. In many cases, the amount of time and effort spent on the shutdown of an event are in direct proportion to the size of the event and its uniqueness. Repeated events, like many of the festivals mentioned in this chapter, have their shutdown schedule refined over many years. It can run quickly and smoothly. All the subcontractors know exactly how to get their equipment out and where they are placed in the order of removal. The event manager of a small event may only have to sweep the floor and turn off the lights.

Most difficulties arise in inaugural events, large events and multi-venue events. In these cases, logistics can be as important after the event as at any other time, and the need for planning is most apparent. As illustrated in Figure 15.14, the management of an event shutdown involves many elements. In project management terminology, this is called the asset handover and project closure. In event management, the most forgotten part is the closure of the project. The tools of project management can be used to manage the shutdown process. The shutdown plan should include a work breakdown structure, a task/responsibility list and a schedule with a critical path, and be subject to risk analysis. It forms part of the overall event project plan.

The on-site issues initially involve the crowd. Whether for a sports event, a conference or a concert, not much major work can be done until the crowd leaves. However, some tasks can be started, such as packing one stage while the crowd's attention is elsewhere. Crowd management at this time is vital because the event management is responsible for the crowd's safety as people leave the venue and make their way home. It is wise to include this issue in the risk management plan. If some members of the crowd want to 'party on', it is smart to plan for this activity well ahead of time so that it can be either countered or allowed to continue safely. Some of the local discos and hotels may welcome the increase in patrons, if told beforehand.

FIGURE 15.14 Event shutdown checklist

Crowd Dispersal
- Exits/transport
- Safety
- Related to programming
- Staggered entertainment

Equipment
- Load -out schedule including correct exists and loading docks
- Shut down equipment using specialist staff (e.g. computers)
- Clean and repair
- Store – number boxes and display contents list
- Sell or auction
- Small equipment and sign off
- Schedule for dismantling barriers

Entertainment
- Send-off appropriately
- Payments – cash
- Thank you letters/awards/recommendations

Human resources
- The big thank you
- Final payments
- Debrief and gain feedback for next year
- Reports
- Celebration party

Liability
- Records
- Descriptions
- Photo/video evidence

Onsite/staging area
- Cleaning
- Back to normal
- Environmental assessment
- Lost and found
- Idiot check
- Site/venue hand-over

Contractors
- Contract release
- Thank you

Finance
- Pay the bills
- Finalise and audit accounts – best done as soon as possible
- Thank donors and sponsors

Marketing and promotion
- Collect press clippings/video news
- Reviews of the event – use a service
- Market research on community reaction

Sponsors and Grants
- Release grants: prompt reports
- Meet sponsors and enthuse for next time
- Government and Politics
- Thank services involved
- Reports to councils and other government organisations

Client
- Glossy report, video, photos
- Wrap up and suggestions for next time

The site may look empty after the event, but the experienced event manager knows that the work has only just begun. The equipment needs to be collected, repaired and stored, or immediately returned to its owners. Small equipment such as hand-held radios are easily lost, so many events have a sign-on/sign-off policy for these items. With large crowds, you can almost guarantee there will be an assortment of lost items. A member of staff needs to walk the site to check whether anything has been left behind — called the 'idiot check' in the music industry. At this point, the event manager realises the value of a torch!

As the site is being shut down, it may also be prepared for the next event. This is a consideration for all the other resources. The equipment may be packed away so it can be easily found and used for the next event. Shutdown thus has a further element: preparation for the next event. Extensive site clean-up is also often required.

The shutdown of an event is the prime security time. The mix of vehicles, movement of equipment and general feeling of relaxation provides a cover for theft. The smooth flow of traffic leaving an event at its conclusion must also be considered. Towing services and the police may need to be contacted. Very large events may require the sale of facilities and equipment at a post-event auction. Some events find that it is more cost-effective to buy or make the necessary equipment and sell it after the event. Finally, it is often left to the person in charge of logistics to organise the final thank-you party for the volunteers and staff.

Back at the event office, there will be at least a few weeks of project closure. This will include acquitting all the contracts, paying the bills and collecting all the records of the event, media clippings and any incident report sheets. These records will assist when all the reports have to be prepared and any funding is acquitted. Although the next step may not be the responsibility of the person in charge of logistics, the event logistics manager will have an important role.

The event is not over until the management of the event has been assessed (Chapter 6). The logistics plan is part of the overall event project plan, so has to be assessed for its effectiveness. It cannot be assessed unless there are written documents or files to compare against the reality of the event logistics. It will be difficult, if not impossible, to suggest real improvements for the next event without these. Too often, in the rush to the next event, the logistics problems are forgotten. The event management produces not just the event but also a way to manage the event.

Checklists are an example of a logistics management system. They represent the micro-management of the event. In the past, many events would have discarded these checklists after the event, yet the checklist is a portable tool — for example, the ticket checklist is common to all events, so it can easily be adapted to a checklist for invitations to a charity event. Checklists should be assessed after the event, along with the rest of the management system.

In placing the checklist as part of a project management system, O'Toole and Mikolaitis (2002, p. 54) state:

> The simple checklist represents the combined experience and knowledge of the corporate event management team. It is the final document output of the work breakdown structure and could be thought of as a list of mini milestones …. It is the fine mesh of the net that stops anything from slipping through and escaping attention before it is too late.

TECHNIQUES OF LOGISTICS MANAGEMENT

The tools used in business and military logistics can be successfully adapted to event logistics. Because an event takes place at a specific time and specific place, the tools of scheduling and mapping are used. The dynamic nature of events and the way the functional areas are so closely linked mean that a small change in one area can result in crucial changes throughout the event. The incorrect placement of an electric generator, for example, can lead to a mushrooming of problems. If the initial problem is not foreseen or immediately solved, it can grow to affect the whole event. This gives initial negotiations and ongoing assessment a special significance in event logistics. The logistics manager needs to be skilled in identifying possible problem areas and needs to know what is not on the list.

We will now consider the role of the logistics managers and their relationship with other functional areas and managers of an event.

The event logistics manager

As mentioned throughout this chapter, the logistics manager has to be a procurer, negotiator, equipment and maintenance manager, human resource manager, map maker, project manager and party organiser. For a small event, logistics can be the direct responsibility of the event manager. Logistics becomes a separate area if the event is large and complex. Multi-venue and multi-day events usually require a separate logistics manager position.

Part of the role of the logistics manager is to efficiently link all areas of the event. Figure 15.15 shows the lines of communication between the logistics manager and various other managers for a large, complex, multi-venue event. It is a network diagram because, although the event manager or director has ultimate authority, decision-making authority is usually devolved to the various managers who work at the same level of authority and responsibility as the event manager.

The information required by the logistics manager from the other festival managers is shown in Table 15.1. The clear communication within this network is also partly the responsibility of the logistics manager. Many of the tools and techniques of the logistics manager are discussed in Chapter 9.

Site or venue map

A map of the event site or venue is a necessary communication tool for the logistics manager. For small events, even a simple map can be an effective tool that obviates

FIGURE 15.15 The lines of communication between the logistics manager and other managers for a multi-venue event

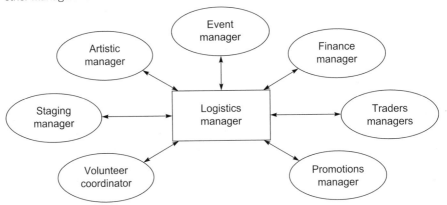

Table 15.1 Information required by the logistics manager from the other festival managers

Position	General Role	Information Sent to Logistics Manager
Artistic Director	Selection and negotiation with artists	Travel, accommodation, staging and equipment requirements
Staging Manager	Selecting and negotiation with subcontractors	Sound, lights and backstage requirements, programming times
Finance Director	Overseeing budgets and contracts	How and when funds will be approved and released and the payment schedule
Volunteers Coordinator	Recruitment and management of volunteers	Volunteers selected to assist and requirements of the volunteers (for example, parking and free tickets)
Promotions Manager	Promotion during the event	Requirements of the media and VIPs
Traders Manager	Selecting suitable traders	Requirements of the traders (for example, positioning, theming, electricity, water and licence agreements)

the need for explanations and can quickly identify possible problem areas. The map for larger festivals can be an aerial photograph with the logistics features drawn on it. For smaller events, it may be a sketch map that just shows the necessary information to the customer. The first questions to ask are 'what is the map for?' and 'who will be reading it?' A logistics site map will contain very different information from that on the site map used for promotional purposes. Of necessity, the map needs to filter information that is of no interest to the logistics plan. Monmonier (1996, p. 25), in his highly respected work on mapping, summarised this concept thus:

> A good map tells a multitude of little white lies; it suppresses truth to help the user see what needs to be seen. Reality is three-dimensional, rich in detail, and far too factual to allow a complete yet uncluttered two-dimensional scale model. Indeed, a map that did not generalize would be useless. But the value of a map depends on how well its generalized geometry and generalized content reflect a chosen aspect of reality.

The three basic features of maps — scale, projection and the key (showing the symbols used) — have to be adapted to their target audience. Volunteers and subcontractors, for example, must be able to clearly read and understand it. The communication value of the site map also depends on where it is displayed. Some festivals draw the map on the back of the ticket or programme.

The checklist for items to be included in a site map can be very detailed. Figure 15.16 shows a standard checklist of the logistics site map for a small festival.

FIGURE 15.16 Site map checklist

- scale and direction (north arrow)
- a list of symbols used on the map (key)
- entrance and exits
- roads and parking
- administration centre
- information booths
- first aid and emergency road access
- lost children area
- electricity and water outlets
- toilets
- lost property
- food and market stalls
- tents and marquees
- equipment storage areas
- off-limit areas and danger spots (e.g. creeks, blind corners)
- green room
- maintenance area
- pathways
- telephones
- ATMs
- media area

With many sporting events, a sketch map on the ticket shows how to find the site, parking and the location of seats and facilities. The back of tickets generally includes a list detailing the behaviour expected of event participants. The festival site shown in Figure 15.8 is a promotional map for the audience, originally presented in full colour with points of interest to the public displayed. For corporate events, a simple map of the venue at the entrance — in particular, showing seating, toilets, food areas and bar — can relieve the staff of a lot of questions! Furthermore, the logistics map for volunteers, staff, performers and all other personnel would provide further details, including the placement of site offices, contractors' compounds and service routes.

NEGOTIATION AND ASSESSMENT

No matter what the size of the event, the mutual agreement on supply and conditions is vital. In particular, the special but changing nature of one-off events requires the techniques of dynamic negotiation to be mastered by the logistics manager. Marsh (1984, p. 1) in his work on negotiation and contracts, defines negotiation as 'a dynamic process of adjustment by which two parties, each with their own objectives, confer together to reach a mutually satisfying agreement on a matter of common interest'.

Logistical considerations need to be covered by the initial negotiations with subcontractors. Agreement on delivery time and removal times are an indispensable part of the timelines as they form the parameters of the critical path.

It needs to be stressed that the management of events in the UK is a dynamic industry. The special nature of many events means that many aspects cannot be included in the initial negotiation. Decisions and agreements need to be continually reassessed. Both parties to the agreement have to realise that the agreement needs to be flexible. However, all possible problems should be unmasked at the beginning, and there are logistics tools to enable this to happen.

Having prepared the schedules and site map, an important tool to use is what Pagonis (1992, p. 194) described as the 'skull session':

Before implementing a particular plan, I usually try to bring together all of the involved parties for a collective dry run. The group includes representatives from all appropriate areas of the command, and the goal of the skull sessions is to identify and talk through all the unknown elements of the situation. We explore all possible problems that could emerge, and then try to come up with concrete solutions to those problems. Skull sessions reduce uncertainty, reinforce the interconnection of the different areas of specialisation, encourage collaborative problem solving, and raise the level of awareness as to possible disconnects [sic] in the theatre.

Goldblatt (2008) called this gap analysis. Gap analysis is studying the plan to attempt to identify gaps that could lead to a weakening in the implementation of the logistics plan. He goes on to recommend using a critical friend to review the plan to look for gaps in your logical thinking.

The identification of risk areas, gaps and 'what ifs' is important in the creation of a contingency plan. For example, as Glastonbury Festival takes place during one of the hottest months of the year, the supply of water was identified as a priority area. For the 1997 festival, a permanent water main was constructed, supplemented by water carts, and drinking water made available to the general public through standpipes. On site, there was also an attempt to encourage water conservation through an association with WaterAid.

CONTROL OF EVENTS LOGISTICS

The monitoring of the logistics plan is a vital part of the overall control of an event. An important part of the plan is the identification of milestones — times when crucial tasks have to be completed. The Gantt chart (Chapter 8) can be used to compare projected performance with actual performance by recording performance times on the chart as the tasks occur. It is a simple monitoring device, with the actual performance written on the chart as the tasks occur.

The aim of the logistics manager is to create a plan to enable the logistics to flow without the need for active control. The use of qualified subcontractors with experience in events is the only way to make this happen. This is where the annual festival with its established relationships to the suppliers has the advantage over the one-off, innovative event. The objective of the event director is to enjoy the event without having to intervene in any on-site problems!

EVALUATION OF LOGISTICS

The ultimate evaluation of the logistics plan is the success of the event and the easy flow of event supply and operations. However, the festival committee, event director and/or the sponsors may require a more detailed evaluation. The main question to ask is whether the logistics met their objectives. If the objectives as set out in the plan are measurable, then this task is relatively straightforward. If the objectives require a qualitative approach, then the evaluation can become imprecise and open to many interpretations.

An evaluation enables the logistics manager to identify problem areas that enables improvement and therefore adds value to the next event (this topic is discussed further in Chapter 16). Techniques used in evaluation are:

- quantitative — a comparison of performance against measurable objectives (sometimes called benchmarking), and
- qualitative — discussion with stakeholders.

The term 'logistics audit' is used for a systematic and thorough analysis of the event logistics. Part of the audit concerns the expectations of the audience and whether they were satisfied. For very large events, the evaluation of the logistics may be contained in the overall evaluation undertaken by an external research company. Evaluation is discussed further in Chapter 18.

The logistics or operations plan

Whether the event is a school class reunion or a multi-venue festival, a written logistics or operations plan needs to be part of the communication within the event. It could range from a one-page contact list with approximate arrival times, to a bound folder covering all areas. The folder for a large event would contain:

- a general contact list,
- a site map,
- schedules, including timelines and bar charts,
- the emergency plan,
- subcontractor details, including all time constraints,
- on-site contacts, including security and volunteers, and
- evaluation sheets (sample questionnaires).

All these elements have been described and discussed in this chapter. These can make up the event manual that is used to stage the event. The manual needs to be a concise document, as it may be used in an emergency. An operations manual may only be used once, but it has to be able to withstand the rigours of the event itself. Some organisations, particularly in the exhibition industry, have a generic manual on their intranet that can be adapted for all their events in any part of the world.

Although this text emphasises the importance of planning, overplanning can be a significant risk, particularly with a special event, as there is often a need to respond and take opportunities when they arise. Artistry and innovation can easily be hampered by a purely mechanistic approach to event creation. As pointed out in the Marine Corps' publication *Logistics* (1997):

> *To deal with disorder, the logistics system must strive for balance. On the one hand, it must estimate requirements and distribute resources based on plans and projections; otherwise the needed support will never be available where and when it is required. On the other, a system that blindly follows schedules and procedures rapidly loses touch with operational realities and inhibits rather than enables effective action.*

The secret is to ensure that the plan is structured sufficiently well to ensure a safe event, while allowing creativity to shine through.

SUMMARY

Military logistics is as old as civilisation itself. Business logistics is a recent science. Events logistics has the advantage of building on these areas, using the tools of both and continually improving on them as the events industry grows. Event logistics provides a framework to manage the operations of the event.

This logistics system can be broken down into the procuring and supply of customers, products and facilities. Once on site, the logistics system concerns the flow around the site, communication and the requirements of the event. At the conclusion of the event, logistics concerns the breakdown of structures, cleaning and managing the evacuation of the site or venue.

For small events, logistics may be the responsibility of the event manager. However, for larger events, a logistics manager may be appointed. The logistics manager's role within the overall event management and his or her relationship with other managers was described earlier. For both small and large events, the tools of business and military logistics are used. The logistics of an event need to be treated as any other area of management and have in-built evaluation and ongoing control. All these elements are placed in a plan that is a part of the overall event plan.

Logistics is an invisible part of events. It enables the customers to focus completely on the event without being distracted by unnecessary problems. It only becomes visible when it is looked for or when there is a problem. It enables the paying customer, the public, client or sponsor to realise and even exceed their expectations.

QUESTIONS

1. What are the logistics areas that need to be contained in the initial agreements with the suppliers to an event?

2. Set out an emergency plan for a small event.

3. List the logistics tasks for (a) a street parade, (b) a product launch and (c) a company party.

4. Discuss the significance of queues at events. What factors do you need to consider?

5. It is often remarked that the best logistics staff come from the military. What are the differences between military logistics and event logistics? What are the advantages of hiring staff with military experience?

6. Develop a spreadsheet for an event so that it can be used in the planning of the logistics.

CASE STUDY: ELECTRICAL SERVICES AT GLASTONBURY FESTIVAL

Aggreko, and the companies they have acquired, have been the main electrical power contractors for the Glastonbury Festival since 1990. This entails providing all the generators, the cabling, electrical distribution (to the highest standards of safety) and lighting, for the main site, all the stages and the market. There are three distinct areas to the operation:

1. *The site*: this involves mainly lighting and the power sources for it. The site lighting performs much the same function as street lighting in a city, highlighting main routes and any obstacles, such as bridges or ditches, and for security. Another major part of this side of the job is toilet lighting. It is a requirement of the council's licence for the event that all the toilets (there are about 1200 of them!) be adequately lit when it is dark. These toilets are clustered in groups (some exceeding 200 individual toilets) all over the 1500 acres of the site, so getting power to them is one of the most challenging parts of the job. There are also vital services such as the site medical centres, water pumps, crew / stewards / contractors / security accommodation areas, catering facilities, and the all important slurry lagoon pumps etc. to be powered. The main site roadways and the vast circular perimeter fence are lit by over 20 watchtowers, each with several floodlights, its own generator. Approximately 23 kilometres of festoon lighting, with a bulb every 5 m support this! The watchtowers, along with many other site functions, now require power for most of the week before the festival and a couple of days after it. The floodlights, stage lighting and countless campfires make the festival site a huge, stunning feature on the Somerset landscape after dark.

2. *The stages*: for all the stages and performance areas, Aggreko provides generators and the cable and distribution. Large amounts of electrical power are needed for the stage lighting systems, PA systems, video screens, lasers, etc. For the main music stages this also involves power for live television and radio outside broadcasts. These supplies are generally larger (3× 400A three phase for main stage lighting) and the distribution much more complex than for site supplies. They are, however, clustered into smaller areas than the site wiring. Stage supplies are backed up with multiple generators in case of failure. All the stages have extensive backstage villages of Portacabin dressing rooms, offices, tented hospitality and catering areas, and loading bays that also need power and lighting.

3. *Market*: The market power for the festival is a major undertaking, organising and providing the power for most of the 600+ stalls. The time scale generally follows that of the site, except that the power is required for food storage (refrigeration) and security (lighting), 24 hours per day from the Monday before the festival to the Monday following. During the operational phase the markets are quite intensive as the large number of users causes issues, with some attempting to use more than they have paid for (causing overloading of sections of the system) and others plugging in faulty equipment leading to tripping of sections. In bad weather conditions (such as the 1998 massive thunderstorms and flooding of 2005) these problems are amplified several times!

Timescale

To install, operate and then remove an installation of this size and complexity in the short time available, while meeting the very high standards of safety required, requires considerable planning and teamwork. The planning really starts almost immediately after one event for the next one with a "Lessons learnt" session. Then once the other summer event season jobs are out of the way, the detailed planning begins again. This is a fairly continuous process, dovetailed with similar planning for other large events, but the rough timescales are as follows:

Six months prior to the event: power requirements for the markets are established. The process commences in January with forms sent out with the pitch applications for stalls at the festival. There then follows a process of collating the returned forms, chasing payments and attempting to anticipate those stall holders who will eventually require power, but are delaying informing us to delay payment! An outline plan is drawn up and the generators and major elements of the cabling and distribution are allocated. Also around this time the budgets for the next event are prepared and reviewed by the company's senior management as there are large sums involved. Initial estimated equipment lists are drawn up and circulated around the business to start the process of preparing the equipment and identifying any potential shortfalls early enough to resolve them. Any new sustainability innovations such as the introduction of Bio Diesel fuelled sets or automatic switching for lighting circuits will be agreed with Glastonbury Festivals and added to the plan during meetings with the Festival management team.

Three months prior to the event: power requests are collated from the other festival area organisers and those who have not yet responded are chased up. Discussions commence with the main subcontractors regarding the supply of men and equipment. Plant is also booked at this stage (e.g., forklift trucks, accommodation and storage cabins). Contracts for the many sub-contract staff involved are also put in place around this time.

Two months prior to the event: detailed construction planning begins – each year's plan is based on the previous year, amended as the power requests come in. The site and performance areas are separated and described, power requirements ascertained and generators allocated. This is completed, in conjunction with the all-important site map, on computerised tables and schedules. About this time we usually have a meeting with Michael Eavis to discuss any special or new points and to agree the budget. With the plans taking shape it is possible to finally confirm the number of generators required, usually about 230 units (including markets) with 25 self-contained lighting tower units ranging from 600 kW to 6 kW. These generators will come from our own fleet in most cases, being collected in the South West from all over the country (and sometimes even from our European depots).

Six weeks before the event: the first part of what will eventually grow into a crew of about ninety electricians / technians / project managers / and assistants arrive on site to start erecting the floodlights and 23 km of festoon lighting and wiring up the accommodation and catering facilities for the other crews arriving. Transport for plant and equipment to, around and from the site are finalised, using around 100 articulated lorries of equipment during the event. The main crew arrives on site – all need to be accommodated and fed for seven weeks in a bare field! Installation begins with site requirements, and the inevitable toilet-chasing as last-minute changes to the plan occur. The on-site office is set up with all the plans and schedules on the walls to act as the nerve centre of the operation. These days the provision of reliable broadband communications is critical to the operation as the site office becomes an integral part of the company's network for the duration to track equipment, e-mail plans etc. Security commences on the gates, and the whole vast contractors operation to lay water pipe, build tents, install toilets, lay temporary roadway, erect fencing begins in earnest.

Two week before the event: the last generators arrive on site and have to be allocated, positioned with trucks and cranes, and wired up and tested for safety. Stage areas need to be made ready for the arrival of the lighting and PA rigs by about the Tuesday of show week.

Doors open! All site licence requirements must be met and are checked by local council staff Over 100,000 people flood onto site so all the safety lighting must be working and all work in public areas needs to be finished as moving around the site become much harder.

Showtime! All systems are up and running. All the generators not on long-range tanks must be refuelled twice a day – each refuelling circuit takes about 12 hours to complete, so it is like

Continued

CASE STUDY: ELECTRICAL SERVICES AT GLASTONBURY FESTIVAL—*CONT'D*

painting the Forth Bridge. The generators will use about 200,000 L of diesel fuel in the next 4 days around a third of it Bio diesel made from waste vegetable and food processing oils. To reduce the risk of a major spillage, on-site storage is kept to about 1.5 days' supply – in separated bunded tanks – with regular tanker deliveries throughout the event. The 24 hour on-call crews attends to any breakdowns or last-minute additions. The other members of the crew get a chance to enjoy the festival, or just catch up on some sleep!

Post-event – the aftermath: immediately after the last band comes off stage any generators wanted urgently elsewhere must be got away before the traffic builds up. Extra lighting is rigged up for the lighting and PA de-rigs. Another area requiring power is the litter recycling machinery. On Monday morning, the clear-up begins. All the wiring and distribution units have to be collected and loaded onto trucks. People who cannot tell the difference between cables and toilets can make this very unpleasant! The lights are taken down and the generators loaded onto a fleet of articulated trucks and returned to the depots. This phase of the operation usually takes about ten days. When the site is clear the crew leave the site and get on to the next job. Some power is left in situ for up to a month more for site crew catering, the fencing crew, etc. Following this, all that remains is to sort out of the paperwork, bills, hire return notes, payments and, of course, collect a cheque from Michael. At this point we look back at the event, take stock and start to plan for next year!

All this adds up to one of the largest jobs of the year for Aggreko's UK operation. For all its size and complexity, the electrical system for the Glastonbury Festival would seem small beer compared to the engineer's responsible for the electrical system of a real city of 177,000. But then, they don't have to build it, use it and remove it all within eight weeks!

For further details about Aggreko, please visit www.aggreko.com.

By Bill Egan, Avonmouth, Bristol. BS11 0QL. Aggreko UK Ltd. Aggreko House, Orbital 2, Voyager Drive, Cannock, Staffs. WS11 8XP

Questions

1. Create a Gantt chart that displays the electrical supply to Glastonbury Festival.
2. What aspects of electricity supply are 'sensitive' (that is, a small change in one area of logistics will have a large effect on the electricity supply to the festival)?
3. Create a risk assessment list for the festival electricity supply that would be used as the basis of a 'skull session'.

CASE STUDY: ULSTER BANK BELFAST FESTIVAL AT QUEEN'S

Introduction

The Ulster Bank Belfast Festival at Queen's reached its 48th anniversary in 2010. Every year, the largest festival of its kind in Ireland brings the best of international art to Belfast and brings international attention to the city's dynamic arts practitioners. The festival covers all art forms, including theatre, dance, classical music, literature, jazz, comedy, visual arts, folk music and popular music, attracting over 45,000 visitors.

Development

In the beginning, there was an enterprising young undergraduate, Michael Emmerson, who started running a small event based on the campus of Queen's University, Belfast. The university, its students and the Belfast public saw that it was good and the infant Belfast Festival at Queen's was born. Ten years later and the festival was 10 times bigger and had already attracted such names as Dizzy Gillespie, Ravi Shankar, Sviatoslav Richter, Laurence Olivier and Jimi Hendrix!

In the 1970s, the festival was a cultural oasis in a landscape dominated by political upheaval and it was to act as a catalyst for the city's future cultural renaissance. By the early 1980s under the directorship of Michael Barnes, a former History lecturer, the festival had expanded into a 2-week-long arts extravaganza across the whole of the city and was hosting everything from Moscow State Ballet and the Royal Shakespeare Company to Dexy's Midnight Runners and the Flying Pickets! Billy Connolly and Rowan Atkinson had visited the festival before they were famous and were welcomed back, while Michael Palin vowed never to take his one-man show anywhere else on earth, such was his love of the event. The dusty archive files lurking in the caverns of the Festival House basement read like a who's who of prominent artists during the latter half of the twentieth century.

By the 47th Ulster Bank Belfast Festival at Queen's in 2009, over 600 artists and crew and events from all four corners of the globe travelled to entertain, enthrall and excite audiences in venues across Belfast.

Accessibility

Drawing on the resources and coordinating events across 33 venues can present a number of challenges, particularly in ensuring that the events are accessible to all members of society, including those with a disability. Belfast Festival has introduced a number of initiatives to address these needs:

- Venue Access: An access information guide has been developed to help patrons find out about a venue's car parking facilities and what facilities there are for patrons with a disability. Alternatively, patrons can contact the Festival Box Office for information. Table 15.2 provides examples of the detail to be included, though it should be noted that available facilities may change and therefore either the website or Festival Box Office will provide current details.
- Visually Impaired: The festival brochure is available in large print, audiocassette, CD and Braille. Furthermore, an audio description is available of selected theatre events.
- Hearing Impaired: Induction loops, a radio microphone system and portable induction loops are available at many of the venues and events. In addition, portable equipment can be booked in advance and Electronic Note Taking and British Sign Language are available upon request.

SUMMARY

Events around the world are increasingly looking at their target markets and identifying how they can make their events accessible to all members of society. In addition, the implementation of the Disability Discrimination Act has provided fresh impetus for exploring this further and making reasonable adjustment to venues or programmes where required. The access information guide included with this case study provides an example of how event organisers can address many diverse needs and ensure that the audience is fully aware of what services and facilities are available at each venue.

For further information about Belfast Festival at Queen's, please visit www.belfastfestival.com. By Ulster Bank Belfast Festival at Queen's.

Questions

1. Belfast Festival at Queen's uses over 33 venues to stage the event. What are the logistical implications of using different venues?
2. The case study particularly demonstrates venue access for disabled visitors. What other aspects of the event would organisers of festivals such as this have to consider?
3. Identify and discuss what issues an event organiser would have to consider for the following events to ensure that they were accessible to all customers:

   a. Large conference (250 delegates) within a hotel
   b. Exhibition (200 exhibition stands, 10,000 visitors) within an exhibition centre
   c. Festival (20,000) on a Greenfield site

Table 15.2 Example of access information

Venue	Wheelchair Access/Venue Entry	Hearing and Sight Disabilities	Parking	Inside Venue	Seating
Grand Opera House	Mobile ramp (must know in advance)	Loop system and headsets available No tactile signage	Parking next door or in Europa multi-storey	Adapted toilets No lift Guide dogs welcome	8 wheelchair spaces available per evening
Ulster Hall	Ramps at side doors	No loop system No tactile signage	Street parking only Lowered pavements outside building	Adapted toilet Chairlift for balcony seats Guide dogs welcome	Recommended ground floor seats but balcony room is available for wheelchairs
City Hall	2 ramps at the front and 1 at the back	Loop system at reception and function rooms Tactile signage	Spaces are available within the grounds	Lifts are available Adapted toilets Guide dogs welcome Wheelchairs available on site	
Waterfront Hall and NTL Studio	Level access into main building and lift access into NTL Studio Accessible phone line	Loop system, infrared system in auditoriums and tactile signage	Badge holders phone in advance for parking. Multi-storey also has spaces	Wheelchairs available on site Lifts and adapted toilets available Guide dogs welcome Lowered counters	Removable seating
Clifton House	Level access into residential home	No loop system No tactile signage	Spaces are available in the grounds	Lift and chairlift (do not need to get out of own chair) Adapted toilets in the residential home (not in board room) Guide dogs welcome	Removable seating

Venue	Access	Loop system / signage	Parking	Lifts / toilets	Seating
Elmwood Hall	No ramps (steps only)	No loop system No tactile signage	Street parking only with a few possible places in the grounds	No adapted toilets Guide dogs welcome	Unfixed seating
Lyric Theatre	Ramp located at side of building	Loop system available No tactile signage	Street parking	A lift and adapted toilets are available Guide dogs welcome	Removable seating
Empire Music Hall	Steps only	No loop system	Street parking	No lifts Adapted toilet available Guide dogs welcome	Loose seating
Ulster Museum	Wheelchair access at main entrance	Loop system at reception No tactile signage	Spaces available in the grounds but museum must be made aware a day in advance	Lifts available Adapted toilets Guide dogs welcome	
Old Museum Arts Centre	Steps only Free entry for friends assisting those with a disability	No loop system or tactile signage	Street parking	No lifts No adapted toilets Guide dogs welcome	
Ormeau Baths Gallery	Ramp located at side of building	No loop system No tactile signage	Street parking	Lift and adapted toilet available Guide dogs welcome	Loose seating
Linen Hall Library	Level access	No loop system No tactile signage	No parking within general area	Lift and adaptable toilets available Guide dogs welcome	
Direct Wine Shipments	No wheelchair access Steps to taster sessions held on 3rd floor	No loop system No tactile signage	Street parking	No lift No adapted toilet	
Belfast Welcome Centre	Level access	Loop system and mini-com system Cassettes and large print brochures	No parking within general area	Lift and adapted toilets available Guide dogs welcome Lowered counters	

Continued

Table 15.2 Example of access information *(Continued)*

Venue	Wheelchair Access/Venue Entry	Hearing and Sight Disabilities	Parking	Inside Venue	Seating
Lanyon building	Level access	No loop system	Spaces available within the grounds	Lifts and toilets available Guide dogs welcome Door controls	Loose seating
Guinness spot	Level access	No loop system	Spaces available within the grounds	Adapted toilets available in the neighbouring Whitla Hall	Loose seating
Whitla Hall	Ramp access	Loop system	Spaces available within the grounds	Adapted toilets No lift Guide dogs welcome	Loose seating
Students Union	Ramp access	Loop system No tactile signage	Street parking	Adapted toilets Lifts available Door controls Guide dogs welcome	Loose seating
Harty Room	Ramp access	No loop system	Street parking	Adapted	Loose seating
QFT	Ramp access	Infrared headsets	Street parking	Adapted toilets and lifts	Removable seating
Drama Studio	Info. – Phone for information				
SARC	Ramp access	No loop system	Spaces available within the grounds	Adapted toilets Lift available	
St Patrick's Church	Temporary ramp access	Loop system	Street parking	Adapted toilets	

Legal issues of event management

LEARNING OBJECTIVES

After studying this chapter, you should be able to:

- explain the central role of event ownership in event management,
- identify and construct the necessary contracts for events and their components,
- understand and be able to comply with the variety of laws, licences and regulations governing event production,
- describe the necessity for and the process of insuring an event.

INTRODUCTION

Underpinning all aspects of an event is the legal framework that ensures all parties are treated fairly and within any applicable law. To complicate matters, the laws relating to events and their management can vary slightly for each country in which the event occurs. As events grow in number and importance to the economy, there will be more laws relating to them. There are some common principles.

This chapter introduces the concepts of event ownership and the crucial duty of care of event management. It discusses the use of contracts (including insurance contracts) that document the relationship between the event and various stakeholders. It is important, therefore, that event and festival management be familiar with the key terms used in contracts. It then continues to discuss the various licences that event managers must obtain, and the duty of care that the event has to its stakeholders.

A key question in event organisation is 'who owns the event?' The legal owner of an event can range from the event coordinator, the management committee, a separate legal entity or the sponsors, but it is important to recognise that the ownership of the event entails legal responsibility and, therefore, liability. The members of an organising committee can be personally held responsible for their event. This is often expressed as 'jointly and severally liable'. The structure of the event administration must reflect this, and the status of various personnel, such as the event coordinator, the subcontractors and other stakeholders, must be clearly established at the outset. Likewise, sponsorship agreements will often have a clause as to the sponsor's liability and, therefore, the extent of their ownership of the event. All such issues need to be carefully addressed by the initial agreements and contracts.

Events Management. DOI: 10.1016/B978-1-85617-818-1.10016-7

The organising committee for a non-profit event can become a legal entity by forming an incorporated association. Such an association can enter into contracts and own property. The act of incorporating means that the members have limited liability when the association incurs debts. However, this does not grant them complete exemption from all liability such as negligence and duty of care. By law, an association must have a constitution or a list of rules. Such documents state the procedures and powers of the association, including auditing and accounting matters, the powers of the governing body and winding-up procedures. In many cases, community and local festival events often do not form a separate incorporated association as they are able to function under the legal umbrella of another body, such as a local council. This gives the event-organising committee considerable legal protection as well as access to administrative support. For a one-off event, this administrative support can save time and resources, because the administrative infrastructure, such as a fax machine, phone lines, secretarial help and legal and accounting advice, is already established.

An apposite event example of this is the annual conference hosted by the Association for Events Management Education (AEME), which is a subject association formed in the UK for events educators. The conference is hosted and convened by a different member organisation each year, but the legal ownership of the event lies with the association, AEME, which has a constitution that covers the legal requirements mentioned above.

Establishing an appropriate legal structure for an event management company is a matter for legal advice. Several structures are possible for an event company, which could operate as a sole trader, a partnership, a charitable trust or a company limited by liability. For example, Figure 16.1 illustrates the legal structure of a sample of festivals, with just over half limited companies and just under half registered as charities (Allen and Shaw, 2001). Each of these legal structures has different liability implications. Legal advice may be required to determine the most appropriate structure for a particular circumstance.

CONTRACTS

Hill and Hill (2005) defined a contract as 'an agreement with specific terms between two or more persons or entities in which there is a promise to do something in return for a valuable benefit known as consideration'. They continued by noting that 'since the law of contracts is at the heart of most business dealings, it is one of the three or four most significant areas of legal concern and can involve variations on circumstances and complexities'. They state that a contract contains the following elements:

- an offer;
- an acceptance of that offer which results in a meeting of minds;
- a promise to perform;
- a valuable consideration (which can be a promise or payment in some form);

FIGURE 16.1 Legal structure of festivals

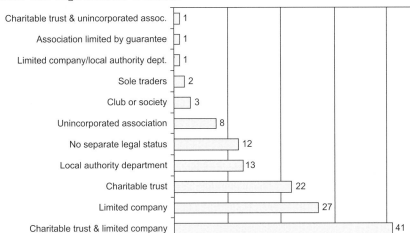

n=137

(Source: Allen and Shaw, 2001, reprinted with permission, British Arts Festivals Association)

- a time or event when performance must be made (meet commitments);
- terms and conditions for performance, including fulfilling promises, and
- performance.

A contract can be either a written or an oral agreement. However, in the world of event management, an oral contract is of little use if problems occur in the future. Therefore, it is appropriate to put all contractual agreements in writing. This may frequently take the form of a simple letter of agreement, not more than a page in length, which incorporates the elements mentioned. However, when large amounts of money and important responsibilities are involved, a formal contract drawn up by lawyers is often necessary. As Goldblatt (2008, pp. 311−314) explained, a typical event industry contract will contain various clauses, including:

- the names of the contracting parties, their details and their trading names;
- details of the service or product that is offered (for example, equipment, enter-tainment, use of land and expert advice);
- the consideration or terms of exchange for such service or product and
- the signature of both parties indicating understanding of the terms of exchange and agreement to the conditions of the contract.

To make this mutual obligation perfectly clear to all parties, the contract would set out all the key elements. These could consist of financial terms (including a payment schedule), a cancellation clause, what to do in case of force majeure (Act of God), insurance, delivery time, the rights and obligations of each party, and an exact description of the goods and services being exchanged.

Contracts and contract terms have been subjected to scrutiny over recent years, due to event management, suppliers, performers and venues being caught out with hidden terms. In order to address this, Chris Hannam (of Stagesafe) developed a sample contract, terms and conditions and notes for use for the Production Services Association for use between service companies, artist management agencies, freelancers and self-employed contractors. The sample contract is presented as Figure 16.2. The terms and conditions that accompany this include areas such as payment terms, insurance requirements for both client and supplier, health and safety commitment, and confidentiality. This is accompanied by a schedule that outlines what both the supplier and the client will provide. Although developed in this specific context, it serves to illustrate a format that could be applied in other areas.

Event management organisations may need a wide range of contracts to facilitate their operation. Some of these are shown in Figure 16.3.

An event of medium size would require a set of formal contracts covering:

- the event company or coordinator and the client,
- the entertainers,
- the venue,
- the supplier (for example, security, audiovisual and caterers) and
- the sponsor(s).

Event management organisations may need a wide range of contracts to facilitate their operation. Some of these are shown in Figure 16.3.

For smaller events these may be arranged by letters of agreement.

Contract management

Contracts lay the foundations for event management. The process of managing contracts is illustrated in Figure 16.4. A common misconception is that once a contract has been negotiated it does not require further action. Event contracts need to be monitored and reviewed if necessary. Changing circumstances, a common feature of event management, can lead to contractual problems. In some areas of an event, particularly large sports events, this can lead to contracts being renegotiated.

Different contracts have different 'styles' and the event manager must be familiar with them. Some of these contracts are discussed in the following text.

Entertainment

A common feature of entertainment contracts is the 'rider', which comprises an amendment or addition to a document. This is an attachment to the contract, usually on a separate piece of paper. Hiring a headline performer may necessitate signing a 20- to 30-page contract. The contract often contains a clause requiring the event company to provide the goods and services contained in the rider, as well as the performance fee. The rider can include such things as a technical specification (for example, size of PA system required, microphone, technician requirements and

FIGURE 16.2 A sample contract

THIS AGREEMENT is made the < *Date* > day of < *Month*................>

BETWEEN < Insert your name or Co name >of:

< Insert your address .... > (The Supplier)

AND < Insert your customers name > of:

< Insert your customers address .... > (The Client).

CONTRACT DETAILS   **CONTRACT NO:** < *Insert your job No* >

EVENT, PRODUCTION OR TOUR:. < *Insert name of job/tour* >

DURATION OF THE AGREEMENT: From: < Insert Start Date > **To:** < Insert Finish Date >

1. The Supplier agrees to supply goods/services in accordance with the Schedule attached hereto or as subsequently agreed in writing by the parties hereto.

2. It is hereby agreed that prior to the signing hereof The Client has had ample opportunity to examine The Supplier's Terms of Business attached hereto and shall be deemed to have unequivocally accepted them.

3. The total contract price shall be < *Insert price and currency* > plus VAT (if applicable)

4. The terms of payment are: < *Insert Payment Terms* >

5. In the event of cancellation of this Agreement by The Client and without prejudice to any rights hereunder or under the Terms of Business attached hereto, The Client will indemnify The Supplier as a result of such cancellation for < .... >% of the contract price. Interest at a rate of <   >% per month is liable to be charged on any outstanding balances.

6. It is a fundamental term of this agreement that the stipulations as to payment contained be fully adhered to by The Client (including an absolute requirement of payment to be made within the times stipulated but subject to the proviso contained in Condition 4) and if for any reason The Client shall be in breach of such stipulations The Supplier shall have the right at its absolute and sole discretion and without prejudice to its other rights hereunder forthwith and without notice to dismantle remove or otherwise bring to an end any works service goods or other things supplied by the supplier hereunder and to terminate forthwith this agreement and be under no further liability hereunder to provide any of the services or goods herein agreed.

Signed for and on behalf of   )

The Supplier   )

Date

Signed for and on behalf of   )

The Client   )

Date

IN ADDITION TO SIGNING THE AGREEMENT, THE CLIENT IS REQUESTED TO INITIAL ALL PAGES OF THIS AGREEMENT, THE TERMS OF BUSINESS AND SCHEDULES, IN THE TOP RIGHT HAND CORNER

(Source: Hannam, 2000)

FIGURE 16.3 Contracts required by an event management organisation

FIGURE 16.4 The contract management process

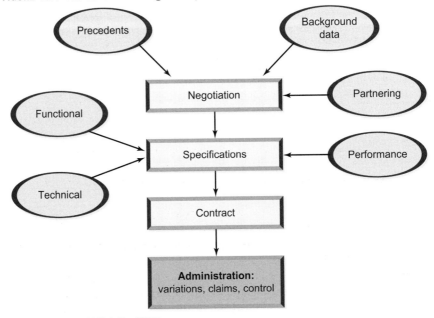

(Source: O'Toole and Mikolaitis, 2002)

lighting), hospitality specification (for example, food, drink and relaxing accommodation) and venue specification (for example, payment terms and insurance requirements) (Kemp, 1995; Vasey, 1998). The event company ignores this at its peril. The rider can be used by the entertainer's agent as a way of increasing the fee in real terms, which can have serious consequences for the budget of an event. For example, a university student union that employs a well-known rock group at a minimal fee for a charity function, for example, would find its financial objectives greatly damaged by a rider stipulating the reimbursement of food, accommodation and transport costs for 30 people.

Another important clause in the entertainment contract is exclusivity. For example, a headline act may be the major attraction for an event. If the act is also performing at a similar event in the same period, for example, the summer festival season, this could easily detract from the uniqueness of the event. A clause to prevent this is therefore inserted into the contract. It indicates that the performer cannot perform within a specified geographic area during the event or for a certain number of days prior to and after the event. The intricacies of an entertainment contract, together with the expense, led Stayte and Watt (1998) to suggest that event managers obtain legal advice from a solicitor experienced in dealing with entertainment/music contracts.

The contract must contain a clause that stipulates that the signatories have the right to sign on behalf of the contracting parties. An entertainment group may be represented by a number of agents. The agents, therefore, must have written proof that they exclusively represent the group for the event.

Venue

The venue contract can have specialist clauses, including indemnifying the venue against damages, personnel requirements and the provision of security staff. The venue contract can also contain the following elements:

- *Security deposit*: an amount, generally a percentage of the hiring fee, to be used for any additional work such as cleaning and repairs that result from the event.
- *Cancellation*: outlining the penalty for cancellation of the event and whether the hirer will receive a refund if the venue is rehired at that time.
- *Access*: including the timing of the opening and closing of the doors, and actual use of the entrances.
- *Late conclusion*: the penalty for the event going over time.
- *House seats*: this is the reserved free tickets for the venue management.
- *Additions or alterations*: the event may require some changes to the internal structures of the venue.
- *Signage*: this covers the signs of any sponsors and other advertising. Venue management approval may be required for all promotional material.
- *Cost:* the cost of the venue for the required time. For events such as conferences held in hotels, the venue may charge a per person per day fee basis that includes

all food, beverage and venue hire, rather than separate rates for each element, which reduces the fixed costs of the conference and makes it easier for the event manager to match expenditure and revenue.

To avoid misunderstandings and potential unforeseen costs, it is prudent to ascertain exactly what facilities are included in the fee. For example, just because there were chairs and tables in the photograph of the venue does not mean that they are included in the hiring cost.

Sponsor

The contract with the sponsor would include all that the sponsee promises to deliver – naming rights, signage, celebrity involvement, media mentions, etc., and the fee (consideration) given in return. Details of how the payment is made (cash or contra) and at what times would also usually be included in the contract. Geldard and Sinclair (1996) advised that among other things, the level of sponsor exclusivity during an event will need to be reflected in the contract between the event committee and the sponsor. Possible sponsor levels are sole sponsor, principal sponsor, major or minor sponsor and supplier. The contract would cover issues related to quality representation of the sponsor such as trademarks and signage, exclusivity and the right of refusal for further sponsorship. It may specify that the sponsor's logo be included on all promotional material or that the sponsor has the right to monitor the quality of the promotional material. Details of what the event will do to inhibit ambush marketing can also be included. Korman (2000) highlighted that sponsors will generally ask for exclusivity within their own brand sector or may demand sole rights to gain full benefit from the event. He further identified that minor sponsors should be managed to ensure that they do not establish a portfolio of rights that may damage public perception of the major sponsorship, and that sponsors are kept to a minimum to ensure that the message is clearly projected. As a result of these issues, the level of sponsorship – sole sponsor, headline sponsor, minor or major sponsor or supplier – needs clearly stating in the contract. The contract would also describe the hospitality rights, such as the number of complimentary tickets supplied to the sponsor.

Broadcast

Broadcast contracts can be very complex, due to the large amount of money involved in broadcasting and the production of related merchandise, such as videos and sound recordings. The important clauses in a broadcast contract address the following key components:

- *Territory or region*: The broadcast area (local, national or international) must be defined. If the attached schedule shows the region as 'World', the event company must be fully aware of the rights it is bestowing on the broadcaster and their potential value.
- *Guarantees*: The most important of these is the guarantee that the event company has the rights to sign for the whole event. For example, some local councils may require an extra fee be paid for broadcasting from their area. Also, performers'

copyright can preclude any broadcast without written permission from their record and publishing companies. Comedy acts and motivational speakers are particularly sensitive about any broadcasts and recordings, and the contract may require explicit permission from them to broadcast their performance.

- *Sponsorship*: This area can present difficulties when different levels of sponsorship are involved. Sometimes the rights of the event sponsor and the broadcaster's sponsors can clash, which can mean some delicate negotiations to resolve the difficulty. This is particularly applicable to sports events, where the match sponsor's products can clash with an individual team member's sponsorship.
- *Repeats, extracts and sub-licences*: These determine the allowable number of repeats of the broadcast, whether the broadcaster is authorised to edit or take extracts from the broadcast and how such material can be used. The event company may sign with one broadcaster, only to find that the rights to cover the event have been sold on for a much larger figure to another broadcaster. In addition, a sub-licence clause may annul many of the other clauses in the contract. The sub-licenser may be able to use its own sponsors, which is problematic if they are in direct competition with the event sponsors.
- *Merchandising*: The contract may contain a clause that mentions the rights to own products originating from the broadcast. The ownership and sale of any of the recordings can be a major revenue source for an event. A recently introduced clause found in these sorts of contracts concerns future delivery systems. Multimedia uses, such as DVDs, CD-ROMs, satellite/cable/on-demand television and now the Internet, are all relatively recent, and new communications technologies continue to evolve, for example, the increasing use of mobile Internet on 3G mobile phones. It is easy to sign away the future rights of an event when the contract contains terms or technologies that are unknown to the event company. It is therefore prudent to seek out specialist legal advice from an entertainment law firm.
- *Access*: The physical access requirements of broadcasting must be part of the staging and logistical plan of the event. A broadcaster can easily disrupt an event by demanding to interview performers and celebrities. It is therefore important to specify how much access the broadcaster can have to the performers and at what times. In this way all stakeholders' needs can be met without disrupting the event.
- *Credits*: This establishes, at the outset, the people and elements that will be listed in the titles and credits.

The broadcaster can offer all kinds of assistance to the event organisation. It has an interest in making the event presentable for television and therefore will often help decorate and light the venue. However, their level of assistance will depend on their stake in the event. For example, Channel 4's involvement in T4 on the Beach (Weston-super-Mare), through their T4 youth brand, has led to many kinds of synergies between the event, the sponsors and the broadcaster.

Constructing a contract

The process of constructing a contract is shown in Figure 16.5. It comprises five key steps:

- *the intention*: preliminary discussions between a potential supplier and event management to establish if the supplier's product and its price are suitable for the event;
- *negotiation*: once a supplier has been deemed to be suitable, discussions take place on price and product enhancements until agreement has been reached to the satisfaction of both parties, which can be formalised in a summary known as a 'heads of agreement';
- *initial acceptance*: the supplier is then advised that their offer is provisionally accepted;
- *agreement on terms*: further discussions may then take place on the fine detail of the agreement, including elements such as payment terms and discounts for meeting volume targets, and
- *signing*: once all details have been agreed they are incorporated in the contract and then signed by responsible officers of the supplier and event management.

This process can be facilitated if the event management has standard contracts for specific services, where the name of the supplier and any special conditions can

FIGURE 16.5 The process of constructing a contract

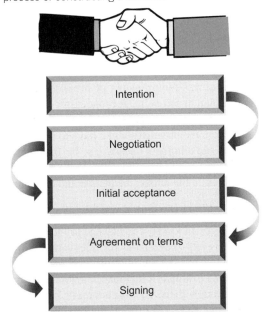

be inserted. This saves the event company time going through unfamiliar contracts from sponsors, suppliers and entertainers, which can be very time-consuming.

For large events and more complex contracts, a 'heads of agreement' is sent after the preliminary negotiations are completed. This is a summary of any important specific points, listing the precise service or product that is being provided. The contract can be renegotiated or terminated with the agreement of all parties. The final version should contain a clause that allows both parties to go to arbitration in the event of a disagreement.

TRADEMARKS AND LOGOS

Another kind of ownership issue for event management is its ownership of trademarks and logos. Protection of trademark ownership is generally covered within legislation, including the Trade Marks Act 1994, the Copyright, Designs and Patents Act 1988 and anti-counterfeit regulations. However, specific legislation has been drawn up to protect the Olympics through the Olympic Symbol etc. (Protection) Act 1995, which specifically prevents the use of their logo, motto and related word by any other party without the permission of the British Olympic Association. This protection is enhanced to cover games-related marks and symbols in relation to the London 2012 Olympics and Paralympics (London 2012, 2004a) through the London Olympic and Paralympics Games Act 2006. This illustrates the importance of the ownership of event symbols.

The event company has to be aware of the risks of misrepresenting their event. There is a danger, when promoting an event, to exaggerate the benefits. Descriptions of the product must always be accurate, as disgruntled consumers may take legal action to gain punitive damages when they feel that advertising for an event has made false claims. The Trade Descriptions Act 1968 can be used to argue such cases. This makes it an offence if a trader:

- applies a false trade description to any goods supplied or offers to supply any goods to which a false trade description is applied and
- makes certain kinds of false statement about the provision of any services, accommodation or facilities.

In the events context, this may involve a music festival advertising that a certain performer will be taking part or implying the support of associations or organisations when this is known not to be true. It may also include a company implying sponsorship approval or affiliation with an event when it is not, for example, through ambush marketing. Couchman and Harrington (2000, p. 2) identified that ambush marketing, sometimes referred to as 'parasitic marketing', can take many forms, but will usually fall into two distinct groups:

(A) Activities traditionally considered piracies — these will usually have a clear-cut remedy in law. They are activities which clearly constitute infringements of the proprietary rights in an event, for example unauthorised use of a registered event

logo on merchandise, false claims to be official suppliers to a particular team or use of copyright broadcast material on a website; and

(B) Other activities — more subtle practices for which the remedy is less clear-cut or may not even exist.

They go on to identify that typical examples of type (B) activities include unauthorised or unofficial merchandise; unauthorised or unofficial publications; unauthorised sales promotion activity or publicity stunts; unauthorised broadcasts/ virtual advertising/web advertising of sports content/live screenings/films/video/ photography/telephone commentary/'sponsored'; on-line text and audio commentary information lines/pager services; and unofficial corporate hospitality. London 2012 (2004a) indicated that the Secretary of State for Culture, Media and Sport had guaranteed that ambush marketing would be specifically addressed by legislation in relation to London 2012 Olympics, a guarantee now expressly supported with the passing of the London Olympic and Paralympics Games Act 2006.

DUTY OF CARE

A fundamental legal principle applied to events is that of taking all reasonable care to avoid acts or omissions that could injure employees, contractors, users, participants and visitors. This is called duty of care and is covered by the area of law known as torts. A tort is a breach of duty owed to other people and imposed by law, and in this it differs from the duties arising from contracts, which are agreed between contracting parties. Unlike criminal law, which is concerned with punishment and deterrence, the law of torts is concerned with compensation. Within the UK, duty of care is enshrined within legislation, including the Occupiers Liability Act 1957 and 1984, Supply of Goods and Services Act 1982 and the Health and Safety at Work etc. Act 1974 (HSE, 1999; Stayte and Watt, 1998). This is summarised in Figure 16.6.

For event management, duty of care means taking actions that will prevent any foreseeable risks of injury to the people who are directly affected by, or involved in,

FIGURE 16.6 The duty of care

The Act sets out the general duties which employers have towards employees and members of the public, and employees have to themselves and to each other.

These duties are qualified in the Act by the principle of *'so far as is reasonably practicable'*. In other words, an employer does not have to take measures to avoid or reduce the risk if they are technically impossible or if the time, trouble or cost of the measures would be grossly disproportionate to the risk.

What the law requires here is what good management and common sense would lead employers to do anyway: that is, to look at what the risks are and take sensible measures to tackle them.

(Source: Health and Safety Executive, 2003, p. 2)

the event. This would include the event staff, volunteers, the performers, the audience or spectators and the public in the surrounding areas.

Another duty of care is to ensure that the noise from an event (particularly music events) does not impinge upon the amenity of the venue's neighbourhood. The UK has an Environmental Protection Act (EPA, 1990) that includes legal powers to deal with annoyance or nuisance to residents caused by noise at venues and events. Local authorities also offer guidance specifically on noise at events and deal with any issues raised by residents, for example, Lambeth Noise Officers in Lambeth Council's Environmental Health Department issued *Guidance on the Control of Noise at Outdoor Events* (2008). In addition, the code of practice from the Noise Council (1995) offers guidance to organisers and environmental health officers. Finally, where event organisers require licences for the event (discussed later) then noise will be considered during the application and would be enforced under the licence conditions. This generally means that police and local authority officers have the power to instruct venues to abate noise after midnight. It behoves event managers to know how the EPA, codes of practice and local authority guidance will affect their event and ensure that they adhere to any requirements. These requirements can usually be obtained from the local council.

The Health and Safety Executive (HSE) has a strategy to improve the safety of workplaces, which encapsulates the concept of duty of care. Working with the Institute of Directors (IoD and HSE, 2009), they have recently produced guidelines for directors and board members, based on essential principles (Figure 16.7).

Managers have always had a duty of care to their employees and people attending their events and could be prosecuted for negligence (Hooker, 2008). However, it is now easier to prosecute companies and organisations with the

FIGURE 16.7 Principles for leading health and safety at work

Strong and active leadership from the top:
- visible, active commitment from the board;
- establishing effective 'downward' communication systems and management structures;
- integration of good health and safety management with business decisions.

Worker involvement:
- engaging the workforce in the promotion and achievement of safe and healthy conditions;
- effective 'upward' communication;
- providing high quality training.

Assessment and review:
- identifying and managing health and safety risks;
- accessing (and following) competent advice;
- monitoring, reporting and reviewing performance.

(Source: IoD and HSE, 2009, p. 1)

recent introduction of the Corporate Manslaughter and Corporate Homicide Act 2007 (HMSO, 2007), which came into effect in April 2008. Under this Act:

> *an offence will be committed where failings by an organisation's senior management are a substantial element in any gross breach of the duty of care owed to the organisation's employees or members of the public, which results in death. The maximum penalty is an unlimited fine and the court can additionally make a publicity order requiring the organisation to publish details of its conviction and fine*

(IoD and HSE, 2009, p. 2).

According to Price (2008), the Act provides a more effective means of holding companies and organisations to account as it removes the requirement to prove individual guilt, rather, it permits collective errors by a number of people to be considered, thus making it possible to punish organisations for systematic failures. As Safeconcerts (2008) noted, in essence 'it means that an organisation will be directly responsible, if any of its business activities result in a gross breach of a duty of care', therefore. it is essential that all managers and employees are trained and fully understand their legal responsibilities for health and safety. As with all areas of legislation, specialist legal advice should be sought when considering individual circumstances.

All event managers need to be conscious of this obligation to provide a safe and healthy environment for their event participants, spectators and staff, to avoid damaging lawsuits as well as other consequences.

DISABILITY DISCRIMINATION

Another area for consideration by event managers is to ensure that events are accessible to all members of society. Considering that over 10 million people within the UK have some form of disability, it makes business (as well as legal) sense to ensure that events are accessible. The Disability Discrimination Act (DDA) 1995 aims to ensure that disabled people are not treated less favourably than other customers (Disability Rights Commission (DRC), 2004). The Act makes it unlawful for a service provider to discriminate against a disabled person by refusing to provide (or deliberately not providing) any service which it provides (or is prepared to provide) to members of the public; or in the standard of service which it provides to the disabled person or the manner in which it provides it; or in the terms on which it provides a service to the disabled person (DRC, 2002, p. 5). The Act includes reference to ensure fair treatment for employees with disabilities. For service providers, including event managers, venues and others involved in the events industry, this means not treating disabled people less favourably than non-disabled people and making reasonable adjustments to services and premises so that disabled people can access them (DRC, 2004, p. 8). Generally, consideration of the needs of disabled people from the very early stages of planning an event will ensure that not only are they accessible for disabled customers but service may also be improved for non-disabled people as well as the event will have been thought through.

There is a wealth of information available for the events industry to assist in ensuring that legal requirements are met. For example, the DRC (2005), subsumed into the Equality and Human Rights Commission in 2007, produced the excellent handbook *Organising Accessible Events*, which has been developed with the input of events industry associations and other stakeholders. It offers advice on areas to consider in all aspects of organising events, from transportation, venue design and layout, through promotional materials, ticketing and bookings, to use of technology and training staff. The Belfast Festival at Queen's case study in Chapter 15 provides a useful example of how one event has approached this.

The DDA along with legislation relating to other forms of discrimination relating to sex, sexual orientation, age, or religious or philosophical beliefs are being brought into one piece of legislation, the Equality Act 2010. The legislation received Royal Assent on 8 April 2010 with the main provisions coming into force in October 2010 and others phased in through to 2013 (Government Equalities Office, 2010).

INSURANCE

Central to any strategy of liability minimisation is obtaining appropriate insurance. Useful suggestions for obtaining appropriate insurance include the following:

- Allow enough time to investigate and arrange the correct insurance. This may include asking for quotes and professional advice. Finding the right insurance broker is the first priority. Figure 16.6 gives details of an on-line method for finding the right insurance provider by using a broker.
- Make sure the event committee or company is fully covered for the whole time — that is, from the first meeting.
- Request all suppliers of products and services show that they have liability cover.
- Be prepared to give the insurance broker all information concerning the event and the companies involved. They may require a list of possible hazards, such as pyrotechnics.
- Be prepared to record the details of any damage or injury. Photographs and videos are helpful.
- Keep all records, as a claimant has 6 years to formulate a claim.
- Do not accept the transfer of liability of the suppliers to the event management.
- Check what is included and excluded in the insurance document. Rain insurance, for example, is specific about the amount and time of the rain. Are the event volunteers covered by the insurance?

- Are additional stakeholders insured? These are companies or individuals covered by the insurance but are not the named insured. The sponsors and the venue, for example, may benefit from the insurance policy.

There are many kinds of insurances that can be taken out for events. These include weather insurance; personal accident insurance for the volunteer workers; property insurance, including money; workers compensation insurance; public liability; and employers' liability. The choice of the particular insurance cover is dictated by the risk management strategy developed by event management, based on legal requirements.

The increase in premiums in all insurance areas has been a shock to the events industry and to many community festivals. Some events have been cancelled. A number of strategies have been implemented to manage this situation:

- *Bulk buying*: Through membership of some associations, for example, British Arts Festivals Association, events and event companies are able to access discounted insurance premiums through group purchasing.
- *Analysing the activities of the event at levels of risk*: The high premium may be the result of one aspect of the event. By changing or eliminating this from the event programme it may reduce the event risk seen by the insurance company.
- *Creating a comprehensive risk management procedure*: Many events that previously ignored risk management have turned to the formal risk management process. This is one positive outcome of the insurance issue. The risk management plan becomes a document used to communicate with the insurance company. Given the experience of insurance companies, it is wise to seek their input on this document.
- *Holding harmless clauses or forfeiting the right to sue*: The attendee signs a contract to the effect that they are voluntarily assuming the risk inherent in the event activity. This requires legal advice to ensure that contracts are enforceable.
- *Insuring offshore*: Some events have gone overseas for insurance. This may cause difficulties as the insurance company will be subject to the law of their country, not UK law.

Event managers are well advised to consult an insurance broker such as Event Assured, Event Insurance Services or Hiscox to ensure that they are not placing the event or themselves in a catastrophic situation where a claim can severely financially damage the event or themselves. April 2010 provided a timely reminder of the value of and need for insurance when a volcano erupted in Iceland — due to weather conditions, the resulting cloud of ash spread across the UK and Europe leading to all flights into or out of UK and European airspace being grounded for 6 days and over 95,000 flights being cancelled. With the timing falling as it did, at the end of the Easter school holidays, this had a major impact on the events industry, with hundreds of thousands of people stranded overseas or unable to travel to or from the UK. This led to the cancellation or postponement of a host of corporate events and prompted

FIGURE 16.8 Event insurance considerations for a crisis

In Case of Emergency ...
1. Notify your insurer immediately if you think you could be affected. A good insurer can help you take the necessary actions to keep the event going. Quick and decisive action could make all the difference.
2. Check your policy to see if you are covered for emergency expenditure. You may be able to claim for these costs without having prior clearance from your insurer.
3. Record keeping is key, both of expenses incurred relating to the event and gross revenue, if insured. Having these details to hand will help should you need to make a claim.

Planning future events ...
4. Organisers of events big and small should have a robust crisis management plan in place. A written plan which details alternative arrangements should the unexpected occur will assist your insurer when assessing the risk and may speed up the process of securing cover for your event.
5. Make sure you have clear contracts (with venues and suppliers, for example) which detail under what circumstances you as the organiser may be able to claim refunds or would be obliged to offer refunds. This will enable insurers to agree claims payments more quickly.
6. Buy your cover early – as soon as you've spent any money on your event. Buying early will cover you for a longer period of time, often at a lower cost than insuring closer to the event date. And if you wait too long to buy your insurance, you may not get all the protection you want.

(Source: Hiscox, 2010)

Hiscox to issue additional guidance for event organisers in the event of travel disruption due to volcanic ash, in this instance, but also generally worth noting for event organisers when planning events (Figure 16.8). On issuing the guidance, Elizabeth Seeger, underwriter at Hiscox noted:

> *We are seeing that some customers are experiencing disruption with international delegates and exhibitors not being able to fly in to attend their events. On the ground level at the event venue, all is working fine but it's getting people in that's difficult.*
>
> *Events may be entirely cancelled if there are key speakers or performers who cannot attend.*
>
> *The chaos caused by the volcanic ash drifting over the UK illustrates how the unexpected can bring months of event planning to a sudden halt.*

REGULATIONS, LICENCES AND PERMITS

There are long lists of regulations that need to be adhered to when staging events. The bigger, more complex or innovative the event, potentially the larger the range of regulations to which it must adhere. To avoid inadvertently contravening any legal regulation that governs the conduct of events, it is necessary to conduct rigorous research to establish what needs to be done. Inquiries with events of a similar nature is a good place to start, and then with local government officials. The correct procedure in one local authority, county or country within the UK may be slightly different in another. The principal rule is to carry out careful research, including investigating similar events in the same area and seeking advice on what permits and licences are necessary to allow an event to proceed.

It is always the responsibility of an event company to find out and comply with all pertinent rules, regulations and licensing requirements. For example, in reviewing the then Public Entertainment Licence application for Glastonbury Festival 2005, the report from the Environmental Health Manager to the licensing authority at Mendip District Council includes input from a wide range of authorities including Mendip District Council, Avon and Somerset Police, Somerset Fire Authority, Westcountry Ambulance Services NHS Trust, Somerset Health Protection Unit, Mendip Primary Care Trust, Environment Agency, Somerset County Highways Authority, Emergency Planning Authority and the local Parish Councils (Kirkwood, 2004).

Many local authorities apply environmental noise control protocols to control the impact of noise on communities, with guidance available from the Noise Council (Noise Council, 1995; HSE, 1999), while the recently updated *Control of Noise at Work Regulations 2005*, which came into force in music and entertainment sectors in April 2008, will reduce the sound levels at which action must be taken to ensure that employees and those exposed to excess noise (for example, sound checks and performances at concerts) are protected (Howden, 2004). The website Sound Advice (www.soundadvice.info) provides a useful source of guidance on the application of this Act to events, entertainment and venues. Event managers must make it a practice to pay particular attention to workplace health and safety regulations.

As an example of the range of regulations that event organisations must comply with, AEO, BECA and EVA (2002, p. A1) identified some of the relevant regulations with which an exhibition must comply during build-up, breakdown and while the exhibition is open (Figure 16.9). The Events Industry Alliance (2009) now produces *eGuide* where up-to-date guidance on current requirements at member venues may be consulted. It should be noted that legislation evolves over time; therefore, it is evident that an exhibition or event manager may need to seek legal, professional or business advice to ensure compliance with all current and relevant regulations, particularly as these are not fixed and may be updated or replaced or additional regulations may be added — organisations such as the HSE, Business Link and industry associations can prove to be a useful source of information in this respect.

The Performing Right Society (PRS) and Phonographic Performance Ltd (PPL) issue licences for the performance of their members' works. They function as a collection society, monitoring and collecting royalties on behalf of their members (music composers and their publishers). So when an event company decides to set fireworks to music, it is not just a matter of hiring a band or pressing 'play' on the sound system.

FIGURE 16.9 Examples of regulations applying to exhibitions

- Electricity at Work Regulations 1998 /EVA Regulations For Stand Electrical Installations
- Environmental Protection Act 1990 / Environment Act 1995
- Health & Safety (First Aid) regulations 1981
- Health & Safety at Work, etc., Act 1974
- Management of Health & Safety at Work Regulations 1999
- Manual Handling Operations Regulations 1992, as amended 2002
- Noise at Work Regulations 1989 (updated 2005)
- Personal Protective Equipment at Work Regulations 1992
- Provision and Use of Work Equipment Regulations 1998
- Reporting of Injuries, Diseases and Dangerous Occurrences Regulations (RIDDOR) 1995
- The Building Regulations
- The Building Standards (Scotland) Regulations 2004
- The Fire Precautions (Workplace) Regulations 1997 as amended 1999
- The Health & Safety (Signs and Signals) Regulations 1996
- The Lifting Operations and Lifting Equipment Regulations (LOLER) 1998
- Workplace (Health, Safety and Welfare) Regulations 1992

(Source: adapted from AEO, BECA and EVA, 2002, p. A1)

Permits and licences are required for many events to take place and for activities associated with this, including the handling of food, entertainment, pyrotechnics, sale of alcohol, street trading and road closures. Licensing differs between England/ Wales and Scotland and Northern Ireland due to different legal frameworks. For example, in England and Wales the Licensing Act 2003 (HMSO, 2003) has established a single integrated system for licensing premises used to supply alcohol, provide regulated entertainment or provide regulated late night refreshment. This new Act has been designed to cut down on red tape by bringing together six existing licensing regimes (alcohol, public entertainment, cinemas, theatres, late night refreshment house and night cafes). Three types of licences available are premises licence, temporary events notice and club premises certificate. Regulated entertainment includes the performance of a play, an exhibition of a film, an indoor sporting event, boxing or wrestling entertainment, a performance of live music, any playing of recorded music, a performance of dance, or entertainment of a similar description to live music, recorded music or dance. The key principles underpinning licensing are to prevent crime and disorder, public safety, prevention of public nuisance and the protection of children. As a result, many events where an audience or spectators are being entertained will be covered by the regulations and will require a licence, even if the audience is not paying for the entertainment. Applications for licences must be made with the appropriate local authority. There are exclusions for some types of events; however, it is advisable to review the specific requirements of the licences to identify these. The Live Music Forum, including representatives of industry, government, local authorities and the Arts Council, small venue operators and others, met from 2004 to 2007 to maximise take-up of the reforms relating to live music, promote live music and monitor and evaluate the impact of the Licensing Act 2003 (DCMS, 2007). Detailed guidance on the Act and the process to follow is available from the Department for Culture, Media and Sport (www.culture.gov.uk) or from the local authority where the event will take place.

In Scotland, under Section 41 of the Civic Government (Scotland) Act 1982 a Public Entertainment or Temporary Public Entertainment licence is required for premises or any place where public entertainment, such as dancing, concerts, a variety show or other entertainment where the public are admitted for payment of an admission fee, or where they are required to buy something to attend, such as a programme. A separate public entertainment licence is not required for licensed liquor premises due to an exemption, but the liquor licence will indicate what entertainment can take place on the premises. The Licensing Section of local authorities in Scotland can provide further information and application forms. Finally, in Northern Ireland indoor and outdoor public entertainment, including singing, dancing, music, and public contests, is licensed under the Local Government (Miscellaneous Provisions) (Northern Ireland) Order 1985. Provision is made for annual or occasional licences. Licences are administered by the building control section of local authorities in Northern Ireland who can provide guidance and application forms.

In July 2007, England and Wales followed Scotland (2006), Northern Ireland (April 2007), the Republic of Ireland (2004) and other countries in Europe and internationally to introduce legislation to control smoking in enclosed public spaces. The Smokefree (Premises and Enforcement) Regulations 2006, introduced under the Health Act 2006, made it illegal for people to smoke in all public enclosed spaces, public transport, work vehicles and workplaces with few exceptions. The introduction was predicted to have a major impact on entertainment venues such as bars, restaurants and nightclubs, where smoking by some was a feature of their social life, however, it appears that people have generally adapted to the new environment. This legislation was introduced to protect employees and the general public from the harmful effects of passive smoking. As well as banning smoking, it requires No Smoking signs to be displayed in all smoke free premises and requires anyone wanting to smoke to go outside (therefore, staff indoor smoking areas were also removed). Useful sources of advice are the government websites www.smokefreeengland.co.uk, www.spacetobreathe.org.uk and www.clearingtheairscotland.com.

The complex area of regulations, licences and permits needs the close attention of event management, particularly as legislation differs across the countries within the UK and overseas. Companies must undertake detailed research into all regulations affecting their event and should allocate time to deal with the results of that research. Government agencies can take a long time to respond to requests and formal processes may have pre-determined timescales that must be adhered to. Therefore, it is imperative to begin early in seeking any permits or licences, and to factor delays and difficulties with obtaining them in the time frame of the event planning process.

SUMMARY

Event managers have a responsibility to understand the legal requirements of event production. Also, they have a duty of care to all involved in the event. Any reasonably foreseen risks to stakeholders have to be eliminated or minimised to avoid legal liability. Therefore, minimising any legal liability is part of the job of event managers. This includes identifying the ownership of the event, careful structuring of the event management, taking out insurance, and adhering to all laws, rules and regulations pertaining to the event. Specific legal issues of concern to the event management team include licensing, contracting, trademarks and trade practices, while the introduction of the Corporate Manslaughter and Corporate Homicide Act 2007 has added weight to existing health and safety legislation. Legal matters can be complex, where the interpretation can differ from council to council and legislation can differ between countries including within the UK, particularly between England/Wales and Scotland or Northern Ireland. The information discussed within this chapter provides a brief overview of issues to consider; however, as regulations and guidelines are subject to constant change, it is highly recommended that any event company seek legal advice when unsure of these matters.

QUESTIONS

1. Explain why it is necessary for an event manager to understand the concept of 'duty of care'.

2. List the areas covered by the contract between an event company and its supplier of audiovisuals.

3. Why do organisations such as PRS PPL exist?

4. What are the elements that should be found in a contract for the supply of a venue for an international conference?

5. Why should a community festival that takes place in a public park take out public liability insurance?

6. What actions can be taken to reduce the cost of overall liability insurance? Should the event company be insured for patrons to be covered after they leave the event?

7. Investigate what licences and permits are needed for a community festival that takes place in a public park that you are familiar with, at which both recorded and live music will be played.

CASE STUDY: RADIO ONE LOVE PARADE, LEEDS, BY LOGISTIK

Background

The Love Parade ran for the first time in the UK in Leeds in July 2000. Following discussions with the Berlin Love Parade organisers, Radio One undertook to organise the dance music-based event in the UK. The event concept involved a parade of 20 floats, sponsored by the leading dance music clubs in the UK, leading to a large, free open-air dance music event. Radio One signed an agreement to use the name 'Love Parade' in the UK and financially underwrote the event – they also promoted it and stimulated interest in the event. Logistik was ultimately tasked with putting together the event, managing it, staging it and running it. A third party was contracted to get support from all the big dance clubs in the UK who bought floats. Leeds City Council's role was as host and to help ensure the event went off well.

The concept

The mission was initially to establish and run a Love Parade in the UK, in association with the German event. Historically, there has been a lot of animosity between Germany and England and events such as this are positive in developing cultural links. The Love Parade in Berlin is well documented – it was established to celebrate the fall of the Berlin Wall, which proved to be an excellent stimulant for running an event. The underlying principle for both the German and UK events was that everybody, regardless of class, money, background or status, had an equal opportunity to attend, join in with the event, and they could do that regardless of their financial position in life. Radio One supported this event wholeheartedly as it was an event open to everyone, clearly relating to their ethos of One Love.

The aims were to hold a free, safe and well-attended event. These were clearly achieved. In addition, the objective, from an organiser's point of view, was to develop the event in such a manner that it could be developed and move on to another city – in 2001 the event moved to Newcastle.

Audience size

In order to determine the potential audiences for the Love Parade, a number of previous events were researched, including the road shows, the Big Sundays, and other events organised by Radio One, together with experience at previous dance events. The resulting audience was estimated at being 250,000 (based on aerial photography and working out the number of people per square meter). This unprecedented audience resulted from two areas. Firstly, there was a high level of support from the youth press as it was unique and it caught the youths' imagination. Secondly, Radio One succeeded in their promotion of it – the event itself caught people's imagination, with a worldwide fellowship of people who love music, love to party, love to have a good time, behave themselves and like to link up with Berlin.

The venue, facilities and staff

The venue for the event changed from the City Centre to Roundhay Park in Leeds 4 weeks before the event, due to concerns expressed by the police over the growth in anticipated audience. Roundhay Park is basically a big open field and as a result, the event site was built from scratch, including a large volume of toilets, food franchises, drinks franchises, bars and standpipes with free water. West Yorkshire Ambulance Service and the Drugs Advisory Group in Leeds provided first aid stations and counselling. Transport was provided with a bus service running up to Roundhay from the City Centre. On site, three free stages and 20 free floats were provided for the audience to watch.

The management structure included a parade manager, site manager, production manager, stage manager, float managers, float stewards, event managers and an event director. The team also included approximately 500 stewards from ShowSec International, a health and safety team,

600 police officers, West Yorkshire Ambulance Service, Drugs Advisory Services and Leeds City Council Cleansing Services. In addition to this, contracts for services were signed with many suppliers.

The licensing and planning process

Planning commenced a year in advance where tacit agreement for the event was obtained from Leeds City Council, followed by the normal system of multi-agency discussion. Within the licensing framework, there was a fairly well-understood set of steps that you go through to get a public entertainment licence. The basis is that a meeting is organised with the multi-agency group where the concept and aims are explained, from which will come hundreds of questions. Following this, a number of submeetings follow with environmental health (sound and toilets), the highways department (road closures) and the police (public order). The process involves risk assessments, safety plans, crowd control statements and mission statements.

Documentation is refined to incorporate the above items and this is then built into the event plan. In this respect, simple is best. While you can write reams of documentation, which can be as detailed as you want it to be, it has to be broadly understood by all those that are involved with the event, not just a key group of people who happen to be in a meeting. All the people involved in the event from the management team to the stewards and the medics have all got to have a good understanding of what's drawn from these meetings, what is being aimed for and what to do in the event of x, y and z. Regardless of the size of the event, you still need a simple plan that everyone understands and can work to. This is the normal process for organising events – clearly it was a lot more complicated for Love Parade due to the scale of the event. Because of the nature of this event, it was very difficult to stick to any sort of well-understood and pre-agreed formulas for getting permissions for the event through Leeds City Council and other agencies. Very quickly people realised that the event that they had agreed to had changed somewhat, because Radio One was the promoter and it was going to be a lot bigger. There was concern in some quarters that they were hosting the equivalent of the Notting Hill Carnival for dance music and peoples' attitudes changed. There was debate within Leeds City Council and with the multi-agency group, led by the police, about how the event could best be licensed and whether it should be licensed at all. The debate went on right up until the actual event – ultimately, it had a public entertainment licence at Roundhay Park (and a drinks licence), however, this was only resolved a few weeks before the event.

As a company, Logistik has insurance for employees, public, professional and hired in plant. In addition, specific insurance was taken out to cover the Love Parade and increased the amounts on the other insurance to cover this size of event. The insurance indemnified everyone involved.

Consultation

Consultation with the local community was limited and not as it should have been due to the short time that was available following the move to Roundhay Park. As organisers, it can be problematic keeping the balance between canvassing opinion and planning the event, when some communities clearly object to events taking place near them, particularly at this scale. Although there was only a short time available before the event, meetings were arranged with a number of community groups, followed by further meetings and correspondence after the event to listen to people's views. Some of these were irate and unreasonable, but a lot of them were good meaning and contributed constructively. The city council also put together a questionnaire that was distributed to the local community to gain feedback. There was a fair amount of consultation afterwards but this did not make up for the fact that there was not enough time to conduct effective consultation beforehand.

Evaluation

Generally, whether the event was a success depends on who is asked – it has to be looked at on balance and in the context of what was achieved. You could ask three different people 'was the

Continued

CASE STUDY: RADIO ONE LOVE PARADE, LEEDS, BY LOGISTIK—*CONT'D*

event a success?' and, depending on their age, outlook on life and geographical position (where they lived), they would give you three completely different answers. If you were under 30 and came to the event specifically to enjoy yourself, you would say it was an absolutely phenomenal success with 250,000 people, no major incidents in terms of injury, people had a really good time, it was a friendly atmosphere and there were no public order problems. If you talked to people who own shops in Leeds, the majority would think it was a success because it brought a huge amount of income into the city – an economic impact of around £15 million was reported purely in relation to the Love Parade. However, if you were resident, living near Roundhay Park, who does not like dance music and does not like their normal everyday life being interrupted, then you would have a completely different view on the success of the event. They probably believe that it was not right for two reasons. Firstly, clearly such a huge event has a massive impact and disrupts people's lives – no matter what you do, that is a consequence of holding this sort of event. Secondly, culturally a lot of older people have a great distrust and dislike of dance music, even the type of people and their motivation for coming along. If you look at it from those people's point of view, they would say it was a terrible event and it should not have been allowed. They were supported by some journalists in the very conservative local press who were outspoken about their opposition to the event and the problems that it caused.

In our view, the event was a success – it went off predominantly well and safely (against a huge amount of opposition) and it showed that if you give young people something to do and put together something that is meaningful to them, they will come along in huge numbers, enjoy themselves and behave themselves. However, Logistik learned a lot from developing this event and there are a number of areas where we can improve for the future. Firstly, we now fully understand the differences between the cultures of the police and the cultures of people who they perceived would be coming to the event. The Leeds Love Parade illustrated that many of the initial fears were unfounded. Secondly, the well-documented funding issue should be resolved with the police at the start of the process. With the experience of Leeds Love Parade, issues raised, including the size of the event, together with the concerns of residents and other stakeholders, will be addressed within the planning stages for future events to ensure that they meet the increasingly stringent requirements of the multi-agency groups.

For further details about Logistik events, please visit www.logistik.co.uk.

By Logistik Ltd.

Questions

1. What characteristics of Leeds do you think lead to it being chosen as the location for the first Love Parade in the UK?
2. What contracts and licences were considered necessary for the event? From what you know of the event, do these measures seem adequate? If not, what other areas of the event might usefully have been covered by written agreements?
3. The increased size of the event affected the perceived risk involved in staging it, leading to the move to Roundhay Park. What could organisers do to control the size of the event?
4. What lessons can be learned regarding the planning of the event, and how would you apply these lessons if you were organising a Love Parade in the future?

CASE STUDY: MARIA ALEXIOU *V* SOCOG (2001)

On 15 September 2000, much of the world watched as athletes, their families, guests, local residents, interstate and overseas visitors, dignitaries, officials, volunteers and the media gathered in Sydney, Australia, to take part in and observe the biggest event in the world – the opening ceremony of the XXVII Olympic Games. Four members of the Alexiou family purchased 'A' category seats for the opening ceremony and for the closing ceremony, athletics and weightlifting, at a total cost of $9337.

At the opening ceremony, the applicants had seats in the second row from the front in the southern stand. They arrived at the Olympic stadium with great expectations about their seating. Sadly, according to their evidence, the seating was 'heartbreaking' and rather than experiencing the event of a lifetime, they were 'shattered', 'devastated' and their 'excitement ended in tears'. One member of the family said 'This evening I looked so forward to became the biggest disap-pointment of my life'.

The Alexious complained that during the opening ceremony large props were 'parked' in front of them; and even though they were close to the athletes and to the performers, they could not see the overall pattern of events because they were not high enough. In short, they argued that they did not have the best seats, which is what they expected category A to be.

SOCOG relied on a written statement from the artistic director and producer of the opening and closing ceremonies, who stated 'In the case of an arena spectacular, there is no "best" seat, or "best view". No matter where you were sitting in the stadium, you got a different viewing perspective, but one position was not "better" than the other.'

SOCOG offered other evidence to show that spectators close to the arena enjoyed a sense of participation in the opening ceremony: the athletes in fact paraded immediately in front of the Alexious' seats; the Olympic torch entered the arena from close to their seats. It was also proposed by SOCOG that people sitting close to the arena had excellent opportunities for involvement with what was happening, and were able to see the details of the athletes, the costumes and the performers.

The Alexious also complained that their seats for the closing ceremony were unsatisfactory – they were in the northern stand 24 rows from the front. In a written statement, Maria Alexiou gave details of her distress: 'My husband had to console me as I had a panic attack when I saw our seating. I was shattered.' Apparently the Alexious expected that they would see each of the performers and floats pass in front of them, which they did not and that accordingly they did not have the best seats in the stadium.

According to SOCOG those seats had uninterrupted views of the entire arena. The artistic director and producer added: 'The performance was arranged so that the audience would have an entertainment experience viewing from all areas of the circular stadium. The views from different parts of the stadium were not the same, but one position did not afford a "better" view than another …. It was a theatrical performance, not a street parade where every piece of equipment performs a "march past" every area of the stadium.'

For the athletics the Alexious again complained that they paid too much money for the seats they obtained because they were in row 49. SOCOG gave evidence that the seating was indeed A category and that there were 77 rows of seating behind where the Alexious sat.

The weightlifting tickets were bought after the other tickets and at a time when most of the better seating had already been sold. All seating for the weightlifting was the same price because it was a small venue. Moreover, SOCOG claimed venue maps were available for review at the place of purchase and the Alexious would therefore have been able to identify the location of available seats before buying them. Nonetheless, the Alexious considered that their seating for the weightlifting was also unsatisfactory because they could not see clearly, in particular the scoreboard.

Continued

CASE STUDY: MARIA ALEXIOU *V* SOCOG (2001)—*CONT'D*

The Alexious brought legal action in the Fair Trading Tribunal of New South Wales (the state of Australia in which Sydney is situated) against SOCOG, on the grounds that SOCOG

- engaged in misleading and deceptive conduct.
- broke its contract or
- engaged in misrepresentation as to the quality or grade of the Alexious' seating at the Sydney Olympic Games.

In essence the Alexious claimed that SOCOG had falsely advertised in that they offered the experience of a lifetime; that they had breached their contract in that they did not give 'the best seats' and they had misrepresented the quality of the seats as A grade when in reality they were inferior. Of greater significance perhaps is one of the remedies they sought. In addition to a refund of all or part of the cost of the tickets they also requested $5000 compensation each for the loss of enjoyment, distress and disappointment they experienced as a result of their expectations not being met. These expectations, it was claimed, arose out of the advertising and ticket category they purchased.

Under Australian, English and European law, for contracts the object of which is to provide entertainment, enjoyment, pleasure or relaxation – which includes contracts for a sporting or cultural event – the aggrieved party may receive compensation for their disappointment and loss of enjoyment upon not receiving that which was promised either in their contract (which includes a ticket) or in any advertising. This compensation is in addition to any refund or compensation for any other loss a person may suffer.

The Court found that the Alexiou family had genuinely suffered distress. Nonetheless, their distress, however severe and however genuine, did not of itself entitle members of the Alexiou family to a full refund of the money they paid to SOCOG for their Olympic Games tickets, nor to any compensation for their loss of enjoyment and mental distress. To be entitled to relief they had to show that SOCOG broke its contract with them, or engaged in misleading or deceptive conduct or a misrepresentation as to the quality of their seating. However, in this case the Tribunal determined on the balance of probabilities (the standard of proof required for a civil hearing) there was insufficient evidence to support a finding that SOCOG had engaged in misleading and deceptive conduct, or that SOCOG engaged in any misrepresentation as to the quality or grade of the Alexious' Olympic Games seating or that there was any breach of contract by SOCOG – they had purchased and received A grade seats with appropriate views. In short, the Alexious did not show that SOCOG was legally responsible for their distress and accordingly were not entitled to any refund or compensation.

Lessons for event

This case makes it clear that event promoters and organisers need to be very careful in what they promise to prospective customers of their events. Contracts to events most certainly fall into the category of contracts for pleasure, entertainment, enjoyment or relaxation. As such it is possible for a disgruntled event spectator or participant to claim loss of enjoyment damages for breach of contract. Some event-based situations which may give rise to such claims include:

1. failure to see the event,
2. failure to receive quality of seats expected,
3. provision of inadequate food,
4. not enough competitors,
5. rowdy spectators and
6. star performer not appearing.

What is crucial for an event patron to succeed in an action for loss of enjoyment is to show that there has been a breach of either a term of the contract or of any promise contained in any event advertising or other promotional material. What is crucial for an event organiser is to keep all promises to patrons.

Paul Jonson, BA (Hons), LLB, GDLS, PhD, Associate Professor, University of Technology, Sydney; Director, Academic Programme, Sport Knowledge Australia.

Questions

1. Did SOCOG have any liability to the Alexiou family?
2. Should SOCOG have refunded the ticket price to avoid going to court?
3. How could SOCOG have managed better the expectations of the Alexiou family?
4. What lessons are there for event managers from the Alexiou case?

Risk management

17

LEARNING OBJECTIVES

After studying this chapter, you should be able to:

- define risk and its relationship to the management of festivals and events,
- understand the context of risk management in the event management process,
- use the tools of risk identification and identify the risks specific to events,
- understand the latest methodologies of risk management,
- understand the core concepts of occupational health and safety.

INTRODUCTION

The Event Management Body of Knowledge (EMBOK, 2006) identified risk management as one of the five knowledge domains necessary for the management of an event. With the growth of the festival and event sector around the world, governments and other key stakeholders realise that they are partially liable for the conduct of events. This is driving the adoption of a formalised risk management procedure for all events. As the number and size of events and festivals increases, so does the public awareness of any mishaps or disasters. Any mistakes made during the planning and execution of major public events such as the Olympics and the Grand Prix reach the press immediately. At the same time it is inevitable that with more events, there is the potential for more mistakes. This is also driving the occupational health and safety acts in each country. The planning of events and festivals can no longer be ignored by the authorities. They realise that an incident at an event is too often a result of incompetence in management; therefore, they want proof of management competency long before the festival or event starts.

A working definition of event risk is any future incident that will negatively influence the event. It could also be described simply as 'possible problems'. Note that this risk is not solely at the event itself. In many texts on events, risk is taken to mean direct safety risk or financial risk, but this definition ignores problems in other areas of event management that may harmfully influence the success of the event. Fraud, for example, is a risk that has surfaced at many events. Misrepresentation of the event by marketing or over promotion is another risk. Each of these risks may result in safety and financial troubles at the event.

Risk, in the event context, may be formally defined as the likelihood and consequence of the event or festival not fulfilling its objectives. Risk management

Events Management. DOI: 10.1016/B978-1-85617-818-1.10017-9

can be defined as the process of identifying these problems, assessing them and dealing with them. Fortunately, risk management may also uncover opportunities. In the past, this may have been done in an informal manner; however, the current management environment demands that the process be formalised. The event team must be able to show that risk management is being employed throughout the project. This chapter outlines the process of risk management. The process is made up of understanding the context of risk, risk identification, evaluation and control. This process can be applied to all the areas of event management.

RISK MANAGEMENT PROCESS

Events are particularly susceptible to risks. A unique venue, large crowds, new staff and volunteers, movement of equipment and general excitement are all a recipe for potential hazards. The event manager who ignores advice on risk prevention is courting disaster and foreshortening his or her career in the event industry. The sensible assessment of potential hazards and preventive action is the basis of risk management, and is a legal requirement under the Management of Health and Safety at Work Regulations 1992. According to the Health and Safety Executive (HSE, 1999, p. 7) risk may be defined as 'the likelihood that harm from a hazard is realised and the extent of it'.

Risk is not necessarily harmful. One reason, among many, that an event company wins the job of organising an event is that competing companies perceive the event to be too risky. The successful company can manage all the risks with its current resources. Risk is the basis of the entrepreneur's business. Without risk, there can be no competitive advantage. Without the appearance of risk, there can be no tightrope walking or extreme games. Part of what makes an event special is the uncertainty — it has not been done before.

The British Standards Institution (BSI, 2002a, p. 7) defines risk management as the:

> *systematic application of management policies, procedures and practices to the tasks of establishing the context, identifying, analysing, evaluating, treating, monitoring and communicating risk*

Every part of event management has potential risks. Various publications exist to assist the event manager in managing risk, including general publications offered by HSE (2006) and guidance developed for exhibitions (AEO, BECA and EVA, 2002; EIA, 2009), music events (HSE, 1999), outdoor events other than pop concerts and raves (NOEA, 1993, 1997), sporting grounds (Department of National Heritage and the Scottish Office, 1997) and crowd safety (HSE, 2000). PAS 51: 2004 (BSI, 2004) has been developed to provide practical guidance for organising all outdoor events and cross-references to existing publications/regulations that event organisers should be aware of. Furthermore, a number of additional publications have been developed specifically for events (Berlonghi, 1990; Hannam, 2004; Kemp and Hill,

2004; Silvers, 2008; Tarlow, 2002). Possibly the best known out of the publications, sometimes referred to as the Purple Guide, is *The Event Safety Guide* (HSE, 1999), which was at the time of writing being reviewed and updated. Designed to provide advice for the safe management of music events, concerts and festivals, the guide separates events into five phases where risk can be assessed:

- *Build-up*: This involves planning the venue design, selection of competent workers, selection of contractors and subcontractors, and construction, for example, of the stage, marquees and fences.
- *Load in*: This involves planning for the safe delivery and installation of equipment and services which will be used at the event, for example, stage equipment used by performers, lighting and sound systems.
- *Show*: This involves planning effective crowd management strategies, transport management strategies and welfare arrangements and planning strategies for dealing with fire, first aid, contingencies and major incidents.
- *Load out*: This requires planning for the safe removal of equipment and services.
- *Breakdown*: This includes planning to control risks once the event is over and the infrastructure is being dismantled, including disposal of waste water and rubbish.

Berlonghi (1990) categorises the main areas of risk as follows:

- *Administration*: The organisational structure and office layout should minimise risk to employees.
- *Marketing and public relations*: The promotion section must be aware of the need for risk management. By their nature, marketers are optimistic about the consequences of their actions and tend to ignore potential risks.
- *Health and safety*: A large part of risk management concerns this area. Loss prevention plans and safety control plans are an important part of any risk management strategy. The risks associated with food concession hygiene and sanitation require specific attention.
- *Crowd management*: Risk management of crowd flow, alcohol sales and noise control (see Chapter 15 on logistics).
- *Security*: The security plan for an event involves careful risk management thinking.
- *Transport*: Deliveries, parking and public transport contain many potential hazards that need to be addressed.

A good risk management strategy will also cover any other operational areas that are crucial to the event and that may need special security and safety precautions, such as ticket sales and other cash points and communications.

Risk management is an integral part of the larger picture of event strategic planning. The event portfolio or event programme of a government or a company undergoes the risk management process. The likelihood and consequence of success or failure is a major consideration in the strategic planning. A portfolio of events and festivals will be subject to a comparison so that the level of support can be ascertained. A consideration in this comparison is the probability of success. Operational risk, such as a melee at a tennis match, will affect the reputation of the event and this may flow into the long-term planning of the event. These areas of strategic planning are described in Chapter 5.

In Chapter 6, the areas of event project management are introduced and risk is one of those areas, but it is not an isolated area. The risk management process cuts right across all the other knowledge areas. In any one of the areas of knowledge and management, the risks must be identified and pre-empted, and their management fully integrated into the event plan. By using a project management approach to the event, risk management becomes an underlying process that is employed continuously in every area of the management. Figure 17.1 identifies nine steps taken to assess the risks associated with staging events.

Figure 17.2 shows the risk management process as explained in this chapter. It begins by the event team understanding the environment or context of risk. This is combined with the expectations of the stakeholders, the constraints of the other event plans and an understanding of risks that are unique to events. The risks are identified and analysed. Once the risks are understood, the action necessary to mitigate the risk is decided. The description of the risk, its analysis and the treatment form the risk register. From the risk register arises critical tasks that become part of the event plans. Once the event occurs this whole process is evaluated and used to assist the next risk management process. Although this diagram is structured as

FIGURE 17.1 Nine steps to risk management

Step 1	Understanding context: Consider event type, management, stakeholders and general environment
Step 2	Identifying risks: Look for the hazards
Step 3	Decision: Decide who might be harmed and how
Step 4	Evaluating the Risk: Evaluate the risks and decide whether the existing precautions are adequate or whether more should be done.
Step 5	Control: Control problems that may arise
Step 6	Mitigating actions: Consider mitigating actions
Step 7	Specific event risks: Consider specific event risks
Step 8	Recording: Record your findings and implement them
Step 9	Review: Review your assessment and update if necessary

(Source: adapted from HSE, 2006, p. 2)

FIGURE 17.2 Risk management process

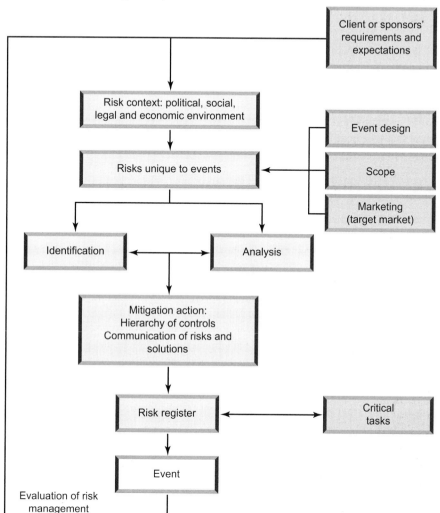

(Source: O'Toole, 2006)

a flow chart, risk management does not follow such a simple step-by-step process. The event team must be aware of risk at all times. This chapter will explain in detail these elements of the risk management process.

A simple example of this is as follows. A risk that is all too common in events is problems with the master of ceremonies (MC). The event team decides that the comedian who has been hired to be the MC could insult the sponsor. They know this because it has happened at other events and the sponsor has been in the press recently. This is the context of the risk. They analyse the risk and decide that it deserves attention. Next they must minimise the risk. The treatment options are numerous:

- tell the comedian not to make jokes about the sponsor,
- revoke the hiring and hire a professional MC or
- tell the sponsor there may be jokes.

These options are placed in the risk register. Whichever event option it decides will need to be acted upon by one of the team. Therefore, the risk register will create a task that is critical. The task of finding an alternative MC, for example, will then be put in the overall project or event plan.

Understanding context

The context of risk management includes the type of event, the management structure, the stakeholder analysis and the general risk environment. Throwing white powder, for example, was considered a major danger at events a few years ago due to the publicity about the anthrax scare. White powder incidents were logged each week around the world — these were hoaxes. However, an incident could cause a stampede if any crowd member thought the powder was anthrax. Today, throwing white powder (as is done during the Indian Holi festival in many cities) might not rate a mention in the press. Terrorism is a major concern for some events. While the attacks on the World Trade Center and Pentagon in 2001 increased the perceived threat in countries previously thought safe from terrorism, it must be remembered that terrorism at events has been a concern since the Munich Olympics. In India, the terrorism threat and reality has been an ongoing concern since 1947. The 2001 attacks in the USA and the numerous violent incidents, such as the bombs in Bali, 2004 attacks in Madrid and the 2005 attacks in the UK, have increased the public perception in western countries of this risk. Some nations deal with terrorism as part of their day-to-day security. Large events, as they attract global media interest, can be a terrorism target. The conclusion is that the surrounding environment, whether it is political, economic, social or cultural, has to be taken into account in the risk management process. The organisational cultures of the client and the event company are also part of the context to be considered.

Some companies or organisations are highly risk averse and would prefer a predictable event that has been tried and tested for many years. These clients prefer the 'franchised' event. A large part of the risk will originate with or involve the stakeholders. A comprehensive stakeholder analysis is a prerequisite for thorough risk management. The stakeholders may also provide the support to deal with the risks. The legislation on duty of care and public liability are further examples of the event environment that will impinge on the risk management process. The financial risk is an example of an ever-changing context. The currency exchange rate, the financial state of the sponsors, fraud and the demands of the shareholders are some of the external developments that can affect the financial viability of the event.

FIGURE 17.3 A risk due to the changes in the regulatory environment

BOSSES PULL THE PLUG ON PARTIES

Bruised by the threat of lawsuits under discrimination and health and safety laws, employers are increasingly often dodging the responsibility of organising office Christmas parties.

The chief executive of the business lobby group Employers First, Garry Brack, painted a grim picture for employers hosting parties under occupational health and safety laws.

'These days you have got to provide a perfectly safe environment for your staff,' he said. 'Can you imagine that is sensible in any set of circumstances?'
Add booze to the mix and it becomes nearly impossible.

'You've got to make sure they don't drink too much; make sure they don't get hurt; make sure they get home safely. Have you got the cab driver's phone number?'

According to Mr Brack, to avoid a discrimination claim if a drunken staff member breaks the law an employer would have to organise training in the lead-up to the event and keep tabs on how much people were drinking at the party.

Despite the difficulties, many Australian employers are still sponsoring parties, defying a trend in Britain.

There, a survey of 3500 company bosses found four out of five would not organise a party in the run-up to Christmas.

Almost all of those questioned in the British survey said festive parties caused arguments among staff and often led to official complaints, and two-thirds said they had sacked a member of staff because of their behaviour.

(Source: O'Malley, 2005)

A comprehensive risk assessment cannot be performed without understanding the context of the event, the risk environment, such as the incidents that have occurred in the past, and the stakeholders' requirements. One must remember this context is changing and therefore needs to be reassessed as the event management progresses.

Figure 17.3 illustrates a risk due to the changing regulatory environment. The office party is almost seen as a fixed part of the corporate calendar. However, an unintended effect of the legislation is the cancellation of what some people might regard as a harmless pursuit. One event company, however, realised an opportunity. It was willing to organise and be responsible for office parties.

Identifying risks

The next stage in the process is identifying the risks. Pre-empting problems requires skill, experience and knowledge. Something that appears safe to some of the event staff may contain hidden dangers. A sponsor's sign at an event may look securely mounted when examined by the marketing manager, but it will require the specialist knowledge of the stagehands to ensure it is secure. As the event manager cannot be an expert in every field, it is best to pool the experience of all the event staff and volunteers by convening a risk assessment meeting. Such a meeting should aim to gather risk management expertise. For large or complex events, an event risk consultant may be hired. The meeting is also an opportunity to train and motivate event staff in the awareness, minimisation and control of risks. Under health and safety regulations, the meeting with staff and their input is mandatory for a safe work environment (HSE, 2008). This is described in the section on consultation.

Identification techniques

Risk can arise anywhere in the management of events. It is essential that the event team has numerous techniques available to it. Several of these techniques, such as using the work breakdown structure (WBS) and fault diagrams, were developed in project management and operation management. Some are common in the military and emergency services, such as scenario development.

- *Work breakdown structure*: Breaking down the work necessary to create an event into manageable parts can greatly assist in the identification of risks. It provides a visual scheme as well as the categorisation of the event into units associated with specific skills and resources. An example of the WBS is found in Chapter 6. Isolating the event areas in this way gives a clear picture of the possible problems. One of the areas of the WBS for an award night, for example, is the work associated with the MC. This question has been posed at many event workshops: 'What could go wrong with the MC?' Some of the problems identified by event manager's experience include being inebriated, not turning up, leaving early, not reading the script, using inappropriate language, having a scruffy appearance, believing they are the main act, being unable to use a microphone and insulting the sponsor. This does not imply that these are common problems; however, an event manager would be foolish to ignore the experience of others. The construction of a WBS assists another area of management − the creation of a risk management plan − and thus illustrates the importance of the project management system to event management. Although the WBS is a necessary tool for risk management, it may not reveal the problems that result in a combination of risks. A problem with the ticketing of an event, for example, may not be severe on its own. If it is combined with the withdrawal of a major sponsor, the result may require the event to be cancelled.
- *Test events*: Large sporting events often run smaller events to test the facilities, equipment and other resources. The Olympics test events were effectively used to iron out any problems before the main event. A test is a self-funded rehearsal. The pre-conference cocktail party, for example, is used to test some aspects of the conference. It can test the venue parking, caterer, sound system and type of performers. Many music festivals will run an opening concert on the night before the first day of the festival, as a means of testing the equipment.
- *Classifying risk and SWOT*: To assist risk analysis, it is useful to have a classification system according to the origin of the risk. Internal risks arise in the event planning and implementation stage. They may also result from the inexperience of the event company. These risks are generally within the abilities of the event company to manage. External risks arise from outside the event organisation and may need a different control strategy. This technique focuses on mitigating the

impact of the risk — dealing with the consequences. The impact of a star football player cancelling, for example, may be minimised by allowing free entry to the event. For this reason, the SWOT analysis is a risk identification technique. The strengths and weaknesses correspond to internal risks, and the opportunities and threats correspond to the external risks.

- *Fault diagram*: Risks can also be discovered by looking at their impact and working backwards to the possible cause. This is called a result-to-cause method. A lack of ticket sales at an event, for example, would be a terrible result. The fault diagram method would go back from this risk through the various event aspects to postulate its cause. The list of causes is then used to manage the risk. Insufficient ticket sales may be traced back to problems in promotion such as wrong information in the press release or incorrect target market. It may be traced to problems in logistics such as incorrectly placed signage or parking problems. In each of the work breakdown categories there can be problems that would result in a lack of ticket sales. In the case of the Grand Prix described in Figure 17.2, the event owners saw a competing event as the cause.

- *Incident report*: Almost all large public events have an incident report document. These may be included in the event manual and are to be filled out by the event staff when there is an incident. The incident data can then be used by agencies to give an event risk profile. This is not to be confused with an accident report book, which is a legal requirement for all events under the Reporting of Injuries, Diseases and Dangerous Occurrences Regulations 1995 (RIDDOR). The ambulance service may have data on medical incidents for events. These data are useful for estimating resources to allocate. By giving the ambulance service key characteristics of an event, such as audience number, alcohol availability, age group and type of event activity, they can predict the type of medical incidents most likely to occur.

- *Contingency plan*: An outcome of the risk analysis may be a detailed plan of viable alternative integrated actions. The contingency plan contains the response to the impact of a risk and involves a decision procedure, chain of command and a set of related actions. An example of contingency planning was the response to the extreme weather conditions on New Year's Eve 2000. As a result of heavy snow and wind, followed by a quick thaw and heavy rain, many events were cancelled. However, the event at Belfast City was transferred from the outdoor venue to Belfast Waterfront (indoors) and the event was a success.

- *Scenario development and tabletop exercises*: The use of a 'what if' session can uncover many risks. A scenario of problems is given to the event team and interested stakeholders. They work through the problems and present their responses. These responses are collated and discussed. These tabletop exercises are surprisingly effective. One tabletop exercise used the scenario of an expected fireworks display not happening at a major New Year's Eve event. All the agencies around the table then responded, describing the consequences as they saw it and their contingency plans. The problems included disappointed crowds, a rush for the public transport and other crowd management issues. Would the event company be able to announce to a crowd of 500,000 what had happened? The fireworks went off as planned in the following year. Two years later, however, the fireworks did not occur. A number of the agencies, such as police, emergency service and railways, were able to use their contingency plans. Major sponsors and government clients may send an event company a number of scenarios and ask for their response. This is a way of testing the competence of the event management.

- *Consultation*: Part of due diligence in planning events is the concept of consultation. The event management team should consult with the various suppliers on their safety plans for the event. It is slightly different for different regions; however, consultation can also be used to strengthen risk identification and analysis. Suppliers have a wealth of information on what can go wrong. Consultation does not imply just asking questions; the event manager must provide relevant information so that the other party can give a considered opinion. This opinion must be taken into account in the planning of the event and risk management. Consultation is further explored in the section on occupational safety and health.

Accurate identification

An essential aspect of risk identification is a way to accurately describe the risks. The risk for an outdoor event is not 'weather'. A beautiful fine day is still 'weather'. Heat or rain may be the risk descriptor. However, this is still not accurate enough. Extreme heat or rain before the event is getting closer to describing the actual risk. The process of describing the risk accurately also enables the event team to think the risk through.

Figure 17.4 illustrates how the seemingly simple risk of rain is, in practice, quite complex. According to the article, which discussed the 14th Tropfest Film Festival in locations around Australia, the film festival would go ahead 'rain, hail or shine'. But the question is 'how much rain and when?' The risk is not a light sprinkle or rain after the event. The risk analysis process demands that the risk is properly described. Note also that the rain at one event was not a disaster for the event company as they had distributed their risk by having events around the country. The lightning was a high risk as the consequence for an outdoor festival with large metal towers is serious. The provision of the DVDs of the finalists is an example of minimising the consequence of the risk. This action covers many other risks, such as judges not showing up on the night. At the same time the festival director minimised another risk, that of the festival being seen as losing its 'grassroots beginnings'. The director deals with this risk with a definitive statement!

Decision

Decide on who may be harmed. This may include, for example:

- people particularly at risk, for example, young workers and trainees, and
- people not familiar with the site, for example, contractors, visitors and members of the public.

FIGURE 17.4 Seemingly simple risks, such as rain, can be quite complex

TROPFEST COPS A LASHING

A severe storm cut the 14th Tropfest film festival abruptly short last night and sent an estimated 35 000 people running for shelter.

With three of the 16 films still to be screened, organisers called off the event, citing safety concerns due to lightning.

The judges — including Toni Collette, Rose Byrne, Guy Pearce, Simon Baker and Phillip Noyce — were drenched in the teeming rain and took shelter in the VIP tents in the Domain.

Earlier in the night, as rain clouds threatened, organisers said the short film festival would go ahead 'rain, hail or shine'.

However, the audience started leaving midway through the program at about 9.30 pm as torrential rain soaked the city.

The festival continued in Melbourne, Canberra, Brisbane, Perth and Hobart, and organisers expect to announce the winner today.

Elsewhere in Sydney, cars floated and roads had to be closed in Penrith as rain overwhelmed the drains. Flooding also closed roads in St Marys and damaged homes in Northmead and Penrith.

Tropfest's program director, Serena Paull, said: 'We've had rain before but never torrential rain like this. There's been a lightning storm and so we can't continue.'

She said the judges would be provided with DVD copies of all 16 finalists to make their decision.

Before the downpour prematurely ended the night, Tropfest's director, John Polson, rejected claims it had lost its grassroots beginnings.

'I think it's crap,' Polson said. 'I think people who say that haven't done their research. The festival hasn't always been about trying to find people who haven't made films before. It's about trying to find the best possible film.' . . .

(Source: Moses, 2006)

Analysis and evaluation of risk

It is clear that there are an infinite number of things that can go wrong and a finite number that can go right. Identifying risk can open a Pandora's box of issues. Risk assessment meetings often reveal the 'prophets of doom' who can bring an overly pessimistic approach to the planning process. This is itself a risk that must be anticipated. The event team must have a method of organising the risks so they can be methodically managed. Once the risks are accurately described, they should be mapped according to:

• the likelihood of them occurring (for example, on a five-point scale from rare to almost certain. Rare means that the incident will occur only in exceptional circumstances; for example, an earthquake in London. The other ratings are unlikely, possible, likely and almost certain. Rain at an event in the Lake District during the spring may be rated as 'almost certain'.)

• the consequence if they do occur (for example, on a five-point scale from insignificant, minor, moderate, major to catastrophic. Insignificant, according to SAI Global, means that the incident would be dealt with by routine operations;

for example, no injuries and no financial loss. Catastrophic means that the consequence would threaten the event and the event organisations; for example, death and huge financial loss) (SAI Global, 2006).

These are often called the dimensions of risk and provide the event team with a tool to rate the risks. A risk that is assessed as catastrophic and almost certain to happen will need immediate action. A risk that is unlikely and insignificant will not be afforded the same attention as risks of a higher rating. Other risk management models include the perception of the risk and its frequency as part of the risk assessment.

An accurate way of describing the risks is essential to clear communication. At a recent risk meeting, for example, the risk of providing 'incorrect information to the media' was identified as 'likely' and the consequence was 'moderate' to 'major'. It was assessed as needing attention and requiring a solution. At another meeting it was found that the decision to possibly cancel the event was being left to the event's general manager (GM). However, during the event, the GM would be in a high-security area with politicians, and difficult to contact. The risk of 'GM impossible to contact' was rated 'certain' and 'catastrophic'. The solution was simple: have security clearance for a 'runner' to be able to communicate between the event team and the GM.

A risk meeting with the staff and volunteers is often the only way to uncover many risks. It is important that the meeting be well chaired and focused, since the time needed for risk assessment must always be weighed against the limited time available for the overall event planning. An effective risk assessment meeting will produce a comprehensive and realistic analysis of the potential risks in a risk register. The risk register is the document output of the risk management process and is further explained in the documentation section later in this chapter.

Control

Once the risks have been evaluated, the event management team needs to create mechanisms to control any problem that can arise. In *Five Steps to Risk Management*, HSE (2006) suggested that managers ask the following questions: can I get rid of the hazard altogether? If not, how can I control the risks so that harm is unlikely? The decisions include:

- changing the likelihood that a problem will occur — this can include avoiding the problem by not proceeding with that aspect of the event. A recent water-ski event, for example, was unable to obtain insurance. The management identified the part of the event that was high risk, a high-speed race, and cancelled it. This enabled the event to go ahead with the necessary level of insurance.
- changing the consequence if the problem does occur — such as contingency planning and disaster plans.
- accepting the risk.
- transferring the risk to another party.

Insurance is an example of changing the consequence by transferring the risk and accepting a smaller risk. The risk that is now accepted is:

- the insurance contract will be honoured (for example, the insurance company could go bankrupt) and
- the event makes enough money to pay for the insurance.

The risk management process can be defined, therefore, as transferring the risks to a part of the event management that has the resources (including skills, experience and knowledge) to handle it. This is an important point because the risk is rarely, if ever, completely eliminated, except by cancelling the event. Once a risk has been identified and a solution planned, its likelihood of occurring and its consequences are reduced.

In his comprehensive manual on risk management for events, Berlonghi (1990) suggested the following risk control strategies:

- *Cancel and avoid the risk*: If the risk is too great, it may be necessary to cancel all or part of the event. Outdoor concerts that are part of a larger event are often cancelled if there is rain. The major risk is not audience discomfort, but the danger of electrocution.
- *Diminish the risk*: Risks that cannot be avoided need to be minimised. To eliminate all possible security risks at an event, for example, may require every patron to be searched. This solution is obviously unworkable at a majority of events and, instead, a risk minimisation strategy will need to be developed − for example, installing metal detectors or stationing security guards in a more visible position.
- *Reduce the severity of risks that do eventuate*: A major part of safety planning is preparing quick and efficient responses to foreseeable problems. Training staff in elementary first aid can reduce the severity of an accident. The event manager cannot eliminate natural disasters but can prepare a plan to contain the effects.
- *Devise back-ups and alternatives*: When something goes wrong, the situation can be saved by having an alternative plan in place. In case the juggler does not turn up to a children's party, for example, the host can organise party games to entertain the children. On a larger scale, back-up generators are a must at big outdoor events in case of a major power failure.
- *Distribute the risk*: If the risk can be spread across different areas, its impact will be reduced if something does go wrong. One such strategy is to widely spread the cash-taking areas, such as ticket booths, so that any theft is contained and does not threaten the complete event income. This does not eliminate the risk, it transfers it to an area that can be managed by the event company − such as security and supervision. Having a variety of sponsors is another way to distribute risk. If one sponsor pulls out, the others can be approached to increase their involvement.
- *Transfer the risk*: Risk can be transferred to other groups responsible for an event's components. Subcontractors may be required to share the liability of an

event. Their contracts generally contain a clause to the effect that they are responsible for the safety of their equipment and the actions of their staff during the event. In Australia, most performing groups are required to have public liability insurance before they can take part in an event.

A more formal system, the hierarchy of controls, has been developed in relation to health and safety, based on the Management of Health and Safety at Work Regulations. This hierarchy provides an order of control measures for risks, based on the principles of eliminating risk, combating risks and minimising risks (HSE, 1997), which is sometimes referred to by the extended mnemonic ERIC PD:

- **ELIMINATE** – Can you get rid of the hazard altogether? If not, how can you control the risks so that harm is unlikely?
- **REDUCE** – Try a less risky option.
- **ISOLATE** – prevent access to the hazard, for example, by guarding.
- **CONTROL** – Organise work to reduce exposure to the hazard, for example, put barriers between pedestrians and traffic.
- **PPE** – Issue personal protective equipment, for example, clothing, footwear and goggles
- **D**iscipline – Of the workforce to work correctly (adapted from HSE, 1997, 2006).

When controlling risk the event team should start at the top of the hierarchy and, if that is not possible, move to the next level of control. The hierarchy of controls is a framework that enables the event team to systematically work through the risks. However, event risk management can be far more complex as some risks require a number of these controls to be used.

Mitigating actions

The following examples of mitigating actions are based on recommendations of the US Emergency Management Institute.

At every event, people will leave some items unattended. Event officials must decide beforehand how to handle unattended packages and have a written plan for all personnel to follow. The issues to consider include: Who will respond? Are dogs trained to identify explosives available? Will the area be evacuated?

Concealment areas are areas where persons may hide or where someone may hide packages or other weapons. The best way to avoid problems in these areas is to map the event venue and identify the areas that could be used as hiding spots. Venue staff can assist in this matter.

Venue and security personnel should work together to conduct a security sweep of the venue. A few areas to address in advance are: How often is security going to go through the event site? What are they looking for? How do they handle incidents? Who is going to do the sweep? Once a sweep of the area has been done the area must be secured.

Each of these mitigating actions, in addition to Berlonghi's strategies, can be reduced to the management of two risk dimensions: likelihood and consequence. A back-up generator is an example of reducing the 'consequence' of a blackout. Checking the capacity of the electricity supply is an example of reducing the 'likelihood' of a power failure.

Risk communication

Effective risk communication includes the following:

- *Understanding the terminology of risk*: The risk needs to be accurately described and understood by all the event staff and volunteers.
- *Open communication channels*: It is a well-known problem at events that staff are hesitant to tell event management that a task has not been completed. If they identify problems there must be a way that this can be communicated to the event management in a timely manner. A system of team leaders may be used with part of their role to collect these data.
- *Informal methods of communication*: Management theorists, such as Peter Drucker (1973), stressed how important these informal methods are to the success of a company. This is true for events. The dinners, chats over coffee or just a friendly talk can greatly assist the communication process. Walking the site is a time-honoured way to find out what is going on.

The formal process of communicating risk includes the distribution of the risk plan. It is the output or deliverable of the risk management process. The plan contains a list of identified risks, their assessment, the plan of action, who is responsible and the timeline for implementation. In the fluid event management environment, a fixed plan may be quickly out of date. A risk management plan of a parade, for example, will have to be revised if there are any additions to the parade, such as horses. For this reason, it is recommended by most project management texts that a live risk register be established. The risk register is a plan that is constantly updated and revised. As new risks are identified they are added to the register. The register has a number of functions:

1. It is a live management tool.
2. It can be used to track risks so they are not forgotten.
3. It is proof of actions for a work-in-progress report.
4. It can be used after the event to help prove competent management.
5. It can be used for the next event to assist risk identification and planning.
6. It can have various levels of access to allow staff and senior management a role in risk management.
7. It can communicate the main issues, simply and clearly.

A live risk register can be put on the intranet or Internet, and is therefore accessible to all members of the event team. At any time, it can be printed off and placed in a report to the various stakeholders. The risk register thus provides a snapshot for the event management process.

Further risk management methodologies

Principles of safe design

As the generic risk management methodology spreads to different industry sectors, it became obvious that many problems were related to how the asset or end product of a project was initially designed.

The British and International Standard BS ISO 31000: 2009 (BSI, 2010b, p. v) on risk management states:

> All activities of an organization involve risk. Organizations manage risk by identifying it, analysing it and then evaluating whether the risk should be modified by risk treatment in order to satisfy their risk criteria.

This suggests that risk management pervades all areas of the event initiation, planning and implementation. The Australian Safety and Compensation Council (2006, p. 6) has applied this to the design stage of a project:

> A safe design approach begins in the conceptual and planning phases with an emphasis on making choices about design, materials used and methods of manufacture or construction to enhance the safety of the finished product.

They describe five principles of safe design, which can be applied to the design of an event, namely:

1. *Person with control*: person who makes the key event management decisions,
2. *Product life cycle*: safe design encompasses all aspects of the event including the after-event outcomes,
3. *Systematic risk management*: using the identification/assess/control process,
4. *Safe design knowledge and capability*: the event team should be trained and competent, and
5. *Information transfer*: the event team needs an effective and timely communication and documentation system for the risk management.

Each of these principles is employed over the phases from pre-design to design completion shown in Figure 17.5. The risk management process of context, identify, analyse, evaluate and control is juxtaposed with the design process. The design process is common in many areas of event management such as staging, theming, programming, marketing and site choice and layout. The figure illustrates how the risk can be embedded in these areas.

An important part of the safe design methodology is the concept of downstream problems that result from upstream risk. It is an excellent metaphor to help the event team realise the consequence of mistakes or seemingly small faults early in the planning of an event. A forgotten phone call to a supplier early in the planning can result in all kinds of problems at the event. Every member of the event team — from the person doing the photocopying to the event director — is responsible for the success of the event. A volunteer who moves a race marker to allow a car to park prior to a marathon race can inadvertently invalidate the whole

FIGURE 17.5 The risk management process from the design perspective

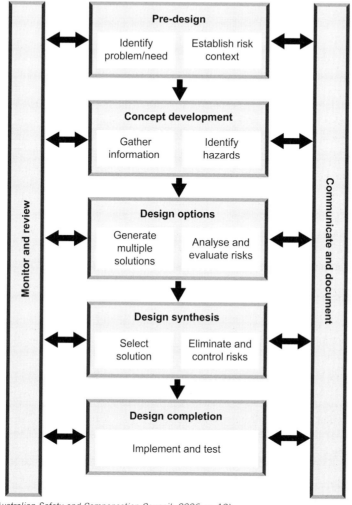

(Source: Australian Safety and Compensation Council, 2006, p. 19)

race. Consider the chain of events: the race marker was returned to a slightly different spot. The race went around that marker quite a few times, significantly shortening the race. All the competitors came in with new 'personal bests' until they realised something was wrong. The shortened race meant that the results were invalid to the world marathon officials. The competitors entered this race as it was a qualifying race for world championships. Therefore, all their months of practice were to no avail. This all occurred because a volunteer wanted to help a motorist.

Hazard analysis and critical control points

A specific application of the generic risk standard to a part of the event industry is found in the food industry. Hazard analysis and critical control points (HACCP) is a methodology that includes consulting, documentation, implementation and internal auditing for the food industry and hospitals. It is important to consider the HACCP methodology as the event caterers will be familiar with it and it illustrates how these tools are used. Food is a major source of risk at events and is covered by food safety and hygiene legislation. As a result, if the event is open to the public it may need to comply with food safety and hygiene legislation and licensing – a local authority would be able to offer advice on this aspect of events. The risk can take many forms. It may be an obvious risk such as the cleanliness of the facilities or a secondary risk arising from a problem in another area of the event management. An example of an often-overlooked secondary risk is the risk of a blackout or power outage. Most event managers would identify the consequence as the sound system not running, lights not working and the elevator stopping mid-floor and trapping people. However, there is also the loss of temperature control for the food. The consequence of a drop in the temperature for food can be classified as major. This simple example illustrates that the food risk management must be linked with the overall event risk management.

The HACCP system consists of the following seven principles (US Food and Drug Administration, 2001):

1. Conduct a hazard analysis.
2. Determine the critical control points (CCPs).
3. Establish critical limit(s).
4. Establish a system to monitor control of the CCP.
5. Establish the corrective action to be taken when monitoring indicates that a particular CCP is not under control.
6. Establish procedures for verification to confirm that the HACCP system is working effectively.
7. Establish documentation concerning all procedures and records appropriate to these principles and their application.

Although these principles were developed for the food industry, the concept of CCPs has application in the wider event context. O'Toole (2006), in describing the event project, identified an 'exposure profile' in the timeline of the event project. The exposure profile identifies critical points over the project when the event team is most exposed to risk. An example is when the main entertainment act has been advertised but the contract has not been finalised. Experienced event companies are adept at minimising this exposure profile by identifying the critical points. They focus on the exposure profile and control the risks.

A similar approach to risk is found in vulnerability profiling and building resilience, which is found in the work of Salter (2005) on preparing for emergencies. This method stresses the process of risk planning, as distinct from the risk plan as a document, and the importance of the community's capacity to deal with hazards. Although this has not been formally applied to events and festivals, the concept of continuously building the capacity of a community to deal with hazards by identifying and minimising hazards through the active process of planning and self-assessment is attractive.

Specific event risks

Many of the risks that are specific to the event industry happen at the event itself. The risks associated with these will vary according to the nature of the event (HSE, 1999). Issues with crowd movement are an obvious area of risk. The consequences of a crowd-related incident can lead to duty of care and criminal liability issues, so they are a high priority in the event manager's mind. However, the risks at the event may be a result of ignoring the risks before the event. For this reason, the risk management must be tracked across all areas of event management. Many of the risks at the event can be tracked back to a lack of time in management. The lack of time is, in reality, an inability to scope or predict the amount of work necessary to carry out the management of the event. The conclusion is that a systematic method must be used. Due to the temporary nature of events, there are numerous risks. For example, Upton (2004) highlights a number of examples of dangerous crowd behaviour at music events, including crowd surges, slam dancing/moshing (where people slam into each other while dancing), crowd surfing (where an individual is lifted above the heads of the crowd and swims or rolls towards the stage) and stage diving (where someone, either a member of the band or audience jumps off the stage into the crowd and is then supported above their heads, possibly turning into a crowd surf). Another example is using volunteers at events which can result in many kinds of risks. Some of the risks listed at a recent workshop relating to volunteers include do not listen, do not turn up, complain and form subgroups, cannot control, no accountability and deplete the asset. The latter refers to a problem with repeat events, when the volunteers are set in their ways and the event needs to change.

This discussion is not exhaustive. It highlights some of the areas specific to events.

Crowd management

Two terms often confused are crowd control and crowd management. As Abbot (2000, p. 105) points out:

> *Crowd management and crowd control are two distinct but interrelated concepts. The former includes the facilitation, employment and movement of crowds, while the latter relates to the steps taken once the crowd has lost control.*

The concept of crowd management is an example of pre-empting problems at the event by preparing the risk management before the event. Many crowd control issues arise from inadequate risk management by the event company. However, there can still be unforeseen risks with crowds. There are many factors that impinge on the smooth management of crowds at an event. The first risk is correctly estimating the number of people who will attend the event. No matter how the site is designed, too many attendees can put enormous strain on the event resources. For example, gatecrashers at Glastonbury Festival 2000 doubled the licensed capacity to an estimated 200,000 people on site. This led to the cancellation of Glastonbury 2001, due to increased safety fears in the wake of the Roskilde tragedy and prosecution of the organiser for alleged breach of the licence. Even at free events, too few attendees can significantly affect the event objectives. For example, the launch of Millennium Square in Leeds on New Year's Eve 2000 saw only hundreds, rather than the anticipated thousands, of visitors attend due to the extreme weather conditions on the evening. Crowd risk management is also a function of the type of audience and their standards of behaviour. A family event will have different priorities in risk management to a rock festival. The expectations of the crowd can be managed with the right kind of information being sent out prior to the event.

The HSE guide, *Managing Crowds Safely* (HSE, 2000), provides general guidance for managing crowd safety in a systematic way, covering the areas of planning, risk assessment, putting precautions in place, emergency planning and procedures, communication, monitoring crowds and review. Crowd management for large events has become a specialist field of study, and there are a number of consultancies in this area. The crowd control issues are amply illustrated by the incidents at large outdoor events such as the Haj. Excellent resources on the study of crowds can be found at www.crowdsafe.com and www.crowddynamics.com.

Alcohol and drugs

Events can range from a family picnic with the audience sipping wine while watching a show, to a New Year's Eve mass gathering of youths and the heavy consumption of alcohol. Under the law, both events are treated the same. The responsible service of alcohol provision in many countries is a method of reducing the likelihood of this risk. Some annual events have been cancelled due to the behaviour problems that arise from selling alcohol. The alcohol risk management procedures can permeate every aspect of some events, including limiting ticket sales, closing hotels early, increasing security and roping off areas. The European Football Championships 2000, hosted jointly by The Netherlands and Belgium, illustrate the negative impact that alcohol can have, with violence, civil disruption, arrests, restaurants and bars closed, and the threat of England team being expelled from the tournament.

A worthy mention is the risk of drugs at events. Many modern events, in particular rave parties, involve risks arising from drug use. Emergency and first-aid services are faced with the quandary of treating the problem and reporting the incident to police. Some rave or dance parties are secret — which is part of the allure — and first-aid services have to decide whether to inform the police of these parties and, therefore, risk the possibility of not being contracted again by the organisers. Another risk related to drug use is the presence of syringes and their safe handling by staff.

Communication

The risks involved in communication are varied as it concerns the event organisation and reporting any risks. Setting up a computer and filing system for the event office can prevent future problems. Easy access to relevant information is vital to good risk management. A standard, yet customised, reporting procedure can also reduce the risk of ineffective communication. Communication can include how the public is informed of the event, signage and keeping attendees informed when they are at the event site. The event manual is an excellent communication device for the procedures, protocol and general event information for staff and volunteers. There can be a risk of too much data obscuring the important information; therefore, it needs to be highly focused.

Stewarding and security

An important consideration for event organisers is how the crowd will be managed and controlled, or more importantly, who will do this. This may range from event stewards and security staff through to volunteer stewards. Stewards are primarily responsible for crowd management, while security may be responsible for the protection of performers, premises or equipment (HSE, 1999). This requires careful thought and planning to ensure that there are sufficient numbers of trained and/or qualified staff performing this role. In addition, as a result of the Private Security Industry Act 2001, paid security and stewards are regulated by the Security Industry Authority. Licences have been implemented to raise standards in the profession by ensuring security staff are trained and meet minimum requirements (including not having a criminal record). As a result of this Act, all staff working as door supervisors or security guards, or the management of these services, will require a Security Industry Association licence. Unpaid volunteers do not currently require a licence. For up-to-date information about the implementation of this Act please visit the Security Industry Association website (www.the-sia.org.uk). BS 8406: 2009 (BSI, 2009) provides a useful code of practice and recommendations for the infrastructure, staffing, operation and management of safety and stewarding at indoor and outdoor events, while BS 7960: 2005 (BSI, 2005) provides a code of practice for door supervisors (security) and BS 7499: 2007 provides a code of practice for static security guards.

Environment

The risk to the environment posed by modern businesses is of increasing concern to the general community. There are dangerous risks such as pollution, spills and effluent leakage, and the more indirect risks that can be minimised by waste recycling and water and energy conservation. The impacts and therefore the priorities for their control will vary over the event project life cycle.

Emergency

An awareness of the nearest emergency services and their working requirements is mandatory for the event management. The reason for using outside emergency services is that the situation is beyond the capabilities of the event staff and needs specialist attention. It is important to understand the chain of command when emergency services arrive. They can be outside the control of the event management staff, who would act purely in an advisory capacity. Emergency services may be called in by any attendee at an event. Commenting on the potential consequences of a major incident, the HSE (1999, p. 31) advises that a multi-agency approach will generally be required, including the event management, policy, fire authority, National Health Service including ambulance service, local authority, local emergency planning officer, stewards and first-aiders. As a result, procedures, demarcation of duties and responsibilities should be agreed in writing with all relevant parties within the planning stage.

EVENT PROFILE

Unforeseen risk – the arrival of six warships

One of the more unusual events in the world was the exchange of East Timor from United Nations control to a newly elected government and the celebrations of independence that accompanied this event. It marked the formation of a new country and involved representatives of more than 80 countries. The major stakeholders were the people of East Timor, the United Nations and the United Nations peacekeeping forces, international media, neighbouring countries (including Indonesia and Australia and their militaries), the independence forces and the anti-independence forces in East Timor, and representatives from the USA, the Catholic Church and the new East Timor government.

The risk management for such an event with a short time frame, high uncertainty and sudden changes had to be performed through multiple meetings and leadership decisions. As there had been an insurgency war between the independence movement and the Indonesian military, it was a surprise when the President of Indonesia, Megawati Sukarnoputri, agreed to attend the celebrations. The Indonesian military wanted to ensure their president had adequate security. Three days before the celebrations the military sent six warships into the area. The warships were visible from the island and, for some East Timorese people, were an ominous reminder of the protracted war. This was a major unforeseen risk. First, the President would be present and, second, the Indonesian military would want to be involved in this celebration of independence from their rule.

According to a report at the time, Jose Ramos Horta (the East Timorese Foreign Minister) said the conclusion from several separate security surveys – conducted by the United Nations, as well as the British, American and Australian intelligence services – was that the risk to visiting delegations during the independence celebrations was 'extremely low'. As a result, he said, 'We did not feel that an advance team comprising six warships was needed to provide security to a head of state'.

Fortunately, a combination of United Nations and East Timorese assurances, and an agreement to reduce the Indonesian military presence to armoured vehicles and helicopters, saved the situation. The last warship left Dili harbour 24 hours before the event. The President's visit went well and the new nation was launched.

Recording

It is advisable that all hazards and actions taken are recorded by all organisations, however, by law only those employing more than five employees are legally required to do so. Records should be suitable and sufficient to demonstrate, should the need arise, that the risk assessment took place, the people affected were identified, significant hazards were dealt with, precautions were taken and the remaining risk was low. Accurate records can assist the event manager in monitoring hazards and provide evidence should this be demanded, for example, in a compensation claim (HSE, 2006).

Review

Evaluating the successes and failures of the risk control strategy is central to the planning of future events. The event company must be a 'learning organisation'. The analysis of, and response to, feedback is essential to this process.

The *Event Safety Guide* provides advice within 33 chapters on specific arrangements for health and safety at music and similar events. The chapter headings, presented in Figure 17.6, can provide organisers with a useful basis for planning their requirements (HSE, 1999, p. 2).

OCCUPATIONAL SAFETY AND HEALTH AND EVENTS

The health and safety of the people at events is the highest priority for any event team. The risks in this part of the event management's responsibilities are enormous — both to the event and to all the key stakeholders. The results of an incident can reverberate

FIGURE 17.6 Checklist for planning risk assessment requirements

- ☐ Planning and management
- ☐ Venue and site design
- ☐ Fire safety
- ☐ Major incident planning (emergency planning)
- ☐ Communication
- ☐ Crowd management
- ☐ Transport management
- ☐ Structures
- ☐ Barriers
- ☐ Electrical installations and lighting
- ☐ Food, drink and water
- ☐ Merchandising and special licensing
- ☐ Amusements, attractions and promotional displays
- ☐ Sanitary facilities
- ☐ Waste management
- ☐ Sound: noise and vibration
- ☐ Special effects, fireworks and pyrotechnics
- ☐ Camping
- ☐ Facilities for people with special needs
- ☐ Medical, ambulance and first-aid management
- ☐ Information and welfare
- ☐ Children
- ☐ Performers
- ☐ TV and media
- ☐ Stadium music events
- ☐ Arena events
- ☐ Large events
- ☐ Small events
- ☐ Classical music events
- ☐ Unfenced or unticketed events, including radio roadshows
- ☐ All-night music events
- ☐ Unlicensed events
- ☐ Health and safety responsibilities

(Source: HSE, 1999, p. iii)

around a country and affect future events and the whole event industry. In South Africa, the crowd crush at the Ellis Park Stadium in Johannesburg directly led to the introduction of the South African National Standard SANS 10366:2004 Health and Safety at Live Events and the Safety at Sports and Recreational Events Bill. According to HSE (1999, p. 7) the key areas to consider for health and safety are:

- *creating a health and safety policy;*
- *planning to ensure the policy is put into practice;*
- *organising an effective management structure and arrangements for delivery of* n *the policy;*
- *monitoring health and safety performance;*
- *auditing and reviewing performance.*

The regulations and legislation concerning occupational safety and health (OSH) in the UK are the responsibility of the UK government. There are two core concepts:

1. duty of care (see Chapter 16)
2. consultation

Consultation

The law sets out employer's duties for consulting with employees in relation to health and safety. The duties are set out in two pieces of legislation, the Safety Representatives and Safety Committees Regulations 1977 (as amended) where employees are in recognised trade unions and the Health and Safety (Consultation with Employees) Regulations 1996 where employees are not in trade unions and are not represented by a trade union. In the former, the employer must consult with the union-appointed health and safety representative, whereas in the latter case, employers may consult directly with individual employees or through an elected health and safety representative (HSE, 2008). According to HSE (2008, p. 3), employers must consult employees on the following in relation to health and safety:

- *the introduction of any measure which may substantially affect their health and safety at work, for example the introduction of new equipment or new systems of work (such as the speed of a process line and shift-work arrangements);*
- *arrangements for getting competent people to help them comply with health and safety laws (a competent person is someone who has sufficient training and experience or knowledge and other qualities that allow them to help an employer meet the requirements of health and safety law);*
- *the information they must give their employees on the risks and dangers arising from their work, measures to reduce or get rid of these risks and what employees should do if they are exposed to a risk;*
- *the planning and organisation of health and safety training; and*
- *the health and safety consequences of introducing new technology.*

The event team must consult with the event stakeholders, such as the suppliers, volunteers and sponsors, on event health and safety. Risk management must be an agenda item at all meetings.

Within the UK, it is a legal requirement for organisations with five employees or more to have a written health and safety policy. Figure 17.7 lists the suggested contents of a safety policy.

Under HSAW events/businesses must have a nominated named person who is responsible for health and safety and for ensuring responsibilities are recorded (HSE, 1999). HSE (1999) recommends that large events also form an event safety management team, what the New Zealand Ministry of Civil Defence and Emergency Management (2004) refers to as an event safety committee (see Figure 17.8). This is a cross-functional team with responsibilities for OSH in each of its department, with potentially members of the local authority and emergency services.

The relevant OSH Acts vary around the world and it is mandatory for an event team to understand the legislation and relevant codes and guidelines to ensure a sustainable events industry. However, there are common concepts. Other countries such as South Africa, Australia and New Zealand have very similar legislation to the UK which applies to events. The core of all the OSH Acts is the risk management procedure as described in this chapter. When this is combined with the relevant codes, guidelines and legislation, it gives the event team a safety framework for events. Furthermore, many local authorities provide guidance on health and safety when organising events in their area (for example, Great Yarmouth Borough Council, 2010).

FIGURE 17.7 Event safety policy

3.2 EVENT SAFETY POLICY

The event safety policy is a document that communicates the values, objectives and broad commitments of the event organiser to conducting a safe event. It represents a high level commitment by the event organiser that sets the tone for how, and to what degree, the system for managing safety will be supported.

3.2.1. What types of things should an event safety policy include?
Some suggested items and themes for inclusion in an event safety policy are:

- statements conveying management commitment;
- continual improvement of safety performance;
- working in consultation;
- objectives or targets for personal injury performance (e.g. number of medical treatments per 1000 spectators);
- compliance with Victorian OHS legislation;
- a commitment toward a high level of event security;
- a reference to the safety of participants, entertainers, members of the public, event staff and contractors;
- competent and trained staff; and
- signed by the CEO.

WorkSafe Victoria's website, www.worksafe.vic.gov.au, should be accessed for more information and future updates.

FIGURE 17.8 Recommended safety committee/event management safety team composition

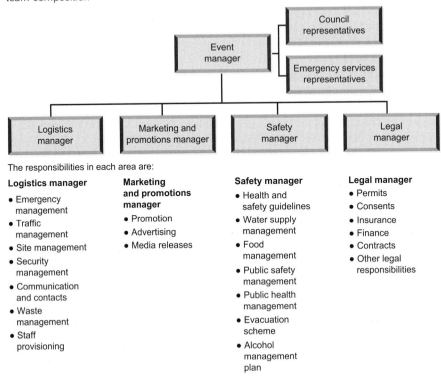

The responsibilities in each area are:

Logistics manager

- Emergency management
- Traffic management
- Site management
- Security management
- Communication and contacts
- Waste management
- Staff provisioning

Marketing and promotions manager

- Promotion
- Advertising
- Media releases

Safety manager

- Health and safety guidelines
- Water supply management
- Food management
- Public safety management
- Public health management
- Evacuation scheme
- Alcohol management plan

Legal manager

- Permits
- Consents
- Insurance
- Finance
- Contracts
- Other legal responsibilities

(Source: New Zealand Ministry of Civil Defence and Emergency Management, 2004, pp. 18–19)

SUMMARY

Risk management is a modern, formal process of identifying and managing risk. It is one of the functions of any event management and the process should be part of the event's everyday organisation. There are risks that are specific to particular events. To correctly identify these risks, knowledge of the unique risks is essential. The risk is more than risks at the event itself. The output of this process is a live risk register that shows the risks and their management schedule. As part of this risk strategy, the management has to understand its legal requirements. It has a duty of care to all involved in an event. Any reasonably foreseen risks have to be eliminated or minimised.

The safety of the event attendees is a prime concern for the event team. Any event comes under the various health and safety acts. Risk management, duty of care and consultation are the three core elements of the recommended methodology. These combine with the codes, legislation and guidelines to provide the safety framework in which the event team must work.

QUESTIONS

1. List the risks to a regional festival arising from these areas:

    a.   local organising committee

    b.   sponsorship

    c.   volunteers

    d.   council politics

    e.   participants in a parade

    f.   computers

    g.   experience of organising group

2. Are corporate events covered by the risk policy of the venue or the client?

3. In the example of the East Timor handover celebrations (see Event Profile on page 614), what other risks can you identify? How can you prepare for unforeseen risks?

4. Event management has been described as 'just solving problems'. To what extent can risk management replace all the other methods of management, such as marketing, logistics and project management, to create an event?

5. Contrast the risks involved in staging an outdoor concert and those involved in producing an indoor food fair. What risk management strategy could be used to reduce or eliminate these risks?

CASE STUDY: 200TH ANNIVERSARY OF THE BATTLE OF TRAFALGAR

The 200th anniversary of the Battle of Trafalgar and the death of the great British naval hero Admiral Lord Nelson were celebrated in 2005. These two defining events have resonated through the years, cementing a sense of British identity. It was fitting then that the Royal Navy should choose to mark the occasion with something special.

A lot has changed in the intervening two centuries, not least the fact that Britain's erstwhile adversaries, France and Spain, are now close allies, partners and confidants. This gave rise to a vision of global scale – invite the navies and merchant vessels of the world to assemble off Portsmouth (home of the British Navy and departure point for Nelson's final voyage) and there celebrate humanity's ongoing relationship with the sea and jointly commemorate all those lost in naval battle from various nations.

The Trafalgar 200 (T200) vision included a wide range of events encompassing land, sea and air and with both military and civilian participation. Chiefs of naval staff were invited from around the globe and Her Majesty Queen Elizabeth II was the guest of honour. Functions ranged in scale from private wreath laying through to mass attendance events with hundreds of thousands witnessing an unprecedented assembly of naval craft from around the world.

Continued

CASE STUDY: 200TH ANNIVERSARY OF THE BATTLE OF TRAFALGAR—*CONT'D*

The principal events were:

- *international fleet review*: Vessels from 40 nations formed the largest international fleet ever assembled, including military, commercial and historic crafts.
- *son et lumiere*: An evocation of a period battle using tall ships and mega-scale lighting and pyrotechnic effects.
- *International Drumhead Ceremony*: A ceremony of remembrance for those lost at sea with royal, political and diplomatic representation.
- *International Festival of the Sea*: A 4-day festival of everything nautical hosted at the imposing Portsmouth Naval Base.
- *HMS Victory dinner*: A reception for Her Majesty the Queen, including a 72-gun salute from the cannons of Nelson's flagship
- *St Paul's service*: A ceremony of remembrance and thanksgiving for all those who took part in the great Battle of Trafalgar.
- *Trafalgar Square spectacular*: Free public show.

Each event produced its own particular logistical and planning challenges and threw up a series of health and safety challenges, some well understood and others unique to the event. Above all, the Ministry of Defence was determined to produce a safe event, enjoyed by thousands, but without undue risk to either the public or participants. To assist with this process, The Event Safety Shop Ltd was appointed to oversee and coordinate safety planning throughout all the shows, through the work of director Tim Roberts as T200 H&S coordinator.

This case study will provide an idea of the complexity of the task, the difficulty in spanning military and civilian cultures and the need to maintain tight security while maximising public access and enjoyment.

It should be stressed that safe delivery of the events was not in any sense the responsibility of Tim Roberts or any other of The Event Safety Shop team. A huge effort was put in by a range of agencies from the Ministry of Defence, local government, commercial partners and individual contractors. Indeed, one of the greatest challenges was simply facilitating and coordinating action among the huge range of health and safety duty holders.

As with any large-scale event, it all started with a health and safety policy. This was written specifically for the event and sought to set out the ground rules and some specific safe working practices for anyone participating in T200. It did not replace or supersede the various health and safety policies held by partner organisations such as Portsmouth Naval Base, the naval fleet or local authority. Instead, the health and safety policy aimed to draw together the work of partner organisations by identifying common objectives and setting out channels for communication and co-operation between organisations that might normally never speak to each other.

Consider the particular risks associated with some of the T200 series of events. Below are some of the more arresting possibilities (however, mundane risks should not be overlooked):

- assembly of hundreds of military vessels from dozens of nations in crowded and heavily tidal waters,
- safe anchorage of these vessels,
- maintaining a security cordon around some of the more sensitive vessels (including nuclear-powered aircraft carriers and submarines),
- managing mass crowds along many miles of seafront,
- planning and operating a ferry service to each of the participating ships to allow crews and VIPs ashore and aboard for visits,
- managing the arrival and departure of crowds with none of the normal ticketing and access controls,

- setting off 72 cannons from aboard the historic (wooden) vessel *HMS Victory* directly at Her Majesty the Queen,
- arranging an air display above nuclear-powered warships,
- inviting 150,000 people into an operational naval base for Europe's biggest maritime party,
- re-creating a Napoleonic sea battle using tall ships,
- transporting, preparing and detonating several tonnes of fireworks in the midst of all the above,
- managing a cast of thousands, including service personnel, veterans, schoolchildren, professional performers, diplomats and royals, and
- dealing with the weather, the international press, the power, stages, fencing, toilets, logistics, etc.

Below are seven key concepts (the seven Cs) that helped identify, address and mitigate the proliferation of risks suggested above:

- *command* – The structure of the organisation and decision making must be clearly established. Many organisations and agencies may feel that they are the ones really in command. One of the first challenges was to ensure that T200 imposed a command structure on the events and their participants.
- *control* – A thorough plan was required for all stages of the shows and everyone knew the role they were to play. Participants, suppliers and service providers were required to adopt specific ways of working. In the instance of the Festival of the Sea, this meant formal health and safety induction sessions for everyone working in the Portsmouth Naval Base, which was something of a shock for some of the suppliers who were normally left to their own devices. This kind of control required on-the-ground safety officers and formal completion or sign-off procedures. Control was also needed for crowds, traffic, public transport, airspace, media and participants.
- *competence* – The right people for the job, whether in a civilian or military context, had to be found. Contractors were required to produce extensive health and safety plans as part of the tendering and contractual process. While causing consternation in some quarters, it meant that issues were addressed early and everyone knew the kind of standards for which the project was aiming.
- *coordination* – The scale and complexity of the tasks faced were enormous; the Festival of the Sea alone required seven professional event safety officers. Coordinating effort between disparate agencies was a substantial part of the safety plan (this is dealt with in greater detail later).
- *co-operation* – This was paramount. Everyone had to put aside any narrow self-interest or territorialism. This was as true for nations assembling in the international fleet as it was for local authorities, police forces and others whose traditional 'patch' may have been encroached upon.
- *communication* – The task of establishing who would talk to whom on which radio frequencies required the work of a specialist team. Imagine then the processes of circulating minutes of critical meetings and ensuring relevant people were kept informed. The Royal Navy had to translate military jargon and acronyms for the civilians and the civilians had to stop using 'production-speak' when trying to describe what was going on. It made for some humorous moments, but a minor misunderstanding could have had serious consequences.
- *contingency* – Planning was conducted at all levels and involved contractors and staff at all levels. Everything from terror strike to typhoons to turnstile failure were considered and planned for.

One of the most valuable experiences was a huge tabletop exercise involving all the key players in which a number of scenarios, from the uncomfortable to the nightmarish, were simulated. Not only did this serve to focus on plans and responses, but it brought together everyone in one room and reinforced that everyone had a common purpose.

Continued

CASE STUDY: 200TH ANNIVERSARY OF THE BATTLE OF TRAFALGAR—*CONT'D*

The job of health and safety coordination required the establishment of a regular safety working group (SWG) that called on subject area specialists from a huge range of disciplines. To keep the agenda manageable, attendance was voluntary unless a question was tabled for a particular sector or someone had something specific to ask. The people planning the air display, therefore, were not forced to attend lengthy discussions of tidal problems.

The SWG rapidly established a relaxed environment for the discussion of virtually any aspect of the events, with input from safety and production professionals for each of the shows. Never underestimate the opportunity to learn from people who have no idea what you do!

The output of the SWG formed the basis for briefings of key staff and managers across all the events. It was also a forum for the presentation and analysis of the mountain of documentation that accompanies any large project.

Perhaps the most valuable aspect of the regular safety group meetings was the building of relationships, partnerships and trust between the stakeholders, or, more specifically, between the safety representatives of these organisations. This was of critical importance and headed off some potential conflicts.

Good safety management occurs because of open discussion about what needs to be done by competent people who have the welfare of public and participants as their prime concern. Though everyone had their own personal and sector agenda, these were pursued in the context of the wider objective to which all parties signed.

A selection of the enforcing authorities who had jurisdiction over some part of the event (for ease of reading the 40 nations who sent vessels have been omitted) is given in Figure 17.9. Every agency adopted the approach of the seven Cs and the events were, for the most part, a model of quiet co-operation.

FIGURE 17.9 A selection of the enforcing authorities who had jurisdiction over some part of the event

Royal Navy

Health and Safety Executive

Fleet Safety

Hampshire Police

Isle of Wight Council

Gosport Council

British Transport Police

City of London Authority

Maritime and Coastguard Agency

Naval Base Commander

Civil Aviation Authority

Portsmouth City Council

Nuclear Installations Inspectorate

Ministry of Defence Policy

Royal Protection

Royal Air Force

Naval Provost Marshal

Westminster Council

Security Services

The result

What did all of the hard work and planning achieve? The results were:

- an excellent series of diverse events with a very high degree of public and guest satisfaction.
- attendance levels in the hundreds of thousands.
- the strengthening of international links. The Festival of the Sea, Drumhead Ceremony and fleet review all sought to forge new links and strengthen old ones and did so with considerable success.
- a high media profile in the UK and overseas.
- the achievement of varying objectives for key stakeholders. Each partner organisation was seeking something slightly different and everyone appeared to get what they needed.
- a significant boost to profile and tourist spending within the region.
- no serious injuries or accidents.
- minimal disruption and impact on local health/emergency service economies. The local economy cannot be expected to pick up the bill for a mega-scale series of events. Careful planning of medical and emergency response teams meant virtually no cost to the local health service.

The T200 series was a unique programme of events, but the core elements of safety planning and delivery apply to any show, whatever the scale, location or content:

- *consider safety at the outset*: Health and safety is not something that can be bought in at the last minute. It is an ethos and attitude that should inform decision making from the outset. Thinking about safety from the beginning saves money and grief.
- *appoint a safety coordinator*: Get a competent person to drive the safety agenda. Depending on the size of the project they may also take on other roles, but when a certain scale is reached a focused professional is needed.
- *plan ahead*: Last-minute decisions tend to be expensive and stressful.
- *coordinate specialist input*: T200 needed specialists on a wide range of subjects, but their input had to be coordinated and filtered. The risk assessments of contractors needed to be vetted, their staff properly briefed and their operations monitored.
- *consult extensively with stakeholders*: A lot of event organisers are distrustful of civil authorities, but structured and open communication allows you to identify shared objectives.
- *develop a robust command framework*: Given the number of things that could have gone wrong, it would have been madness to plan a response to every potential scenario. Instead, effort should be focused on setting up a clear decision-making structure with good communications and access to outside help if needed. An effective command structure should be able to deal with anything that is thrown at it.
- *involve staff at all levels of the organisation*: People have got to buy into the health and safety agenda. It must be seen as a way of getting the job done effectively and efficiently rather than the imposition of a set of arbitrary rules by people who do not know what they are talking about.
- *do not lose sight of the everyday risks*: It is easy to become fascinated by 'big danger'. The problem is that it is too easy to become fixated by the possibility of the RAF crashing into the side of the French nuclear carrier, sparking meltdown, Armageddon and a nuclear winter. In reality, it is likely to be the trips and falls on seafront steps that generate the casualties.

Tim Roberts, T200 H&S coordinator.

Questions

1. The importance of tabletop exercises and using scenarios are emphasised in this case study. Discuss why this is so effective. List some likely scenarios.
2. The risk management was performed from a health and safety perspective. What other risks can be identified in marketing, finance and administration? Which of these risks would flow on to risks in the safety area?
3. Discuss the importance of the human side of risk management. Compare the case study to the comments from Drucker and Salter in the chapter.

CASE STUDY: EVENT RISK MANAGEMENT AT LEEDS NEW YEAR'S EVE 2003

Most major cities in the UK, since the turn of the century, have staged some kind of New Year's Eve event for their residents and visitors. These events range in scale from a simple fireworks display to, what is probably the world's largest New Year's Eve party, Edinburgh's Hogmanay.

Such events offer the organiser some unique challenges in the staging of these events, particularly with regards to risk management:

- Staged in the middle of winter, with night-time temperatures normally below or only just above freezing. NB: In 2000 and 2003 New Year's Eve events in Edinburgh, Liverpool and Newcastle have had to be cancelled due to extreme weather.
- They are large events, almost exclusively staged in city centres, as opposed to Greenfield sites.
- The demographic of the audience is predominantly made up of 18- to 35-year olds; as such the consumption of alcohol is widespread, as people seek to 'toast the New Year'.
- Events normally feature a countdown, followed by a 'midnight moment' which can involve anything from fireworks, confetti and the singing of 'Auld Laing Syne'.
- The event organiser will need to consider all the above and incorporate various control measures, which will need to be put into place as a part of the event risk management process.

Background

Prior to New Year's Eve 2000, the city of Leeds had not staged a major New Year's Eve event. Revellers seeking a 'gathering point' to see in the New Year, used to congregate in City Square, a small square not that suitable for events. This was due to the Square technically being a roundabout, bordered on three sides by a busy road and the fact that it contained numerous statues and other street furniture, which in the run up to midnight soon became a vantage point for revellers. During the mid-1990s, things got so bad at City Square that a Medical and Police Unit was positioned at the Square, as effectively the gathering of revellers had become an 'un-managed' event.

Having been widely criticised by the press and the public for the largely low-key community-led celebrations laid on during at Millennium Eve (1999), and the fact that Leeds had a brand new public square, Millennium Square, to stage large-scale events, the decision was taken to create an event for New Year's Eve 2000.

Unfortunately, the weather was so bad across much of Northern England on 31 December 2000 that the Leeds event, which incorporated the opening of the Millennium Square had to be curtailed, with only fireworks being successfully staged due to widespread blizzards. New Year's Eve events were then successfully staged in 2001, 2002 and 2003. The events quickly became very successful, with a number of interesting issues coming about, due to the staging of the event, as revellers were encouraged to join in the celebrations in a managed, rather than un-managed environment as previously:

- City Square was no longer seen as the gathering point for revellers in the city centre.
- West Yorkshire Police reported a dramatic reduction in arrests made across the city centre, while West Yorkshire Ambulance Service reported a reduction in city centre casualties.
- Public transport was laid on to all areas of the city until 0230 hours, which made the event more accessible and reduced the pressure on taxi services, as prior to 2000, bus services stopped at 1900 hours or before.
- Images of the event we used widely in local media, and the event became billed as 'York-shire's largest New Year's Eve Party', which as a result saw audiences attending the event from across the region, staying overnight in the city's hotels.

- The city centre attracted a much wider demographic, including families and children as opposed to just being the preserve of 18- to 35-year olds. This was further encouraged through the programming of entertainment, such as street performers, the use of tribute acts with wide appeal such as 'Robbing Williams' or 'Beatlemania' and the development of a fun fair adjacent to the event, which added to the celebratory atmosphere. Alcohol and food were also widely available at the event.
- By making the event free and no ticket required, it increased accessibility and prevented the problem encountered when giving free tickers away of potential capacity not being reached due to people deciding not to attend the event due to a change in plans or bad weather for example. This also results in non-ticket holders and visitors to the city not being frustrated by their lack of ticket, enabling then to still experience the event.

The risk management process

The event was becoming a victim of its own success, as more and more people sought to join in the celebrations. The licensed event capacity was increased each year to a maximum in 2003 of 12,000, which included the use of adjoining streets to maximise capacities. In addition, given the nature of the event, organisers were experiencing a significant ingress of people to the Square from 2330 hours until just before midnight, as people left neighbouring bars and clubs to join the celebrations and see the fireworks display.

The issue of potential overcrowding is just one of the many issues the event management team had to consider in the development of their risk assessments for the event. The risk assessment ended up being a 36-page document, excluding the fireworks display, which due to its specialist nature was provided by the fireworks display provider.

In managing and recording the risk of overcrowding, the first stage is to identify that the potential hazard of overcrowding exists, and identify what the risk, so in this case the risk would be potential crushing, pushing, crowd collapse and ultimately resulting in serious injury or potential death.

The next stage is to rate the risk, first by estimating potential numbers involved, which for an incident as serious as overcrowding could be as high as 500. Then a further rating of the risk is calculated by grading the severity × the probable frequency. Table 17.1 illustrates the severity and frequency scales used.

Therefore, using the example of overcrowding, the maximum score would be 36 [the chance of fatalities (6) × happening frequently (6)]. This alone, or in reality any score over about 20, would tell the event manager that the activity should not be staged. Some risk assessments just stop here, as risk assessments can adopt many different styles. However, best practice has identified the need to then introduce 'control measure(s)'. For example, control measures put into place for New Year's Eve to prevent overcrowding included:

- The use of video screens to increase visibility of the stage and key elements of the event – the use of screens can also greatly assist in letting the audience know when the midnight moment

Table 17.1 Severity and frequency scales

Severity		Probable Frequency	
Trivial	1	Improbable	1
Minor	2	Unlikely	2
Major – single	3	Possible – happens	3
Major – multiple	4	Happens occasionally	4
Hospitalisation	5	Happens periodically	5
Fatality	6	Happens frequently	6

Continued

CASE STUDY: EVENT RISK MANAGEMENT AT LEEDS NEW YEAR'S EVE 2003—*CONT'D*

Table 17.2 Example of headings used in an event risk assessment

Hazard	Risk	Potential Numbers	Severity Rating × Likelihood = Primary Risk Based on No Controls	Control Measures	Severity Rating x Likelihood = Residual Risk Based on No Controls	Comments

actually is, all it takes is one group of people with a watch 3 or 4 minutes fast and the spontaneity of the moment can be lost.

- The use of barrier dumps and stewards at key ingress points to the Square to block the roads if there is a danger of capacity being reached. Such a plan was actually put into place at the 2002 event.
- The identification of possible vantage points, anything from bus shelters to walls, and to control access to such points to prevent climbing, by either stewards or barriers/fencing.
- The use of event communications such as CCTV and radios to inform the event manager of crowd density and spread across the site. For example, Millennium Square normally fills from the east, as this is the area where most pubs and bars are. This can result in the east of the Square being full, while to the west, the crowd is less dense. This information can then be relayed to stewards who would close certain approach routes and advise audience goers of alternative routes to the event.

After you have considered control measures such as these, you then rate the risk again, which should come up with a much lower figure thanks to the control measures you have put into place. A table can be used to assist this process (Table 17.2).

While this formula might appear simple and to some extent of common sense, it is recording of the potential for risk and the measures put into place that the risk assessment is designed to cover.

Risk assessments should also be used to consider issues throughout the 'on site' period, for example, such as how to manage the use of plant and machinery in a public space, or issues to consider such as the use of electricity in the open air. Therefore, risk assessments should ideally be broken down into sections for ease of use, for example, build and breakdown, venue, audience and performance.

Individual risk assessments should be obtained from each supplier providing equipment or services at the event (in some cases alongside a method statement, which actually details how they will undertake the task). This, therefore, allows the event manager to then cross-reference documents in the completion of the event risk assessment.

SUMMARY

Although risk assessments are time-consuming documents to produce, particularly when the event manager has many other tasks to complete prior to an event, they should never be generic (that is, not off the shelf, being specific to the event being staged in each venue they are performed at). They should also be considered a 'working document' with amendments being included up to show day in some instances, although the licensing authority normally requires at least a draft version several weeks before the event.

If the event manager or licensing authority, when dealing with a large commercial event such as a festival, does not feel competent in the writing or reviewing of risk assessments, or in undertaking the role of event safety officer (the person who implements control measures and oversees event safety on site), then several companies now independently offer such a service such as Capita Symonds, who can independently provide such services to the event organiser.

For further information about events in Leeds, including Millennium Square, please visit: www.leeds.gov.uk/Leisure_and_culture/Leeds_entertainment_and_events_guide.aspx.

By Patrick Loy, former Events Manager at Leeds City Council (2000–2004). Currently working for Events for London and managing a wide variety of events on Trafalgar Square (including London's New Year's Eve celebrations).

Questions

1. What were the unique features of this event and how did this contribute to the risk assessment?
2. Draw the risk management process in a step-by-step diagram. Describe how this was applied to the New Year's event.
3. Identify what other management techniques could be used to control crowds at events such as this.

Evaluation and research

18

LEARNING OBJECTIVES

After studying this chapter, you should be able to:

- describe the role of evaluation in the event management process,
- discuss the nature and purpose of post-event evaluation,
- understand and discuss the evaluation needs of event stakeholders,
- identify and use a range of sources of data on events,
- create an evaluation plan for an event,
- apply a range of techniques, including the design of questionnaires and conduct surveys to evaluate events,
- understand how to analyse data on events,
- prepare a final evaluation report,
- use event profiles to promote the outcomes of events and to seek sponsorship,
- apply the knowledge gained by the post-event evaluation process to the future planning of an event.

INTRODUCTION

Event evaluation is critical to the event management process. It is the final step in the planning process, where the goals and objectives set at the start of an event are used as benchmarks to determine its final outcomes and success. It enables event managers to evaluate their own processes and to communicate event outcomes to key stakeholders. As events become more central to our economy and involve considerable investment by host organisations and governments, it is becoming increasingly important to accurately evaluate their outcomes. While economic evaluation dominates much of the field of evaluation literature and practice, the triple bottom line of economic, social and environmental impacts is increasingly recognised by governments and researchers alike.

The events industry is still young, and is struggling in some areas to establish legitimacy and acceptance as a profession. One of the best means for the industry to gain credibility is for events to be evaluated honestly and critically, so their outcomes are known, their benefits acknowledged and their limitations accepted. However, event evaluation serves a much deeper purpose than just 'blowing the trumpet' for events. It is at the very heart of the process where insights are gained,

Events Management. DOI: 10.1016/B978-1-85617-818-1.10018-0

lessons are learnt and events are perfected. Event managers need to be aware of and utilise both primary and secondary research sources in the planning and evaluation of events. Event evaluation, if properly utilised and applied, is the key to the continuous improvement of events and to the standing and reputation of the event industry. As such, it should be a high priority for all event managers to properly evaluate their events and to disseminate this evaluation to their stakeholders and interested groups. If done well, this will not only enhance the reputation of their events, but also their own reputation as professional event managers.

WHAT IS EVENT EVALUATION?

Event evaluation is the process of critically observing, measuring and monitoring the implementation of an event in order to assess its outcomes accurately. Evaluation is a continuous process that takes place throughout the life of an event. It enables the creation of an event profile that outlines the basic features and important statistics of an event. It also enables feedback to be provided to event stakeholders, and plays an important role in the event management process by providing a tool for analysis and improvement. However, it has three key phases:

- pre-event evaluation, also known as feasibility studies, which takes place before the event in order to ascertain whether it is viable to stage it. This was discussed in Chapter 5 under the heading of 'Evaluating the event concept'.
- the monitoring and control process, which takes place during the implementation of the event in order to ensure that it is on track and to take remedial action if required. This process was discussed in Chapter 6 on project management and events.
- post-event evaluation, which focuses on the measurement of event outcomes and on ways in which the event can be improved.

This chapter will focus on the post-event evaluation phase and process.

EVENT IMPACTS AND EVALUATION

An important aspect of event evaluation is the calculation of event impacts, both positive and negative, short term and long term, on their stakeholders and the wider host community. This is particularly important for government stakeholders, who are interested in the bigger picture of the impacts of an event on the host city, region or nation as was discussed in Chapter 3. Such assessment will often focus on economic impacts, as governments and funding bodies require evidence of what the event has achieved in relation to the investment of taxpayers' funds. Governments also use such assessments to conduct a cost–benefit analysis in order to compare the outcomes of investment in events with other potential uses of resources. Economic impact studies are also used by governments to prioritise which events to support, as was discussed in the case of UK Sport in Chapter 3.

Given this emphasis by government on the economic dimension of events, it is not surprising that the study of economic impacts dominates both evaluation practice and the academic literature on events (Raybould et al., 2005; Wood et al., 2006). In a comprehensive review of the academic literature, Sherwood et al. (2005) analysed the content of a total of 224 refereed journal articles and event-related conference papers. As might be expected, the most frequent focus was on economic impacts (28.1%), followed by social impacts (19.6%), event management (13.4%) and tourism impacts (12.9%). Only two articles in the study focused on the environmental components of events. The researchers noted a growing unease in host communities with this emphasis on economic evaluation, noting that the failure to adequately address social and environmental impacts may lead to a misrepresentation of the long-term contribution of events to the host community.

A counter-trend has been a growing emphasis on the wider social and cultural impacts of events, highlighting aspects such as social capital (Hilbers, 2005), host community perceptions of event impacts (Fredline et al., 2005), community engagement in events (Harris, 2005) and methods of evaluating social impacts (Wood et al., 2006).

Raybould et al. (2005) have developed a holistic triple bottom-line approach to the economic, social and environmental impacts of events. They identified key performance indicators in each of the three domains and suggested a technique for examining them holistically by providing a framework for dealing with the inevitable trade-off between positive and negative impacts within the three domains.

For economic impacts, they suggested using traditional indicators such as the net income as a ratio over the expenditure necessary to host the event, the financial yield of visitors and the net benefits per person of the event to the host community. For social impacts, they proposed using a range of indicators, such as the percentage of locals who attend, volunteer for or are employed by the event; the percentage of local businesses contracted to supply goods and services; the value of access to new facilities developed or access to facilities denied to locals during the event; crime reported associated with the event; crowd management incidents; traffic counts or dollar value of time lost in traffic; and the quantity and quality of media exposure generated by the event. For environmental impacts, they suggested indicators such as the energy consumed at the venue and in transport to the event, water consumed at the event, waste water recycled, waste generated at the event and waste recycling.

Much work needs to be done to perfect indicators and measurement techniques for each of the three domains, and to find adequate means to document and record them. However, such approaches may ultimately provide a fuller and more accurate evaluation of the impacts of events on their communities.

POST-EVENT EVALUATION

Post-event evaluation is concerned primarily with measuring the success of an event in terms of its objectives by collecting and analysing relevant data from the event. It is also concerned with evaluating the process of organising the event, and feeding back lessons and observations learnt from this into the ongoing event management process. Post-event evaluation can also build up a picture of the event, facilitating the communication of its outcomes to key stakeholders. Silvers (2004), Shone and Parry (2010) and Van Der Wagen (2008) identified a number of important functions of post-event evaluation. These include:

- measurement of event outcomes,
- creation of a demographic profile of the event audience,
- identification of how the event can be improved,
- enhancement of event reputation and
- evaluation of the event management process.

These functions are further elaborated.

Measurement of event outcomes

In the planning phase, key goals and objectives are identified in relation to the event. These become important benchmarks, sometimes known as key performance indicators, which enable the success of the event to be measured in relation to its outcomes. For example, a community festival may set clear objectives in relation to the number of people attending, the level of audience satisfaction and the financial performance of the event. For major events, the event objectives and the means to measure them may be much more complex, involving benchmarks such as economic impacts, media coverage, tourism outcomes and sponsor benefits. For corporate events, important benchmarks might include levels of staff motivation, product awareness or sales generated. In each case, these are the agreed criteria by which the success of the event will be judged and the evaluation process will need to establish reliable ways to measure them and report back to stakeholders.

Creation of a demographic profile of the event audience

For future planning purposes, it will be useful to establish not only the number of people who attended the event, but also where they came from, how they heard about it and demographic details such as age range, gender, levels of education and income. Establishing an accurate demographic profile of the audience will enable marketing strategies to be refined and the spending of marketing funds to be better targeted.

Identification of how the event can be improved

Another important function of event evaluation is the identification of what worked and what did not, providing a sound basis for improved planning in the case of ongoing events. For example, the Parkes Elvis Festival in the central west of New South Wales conducts an annual survey of visitors to the festival in association with a university research partner. In addition to tourism and demographic information, the survey seeks to obtain opinions of visitors to the festival by asking them what they enjoyed most about the festival and what improvements could be made. The information gained from this study has led to improvements to the festival pro-gramme and organisation such as the extension of trading hours of outdoor activities, the upgrading of the festival parade, the improvement of signage and the inclusion of new activities in the programme.

Enhancement of event reputation

Capturing and disseminating the achievements of an event can assist greatly in building its reputation and credibility. Thus, some events make extensive use of their final reports to gain media exposure and support. This becomes critical when the reputation of an event has been damaged by negative publicity, as was the case with the death of a young woman in the mosh pit at the Big Day Out music festival in 2001. Other events use the reporting of event outcomes to gain public acceptance, as the Sydney Gay and Lesbian Mardi Gras has done by issuing frequent reports of the economic impacts of the event. Governments also report regularly on the economic impacts of major events in order to gain political advantage by demonstrating the benefits of the events as a result of their investment and support.

Evaluation of event management processes

Another key purpose of post-event evaluation is to examine the processes used by the event manager in the planning and conduct of the event. By careful analysis of these processes the event manager will improve not only the outcomes of the event but also their own skills and techniques in managing it, as was discussed in Chapter 6. The use of computers allows the event manual to be reviewed, refined and used for the next incarnation of the event. Important questions to consider are whether the budget and resources were adequate, whether the critical path timeline was sufficient and whether key documents such as marketing, operations and risk management plans, policies and procedures and checklists can be revised and updated for future use. In this way, by evaluating the processes of organising the event, event managers can improve and refine their own professional skills and practices.

KNOWLEDGE MANAGEMENT

This refinement of the skills and practices of event management has led to the development of the field of event knowledge management. The staging of major events and conferences has now become so complex that event managers and organising bodies cannot afford to start from scratch in the planning of events. They must start from what has been learnt from the previous staging and history of the event and build on this to further develop the event's management practices and profile. Multi-sport events such as the Olympic and Commonwealth Games, and individual championships such as the FIFA World Cup and the FINA World Swimming Championships, have developed a formal process for the transfer of knowledge from one event to the next. The International Olympic Committee has established the Olympic Games Knowledge Service in Lausanne, Switzerland, responsible for making the expertise gained from previous Olympic Games available to bidding cities and future Olympic host cities. The process was formalised by the payment of Australian $5 million to the Sydney Organising Committee for the Olympic Games for the intellectual property of the Sydney Olympics (Halbwirth and Toohey, 2005).

Innovations in marketing, programming and staging, as well as improvements in operational issues such as crowd control, risk management and security, quickly ripple through the industry and become universally used and accepted. The process of the transfer of knowledge takes place partly through the documentation of the event and partly through the skills and experience of key event personnel, who become highly sought after because of their successful track record in organising events. Thus, many of the personnel from the Sydney Olympic Games have played key roles in Olympics in Athens and Beijing, Commonwealth Games in Manchester and Delhi, and Asian Games in Doha and Guangzhou. For example, Di Henry, who successfully organised the torch relay for the Sydney Olympic Games in 2000, went on to organise the torch relays for the Commonwealth Games in Manchester in 2002 and Melbourne in 2006. Andrew Walsh, who directed the opening ceremony for the Rugby World Cup in Sydney in 2003, went on to become executive producer for the opening and closing ceremonies of the Olympic Games in Athens in 2004. Major corporate events and conferences now also formalise the transfer of knowledge process, with the development of standard procedures and manuals for their events in order to achieve consistency and to build a body of knowledge and best practice in relation to their events.

Post-event evaluation, then, serves a variety of purposes in relation to events. In addition to assessing event outcomes, it also feeds observations and information back into the event management cycle, leading to a process of continuous improvement (see Figure 18.1). This applies to individual repeat events, where the lessons learnt from one event can be incorporated in the planning of the next. It also applies to the general body of events knowledge, where the lessons learnt from individual events contribute to the overall knowledge and effectiveness of the events industry.

THE EVENT EVALUATION PROCESS

The event evaluation process has five major stages:

- planning and identification of event data required,
- data collection,

FIGURE 18.1 Evaluation and the event management process

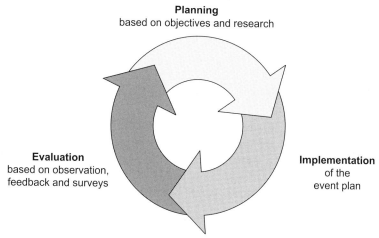

- data analysis,
- reporting and
- dissemination.

The process must be planned from the outset of the event and will involve the commitment of resources including staff, time and budget. As the collection of data can be expensive, budget will sometimes be a limiting factor in the design of the event evaluation process.

Planning and identification of event data required

The first step is to define the purposes of the evaluation and, therefore, what data will need to be collected. From the purposes listed above, it is evident that there will often be a number of complementary agendas in relation to the needs of different stakeholders in events:

- The host organisation will want to know what the event achieved. Did the event come in on budget and on time? Did it achieve its objectives? How many people attended and were their expectations met?
- The event sponsor may have other measures. Was the level of awareness of the product or service increased? What penetration did the event advertising achieve? What media coverage was generated? What was the demographic profile of the people who attended?
- Funding bodies will have grant acquittal procedures to observe and will usually require audited financial statements of income and expenditure, along with a report on the social, cultural or sporting outcomes of the event.

- Councils and government departments may want to know what the impact was on their local or state economies.
- Tourism bodies may want to know the number of visitors attracted to the area and what they spent, not only on the event, but also on travel, shopping and accommodation.

All these complementary and overlapping agendas must be taken into account in determining the purposes of the evaluation.

Once the purposes of the evaluation have been defined, the data that need to be collected can be identified and listed. These can be grouped into matching areas or subsets; for example, one group of data may relate to attendance and demographic profile, another to audience response and satisfaction levels, another to media coverage and another to sponsor outcomes. The fuller and more specific the identification of data required, the easier it will be to plan the collection of the data.

What to evaluate?

Events have both tangible and intangible impacts. Surveys most commonly measure tangible impacts such as economic costs and benefits, as these can most easily be measured. However, it is also important to evaluate the intangible impacts of events, even if this evaluation needs to be more narrative based or descriptive. Some of the intangibles that are hard to measure include the impacts on the social life and well-being of a community, the sense of pride engendered by events and the long-term positioning of a place or tourist destination.

The parade and events staged for the London gay and lesbian communities as Pride London, and its predecessor London Mardi Gras, has been a focus for Gay Rights and Pride. The Bradford Mela aims to celebrate Asian cultures and educate other residents, fostering a culture of racial tolerance. The Eisteddfod Festival, alternating between north and south Wales each year, has provided a strong focus for Welsh national identity. While events such as these have undoubted social worth, it may be difficult and perhaps even counterproductive to quantify this in anything other than descriptive terms. Nevertheless, their cultural meaning and social impacts would need to be taken into account in any serious evaluation of their community impacts.

Qualitative and quantitative data

It is important at this stage to distinguish between two different types of data, both of which will often be involved in the event evaluation process.

Qualitative data are based on individual perceptions and responses and are often obtained through informal and in-depth interviews, focus groups, staff feedback and participant observation. They can provide valuable insights, but are often anecdotal and lend themselves to narrative rather than statistical analysis.

By contrast, quantitative data are measurable and subject to statistical analysis. They are often collected via box office receipts, financial records, surveys, etc. and lend themselves to conclusions based on statistical analysis. The City of Edinburgh Council, together with other stakeholders in the Edinburgh Festivals (including the organisers and the Scottish Tourism Board), use the economic impacts of the Edinburgh Festivals very effectively in promoting support for, and acceptance of, the events. Other councils, tourist boards and regional development agencies have also quickly recognised the value of such data. For example, Bournemouth Borough Council (2008) indicated a £24 million impact from their Air Festival, and in a press release announcing the 2009 event, Visit York (2009) indicated an economic impact of £2.8 million for Illuminating York 2008. Similarly, Welcome to Yorkshire and Yorkshire Forward have used economic impact studies to underline the contribution of events such as the International Indian Film Academy (IIFA) Awards in 2007, sometimes referred to as the 'Bollywood Oscars', to the regional economy, with an estimated return on investment of £2 million (Ruddick, 2008).

Both forms of data can play a valuable role in the event evaluation process, but their use will need to be carefully balanced in order to provide a total picture of the event. In addition, care should be taken that an appropriate methodology is followed to ensure that the resulting data are valid.

Data collection

Each of the subsets listed above will now require consideration as to how the data are to be collected and analysed. Silvers (2004) and Veal (2006) suggested several main sources of data on events and these are discussed here.

Event documentation

The process of organising the event will provide many opportunities for the collection of significant data.

- *Financial performance*: The event budget and final balance sheet will provide detailed information on income and expenditure and profit or loss of the event. This can be compared with previous costs of staging the event and may require interpretation with regard to variance; for example, downturns in the economy, or currency exchange fluctuations in relation to international events or visiting performers.
- *Paid attendance*: For a ticketed event, box office reports or participant registration lists will generally provide information with regard to event attendance. Ticket sales reports may provide other valuable information such as gender analysis and postcode breakdowns.
- *Crowd size*: For free-entry events, police crowd estimates, and public transport and car park figures can be helpful in calculating attendance numbers. Other tools such as judging the percentage of the venue filled in relation to its known capacity and photographic surveys taken at regular intervals can help to estimate attendance.

- *Demographic information*: If participants are required to fill in an event registration form, this can be designed so that valuable demographic information is captured, such as age, gender, point of origin, spending patterns and so on.
- *Performance statistics*: An examination of contracts will reveal number of performers engaged in, say, a multi-site festival over several days.
- *Merchandise sales*: Sales records will provide data on the sale of merchandise and the contribution of these sales to the income of the event.
- *Safety profiles*: Accurate recording of first-aid treatments, on-site incidents, etc. will help to establish risk management and safety profiles of the event.

These are just some examples of the useful data that can be compiled from the event documentation in order to build up a picture of the event. Organisers of the Australian Masters Games, for example, are required to provide a detailed profile of the event, including the number of participants and their partners, the number and type of competitions/functions that were conducted, the marketing and risk management strategies employed and detailed statements of income and expenditure. The profiles of previous events are of immense value to the organisers of future Games events.

Media monitoring

Media coverage is an important aspect of an event. This coverage can be either positive or negative, depending on the event outcomes, the impact on the community and the kind of relationship built up with the media. It is important to monitor and record this coverage as part of the event documentation. If the event is local, it may be possible to do this by keeping a file of newspaper articles and by listening and looking for radio and television interviews and news coverage. For larger events, it may be necessary to employ a professional media-monitoring organisation that can track media coverage from a variety of sources. They will usually provide copies of print media stories and transcripts of radio interviews and news coverage. Audiotapes and videotapes of electronic coverage can be obtained for an additional charge. This coverage provides an excellent record of the event and can be used effectively in profiling the event for potential sponsors and partners.

A further issue is content analysis of the media coverage, as this is not always positive. Negative media coverage can affect the reputation of the event and by implication negatively impact on stakeholders, such as host organisations and sponsors.

Some media monitors attempt to place a monetary value on positive media coverage, usually valuing it at around three times the cost of equivalent advertising space, on the grounds that editorial is likely to be better trusted by consumers and is therefore worth more. Such valuations should be regarded as approximate only, but may provide a useful comparative assessment of media coverage. An initial media evaluation of Manchester International Festival 2009 valued the total media coverage of the event at £19.9 million (Bernstein, 2009), while IIFA Awards 2007 achieved broadcast value for Yorkshire of £40 million, with 500 million viewers in 110 countries (Ruddick, 2008).

Event observation

Another means of collecting data is by structured and detailed observation of the event. This may involve the event manager as well as staff, attendees and key stakeholders in the event.

Management observation

There is no substitute for direct observation of the event (sometimes called 'management by looking around'). Knowing the event and its objectives well, the event manager is in a good position to observe aspects such as general ambience, performance quality, audience response, crowd flow, etc., which can make or break an event from the point of view of participants. They will also be well placed to observe the levels of performance of contractors and staff, and defects in site design or event operations, which may constitute important lessons to be learnt from the event.

Staff observation

Staff members are also in a good position to critically observe the event and their observations and reports may provide information on a number of important aspects of the event. However, staff will provide more accurate and useful data if they are trained to observe these issues and are given a proper reporting format, such as checklists to evaluate items such as attendance figures, performance quality and audience reaction. Security staff may be required to report on crowd behaviour, incidents, disturbances and injuries.

Stakeholder observation

Other key players in an event, such as venue owners, councils, sponsors, vendors, police and first-aid officers, can often provide valuable feedback from their various perspectives.

- *Venue owners* may be able to compare the performance of the event with their normal venue patterns and comment usefully on matters such as attendance figures, parking, access, catering and facilities.
- *Police* may have observed aspects such as crowd behaviour, traffic flow and parking and may have constructive suggestions for future planning.
- *Councils* may be aware of disturbances to the local community or difficulties with street closures or compliance with health regulations.
- *Sponsors* may have observations based on their own attendance at the event, or may have done their own surveys of audience reaction, awareness levels and media coverage.
- *Vendors* may have information on the volume of sales or the waiting time in queues that will be valuable in planning future catering arrangements.

- *First-aid providers* may provide statistics on the number and seriousness of injuries such as cuts, abrasions or heat exhaustion that will assist in future planning of safety and risk management.

All these key stakeholders may have observations on general planning issues such as signage, access, crowd management, communication and the provision of facilities that will have implications for improvement of the event. It is important that their observations are recorded and incorporated into the evaluation and planning stages of the event management process.

De-brief meetings

A valuable opportunity for feedback on the event management process is provided by the de-brief meeting. This should be held as soon as practical after the event, while memory and impressions of the event are still fresh. Staff members, contractors, public authorities, such as police and ambulance, and other key stakeholders may be invited to the de-brief meeting. For larger events, the process might even be conducted as a series of meetings devoted to individual aspects of the event such as operations and marketing. Participants should be given notice of the meeting prior to the event, so that they are aware that their observations will be welcomed and noted. For the best results, an agenda should be prepared and circulated and the meeting should be carefully chaired and not allowed to ramble or descend into blame or recrimination. A well run de-brief meeting can make a major contribution to the understanding of what went well and what did not, any significant risk factors that were revealed and any implications for the future improvement of the event. The topics to be addressed at the meeting will be determined by the nature and size of the event. However, the checklist in Figure 18.2 is a useful starting point.

Focus groups

Focus groups can provide a good opportunity to test participant reactions to an event and to obtain in-depth perceptions of particular stakeholder groups. They are normally directed discussions involving a small group of 8–12 people with similar demographics, conducted by professional interviewers in a relaxed environment. The event manager or his or her representative may be an observer and is sometimes hidden by a two-way mirror so as not to intrude in the process. The focus group can provide a detailed, directed discussion and is a useful tool to explore participant attitudes, opinions and motivations.

Surveys

It would be ideal to seek the opinions and responses of all attendees of an event, but for most large events this task would be too costly and impractical. Survey techniques involve seeking the opinions and responses of a representative sample of total attendees in order to obtain vital and accurate data on the event. The better the design of the questionnaire form used and the more rigorous the survey process, the more accurate will be the results obtained.

FIGURE 18.2 Event evaluation checklist

CHECKLIST FOR EVENT EVALUATION			
Aspect	Satisfactory	Requires attention	Comments
■ Timing of the event ■ Venue ■ Ticketing and entry ■ Staging ■ Performance standard ■ Staffing levels and performance of duties ■ Crowd control ■ Security ■ Communications ■ Information and signage ■ Transport ■ Parking ■ Catering facilities ■ Toilets ■ First-aid ■ Lost children ■ Sponsors acknowledgement ■ Hosting arrangements ■ Advertising ■ Publicity ■ Media liaison			

Surveys can range from simple feedback forms targeting event partners and stakeholders to detailed audience or visitor surveys undertaken by trained personnel. The scale of the survey will depend on the needs and resources of the event. Simple feedback forms can usually be designed and distributed using the event's own internal resources. They may seek to record and quantify basic data, such as the expenditure of event partners, or feedback from local retailers and accommodation providers as to the effect of the event on their levels of business activity. In their study of local authorities' event-based tourism, Thomas and Wood (2003) found that visitor feedback/surveys were the most popular methods of evaluation undertaken by more than 60% of responding authorities.

Surveys are used to ascertain reliable statistical information on audience profiles and opinions, and visitor patterns and expenditure. They may be implemented by direct interviews with participants or may rely on participants filling in written questionnaires. They may be undertaken face to face, or by telephone, mail or e-mail. Face-to-face interviews will usually generate a higher response rate, but techniques such as a competition with prizes as incentives for participation may improve the response rate of postal or e-mail surveys.

Undertaking effective surveys requires expertise and considerable organisational resources. For event organisers with limited in-house experience and expertise, professional assistance can be called on for tasks ranging from the design of questionnaire forms to the full implementation of the survey process. Professionally prepared generic templates and questionnaires are also available to assist the event manager in this process — see, for example, the *Encore: Festival and Event Evaluation Kit* (Jago, 2006) discussed later in this chapter, eventIMPACTS, and the *APEX Post-Event Report Template* (Convention Industry Council, 2005).

In the case of repeat events, event organisers may wish to repeat the same survey each year in order to compare successive events and to establish trends, or they may want to embark on more ambitious research programmes surveying different aspects of the event each year. Whatever the scale and approach that is decided on, experts such as Getz (2005), Jago and Dwyer (2006), Veal (2006) and the publication by the UK Sport (1999c) suggest certain basic factors that should be kept in mind. These are:

- *purpose*: Clearly identify the purpose and objectives of the survey. A clearly stated and defined purpose is most likely to lead to a well-targeted survey with effective results.
- *survey design*: Keep it simple. If too much is attempted by the survey, there is a danger that focus will be lost and effectiveness reduced. Questions should be clear and unambiguous and should be tested by a pilot study before the actual survey.
- *language*: Questions should use a suitable vocabulary and be grouped around topics. Avoid using 'leading' questions that encourage pre-conceived answers, and the use of biased or emotive language.
- *open versus closed questions*: An open question is one that invites the interview subject to answer without prompting a range of responses. A closed question is one where the interview subject is offered a range of answers to choose from, such as rating an item on a scale of 1—5 or on a range of poor to excellent. Open questions can provide a greater opportunity for the respondent to express their opinion, but are harder to quantify. Closed questions are more restricted, but lend themselves to easier coding and analysis. A good questionnaire form should seek an appropriate balance between open and closed questions.
- *size of sample*: The number of participants must be large enough to provide a representative sample of the audience. The sample size will depend on the variability in the population to be sampled, the level of precision required and the available budget. If in doubt, seek professional advice on the size of the sample.
- *randomness*: The methodology employed in the selection of participants must avoid biases of age, sex and ethnicity. A procedure such as selecting every tenth person who passes by a specified point may assist in providing a random selection. With multi-venue and multi-day events, care should also be taken that the survey process is spread evenly across venues and days of the event in order to provide a truly random sample of participants.

- *support data*: The calculation of some outcomes will depend on the collection of support data. The calculation of total visitor expenditure, for example, will require accurate data on the average expenditure of visitors as well as support data on the number of visitors to the event. Then the spending pattern revealed by the survey can be multiplied by the number of visitors to provide an estimate of the total visitor expenditure for the event.

Secondary data

In addition to the data collected from the above sources, other data may be available which were collected for some other (primary) purpose, but which may be useful in evaluating some aspect of the event. These are known as secondary data (Veal, 2006). Examples include:

- research bureaus
- web searches
- journal databases
- reports from previous events

Research bureaus

There are many publicly and privately funded research organisations that will provide access to valuable data either free of charge or for a modest fee. The Office of National Statistics (www.statistics.gov.uk), for example, produces detailed information on a wide variety of topics, including Australian social trends, census statistics and how British people spend their leisure time. They also provide useful information on a range of social and cultural trends including topics such as attendance at cultural events, reasons for attending the arts and children's participation in cultural and leisure activities (see, for example, 'Taking Part: England's survey of culture, leisure and sport' produced quarterly by the Department of Culture, Media and Sport).

VisitBritain, Northern Ireland Tourist Board, VisitScotland and Visit Wales commission and provide access to national and international visitor surveys, which provide accurate data on visitor patterns and expenditure on a wide range of activities, including travel, accommodation and attendance at some types of events. The arts councils collect and disseminate data relating to arts-related events. The Business Visits & Events Partnership (www.businessvisitsandeventspartnership. com) produces and disseminates research relating to aspects of business visits, events and business tourism.

Web searches

A web search of similar events will produce a surprising amount of data, including how other event managers have approached the issues of event coordination, programming, promotion, logistics and evaluation. Some will even include copies of their event reports, providing detailed information on event outcomes such as attendance and economic impacts.

Journal databases

Also found on the web are journal databases that will enable event managers to track down research articles in tourism-, leisure-, marketing- and event-specific journals, which can be of great assistance in researching, planning and evaluating an event. Some of these articles may be accessed directly from the web or through public and university libraries. Articles can be found on a wide range of event issues, including marketing, sponsorship, audience motivation and satisfaction, event impacts, risk management, harm minimisation, event operations and evaluation.

By undertaking a thorough scan of relevant secondary research, the event manager can proceed from an informed and knowledgeable position and can often save time and money in devising a primary research and evaluation plan for an event.

Research reports from previous events

If the event has been conducted before, then previous event reports and/or discussions with their organisers or staff may be of great assistance to the event manager. Each Commonwealth Games, for example, is required to provide a detailed post-games report, including the number of event participants and their partners, the number and type of competitions/functions that were conducted, the marketing strategies employed and detailed statements of income and expenditure of the event. The report from the 2002 Manchester Commonwealth Games has provided the basis for a useful on-line resource (now available through http://web.archive.org/web/20071022064134/ www.gameslegacy.com) including the full reports, while a similar level of information is also available for Sydney Olympics (www.gamesinfo.com.au). By studying these previous event reports carefully, the event manager can form a fairly accurate profile of the event, including likely predictions of attendance figures and budgets. The specifics of the host city's planned event will need to be taken into account, including charac-teristics and aspects of the location that are likely to influence the event outcomes.

Studies of similar events, or discussions with their event managers, may prove rewarding, particularly if the event has not taken place before. A new food and wine festival, for example, may be expected to have a similar profile to other existing food and wine festivals, allowing for differences of location, market, etc. A conference for one industry group or association may be expected to behave in similar ways to previous conferences for similar groups or associations. By studying carefully what has gone before, an astute event manager may be able to develop a template that may need fine-tuning and adjustment, but will provide valuable insights into the likely profile of a new event.

Data analysis

Much of the data from sources such as event documentation and observation listed above can be analysed manually in order to identify key event outcomes such as attendance and financial results. These data may need some degree of interpretation, for example, by comparing them with stated event objectives or with similar data from previous events.

Data from surveys will need to be analysed in order to reveal useful statistics and trends. This can be done using a spreadsheet package such as Microsoft Excel, or PASW Statistics (formerly known as SPSS), a statistical software package used widely by event and tourism academic researchers. This will enable the calculation of frequencies (for example, what percentage of respondents rated the event as poor, average, good, very good or excellent) and of means or averages of variables such as the average spend by visitors to the event. These packages also enable statistical information to be presented graphically, for example, the use of line graphs, bar charts or pie charts.

If open questions have been used in the survey, these will need to be coded or categorised so that their frequencies can be calculated. They may best be reported using a narrative rather than a statistical format.

Reporting

Once the relevant data have been collated and analysed, then comes the task of writing and preparing the event report. The first consideration is for whom the report is intended. Reviewing the purposes of the evaluation discussed at the beginning of this chapter may prove useful. This may influence the style of writing, the amount of detail and the overall presentation of the report. In some cases a number of versions of the report may have to be prepared for different audiences, such as the host organisation, government, sponsors and the media, though the core of the report will remain constant. Veal (2006) distinguished between the report as a narration, telling the story of the event and its achievements, and the report as a record, creating a formal and definitive account of the event process and outcomes. The narrative one will need to be largely descriptive, focusing on key points and interpreting the data to create a cohesive picture of the event. It may be argued that evaluation is to some degree subjective, but nonetheless the writer should try to reflect the event as accurately as possible, quoting relevant data to support conclusions and assumptions. Quotations from attendees, media reports, photographs and copies of flyers, posters and programmes may all help to communicate the flavour and atmosphere of the event.

The function of the report as the record of the event will lend itself to the use of statistics to create an accurate profile of the event, supported by appropriate detail through the use of tables, graphs, etc. Any outcomes noted, such as economic or tourism impacts, should be supported by a description of the methodology used to evaluate them and the number of survey responses obtained. Both the narrative and record functions of the event report combine to present a useful basis for reporting to stakeholders and for planning the next event.

Dissemination

The final step in the post-event evaluation process is to disseminate the event report to relevant stakeholder groups. This may be done by face-to-face meetings with key stakeholders such as the host organisation, government and sponsors, where the content of the report can be verbally communicated and discussed. For the host organisation this may represent an important closure and for sponsors it may give rise to a discussion on continued involvement with the event. It is worth considering additional formats of the report, for example, a PowerPoint presentation may be prepared for face-to-face presentations, or a media release may be prepared to accompany distribution of the report to the media. If the event report is well written and carefully distributed, it can be an important tool for enhancing the reputation and future prospects of the event. Figure 18.3 provides an example of a media release following the Manchester World Sport 08.

MEASURING VISITOR EXPENDITURE

All event managers will be familiar with constructing a simple financial balance statement of the income and expenditure of events. Until recent times, this form of reporting was considered sufficient as most events were evaluated on the basis of their inherent social, cultural or sporting value to the local community. However, the growing involvement of governments, tourism and arts bodies, companies and sponsors has brought with it an increasing need to consider the wider impacts of events.

The impacts of events on the economy are based primarily on the expenditure of visitors to the event from outside the host community. UK Sport (1999c, p. 12) defined the economic impact as, 'the total amount of additional expenditure generated within a city, which could be directly attributable to the event'. They have published simple guidelines for measuring the economic impact of sports events, which can be applied to other events. Their publication outlines a basic methodology (illustrated in Figure 18.4) and includes sample questions for the visitor survey (Figure 18.5). This is discussed subsequently. Since publication in 1999, the area of event impacts research has developed and the tools available to event organisers have increased significantly.

Phase 1: pre-planning

This involves planning the data collection strategy, including the likely respondents. Points to consider include:

- How many of each respondent group will attend?
- When will they be arriving?
- Where will they be staying?
- When to conduct the survey?
- Any unique circumstances, for example, children involved therefore limited funds?

FIGURE 18.3 Manchester World Sport 08 events — £23 million of economic impact generated for the city

Recently completed research has confirmed that the biggest year of international sport ever in Manchester attracted over 317,000 visitors to the City and generated £23 million of net economic impact to the Manchester area, along with providing social and participatory benefits for community and youth groups across the city and the Northwest.

Manchester City Council and its major sports events partners commissioned Ipsos MORI North, in conjunction with Experian, to undertake a research study to assess the economic benefits associated with each of the Manchester World Sport 08 events, along with the collective impacts across the city's biggest series of sporting events ever and the most significant year of world sport for Manchester since the XVII Commonwealth Games in 2002.

The study, which included primary research with spectators, revealed that the events supported a total of 499 full-time equivalent jobs in the Manchester area and that for almost all of the attendees across all of the events, the sport was the only or one of the main reasons for coming to Manchester. 11% of attendees were first time visitors to Manchester and of those, 85% enjoyed their experience of the city so much, they are likely to return within the next three years.

The 9th FINA World Swimming Championships 2008 and the UEFA Cup Final 2008 contributed £7million and £11million of net impact across Manchester, respectively. Councillor Mike Amesbury, Manchester City Council's Executive Member for Culture and Leisure, said:

"Manchester connects all its major events to the city's Sports Development and Community Sports programme, one of the most successful in the country.

"The hugely positive impacts of Manchester World Sport 08 demonstrate the Council's commitment to delivering social benefits to residents by maximising opportunities for inclusion and participation, while harnessing the considerable contribution that major sports events can make to the local economy."

Manchester won the accolade of world's top Sport City at the SportBusiness Sports Event Management Awards in November 2008, ahead of Melbourne, Berlin, Doha, Moscow and New York. Many of the individual MWS08 events were acknowledged as being groundbreaking and won awards for excellence, including the 9th FINA World Swimming Championships 2008 (25m) which saw two temporary swimming pools constructed in the MEN Arena and the sport itself being presented in a more theatrical manner.

In addition, the BUPA Great Manchester Run became the first 10k event in Europe and only the second in the world to be categorised as one of the world's leading road races with the award of the International Association of Athletics Federations (IAAF) Gold Label status.

Several of the Manchester World Sport 08 events were key to the preparation of Team GB's Olympians and Paralympians ahead of success at the 2008 Bejing games. Rebecca Adlington, Sir Chris Hoy and David Weir all won gold in Manchester last year before going on to further glory at the Olympics.

Events are a key component of Manchester City Council's Marketing Strategy. The MWS08 series was also closely aligned to the strategies of the other MWS08 key stakeholders and partners: NWDA; UK Sport; Marketing Manchester; and MEN Media, part of GMG Regional Media - with major sport events having a wider role in ensuring that Manchester's burgeoning reputation as a global sports city is maintained, particularly in the run-up to London 2012.

Complementing the MWS08 benefits to the city's international reputation and economy, Manchester residents and in particular the city's schools and community groups, were able to take part in a series of related activities and competitions that ran alongside each event and had the chance to use the numerous sports facilities at Sportcity.

Continued

FIGURE 18.3 *Continued*

Peter Mearns, Executive Director for Marketing and Communications at the NWDA said:
"This level of economic impact shows just how important major sporting events are to the regional economy. It is a fantastic figure obtained from Manchester hosting a unique number of high-quality international sporting events and world championships.
"I am delighted the NWDA has been a key player in attacting and supporting these events, which have provided a huge boost in visitor numbers and economic benefit not only for Manchester but the wider region."

Andrew Stokes, chief executive of Marketing Manchester, the agency charged with promoting the city on a national and international stage, said:
"Tourism is a £5.6bn industry in Greater Manchester and the sports events of 2008 are a great example of how the sector contributes both financially and culturally to the city-region. What is important now is to build on this success and continue to bring world championship sports events to Manchester."

Simon Morton, Senior Events Consultant at UK Sport, said:
"UK Sport brings strategically important international sporting events, like last year's World Swimming and Track Cycling Championships, to the UK in order to boost the performance of our athletes. These events, hosted in Manchester, played a significant role in preparing British athletes for success at the Olympic and Paralympic Games, as seen in Beijing last summer.
"The city of Manchester will continue to play a key role in our World Class Events Programme throughout the coming years, as we prepare British athletes, volunteers, and officials for our home Games in London in 2012."

Mark Dodson, Chief Executive Officer, GMG Regional Media said:
"We were proud to support these events which shone a spotlight on Manchester and its vibrant sport scene. Our editorial sports team dedicated many pages of coverage in our print media and Channel M promoted events to a wide audience across the region. Our partnership underlines our commitment to bringing the best sports coverage to the community across the range of media platforms."

The Manchester World Sport 08 events were:
UCI Track Cycling World Championships: 26 – 30 March
9th FINA World Swimming Championships 2008 (25m): 9 – 13 April
Paralympic World Cup: 7 – 11 May
UEFA Cup Final 2008: 14 May
BUPA Great Manchester Run: 18 May
Hi-Tec World Squash Championships Manchester 2008: 11 – 19 October

Manchester is continuing to present international sport in 2009 with major events, including:
BUPA Great Manchester Run;
BT Paralympic World Cup;
Standard Bank Cup Argentina vs England Rugby Union International;
LEN European Women's Water Polo Trophy;
BTCB British International Taekwondo Open Championship;
Co-operative World Netball Series;
UCI Track Cycling World Cup Classic
and the UCI Paracycling World Championships.

For information on Manchester World Sport visit www.manchesterworldsport.com

(Source: Manchester City Council, 2009)

FIGURE 18.4 Five-phase approach to economic impact evaluation

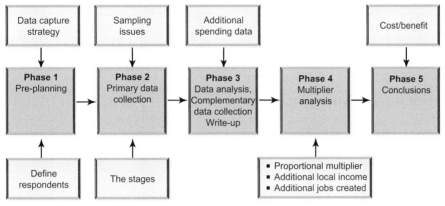

(Source: adapted from UK Sport, 1999c)

Phase 2: primary data collection

This phase involves data gathering using the survey questionnaire. UK Sport highlights the fact that each event is unique; therefore, the survey questionnaire will need to be adapted in order to meet the objectives of the event and to achieve meaningful data. The objectives and stages of the research method are:

- To quantify the number of people from outside the host city who will be staying overnight in the host city and from this subsample to quantify how many are staying in commercially provided accommodation.
- To quantify how many nights those staying in commercial accommodation will spend in the city and how much per night such accommodation is costing.
- To quantify for both those staying overnight and day visitors the amount spent per day on six standard categories of expenditure.
- To quantify how much in total people have budgeted to spend in a host city and on how many other people this expenditure will be made.
- To establish the proportion of people whose main reason for being in the host city is the event under investigation.
- To determine if any respondents are combining their visit to the host city with a holiday, so that the spending associated with the holiday, and the location of the spending, can be used to estimate any wider economic impact in other cities or regions due to staging of the event (UK Sport, 1999c, p. 12).

Phase 3: data analysis, complementary methods and writing up

The data collected by the survey questionnaire should be analysed using a statistical package (for example, SPSS), or a spreadsheet package (for example, Microsoft Excel). The data should be analysed by using three filters. First, is the respondent a local or visitor? Second, which group do they belong to? Finally, based on their group type, are they a day visitor or staying overnight?

FIGURE 18.5 Visitors Survey

[*Event Name*] Visitors' Survey

We are asking for your help. We are looking to establish the economic importance of this event. We would be grateful if you could complete the following survey. Information provided will be treated in the strictest confidence. No individual responses will be identified.

1. Please state nationality

2. Where do you live? (please specify town or city)

3. Which of the following are you?

   Athlete   1 ☐   Coach   2 ☐
   Official   3 ☐   Journalist/media   4 ☐
   Spectator   5 ☐

   If you are a resident of Cityville thank you very much for your co-operation, however your assistance is no longer required. Please return this form to a research steward

4. Are you attending the event alone?

   Yes 1 ☐   No 2 ☐

   If YES: please go to QUESTION 5a

   If NO: How many other ADULTS (over 16) are there in your party today?

   If NO: How many CHILDREN (15 and under) are there in your party today?

5a. In which TOWN/CITY are you staying tonight?

5b. Is this -

   At Home?   1 ☐
   With Friends/Relatives?   2 ☐
   A Guest House?   3 ☐
   An Hotel?   4 ☐
   A Camp Site?   5 ☐
   Other?   6 ☐

   If Other: please specify _____

For Official Use Only

Date
   ☐ 27th June
   ☐ 28th June
   ☐ 29th June

Gender
   ☐ 1 Male
   ☐ 2 Female

1. ☐ 1   British
   ☐ 2   Other European
   ☐ 3   North American
   ☐ 4   South American
   ☐ 5   African
   ☐ 6   Asian
   ☐ 7   Other
   ☐ 99 Missing

2. ☐ 0   Sheffield
   ☐ 1   Yorkshire
   ☐ 2   North
   ☐ 3   Midlands
   ☐ 4   South
   ☐ 5   Other UK
   ☐ 6   Western European
   ☐ 7   Central European
   ☐ 8   Eastern European
   ☐ 9   North America
   ☐ 10 South America
   ☐ 11 African
   ☐ 12 Australia
   ☐ 13 Other
   ☐ 99 Missing

5a. ☐ 1   Sheffield
    ☐ 2   Yorkshire
    ☐ 3   North
    ☐ 4   Midlands
    ☐ 5   South
    ☐ 6   Other UK
    ☐ 7   Other
    ☐ 99 Missing

FIGURE 18.5 *Continued*

6. How many nights are you staying in CITYVILLE? [   ]

   If you are NOT STAYING OVERNIGHT in CITYVILLE,
   please go to QUESTION 8.

7. If you are STAYING OVERNIGHT in CITYVILLE:
   How much are you spending on ACCOMMODATION
   PER NIGHT? [   ]

8. How much will you spend in CITYVILLE TODAY on the
   following -

   Food & Drink?   £ [   ]
   Entertainment?   £ [   ]
   Travel?   £ [   ]
   Programmes/Merchandise?   £ [   ]
   Shopping/Souvenirs?   £ [   ]
   Other? (Parking, petrol, etc.)   £ [   ]

9a. How much have you budgeted to spend in TOTAL during
    your stay in CITYVILLE?

   Total Expenditure   £ [   ]

9b. Does this include expenditure on others?

   Yes 1 ☐   No 2 ☐

   If YES: How many others is this expenditure for? [   ]

10. Is the EVENT the main reason for you being in
    CITYVILLE today?

   Yes 1 ☐   No 2 ☐

11. Are you combining your visit to the EVENT with a
    holiday?

   Yes 1 ☐   No 2 ☐

   If YES: Where are you going? [   ]

   For how long? [   ]

   Can you provide us with a rough idea of your total budget
   for this part of your trip?   £ [   ]

   Thank you for taking the time to complete this survey.
   Please return this form to a research steward.

(Source: adapted from UK Sport, 1999c)

In addition to questionnaire analysis, it is useful to use complementary methods in order to understand the significance of the findings. This may take the form of observing the event or qualitative interviews with the event organiser and other stakeholders, including local hotels, restaurants and shops. The final area of data to collect, sometimes referred to as 'organisational spend', is additional expenditure in the host area directly attributable to the event but not collected by the questionnaire. Once the data are collected from the sources discussed above, the final writing up of the report can begin.

Phase 4: multiplier analysis

The data collected may be analysed further, depending on the needs of the host organisation or other stakeholders. Multiplier analysis involves calculating the amount of additional income retained in the city after allowing for 'leakage' from the local economy, for example, to suppliers or staff from outside the area. Use of multipliers has been discussed by various authors, including Hall (1997) and Getz (1997), who warn that caution is required in calculating multipliers as it can lead to the impacts being exaggerated. UK Sport suggests that one of the most common methods used is the proportional income multiplier, illustrated in Figure 18.6.

Phase 5: conclusions

The final phase involves an evaluation of the costs of staging the event, compared with the benefits. However, it should be remembered that events might make a direct

FIGURE 18.6 Economic impact equations

(a) $\dfrac{\text{Direct impact } + \text{Indirect impact } + \text{Induced impact}}{\text{Initial visitor expenditure}} = \text{Proportional income}$

(b) Proportional income $\times$ Local multiplier (e.g. 0.20) = Additional local income

(c) $\dfrac{\text{Additional local income}}{\text{Average annual full-time wage}} = \text{Additional jobs created}$

(full-time equivalent job years)

Direct impact – Total expenditure by visitors (hotels, food, etc.) stays in the local economy from locally produced goods and services. Additional wages, salaries and profits for local business were direct recipients of the visitor expenditure.

Indirect impact – Benefit from visitor expenditure, but not directly received (e.g. suppliers to hotels and restaurants).

Induced impact – Benefit from respending of visitor expenditure in local economy.

(Source: adapted from UK Sport, 1999c)

loss at the time of the event, with rewards achieved in the longer term. Data from studies such as this will allow stakeholders (such as local authorities or regional development agencies) to evaluate their economic development policies for growth in tourism, leisure and sports. For example, the World Student Games in 1991 left Sheffield with a political argument due to a direct loss of £10.4 million; however, in the longer term, Sheffield benefited from an investment of £147 million in new and refurbished facilities that are still providing income to the city today through major events (Bramwell, 1997).

The methodology takes into account the complexity of estimating the number of visitors from outside the region. It seeks to distinguish visitors attracted by the event or who have extended their visit because of the event, from those who would have visited the region anyway. In the case of an event that extends for more than one day or that has multiple events, it also takes into account the need to identify the number of days or events attended, and to weigh this in calculating the results of the survey.

The survey form allows distinction between residents and non-local residents. This is important as it is generally accepted that local residents spending money at events does not usually lead to an increase in local income, as local residents would have spent money whether the event took place or not. This is sometimes referred to as 'deadweight expenditure' (UK Sport, 1999c).

Calculating the economic impact of events is a complex task involving many factors. However, by applying the guidelines and the survey shown in Figure 18.4, a simple and useful snapshot of the economic impact of an event can be readily obtained.

Event evaluation toolkits

Arts Council England has funded a range of projects relating to arts evaluation, which has application for festivals. Reeves (2002) provided an overview of arts impacts research based on the literature available, focusing on the economic and social aspects. One of the objectives of the study was to develop a practical resource to assist practitioners with effective evaluation. Further work commissioned as the 'National Arts Information Project: Evaluation Toolkit' (Comedia, 2003) included an extensive practical overview of evaluation together with supporting evaluation tools developed in Microsoft Excel — participant and audience questionnaires and a project data template. The idea of the evaluation toolkit had also been explored by other arts organisations within the UK and overseas. Arts Council of Northern Ireland (Jackson, 2004) focused on the evaluation of social impacts on participants of arts groups working in community and voluntary sectors. Furthermore, a range of guidance and toolkits have been developed for people and organisations to evaluate funded arts projects. A current initiative, Evaluation Support Scotland (www.evaluationsupportscotland.org.uk), provides case studies, guides and templates.

As discussed in Chapter 3, UK Sport, working with other partners, has developed a full on-line toolkit for event impact evaluation, eventIMPACTS, that builds on their work in UK Sport (1999c) outlined earlier. Their website, www.eventimpacts.

com provides a valuable resource, including case studies and offers a methodology, tools and techniques, which can be applied to a range of sporting, tourism and cultural events and festivals.

Encore: Festival and Event Evaluation Kit

One example of these evaluation toolkits is the *Encore: Festival and Event Evaluation Kit*. Encore has been developed to facilitate the task of evaluating community events. It is produced and distributed by the Cooperative Research Centre for Sustainable Tourism in Australia and distributed internationally by IFEA, the International Festival and Events Association. The kit provides a standardised, user-friendly, computerised tool for the evaluation of festivals and events. It consists of four key modules (Jago, 2006):

- Demographic module
- Economic module
- Marketing module
- Additional questions module

Demographic module

This module enables the user to assess the demographic profile of festival and event attendees, competitors and exhibitors. Questions are chosen that relate to aspects such as gender, age, education and income. Once the data are collected and entered, a number of demographic-related reports can be produced automatically in tabular and graphic formats.

Economic module

This module calculates the direct in-scope expenditure that results from the event in a given region. This refers to the amount of new money attracted to the host region that would not have entered the region if the event had not been held. Direct in-scope expenditure can be fed directly into a computable general equilibrium (CGE) model or an input/output model to assess the flow-on effect on the local economy and produce an economic impact figure for the event. It is calculated by assessing:

- the expenditure of visitors from outside the region to the event and
- the event-related income generated by the organisers from outside the region and spent within the region.

The region must first be clearly defined, usually as a city name or a regional description. The event expenditure of locals within the region will not be counted, as it is assumed that this money would have been spent on other goods or services had the event not been held.

The expenditure of visitors from outside the region whose primary purpose was not to attend the event is also excluded, as it is assumed that they would have visited the region even if the event had not been held. An exception would be if the event had caused them to extend their visit, in which case their expenditure for the extended period of their visit would be counted.

The event organiser may wish to collect these data for other purposes, but they are not included in the direct in-scope expenditure of the event.

Marketing module

This module enables users to assess marketing-related issues by asking event participants questions that identify their motives for attending the event, how they heard about it, what they liked and disliked, their levels of satisfaction and whether they are likely to return to the next event.

Additional questions module

This module enables users to frame their own questions and to collect data on specific elements that may be unique to a particular event. This option increases the flexibility of Encore and enables users to customise the evaluation to their own needs.

Tools within Encore

Encore includes three tools:

- a survey instrument to collect data from festival or event attendees. Once questions have been selected or new questions entered, Encore can automatically prepare and print a questionnaire based on these questions and a template for the data entry.
- a calculation of the level of in-scope expenditure attributed to the event
- a reporting tool, which presents the results of each of the visitor survey questions in both tabular and graphic form.

Using this fairly simple process (see Figure 18.7), a comprehensive event evaluation can be conducted economically and effectively. Using Encore evaluation kit has the added value that it has been vetted by Australian state government treasuries.

SUMMARY

Event evaluation is a process of measuring and assessing events throughout the event management cycle. It provides feedback that contributes to the planning and improvement of individual events and to the events industry's pool of knowledge.

Feasibility studies identify the likely costs and benefits of an event, and help to decide whether to proceed with it. Monitoring the event establishes whether it is on track and enables the event manager to respond to changes and adjust plans. Post-event evaluation serves a number of purposes, including measuring the success of the event in relation to its objectives, and analysing and reflecting on it in order to feed lessons learnt from the event back into the ongoing event management process. The exact nature of this evaluation will depend on the perspectives and needs of the

FIGURE 18.7 The festival/event evaluation process

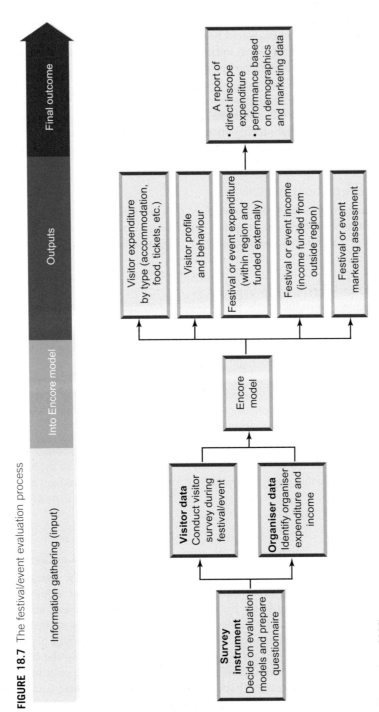

(Source: Jago, 2006)

stakeholders. The event manager needs to be aware of both primary and secondary research sources and techniques.

Good evaluation is planned and implemented from the outset of the event management process, with all participants made aware of its objectives and methodology. As well as tangible impacts, events have intangible benefits which cannot always be quantified, and may need to be recorded on a narrative or descriptive basis. These include social and cultural impacts on a community, and the long-term profile and positioning of a tourism destination. It involves deciding on the purpose of the evaluation, and then identifying and collecting data from a number of sources including event documentation, observation, de-brief meetings, focus groups and surveys. A good evaluation plan will strive to create the right balance between qualitative and quantitative data in order to provide a full and accurate picture of the event. Surveys are an important tool for providing quality data on the event and rely for their success on well-designed questionnaires and a rigorous survey process.

Calculating the economic impact of an event can be complex and expensive, but a simple methodology is available to carry out a basic study, and further guidance is available through toolkits such as eventIMPACTS and Encore. A key factor in calculating this impact is the measurement of visitor expenditure through the use of visitor surveys. The media coverage of an event should be monitored in house, or by using professional media monitors.

Once information is gathered from all sources, an event evaluation report should be compiled and distributed to all stakeholders. This report can serve to enhance the future reputation and success of the event, provide the basis for media releases that promote the outcomes of the event, and can be used for future planning and seeking of sponsorship. In finalising the event, it is important to tidy up loose ends and to feed lessons learnt from the event back into the event management process.

QUESTIONS

1. Identify a major event in your area with which you are familiar. Identify and list the purposes that the event might have in undertaking a post-event evaluation.

2. Identify a major event and then design an evaluation plan that will provide a profile of the event and form the basis of a report to key stakeholders.

3. Imagine that you are employing staff to work on a particular event. Design a report sheet for them to record their observations of the event. Decide what aspects you want them to observe and what benchmarks you want them to use.

4. Select an event that you are familiar with, and identify the stakeholders that you would invite to a final evaluation meeting. Write an agenda for the meeting that will encourage well-organised feedback on the event.

5. For a small to medium-sized corporate event or seminar, design a questionnaire to provide participant feedback on the event.

6. Obtain copies of three evaluation reports from libraries, event organisations or the Internet. Compare and contrast the methodology, style and format of these reports.

7. Identify a high-profile event in your region, and monitor as closely as you can the media coverage generated by the event, including print media, on-line, radio and television. Make a list of all the media items that you were able to identify.

8. Choose an event that you have been involved in organising, or were able to observe closely. Assemble as much data as you can on the event and use these data to create a written profile of the event. Using this written profile as a basis, draft a media release that outlines the outcomes of the event and the benefits to the local community.

CASE STUDY: MTV EUROPE MUSIC AWARDS 2003

The starring performance of Edinburgh in the 10th anniversary MTV Europe Music Awards won Scotland priceless worldwide exposure and an £8.9 million jackpot in direct economic benefit. Figures announced in March 2004 by Scotland's Tourism Minister, Frank McAveety, reveal that the rock and pop extravaganza delivered more than double the original estimate of economic benefit to the city and Scotland. It was anticipated when MTV Europe announced Edinburgh would host the 2003 'Oscars' of the music world that they would be worth £4.2 million to the economy. The real benefits are identified in an economic study of the event undertaken by independent consultants SQW on behalf of the public sector partners, Scottish Enterprise, City of Edinburgh Council and EventScotland, who supported the Awards with funding of £750,000.

The breakdown of where the benefits were realised in hosting the show, which attracted a galaxy of the world's hottest music talent, indicates that:

*   Edinburgh gained £6.4 million extra expenditure,
*   Lothians benefited by £300,000 and
*   Scotland benefited from another £2.2 million of additional spend, giving a total of £8.9 million,

MTV Europe's free performance in Princes Street Gardens, arranged as a thank you to Edinburgh and Scotland, and the first time MTV Europe has undertaken such a production, generated £1.3 million.

Television and media evaluation

The show, hosted by Christina Aguilera and featuring Beyoncé, Kylie Minogue, Justin Timberlake, Travis and a host of other stars, was beamed around the world in 77 hours of programming by MTV's global networks. MTV's viewing audiences showed a remarkable increase over the previous year. Even Spain, which was host to the show in Barcelona in 2002, increased its viewing figures. The UK audience was up 200%, Sweden increased by 25%, Spain increased by 45% and America recorded a 38% rise to its highest ever level for the show.

The study also identified the value of television and print media coverage of the event.

*   MTV's global networks screened 77 hours of coverage worth an estimated £8.6 million.
*   Worldwide print media coverage in 2094 articles carried by 928 publications in 19 countries has an estimated value of £4.8 million.

Supplier evaluation

Hotels in Edinburgh received bookings valued at £2.2 million with 2360 more rooms being sold across the week of the event compared with the same week in 2002. Occupancy levels for the night of the event were 26% up at 93% while occupancy for the week rose by 9.4%–83% compared with the same period in 2002.

During the show, the city and Scotland received 45 celebrity endorsements which the report says have 'a huge value' in reaching younger audiences and raising the profile of Edinburgh and Scotland as a tourist destination and place to live and work.

Retailers provided mixed feedback on the impact of the event with 37% recording an increase in business, 37% reporting no impact while 26% said it had a negative effect on them. But 62.5% said the Awards would provide long-term benefit.

Encouraging the use of local suppliers by MTV Networks Europe in supporting the production of the event was a key objective of the public sector's funding for the project. This resulted in more than 50% of suppliers being Scotland based, the highest involvement of local companies in the 10-year history of the MTV Europe Music Awards. The study reveals that these companies between them earned a total of £1883 million.

Evaluation of perceptions

Both MTV Europe and the public sector commissioned reports on people's perceptions of the Edinburgh event. Those questioned for MTV placed the appeal of the event above the Brit Awards and the Oscars. Their report discovered that many attendees had been offered up to £1000 for their tickets. The public sector study found that among corporate guests, journalists and the stars' agents, 83% rated the Edinburgh event the best they had ever attended. MTV Europe proclaimed the event their best ever and presented Edinburgh and Scotland with a special MTV Award, normally given only to the winning performers, in recognition of the support they received.

Views of key stakeholders

Commenting on the findings, Scotland's Minister for Tourism, Culture and Sport, Frank McAveety, said: 'Edinburgh and Scotland have benefited immensely by having the MTV Awards here. This was a hugely successful event, with the short term major economic benefits twice as high as was forecast. And we should not forget the long term benefits we can expect as this occasion delivered a global profile for Scotland as a world class location for tourism and business. We can now look forward to building on this success to attract other world class events.'

Jim McFarlane, Chief Executive, Scottish Enterprise Edinburgh and Lothian, said: 'These results are a well earned tribute to the creativity, innovation and excellence of effort invested by everyone involved in the production of a star studded event that has promoted Edinburgh and Scotland around the world. The headline figures are really just the tip of the iceberg in measuring the value of the MTV Europe Music Awards 2003. The lasting impact will come from realising the benefits of the exposure to a young, increasingly mobile global audience and the endorsement of the city and Scotland as a world class location by universally recognised celebrities. The Awards were a challenge which we met. The standard has been set and the bar raised in terms of what we must seek to achieve in attracting international events of every nature. A prime lesson that can be learned from the success of the MTV Europe Music Awards 2003 is the effectiveness of real partnership working that has a "can do" attitude.'

Council Leader Donald Anderson said: 'It is a tribute to the huge success of the MTV Europe Music Awards that the economic findings have more than doubled from the original estimate. An £8.9 million boost to the Scottish economy, of which more than 70% has gone directly to Edinburgh's economy, is a very significant return. It is clear from these findings that through MTV's visit to the city and the resulting worldwide media coverage we have reached new audiences, showing that Edinburgh is among the world's top destinations for visitors and conferences and events of this scale. MTV gave Edinburgh and one billion viewers worldwide a fantastic party and it was an unforgettable experience that has left a lasting legacy for the city and its people.'

David Williams, Chief Executive, EventScotland, added: 'These are very positive results reflecting the strength of both public and private sector partnerships, and the economic benefits associated with major events. We will use the example of the MTV Europe Awards 2003 when

Continued

CASE STUDY: MTV EUROPE MUSIC AWARDS 2003—*CONT'D*

bidding for other events, to demonstrate Scotland's experience and capability of staging world class events.'

Richard Godfrey, Executive Producer, MTV Europe Music Awards, said: 'MTV Europe is delighted that Scotland has enjoyed such huge economic benefit as a result of the show coming to Edinburgh – this news duly caps the best ever MTV Europe Music Awards. Edinburgh was the perfect location for a show of this scale and the success the show was built on our fantastic partnerships with Edinburgh and Scotland. Scotland is a world-class destination for high-profile events.'

SUMMARY

Evaluation is key to ensuring that lessons are learnt from events and that the wider implications and impacts can be fully assessed. EventScotland, Scottish Enterprise Edinburgh and Lothian, City of Edinburgh Council and the Scottish Executive were keen to ensure that a range of perspectives on the MTV Music Awards were evaluated in order to gain an understanding of the true value in hosting events of this type and to inform the wider events policy for Scotland. Evaluating the 10th MTV Europe Music Awards provided some very useful insights and data which have demonstrated the impact and also the capacity of Scottish suppliers to deliver world-class events.

For further information about MTV, please visit www.mtveurope.com. To access the full impact evaluation report, please visit www.scottish-enterprise.com.

By Scottish Enterprise Edinburgh and Lothian, City of Edinburgh Council and EventScotland.

Questions

1. Identify the benefits of hosting an event such as this to Edinburgh and the wider region.
2. Discuss what activities the stakeholders in this event could undertake in order to maximise the benefits of hosting the event.
3. Identify which methods of evaluation were demonstrated in this case study.
4. Identify and discuss other methods of evaluation that may have been appropriate.
5. Investigate and discuss what support is available for attracting events to Edinburgh and Scotland.

CASE STUDY: T IN THE PARK

From its beginnings at Strathclyde Country Park in 1994 to what will undoubtedly be the most successful year to date, in the lush environs of Balado in 2008, T in the Park has grown in size and influence to become one of the most important and critically acclaimed music events on the international festival circuit.

Now attracting over 85,000 music fans from all over the globe each day, T in the Park is consistently a sell out success. This popularity can be attributed to the festival's unique atmosphere, the legendary Balado crowd, unrivalled the world over and an annual line-up that is one of the most exciting on the planet.

With over 180 artists performing across 11 stages over 3 days, T in the Park consistently attracts the finest international talent from the Red Hot Chili Peppers, The Who, Green Day, The Killers, Foo Fighters, REM, Oasis, Radiohead, to home-grown heroes Franz Ferdinand, Primal Scream, Amy Macdonald, The View and The Fratellis.

History

T in the Park was established when DF Concerts, one of UK's leading concert promoters, teamed up with Scotland's favourite pint Tennent's Lager, who had a history of supporting the Scottish live music scene in the late 1980s. DF Concerts had for some time been considering the development of Scotland's first large-scale, multi-stage music event to act as an annual focal point for the music scene, and Tennent's were keen to further increase its support of live music.

The first T in the Park took place at Strathclyde Country Park in 1994, with DF Concerts teaming up with MCD Promotions of Eire to create a sister company Big Day Out Ltd to promote the event. The festival was an artistic success, and while financially it was less successful, it fired the enthusiasm of the 17,000 fans that turned up each day, and subsequent years have been greeted with ever-increasing popularity and acclaim.

Development

In 1997, when the festival's original site was developed as a supermarket, Balado Activity Centre, near Kinross, provided an excellent alternative at the very heart of Scotland. This relocation has made T in the Park more accessible for fans travelling from remote parts of Scotland, as well as being convenient for all major cities and other parts of the UK. This shift is now reflected in the increasingly diverse T in the Park audience, with more than 45% of ticket buyers coming from outwith Scotland, making the event one of the country's biggest annual tourist attractions (and fifth biggest town in Scotland for the duration of the weekend!).

Now in its 16th year, the festival's progressive attitude has seen it develop into a benchmark event, held up not only in the UK, but in Europe and beyond. Its inception has led to the development of a strong and sustained outdoor live events industry in Scotland with its model inspiring the emergence of other successful UK festivals, such as V. T in the Park's sustained development in both size and status has allowed DF Concerts to effectively combine the creative and business elements needed to produce an event with both financial stability and music industry prestige, ensuring that it attracts the very best artists to Scotland each year.

The success of DF Concerts' ongoing relationship with founding partners Tennent's Lager has ensured that T in the Park has developed in both size and stature and has gone on to become recognised as one of the key players in the global music calendar. Worldwide media attend the event in significant numbers, further underlining the festival's international profile.

On-site activity at T in the Park has seen many changes over the years, with 75% of the audience now opting for the 'true festival experience' of camping on site for the whole weekend, compared to just 5% in 1994 – making it the largest camp site in Scotland. In addition to the diverse range of stages, tents, Silent Disco and other on-site entertainment, the site also boasts a funfair, global food village and a range of additional bars and entertainment.

Other event initiatives introduced in 2007 included 'Healthy T', an area which sought to redress the notion that festival food is unhealthy and unappealing. The area offered such delights as a juice bar, stovies, oysters and mussels and saw demonstrations by celebrity chefs The Hairy Bikers and Scots Michelin starred chef Martin Wishart over the course of the weekend, along with other top Scottish chefs.

T Break has been working with new Scottish talent since 1996 and is now an established and well-respected highlight of the Scottish musical calendar. T Break is a Tennent's Lager initiative which, over the past decade, has supported thousands of aspiring musicians, including the likes of The Cinematics, Lizard King's hottest new signing Drive-By Argument and Biffy Clyro, all of whom regularly acknowledge the importance of the platform which T Break provided for them as they launched their career. Along with the Ceilidh Tent, the T Break Stage makes T in the Park the only UK festival to have two stages dedicated entirely to home-grown talent.

Also new in 2007 was the introduction of TicketExchange launched by DF Concerts and Ticketmaster for T in the Park, aimed at countering ever-increasing activity on unauthorised Internet resale sites. TicketExchange is the only legitimate resale site authorised by T in the Park and offers fans protection from potentially fraudulent sellers. Working in tandem with the ticket bar code scanning system AccessManager introduced in 2005, these measures highlight T in the Park's ongoing commitment to act as a forerunner in innovative practice in the fight against touting.

Continued

CASE STUDY: T IN THE PARK—*CONT'D*

The year 2008 saw the introduction of many new exciting initiatives which continued to ensure that the T experience was the ultimate in festival fun for fans.

Three days proved just not enough for T in the Park fanatics so when faced with the chance to make it last that little bit longer, thousands jumped to have an extra night's camping. Thursday night gave revellers pick of the first pitches and a chance to get themselves into the party spirit early with the Silent Disco, Boombus, Cinema, Duracell Power House Club, bars and a fairground.

Tennent's literally took the weight off camper's shoulders this year as they provided a pre-order service 'Be Chilled' that allowed campers to pre-order chilled cans of lager for collection, at their convenience on arrival at T in the Park.

Introduced for the first time, yet another welcome addition was Fancy Dress Friday, which, in 2008, exceeded all expectations as thousands embodied the community spirit of T in the Park, coming together dressed in anything and anyone that took their fancy. Bananaman seemed to replicate camp site wide, and a sea of superhero's over lapped the site. The resultant winners literally embodied T dressing as Tennent's cans with fine-stitch detail to boot.

You arrive at T in the Park. Your bed's set up, there are chocolates on your pillow and you head to the spa before taking to the Main Stage. Sounds like a dream? Well 2008 saw this become the reality for many as luxury camping took to the fields of Balado. Following the government decision not to pass legislation against ticket touting, T in the Park organisers were aware that some people may be willing to pay a great deal of money for tickets through the secondary market (that is, tout sites). T was keen to offer a reliable alternative for those considering going down this route by offering a guaranteed ticket package for the event. Featuring a range of bespoke tipi accommodation including the dream features mentioned above alongside access to hospitality, a special catering area, luxury toilets and shower facilities. With treatment like that it's a wonder they were not being dragged to the stage mistaken for stars!

Sustainable festival

T in the Park is more concerned about its impact on the environment than ever before and has taken many steps to exercise a greener approach. One of only two CarbonNeutral events in the UK (the other being DF Concerts' Connect festival), T in the Park is the largest CarbonNeutral festival in the world and continues year on year to reduce its impact on the environment through its working practices, for example, using low-energy light bulbs and a carefully considered fuel system.

T in the Park also canvasses the support of its attendees. The beautiful Balado site sits near Loch Leven, a Site of Special Scientific Interest which means all T in the Parkers are encouraged to bring phosphate-free soap to site. Citylink's bus services are advocated as the greenest way to travel to the event and once there, T in the Park asks for festival-goers assistance to recycle what they can at the recycling points provided.

This request has not gone unheeded with 95% of the audience believing that it is fairly or very important that the event is as green as possible. Participation in 2009's cup recycling scheme has increased – the initiative introduced in 2006 was expanded in 2007; a 10p deposit, added to the price of each pint, was returned when the cup was returned to a designated recycling point. A huge success, over 75% of cups were returned meaning that the co-operation of T in the Parkers made a huge difference to the overall tidiness of the site, and of course the environment.

Evaluation

Despite the large crowds that descend on Balado each year, the event enjoys an extremely warm and positive reception from the local council and surrounding communities and in 2006 became the only festival in the UK to be awarded a 3-year licence for the second time.

The importance of T in the Park to Scotland was recognised by Jack McConnell who visited the event in its 10th year in 2003 and said: 'It is great to see so many young people enjoying themselves. The festival is very valuable to the Scottish economy and it symbolises the modern Scotland we want to portray.' Motions have been passed in Parliament, the past 2 years running to congratulate T in the Park on its success in the UK Festival Awards, with the event receiving unanimous cross-party support.

SUMMARY

With 15 years of success behind it and yet another weekend of the very best music and unique atmosphere ahead, T in the Park can most definitely claim to be one of the British music industry's greatest success stories.

Finally, testament to the excellent event management of DF Concerts, T in the Park also won a raft of awards recognising achievements in the event overall and its approach to sustainable issues, including Greener Festival Award (AGreenerFestival.com, 2008 and 2009); Best Toilets (UK Festival Awards 2009); Best Line Up (publicly voted) (UK Festival Awards 2008); C4 Festival of the Year (publicly voted) (Vodafone Live Awards); Green'n'Clean Award (Yourope – European Festival Association Awards 2008); and 'Event Grand Prix', 'Green Award' and 'Best Large Festival' (Scottish Event Awards 2008). Tennent's Lager's commitment and successful involvement in T in the Park has also yielded many awards, among these the prestigious Hollis Award for Sponsorship Continuity in 2003, which not only saw a fitting tribute to T in the Park's 10th year, but saw the event beat Nationwide (Football Association and England Team), HSBC (ITV Drama Premieres), and Ford (UEFA Champions League) for the title.

For further information about T in the Park, please visit www.tinthepark.com.

By DF Concerts and Tennent's Lager.

Questions

1. What do you see as the successful components of this festival which have seen it grow so quickly and result in tickets being sold out?
2. T in the Park has developed over the years to ensure that it can compete on the international stage. What evaluation methods would you propose the organisers undertake to ensure that T in the Park remains a must-see festival?
3. What criteria would you suggest for the success of the event to be measured from the organiser's and other stakeholders' perspectives?
4. What questions would you include in a visitor's survey for T in the Park to obtain the data identified in question 3?
5. The organisers have introduced a range of initiatives to increase the sustainability of T in the Park. What other initiatives and activities do you believe that they could introduce to continue this journey?

References

A Greener Festival Ltd (2010). *Welcome*. (Internet) Available from <www.agreenerfestival. com> (accessed 1 May 2010).

Abbot, J. (2000). The importance of proper crowd management and crowd control in the special events industry. In *Events Beyond 2000 — Setting the Agenda. Proceedings of the Conference on Evaluation, Research and Education, 13—14 July* (J. Allen, R. Harris, L. K. Jago and A. J. Veal, eds). Sydney, Australian Centre for Event Management, University of Technology.

Adams, J. S. (1965). Inequity in social exchange. In *Advances in Experimental Social Psychology* (L. Berkowitz, ed.) New York, Academic Press.

Advantage West Midlands (2004). *Motor Show Set To Boost Tourism by £5 Million*. (Internet) Press Release, 16 January. Available from <http://www.advantagewm.co.uk/ news/motor-show-set-to-boost-tourism-by–5-million.html> (accessed 5 August 2005).

Aguilar-Manjarrez, R., Thwaites, D. and Maule, J. (1997). Modelling sports sponsorship selection decisions. *Asia-Australia Marketing Journal*, **5**(1), 9—20.

Aitchison, C. and Pritchard, A. (eds) (2007). *Festivals and Events: Culture and Identity in Leisure, Sport and Tourism*. Festivals and Events: Beyond Economic Impacts, Volume 4. Eastbourne, Leisure Studies Association.

Aitken, J. (2006). General Manager, Events and Marketing, Sydney Royal Easter Show, Royal Agricultural Society of New South Wales. *Personal Communication*, June.

Ali-Knight, J. and Chambers, D. (eds) (2006). *Festivals and Events: Beyond Economic Impacts: Volume 2: Case Studies in Festival and Event Marketing and Cultural Tourism*. Eastbourne, Leisure Studies Association.

Ali-Knight, A., Robertson, M., Fyall, A. and Ladkin, A. (2009). *International Perspectives of Festivals and Events: Paradigms of Analysis*. Oxford, Elsevier.

All England Lawn Tennis Club (2009). *AELTC Local Community Programme* (Internet) Available from <http://www.wimbledon.org/en_GB/about/infosheets/aeltc_community. html> (accessed 22 November 2009).

Allen, J. (2002). *The Business of Event Planning*. Ontario, John Wiley & Sons Canada Ltd.

Allen, J. (2003). *Event Planning Ethics and Etiquette: A Principled Approach to the Business of Special Event Management*. Ontario, John Wiley & Sons Canada Ltd.

Allen, J. (2004). *Marketing Your Event Planning Business: A Creative Approach to Gaining the Competitive Edge*. Ontario, John Wiley & Sons Canada Ltd.

Allen, J. (2005). *Time Management for Event Planners*. Ontario, John Wiley & Sons Canada Ltd.

Allen, J. (2007). *The Executive's Guide to Corporate Events & Business Entertaining*. Ontario, John Wiley & Sons Canada Ltd.

Allen, J. (2009). *Event Planning: The Ultimate Guide to Successful Meetings, Corporate Events, Fundraising Galas, Conventions, Conferences, Incentives and Other Special Events*. 2nd edn. Ontario, John Wiley & Sons Canada Ltd.

Allen, K. and Shaw, P. (2001). *Festivals Mean Business: The Shape of Arts Festivals in the UK*. London, British Arts Festival Association.

Allsop, K. (2004). How the Broncos "do" Sponsorship. *Presentation at Queensland University of Technology*, 19 April 2004.

American Marketing Association (2010). AMA Dictionary. (Internet) Available from <http://www.marketingpower.com/_layouts/dictionary.aspx> (accessed 24 April 2010).

Amis, J. and Cornwell, T.B. (eds) (2005). *Global Sport Sponsorship*. Oxford, Berg.

Anon (1998). *Bear Necessities. Electronic Telegraph*, Issue 1310, 26 December. (Internet) Available from <http://portal.telegraph.co.uk/html Content.jhtml? html=%2Farchive% 2F1998%2F12%2F26%2Fsogile26.html> (accessed 8 February 2001).

Anon (2000). *Rugby World Cup 1999 Economic Impact Evaluation: Summary Report*. Edinburgh, Segal Quince Wicksteed Limited and System Three.

Anon (2004). NPower ties with cancer charity. *Marketing*, 4 August, 8.

Anon (2005a). IVCA Estimates Industry Worth £2.8 billion. (Internet) AVInteractive, 21 July. Available from <http://www.avinteractive.co.uk/news/search/820231/Ivca-Estimates-Industry-Worth-28bn/> (accessed 1 May 2010).

Anon (2005b). *Tetley's 'Official Beer' Status of Super League Clubs*. (Internet) 8 February, *Sponsorship News*. Available from <http://www.sponsorshipnews.com/svga/archive. cfm?id=1106> (accessed 3 August 2005).

Anon (2005c). *Tiger Beer to Sponsor Cult Asian Filmfest*. (Internet) Event, April. Available from <http://www.eventmagazine.co.uk/news/search/824715/Tiger-Beer-sponsor-cult-Asian-filmfest/> (accessed 1 May 2010).

Anon (2010). *Over 1,200 Athletes Get Food Poisoning at Event in Dominican Republic*. (Internet) Latin American. Herald Tribune, 26 April Available from <http://www.laht. com/article.asp?ArticleId=355962&CategoryId=13002> (accessed 27 April 2010).

Ansoff, I. (1957). Strategies for diversification. *Harvard Business Review, September–October*, 113–124.

Armstrong, M. (1999). *A Handbook of Human Resource Management Practice*. 7th edn. London, Kogan Page.

Armstrong, M. (2006). *A Handbook of Human Resource Management Practice*. 10th edn. London, Kogan Page.

Arnold, A., Fischer, A., Hatch, J. and Paix, B. (1989). The Grand Prix, road accidents and the philosophy of hallmark events. In *The Planning and Evaluation of Hallmark Events*, (G. J. Syme, B. J. Shaw, D. M. Fenton and W. S. Mueller, eds). Avesbury, Aldershot.

Arts Council of England (1999). *Guidance Notes on Carrying out Audience/Visitor Surveys*. London, Arts Council of England.

Association of Exhibition Organizers, British Exhibition Contractors Association and Exhibition Venues Association (AEO, BECA and EVA) (2002). *The Guide to Managing Health and Safety at Exhibitions and Events*, Berkhamsted. AEO, BECA and EVA.

Association Planner (2009). London: Gastro (2009). Who won the bid? THEPLANNER.BE, Ghent. (Internet) Available from <http://www.associationplanner.be/file.php?page=file& N=287> (accessed 18 October 2009).

Athens Environmental Foundation (2004). *World Conference on Sport and the Environment at Nagano 2001, Athens Environmental Foundation 2004*, World conference on sport and the environment at Nagano, Japan 2001, www.athensenvironmental.org.

Australian Safety and Compensation Council (2006). *Guidance on the Principles of Safe Design for Work*, Commonwealth of Australia, Canberra.

Axelsen, M. and Arcodia, C. (2004). Motivations for attending the Asia–Pacific Triennial Art Exhibition. In *Paper presented at the 14th International Research Conference of the Council for Australian University Tourism and Hospitality Education*, 10–13 February, Brisbane.

Ayaya (2002). *At Tournament End, Converged Network Built by Avaya Scores FIFA World Cup Firsts*. (Internet) Press Release, 11 July. Available from <http://www.avaya.com/gcm/

master-usa/en-us/corporate/pressroom/pressreleases/2002/pr-020711.htm> (accessed 1 May 2010).

Backman, K. F., Backman, S. J., Muzaffer, U. and Sunshine, K. (1995). Event Tourism: an examination of motivations and activities. *Festival Management and Event Tourism*, **3**(1), 26–34.

Baker Associates (2008). *Glastonbury Festival 2007: Economic Impact Assessment*. Mendip, Mendip District Council/Glastonbury Festivals Ltd. (Internet) Available from <http://www.mendip.gov.uk/Download.asp?path=%2FDocuments%2FFinal+ReportLOWRES%2Epdf> (accessed 12 April 2010).

Baker, R. (2010). *Asos.com to Sponsor Capital FM Summertime Ball*. Marketing Week, 8 April (Internet) Available from <http://www.marketingweek.co.uk/asoscom-to-sponsor-capital-fm-summertime-ball/3012026.article> (accessed 24 April 2010).

Baker, D. A. and Crompton, J. L. (2000). Quality, satisfaction, and behavioural intentions. *Annals of Tourism Research*, **27**(3), 785–804.

Ball, S. (2000). Thank you for the music. *Access All Areas*, May, 15, 32.

Bank of Scotland Corporate (2009a). *Sponsorship Criteria*. (Internet) Chester, Bank of Scotland. Available from <http://www.bankofscotland.co.uk/corporate/sponsorship/criteria.html> (accessed 18 November 2009).

Bank of Scotland Corporate (2009b). *Corporate Sponsorship Request Form*. (Internet) Chester, Bank of Scotland. Available from <http://www.bankofscotland.co.uk/corporate/pdf/sponsorship.pdf> (accessed 18 November 2009).

Barclays Capital (2005). *Barclays Climbs the Leader Board in Golf Sponsorship*. (Internet) London, Barclays Capital Communications. Available from <http://www.barclaysscottishopen.co.uk/images/generic/sponsorship.pdf> (accessed 22 August 2005).

Barnes, P. (1999). Bournemouth makes Labour's part swing. *Access All Areas*, October, (44), 3.

Barry, T. (1986). *Marketing — An Integrated Approach*. Chicago, The Dryden Press.

Bath and North East Somerset District Council (B&NES) (1999). *Bath Festivals Trust: Annual Report and Service Specification 1999–2000*. (Internet) Bristol, Bath and North East Somerset District Council. Available from <http://www.bathnes.gov.uk/Committee_Papers/CCL/cl990322/14bathre.htm> (accessed 20 October 2009).

Bath and North East Somerset District Council (B&NES) (2000). *Bath and North East Somerset Arts Impact Assessment*. (Internet) Bristol, Bath and North East Somerset District Council. Available from <http://www.bathnes.gov.uk/Committee_Papers/CCL/cl000124/14app.htm> (accessed 20 October 2009).

Bath Festivals Trust (2007). *Summary Information Return 2007 Of Aims, Activities and Achievements*. (Internet) Available from <http://www.charitycommission.gov.uk/SIR/ENDS17%5C0000801617_SIR_07_E.PDF> (accessed 18 April 2010).

Battle, R. (1988). *The Volunteer Handbook*. Austin, Texas, Volunteer Concepts.

Baum, T., Deery, M., Hanlon, C., Lockstone, L. and Smith, K. (eds) (2009). *People and Work in Events and Conventions: A Research Perspective*. Wallingford, CABI.

BBC (2004). *First Artists Announced for Beautiful Night*. (Internet) Press Release, 6 March. Available from <http://www.bbc.co.uk/pressoffice/pressreleases/stories/2004/03_march/06/beautiful_night.shtml> (accessed 20 October 2009).

BBC News (2002a). *The Golden Jubilee*. (Internet) BBC News In Depth, 8 October. Available from <http://news.bbc.co.uk/1/hi/in_depth/uk/2002/the_golden_jubilee/default.stm> (accessed 20 October 2009).

BBC News (2002b). *Palace Pop Spectacle Wows Jubilee Crowds.* (Internet) BBC News UK Edition, 4 June. Available from <http://news.bbc.co.uk/1/hi/entertainment/music/3116113.stm> (accessed 20 October 2009).

BBC News (2003). *Fans Go Wild for Robbie.* (Internet) BBC News UK Edition, 2 August. Available from <http://news.bbc.co.uk/1/hi/uk/2022995.stm> (accessed 12 April 2010).

BBC News (2005). *Dome to Reopen as Concert Arena.* (Internet) BBC News UK Edition, 25 May. Available from <http://news.bbc.co.uk/1/hi/entertainment/arts/4578753.stm> (accessed 12 April 2010).

BBC News (2010). *Celtic Connections Festival Hits Economic High Note.* (Internet) BBC News, 8 April. Available from <http://news.bbc.co.uk/1/hi/scotland/glasgow_and_west/8609880.stm> (accessed 12 April 2010).

BDS Sponsorship Ltd (2010). *The Definition of Sponsorship.* (Internet) Available from <http://www.sponsorship.co.uk/in_sponsorship/in_sponsorship.htm> (accessed on 27 March 2010).

Beardwell, I. and Holden, L. (2001). *Human Resource Management: A Contemporary Perspective.* 3rd edn. London, Pearson Education.

Beardwell, I., Holden, L. and Claydon, T. (2003). *Human Resource Management: A Contemporary Perspective.* 4th edn. London, Pearson Education.

Belch, G. and Belch, M. (2004). *Advertising and Promotion: An Integrated Marketing Communications Perspective*, 6th edn. McGraw-Hill, Boston.

Belfast City Council (2000a). *Events Unit Performance Improvement Business Plan.* (Internet) Belfast, Belfast City Council, 10 April. Available from <http://www.development.belfastcity.gov.uk/Press/performanceimpbusplan.pdf> (accessed 3 August 2005).

Belfast City Council (2000b). *Events Unit Strategic Vision.* (Internet) Belfast, Belfast City Council Development Department, 1 February. Available from <http://www.development.belfastcity.gov.uk/Press/eventsunitstratvision.pdf> (accessed 3 August 2005).

Belfast City Council (2005). *Events.* (Internet) Belfast, Belfast City Council. Available from <http://www.development.belfastcity.gov.uk/ourwork/Events/index.asp> (accessed 3 August 2005).

Belfast City Council (2010). *Events Funding.* (Internet) Belfast, Belfast City Council. Available from <http://www.belfastcity.gov.uk/supportforsport/events.asp> (accessed 16 December 2010).

Belfast Visitor and Convention Bureau (2010). *About Us.* (Internet) Available from <http://www.gotobelfast.com/about_us.aspx> (accessed 20 April 2010).

Beniger, J. (1986). *The Control Revolution.* Cambridge, Harvard University Press.

Berlonghi, A. (1990). *Special Event Risk Management Manual.* Mansfield, Ohio, Bookmasters.

Bernstein, H. (2009). *Manchester International Festival 2009.* Manchester City Council Executive Report for Information. 10 September, (Internet) Manchester, Manchester City Council. Available from <http://www.manchester.gov.uk/egov_downloads/International Festival2009.pdf> (accessed 12 April 2010).

Berridge, G. (2007). *Events Design and Experience.* Oxford, Butterworth-Heinemann.

Bigwood, G. and Luehrs, M. (2009). *COP15 United Nations Climate Conference, Copenhagen: Event Sustainability Report. Copenhagen, Copenhagen Sustainable Meetings Coalition.* (Internet) Available from <http://www.csmp.dk> (accessed 1 May 2010).

Bigwood, G. and Luehrs, M. (2010). *Copenhagen Sustainable Meetings Protocol. Copenhagen, Copenhagen Sustainable Meetings Coalition.* (Internet) Available from <http://www.csmp.dk> (accessed 1 May 2010).

Birch, R. (2004). *Master of Ceremonies.* Sydney, Allen & Unwin.

Blakey, P., Metcalfe, M., Mitchell, J. and Weatherfield, P. (2000). Sports events and tourism: effects of motor car rallying on rural communities in mid wales. In *Reflections on International Tourism: Developments in Urban and Rural Tourism* (M. Robinson, N. Evans, P. Long, R. Sharpley and J. Swarbrooke, eds). Sunderland, Centre for Travel and Tourism with Business Education Publishers.

Blicher-Hansen, L. (2007). *Event Denmark Strategy,* unpublished case study.

Blue Green Meetings (2010). *Links and Resources.* (Internet) Available from <http://www.bluegreenmeetings.org/Links.htm> (accessed 1 May 2010).

Blyth, A. (2003). Joining the throng. *New Media Age,* July, 31.

Blythe, J. (2009). *Principles and Practices of Marketing.* 2nd edn. Andover, Cengage Learning.

Bold, B. (2005). *CreditExpert Sponsors Bennett Arron's Edinburgh Show.* (Internet) *Brand Republic*, 4 August. Available from <http://www.brandrepublic.com/news/search/article/489395/creditexpert-sponsors-bennett-arrons-edinburgh-show/> (accessed 16 August 2005).

Bond, C. (2005). *Showcase: Nokia Urban Music Festival.* (Internet) Event, May, 19. Available from <http://www.eventmagazine.co.uk/news/search/479197/Showcase-Nokia-Urban-Music-Festival/> (accessed 1 May 2010).

Boscombe Arts Festival (2006). *About Us.* (Internet) Available from <http://barfruit.co.uk/boscombeartsfestival/about.php> (accessed 16 April 2010)

Bournemouth Borough Council (2008). *£24million Benefits of Air Festival make the case for Future Events.* Bournemouth, Bournemouth Borough Council. (Internet). Available from: http://www.bournemouth.gov.uk/News/press_office/Press_Releases/December2008/future_airfestival.asp (accessed 11 November 2009).

Bowdin, G. A. J. and Church, I. J. (2000). Customer satisfaction and quality costs: towards a pragmatic approach for event management. In *Events Beyond 2000 − Setting the Agenda. Proceedings of the Conference on Evaluation, Research and Education, 13−14 July* (J. Allen, R. Harris, L. K. Jago and A. J. Veal, eds). Sydney, Australian Centre for Event Management, University of Technology.

Bradford Festival (2000). *Bradford Festival 2000 Review.* Bradford, Bradford Festival.

Bradner, J. (1995). Recruitment, Orientation, Retention. In *The Volunteer Management Handbook* (T. Connors, ed.) New York, John Wiley and Sons.

Bramwell, B. (1997). Strategic planning before and after a mega-event. *Tourism Management*, **18**(3), 167−176.

Brassington, F. and Pettitt, S. (2006). *Principles of Marketing.* 4th edn. Harlow, Financial Times Prentice-Hall.

British Arts Festivals Association (BAFA) (2001). *New Research Shows that Festivals Mean Business.* (Internet) London, British Arts Festivals Association press release, March.

British Association of Conference Destinations (BACD) (2004). *The British Conference Venues Survey* 2004. Birmingham, British Association of Conference Destinations.

British Federation of Festivals for Music, Dance and Speech (BFF) (2005). *General Information.* (Internet) Macclesfield, British Federation of Festivals for Music, Dance and Speech. Available from <http://www.festivals.demon.co.uk/geninfo.htm> (accessed 3 August 2005).

British Standards Institution (BSI) (2002). BS IEC 62198:2001. *Project Risk Management — Application Guidelines*. London, BSI.

British Standards Institution (BSI) (2004). PAS 51:2004. *Guide to Industry Best Practice for Organizing Outdoor Events*. London, BSI.

British Standards Institution (BSI) (2005). BS 7960:2005. *Door Supervisors — Code of Practice*. London, BSI.

British Standards Institution (BSI) (2006). BS 8900:2006. *Guidance for Managing Sustainable Development*. London, BSI.

British Standards Institution (BSI) (2007). BS 7499:2007. *Static Site Guarding and Mobile Patrol Services — Code of Practice*. London, BSI.

British Standards Institution (BSI) (2009a). BS 8901:2009. *Specification for a Sustainability Management System for Events*. London, BSI.

British Standards Institution (BSI) (2009b). Overview BS 8901:2009. *Specification for a Sustainability Management System for Events*. London, BSI. (Internet) Available from <http://shop.bsigroup.com/ProductDetail/?pid=000000000030196056> (accessed 28 April 2010).

British Standards Institution (BSI) (2009c). BS 8406:2009. *Event Stewarding and Crowd Safety Services – Code of Practice*. London, BSI.

British Standards Institution (BSI) (2010a). BS 8901:2010. *Sustainability Management Systems for Events*. London, BSI. (Internet) Available from <http://www.bsigroup.co.uk/en/Assessment-and-Certification-services/Management-systems/Standards-and-Schemes/BS-8901> (accessed 28 April 2010).

British Standards Institution (BSI) (2010b). BS ISO 31000:2009. *Risk Management — Principles and Guidelines*. London, BSI.

British Tourism Authority (2005). *Business Tourism: International Marketing Opportunities 2005–2006*. London, British Tourism Authority.

Brody, R. and Goodman, M. (1988). *Fund-raising Events: Strategies and Programs for Success*. New York, Human Sciences Press Inc.

Brooks, I. and Weatherston, J. (2000). *The Business Environment: Challenges and Changes*. 2nd edn. Harlow, Financial Times Prentice-Hall.

Brooks, F. and Landry, C. (2002). *Good Times: The Economic Impact of Cheltenham's Festivals*. Stroud, Comedia.

Brown, T. J. and Dancin, P. A. (1997). The company and the product: corporate associations and consumer product responses. *Journal of Marketing*, **61**(1), 68–84.

Buckler, B. (1998). Practical steps towards a learning organisation: applying academic knowledge to improvement and innovation in business performance. *The Learning Organisation*, **5**(1), 15–23.

Burgan, B. and Mules, T. (2000). Event Analysis — understanding the divide between cost benefit and economic impact assessment. In *Events Beyond 2000: Setting the Agenda — Event Evaluation, Research and Education Conference Proceedings* (J. Allen, R. Harris, L. K. Jago and A. J. Veal, eds). Sydney, Australian Centre for Event Management, University of Technology.

Burke, R. (2003). *Project Management: Planning and Control Techniques*. 4th edn. Chichester, John Wiley & Sons.

Business Tourism Partnership (2004). *Why The Fuss Over The Olympics Or New Gaming Laws When UK Business Tourism Generates £19bn A Year?! Press Release*, 15 November 2004. London, Business Tourism Partnership.

Business Visits and Events Partnership (BVEP) (2007). *Business Tourism Briefing*. London, Business Visits and Events Partnership.

CACI (2006). *Acorn: The Smarter Consumer Classification: User Guide*. London, CACI Limited.

Cake (2005). *19 More Reasons to be at V*. (Internet) Press Release, 8 March. Available from <http://www.vfestival.com/vfestival/pressreleases/oasis.pdf> (accessed 22 August 2005).

California Traditional Music Society (2003). *CTMS Volunteer Survey — 2003*. (Internet) Available from <http://www.ctmsfolkmusic.org/pdf/festival/2003/Solstice/Volsurvey.pdf> (accessed 24 August 2005).

Cambridge Policy Consultants (2002). *The Impact of the Manchester 2002 Commonwealth Games Executive Summary*. (Internet) Available from <http://www.sportdevelopment.org.uk/manimpactcpc.pdf> (accessed 1 May 2010).

Campbell, N. (2001). Future legacies — OCA's environmental initiatives. *Proceedings from the Seminar 'Passing the Torch: Sustainable Development Lessons and Legacies from the 2000 Sydney Olympic Games', Macquarie University Graduate School of Environment*, 9 March 2001. Retrieved 19 February 2005 from CD Sustainable development principles in action: learning from the Sydney 2000 experience. Ottawa, Canada, Green & Gold Inc.

Canadine, I. C. (2001). *Transport, Logistics and All That!* (Internet) Corby, The Chartered Institute of Logistics and Transport (UK). Available from <http://www.ciltuk.org.uk/pages/whoweare> (accessed 7 April 2005).

Canadian Tourism Human Resource Council (CTHRC) (2009). *International Occupational Standards for Event Management*. Ontario, Canadian Tourism Human Resource Council.

Carling, P. and Seeley, A. (1998). *The Millennium Dome*. House of Commons Library Research Paper 98/32, 12 March. London, House of Commons Library Business and Transport Section.

Carlsen, J. and Millan, A. (2002). The links between mega-events and urban development: the case of the manchester 2002 commonwealth games. In *Events and Place-making: Proceedings of International Research Conference Held in Sydney 2002* (L. Jago, M. Deery, R. Harris, A. Hede and J. Allen, eds). Sydney, Australian Centre for Event Management.

Carlsen, J. and Taylor, A. (2003). Mega-events and urban renewal: the Case of the Manchester 2002 Commonwealth Games. *Event Management*, **8**(1), 15–22.

Carroll, L. (1977) (first published 1865). *Alice's Adventures in Wonderland*. London, Puffin Books.

Carter, B. (2004). *O2 Sponsors Live Music to Boost Appeal to Youth*. (Internet) *Marketing*, 8 April. Available from <http://www.marketingmagazine.co.uk/news/207277/O2-sponsors-live-music-boost-appeal-youth?DCMP=ILC-SEARCH> (accessed 1 May 2010).

Cartwright, G. (1995). *Making the Most of Trade Exhibitions*. Oxford, Butterworth-Heinemann.

CAT Publications Ltd (2010). *M&IT Industry Awards Sponsors*. (Internet) Available from <http://www.meetpie.com/modules/eventmodule/mit/default.aspx?url=events_mit_sponsors> (accessed 12 April 2010).

Catherwood, D. W. and Van Kirk, R. L. (1992). *The Complete Guide to Special Event Management: Business Insights, Financial Advice, and Successful Strategies from Ernst and Young, Advisors to the Olympics, the Emmy Awards and the PGA Tour*. New York, John Wiley & Sons.

Chaloner, H. (1998). *A Quality of Light Boosts Cornwall's Economy.* (Internet) Available from <http://www.southwesttourism.co.uk/prodev/light.htm> (accessed 8 January 2001).

Chartered Institute of Marketing (CIM) (2005). *Marketing Glossary.* (Internet) Maidenhead, Chartered Institute of Marketing. Available from <http://www.cim.co.uk/cim/ser/html/infQuiGlo.cfm?letter=M> (accessed 3 August 2005).

Chernushenko, D. (1994). *Greening Our Games: Running Sports Events and Facilities That Won't Cost the Earth.* Ottawa, Canada, Centurion.

Chisnall, M. (1995). *Consumer Behaviour.* 3rd edn. London, McGraw-Hill.

City of Edinburgh Council (2000a). *Minutes: The City of Edinburgh Council: Appendix 1,* 24 August.

City of Edinburgh Council (2000b). *Edinburgh Launches Hogmanay Programme for 2000/2001.* City of Edinburgh Council Press Release, 23 November.

City of Edinburgh Council (2000c). *Edinburgh's Hogmanay Traffic and Safety Arrangements Announced.* City of Edinburgh Council Press Release, 15 November.

City of Edinburgh Council (2002). *Planning Guide: Events in Edinburgh.* April. (Internet) Edinburgh, City of Edinburgh Council. Available from <http://download.edinburgh.gov.uk/events/planning%2Bguide%2B2.pdf> (accessed 1 May 2010).

City of Edinburgh Council (2005). *Summary of Economic Impact Study: Edinburgh's Year Round Festivals 2004–05.* Edinburgh, City of Edinburgh Council.

City of Edinburgh Council (2006). *Edinburgh's Winter Festivals Annual Review 2005–06.* Edinburgh, City of Edinburgh Council, 3.

City of Westminster (2000). *Preferred Practice Notes: Risk Assessment in Event and Filing Activities.* (Internet) London, City of Westminster. Available from <http://www.westminster.gov.uk/leisureandculture/artsandentertainment/events/upload/5711.pdf> (accessed 1 May 2010).

City of Westminster (2005). *Guidance Notes for Organisers Proposing Events in the City of Westminster on the Public Highway or in Council Managed Areas of the City.* (Internet) London, City of Westminster. Available from <http://www3.westminster.gov.uk/docstores/formsguidance_store/634-Major%20Event%20Guidance%20Notes%202005.pdf> (accessed 9 August 2005).

Clark, R. (2000). *Australian Human Resources Management.* 3rd edn. McGraw-Hill, Sydney.

Clark, G. (2008). *Local Development Benefits from Staging Major Events.* Paris, OECD.

Clulow, J. (2007). *Dragon Festival Organizers Respond to Criticism.* (Internet) Available from <http://www.newcastle-emlyn.com/dragon-festival-organizers-respond-to-criticism> (accessed 24 April 2010).

Cohen, H. (2005). *Not Your Grandfather's Sponsorships.* ClickZ, January 20. Available from <http://www.clickz.com/3461291> (accessed 2 May 2010).

Comedia (2003). *National Arts Information Project: Evaluation Toolkit.* London, Arts Council of England.

Comfort, J. (1996). *Effective Meetings.* Oxford, Oxford Business English Skills.

Commonwealth Games Legacy Manchester (2002a). *Post Games Report,* 5, 51. <http://www.gameslegacy.com>.

Commonwealth Games Legacy Manchester (2002b). *The XVII Commonwealth Games 2002 Manchester: Regeneration/Legacy,* <http://www.gameslegacy.com>.

Commonwealth Games Legacy (2003). *The XVII Commonwealth Games 2002 Manchester: Regeneration/Legacy,* <http://web.archive.org/web/20071027061444/www.gameslegacy.com/cgi-bin/index.cgi/27> (accessed 12 April 2010).

Communications Agencies Federation (2003). *The Client Brief: A Best Practice Guide to Briefing Communications Agencies*. (Internet) London, Communications Agencies Federation. Available from <http://www.clientbrief.info> (accessed 1 May 2010).

Convention Industry Council (CIC) (2005a). *APEX Industry Glossary*. (Internet) Available from <http://glossary.conventionindustry.org/> (accessed 14 January 2010).

Convention Industry Council (CIC) (2005b). *APEX Post-event Report Template*. (Internet) Available from <http://glossary.conventionindustry.org/> (accessed 14 January 2010).

Conway, L. (2000). *The Tobacco Advertising and Promotion Bill*. House of Commons Research Paper 00/97, 20 December. (Internet) London, House of Commons Library. Available from <http://www.parliament.uk> (accessed 13 January 2010).

Cook, N. and Morse, P. (2004). *The Environmental Impacts of the Notting Hill Carnival 2004*. (Internet) Overview and Scrutiny Committee on Environmental Services, Environmental Health and Planning Policy, 1st November. London, The Royal Borough of Kensington and Chelsea. Available from <http://www.rbkc.gov.uk/committeedocuments/pages/document.aspx?id=14981> (accessed 22 January 2010).

Cordingly, S. (1999). *Managing Volunteers*. (Internet) Available from <http://www.fuel4arts.com.au> (accessed 22 August 2005).

Cornwell, T., Roy, D. and Steinard II, E. (2001). Exploring managers' perceptions of the impact of sponsorship on brand equity. *Journal of Advertising*, **30**(2), 41−51.

Cornwell, T., Weeks, C. and Roy, D. (2005). Sponsorship-linked marketing: opening the black box. *Journal of Advertising*, **34**(2), 21–43.

Cornwell, T., Humphreys, M., Maguire, A., Weeks, C. and Tellegen, C. (2006). Sponsorship linked marketing: the role of articulation in memory. *Journal of Consumer Research*, **33**(3), 312–321.

Couchman, N. and Harrington, D. (2000). *Preventing Ambush/Parasitic Marketing in Sport*. (Internet) Sports and Character Licensing, (4), Available from <http://www.townleys.co.uk/ambush%20marketing.htm> (accessed 31 January 2001).

Coulson, C. and Coe, T. (1991). *The Flatter Organisation: Philosophy and Practice*. Corby, Institute of Management.

Council of the European Union (2006). *Brussels European Council 15/16 JUNE 2006: Presidency Conclusions*. Brussels, Council of the European Union.

Cowan, D. (2005). *An Evidence Based Case for Arts Sponsorship*. London, Arts and Business.

Cowell, D. (1984). *The Marketing of Services*. London, Heinemann.

Cragg Ross Dawson (2007). *The Olympic Legacy: Qualitative Research Into Public Attitudes*. London, Cragg Ross Dawson.

Cravens, D., Merrilees, B. and Walker, R. (2000). *Strategic Marketing Management for the Pacific Region*. Sydney, McGraw-Hill.

Crawford, D. (2000). *Environmental Accounting for Sport and Public Events: A Tool for Better Decision Making*. (Internet) *Sustainable Sport Sourceline*, May. Available from <http://www.greengold.on.ca/newsletter/index.html> (accessed 22 January 2010).

Crimmins, J. and Horn, M. (1996). Sponsorship: from management ego trip to marketing success. *Journal of Advertising Research*, **36**(4), 11–21.

Crofts, A. (2001). *Corporate Entertaining as a Marketing Tool*. Chalford, Management Books 2000 Ltd.

Crompton, J. (1993). Understanding a business organisation's approach to entering a sponsorship partnership. *Festival Management and Event Tourism*, **1**(3), 98−109.

Crompton, J. (1994). Benefits and risks associated with sponsorship of major events. *Festival Management and Event Tourism*, **2**(2), 65−74.

Crompton, J. (1995). Factors that have stimulated the growth of sponsorship of major events. *Festival Management and Event Tourism*, **3**(2), 97−101.

Crompton, J. L. and McKay, S. L. (1994). Measuring the impact of festivals and events: some myths, misapplications and ethical dilemmas. *Festival Management and Event Tourism*, **2**(1), 33−43.

Crompton, J. and McKay, S. (1997). Motives of visitors attending festival events. *Annals of Tourism Research*, **24**(2), 425−439.

Crompton, R., Morrissey, B. and Nankervis, A. (2002). *Effective Recruitment and Selection Practices*. 3rd edn. Sydney, CCH Australia.

Culture, Media and Sport Committee (2000). *Marking the Millennium in the United Kingdom: Eight Report from the Culture, Media and Sport Committee Session 1999−2000*. (Internet) London, HMSO. Available from <http://www.publications. parliament.uk/pa/cm199900/cmselect/cmcumeds/578/57802.htm> (accessed 22 January 2010).

Culture, Media and Sport Committee (2008). *Ticket Touting: Second Report from the Culture, Media and Sport Committee Session 2007−8*. (Internet) London, The Stationary Office Limited. Available from <http://www.publications.parliament.uk/pa/cm200708/ cmselect/cmcumeds/202/202.pdf> (accessed 28 August 2009).

Dale, M. (1995). Events as image. In *Tourism and Leisure − Perspectives on Provision* (D. Leslie, ed.), vol. 2. Brighton, LSA.

Davidson, R. (2002). *Making the Most of Our Business Visitors*. (Internet) London, Business Touirsm Partnership. Available from <http://www.businesstourismpartnership.com/pubs/ makingthemost.pdf> (accessed 5 August 2005).

Davidson, H. (2004). *Manchester International Festival Proposal*. (Internet) Press Release, 12 January, Manchester, Manchester City Council. Available from <http://www. manchester.gov.uk/news/2004/jan/festival.htm> (accessed 9 August 2005).

Davidson, R. and Cope, B. (2003). *Business Travel: Conferences, Incentive Travel, Exhibitions, Corporate Hospitality and Corporate Travel*. Harlow, Financial Times Prentice Hall.

Davidson, R. and Rogers, T. (2006). *Marketing Destinations and Venues for Conferences, Conventions and Business Events*. Oxford, Butterworth-Heinemann.

Davies, J. (1996). The buck stops where? The economic impact of staging major events, *Paper Presented to the Australian Events Conference*, Canberra.

Day, J. (2002). Global sponsorship market soars. (Internet) *Media Guardian*, 15 January. Available from <media.guardian.ac.uk> (accessed 22 January 2010).

De Groote, P. (2005). Economic and tourism aspects of the Olympic Games. *Tourism Review*, **60**(1), 12−19.

De Pelsmacker, P., Geuens, M. and Van den Bergh, J. (2004). *Marketing Communications − A European Perspective*. 2nd edn. Harlow, Financial Times Prentice Hall.

De Smet, L. (1999). Enter the Dragon. *Access All Areas*, September, 20−21.

Dean, J., Goodlad, R. and Hamilton, C. (2001). *Toolkit for Evaluating Arts Projects in Social Inclusion Areas: A Report to the Scottish Arts Council*. Edinburgh, Scottish Arts Council.

Deeley, P. (1998). *Old Trafford in Crackdown on Rowdy Element*. (Internet) Daily Telegraph, 1 July. Available from <http://static.cricinfo.com/db/ARCHIVE/1998/RSA_IN_ENG/

ARTICLES/OLD_TRAFFORD_CRACKDOWN_01JUL1998.html> (accessed 22 January 2010).

Denvir (2009). *Enjoy the Taste of Scotland: Get to Know Your Locals. Marketing Excellence Awards.* (Internet) Available from <http://www.tunaweb.com/meas08/casestudy/Event%20Excellence%20Tesco%20ETTOS.pdf> (accessed 20 April 2010).

Department for Culture, Media and Sport (DCMS) (1999). *Tomorrow's Tourism: A Growth Industry for the New Millennium.* London, Department for Culture, Media and Sport.

Department for Environment, Food and Rural Affairs (DEFRA) (2007). *Sustainable Events Guide.* London, Department for Environment, Food and Rural Affairs.

Department for Culture, Media and Sport (DCMS) (2007a). *Our Promise for 2012: How the UK will benefit from the Olympic Games and Paralympic Games.* (Internet) London, Department for Culture, Media and Sport. Available from <http://www.culture.gov.uk/reference_library/publications/3660.aspx> (accessed 22 December 2009).

Department for Culture, Media and Sport (DCMS) (2007b). *Live Music Forum.* (Internet) London, Department for Culture, Media and Sport. Available from <http://www.culture.gov.uk/what_we_do/creative_industries/4117.aspx> (accessed 28 November 2009).

Department for Culture, Media and Sport (DCMS) (2008b). *Before, During and After: Making the Most of the London 2012 Games.* (Internet) London, Department for Culture, Media and Sport. Available from <http://www.culture.gov.uk/reference_library/publications/5161.aspx> (accessed 22 December 2009).

Department for Culture, Media and Sport (DCMS) (2008b). *Winning: A Tourism Strategy for 2012 and Beyond.* (Internet) London, Department for Culture, Media and Sport. Available from <http://www.culture.gov.uk/images/publications/tourismstrategyfor2012_fullreport.pdf> (accessed 22 April 2010).

Department for Culture, Media and Sport (DCMS) (2009). *Consultation on Ticketing and Ticket Touting.* (Internet) London, Department for Culture, Media and Sport. Available from <http://www.culture.gov.uk/reference_library/consultations/5884.aspx> (accessed 28 November 2009).

Department of National Heritage and the Scottish Office (1997). *Guide to Safety at Sports Grounds.* 4th edn. London, HMSO.

Department for Culture, Arts and Leisure (DCAL) (2009). *Guidance Notes for Funding Under the Major Events Fund 2010–2011.* (Internet) Available from <http://www.dcalni.gov.uk/index/events_unit/grant_funding_programme_.htm> (accessed 16 December 2009).

Destination Sheffield (1995). *An Event-led City and Tourism Marketing Strategy for Sheffield.* Sheffield, Destination Sheffield.

Dibb, S., Simkin, L., Pride, W. M. and Ferrell, O. C. (2006). *Marketing: Concepts and Strategies.* 5th Euro. edn. Boston, Mass. Houghton Mifflin.

Dickman, S. (1997). Issues in arts marketing. In *Making It Happen: The Cultural and Entertainment Industries Handbook* (R. Rentchler, ed.) Melbourne, Centre for Professional Development.

Dinsmore, P. C. (1998). *Human Factors in Project Management.* New York, AMACOM.

Disability Rights Commission (DRC) (2002). *Code of Practice: Rights of Access: Goods, Facilities, Services and Premises.* Stratford-upon-Avon, Disability Rights Commission.

Disability Rights Commission (DRC) (2004). *Organising Accessible Events.* Stratford-upon-Avon, Disability Rights Commission.

Dolphin, R. (2003). Sponsorship: perspectives on its strategic role. *Corporate Communications: An International Journal*, **8**(3), 173–186.

Drucker, P. (1973). *Management*. New York, Harper and Row.

Dukes, C. J. (2004). *Big-Time Tennis Comes to Beijing*. Business Beijing, Issue 98. Beijing, Beijing This Month Publications.

Duncan, T. (2002). *IMC: Using Advertising and Promotion to Build Brands*. Boston, McGraw-Hill Irwin.

Dyson, J. R. (2007). *Accounting for Non-accounting Students*. 7th edn. Harlow, Financial Times Prentice-Hall.

EdComs Ltd (2007). *London 2012 Legacy Research: Final Report*. November. London, EDComs.

Edinburgh Festival Fringe (2002). *Edinburgh Festival Fringe Annual Report 2002*. Edinburgh, Edinburgh Festival Fringe.

Edinburgh Fringe Festival (2005). *More About the Fringe 2004 Economic Impact Study Results* <http://www.edfringe.com> (accessed 12 December 2006).

Edinburgh International Book Festival (2010). *About The Edinburgh International Book Festival*. (Internet). Available from <http://www.edbookfest.co.uk/about/index.html> (accessed 2 April 2010).

Edinburgh International Festival (EIF) (2000). *Edinburgh International Festival Annual Review 1999*. Edinburgh, EIF.

Edinburgh International Festival (EIF) (2001). *Edinburgh International Festival Annual Review 2000*. Edinburgh, EIF.

Edinburgh International Festival (EIF) (2005). *Edinburgh International Festival Annual Review 2004*. Edinburgh, EIF.

Edinburgh International Book Festival (2010). *About Connecting to Music*. (Internet) Edinburgh, Bank of Scotland. Available from <http://www.eif.co.uk/connectingtomusic/G87_About_Connecting-to-Music.php> (accessed 12 April 2010).

Edinburgh International Festival Society (2010). *Report and Financial Statements for the Year Ended 31 October 2009*. Edinburgh, Edinburgh International Festival Society.

Elliot, T., Phipps, L. and Harrison, S. (2009). *Accessible Events: A Good Practice Guide for Staff Organising Events in Higher Education*. York, TechDis.

Ellery, S. (2004). *Hospitality — Summer Attractions*. PR Week, March, 5.

Elstad, B. (2003). Continuance commitment and reasons to quit: a study of volunteers at a jazz festival. *Event Management*, **8**(2), 99–108.

EMBOK (2006). *Event Management Body of Knowledge*. (Internet) Available from <http://www.embok.org> (accessed 12 April 2010).

Encyclopedia Britannica (2009). *Music Festival*. (Internet) Encyclopedia Britannica Online. Available from <http://www.britannica.com/EBchecked/topic/399021/music-festival> (accessed 27 September 2009).

English Sports Council (1999). Memorandum Submitted by the English Sports Council. In *Fourth Report: Staging International Sporting Events*. *Volume II Minutes of Evidence* (Select Committee on Culture, Media and Sport). London, The Stationery Office.

English Tourism (1999). *Tourism and Sport in England*. Media brief, July. London, English Tourism.

Environment News Service (2004). *WWF Gives Athens Olympics No Green Medals*. 16 July. (Internet). Available from <http://www.ens-newswire.com/ens/jul2004/2004-07-16-05.asp> (accessed 5 May 2010).

Evans, G. (1996). Planning for the British Millennium Festival: establishing the visitor baseline and a framework for forecasting. *Festival Management and Event Tourism*, **3**(3), 183–196.

Event Assured (2005). *Risk Check List for Event Organisers — Risk and Your Event.* (Internet) Event Assured Advice Centre, 28 April. Available from <http://www.event-assured.com/> (accessed 17 July 2005).

Events Edinburgh (2010). *Edinburgh International Children's Festival.* (Internet) Edinburgh, The City of Edinburgh Council. Available from <http://eventsedinburgh.org.uk/visitors_event_listing.html&event_id=46> (accessed 18 April 2010).

Events Industry Alliance (EIA) (2009). *eGuide. EIA, Berkhamsted.* (Internet) Available from <http://www.aeo.org.uk/files/eguide_29.4.10.pdf> (accessed 10 June 2010).

Event Marketing Support Unit (2010). *Achieving Our Potential: Event Marketing Support Scheme.* (Internet) Cardiff, Event Marketing Support Unit. Available from <http://www.wtbonline.gov.uk/topics/tourism/marketing/majorevents/?lang=en> (accessed 22 April 2010).

Event South West (2008). *Event Strategy.* (Internet) Plymouth, Event South West. Available from <http://www.eventsouthwest.co.uk> (accessed 26 April 2010).

Events Tasmania (2005). *National and Special Interest Event Grant Programs.* (Internet). Available from <http://www.eventstasmania.com/Events_National.pdf> (accessed 17 August 2005).

Events Tasmania (2006a). *Strategic Plan 2006–10.* Hobart, Events Tasmania.

EventScotland (2010). *National Events Programme.* Edinburgh, EventScotland.

Eventia (2010). *Eventia One Future.* (Internet) Available from <http:///www.eventia.org.uk/html/article/csr-home> (accessed 28 April 2010).

Event Knowledge Services (EKS) (2010). *EKS Evolution and Origins.* Lausanne, EKS. Available from <http://www.eks.com/SITE/ABOU/ABOU01/index.html> (accessed 01 May 2010).

Exhibition Audience Audits Ltd (2005). *UK Exhibition Facts*, Volume 16. North Seaton, Exhibition Venues Association.

Exhibition Industry Alliance (EIA) (2007). *Vital Statistics: Highlights Events' Successes*, 8 February. Berkhamsted, Exhibition Industry Alliance.

Exhibition Liaison Committee (1995). *The Exhibition Industry Explained.* London, Exhibition Liaison Committee.

Farrelly, F. and Quester, P. (2003). The Effects of Market Orientation on Trust and Commitment — the case of the sponsorship business to business relationship. *European Journal of Marketing*, **37**(3/4), 530–553.

Farris, P., Bendle, N., Pfeifer, P. and Reibstein, D. (2006). *Marketing Metrics: 50+ Metrics Every Executive Should Master.* New Jersey, Pearson Education.

Faulkner, B. (1993). *Evaluating the Tourism Impact of Hallmark Events.* Occasional Paper No. 16. Canberra, Bureau of Tourism Research.

Fenich, G. (2008). *Meetings, Expositions, Events & Conventions: An Introduction to the Industry.* 2nd edn. Upper Saddle River, Prentice Hall.

Ferguson, T. (2004). Suncorp Sponsorship Manager. *Personal Communication*, 10 March.

Ferguson, B. (2005). Audiences to get a starring role with text rating, *Edinburgh Evening News*, 25 July, 9.

FINA (2007). *Kelloggs Confirmed as Official Cereal of World Swimming Championships!* Press Release, 5 September. (Internet) Available from <http://www.visitmanchester.com/

sport-talks/ShowMediaFile.aspx?id=22&documentId=76&mode=binary> (accessed 12 April 2010).

Flashman, R. and Quick, S. (1985). Altruism is not dead: a specific analysis of volunteer motivation. In *Motivating Volunteers* (L. Moore, ed.) Vancouver, Vancouver Volunteer Centre.

Fleming, S. and Jordan, F. (eds) (2006). *Events and Festivals: Education, Impacts and Experiences*. Festivals and Events: Beyond Economic Impacts, Volume 3. Eastbourne, Leisure Studies Association.

Focused Performance (2006). *Unconstrained Quotes*. www.focusedperformance.com. (accessed 20 May 2006).

Formic Media (2009). *SEM Glossary*. (Internet) Available from <http://www.formicmedia.com/sem-glossary.htm> (accessed 18 April 2010).

Fredline, L., Deery, M. and Jago, L. K. (2005). Testing of a compressed generic instrument to assess host community perceptions of events: a case study of the Australian Open Tennis Tournament. In *The Impacts of Events: Proceedings of International Event Research Conference Held in Sydney in July 2005* (J Allen, ed.). Sydney, Australian Centre for Event Management.

Fuller, M. (1998). *Basingstoke Arts Festival Feasibility Study: Report of the Director of Arts, Countryside and Community*. (Internet) Hampshire, Hampshire County Council Recreation and Heritage Committee, 15 January. Available from <www.hants.gov.uk/> (accessed 15 November 2000).

FxPro (2010). *FxPro Becomes Major Sponsor of World Rally Championship*. FxPro, Limassol. (Internet) Available from <https://www.fxpro.com/news/2010-02-13> (accessed 12 April 2010).

Garcia, B., Melville, R. and Cox, T. (2010). *Creating an Impact: Liverpool's Experience as European Capital of Culture*. (Internet) Liverpool, Impacts 08. Available from <http://www.liv.ac.uk/impacts08/Papers/Creating_an_Impact_-_web.pdf> (accessed 28 March 2010).

Gartside, M. (1999). Cornwall 'bungles' total eclipse. *Access All Areas*, September, 1−2.

Gaur, S. and Saggere, S. (2004). *Event Marketing and Management*. New Delhi, Vikas.

Geldard, E. and Sinclair, L. (2002). *The Sponsorship Manual: Sponsorship Made Easy*. 2nd edn. Victoria, Australia, Sponsorship Unit.

George, W. and Berry, L. (1981). Guidelines for the advertising of services. *Business Horizons*, July−August, 52−6.

Getz, D. (1991). *Festivals, Special Events and Tourism*. New York, Van Nostrand Reinhold.

Getz, D. (2005). *Event Management and Event Tourism*. 2nd edn. New York, Cognizant Communications Corporation.

Getz, D. (2007). *Event Studies: Theory, Research and Policy for Planned Events*. Oxford, Butterworth-Heinemann.

Getz, D. and Wicks, B. (1994). Professionalism and certification for festival and event practitioners: trends and issues. *Festival Management and Event Tourism*, **2**(2), 108−109.

Getz, D., O Neill, M. and Carlsen, J. (2001). Service quality evaluation at events through service mapping. *Journal of Travel Research*, **39**(4), 380−390.

Giddens, A. (1990). *The Consequences of Modernity*. Cambridge, Polity Press.

Giddings, C. (1997). *Measuring the Impact of Festivals — Guidelines for Conducting an Economic Impact Study*. National Centre for Culture and Recreation Studies, Canberra, Australian Bureau of Statistics.

Glasgow City Marketing Bureau (2009). *About Glasgow River Festival*. (Internet) Available from <http://www.glasgowriverfestival.co.uk/> (accessed 12 April 2010).

Glasgow City Council (2010). *A Games Legacy for Glasgow*. Glasgow, Glasgow City Council. (Internet) Available from http://www.glasgow.gov.uk/en/AboutGlasgow/AGamesLegacyForGlasgow/ (accessed 23 February 2010).

Glastonbury Festivals Ltd (2000). *Recycling Crew: Information, Terms and Conditions*. Pilton, Glastonbury Festivals Ltd.

Global Forum for Sports and Environment (G-ForSE)(2004). Athens — UNEP sign MOU. (Internet) Available from <http://www.g-forse.com/archive/news283_e.html> (accessed 5 May 2010).

Goh, F. (2003). Irish festivals, Irish life: the facts and how to use them. *Presentation at the 2003 Irish Festivals Association Conference*. (Internet). Available from <http://www.aoifeonline.com> (accessed 17 July 2005).

Goldblatt, J. (1997). *Special Events: Best Practices in Modern Event Management*. 2nd edn. New York, John Wiley & Sons.

Goldblatt, J. (2000). A future for event management: the analysis of major trends impacting the emerging profession. In *Events beyond 2000 — Setting the Agenda. Proceedings of the Conference on Evaluation, Research and Education, 13—14 July* (J. Allen, R. Harris and L. Jago, eds). Sydney, Australian Centre for Event Management, University of Technology.

Goldblatt, J. (2008). *Special Events: Event Leadership for a New World*. 5th edn. Hoboken, John Wiley & Sons.

Goldblatt, J. and Perry, J. (2002). Re-building the community with fire, water and music: the waterfire phenomenon. In *Events and Place-making: Proceedings of International Research Conference Held in Sydney 2002* (L. Jago, M. Deery, R. Harris, A. Hede and J. Allen, eds). Sydney, Australian Centre for Event Management.

Good Relations Unit (2010). *Current Projects*. (Internet) Belfast, Belfast City Council. Available from <http://www.belfastcity.gov.uk/goodrelations/projects.asp> (accessed 22 April 2010).

Government Equalities Office (2010). *Equality Act 2010*. (Internet) Available from <http://www.equalities.gov.uk/equality_act_2010.aspx> (accessed 28 April 2010).

Government Office for the South West (2010). *Greener Events: A Guide to Reducing the Environmental Impacts of Conferences and Seminars*. Bristol, Government Office for the South West.

Graham, S., Neirotti, L. D. and Goldblatt, J. J. (2001). *The Ultimate Guide to Sports Event Management and Marketing*. 2nd edn. New York, McGraw-Hill.

Grant, R. (2005). *Contemporary Strategy Analysis*. Melbourne, Blackwell.

Gray, C. and Larson, E. (2000). *Project Management: The Managerial Process*. Boston, McGraw-Hill International.

Great Yarmouth Borough Council (2010). *Public Events: A Safety Guide*. Great Yarmouth, Great Yarmouth Borough Council. Available from <http://www.great-yarmouth.gov.uk/hs-public-events.pdf> (accessed 28 April 2010).

Greaves, S. (1996). Post Millennium Motivation. *Conference and Incentive Travel*, July—August, 46—48.

Greaves, K. (1999). Tailor-made for business. *Marketing Event*, October, 45—50.

Green Meetings Industry Council (2007). *Green Meetings Good for Business*. (Internet) Available from <http://web.archive.org/web/20071101081451/www.greenmeetings.info/goodforbusiness.htm> (accessed 5 May 2010).

Green Games Watch 2000 (2004). *About Us*. (Internet) Available from <http://pandora.nla.gov.au/nph-arch/2000/S2000-Sep-12/http://nccnsw.org.au/member/ggw/about/index.html> (accessed 5 May 2010).

Greenpeace (2003). *The Greenpeace Olympic Environmental Guidelines*. New South Wales, Greenpeace. (Internet) Available from <http://www.greenpeace.org/australia/resources/reports/general/greenpeace-olympic-environment> (accessed 5 May 2010).

Grey, A. M. and Skildum-Reid, K. (2003). *The Sponsorship Seeker's Toolkit*. 2nd edn. Sydney, McGraw-Hill.

Gronroos, C. (1990) *Services Marketing and Management*. Lexington, Massachusetts, Lexington Books.

Gronroos, C. (1994). From marketing mix to relationship marketing: towards a paradigm shift in marketing. *Asia-Australia Marketing Journal*, **2**(1), 9–29.

Gwinner, K. (2005). Image transfer in global sport sponsorship: theoretical support and boundary conditions'. In *Global Sport Sponsorship* (J. Amis and B. Cornwell, eds). New York, Berg, 191–206.

Gwinner, K. and Bennet, G. (2007). The impact of brand cohesiveness and sport identification on brand fit in a sponsorship context. *Journal of Sports Management*, **22**(4), 410–426.

Halbwirth, S. and Toohey, K. (2001). The Olympic Games and Knowledge Management: a case study of the Sydney Organising Committee of the Olympic Games. *European Sport Management Quarterly*, **1**(2), 91–111.

Hall, C. M. (1989). Hallmark events and the planning process. In *The Planning and Evaluation of Hallmark Events* (G. J. Syme, B. J. Shaw, D. M. Fenton and W. S. Mueller, eds). Aldershot, Avebury.

Hall, C. M. (1992). *Hallmark Tourist Events — Impacts Management and Planning*. London, Belhaven Press.

Hall, C. M. (1997). *Hallmark Tourist Events: Impacts, Management and Planning*. Chichester, John Wiley and Sons.

Hall, C. M. and Selwood, J. H. (1995). Event tourism and the creation of a postindustrial portscape: the case of Fremantle and the 1987 America's Cup. In *Recreation and tourism as a catalyst for urban waterfront development: an international survey* (S. J. Craig-Smith and M. Fagence, eds). Westport, Connecticut, Praeger Publishers.

Hanlon, C. and Jago, L. (2000). Pulsating sporting events. In *Events Beyond 2000 — Setting the Agenda. Proceedings of the Conference on Evaluation, Research and Education, 13–14 July* (J. Allen, R. Harris, L. K. Jago and A. J. Veal, eds). Sydney, Australian Centre for Event Management, University of Technology, 93–104.

Hanlon, C. and Cuskelly, G. (2002). Pulsating major sport event organisations: a framework for inducting managerial personnel. *Event Management*, **7**(4), 231–243.

Hanlon, C. and Jago, L. (2009). Managing Pulsating Major Sporting Organisations. In *Events Beyond 2000 — Setting the Agenda* (T. Baum, M. Deery, C. Hanlon, L. Lockstone and K. Smith, eds). People and Work in Events and Conventions: A Research Perspective. Wallingford, CABI, 93–107.

Hannagan, T. (2008). *Management Concepts and Practices*. 5th edn. London, Financial Times Prentice Hall.

Hannam, C. (2000). *Sample Contract Terms and Conditions*. Kingston upon Thames, Production Services Association.

Hannam, C. (2004). *Heath and Safety Management in the Live Music and Events Industry*. Cambridge, Entertainment Technology Press.

Hardman, R. (1995). *Youth Sets the Tone for Peace in Hyde Park*. (Internet) Electronic Telegraph, 8 May. Available from <http://www.telegraph.co.uk> (accessed 8 April 2001).

Harris, R. and Griffin, T. (1997). *Tourism Events Training Audit*. Sydney, Tourism New South Wales Events Unit.

Harris, R. and Jago, L. (1999). Event education and training in Australia: the current state of play. *Australian Journal of Hospitality Management*, **6**(1), 45−51.

Harris, R. and Allen, J. (2002). *Regional Event Management Handbook*. Sydney, Australian Centre for Event Management, University of Technology.

Harris, R. and Allen, J. (2006). *Community Engagement and Events: A Study for artsACT*, unpublished report. Sydney, Australian Centre for Event Management.

Harrison, D. and Hastings, C. (2000). *High Spirits and Bright Lights Till Dawn*. (Internet) Electronic Telegraph, 2 January, Issue 1682. Available from <http://www.telegraph.co.uk> (accessed 5 February 2001).

Harrison, P. (2004). *Sponsorship — Cutting Through the Hype*. (Internet) New South Wales, The Australia Council for the Arts. February. Available from <http://www.fuel4arts.com> (accessed 20 August 2005).

Harrogate International Festival (2004a). *Volunteer Event Steward Application Form*. (Internet) Harrogate, Harrogate International Festivals Ltd.

Harrogate International Festival (2004b). *Volunteer Event Steward Job Description*. (Internet) Harrogate, Harrogate International Festivals Ltd.

Harrowven, J. (1980) *Origins of Festivals and Feasts*. London, Kaye & Ward.

Haymarket Land Events LLP. (2005). *Town & Country Festival 05*. Stoneleigh Park, Haymarket Land Events LLP.

Health and Safety Executive (HSE) (1997). *Successful Health and Safety Management*. 2nd edn. HSG63. London, HSE.

Health and Safety Executive (HSE) (1999). *The Event Safety Guide*. Norwich, HSE Books.

Health and Safety Executive (HSE) (2000). *Managing Crowds Safely*. Norwich, HSE Books.

Health and Safety Executive (HSE) (2003). *Health and Safety Regulation. A Short Guide*. HSC13(rev 1) 08/03. London, HSE.

Health and Safety Executive (HSE) (2006). *Five Steps to Risk Management*. Revision 2. London, HSE.

Health and Safety Executive (HSE) (2008). *Consulting Employees on Health and Safety: A Brief Guide to the Law*. London, HSE.

Hede, A.-M., Jago, L. and Deery, M. (2003). Satisfaction-based cluster analysis of theatre event attendees: preliminary results. *Paper Presented at the 13th International Research Conference of the Council for Australian University Tourism and Hospitality Education*, 5−8 February, Coffs Harbour, New South Wales.

Hemmerling, M. (1997). What Makes an Event a Success for a Host City, Sponsors and Others? *Paper Delivered to The Big Event New South Wales Tourism Conference*, 5−7 November, Wollongong, Australia.

Henderson, P. and Chapman, A. (1997). Thousands are left stranded. *Mail on Sunday*, 6 April, 2−3.

Hertzberg, F. (1968). One more time: how do you motivate employees? *Harvard Business Review*, **46**(1), 361−367.

Heskett, J., Sasser, W. and Schelesinger, L. (1997). *The Service Profit Chain*. New York, Free Press.

Hicks, H. and Gullet, C. (1976). *The Management of Organisations*. Tokyo, McGraw-Hill Kogakusha Ltd.

Higgins, C. (2004). *Edinburgh Festival Faces New Rival: Manchester to Launch Big-budget Arts Event*. (Internet) The Guardian, 9 November. Available from <http://www.guardian.co.uk/arts/news/story/0,11711,1346606,00.html> (accessed 9 August 2005).

Hilbers, J. (2005). Research and evaluation of "Communities Together" Festivals and Celebrations Scheme 2002–04: building community capacity. In *The Impacts of Events: Proceedings of International Event Research Conference Held in Sydney in July 2005* (J. Allen, ed.). Sydney, Australian Centre for Event Management.

Hill, G. and Hill, K. (2005). *Contract, The People's Dictionary*. (Internet) New York, Fine Communications. Available from <http://dictionary.law.com> (accessed 12 April 2010).

Hill, C., Jones, G., Galvin, P. and Haidar, A. (2007). *Strategic Management*, 2nd edn, John Wiley & Sons, Brisbane.

Hiller, H. and Moylan, D. (1999). Mega-events and community obsolesence: redevelopment versus rehabilitation in Victoria Park East. *Canadian Journal of Urban Research*, **8**(1), 47–81.

Hinch, T. and Higham, J. (2004). Sport tourism development. In *Aspects of Tourism* (C. Cooper, ed). Clevedon, Channel View Publications.

Hiscox (2010). *Volcanic Ash Casts Cloud Over Planned Events*. Press Release, 19 April. (Internet) Available from <http://www.hiscox.com/en/news/press-releases/2010/19-04-10.aspx> (accessed 20 April 2010).

Hjalager, A. M. (1996). Tourism and the environment: the innovation connection. *Journal of Sustainable Tourism*, **4**(4), 201–207.

HM Government (2005). *Opportunity Age – Opportunity and Security Throughout Life*. London, HMSO. (Internet) Available from <http://www.dwp.gov.uk/opportunity_age/> (accessed 9 August 2005).

HMSO (2003). *Licensing Act 2003*. London, The Stationery Office Limited.

HMSO (2007). *Corporate Manslaughter and Corporate Homicide Act 2007*. (Internet) London, The Stationery Office Limited.

Hoffman, K.D., Bateson, J.E.G., Wood, E.H. and Kenyon, A.J. (2009). *Services Marketing: Concepts, Strategies & Cases*. London, Cengage Learning EMEA.

Holder, C. (2001). Case study: Notting Hill Carnival. In *Events Management* (G. Bowdin, I. McDonnell, J. Allen and W. O'Toole, eds). Oxford, Butterworth-Heinemann.

Holmes, K. and Smith, K. (2009). *Managing Volunteers in Tourism: Attractions, Destinations and Events*. Oxford, Butterworth-Heinemann.

Hooker, J. (2008). *The Corporate Manslaughter Act – Is Your Business Prepared? Myvenues.co.uk* (Internet) Avaiable from: <http://www.myvenues.co.uk/news/Industry/The-Corporate-Manslaughter-Act-%E2%80%93-is-your-business-prepared_/759/> (accessed 22 April 2010).

Home Office (2000). *Dealing with Disaster*. 3rd edn. London, Home Office Communication Directorate. (Internet). Available from <http://www.homeoffice.gov.uk/docs2/dwdrevised.pdf> (accessed 3 August 2005).

Horne, J. and Manzenreiter, W. (eds) (2006). *Sports Mega-Events: Social Scientific Analyses of a Global Phenomenon*. Oxford, Blackwell Publishing Limited.

Howden, N. (2004). Extreme Noise Terror. *Access All Areas*, October, 7.

Howey, J. (2000). *Outdoor Events Policy — Royal Victoria Park*. (Internet) Bath and North East Somerset Council Community, Culture and Leisure Committee, 13 July. Available from <http://www.bathnes.gov.uk/Committee_Papers/CCL/cl000710/13events.htm> (accessed 3 August 2005).

Hoyle, L.H. (2002). *Event Marketing: How to Successfully Promote Events, Festivals, Conventions and Expositions*. New York, John Wiley & Sons Inc.

Hughes, H. (1993). Olympic tourism and urban regeneration. *Festival Management and Event Tourism*, **1**(4), 157–162.

Humphries, D. (2000). Benefit to economy is unseen. *The Sydney Morning Herald*, 23 August, 8.

Hunn, C. and Mangan, J. (1999). Estimating the economic impact of tourism at the local, regional, state or territorial level, including consideration of the multiplier effect. In *Valuing Tourism: Methods and Techniques* (K. Corcoran, A. Allcock, T. Frost and L. Johnson, eds). Canberra, Bureau of Tourism Research.

Hurley, L. (2005). TBA goes global. *Special Events*, 1 September. <http://specialevents.com/corporate/events_tba_goes_global_20050824/> (accessed 14 March 2010).

ICC Cricket World Cup (2003). *Volunteers 2003 Training Manual*. Johannesburg, South Africa, ICC Cricket World Cup Organising Committee.

Imaginate (2010). *Welcome to Imaginate*. (Internet) Available from <http://www.imaginate.org.uk/corporate/index.php> (accessed 18 April 2010).

IMIE Ltd (2008). *Key Show Facts*. London, IMIE Ltd.

Institute of Fundraising (2002). *Outdoor Fundraising in the UK*. London, Institute of Fundraising.

Institute of Directors and Health and Safety Executive (2009). *Leading Health and Safety at Work*. Suffolk, HSE.

International Association for Public Participation (2007). *IAP2 Core Values for Public Participation*. <http://www.iap2.org>. (accessed 18 March 2010).

International Congress and Convention Association (ICCA) (2009). *Statistics Report: The International Association Meetings Market 1999–2008*. Amsterdam, International Congress and Convention Association.

International Chamber of Commerce (ICC) (2003). *International Code on Sponsorship*. (Internet) Commission on Marketing and Advertising, Paris, ICC, 17 September. Available from <http://www.iccwbo.org/id926/index.html> (accessed 23 November 2009).

International EMBOK Executive (2005). *Event Management Body of Knowledge (EMBOK)*. (Internet). Johannesburg, International EMBOK Executive. Available from http://www.embok.org> (accessed 12 November 2009).

International Visual Communications Association (2008). *What is the Visual Communications Industry?* (Internet) Available from <http://www.ivca.org/about/about-the-industry.html> (accessed 20 April 2010).

International Olympic Committee (2004). *The IOC, the Environment and Sustainable Development*. Lausanne, International Olympic Committee.

International Olympic Committee (2006). *Building a Positive Environmental Legacy Through the Olympic Games*. Lausanne, Switzerland, Commission on Sport and the Environment.

International Olympic Committee (IOC) (2009a). *100 years of Olympic Marketing*. (Internet) Lausanne, International Olympic Committee. Available from <http://www.olympic.org/en/content/The-IOC/Commissions/Marketing/Evolution-of-Marketing/> (accessed 23 November 2009).

International Olympic Committee (2009b). *The Environment and Sustainable Development.* Lausanne, International Olympic Committee. (Internet) Available from <http://www. olympic.org/Documents/Reference_documents_Factsheets/Environment_and_substainable_ developement.pdf> (accessed 5 May 2010).

International Organization for Standardization (ISO) (2010). *ISO to Develop Sustainable Event Standard in Run-up to 2012 Olympics.* Press Release1281. (Internet) Available from <http://www.iso.org/iso/pressrelease.htm?refid=Ref1281> (accessed 30 April 2010).

Jackson, A. (2004). *Evaluation Toolkit for the Voluntary and Community Arts in Northern Ireland.* Bath, Annabel Jackson Associates.

Jackson, J., Houghton, M., Russell, R. and Triandos, P. (2005). Innovations in measuring economic impacts of regional festivals: a Do-It-Yourself kit. *Journal of Travel Research,* **43**(4), 360−367.

Jago, L. (2006). *Encore Festival and Event Evaluation Kit, Draft Document Prepared for CRC for Sustainable Tourism,* Melbourne.

Jago, L. K. and Shaw, R. N. (1998). A Conceptual and differential framework. *Festival Management and Event Tourism,* **5**(1/2), 21−32.

Jago, L. and Dwyer (2006). *Economic Evaluation of Special Events: A Practitioner's Guide.* Altona, Victoria, Common Ground Publishing.

Jago, L., Chalip, L., Brown, G., Mules, T. and Ali, S. (2002). The role of events in helping to brand a destination. In *Events and Place-making: Proceedings of International Research Conference Held in Sydney 2002* (L. Jago, M. Deery, R. Harris, A. Hede and J. Allen, eds). Sydney, Australian Centre for Event Management.

Jago, L., Chalip, L., Brown, G., Mules, T. and Ali, S. (2003). Building events into destination branding: insights from experts. *Event Management,* **8**(1), 3−14.

James, B. (1972). *Integrated Marketing.* Penguin, Hammondsworth.

Janiskee, R. (1996). Historic houses and special events. *Annals of Leisure Research,* **23**(2), 398−414.

Jeff Kline (Hurley, 2005). *Executive Vice President of Business Affairs at California based TBA Global Events.*

Jeffries-Fox, B. (2005). *A Guide to Measuring Event Sponsorships.* London, Institute for Public Relations.

Jobber, D. (2007). *Principles and Practice of Marketing.* 5th edn. Maidenhead, McGraw-Hill International (UK) Ltd.

Johnson, G. and Scholes, K. (2001). *Exploring Corporate Strategy,* 6th edn. Hemel Hempstead, Prentice Hall Europe.

Johnson, G., Scholes, K. and Whittington, R. (2008). *Exploring Corporate Strategy.* 8th edn. Harlow, Financial Times Prentice-Hall.

Johar, G.V. and Pham, M.T. (1999). Relatedness, prominence and constructive sponsor identification. *Journal of Marketing Research,* **36**(3), 299–312.

Joint Meetings Industry Council (JMIC) (2005). *Profile and Power: A Strategic Communications Plan for Building Industry Awareness and Influence.* Brussels, Joint Meetings Industry Council.

Jones, C. (2000). *It's Time for a Dressing Down at Stuffy SW19.* (Internet) *Evening Standard,* 7 June. Available from <http://www.findarticles.com/p/articles/mi_qn4153/is_20000607/ ai_n11933808> (accessed 3 August 2005).

Jones, C. (2001). A level playing field? sports stadium infrastructure and urban development in the United Kingdom. *Environment and Planning*, **33**, 845–861.

Jones, C. (2002). The stadium and economic development: cardiff and the Millennium Stadium. *European Planning Studies*, **10**(7), 819–829.

Jones, M. (2010). *Sustainable Event Management*. London, Earthscan.

Judd, D. (1997). *Diamonds are Forever? Kipling's Imperialism*. (Internet) History Today, **47**(6), June, 37–43. <http://www.historytoday.com/MainArticle.aspx?m=13843&amid=13843> (accessed 23 November 2009).

Jung, M. (2006). Determinants of Exhibition Service Quality as Perceived by Attendees. *Journal of Convention & Event Tourism*, **7**(3 & 4), March 2006, 85–98.

Jura Consultants and Gardiner & Theobold (2001). *Millennium Festival Impact Study*. Edinburgh, Jura Consultants and Gardiner & Theobold Management Consultancy.

Kaless, S. (2003). *Looking at the Numbers Game*. (Internet) News, 24 November. Available from <http://www.rwc2003.irb.com/EN/Tournament/News/sk+24+11+stats.htm> (accessed 24 November 2009).

Kaye, A. (2005). China's convention and exhibition center boom. *Journal of Convention & Event Tourism*, **7**(1), 5–22.

Kearney, A. (2006). *Building a Legacy — Sports Mega Events Should Last a Lifetime*, Kearney.

Keep America Meeting (2009). *Keep America Meeting*. (Internet) Available from <www.keepamericameeting.com> (accessed 20 April 2010).

Keep Britain Talking (2009). *Keep Britain Talking*. (Internet) Available from <http://www.keepbritaintalking.co.uk> (accessed 20 April 2010).

Kelly, M. (2003). *Feature Article*. Venue Managers Association News, 22 November.

Kemp, C. (2000). *Music Industry Management and Promotion*. 2nd edn. Kings Ripton, ELM Publications.

Kemp, C. and Hill, I. (2004). *Heath and Safety Aspects in the Live Music Industry*. Cambridge, Entertainment Technology Press.

Kerwood, P. (2009). Joining the social media conversation — connect, communicate, co-operate and collaborate. *Event Magazine*, 16 June. (Internet) Available from <http://community.eventmagazine.co.uk/blogs/peterkerwood/archive/2009/06/16/joining-the-social-media-conversation-connect-communicate-co-operate-and-collaborate.aspx> (accessed 18 April 2010).

Keung, D. (1998). *Management: A Contemporary Approach*. London, Pitman Publishing.

Kirkwood, J. (2004). *Application for Occasional Public Entertainment Licence for Glastonbury Festival 2005*. (Internet) Mendip, Mendip District Council, 6 December. Available from <http://www.mendip.gov.uk/committeemeeting.asp?id=SX31F-A780B5E2> (accessed 23 November 2009).

Korman, A. (2000). *Basic Guide to Sponsorship Contracts*. (Internet) London, Townleys Solicitors. Available from <http://www.sponsorshiponline.com> (accessed 17 July 2005).

Kotler, P. and Armstrong, G. (2010). *Principles of Marketing*, Thirteenth Global Edition. Upper Saddle River, NJ, Pearson Education Inc.

Kotler, P., Wong, V., Saunders, J. and Armstrong, G. (2008). *Principles of Marketing*. 5th Euro edn. London, Pearson Education Limited.

Kotler, P., Bowen, J. and Makens, J. (2010). *Marketing for Hospitality and Tourism*. 5th edn. Upper Saddle River, NJ, Pearson Education Inc.

Kover, A.J. (2001). The sponsorship issue. *Journal of Advertising Research*, **41**(1), January/February, 5.

KRONOS (1997). *The Economic Impact of Sports Events Staged in Sheffield 1990–1997*. Destination Sheffield, Sheffield City Council and Sheffield International Venues Ltd.

Kyriakopoulos, V. and Benns, M. (2004). Passing the Torch to Athens, *The Sun-Herald*, 22 February.

Lagae, W. (2005). *Sport Sponsorship and Marketing Communications: A European Perspective*. Harlow, Financial Times Prentice Hall.

Lake District National Park Authority (1999). *Lake District National Park Management Plan*. Cumbria, Lake District National Park Authority.

Lambeth Environmental Health (2008). *Guidance on the Control of Noise at Outdoor Events*. London, Lambeth Council. (Internet) Available from <http://www.lambeth.gov.uk/Services/Environment/Pollution/GuidanceControlNoiseOutdoorEvents.htm> (accessed 10 April 2010).

Langen, F. and Garcia, B. (2009). *Measuring the Impacts of Large Scale Cultural Events: A Liturature Review. Liverpool, Impacts 08*. (Internet) Available from <http://www.liv.ac.uk/impacts08/Publications/publications.htm> (accessed 20 March 2010).

Leeds Rhinos (2010). *Sponsors. Leeds, Leeds Rugby Ltd*. (Internet) Available from <http://www.therhinos.co.uk/club/sponsors/index.php> (accessed 12 April 2010).

Lee, S., Ryder, C. and Shin, H. J. (2003). An investigation of environmental motivation factors among minor League Baseball Fans. (Internet) *The Sport Journal*, **6**(3). Available from <http://www.thesportjournal.org/article/investigation-environmental-motivation-factors-among-minor-league-baseball-milb-fans> (accessed 24 November 2009).

Lenskyj, H. (1998). Sport and corporate environmentalism: the case of the 2000 Olympics. *International Review for the Sociology of Sport*, **33**(4), 341–54.

Levitt, T. (1980). Marketing Myopia. In *Marketing Management and Strategy* (K. Kotler and C. Cox, eds). Englewood Cliffs, New Jersey, Prentice-Hall.

Lewis, D. (2007). Freak Storm: sideshow alley to shake up the Show. *Sydney Morning Herald*, 4 April, 3.

Lieberman, A. with Esgate, P. (2002). *The Entertainment Marketing Revolution*. Upper Saddle River, New Jersey, Financial Times Prentice Hall.

Lilley III, W. and DeFranco, L. J. (1999a). *The Economic Impact of Network Q Rally of Great Britain*. Washington, D.C., InContext Inc.

Lilley III, W. and DeFranco, L. J. (1999b). *The Economic Impact of the European Grand Prix*. Washington, D.C., InContext Inc.

Linton, I. and Morley, K. (1995). *Integrated Marketing Communications*. Oxford, Butterworth-Heinemann.

Litherland, S. (1997). Expose yourself live. *Marketing Event*, June, 41–42.

Live 8 (2005). *The Long Walk to Justice*. (Internet). Available from <http://www.live8live.com/whattodo/index.shtml> (accessed 23 November 2009).

Liverpool Culture Company (2005a). *Culture Uncovered – Your Questions Answered*. (Internet) Liverpool, Liverpool Culture Company. Available from <http://www.liverpoolculture.com/archive/index.asp?tcmuri=tcm:79-55942&ipage=1&m=May&y=05> (accessed 23 November 2009).

Liverpool Culture Company (2005b). *Liverpool 2008.* (Internet) Liverpool, Liverpool Culture Company. Available from <http://www.liverpoolculture.com/about/> (accessed 23 November 2009).

Liverpool Culture Company (2005c) *Executive Summary of Liverpool's Bid for European Capital of Culture 2008.* (Internet) Liverpool, Liverpool Culture Company. Available from <http://www.liverpool08.com/Images/tcm21-32519_tcm79-56880_tcm146-122188.pdf> (accessed 10 March 2010).

Liverpool Culture Company (2005c). *Liverpool Culture Company 2004–5 Review: 2005–6 Delivery Plan.* Liverpool, Liverpool Culture Company.

Lloyds TSB Scotland (2005). *Lloyds TSB Scotland.* Entry for Marketing Excellence Awards Scotland 2005. London, Marketing Society.

Local Government Association of New South Wales (2006). Hosting the 2008 Annual Conference. (Internet) Available from <http://www.lgsa-plus.net.au/resources/documents/hosting_2008_lga_conference_230606.pdf> (accessed 16 April 2010), 1–3.

Lock, D. (2007). *Project Management.* 9th edn. Aldershot, Gower.

London 2012 (2004a). *London 2012 Candidate File.* London, London 2012 Ltd.

London 2012 (2004b). *London 2012 Candidate File: Volume 3 Theme 12: Security.* London, London 2012 Ltd.

London 2012 (2007). *London 2012 Launches Sustainability Plan.* Press Release, 26 November. London, The London Organising Committee of the Olympic Games and Paralympic Games Limited. (Internet) Available from <http://www.london2012.com/press/media-releases/2007/11/london-2012-launches-sustainability-plan.php> (accessed 16 April 2010).

London 2012 (2009a). *London 2012 Publishes Sustainability Guidelines for Corporate and Public Events.* Press Release, 25 February. London, The London Organising Committee of the Olympic Games and Paralympic Games Limited. (Internet) Available from <http://www.london2012.com/press/media-releases/2009/02/london-2012-publishes-sustainability-guidelines-for-corporate-and-public-eve.php> (accessed 16 April 2010).

London 2012 (2009b). *Sustainability Guidelines – Corporate and Public Events.* 1st edn. London, The London Organising Committee of the Olympic Games and Paralympic Games Limited. (Internet) Available from <http://www.london2012.com/documents/locog-publications/london-2012-sustainability-events-guidelines.pdf> (accessed 16 April 2010).

London 2012 (2009c). *Towards a One Planet 2012: Sustainability Plan*, 2nd ed. London, The London Organising Committee of the Olympic Games and Paralympic Games Limited. (Internet) Available from <http://www.london2012.com/documents/locog-publications/london-2012-sustainability-plan.pdf> (accessed 16 April 2010).

London 2012, WWF and BioRegional (2005). *Towards a One Planet Olympics: Achieving the first sustainable Olympic Games and Paralympic Games.* London, London 2012 Ltd.

London Assembly (2010). *A 2012 Legacy for London and Londoners.* London, London Assembly. (Internet) Available from <http://www.london.gov.uk/priorities/london-2012/benefits-and-legacy> (accessed 22 December 2009).

London Development Agency (2003). *The Economic Impact of the Notting Hill Carnival.* London, London Development Agency.

London International Exhibition Centre PLC (2000). *Planning, Designing and Constructing your Exhibition: ExCel Rules and Regulation.* Version 14. London, London International Exhibition Centre PLC.

London Marathon (2010a). *History of the London Marathon*. (Internet) Available from <http://www.virginlondonmarathon.com/marathon-centre/history-london-marathon/charity-history/> (accessed 21 December 2009).

London Marathon (2010b). *Be a Record Breaker!* (Internet) Available from <http://www.virginlondonmarathon.com/news-and-media/news-and-media/be-record-breaker/> (accessed 21 December 2009).

London Mardi Gras (2000). *Statement of Values for the Pride March and Parade*. (Internet) London, London Mardi Gras. Available from <http://www.londonmardigras.com/newmaster/pages/statementvalues.htm> (accessed 20 December 2000).

London Organising Committee for the Olympic Games (2006). *World Experts Back London 2012 Plans for First Sustainable Olympic Games in Countdown to World Environment Day*. www.london2012.com, (accessed 2 May 2010).

Lord Mayor's Show (2010). *History of the Show*. (Internet) Available from <http://www.lordmayorsshow.org/hist/index.shtml> (accessed 06 February 2010).

Lovelock, C. and Wirtz, J. (2004). *Services Marketing: People, Technology, Strategy*. 5th edn. Upper Saddle River, NJ, Pearson Prentice-Hall.

Lovelock, C. and Wirtz, J. (2011). *Services Marketing: People, Technology, Strategy*. 7th edn. Upper Saddle, NJ, Pearson Prentice-Hall.

Lulewicz, S. (1995). Training and Development of Volunteers. In *The Volunteer Management Handbook* (T. Connors, ed.). New York, John Wiley & Sons.

Lynch, R. (2009). *Strategic Management*. 5th edn. Harlow, Financial Times Prentice Hall.

Lyon, M. (2004). *A Planning Guide for Venue Finding Agencies, Meetings and Event Planners and Conference and Exhibition Managers*. Version 2. (Internet) Warwick, Write Style Communications Ltd. Available from <http://www.write-style.co.uk/pdfs/SiteInspectionHandbook.pdf> (accessed 2 August 2005).

Machiavelli, N. (1962). *The Prince*. (Trans. L. Ricci). Chicago, Mentor Classics.

Made-Up Textiles Association (MUTA) (2009). *Safe Use and Operation of Marquees and Temporary Structures*. (Internet) Tamworth, Made-Up Textiles Association. Available from <http://www.performancetextiles.org.uk/public/downloads/mutamarq.pdf> (accessed 9 February 2010).

Magherafelt District Council (2010). *Events and Festivals Grants 2010/11*. (Internet) Available from <http://www.magherafelt.gov.uk/grants/index.php> (accessed 20 April 2010).

Major Events Investigative Committee (2001). *Future Major Events In London: Final Report of the Major Events Investigative Committee*. March. London, Greater London Authority London Assembly.

Mallen, C. and Adams, L. J. (2008). *Sport, Recreation and Tourism Event Management: Theoretical and Practical Dimensions*. Oxford, Butterworth-Heinemann.

Malouf, L. (1999). *Behind the Scenes at Special Events*. New York, John Wiley & Sons.

Manchester 2002 (2003). *2002 Manchester The XVII Commonwealth Games: Post Games Report*. London, Commonwealth Games Federation.

Manchester City Council (2005). *Regeneration in Manchester Statement: Regeneration Initiatives — East Manchester*. (Internet) Available from www.manchester.gov.uk, (accessed 03 December 2005).

Manchester City Council (2006). *A Guide to Greening Your Event*. Manchester, Manchester City Council Green City Team.

Manchester City Council (2009). *Manchester World Sport 08 Events – £23 Million of Economic Impact Generated for the City.* Press Release, 27 May 2009. (Internet) Available from <http://www.manchester.gov.uk/news/article/4763/manchester_world_sport_08_events-23_million_of_economic_impact_generated_for_the_city> (accessed 15 February 2010).

Manly Daily (2006). Filmmakers get professional help. 11 August.

Mannell, R. and Iso-Ahola, S. (1987). Psychological nature of leisure and tourism experience. *Annals of Tourism Research,* **14**(3), 314–29.

Marketing Manchester (2004). *Northwest Conference Bidding Unit.* (Internet). Available from <http://www.conference.visitmanchester.com/conference/bidding.shtml> (accessed 3 August 2005).

Marketing Birmingham (2010). *Meet Birmingham.* (Internet) Available from <http://www.meetbirmingham.com> (accessed 20 April 2010).

Marsh, P. D. V. (1984). *Contract Negotiation Handbook.* 2nd edn. Aldershot, Gower.

Maslow, A. (1954). *Motivation and Personality.* New York, Harper and Row.

Masterman, G. (2007). *Sponsorship for a Return on Investment.* Oxford, Butterworth-Heinemann.

Masterman, G. (2009). *Strategic Sports Event Management: Olympic Edition.* 2nd ed. Oxford, Butterworth-Heinemann.

Masterman, G. and Wood, E. (2005). *Innovative Marketing Communications: Strategies for the Events Industry.* Oxford, Butterworth-Heinemann.

Material Marketing & Communications Ltd (2005). *T In The Park.* (Internet) Entry for Marketing Excellence Awards Scotland 2005. Available from <http://www.tunaweb.com/MarketingAwardsScotlandNominees/casestudies/Comms-SE-TinthePark.pdf> (accessed 24 August 2005).

Matthews, D. (2008a). *Special Event Production: The Process.* Oxford, Butterworth-Heinemann.

Matthews, D. (2008b). *Special Event Production: The Resources.* Oxford, Butterworth-Heinemann.

Maughan, C. and Bianchini, F. (2003). *Festivals and the Creative Region.* Nottingham, Arts Council England.

Mayor of London (2005). *Trafalgar Square Festival 2005.* (Internet) Available from <http://www.london.gov.uk/mayor/trafalgar_square/tsaf-05/index.jsp> (accessed 9 August 2005).

Mayor of London (2008). *Five Legacy Commitments.* London, Greater London Authority. (Internet) Available from <http://legacy.london.gov.uk/mayor/olympics/docs/5-legacy-commitments.pdf> (accessed 22 December 2010).

Mayor's Carnival Review Group (2004). *Notting Hill Carnival: A Strategic Review.* London, Greater London Authority.

McCarthy, E. J. (1960). *Basic Marketing: A Managerial Approach.* Homewood, Illinois, Irwin.

McCrindle, M. with Wolfinger, E. (2009). *The ABC of XYZ: Understanding Global Generations.* Sydney, University of New South Wales Press Ltd.

McCurley, S. and Lynch, R. (1998). *Essential Volunteer Management.* 2nd edn. London, Directory of Social Change.

McDermott, S. (2006). *Why Track Blogs?* (Internet). Available from: <http://www.attentio.com/blog/2006/02/19/24/> (accessed 2 May 2010).

McDonnell, I. (1999). The intefrag marketing continuum: a tool for tourism marketers. *Journal of Travel and Tourism Marketing,* **8**(1), 22–39.

McDaniel, S. (1999). An investigation of match-up effects in sport sponsorship advertising: the implications of consumer advertising schemas. *Psychology and Marketing*, **16**(2), 163–84.

McDonald, M. (2002). *Marketing Plans: How to Prepare Them, How to Use Them*. Oxford, Butterworth-Heinemann.

McDuff, N. (1995). Volunteer and Staff Relations. In *The Volunteer Management Handbook* (T. Connors, ed.). New York, John Wiley and Sons.

McKay, G. (2000). *Glastonbury: A Very English Fair*. London, Gollancz.

McLuhan, R. (2000). 20 Ways to Cut Costs. *Marketing Event*, March, 43–44.

Meenaghan, T. (2001a). Understanding sponsorship effects. *Psychology and Marketing*, **18**(2), 95–122.

Meenaghan, T. (2001b). Sponsorship and advertising: a comparison of consumer perceptions. *Psychology and Marketing*, **18**(2), 191–215.

Meetings Industry Association (MIA) (2009). *An Introduction to AIM for Venues & Suppliers*. (Internet) Available from <http://www.mia-uk.org/default.asp?PageID=527&n=AIM +2D+Main> (accessed 18 March 2010).

Meeting Professionals International (MPI) (2010). *MPI Global Training for Meetings and Events*. (Internet) Available from <http://www.mpiweb.org/Education/GlobalTraining/Programs/About.aspx> (accessed 18 March 2010).

meetEngland (2010a). *About Us*. (Internet) Available from <http://www.meetengland.com/Home/About-Us.aspx> (accessed 20 April 2010).

meetEngland (2010b). *Conventions and Conference Support*. (Internet) Available from <http://www.meetengland.com/Useful-Information/Conventions-and-Conference-Support.aspx> (accessed 20 April 2010).

Melbourne Commonwealth Games (2006). *Melbourne 2006 Workforce Privacy Policy*. <http://www.melbourne2006.com.au> (accessed 24 March 2010).

Mellor, P. (2000). The Core Debate. *Access All Areas*, November–December, 16.

Merlin Entertainments Group (2009). *Welcome*. (Internet) Available from <http://www.merlinvenues.com> (accessed 20 January 2010).

Mermiri, T. and South, J. (2009). *Private Investment in Culture 2007/08*. (Internet) London, Arts and Business. Available from <http://www.aandb.org.uk/Central/Research/Other-projects/Private-investment-culture-recession.aspx> (accessed 12 April 2010).

Middleton, V. T. C. (1995). *Marketing in Travel and Tourism*. Oxford, Butterworth-Heinemann.

Midlands Environmental Business Club Limited (2002). *SEXI: The Sustainable Exhibitions Industry Project*. Birmingham, Midlands Environmental Business Club Limited.

Millennium Commission (2000). *Celebrating the Year 2000*. (Internet). Available from <http://www.millennium.gov.uk/lottery/festival.html> (accessed 24 August 2005).

Millennium Commission Press Office (2000). *August Bank Holiday Sees High Point for Millennium Festival*. (Internet) Millennium Commission Press Release, 23 August. Available from <http://www.millennium.gov.uk/cgi-bin/item.cgi?id=1286andd=11andh=24andf=46anddateformat=%25o-%25B-%25Y> (accessed 3 August 2005).

Mintel (2000). *Music Concerts and Festivals*. London, Mintel International Group Ltd.

Minton, A. and Rose, R. (1997). The effects of environmental concern on environmentally friendly consumer behavior: an exploratory study. *Journal of Business Research*, **40**(1), 37–48.

Mintzberg, H. (1994). *The Rise and Fall of Strategic Planning*. New York, Prentice Hall.

Mintzberg, H. (2003). *The Strategy Process*. 4th edn. Harlow, Pearson Education.

Mintzberg, H., Quinn, J. and Voyer, J. (1995). *The Strategy Process.* New Jersey, Prentice Hall.

Mohr, K., Backman, K., Gahan, L. and Backman, S. (1993). An investigation of festival motivations and event satisfaction by visitor type. *Festival Management and Event Tourism*, **1**(3), 89–97.

Monmonier, M. (1996). *How to Lie with Maps.* 2nd edn. Chicago, University of Chicago Press.

Monroe, J. C. (2006). *Art of the Event: Complete Guide to Designing and Decorating Special Events.* Hoboken, NJ, Wiley.

Moore, L. (1985). *Motivating Volunteers.* Vancouver, Vancouver Volunteer Centre.

Morgan, M. (1996). *Marketing for Leisure and Tourism.* London, Prentice-Hall.

Morrow, S. S. (2002). *The Art of the Show.* 2nd edn. Dallas, IAEM Foundation.

Moses, A. (2006). *Tropfest Cops a Lashing.* Sydney Morning Herald, 27 February, www.smh. com.au (accessed 28 April 2010).

Moseley, T. (2010). *Free Tickets for Blackburn Rovers v Birmingham City Game Snapped Up.* (Internet) Lancashire Telegraph, 2 March. Available from <http://www.lancashiretelegraph. co.uk/news/5033900.Free_tickets_for_Blackburn_Rovers_v_Birmingham_City_game_ snapped_up> (accessed 18 April 2010).

Motor Sports Association (1999). *MSA Report Reveals Economic Impact of World Rally Championship (1999).* (Internet) Slough, Motor Sports Association press release, 19 November. Available from <http://www.ukmotorsport.com/networkq/1999/9914.html> (accessed 3 August 2005).

Motorsport Industry Association (MIA) (2003). *The Economic Impacts of the 2002 FIA Foster's British Grand Prix.* July. Stoneleigh Park, Motorsport Industry Association.

Mules, T. (1993). A special event as part of an urban renewal strategy. *Festival Management and Event Tourism*, **1**(2), 65–67.

Mules, T. (1998). Events tourism and economic development in Australia. In *Managing Tourism in Cities* (D. Tyler, Y. Guerrier and M. Robertson, eds). New York, John Wiley & Sons.

Mules, T. (1999). Estimating the economic impact of an event on a local government area,- Region, State or Territory. In *Valuing Tourism: Methods and Techniques* (K. Corcoran, A. Allcock, T. Frost and L. Johnson, eds). Canberra, Bureau of Tourism Research.

Mules, T. and McDonald, S. (1994). The economic impact of special events: the use of forecasts. *Festival Management and Event Tourism*, **2**(1), 45–53.

Mullins, L. J. (1999). *Management and Organisational Behaviour.* 5th edn. London, Financial Times, Pitman Publishing.

Mullins, L. J. (2005). *Management and Organisational Behaviour.* 7th edn. London, Financial Times, Pitman Publishing.

Muñoz, F. (2006). Olympic urbanism and Olympic villages: planning strategies in Olympic host cities, London 1908 to London 2012. In *Sports Mega-Events: Social Scientific Analyses of a Global Phenomenon* (J. Horne and W. Manzenreiter, eds). Oxford, Blackwell Publishing Limited.

Muthaly, S. K., Ratnatunga, J., Roberts, G. B. and Roberts, C. D. (2000). An event based entrepreneurship case study of futuristic strategies for Sydney 2000 Olympics. In *Events Beyond 2000 – Setting the Agenda. Proceedings of the Conference on Evaluation, Research and Education, 13–14 July* (J. Allen, R. Harris, L. K. Jago and A. J. Veal, eds). Sydney, Australian Centre for Event Management, University of Technology.

Myhill, M. (2005). *Return on Investment: The Bottom Line.* Meetingsnet, 1 September. <http://meetingsnet.com/checklistshowto/budget/insurance_return_investment_bottom> (accessed 28 April 2010).

National Fairground Archive (2007). *Charter Fairs — A History.* (Internet) Sheffield, University of Sheffield. Available from <http://www.nfa.dept.shef.ac.uk/history/charter/history.html> (accessed 3 January 2010).

National Heritage Committee (1995). *Fifth Report Bids to Stage International Sporting Events, HC (1994–95) 493.* London, HMSO.

National Maritime Museum (2005). *What is SeaBritain 2005?* (Internet) Available from <http://www.seabritain.com/server.php?show=nav.00400q> (accessed 9 August 2005).

National Outdoor Events Association (NOEA) (1993). *Code of Practice for Outdoor Events: Other than Pop Concerts and Raves.* Wallington, NOEA.

National Outdoor Events Association (NOEA) (1997). *Code of Practice for Outdoor Events: Other than Pop Concerts and Raves: Amendments and Updates.* Wallington, NOEA.

National Readership Surveys Limited (NRS) (2008). *Social Grade — Definitions and Discriminatory Power.* London, NRS Ltd. (Internet) Available from <http://www.nrs.co.uk/lifestyle.html> (accessed 15 November 2009).

National Readership Surveys Limited (NRS) (2009). NRS Readership Estimates*: Newspapers and Supplements: AIR — Latest 12 Months — July 2008 — June 2009.* London, NRS Ltd. (Internet) Available from <http://www.nrs.co.uk/toplinereadership.html> (accessed 15 November 2009).

National Rural Health Alliance, Services for Australian Rural and Remote Allied Health (SARRAH) Conference (2006). *Conference Mission Statement.* www.ruralhealth.org.au.

National Statistics (2009). *Population Change.* 27 August 2009 (Internet). Available from <http://www.statistics.gov.uk/cci/nugget.asp?id=950> (accessed 10 October 2009).

Neal, C., Quester, P. and Hawkins, H. (2002). *Consumer Behaviour.* 3rd edn. Sydney, McGraw-Hill.

Neeb, S. (2002). Green Games — the environmental efforts of the International Olympic Committee and the Lillehammer Olympic Organising Committee. In *The legacy of the Olympic Games 1984–2000, IOC Olympic Museum and Studies Centre and the Olympic Studies Centre of the Autonomous University of Barcelona* (M. Moragas, C. Kennet and N. Puig, eds). Lausanne, International Olympic Committee, 159–183.

Neighbourhood Arts Unit (1991). *Community Festival Handbook.* Melbourne, City of Melbourne.

NetAid.org (1999). *Netaid.org Web Site Sets World Record for Largest Internet Broadcast; More than One Thousand Organizations Join Initiative to Fight Extreme Poverty.* 12 October. (Internet) Available from <http://www.cisco.com/netaid/pressroom.html> (accessed 4 May 2005).

Newcastle Gateshead Initiative (2010). *Culture10.* (Internet) Available from <http://www.newcastlegateshead.com/culture10.php> (accessed 20 April 2010).

New Leisure Markets (1995). *Festivals and Special Events.* New Local Authority Leisure Markets Headland, Cleveland, Business Information Futures Ltd.

New Zealand Ministry of Civil Defence and Emergency Management (2003). *Safety Planning Guidelines for Events.* Wellington, New Zealand.

Newham Leisure Services (2000). *Reasons to be Cheerful: Newham's Local Culture Strategy.* London, Newham Leisure Services.

Nightingale, J. (2009). The orientation of map boards. *Event Management,* **13**(2), 133–7.

Nindi, P. (2005). *National Carnival Arts Strategy 2005–2007*. London, Arts Council England.

Niersbach, W. (2006). *An XXL World Cup for the Media*. News 15 FIFA World Cup Germany 2006. Lausanne, FIFA.

Noe, R., Hollenbeck, J., Gerhart, B. and Wright, P. (2003). *Human Resource Management*. 4th edn. New York, McGraw Hill.

Noise Council (1995). *Code of Practice on Environmental Noise Control at Concerts*. London, Chartered Institute Environmental Health Officers.

North West Arts Board (1999). *No Difference, No Future! Action for Cultural Diversity in Greater Manchester*. Manchester, North West Arts Board. (Internet) Available from <http://www.arts.org.uk/directory/regions/north_west/report_cult_div.html> (accessed 12 July 2000).

Northern Ireland Events Company (NIEC) (2005). *Background*. (Internet) Available from <http://www.nievents.co.uk/about/default.asp> (accessed 9 August 2005).

Northern Ireland Tourist Board (NITB) (2003). *Tourism in Northern Ireland: A Strategic Framework for Action 2004–2007*. Belfast, Northern Ireland Tourist Board.

Northern Ireland Tourist Board (NITB) (2008). *Planning Our Routre to Success: Northern Ireland Tourist Board Corporate Plan 2008–2011*. Belfast, Northern Ireland Tourist Board.

Northern Ireland Tourist Board (NITB) (2010). *Northern Ireland Conference Support Programme*. Belfast, Northern Ireland Tourist Board.

Northern Lights Festival Boreal (2006). *Mission Statement*. www.nlfbsudbury.com.

Northwest Development Agency (NWDA) (2007). *The Strategy for Tourism in England's Northwest*. (Internet) Warrington, Northwest Development Agency. Available from <http://www.nwda.co.uk/pdf/tourism_strategy0310.pdf> (accessed 24 April 2010).

Notman, S. (1999). *BEIC Topic Report: The Tourism Sector in Birmingham*. Birmingham, Birmingham Economic Information Centre.

Nurse, K. (2003). Festival tourism in the Caribbean: an economic impact assessment. In *Proceedings of the Fifth Annual Caribbean Conference on Sustainable Tourism Development*, Caribbean Tourism Organisation.

O'Connor, J. and Galvin, E. (1997). *Marketing and Information Technology: The Strategy, Application and Implementation of IT in Marketing*. Harlow, Pearson Education.

O'Malley, N. (2005). *Bosses Pull the Plug on Parties*. The Sydney Morning Herald, 1 November, www.smh.com.au.

O'Neill, S. (2000). *Geldoff Fury as Can't-do Culture Kills New Year Fireworks*. (Internet) Daily Telegraph, issue 2006, 21 November. Available from <http://www.telegraph.co.uk> (accessed 6 February 2001).

O'Neill, M., Getz, D. and Carlsen, J. (1999). Evaluation of service quality at events: The 1998 Coca-Cola Masters surfing event at Margaret River, Western Australia. *Managing Service Quality*, **9**(3), 158–166.

O'Toole, W. (2000). Towards the integration of event management best practice by the project management process. In *Events Beyond 2000 – Setting the Agenda. Proceedings of the Conference on Evaluation, Research and Education, 13–14 July* (J. Allen, R. Harris, L. K. Jago and A. J. Veal, eds). Sydney, Australian Centre for Event Management, University of Technology.

O'Toole, W. (2004). *Event Project Management System*. Sydney, EPMS.net. (Multimedia: CD-ROM).

O'Toole, W. (2006). *Event Project Management System*. Sydney, EPMS.net. (Multimedia: CD-ROM).

O'Toole, W. and Mikolaitis, P. (2002). *Corporate Event Project Management*. New York, John Wiley & Sons.

Office for National Statistics (ONS) (2003). *All People Aged 16 and Over in Households: Census 2001, National Report for England and Wales — Part 2: Table S066 Sex and Approximated Social Grade by Age*. (Internet) London, Office for National Statistics. Available from <http://www.statistics.gov.uk/StatBase/Expodata/Spreadsheets/D7534.xls> (accessed 12 November 2009).

Office for National Statistics (ONS) (2004). *Socio-economic Classification of Working-age Population, Summer 2003: Regional Trends 38*. 1 March. London, Office for National Statistics. (Internet) Available from <http://www.statistics.gov.uk/STATBASE/Expodata/Spreadsheets/D7665.xls> (accessed 9 August 2009).

Office for National Statistics (ONS) (2005). *The National Statistics Socio-economic Classification User Manual*. London, Office for National Statistics. (Internet) Available from <http://www.statistics.gov.uk/methods_quality/ns_sec/downloads/NS-SEC_User_2005.pdf> (accessed 12 November 2009).

Office of Commonwealth Games Coordination (n.d.). *2006 Melbourne Commonwealth Games: The Environment Strategy*. Melbourne: Office of Commonwealth Games Coordination.

One NorthEast (2007). *North East England Festival and Events Strategy*. Newcastle Upon Tyne, One NorthEast.

One NorthEast (2009). *North East Key Players Invest in Learning and Skills as the Class Awards are Launched*. (Internet) Newcastle Upon Tyne, One NorthEast. Available from <http://www.onenortheast.co.uk/object/display.cfm?serv=1&id=4102> (accessed 24 April 2010).

One North East Tourism Team (2010). *The Online Toolkit for Festival and Events Organisers: Legislation*. (Internet) Newcastle Upon Tyne, One North East. Available from <http://www.tourismnortheast.co.uk/pages/information-sheets/required-permissions-and-legislation/legislation> (accessed 28 April 2010).

Oittinen, A. (2003). *The Olympic Movement and the Olympic Games, an Environmental Perspective*. Olympia, International Olympic Academy.

Owen, J. and Holliday, P. (1993). *Confer in Confidence: An Organiser's Dossier*. Broadway, Worcester, Meetings Industry Association.

Oxford Interactive Encyclopedia (1997). *Folk Festival*. San Francisco, The Learning Company, Inc.

PA Cambridge Economic Consultants (1990). *An Evaluation of Garden Festivals*. London, HMSO.

Page, W. and Carey, C. (2009). *Economic Insight 15 — Adding up the Music Industry for 2008*, 20 July. London, PRS for Music. (Internet) Available from <http://www.prsformusic.com/economics> (accessed 1 October 2009).

Pagonis, W. G. (1992). *Moving Mountains Lessons in Leadership and Logistics from the Gulf War*. Boston, Harvard Business School Press.

Palmer, G. and Lloyd, N. (1972). *A Year of Festivals: British Calendar Customs*. London, Frederick Warne.

Parasuraman, A., Zeithaml, V. and Berry, L. (1988). SERVQUAL: a multiple-item scale for measuring consumers' perceptions of service quality. *Journal of Retailing*, **64**(1), 22–37.

Peach, E. and Murrell, K. (1995). Reward and recognition systems for volunteers. In *The Volunteer Management Handbook* (T. Connors, ed.), New York, John Wiley & Sons.

Pearce, L. (2003). *Open Seeks New Sponsor After Heineken Decision*. The Age, 31 December. (Internet) Available from <http://www.theage.com.au/articles/2003/12/30/1072546528779.html> (accessed 18 April 2010).

Pembroke Festival (2004). *Welcome to the 2004 Pembroke Festival Music Programme!* (Internet) Available from <http://www.pembrokefestival.org.uk/content/2004/index.htm> (accessed 10 May 2005).

People 1st (2010). *Labour Market Review of the Events Industry*. Harlow, People 1st.

Performance Research (2000). *British Football Fans Can't Recall Euro 2000 Sponsors*. (Internet) London, Performance Research. Available from <http://www.performanceresearch.com/euro-2000-sponsorship.htm> (accessed 12 April 2010).

Performance Research (2001). *Independent Studies*. Henley on Thames, Performance Research.

Performance Research (2004). *Ninth Annual IEG/Performance Research Sponsorship Decision-Makers Survey*. (Internet). Available from <http://www.performanceresearch.com/sponsor-survey.htm> (accessed 12 April 2010).

Performance Research (2009). *Ninth Annual IEG/Performance Research Sponsorship Decision-Makers Survey*. (Internet) Available from <http://www.performanceresearch.com/sponsor-survey.htm> (accessed 12 April 2010).

Perreault, W., Cannon, J. P. and McCarthy, E. J. (1987). *Basic Marketing*. 16th edn. Homewood, IL, Irwin.

Perry, M., Foley, P. and Rumpf, P. (1996). Event management: an emerging challenge in Australian education. *Festival Management and Event Tourism*, **4**(1), 85–93.

Phillips, J. J., Breining, M. T. and Phillips, P. P. (2008). *Return on Investment in Meetings & Events: Tools and Techniques to Measure the Success of all Types of Meetings and Events*. Oxford, Butterworth-Heinemann.

Picard, D. and Robinson, M. (eds) (2006). *Festivals, Tourism and Social Change: Remaking Worlds*. Clevedon, Clear Channel Publications.

Pickett, B. (2002). *As Cingular Ads Parody, Not All Sponsorships Fit the Brandbuilding Bill*. (Internet) National Hotel Executive, September. Available from <http://www.brandchannel.com/images/papers/sponsorshipBC.pdf> (accessed 12 April 2010).

Pickton, D. and Broderick, A. (2005). *Integrated Marketing Communications*. 2nd edn. Harlow, Pearson Education Ltd.

Pine II, B. J. and Gilmore, J. H. (1999). *The Experience Economy: Work is Theatre & Every Business a Stage*. Boston, Harvard Business School Press.

Pitts, R. and Lei, D. (2006). *Strategic Management*. Mason, Thomson.

Planet Drum (2004a). *Environmental "Greenwashing" of the 2002 Winter Olympic Games*. (Internet) Available from <http://www.planetdrum.org/background_2002.htm> (accessed 5 May 2010).

Planet Drum (2004b). *Environmental Recommendations go Unheeded by Olympics Organizers*. <http://www.planetdrum.org/slo_recommendations.htm> (accessed 5 May 2010).

Policy Studies Institute (PSI) (1992). *Arts Festivals*. Cultural Trends, 15. London, Policy Studies Institute.

Port Fairy Folk Festival (2006). *The Committee*. www.portfairyfolkfestival.com.

Porter, M. (1990). *Competitive Advantage of Nations*. New York, Free Press.

Price, J. (2008). *Corporate Manslaughter Act*. London, National Council for Voluntary Organisations (Internet) Available from <http://www.ncvo-vol.org.uk/policy-research-analysis/policy/charity-law-regulation/corporate-manslaughter-act> (accessed 26 April 2010).

PricewaterhouseCoopers (2001). *E-commerce Impact Study for the Exhibition and Conference Sector.* Final report, September 2001. London, DTI.

PricewaterhouseCoopers (2002). *2002 Sustainability Report.* Boston, PricewaterhouseCoopers.

Project Management Institute (2008). A *Guide to the Project Management Body of Knowledge (PMBOK® Guide).* 4th edn. Pennsylvania, Project Management Institute.

Quainton, D. (2009). Social networking: find your wings, or get left behind. *Event Magazine*, 1 June. (Internet) Available from <http://www.eventmagazine.co.uk/news/features/909373/Social-networking-Find-wings-left-behind> (accessed 18 April 2010).

Raj, R., Walters, P. and Rashid, T. (2009). *Events Management: An Integrated and Practical Approach.* London, Sage.

Rao, V. and Steckel, J. (1998). *Analysis for Strategic Marketing.* Reading, Massachusetts, Addison-Wesley.

Raybould, M., Fredline, L., Jago, L. and Deery, M. (2005). Triple bottom line event evaluation: a proposed framework for holistic event evaluation. In *The Impacts of Events: Proceedings of International Event Research Conference Held in Sydney in July 2005* (Allen, ed.). Sydney, Australian Centre for Event Management.

Redmond, A. (2005). *Convention Bureau.* (Internet) Glasgow, Glasgow City Marketing Bureau. Available from <http://www.seeglasgow.com/convention-bureau> (accessed 9 August 2005).

Reeves, M. (2002). *Measuring the Economic and Social Impact of the Arts.* London, Arts Council of England.

Reid, F. (1995). *Staging Handbook.* 2nd edn. London, A. & C. Black.

Renault (2003). *Renault UK Sponsor of Cirque du Soleil's Saltimbanco Season.* (Internet). Press Release, 17 January. Available from <http://www.carpages.co.uk/renault/renault_sponsor_cirque_du_soleils_saltimbanco_season_17_01_03.asp?switched=on&echo=10757702> (accessed 22 July 2005).

Resource NSW (2003). *7 Steps to a Waste Wise Event.* www.wastewiseevents.resource.nsw.gov.au (accessed 22 December 2005).

Rice, J. (2007). *Co-creation.* (Internet) Available from <http://brand.blogs.com/mantra/2006/05/cocreation.html> (accessed 2 May 2010).

Richards, G. and Wilson, J. (2002). The links between mega events and urban renewal: the case of the manchester 2002 Commonwealth Games. In *Events and Place-making: Proceedings of International Research Conference Held in Sydney 2002* (L. Jago, M. Deery, R. Harris, A. Hede and J. Allen, eds). Sydney, Australian Centre for Event Management.

Rifon, N., Choi, S., Trimble, C. and Li, H. (2004). Congruence effects in sponsorship. *Journal of Advertising*, **33**(1), 29–42.

Ritchie, J. R. B. (1984). Assessing the impact of hallmark events. *Journal of Travel Research*, **23**(1), 2–11.

Ritchie, B. (2000). Turning 16 days into 16 years through Olympic legacies. *Event Management*, **6**(3), 155–165.

Robbins, S. and Coulter, M. (1999). *Management.* 6th International edn. Upper Saddle River, New Jersey, Prentice-Hall.

Robertson, M. (ed.) (2006). *Sporting Events and Event Tourism: Impacts, Plans and Opportunities.* Festivals and Events: Beyond Economic Impacts, Volume 1. Eastbourne, Leisure Studies Association.

Robertson, D. and Pope, N. (1999). Product bundling and causes of attendance and non-attendance in live professional sport: a case study of the Brisbane Broncos and the

Brisbane Lions. (Internet) *The Cyberjournal of Sports Marketing*, **3**(1). Available from <http://www.ausport.gov.au/fulltext/1999/cjsm/v3n1/robertson&pope31.htm> (accessed 24 August 2005).

Robertson, M. and Frew, E. (eds) (2008). *Events and Festivals: Current Trends and Issues.* London, Routledge.

Robertson, M., Rogers, P. and Leask, A. (2009). Progressing Socio-Cultural Impact Evaluation for Festivals. *Journal of Policy Research in Tourism, Leisure and Events*, **1**(2), July, 156–169.

Robinson, G. (2000). *The Creative Imperative: Investing in the Arts in the 21st Century.* New Statesman Arts Lecture 2000, Banqueting Hall, Whitehall, 27 June. London, Arts Council of England.

Robinson, L. S. and Callan, R. J. (2001). The U.K. conference and meetings industry: development of an inventory for attributional analysis. *Journal of Convention and Exhibition Management*, **2**(4), 65–80.

Robinson, L. S. and Callan, R. J. (2002a). A qualitative gambit to formulate a foundation for the appraisement of service quality in the U.K. meetings industry. *Journal of Convention and Exhibition Management*, **3**(4), 1–16.

Robinson, L. S. and Callan, R. J. (2002b). Professional U.K. conference organizers' perceptions of important selection and quality attributes of the meetings product. *Journal of Convention and Exhibition Management*, **4**(1), 1–18.

Robinson, L. S. and Callan, R. J. (2005). UK conference delegates' cognizance of the importance of venue selection attributes. *Journal of Convention and Event Tourism*, **7**(1), 77–91.

Roche, M. (1992). Mega-events and micro-modernisation: On the sociology of new urban tourism. *British Journal of Sociology*, **43**, 563–600.

Roche, M. (2000). *Mega-Events and Modernity: Olympics and Expos in the Growth of Global Culture.* London, Routledge.

Rock Eisteddfod Challenge (2010). *History.* (Internet) Available from <www.rockchallenge.com.au> (accessed 2 May 2010).

Rogers, T. (2003). *Business Tourism Briefing: An Overview of the UK's Business Tourism Industry.* London, Business Tourism Partnership.

Rogers, T. (2008). *Conferences and Conventions: A Global Industry.* 2nd edn. Oxford, Butterworth-Heinemann.

Rogers, T. (2010). *UK Conferences and Meetings: Where Are We Now? Destination World News*, Issue 34, March 2010. (Internet) Available from <http://www.destinationworld.info/newsletter/feature69.html> (accessed 23 April 2010).

Rolfe, H. (1992). *Arts Festivals in the UK.* London, Policy Studies Institute.

Rose, D. and O'Reilley, K. (1998). *The ESCR Review of Government Social Classifications.* London, Office for National Statistics/Economic and Social Research Council.

Roskilde Festival (2006). *Roskilde Organisational Structure.* www.roskilde-festival.dk.

Roslow, S. Nicholls, J. and Laskey, H. (1992). Hallmark Events and Measures of Reach and Audience Characteristics. *Journal of Advertising Research*, July–August, 53–59.

Rowley, J. and Williams, C. (2008). The impact of brand sponsorship of music festivals. *Marketing Intelligence & Planning*, **26**(7), 781–79.

Roy, D. and Cornwell, T. B. (2004). The effects of consumer knowledge on responses to event sponsorships. *Psychology and Marketing*, **21**(3), 185–207.

Royal Bank of Scotland (2003). *Royal Bank of Scotland Staff Turn up and Try it Themselves*. (Internet) Press Release 31 July. Available from <http://www.rbs.com/media03.asp?id=MEDIA_CENTRE/PRESS_RELEASES/2003/JULY/31_ED_FESTIVAL> (accessed 21 August 2005).

Royal Bank of Scotland (2004). *Royal Bank Lates — The Quintessential Festival*. (Internet) Press Release 1 April. Available from <http://www.rbs.com/media/news/press-releases/2004-press-releases/2004-04-01royal-bank-lates–th.ashx> (accessed 16 December 2009).

Royal, C. G. and Jago, L. K. (1998). Special events accreditation: the practitioner's perspective. *Festival Management and Event Tourism*, **5**(4), 221–30.

Ruddick, A. (2008). *Yorkshire in Global Spotlight*. Press Release 3 June. (Internet) Available from <http://www.welcometoyorkshire.net/News—Events/Press-Release-Archive/News-Example-3.aspx> (accessed 15 February 2010).

Saga Group Ltd. (2010). *Saga's Sponsorship Strategy*. (Internet) Available from <http://www.saga.co.uk/corporate/sponsorship.asp> (accessed 12 April 2010).

Safeconcerts (2008). *Corporate Manslaughter and Corporate Homicide Act 2007*. (Internet) 20 March. Available from <http://www.safeconcerts.com/crowdsafety/corporate-manslaughter-act.asp> (accessed 18 April 2010).

SAI Global (2006). *Risk Management for Events*. Sydney, SAI Global Assurance Services.

Saleh, F. and Ryan, C. (1993). Jazz and Knitwear: factors that attract tourists to festivals. *Tourism Management*, August, 289–297.

Salford Film Festival (2010). *Mission Statement and Aims*. (Internet) Available from <http://www.salfordfilmfestival.org.uk/p.asp?ID=10> (accessed 12 March 2010).

Salter, J. (2005). Emergency planning capability assessment. In *Civil Care and Security Studies* (R. Gerber and J. Salter, eds). Armidale, NSW, Kardoorair.

Schlegelmilch, B., Bohlen, G. and Diamantopoulos, A. (1996). The link between green purchasing decisions and measures of environmental consciousness. *European Journal of Marketing*, **30**(5), 35–55.

School of Volunteer Management (2001). *Rights and Responsibilities of Volunteers and Voluntary Organisations*. Sydney, School of Volunteer Management.

Schrieber, A. (1994). *Lifestyle and Event Marketing: Building the New Customer Partnership*. New York, McGraw-Hill.

Schwartz, A. (2010). *Vancouver Held the Greenest Olympic Games, but the Sochi in 2014 Could be the Dirtiest*. Fast Company, 3 March (Internet) Available from <http://www.fastcompany.com/1569772/will-the-vancouver-games-remain-the-greenest-winter-olympics-ever> (accessed 20 April 2010).

Scottish Courage (2005). *The Strongbow Rooms*. (Internet). Entry for Marketing Excellence Awards Scotland 2005. Available from <http://www.tunaweb.com/MarketingAwardsScotlandNominees/casestudies/Comms-SE-StongbowRooms.pdf> (accessed 24 August 2005).

Scottish Executive (2002). *Scotland's Major Events Strategy 2003–2015: Competing on an International Stage*. (Internet). Available from <http://www.scotland.gov.uk/publications> (accessed 18 April 2010).

Scottish Exhibition and Conference Centre (SECC) (2005). SECC Successfully Hosts ERS. *Scene*, Issue 1, 4.

Scottish Government (2010). *A Games Legacy for Scotland*. Edinburgh, Scottish Government. (Internet) Available from <http://www.scotland.gov.uk/gameslegacy> (accessed 13 February 2010).

Scottish Golf Environment Group Ltd (SGEGL) (2008). *Green Event Guidelines*. St Andrews, Scottish Golf Union.

SeaBritain 2005 PressOffice (2004). *SeaBritain 2005 — Take a Fresh Look at the Sea*. Press Release, 1 October. <http://www.seabritain2005.com/server.php?show=ConWebDoc.116> (accessed 9 August 2005).

Seekings, D. (1999). *How to Organize Effective Conferences and Meetings*. London, Kogan Page.

Select Committee on Culture, Media and Sport (1999). *Fourth Report: Staging International Sporting Events*. May. London, The Stationery Office.

Select Committee on Culture, Media and Sport (2001). *Third Report: Staging International Sporting Events*. London, The Stationery Office.

Selwood, H. J. and Jones, R. (1993). The America's Cup in retrospect: the aftershock in Fremantle. In *Leisure and Tourism: Social and Environmental Change: Papers from the World Leisure and Recreation Association Congress* (A. J. Veal, P. Jonson and G. Cushman, eds). Centre for Leisure and Tourism Studies, University of Technology, Sydney, 656—60.

Shani, D. and Sandler, D. (1998). Ambush Marketing: is confusion to blame for the flickering of the flame? *Psychology and Marketing*, **15**(4), 367—83.

Shaw, R., Seminik, R. and Williams, R. (1981). *Marketing — An Integrated Analytical Approach*, South Western Publishing, Cincinnati.

Sherwood, P., Jago, L. and Deery, M. (2005). Unlocking the triple bottom line of special event evaluations: what are the key impacts? In *The Impacts of Events: Proceedings of International Event Research Conference Held in Sydney in July 2005* (Allen, ed.), Australian Centre for Event Management, Sydney.

Shimp, T. (2010). *Advertising, Promotion and Supplemental Aspects of Integrated Marketing Communication*. 8th edn. Mason, Ohio, South-Western Cengage Learning.

Shone, A. (1998). *The Business of Conferences*. Oxford, Butterworth-Heinemann.

Shone, A. with Parry, B. (2001). *Successful Event Management*. Continuum, London.

Shone, A. and Parry, B. (2010). *Successful Event Management*. 3rd edn. London, Cengage Learning.

Shropshire Council (2010). *Local Grants*. Telford, Shropshire Council. (Internet) Available from <http://www.shropshire.gov.uk/economicdevelopment.nsf> (accessed 24 April 10).

Silvers, J. R. (2004a). Global knowledge domain structure for event management. In *Las Vegas International Hospitality and Convention Summit* (Z. Gu, ed.), Las Vegas, Nevada, UNLV.

Silvers, J. (2004b). *Professional Event Coordination*. Hoboken, New Jersey, John Wiley & Sons Inc.

Silvers, J. (2008). *Risk Management for Meetings and Events*. Oxford, Butterworth-Heinemann.

Silvers, J. (2010). *Event Management Body of Knowledge Project: The Event Genre of Event Management*. 1 January (Internet) Available from <http://www.juliasilvers.com/embok.htm> (accessed 26 April 2010).

Skinner, B.E. and Rukavina, V. (2003). *Event Sponsorship*. Hoboken, New Jersey, John Wiley and Sons Inc.

Silvers, J., Bowdin, G., O'Toole, W. and Nelson, K. (2006). Towards an International Event Management Body Of Knowledge (EMBOK). *Event Management*, **9**(4), 185—198.

Slack, N., Chambers, S. and Johnston, R. (2010). *Operations Management*. 6th edn. Harlow, Financial Times Prentice-Hall.

Sleight, S. (1989). *Sponsorship: What It Is and How to Use It*. Maidenhead, McGraw-Hill.

Slice (2000). *Creamfields 2000*. (Internet) London, Slice. Available from <http:// www.slice. co.uk/creamfields00_sitemap.html> (accessed 2 February 2001).

Sloman, J. (2006). *Project Management (Course Notes)*. Major Event Management Program 9–14 June, Sydney, Sport Knowledge Australia.

Smith, A. and Jenner, P. (1998). The impact of festivals and special events on tourism. *Travel and Tourism Analyst*, **4**, 73–91.

Smith, J. and Taylor, J. (2004). *Marketing Communications: An Integrated Approach*. 4th ed., Kogan Page, London.

Society of Motor Manufacturers and Traders (SMMT) (2004). *Motor Show Matters to the West Midlands*. (Internet) London, Society of Motor Manufacturers and Traders, Press Release 29 September. Available from <http://www.smmt.co.uk/news/> (accessed 18 April 2010).

Sodexho Prestige (2004). *The National Corporate Hospitality Survey*. Alperton, Sodexho Prestige.

Solis, B. (2010). *Defining Social Media 2006–2010*. 7 January (Internet) Available from <http://www.briansolis.com/2010/01/defining-social-media-the-saga-continues> (accessed 18 April 2010).

Sonder, M. (2005). *Event Entertainment and Production*. Hoboken, New Jersey, John Wiley & Sons, Inc.

Sorin, D. (2003). *The Special Events Advisor*. Hoboken, New Jersey, John Wiley & Sons Inc.

South East Arts (1998). *A Festival's Strategy for the South East*. London, England's Regional Arts Boards.

SponsorMap (2008). *Understanding Sponsorship*. (Internet). Available from <http://www. sponsormap.com/defining-sponsorship/> (accessed 12 April 2010).

SponsorMap (2009). *Global Sponsorship Spend Remains Positive for 2009*. (Internet). Available from <http://www.sponsormap.com/global-sponsorship-spend-remains-positive-for-2009/> (accessed 12 April 2010).

Sponsorship Consulting Limited (2005). *Accenture – A Case Study*. (Internet). London, Sponsorship Consulting Limited. Available from <http://www.sponsorshipconsulting.co. uk/case_Accenture.htm> (accessed 23 August 2005).

Sport Industry Research Centre (SIRC) (2005). *Tour of Britain Economic Impact Report*. Surrey, Tour of Britain.

Sports East South East (2006). *Major Sports Events Strategy for the South East Region*. Kent, Sports East South East.

SQW Ltd and TNS Travel and Tourism (2005). *Edinburgh Festivals 2004–2005 Economic Impact Survey Stage 1 Results*. Edinburgh, The City of Edinburgh Council, Scottish Enterprise Edinburgh and Lothian, EventScotland and VisitScotland.

Stayte, S. and Watt, D. (1998). *Events: From Start to Finish*. Reading, ILAM.

Stephenson, G. (2005). *Arts and Culture in Northern Ireland: 2004 Baseline Survey*. Belfast, Arts Council of Northern Ireland.

Stone, R. (2007). *Human Resource Management*. 6th edn. John Wiley & Sons Australia, Brisbane.

Stoner, J. A. F., Freeman, R. E. and Gilbert, D. R., Jr (1995). *Management*. 6th edn. Englewood Cliffs, New Jersey, Prentice-Hall.

Strauss, N. (2000). The last 10 per cent is the toughest. *BioCycle*, January, 35.

Strauss, J., El-Ansary, A. and Frost, R. (2006). *E-marketing*. 4th edn, Pearson Education International, New Jersey, 341.

Strauss, J. and Frost, R. (2009). *E-Marketing*. 5th edn. Upper Saddle River, New Jersey, Pearson Education Inc.

Sudhaman, A. (2004). Game, set and client match. *Media Asia*, 9 May, 28–29.

Summerfield, C. and Gill, B. (2005). *Social Trends*. No. 35. (Internet) Basingstoke, Palgrave Macmillan. Available from <http://www.statistics.gov.uk/downloads/theme_social/ Social_Trends35/Social_Trends_35.pdf> (accessed 13 January 2010).

Sunshine, K., Backman, K. and Backman, S. (1995). An Examination of Sponsorship Proposals in Relation to Corporate Objectives. *Festival Management and Event Tourism*, **2**(3/4), 159–166.

Supovitz, F. (2005). *The Sports Event Management and Marketing Playbook*. Hoboken, New Jersey, John Wiley & Sons Inc.

Supply Chain Inventory Management Forum (2003). *Glossary of Supply-Chain Inventory Management Terms*. (Internet) Corby, Chartered Institute of Logistics and Transport (CILT) Available from <http://www.ciltuk.org.uk/process/glossary.asp> (accessed 21 July 2005).

Sussex Arts Marketing (2004). *Brighton Festival 2004: Everyone Benefits* …. Brighton, Sussex Arts Marketing. (Internet) Available from <http://www.brightonfestival.org/ impact> (accessed 12 April 2010).

Sussex Arts Marketing and the University of Brighton (2008). *Festivals Mean Business III: A Survey of Arts Festivals in the UK*. London, British Arts Festivals Association.

Sustainability Victoria (2006). *Waste Wise Events*. Melbourne, Sustainability Victoria.

Sustainability Victoria (2007). *Wangaratta Jazz Festival Case Study*. (Internet) Available from <http://www.sustainability.vic.gov.au/resources/documents/01432_Case_study_ TAC_Wanga.pdf> (accessed 5 May 2010).

Sustainable Development Commission (SDC) (2010). *Watchdog*. (Internet) London, Sustainable Development Commission. Available from <http://www.sd-commission.org. uk/pages/watchdog.html> (accessed 1 May 2010).

Sydney (2000). *Environmental Guidelines. Sustainable Development Principles in Action: Learning from the Sydney 2000 Experience*. CD-ROM resource. Sydney, Green and Gold Inc.

Tambe, R. (2004). *Corporate Hospitality*. London, Key Note Ltd.

Tapscott, D. (2009). *Grown Up Digital: How the Net Generation is Changing Your World*. New York, McGraw-Hill.

Tarlow, P. (2002). *Event Risk Management and Safety*. New York, John Wiley & Sons Inc.

Tarradellas, J. and Behnam, S. (2000). *Olympic Movement's Agenda 21: Sport for Sustainable Development*. Lausanne, Switzerland, International Olympic Committee, Sport and Environment Commission.

Tassiopoulous, D. (ed.) (2010). *Event Management: A Developmental & Managerial Approach*, 3rd edn. Claremont, Juta Publishing (Academic).

The Association for Festival Organisers (AFO) (2003). *A Report into the Impact of Folk Festivals on Cultural Tourism*. Matlock, The Association for Festival Organisers.

The Association for Festival Organisers (AFO) (2004). *The Impact of Folk Festivals*. Matlock, The Association for Festival Organisers.

The Chambers Dictionary (1998). Edinburgh, Chambers Harrap Publishers Ltd.

The Chartered Institute of Purchasing and Supply (CIPS) (2007). *Event Management*. Stamford, The Chartered Institute of Purchasing and Supply.

The Clapham Festival of Music and the Arts (2010). *Education and Outreach*. (Internet) Available from <http://claamfest.org/educationandoutreach.htm> (accessed 18 April 2010).

The Comptroller and Auditor General (2000). *The Millennium Dome*. London, The Stationery Office.

The Dana Foundation (2005). *Brain Awareness Week*. (Internet). Available from <http://www.dana.org/brainweek> (accessed 12 April 2010).

The Guardian Hay Festival (2010). *Sponsor The Festival*. (Internet). Available from <http://www.hayfestival.com/portal/sponsorship.aspx> (accessed 12 April 2010).

The NEC Group (2004). *Textile Show Gives Massive Boost to Region*. (Internet) Press Release, 16 March. Available from <http://www.necgroup-sport.com/media/PressRelease.asp?i=675> (accessed 3 August 2005).

The NEC Group (2005a). *The Lions Club*. The NEC Group Hall of Fame. (Internet). Available from <http://www.necgroup.co.uk/corporate/halloffame/lions-club.asp> (accessed 3 August 2005).

The NEC Group (2005b). *Factsheet 1 — The NEC Group — Introduction and Background*. (Internet). Available from <http://www.necgroup.co.uk/media/pdfs/facts1.pdf> (accessed 3 August 2005).

The Right Solution (2005). *UK Conference Market Survey*. Wellingborough, Meetings Industry Association.

The Scottish Traditional Boat Festival (2010). *Welcome*. (Internet) Available from <http://www.scottishtraditionalboatfestival.co.uk> (accessed 16 April 2010).

The Theatre Shop Conference (2002). *Panel Discussion: Programming Criteria Used By International Festivals*. (Internet). Available from <http://www.fuel4arts.com> (accessed 24 August 2005).

Theodoraki, E. (2007). *Olympic Event Organization*. Oxford, Butterworth-Heinemann.

Thomas, R. and Wood, E. (2003). Events-based tourism: a survey of local authority strategies in the UK. *Local Governance*. **29**(2), 127–136.

Thompson, J. L. (1997). *Strategic Management: Awareness and Change*. 3rd edn. London, International Thompson Business Press.

Thompson, J. L. with Martin, F. (2005). *Strategic Management: Awareness and Change*. 5th edn. London, Thomson Learning.

Thrane, C. (2002). Music quality, satisfaction and behavioural intentions within a jazz festival context. *Event Management*, **7**(3), 143–50.

Thorley, C. (2009). *Strongbow's Experiential Bowtime Bar Back for V Festival*. Event, 22 June (Internet) Available from <http://www.eventmagazine.co.uk/news/914771/Strongbows-experiential-Bowtime-Bar-back-V-Festival> (accessed 12 April 2010).

Toffler, A. (1999). *Future Shock*. New York, Bantam Books.

Toohey, K. (2001). *Official Report of the Games of the XXVII Olympiad*. Sydney, Sydney Organising Committee for the Olympic Games.

Toohey, K. and Halbwirth, S. (2001). *The Sydney Organising Committee of the Olympic Games and Knowledge Management: Learning from Experience*. www.sprig.org.uk, p. 4.

Torkildsen, G. (2005). *Leisure and Recreation Management*. 5th edn. Abingdon, Routledge.

Tourism Works (1996). *Economic Impact of the European Championships 1996 on the City of Leeds: An Image Volume Value Study*. Leeds, Leeds City Council.

Travers, T. (1998). *The Wyndham Report*. London, Society of London Theatre.

Tribe, J. (1997). *Corporate Strategy for Tourism.* London, International Thompson Business Press.

Tum, J., Norton, P. and Wright, N. (2005). *Managing Event Operations.* Oxford, Elsevier Butterworth-Heinemann.

UK Sport (1998). *Public Opinion Survey − Importance and Measure of UK Sporting Success.* London, UK Sport.

UK Sport (1999a). *A UK Strategy: Major Events − A 'Blueprint' For Success.* London, UK Sport.

UK Sport (1999b). Memorandum submitted by the United Kingdom Sports Council. In *Fourth Report: Staging International Sporting Events. Volume II Minutes of Evidence* (Select Committee on Culture, Media and Sport). London, The Stationery Office.

UK Sport (1999c). *Major Events: The Economics − A Guide.* London, UK Sport.

UK Sport (2000). *Major Events Blueprint: Measuring Success.* London, UK Sport.

UK Sport (2002). *Practical Environmental Guidelines.* London, UK Sport.

UK Sport (2004). *Measuring Success 2: The Economic Impact of Major Sports Events.* London, UK Sport.

UK Sport (2005). *Major Sports Events: The Guide.* London, UK Sport.

UK Sport (2006). Measuring Success 2 — The Economic Impact of Major Sports Events. www.uksport.gov.uk.

UK Sport (2007). *Measuring Success 3: The Economic Impact of Six Major Sports Events Supported by the World Class Events Programme in 2005 & 2006.* London, UK Sport.

Ukman, L. (1995). *Successful Proposals.* (Internet). Available from <http://www.sponsorship.com/forum/success.html> (accessed 25 April 2001).

United Nations (1992). *Agenda 21: Programme of Action for Sustainable Development.* New York, United Nations Department of Public Information.

United Nations Environment Programme (UNEP) (2004). *Agreement to Boost Environmental Awareness at Summer Olympics.* (Internet) Available from <http://www.unep.org/documents.multilingual/default.asp?documentid=399&articleid=4511&l=en> (accessed 5 May 2010).

United Nations Education, Scientific and Cultural Organisation (UNESCO) (2005). *UN Decade of Education for Sustainable Development 2005−2014: The DESD at a Glance.* Paris, UNESCO − Education for Sustainable Development.

United Nations Environment Programme (UNEP) (2006). *Football World Cup Scores Green Goal: The United Nations Environment Programme (UNEP) and the Competition Organisers sign historic partnership agreement 'Green Goal'.* (Internet) Available from <http://www.unep.org/documents.multilingual/default.asp?documentid=452&articleid=4918&l=en> (accessed 5 May 2010).

US Food and Drug Administration (1997). *Hazard Analysis and Critical Control Point Principles and Application Guidelines.* www.cfsan.fda.gov (accessed 14 April 2010).

Uysal, M., Gahan, L. and Martin, B. (1993). An examination of event motivations. *Festival Management and Event Tourism,* **1**(1), 5−10.

Van Der Wagen, L. (2007). *Human Resource Management for Events: Managing the Event Workforce.* Oxford, Butterworth-Heinemann.

Van Der Wagen, L. (2008). *Event Management for Tourism, Cultural, Business and Sporting Events.* 3rd edn. Frenchs Forest, Pearson Education Australia.

Vanneste, M. (2008). *Meeting Architecture, a Manifesto*. Turnhout, Meeting Support Institute.

Vasey, J. (1998). *Concert Tour Production Management*. Boston, Focal Press.

Veal, A. (2006). *Research Methods for Leisure and Tourism*. 3rd edn. Harlow, Pearson Education Limited.

Victorian Government (2006). *Ten Year Tourism and Events Industry Strategy*. Melbourne, Victorian Government Department of Innovation, Industry and Regional Development. <http://www.diird.vic.gov.au>.

Victorian Auditor-General (2007). *State Investment in Major Events*. Melbourne, Victorian Auditor-General's Office.

Verwey, P. (1999). *Sample Audience Survey Questions*. London, Arts Council of England.

Victorian Government, Department of Innovation, Industry and Regional Development. (2006). *Ten Year Tourism and Events Industry Strategy*. www.diird.vic.gov.au.

ViewLondon.co.uk (2005). *What's On: BBC Henry Wood Promenade Concerts — Week Seven*. (Internet) Available from <http://www.viewlondon.co.uk/whats_on_31109.html> (accessed 22 August 2005).

Vignette (2004). *Vignette Powers Record-Setting Performance of Athens 2004 Olympics Web Site*. (Internet) Case Study: Publishing and Entertainment. Available from <http://www.vignette.com/Downloads/CS_Athens2004.pdf> (accessed 10 January 2010).

Viljoen, J. and Dann, S. (2000). *Strategic Management*. 3rd edn. Longman, Sydney.

Virgin Radio (2004). *Wall's Ice Cream — Live to Play*. (Internet). Available from <http://www.virginradio.co.uk/music/vfestival2004/walls.html> (accessed 23 August 2005).

VisitBritain (2010). *VisitBritain 2010–11 Business Plan*. London, VisitBritain. (Internet) Available from <http://www.visitbritain.org/Images/BusinessPlan2010-11_tcm139-186939.pdf> (accessed 20 April 2010).

Visit York (2009). *Explosion of Light Illustrations to Transform York's Ancient Tower*. Press Release 1 October. York, Illuminating York Festival. (Internet) Available from http://illuminatingyork.org.uk/resourses/PRESS%20RELEASE%20FINAL%20Walls%20of%20Light.pdf (accessed 15 February 2010).

Vroom, V. (1964). *Work and Motivation*. New York, John Wiley & Sons.

Waitt, G. (2003). Social Impacts of the Sydney Olympics. *Annals of Tourism Research*, **30**(1), 194–215.

Wales Event Recycling Project (2008). *Wales Events Recycling Guide*. 2nd edn. Cardiff, Waste Awareness Wales. (Internet) Available from <http://www.wasteawarenesswales.org.uk/1662.file.dld> (accessed 23 February 2010).

Wales Tourist Board (WTB) (2000). *Achieving Our Potential: A Tourism Strategy for Wales*. Cardiff, Wales Tourist Board.

Wallis, N. (2003). Analysis — festivals find their place in the sun. *Event*, November/December, 10.

Weber, K. and Chon, K. (eds) (2002). *Convention Tourism: International Research and Industry Perspectives*. New York, The Haworth Hospitality Press.

Weed, M. (2008). *Olympic Tourism*. Oxford, Butterworth-Heinemann.

Wells, W. D. and Gubar, G. (1966). Lifecycle concepts in marketing research. *Journal of Marketing Research*, **3**, 355–63.

Welsh, J. (2003). *Reinventing Sponsorship*. (Internet) Number 22 (Spring). Available from <http://welshmktg.com/WMA_reinventing_sponsorship.pdf> (accessed 12 April 2010).

Wendroff, A. L. (2004). *Special Events: Proven Strategies for Nonprofit Fundraising.* Hoboken, New Jersey, John Wiley & Sons Inc.

Westerbeek, H., Smith, A., Turner, P., Emery, P., Green, C. and van Leeuwen, L. (2006). *Managing Sport Facilities and Major Events.* London, Routledge.

Wilshire Council (2009). *Good Hygiene Practices for Catering at Outdoor Events.* Trowbridge, Wiltshire Council.

WIMFEST (2004). *Our Vision.* (Internet). Available from <http://www.wimfest-liverpool.com/vision.php> (accessed 1 August 2005).

Windsor Festival (2010). *About Windsor Festival.* (Internet). Available from <http://www.windsorfestival.com/about/> (accessed 12 April 2010).

Wisconsin Department of Natural Resources (2001). *Special Events: Recycling and Waste Management.* (Internet) Available from <http://dnr.wi.gov/org/aw/wm/publications/anewpub/CE281.pdf> (accessed 5 May 2010).

Wood, H. (1982). *Festivity and Social Change.* London, Leisure in the Eighties Research Unit, Polytechnic of the South Bank.

Wood, E. (2002). Events, civic pride and attitude change in a post-industrial town: evaluating the effect of local authority events on residents' attitudes to the Blackburn region. In *Proceedings of the Events and Place-Making Conference* (L. Jago, M. Deery, R. Harris, A. Hede and J. Allen, eds). Sydney, Australian Centre for Event Management, University of Technology.

Wood, E. (2005). Measuring the Economic and Social Impacts of Local Authority Events. *International Journal of Public Sector Management,* **18**(1), 37–53.

Wood, J., Chapman, J., Fromholtz, M., Morrison, V., Wallace, J., Zeffane, R., Schermerhorn, J., Hunt, J. and Osborn, R. (2004). *Organisational Behaviour: A Global Perspective.* 3rd edn. Brisbane, John Wiley & Sons Australia.

Wood, E. H., Robinson, L. S. and Thomas, R. (2006). Evaluating the social impacts of community and local government events: a practical overview of research methods and measurement tools. In *Events and Festivals: Education, Impacts and Experiences* (F. Jordan, and S. Fleming, eds). Eastbourne, Leisure Studies Association.

Worcester Festival (2005). *Welcome to Worcester Festival 2005.* [Internet] Available from <http://www.worcesterfestival.co.uk/about_the_festival.asp/> (accessed 13 March 2010).

World Commission on Environment and Development (1987). *Our Common Future.* New York, Oxford University Press.

World Wide Fund for Nature (2004). *Environmental Assessment of the Athens 2004 Olympic Games.* (Internet) Available from <assets.panda.org/downloads/olympicsscorecardenglish.doc> (accessed 5 May 2010).

Wunsch, U. (ed.) (2008). *Facets of Contemporary Event Management – Theory & Practice for Event Success.* Bad Honnef, Verlag K.H. Brock.

Xerox Corporation (1998). *Guide to Waste Reduction and Recycling at Special Events.* New York, Xerox Corporation.

Yeoman, I., Robertson, M., Ali-Knight, J., Drummond, S. and McMahon-Beattie, U. (eds) (2004). *Festival and Events Management: An International Arts and Cultural Perspective.* Oxford, Elsevier Butterworth-Heinemann.

Yorkshire Tourist Board (2000). *Love Parade at Roundhay Park, Leeds: Event Evaluation.* York, Yorkshire Tourist Board Research Services.

Yorkshire Forward (2009). *YF Sponsors Key Biomed Conference.* (Internet) Available from: <http://www.yorkshire-forward.com/news-events/news/local-news/yf-sponsors-key-biomed-conference> (accessed 24 April 2010).

Younge, G. (1999). *New Beat to Saving the World from Debt.* (Internet) Guardian Unlimited, 15 February. Available from <http://www.guardianunlimited.co.uk> (accessed 15 April 2001).

Zeithaml, V., Parasuraman, A. and Berry, L. (1990). *Delivering Quality Service: Balancing Customer Perceptions and Expectations.* New York, Free Press.

Zhang, A. (2008). *China After the Olympics: Lessons from Beijing.* (Internet) Available from <http://www.greenpeace.org/raw/content/china/en/press/reports/green.pdf> (accessed 14 April 2010).

Index